A Place in Politics

JAMES P. WOODARD

A Place in Politics

São Paulo, Brazil, from Seigneurial Republicanism

to Regionalist Revolt

DUKE UNIVERSITY PRESS   DURHAM AND LONDON   2009

© 2009 Duke University Press
All rights reserved
Printed in the United States of America
on acid-free paper ∞
Designed by C. H. Westmoreland
Typeset in Arno with Chaparral display
by Keystone Typesetting, Inc.
Library of Congress Cataloging-in-
Publication information appear on the last printed
page of this book.
Duke University Press gratefully acknowledges the
support of Montclair State University,
which provided funds toward the production of this book.

For Tom and Felicity Skidmore

Contents

Acknowledgments

My first debt is to Tom and Felicity Skidmore, to whom this work is dedicated. Looking back, I can't bring myself to imagine a graduate apprenticeship without the two of them and their great personal and intellectual generosity. At best it would have been less lively, less interesting.

From the beginning, Felicity and Tom not only opened their homes and hearts to me, but also to Kim, who has herself, at every stage, made this work possible. It is her book too.

R. Douglas Cope was a model teacher, mentor, and—all too briefly— colleague. That he came to this project from far afield never prevented him from contributing meaningfully to the making of what I hope is a work that he can look upon with some pride.

The necessarily solitary work of research and writing, sometimes steadily, at other times in fits and starts, has been punctuated, happily, by conversation and correspondence with Barbara Weinstein, who saw some merit in what I was trying to do at an earlier stage than nearly any other North American could have. These exchanges with her, as the third member of my doctoral committee, as a colleague, and as a friend, have been sustentative.

Joseph Love, having read a small portion of a related work, generously offered to read the dissertation just a few months after its defense. His careful, incisive comments proved every bit as important to the making of this book as his *São Paulo in the Brazilian Federation* had been to the making of the dissertation itself.

The formal editorial process has been overseen by Valerie Milholland, the doyenne of English-language historical publishing on Brazil. I thank her for her support. Pam Morrison, also of Duke University Press, is deserving of thanks as well, not least for her patience while I wrestled with the copyedited manuscript. It is a better book for her efforts.

My debts to librarians and archivists are immense. In the United States, the inter-library loan specialists at Brown University, Harvard

University, the University of Maryland, Emory University, and Montclair State University are each deserving of mention, as are the staffs of the New York Public Library, the United States National Archives, and the Library of Congress's Newspaper Division and its Hispanic Reading Room. Special thanks are due to Maria Leal of the Oliveira Lima Library and to the funders and functionaries of the Cambridge Public Library, where I spent many more hours than I care to count scrolling through microfilm brought back from Brazil.

In Brazil my archival and bibliothecarial debts are similarly legion. In Rio de Janeiro, the personnel of the Casa de Rui Barbosa and the Centro de Pesquisa e Documentação da História Contemporânea do Brasil provided world-class service; their counterparts at the Biblioteca Nacional and the Museu da República were patient and helpful. At the Universidade Estadual de Campinas, the staffs of the Arquivo Edgard Leuenroth and the Centro de Documentação Cultural Alexandre Eulalio helped me uncover some truly remarkable material. Back in the city of São Paulo, I was graciously received at the Arquivo do Estado de São Paulo, the Biblioteca Mário de Andrade, the Biblioteca Presidente Kennedy (now the Biblioteca Prefeito Prestes Maia), the Centro de Documentação e Memória da Universidade Estadual Paulista, and the Istituto Italiano di Cultura, as well as at various libraries in the Universidade de São Paulo system, most notably those of the São Paulo Law School and the Instituto de Estudos Brasileiros.

My greatest debts were incurred at the Instituto Histórico e Geográfico de São Paulo. Brás Ciro Gallotta allowed me access to the IHGSP's manuscript materials afternoon after afternoon, including on days when its reading room was closed to the general public, for which I remain deeply grateful. Thanks are also due to the other members of the Instituto's staff, not least Dona Eva, who endeavored to keep me caffeinated.

The financial support that allowed me to take on this research was provided by the Watson Institute for International Studies and the Brown University Graduate School. These two institutions also contributed to my upkeep while I was writing the dissertation, as did the Department of History at Brown University. The penultimate draft of the book was prepared while I was engaged all but full-time on another project, as a fellow at Emory University's Center for Humanistic Inquiry. Similarly late (but by no means tardy) support was provided by Montclair State University's Office of Research and Sponsored Programs.

Over the last five years Elizabeth Johnson and Reese Ewing have welcomed me into their home whenever I needed to be in São Paulo. They are as kind and generous a pair of friends as Kim and I have had.

My colleague Jeff Strickland helped get me started on the preparation of maps for this volume. Elsewhere, I am more than willing to share the blame for any errors, but in this particular instance I must insist they are mine alone.

I would have given much less thought to the problem of maps had it not been for the insistence of one of Duke University Press's anonymous readers, whom I hope I have not disappointed. Preparing the maps helped refocus my mind's eye as far as the geographic categories that I use are concerned; each of Duke's readers spurred similar rethinkings of aspects of this project, and much else besides.

Further favors, email exchanges, bits of advice, and *bate-papos* contributing to the making of this work stretch back nearly a decade. It would be impossible for me to list everyone who so contributed, but it would be in poor form not to try. Here goes, in no particular order: Matthew Kadane, Claire Lesemann, Zachary Morgan, Jeffrey Lesser, Amy Chazel, Oliver Dinius, Jerry Dávila, Maria Helena Machado, John Monteiro, Gregg Bocketti, Joel Wolfe, John Coatsworth, Tamera Marko, João Felipe Gonçalves, Ben Penglase, Erika Grinius, Peter Beattie, Roger Kittleson, Erica Windler, Magda Völker, Josh Zeitz, Tony Jensen, Yoko Sato, Jens Hentschke, Vania Regina Lopes, Luigi Biondi, Christopher Frazer, Brian Bockelman, Célio Debes, Jacques Roberto Galvão Bresciani, Délio Freire dos Santos, Ori Preuss, Luiz Valente, Lowell Gudmundson, Andrew Kirkendall, Alexandre Hecker, Susan Goscinski, Michael Whelan, and Jonathan Evans.

I would also like to recognize my family: my sister, Barbara Montero; my parents, Robert and Patricia; and my in-laws, Elliott and Debbie Freer, who have been hosting me in the Washington, D.C., area since this project's inception. My grandparents, George Michael Cohan Jr. and Barbara Myers Cohan, did not live to see the work's conclusion; I'd like to think they'd be, as always, proud and more than a little amused.

My debt to Louis A. Pérez Jr., my undergraduate mentor at the University of North Carolina, is acknowledged only obliquely in the introduction that follows. It is almost definite that I would not have pursued graduate study in history had it not been for his example and encouragement, and it is certain that I would not have been as well prepared. The next book will be for him.

A Note on the Orthography
of Brazilian Portuguese

Orthographic reforms have made present-day written Brazilian Portuguese distinct from the language as written during much of the history of Lusophone South America. Changes in the accepted spelling of certain sounds are particularly prevalent in the names of people and places, a vexing problem for historians that different scholars have attempted to deal with in different ways. I have adopted what I believe to be an acceptable way of dealing with this issue and have striven to be consistent with its application. Place names have been updated in accord with the Instituto Brasileiro de Geografia e Estatística's usage (thus Ytú is now Itu). Personal suffixes have been updated as well (Netto and Junior are now Neto and Júnior), while surnames have been left in their original spelling (Moraes rather than Morais, for example). I have updated given names in cases where orthographic changes require adding diacritical marks (Antonio is now Antônio, Mario is now Mário), but not where changes in lettering would be in order (Arthur, not Artur; Moacyr, not Moacir; Theodoro, not Teodoro). Exceptions are made in cases in which the person in question is known to have used a different spelling in his lifetime (as was the case for Clovis Ribeiro, who did not add the accent mark, and for Afonso Schmidt, who dropped an "f"); a similar exception is made for Julio Mesquita, who died before these orthographic reforms were put into effect, but whose family has continued to use the original spelling in subsequently published works, as well as on the masthead of *O Estado de S. Paulo*.

The above rules have been applied to the text. In direct quotations and in nontextual citations (in the bibliography and in citations in the endnotes), original spellings have been maintained.

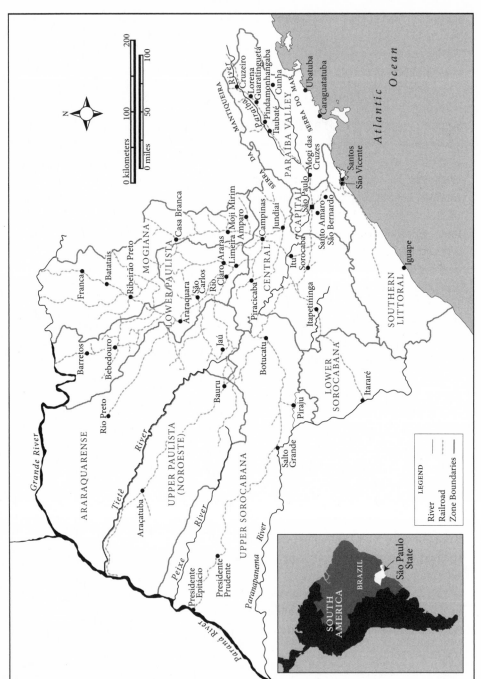

Map 1. Geographic zones, railway lines, and selected county seats of São Paulo state, 1930.

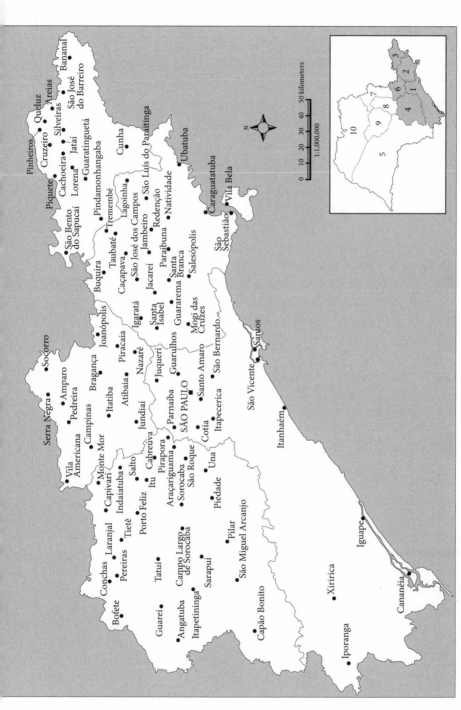

Map 2. São Paulo state electoral districts and county seats, 1926: districts 1–4 and 6. Based on tables in Repartição de Estatística e Archivo de São Paulo, *Divisão judiciaria e administrativa e districtos eleitoraes do estado de São Paulo em 1926* (São Paulo: Officina do *Diario Official*, 1927), 47–48.

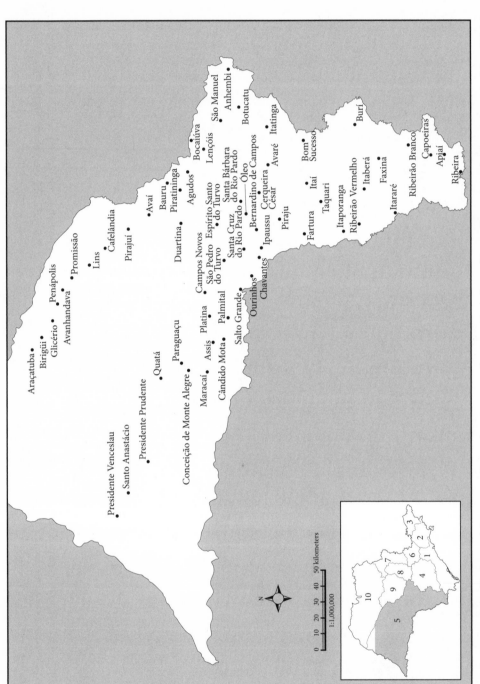

Map 3. São Paulo state electoral districts and county seats, 1926: district 5. Based on tables in Repartição de Estatística e Archivo, *Divisão judiciaria e administrativa e districtos eleitoraes do estado de São Paulo em 1926, 47–48.*

Map 4. São Paulo state electoral districts and county seats, 1926: districts 7–10. Based on tables in Repartição de Estatística e Archivo, *Divisão judiciaria e administrativa e districtos eleitoraes do estado de São Paulo em 1926*, 48.

Introduction

As a subject, São Paulo—province and provincial center to 1889, state and state capital thereafter, section and city throughout—has long inspired metaphor, superlative, simile, and metonym. Passing through in 1889–90, a North American visitor described the region as "the garden of Brazil" and the country's "most highly-favored portion." Ten years later, another U.S. correspondent referred to its capital as a "Yankee City of Brazil," an appellation echoed at a dozen-year lag by a visitor from Colombia (he may not have seen the appellative itself as entirely complementary), who also described "the beautiful City of Sao Paulo" as "one of the most magnificent cities of the Western Hemisphere, surpassing those of Europe and the United States in the breadth of its avenues and in its tropical luxuriance." Approaching the city in 1927, Rudyard Kipling saw "several immense Madrids breaking half the horizon"; within the city limits, he found "cars and lorries mov[ing] everywhere, like electrons in the physics primers." Three years later, Paul Vanorden Shaw—born in the city of São Paulo to North American parents in 1898—described the state as "the economic foundation of the entire nation" and "the motor" of Brazil. The Viennese exile Stefan Zweig opted for the anatomical over the architectural or mechanical: for him, São Paulo was Brazil's "centre of muscles, its organ of strength." As for metonymy, as early as 1906 visitors were repeating a turn of phrase that would long infuriate Brazilians from elsewhere in the federation: "São Paulo is Brazil."[1]

Whether second-hand or spontaneous, and leaving aside the responses of other Brazilians (many of whom were themselves given to celebration of things *paulista* in not unsimilar terms), one thing is clear: there was much to be impressed by in São Paulo during these years.[2] For by the 1880s, São Paulo was already Brazil's greatest export producer; by the 1910s, it was its greatest industrial center; and, by the close of the 1930s, it was its most populous unit.

During these same years, São Paulo played host to some of Brazil's most important political, intellectual, and social movements. From the 1870s through the 1880s, it was home to Brazil's most noteworthy movement of antimonarchical opposition, which sought to replace the country's centralized "imperial" government with a federal republic. During these same decades, the province was also the proving ground for the greatest of Brazil's antislavery campaigns. With the victory of the two good causes between 1888 and 1889, the state came into its own in political terms, and over the course of the next four decades, four Brazilian presidents would emerge directly from its political machine. Only once would its chosen candidate fail, in 1909–10, when the São Paulo state machine backed Ruy Barbosa, a son of the northeastern state of Bahia, in what is remembered as the country's first contested presidential election.

Beginning in the 1880s, São Paulo also served as the destination of choice for the greatest number of immigrants seeking Brazilian shores. These immigrants and the expansion of public education helped to rank São Paulo among Brazil's most literate provincial units. By the turn of the twentieth century, São Paulo was also Brazil's most lettered unit, home to ever-increasing numbers of morning and afternoon newspapers, weekly and monthly reviews, and almanacs and other annuals. Beginning at around the same time, paulista men and women of letters made what now appear to be a series of bids to become Brazil's most literary unit: in their literatures of heritage and heraldry, of folkloric naturalism, and of cosmopolitan modernism.

While the aesthetically minded gathered in São Paulo salons, practical men of affairs met in the halls of the state's associational bodies, from its early, but still extant, business-and-industry "commercial associations" to its industrial-interest "centers." For and by the associative among paulista workers were analogous groupings: mutual aid societies, workingmen's federations, and—by the close of the 1920s—at least one intensely politicized trade union.

The activists who led the latter group were, at least in theory, militantly internationalist in orientation, but movements characterized by narrower loyalties were to be found in São Paulo as well. In the 1910s, mobilizationist nationalism enjoyed its vogue, not only in the state capital, but in the interior as well. In 1924, mobilization of another sort came to the state unexpectedly, in the form of a military rebellion led by mostly young, mostly junior officers whose troops captured and held the city of São Paulo and much of the rest of the state for weeks. Two years later, the state capital was the site chosen for the founding of the age's most important civilian opposition movement, a political party that challenged the state's republican machine in liberal, constitutionalist terms. Four years on, in 1930, the new party's leaders tied their fortunes to extra-regional machine politicians in what has come to be known and renowned as the "Revolution of 1930."

Throughout these years, São Paulo—city and section—was setting and subject for the elaboration of a deep and abiding sense of regional difference and distinctiveness. This peculiar tradition, elements of which were taken up by outsiders beginning in the nineteenth century, received its most prolonged, emphatic statement in the assembly and remembering of what has come to be called the "Constitutionalist Revolution" of 1932, Brazil's last great regionalist revolt.

For all of their importance, excitement, and dynamism, the politics of these years have yet to receive their historiographical due. To be sure, they have long been pointed to as formative in the making of modern Brazil, but their examination in bits and pieces (a party or person here, a municipality or magazine there), while yielding very fine monographs that have made signal contributions to our existing body of knowledge, has left the problem of broad interpretation virtually untouched.

At the broadly interpretive level, the case could be made that in no other period of Brazilian history is the literature as thick with cliché and received wisdom. Indeed, in reading about politics in Brazil from the late nineteenth century through the early decades of the twentieth one quickly comes up against layers of verities, understandings that have proven remarkably durable, not only in what public imagination can be said to exist, but also in the works of professional historians.

Republicanism may again be taken as a starting point. Republican politics, so the story goes, was the exclusive preserve of a comfortable few (in São Paulo, rendered variously as the "coffee aristocracy," the "coffee bourgeoisie," or the "coffee oligarchy"). Beyond tending to the narrow economic interests of this privileged group, republicanism had only the most tenuous connections, if any at all, to other spheres of human activity, cultural, intellectual, and social. The resulting political culture was exceedingly thin in content and extremely limited in its reach.

Political opposition is attributed to conflict among these comfortable few (thus the unintentionally oxymoronic "dissident oligarchs") or to a deus ex machina summoned from elsewhere (a "rising middle class," a presumed institutional ethos peculiar to Brazil's military, the emergence of industrial capitalism). Whichever the scenario, with the partial exception of works relying on the no less ghostly and mechanistic explanatory device of "nationalism," the resulting politics is understood as having been as thin in content and limited in appeal as that it opposed.

When one gets to the grander dates of national history, the tendency toward reification of particular period-portraits of the past becomes even more marked. Ruy Barbosa's campaign for the Brazilian presidency in 1909–10 was one fool's errand (and its 1919 sequel unworthy of mention, much less serious consideration). The labor militancy of the late 1910s was heroic and important on its own, but had no influence upon republican politics. That the great military rebellion of 1924 occurred in São Paulo meant little; it may well have occurred in Piauí for all of its involvement with and influence upon paulista society. And 1930, 1930 was the greatest of partings-of-waters, after which everything was forever changed and the past no longer held any sway over the future, at least in matters political.

Evidence unearthed in the monographic work of the last ten years calls into question certain of these understandings. We now know, for example, that men of the middle (not coffee aristocrats, coffee bourgeois, or coffee oligarchs) occupied leading positions in the local republican parties of places like Rio Claro in the early decades of the twentieth century. However, the weight of received wisdom is such that even findings like these are pressed into the existing interpretive framework and the resulting works are catalogued at Brazil's National Library under the subject heading "Brazil—coffee oligarchy," without having made any impression on more general understandings of paulista politics.[3]

Given this situation, it is more than apparent that the further accumulation of monographs will not force a rethinking of the political history of São Paulo from the 1880s through the first third of the twentieth century any time soon. Rather, a broad reinterpretation, one bringing together synthesis and original research, is in order.

Origins and Expectations

A thoroughgoing reinterpretation of paulista history through the early 1930s was among the furthest things from my mind at this project's inception. Indeed, had I known where my work would lead, I would like to think that I would have had the good sense to acquire a different interest, perhaps to choose another calling.

My initial goals were nothing if not more modest. I sought to map the participation of ordinary paulistas ("nonelites" was my inelegant term) in what could be, and indeed was, seen as a set of "liberal-constitutionalist" or "liberal-reformist" movements, the best documented of which was the Democratic Party of São Paulo, founded in 1926. Whistling while I worked, and repeating to myself more than once, "There can be no high politics without a good deal of low politics," I set about collecting my raw material.[4] The documentation did not disappoint. Indeed, I soon found more and better material than I had dared hope. But as I looked ahead to writing, and in so doing connect my findings to the existing scholarship, I was increasingly troubled.

The more I learned about reformist "low politics," the less satisfactory the existing interpretations of the reformist movements themselves seemed. The same was true of incumbent politics, only more so. Indeed, it became clear that not only was the extant scholarship on paulista politics insufficient as background for the kind of study I had set out to write, it was itself deficient in certain important respects.[5]

As I turned from my original, monographic point of inquiry to a broader course of study, new problems presented themselves. Once-key concepts and conceptions revealed themselves to be useless (my own "nonelites," to begin with) or worse (*coronelismo*, for example).[6] Understanding paulista politics demanded a better understanding of the press; in turn, "the press" itself became a portmanteau that demanded unpacking. Where before I had envisioned my original research as being limited in geographic scope to the state capital and a few secondary cities, I now found myself ranging over all of São Paulo: capital, coast, and countryside. Most importantly, and most interestingly to me, were the people whose stories emerged in the documentation and confounded existing understandings of Brazilian republicanism, including my own: election-day entrepreneurs, small-town reformers, rabble-rousing beat reporters.

Context and Comparisons

In considering late-nineteenth-century and early-twentieth-century São Paulo within its Brazilian context, a number of facts present themselves. The first couple of these may seem both banal and redundant, but they bear restatement.

First, of course, is São Paulo's importance in economic and political terms. One can, I hope, write critically about aspects of a region's self-image without losing sight of the same region's actual import.

Second is the appropriateness of the provincial unit (the state) as the scale of analysis during this time period. The extreme federalism of Brazil's post-imperial system makes this fact plain for those scholars . interested in administration and government, but the usefulness of the state-level approach does not end there. In an age in which sectional identities were as deeply held as or more deeply held than national loyalties, in which there was only one institution that was truly national in scope (the army, an institution that was also decidedly unpopular, in almost any sense of the word), and in which extra-local exchange—commercial, intellectual, and social—occurred overwhelmingly on a regional basis, national history is elusive and local history incomplete. The seeming exception comes in studies of the city of Rio de Janeiro, which are, of course, completely local.[7]

Third, there is São Paulo's status as setting for so many of Brazil's most important developments from the making of nineteenth-century republicanism through the outbreak of the regionalist revolt of 1932. Some of these developments were solely paulista in scope, but national in importance. Other social, intellectual, and political movements arose most dramatically in the paulista context, but were experienced elsewhere as well: labor militancy and aesthetic modernism are two of the most celebrated examples. Another example, the reformist party politics of the 1920s, is often thought of as being uniquely or especially paulista, but its leaders found allies and imitators in states throughout Brazil.[8]

It is almost unnecessary to add that further parallels may be found still farther afield. São Paulo's republican machine, with its managed elections and patronage appointments, possessed analogues from Buenos Aires to Brooklyn. Not for nothing is there a Spanish cognate for the Portuguese-language term, *chefe político*, and an English equivalent for both. Likewise, the comparison between Brazilian ruyismo and Mexican maderismo is now four decades old; via maderismo, the same comparison was made to U.S. progressivism, Argentine Radicalism, and Uruguayan batllismo, among other movements, and has since been extended to the Radicalism of France's Third Republic.[9]

Prolonged ruminations on these and like comparisons are fewer than they might be in the pages that follow, for various reasons. At one point in my work, I had the grandest expectations of stepping out from São Paulo and extending comparisons from Rio de Janeiro to the Río de la Plata, whence from Córdoba to Coahuila, then to the Atlantic crossings of the Progressive-Era United States and Third-Republic France. The old parallels are still there to be drawn, between republican machines of widely varied hue and between reformist movements of similarly varied aspect, as are some comparisons that have not, to my knowledge, been made (between Getúlio Vargas and Hipólito Yrigoyen, for example), but I no longer believe that I am the one to make them at any length, at least not in this particular work, for combining research-driven revisionism and high-flying comparativism is a tricky task. Readers will detect few parallels of approach or outlook between this work and Florencia Mallon's *Peasant and Nation*, aside from the authors' starting points in what seems increasingly quaint to call "political history from below," but I think that Mallon was absolutely right to make her comparative case on the basis of more or less equivalent archival diggings.[10] Without having built the kind of mental map of Rio de Janeiro or Buenos Aires that I have assembled for the city and state of São Paulo (and for the state's subregions), I could not be sure that I was not committing the fallacy of comparing my own understandings of paulista politics with the kinds of hoary received wisdom that were so clearly inapplicable in my own area of specialization.

My reluctance to engage in extended comparisons between my findings on São Paulo and the existing literatures on other regions, countries, and cultures should not be taken to mean that I consider the paulista case to be sui generis or that I have not found inspiration, succor, and support in these literatures throughout the formulation of this work. On the contrary, even my belief in the merit of this particular approach has been encouraged by my experience outside of the archives and arcana of paulista history. Although I lived in Brazil as a child, my introduction to the historian's craft did not begin with the study of the South American giant. Instead, I cut my historiographical teeth on a tradition that rightly insists on the worthiness of studying, on its own terms, the complex history of another land of the future. On that basis, too, it seemed to me that the history of the Brazilian state of São Paulo was worthy of careful, attentive, solitary study.

Project and Projections

The result of such a course of study is a work that aims to make a series of contributions to the historiography of modern Brazil and, it is hoped, to understandings of modern politics and political and cultural change more broadly. These contributions begin with a reconsideration of republicanism in São Paulo.

Paulista Republicanism Reconsidered

The much-mentioned "coffee oligarchy" finds scant purchase in the chapters that follow. Instead, one finds a set of political structures and practices that displayed a statewide unity, including in areas where little or no coffee was to be found.

These structures and practices showed a marked continuity with those of the preceding political dispensation, a fact that will be of little apparent surprise to most scholars, but that bears repeating in this context, as does their comparability to analogous arrangements the world over. As in Richard Graham's neo-Namierite nineteenth-century Brazil (and in Lewis Namier's own eighteenth-century England), the structure of politics in São Paulo during these years was characterized by patronage and personalism, fraud and favor, corruption and clientele-building.[11]

There are, however, distinctions to be made. More than its predecessor regime, and perhaps more than many similar sets of political and administrative arrangements, the paulista machine of the late nineteenth century and the early twentieth was characterized by the thorough interweaving of party and government. Where there had been two parties of government, there was now one, and while the national head of state had stood above both parties, the state executive now emerged from the single party in the field. In what might seem a paradox at first glance, conflict within this one-party system was every bit as heated as it had been under the previous regime, in contests between and among in- and out-of-power factions ranging territorially from the paulista littoral to the furthest reaches of frontier settlement.

These patterns of incumbency and opposition, and the means by which the two positions were exchanged, involved a far greater number and variety of players than has heretofore been imagined. Teamsters, tax collectors, folk healers, factory foremen, judges, builders, postmen, police delegates, professors of law, solicitors, schoolteachers, state's attorneys, coffee merchants, claim jumpers, Indian killers, land developers, small-town scribblers, neighborhood newspapermen—all played their parts. The relationships that tied these players together involved complex processes of give-and-take, the take increasing with the exaltedness of the particular player in question.

Republican Political Culture

In outlining the structure of republican politics in São Paulo, I was able to draw upon a sizeable body of work, ranging from the recently classic to the remote and obscure.[12] Examining republican political culture—the

ideals, imagery, symbols, stories, and language of paulista republicanism—required that I go it alone. What studies we have of political culture
in Brazil, and there are some very fine ones, have taken as their setting
the country's nineteenth-century margins or its mid-twentieth-century
capital, while the political culture of republican São Paulo has gone
unexamined.[13]

Undertaking such an examination, one soon finds that republican
political culture was neither so thin in content nor as limited in appeal as
has been supposed. Its sources were manifold: classical and modern
republican precedent, gendered notions of honor and community standing, nineteenth-century civilizational optimism, Portuguese-derived municipalism. Perhaps most importantly, and almost certainly most potent-
ly, there was São Paulo's distinct patriotic tradition, which encompassed
a sense of regional difference approaching, and at points becoming,
outright chauvinism.

These aspects of paulista political culture found expression in legislative addresses, post-electoral processions, and newsprinted comment on
the events of the day. That appeals to certain elements of republican
tradition were most often made in a spirit of purest cynicism is clear, but
further tenets were widely shared and deeply held.

Particular aspects of republican political culture were likewise subject
to capture by paulistas who were openly critical of the structure and
practice of republican politics in their society, often with at least one eye
on really existing republicanism elsewhere. These critics had recourse to
a republican ideal that was liberal, popular, and potentially democratic,
even as they disagreed among themselves as to what liberalism or popular sovereignty, to take two examples, might actually mean. The critical, cosmopolitan appeal to reform was thus intrinsic to the republican
tradition.

Culture, Criticism, Opposition

The capture of aspects of republican political culture by the opponents
of particular republican power-holders and by critics of republican
politics-as-practiced was especially evident from the later 1910s onward.
Among the challengers were idealistic students, ambitious newspapermen, insurgent workers, rebellious military officers, disaffected patricians, and out-and-out political novices—angry planters, anxious ur-
banites—each of which appealed to elements of the republican tradition,
to some degree or another, to greater or lesser effect.

Even as familiar patriotic, republican ideals and imagery were re-

hearsed, so too did the existing republican idiom expand with the incorporation of new ideas and points of emphasis. The idea of the secret
ballot, borrowed from post-Saenz Peña Argentina, was one such neolo-
gism. It was joined by war-era mobilizationist nationalism, concern for
what was called the "social question," and appeals to interest group
representation, among other elements.

Bundled together or picked apart, these ideas inspired and informed,
to greater and lesser degrees, anti-machine movements through at least
the 1920s. Among these movements, each of which further added to the
warp and weft of paulista political culture, were Ruy Barbosa's twilight
campaign for the presidency in 1919, the efforts at mobilization surrounding the military revolt of July 1924, and the founding and subsequent campaigning of the Democratic Party.

São Paulo's republican host endured these varied challenges. Indeed,
its younger, sprier leaders made some attempts to learn from them.
Throughout, contenders old and young struggled among themselves in
the contests for patronage, party leadership, and prestige that defined the
structure of republican politics.

Republic and Public

The leaders of the state's republican machine may have held the balance
of formal political power through the late 1930s, but the exertions of their
disparate challengers were at least as important in the longer term. Not
only did the critics and counterparties of the 1910s and 1920s contribute
to the deepening and diffusion of São Paulo's regionally distinct political
culture, they converged upon and contributed to shaping a broader and
more participatory public sphere, one that may have been put to ends
that present-day sensibilities find off-putting but that was nevertheless
impressive in its time and place and that, despite its many exclusions and
other ugly facets, was not without its democratic potentialities.

Hilda Sabato, who has contributed more than any other scholar to the
adoption of the "public sphere" concept by historians of Latin America,
has also noted great variance in its use among historians in general.
"Historians," she writes, "have frequently made a rather eclectic use" of
the idea. This work, like Sabato's own, is no exception. Indeed, in both
cases the term "elastic" might be more apt than "eclectic."[14]

In her fullest, most recent statement on the subject, Sabato identifies a
public sphere as having come into existence in Buenos Aires in the 1860s
and 1870s, where it "became a space of mediation between civil society

and the state, and for the participation of vast sectors of the population in the public life of the city." This *porteño* public sphere was a "new and expanding space, [in which] different groups and sectors of society voiced their opinions and represented their claims directly, avoiding the specifically political path."[15] Encompassing certain institutions, "the different types of associations, the press," it excluded others: "political institutions such as the parties or Congress," which "were closely tied to the state, and may be understood as part of its sphere of action."[16]

The public sphere upon which the anti-machine contenders of São Paulo's 1910s and 1920s converged was also an "expanding space" in which "different groups and sectors of society voiced their opinions and represented their claims." It, too, spanned a vibrant print culture and a rich associational life. But there are important distinctions to be made. Unlike its porteño analogue, the paulista public sphere included politics as they were understood to exist, the politics of party, faction, and election—or, at least, of certain kinds of party, faction, and election.[17] Where the Sabatian public sphere was characterized by comity and affected unanimity, São Paulo's public sphere afforded room for conflict within and between distinct groups. Indeed, at points its opinion leaders countenanced degrees of disorder that would have been beyond the porteño pale.[18] Another distinction concerns questions of scale and scope: while Sabato's public sphere was strictly municipal, São Paulo's encompassed a much greater geographic area; its center was the state capital, but it included a vast hinterland. As a result, and in more ways than one, the paulista public sphere was regional, a fact that also distinguishes it from another national-capital counterpart, that of the city of Rio de Janeiro.[19]

A public sphere, of course, demands a public. Here, too, differences may be found with the Sabatian model. Sabato asserts that her porteño public sphere was "new and expanding," but otherwise one is left with little sense of change, still less of genesis. *The* or *a* public sphere appears in Buenos Aires in the 1860s and lasts through the 1870s, only to disappear at some point thereafter. Its basis or character is elusive: in an early interpretive piece Sabato labeled it "bourgeois," linking its emergence to Buenos Aires's "increasingly bourgeois character" and explaining "because in Buenos Aires the public sphere was largely organized by bourgeois and petit-bourgeois elements"; now it is undone after 1880 as "Buenos Aires turned decidedly modern, capitalistic, and—in the word of José Luis Romero—'bourgeois.' "[20] Despite Sabato's interest in citizenship as a category of social-science analysis, she does not delve particularly deeply into how the "citizen" (or the member of the public) was envisioned in the period under study.[21]

The anti-machine politics of São Paulo's 1910s and 1920s would have been inconceivable without the growth of an actual public over the first three decades of the twentieth century. Population growth, an increase in the number of readers, and the expansion of the range and reach of press outlets and the variety of associational groupings, were among the markers and manifestations of this development, which had its roots in the nineteenth century but which was experienced with increasing urgency after the turn of the twentieth. As to the character of this public, it included men and women from a fairly wide cross-section of paulista society, but its exemplar—its "model citizen"—was represented as literate, modern, and respectable, of middling or better means (but not idly rich), viriliously male, and (often, but not always) white. The politics of the 1910s and 1920s, old and new, displayed an ongoing, take-and-give relationship with these representations of the paulista public, appropriating them and elaborating upon them by turn.

From the Social History of
Politics to a Political History of Society

Historians, particularly historians at the beginning of their careers, are faced with tremendous incentives to assert scholarly innovation, even to the extent of imagining that they have rediscovered gravity. One result is that scholars only too ready to identify invented traditions in the historical past find themselves attempting to pass off such invented novelties as the "new political history" in their professional present.

In this work, at the risk of being barred from more than one imagined community, I have endeavored to resist the temptation to claim conceptual or methodological novelty. Rather, my goal has been, in Emilia Viotti da Costa's words, "to conceive [a history] in which politics . . . is seen in connection with other aspects of human life," in particular "the interconnections among economic, social, political, and ideological institutions and structures," a statement of purpose first set in type more than twenty years ago and anticipated by work going back decades earlier, including work by Viotti da Costa herself and by scholars rooted in distinctly different traditions, historiographical and otherwise.[22]

Affinity is not identity. As should be clear from the foregoing, I have accorded culture a good deal more attention and a greater measure of autonomy than Viotti da Costa might have, at least until the relatively recent past.[23] As far as the paulista politics of the first third of the twentieth century are concerned, cultural conflict (in the form of rival claims to certain traditions and challenges fired by particular political ideas) was in almost every instance more important than conflict issuing forth from distinct economic interests. By the same token (and taking only one example), the relative success of the Democratic Party for the first few years after its founding had a good deal more to do with cultural capital than it did with coffee capital. Taking a longer chronological view, among the most important aspects of the politics of these years were ongoing efforts to define São Paulo as a society, efforts that were, by their very nature, cultural.

Returning to the comparison with Viotti da Costa's work, I have also been at pains to emphasize the experiences of individual human lives to a greater extent than she did, at least in the first edition of her *Brazilian Empire*. This emphasis is more than a holdover from my original envisioning of a social history of a certain kind of politics (though it may be that, too); it is also an inextricable part of a larger attempt to restore a sense of perspective and of possibility missing from much of what has been written on the politics of these years. The fools' errands subsequently scoffed at by historians were not seen as such in their time. Even in disappointment, disillusionment, and defeat were contained lessons for the future and the lineaments of conflicts to come.

In looking at these individual human lives in their local and regional contexts, influenced by national and international developments, I have attempted, through most of the text, to enmesh analysis and narrative. This approach was the only one I found that served to recreate the feeling of movement apparent in the evidence left by actual participants without losing track of important institutional and cultural continuities, the weight of which are more than attested to by the mood of most subsequent scholarship.

Six chapters follow, beginning with one designed to situate readers amid the places and people that made up São Paulo between the 1890s and the 1930s. Of the five chapters of greater heft, chapter 2, "A Republic of Layers," offers an extended, but still introductory, interpretation of paulista republicanism as a structure, as a set of practices, and as a political culture from the 1890s onward. In looking at republican political culture, in particular, special attention is paid to the cosmopolitan and reformist strains that grew up alongside official republicanism. The resulting ambivalence and potential for conflict is further explored in the context of the 1909–10 presidential campaign, which, arguably foolhardy, was no one man's errand.

So much for chapter 2, if not its republic of layers. The remaining four chapters unfold more or less in chronological order. Chapter 3 takes as its starting point the mid-1910s, when the cosmopolitan strains of paulista republicanism, and the cosmopolitan nature of paulista society more generally, meant that affairs abroad, from Argentine democratization to Europe's self-immolation across the Atlantic, would command considerable attention throughout São Paulo, from belle-lettered opinion-makers to guttersnipe news-gatherers, well-heeled readers to streetwise rowdies. As the European war staggered to its standstill, these developments intersected with events at home, all of which, in turn, came to influence the formal politicking of the years 1918–19, which featured an ideologically inspired opposition, with the 1919 campaign for the national presidency as its exemplar and apogee.

Venality, violence, and internal weakness condemned the movements of the late 1910s to insuccess, to the great satisfaction of the kingpins of the state's political machine. The latter group, however, found itself facing a more serious threat in the military revolt of July 1924. The rebels of 1924, in addition to driving the state government from the city of São Paulo, attracted allies of conviction and of convenience throughout the state and deepened ongoing debates regarding the potential reform of Brazilian and especially paulista politics. In the longer term, the rebel officers themselves became iconic figures for all manner of opponents of the existing political order. These connections between the rebellion of 1924 and the society and politics of São Paulo are the subject of chapter 4.

Chapter 5 deals with the Democratic Party of São Paulo, which was among the most important institutional spinners of the military-rebel mythos. A broad and often fractious host, the Democratic Party represented the temporary coming together of several distinct varieties of criticism and opposition, which together mounted an important but ultimately unsuccessful challenge to the republican machine, with several notable longer-term effects.

In 1929–30—the years covered by chapter 6—events abroad and out-of-state again exerted their influences upon paulista politics, though hardly in the simplistic fashion that the existing literature presents. Interregional brinkmanship, economic collapse, and military conspiracy each played a part, to be sure, but so did São Paulo's existing structures of politics and patterns of conflict.

A conclusion draws together some of the most important motives and meanings of paulista politics between the 1890s and the early 1930s, including the many ways in which São Paulo's pre-1930 political experiences prefigured and paved the way for the regionalist revolt of 1932. Appended to this conclusion is an epilogue hazarding a discussion of selected aspects of São Paulo's subsequent history. As one of my subjects might have remarked, *pro brasilia fiant eximia.*

1 São Paulo as a Developing Society

The political conflicts of the first third of the twentieth century are incomprehensible without a basic description of São Paulo as a place and a brief discussion of its people. Both were shaped by a welter of overlapping changes in the society, the economy, and the land of the southeastern Brazilian state. Beginning early in the nineteenth century, coffee production spread throughout São Paulo in successive waves of boom and bust, from the areas of initial cultivation in the eastern third of the state through the virgin soils of the central plateau. Economic expansion and stagnation, demographic change, and the growth of the transportation network led to the creation of distinct subregions within the state. At the same time, native-born paulistas, immigrants from abroad, and migrants from elsewhere in Brazil came together in the making of a society that was cosmopolitan yet distinct. Among these men and women were the individuals and groups who would also make the political conflicts of the 1910s and 1920s.

Places

The state of São Paulo occupies nearly 96,000 square miles (248,209 square kilometers), a landmass slightly larger in area than those of the states of New York and Pennsylvania combined. It has a coastline of approximately 370 miles (600 kilometers), more or less at the center of which lies the port city of Santos, the littoral's sole urban center of note. Although it lies almost entirely below the tropic of Capricorn, São Paulo's coastal area—a narrow band of land between the south Atlantic and the coastal escarpment known as the Serra do Mar—is characterized by a tropical climate, with high temperatures and heavy rainfall.

Moving up and over the coastal escarpment, the state is dominated by a vast plateau that slopes westward toward the Paraná River, which marks the state line with Mato Grosso. The plateau has milder average temperatures than the coast but still receives ample rainfall. Its expanse is well watered by a number of river systems that flow westward into the Paraná, which itself runs into the Río de la Plata system. These river systems made São Paulo's agricultural dynamism possible and, as a source of hydraulic and hydroelectric power, greatly contributed to its industrial growth. They are not, however, particularly suitable for navigation, which meant that the territorial integration of São Paulo would be achieved by railroad rather than riverboat.

The only major exception to the generally westward slope of the land is to be found in the eastern corner of the state, known historically as the "North" (if São Paulo's coastline ran north-south, it would be the northernmost portion of the state),[1] now known as the "Eastern Cone."[2] Its central feature is the Paraíba River, which runs eastward into Rio de Janeiro state in a valley formed by the coastal escarpment and the Serra da Mantiqueira.

The lay of the land, patterns of human settlement, changes in political administration, and the development of a railway network served to make São Paulo a province, then a state, characterized by distinct subregions. Scholars are in wide agreement on this matter. Where they differ is how these subregions are best categorized.[3] In his pioneering study of elite politics in São Paulo, Joseph L. Love adopted José Francisco de Camargo's ten-zone system; I have done the same, based on this precedent and on the degree to which the system can be shown to overlap with the administrative organization developed for state elections beginning in 1905.[4]

The first of these ten zones is dominated by the state capital, the city of São Paulo, located to the northwest of Santos beyond the Serra do Mar. It was founded as a Jesuit village in the mid-sixteenth century but soon became a secular settlement (*vila*), the base for slave-hunting expeditions (*bandeiras*) that ventured deep into the hinterland in search of Indian captives.[5] In the early nineteenth century, it acquired one of Brazil's two law schools, making it a cultural and sociopolitical center of considerable importance.[6] As coffee expanded to the north and west, bringing railroads in its wake, São Paulo grew in economic importance, as the city through which these railways were linked to the export markets of Santos and as an important commercial center in its own right.[7] Industry followed; by the early 1910s, placards on the city's streetcars were proclaiming São Paulo to be "the largest industrial center in South America."[8] As these processes continued, the state capital was the site of spectacular demographic growth, its population more than doubling with each census: 31,385 in 1872, 64,934 in 1890, 239,820 in 1900, 579,033 in 1920, and 1,326,261 in 1940.[9]

The remainder of the capital zone was made up of a handful of counties (*municípios*) containing settlements that were first tied to the state capital through truck farming for the urban market. Later, in cases like São Bernardo (an "industrial center of the first order" by the early 1920s) and, less dramatically, Santo Amaro, some of these counties became important as areas into which the city's industries could expand.[10]

The state's second zone is dominated by the Paraíba Valley, but it also includes the uplands that flank the valley as well as the northern third of the paulista coast. Historically, this area has had more in common with southern Minas Gerais and with western Rio de Janeiro than with the rest of São Paulo (in 1888, one of its representatives proposed that it be merged with these regions to create a new province); like southern Minas and western Rio de Janeiro state it looked to the national capital (the city of Rio de Janeiro) as its metropolis. In the early nineteenth century, the valley itself became a center for coffee growing, from which the beans were brought to northern São Paulo ports like Caraguatatuba and Ubatuba by muleteers, then exported from the port of Rio de Janeiro. In the 1870s, the coming of what would come to be called the Central do Brasil Railroad meant that planters could send their coffee directly to Rio's export market by rail.[11]

By the time the rails arrived, however, the Paraíba Valley—on both sides of the Rio-São Paulo boundary—was showing signs of decline. Coffee growing was punishing to the land; as the bushes leached nutrients out of the valley's soils, coffee yields declined. To the "push" of coffee's collapse was added the "pull" of boom times elsewhere in the state, and the Paraíba Valley zone, which had been the most populous of the state's ten zones during every census taken between 1836 and 1886, began to experience demographic as well as economic decline.[12] By the 1910s, José Bento Monteiro Lobato, born in the Paraíba Valley town of Taubaté in 1882, was already holding forth on its "Dead Towns."[13] It should be noted, however, that the region's declining economic and demographic fortunes were relative rather than absolute and not as uniformly dismal as Lobato's faithful readers might believe. While upland counties like Cunha did slide back into mostly subsistence agriculture and the northern coast experienced continued stagnation, industry was not unknown in the valley's towns and some of its counties saw successful experiments in non-coffee agriculture, livestock raising, and dairy production.[14]

It was in the central zone that coffee had its first boom on the western plateau, though not all of the land in the zone is suitable for coffee cultivation. The central zone includes some of the state's most important interior cities, most notably Campinas (which, thanks to coffee was larger and more populous than the state capital for a brief period in the late nineteenth century), but also including Jundiaí, Piracicaba, Itu, and Sorocaba.[15]

In the central zone, coffee was most important in the area that runs northward from Jundiaí to Campinas and west to Piracicaba, though it never wholly replaced cane cultivation even here. The southern and western portions of the central zone were not as well suited to coffee growing. In the area between Sorocaba and Itapetininga, cane, cattle, and some coffee were produced from the nineteenth century into the twentieth century, a span of time that also saw periodic booms in cotton cultivation. As the twentieth century progressed, both parts of the central zone also saw increased diversification into the production of food-stuffs for domestic consumption; in coffee areas, this process accompanied the decline of local yields.[16]

Along with the diversification of agriculture in the countryside, the central zone also saw the growth of industry in its cities. Sorocaba vied with the *paulistano* district of Lapa for the title of "*Manchester paulista*," while Campinas, Jundiaí, and Piracicaba each became known as an "industrial center of the first order." Itu, for its part, was also deemed to be an "industrial center."[17] Partly as a result, the central zone came to have more counties in which the population was split between the county seat and outlying areas, unlike the pattern existing in much of the rest of the state in which the portion of the population living in the countryside dwarfed that living in cities and towns.[18]

The fourth geographic zone of the state of São Paulo is the Mogiana, named for the planter-financed Mogiana Railroad, which was built running north out of Campinas, reaching Moji Mirim in 1875, Ribeirão Preto in 1883, and the Minas Gerais state line four years later.[19] It may be further divided into two subzones: the lower Mogiana, based around Moji Mirim, and the upper Mogiana, based around Ribeirão Preto. The latter subzone was the most important coffee-growing area in the world in the late nineteenth century and the early twentieth, producing three successive "Kings of Coffee."[20]

The lower-Paulista zone (named for the "lower" trunk of the Paulista Railroad) is the fifth of São Paulo's ten subregions. Like the railway line for which it is named, the zone begins in the rich agricultural lands of

Limeira, Rio Claro, and Araras (major coffee-producing counties in the late nineteenth century and the early twentieth), runs northwest through São Carlos to Araraquara (where the railhead of the Paulista Railroad arrived in 1885), and then north to Barretos. The latter county became a major stock-raising center and saw the founding of massive, industrial-style slaughterhouses (*frigoríficos*) for processing cattle on the hoof into chilled beef.[21]

The Araraquarense zone was named for the railroad that left the lower-Paulista county of Araraquara and cut northwest through São Paulo toward Mato Grosso, though it should be kept in mind that the zone, in its southern reaches, was also served by the Paulista and Dourado railroads. The Araraquarense's coffee trees had only begun to bear fruit around 1905, but the bonanza was already beginning. By 1920, eight years after the arrival of the railhead, the Araraquarense county of Rio Preto had 127,000 inhabitants (in 1886, by comparison, the entire zone had only 33,000 inhabitants). In the shadow of its coffee trees (sometimes quite literally), pluriculture was also emerging, as was a tiny industrial sector.[22]

The seventh zone is known as the upper Paulista or the Noroeste. Until 1912, it contained only one county, Bauru. Indeed, at the turn of the twentieth century, all points to the west of Bauru were relatively un-known and described as "lands inhabited by wild Indians" or as "unex-plored territory" on maps of São Paulo. This situation changed rapidly with the building of the Noroeste do Brasil Railroad from Bauru to the Paraná River during the years 1905–10. The Coroado and Kaingangue resisted as best they could, but railwaymen, settlers, and land developers were relentless in their war against the "savages" (*bugres*). Eventually, apparently well-meaning agents of the Indian Protection Service (SPI) effected a peace with the Kaingangue, but—following familiar patterns— their settlement of the nomadic tribesmen into villages served to further the interests of settlers and developers, the latter of whom had strong political ties and could manipulate the SPI to further benefit themselves. In the wake of pacification, the zone was flooded by settlers, with its population increasing 350 percent between 1920 and 1934.[23]

The settlement of the eighth zone, the upper Sorocabana, which stretches almost due west from Botucatu to the town of Presidente Epitácio, on the Paraná River, was very similar to that of the Noroeste. Like the Noroeste, this region was largely unexplored and its settlement was carried out at the expense of the native population. Also like the Noroeste, its settlement was brought by the expansion of the railroad rather than vice versa, as had been the case elsewhere. The expansion of the upper Sorocabana railroad, however, proceeded more slowly than that of the Noroeste: the railhead stood at Botucatu in 1889, Salto Grande in 1909, Presidente Prudente in 1919, and Presidente Epitácio in 1922.[24]

The lower Sorocabana is the ninth of São Paulo's subregions. Wedged between Paraná, the upper Sorocabana, the central zone, and the southern coast, it was not, strictly speaking, a pioneer zone. It had long been explored and was already settled, albeit sparsely. The lower Sorocabana railway reached Itararé, on the Paraná state line, in 1909, thereby connecting São Paulo with the rail routes of southern Brazil and giving the town of Itararé considerable strategic importance. The ninth zone has historically been characterized by mixed pastoral and agricultural production; coffee has never flourished there, as the climate is generally too cool, but cotton will grow in the lower Sorocabana and has at points been an important local crop.[25] During the early decades of the twentieth century its relative underpopulation and its status as São Paulo's gateway to southern Brazil gave the lower Sorocabana the feeling of a frontier, but it was that of a semi-permanent one that lacked the dynamism of the moving frontiers of the Noroeste and upper Sorocabana.

The tenth zone runs from the city of Santos down the coastline and through the south-central tip of the state. It is known as the southern littoral, though by 1929 it included three counties that were entirely landlocked (Xiririca, Iporanga, and Jacupiranga).[26] It was here that Portuguese colonization had begun, at São Vicente, in 1532.[27] As late as 1886, the census still identified the decadent port of Iguape as its most important population center. Thereafter, however, Santos overtook Iguape, benefiting from the spread of coffee trees throughout the western plateau, the fruits of which crossed its docks for export.[28] By the early 1920s, the county of Santos boasted 102,589 inhabitants (most of whom lived within the city limits), a bustling commercial exchange, large service and administrative sectors, and some industry, while Iguape had under 40,000 inhabitants, only 10 percent of whom lived in the town itself, where they might be startled to come upon one of the town's four automobiles while making their way to market. By this point, rice and manioc were king in Iguape, and the county's interior was home to a considerable number of immigrant small farmers, including two colonies of Japanese immigrants. The southern littoral zone, in short, with the exception of the area around Santos, was and to a considerable extent remains, quite literally, a backwater.[29]

The counties of the southern littoral, however, ranked with the most important population center in the state in one important regard. Together with the capital zone, the southern littoral formed the first of São Paulo's ten state electoral districts. Whether by accident or design, its backwater counties were thus perfectly positioned to serve as a counter to independent-minded urban voters, a point that was not lost on state-level power-holders.[30]

The Paraíba Valley, for its part, retained a degree of political importance out of proportion to its declining economic and demographic fortunes. It was the site of two of the state's ten electoral districts (the second, based in Taubaté, and the third, centered around Guaratinguetá) and was the only one of São Paulo's ten geographic zones to form its own federal electoral district.[31]

The fourth state electoral district overlapped nearly exactly with the portion of the central zone that runs west from the capital zone through Itu and Sorocaba to Angatuba and Capão Bonito. The historic city of Itu, where the state Republican Party had been founded in 1873, was nominally the seat of the fourth district, but from the early 1890s through 1930 real power in the zone rested in the former muleteering entrepôt of Itapetininga, home of the Prestes clan.[32]

The fifth electoral district was the largest in geographic terms and, by the mid-1920s, included the greatest number of individual counties. It included the two great frontier zones, the Noroeste and the upper Sorocabana, as well as the lower Sorocabana.[33]

The northeastern portion of the central zone made up the bulk of the sixth electoral district. The district's seat was Campinas, the coffee center that had briefly overtaken the state capital in population during the late nineteenth century, and it also included the railroad way-station and industrial town of Jundiaí.[34]

The seventh district overlapped more or less with the lower Mogiana subzone. Along with Moji Mirim, its seat, it included the town of Casa Branca (which boasted a normal school beginning in the 1910s) and several important coffee counties.[35]

The southern portion of the lower Paulista zone, including Limeira, Rio Claro, and Araras, made up the greatest part of the eighth electoral district. Limeira was the district seat, but its most important city was central-zone Piracicaba, the birthplace of many of São Paulo's most distinguished politicians of the late nineteenth century and the early twentieth.[36]

The ninth electoral district began to the west of the eighth electoral district and ran in a northwesterly direction to Novo Horizonte. It included the central portion of the lower Paulista zone and the southern half of the Araraquarense zone. Its seat was São Carlos, but it also included the important cities of Jaú and Araraquara.[37]

The last of the state's electoral districts, the tenth, was among its most crucial. It included nearly all of the upper Mogiana subzone (Ribeirão Preto was its seat), as well as the northern portions of the lower Paulista and the Araraquarense zones, including the cities of Barretos and Rio Preto.[38]

People

Regionalist dogma once held that São Paulo and, indeed, all of Brazil owed its progress to the special qualities of an intrepid "race of giants" known as *bandeirantes* who, following the settlement of São Paulo in the sixteenth century, explored the outer reaches of Brazilian national territory, tamed the land, and laid the basis for a new civilization.[39] In the first third of the twentieth century, would-be aristocrats attempting to tie their names to this narrative came up with terms like "paulista of 400 years" (*paulista de quatrocentos anos*) or "four-hundred-er" (*quatrocentão*) to describe their (largely imaginary) links to the tradition. Left unacknowledged in this tradition is that, from the very beginning of European colonization, immigrants, internal migrants, travelers, traders, and slaves made the greatest contributions to the settlement of the region and to the social formation of São Paulo in the late nineteenth century and the early twentieth.

The bandeirantes can be shown to have existed, to be sure. The descendants of Portuguese settlers, they roamed the interior of South America in search of riches. But patriotic historians tend to downplay the fact that enslaved Indians were their greatest source of wealth and the porters and bowmen that made these journeys of conquest possible. Moreover, in the regionalist lore of the early twentieth century, "the bandeirante is always white" (to paraphrase a northeastern saying of the same period), but many of them were in fact of mixed European (including Spanish, Italian, and German, in addition to Portuguese) and Indian parentage. These *mamelucos*, as the descendants of these unions were called, lived in a sociocultural milieu that was formed out of elements from both Europe and America in which the Indian language, Tupi, was universally used.[40]

rise, in the second cycle of regional growth, native paulistas made ~trikes of gold in Minas Gerais, but it was new Portuguese ₅rants, black slaves, and imported mining techniques that made the ₋nines prosper. And, though the demand brought by the mining boom made the area around Sorocaba a key center in the trade in livestock, in particular mules, the animals in question were raised by non-paulistas in the far south.[41]

Initial settlement of the areas that would become the upper Mogiana and the upper Sorocabana were likewise accomplished by non-paulistas, *mineiros* who raised livestock and grew staple crops in the years before the coffee boom reached the far north and far west of São Paulo.[42] Indeed, even prior to the massive changes heralded by abolition, the spread of coffee itself resulted from the interplay of geography and local entrepreneurship with capital, expertise, and, not least, enslaved labor brought to São Paulo from abroad and from elsewhere in Brazil.

Even the one development that more than any other single factor contributed to the regional preeminence and national standing of the state-capital-to-be was achieved by imperial fiat rather than by local initiative. The early-nineteenth-century founding of the law school on São Paulo's Largo de São Francisco gave the provincial city a stature all out of proportion to its size or socioeconomic importance (without which it is possible to imagine the provincial capital moving to Campinas in the 1870s or 1880s), making it a point of destination for aspiring elites from throughout newly independent Brazil and creating the basis for a local intelligentsia.[43]

Moving from the relatively distant past of the colonial and early national periods to the social formation of São Paulo in the late nineteenth century and the early twentieth, the state (as it was referred to administratively beginning in 1889) continued to be shaped by the movement of people, technology, and capital from within and without. This interaction of money, men, mechanics, and land forms the immediate background to the politics of the 1910s, 1920s, and 1930s.

Renato Jardim arrived on São Paulo's central plateau in 1889. In his memoir of the period, he describes himself as part of a larger exodus out of Rio de Janeiro's exhausted coffee counties and into what would be called the Mogiana zone. This exodus was not only made up of agriculturalists, it also included urban tradesmen and professionals seeking their fortunes. The newcomers were not only *fluminenses*, they were also Italians, Portuguese, Spaniards, paulistas from older zones, *nortistas*, and "brasileiros," as the Italian immigrants referred to Afro-Brazilians. With them came the "easy money" of the speculative bubble of the early 1890s.[44]

The degree of migration from elsewhere in Brazil, particularly by middling folks on the make like those described by Jardim, should not be slighted (many such outsiders, including Jardim, would become involved in politics in the years that followed), but the greatest part of the influx was made up of foreigners, who formed the principal labor force of the state's coffee plantations. Italians were the largest single group, followed by Spaniards and Portuguese. Central and eastern Europeans also came, joined later by Syro-Lebanese and Japanese.

These immigrants were brought to replace the former slaves, who were thought to be unsatisfactory workers and who had little desire to continue the work of slavery. The former slaves were thus largely excluded from the development of the *colonato*, a form of labor that combined wage work with profit-sharing and/or land-use incentives. While lucky immigrant workers (*colonos*) might save and one day buy a family-sized plot of land, there is little indication that Afro-paulistas in any numbers could have aspired to the same. The best that most Afro-paulistas could hope for in the countryside was work as hired hands (*camaradas*) or absorption into the semi-peasantry known as *caipiras*. They were likewise at a disadvantage in seeking employment in the city, where many joined the ranks of the urban poor.[45]

Immigrants were the sought-after laborers, in the countryside and in the city. On the state's plantations, resident immigrant families tended a set number of trees, weeding around them, and in return they were paid a small wage, given access to pasturage, and allowed to plant grains between the rows of coffee bushes. They were also responsible for the harvest, at which time they might expect a share of the yield or profits.[46] In the state capital and its satellites, immigrant labor formed the bulk of the industrial working class, particularly in textiles. Concentrated in outlying neighborhoods like Brás and Bom Retiro, or undesirable pockets closer in, like Bexiga, these men, women, and children labored long days in often unsafe conditions.[47]

Other immigrants were more fortunate. Some came from better-off backgrounds in their home countries and thus were able to bring a marketable skill or some savings with them to Brazil; others were able to save some money as colonos or in petty trading. These middling immigrants came to play important roles in the development of commerce and services in the cities and towns, as merchants, clerks, barbers, cobblers, tailors, seamstresses, and bakers, running corner stores, workshops, bars, trattorias, and other small businesses. The greatest of São Paulo's industrialists, Francisco Matarazzo, started out as a petty trader; this relatively fortuitous start, an undeniable ruthlessness, and a keen eye for the good connection, along with the more mundane values of hard work and thrift, made him an industrial giant.[48] It was many little men like the young Matarazzo who more than any other single group served to give the turn-of-the-century state capital its feeling of *italianità*.

Most of the population did not live in the state capital, or in any of the state's greater cities or larger towns for that matter. The majority of paulistas lived in the countryside. That this was true, however, does not imply rural stasis or uniformity. In addition to planters and colonos, the agricultural zones of the state saw a significant amount of investment in coffee by urban folks who practiced nonagricultural professions in cities and towns.[49] On the settled side of coffee's "hollow frontier" or on other lands unsuited for the planting of new bushes, state-sponsored colonization projects made for communities of immigrant small farmers, as in Jundiaí and Iguape, respectively.[50] Beyond the railhead, the ambitious might carve out small plots, while coffee agriculture's boom-and-bust cycles and harsh punishment of the land periodically made settled lands available.

The variety of farming that existed in São Paulo is clear in the language that was used to describe those individuals involved in agriculture. Simply put, there was more to rural society than planters (*fazendeiros*) and immigrant laborers (*colonos*). There were also hired hands (*camaradas*), who performed tasks such as fence building or clearing brush in return for cash payments, and semi-peasant cultivators (*caipiras, roceiros*), who eked out miserable existences in hilly, marginal areas located across the state, places like Bofete, Cunha, and Nazaré. There were also small farmers who held title to their lands, who were referred to as *sitiantes* or, more rarely (though the term seems to have gained greater currency in the 1930s), *pequenos lavradores*.

The terms *lavrador* and *lavoura* could themselves be used in different ways. Lavoura could refer generically to "agriculture"; it could refer to all those people involved in agriculture, from the mightiest absentee planter to the lowliest immigrant laborer; and it could be appropriated by certain groups, as by the self-appointed spokesmen of large-scale coffee planters, who sometimes referred to the planters as "the lavoura." Conversely, the term lavrador could refer to any landholding agriculturalist, in which case the umbrella term "lavradores" would include both fazendeiros and sitiantes, or it could refer to a landowning agriculturalist whose holdings did not justify the extravagant title of "fazendeiro" or the diminutive label of "sitiante."

In describing the social structure of São Paulo state as a whole, both rural and urban, contemporaries most often relied on a binary model that divided society into the "propertied classes" (*classes conservadoras*) and the "popular classes" (*classes populares*). The former were made up of landholding agriculturalists, industrialists, bankers, merchants, and rentiers, while the collar-and-tie middle class, tradesmen, urban laborers, and unpropertied folks of all stripes were labeled "populares." The position of liberal professionals in this schema was not always clear. In some contexts, they were placed in a category apart, as the "liberal classes" (*classes liberaes*). In others, high-status liberal professionals, in particular law professors and well-educated newspaper editors-proprietor, were counted among the classes conservadoras while lower-status liberal professionals (pharmacists, dentists, beat reporters) were lumped in with the populares.[51]

As the twentieth century began, however, it was becoming increasingly apparent that this binary system of categorization was no longer adequate for describing the socioeconomic realities of Brazilian society. As a result of this realization and the influence of foreign fashion, the now-familiar tripartite division of society into upper, middle, and lower classes was coming into increasing use.[52]

It is the latter way of writing about society that is used here, as has long been done to good effect by historians and other chroniclers of early-twentieth-century Brazil.[53] It scarcely needs adding that the use of this model to describe paulista society between the 1890s and the 1930s does not imply acceptance of tired teleologies, whether of Whig, modernizationist, or vulgar-Marxist provenance.

In this tripartite model, a tiny upper class of absentee planters, large merchants, prominent bankers, powerful industrialists, and grand rentiers stood at the apex of paulista society, with many of its members fitting two or more of these descriptions. This upper class also included higher-status liberal professionals with significant investments in agriculture, commerce, finance, industry, and urban real estate. Although it was quite an incestuous group, it was by no means one shut off to new blood. The newspaper publisher Julio Mesquita, born to modest Portuguese immigrants, qualified on the basis of good book learning and a better marriage, while Francisco Matarazzo's vast wealth opened nearly all doors for the former *carcamano*. Typically, members of this exclusive stratum lived in one of the more chic neighborhoods of the state capital

(Avenida Paulista and Higienópolis were favorites) or at least maintained a home somewhere in the city of São Paulo so that they might participate in the events sponsored by its social clubs. Some, however, spent a good deal of time in their country homes, where they could give themselves over to the simple pleasures of watching their wealth grow and lording over their country cousins.[54]

Immediately below the paulista upper class was an extremely heterogeneous intermediate group. At its upper ranks, this group included high-status liberal professionals of good backgrounds (typically law-degree holders, although medicine was gaining in respectability and some of the state's leading families had sons who were trained as physicians), who lived in the state capital and might socialize with and even marry into the upper class.

In interior counties, liberal professionals whose practices were purely local, resident planters and industrialists, local merchants and businessmen, and upper-level civil servants might count themselves as members of the municipal "élite" (in the sense that the word is used in the society pages), but when visiting the state capital they counted their change and did not grace the halls of the city's exclusive social clubs unless they had been invited by a member. They were men of the middle, and their compatriots in the outlying districts of the state capital—the industrialists of Itaquera, the officialdom of Osasco—occupied a similar social position.

In the state capital and other large, socially differentiated urban centers, there was another tier of middling folks. It included nonmanual government functionaries, clerks, bookkeepers, tellers, and other salaried employees; tailors, joiners, and other tradesmen and small businessmen; and lower-status liberal professionals such as schoolteachers, pharmacists, and dentists. As a group, these city folk possessed an agrarian analogue in the middling farmers of the paulista interior, boorish company, perhaps, but their peers in socioeconomic terms.

There was little difference, in terms of earnings or background, between the lower reaches of the intermediate group (such as commercial employees) and the upper reaches of the paulista working class, a stratum best represented by the state's railwaymen and the skilled laborers of the construction industry. Both of the latter two groups were composed of mostly literate, largely Brazilian-born men who shared a certain sense of social respectability. Severino Gonçalves Antunha, a labor militant in the port city of Santos, would later contrast the stevedores of his hometown (barefoot and given to drink was how he remembered them) with the skilled construction workers "who ate lunch on the job, had a coffee break, changed clothes for work, wore shoes" and "who had a lower percentage of illiterates," "read something or other," and thought of themselves as artisans.[55] Not coincidentally, it was workers like these who founded the local workingmen's federation, "with its night school, [and] its reading room, where anarchist books were found alongside didactic publications, [and] newspapers from São Paulo, from Rio de Janeiro, from Buenos Aires or from Barcelona."[56] Movement between these upper reaches of the paulista working classes and the lower rungs of the middle classes was not unheard of, nor was it always to one's financial benefit: when Jacob Penteado left his job as a skilled worker at a glassworks to become a postman (as a government employee, he was thus able to avoid military service), his earnings shrunk from 11$000 per day to 150$000 per month and he had to reign in the relatively high-living ways of an unmarried skilled worker for the frugal habits of a petty functionary.[57]

To be a part of the rank and file of the industrial working class was another matter. Work in textile factories, whether in the state capital and its suburbs, or in the central zone or the Paraíba Valley, was monotonous and potentially dangerous, and it was made still more hazardous and humdrum by ten- and twelve-hour shifts. It required little skill and could be done by women and children, which allowed industrialists to pay their employees even less. Literacy was not required either, nor was the ability to speak Portuguese, still less the sense of respectability that a railway-man or a skilled tradesman in construction might lay claim to. Indeed, such an evident sense of self-worth was likely to be a liability in the textile factories, in which abusive treatment by foremen was a common complaint.[58] The textile labor force of the plateau and the Paraíba Valley thus formed an equal-opportunity analogue to Severino Antunha's stevedores.[59]

It was once the accepted wisdom in the field that the lot of a laborer at the lowest reaches of the paulista urban working class was still marginally better (or less dreadful) than that of an immigrant coffee-tender in the interior. Now, however, the consensus seems to be that the colonato afforded many immigrant families the opportunity to acquire their own pieces of land, itself an indicator of significant social mobility, and gave them a degree of leverage vis-à-vis coffee planters, who found themselves competing with one another for colonos.[60] My own research on politics led me to much anecdotal evidence supporting the revisionist view: Italian-surnamed agriculturalists of all descriptions (including fazendeiros) were to be found in counties throughout the state, and the countryside witnessed a great deal of geographic mobility on the part of colonos themselves, who were able to move around in search of better pay and working conditions and who blurred the lines between rural labor, truck farming, and petty commerce.

There were still other ill-defined "types" at or near the bottom of paulista society, who often had limited interactions with the cash nexus. The caipira or roceiro, whose regular demands of the market (sometimes obtainable by barter) did not go much further than salt, matches, and cane liquor, was a case in point. A hired hand (camarada) on a given plantation or ranch, though he was paid by the task, might be a somewhat respected figure (he might have rights to a small plot of land where he or his family raised subsistence crops or even some livestock of their own), but the camarada could also be a rural itinerant who took care of jobs for which colonos were deemed too valuable or that colonos considered to be beneath them.

In the cities, an uncounted number of men and women performed similarly demeaning tasks. Scant research exists on these street sweepers, trash collectors, porters, washerwomen, and peddlers, although a recent monograph makes it clear that many if not most of them would likely have been considered non-white.[61]

Necessarily static, this sketch of São Paulo's social structure overlooks the degree of movement between city, town, and countryside. It also leaves aside the question of self-identification on the basis of class, occupation, religion, ethnicity, region, and nation, themes that will reemerge, to a greater or lesser extent, in the chapters that follow.

Among the groups or networks that bridged two or more of the social strata laid out above, one does deserve mention here (another such network, the structure of state politics, receives ample consideration in the following chapter, and the network-producing practices of patronage are a staple of the literature). I referred to it above as the state's intelligentsia. It was composed of men and women (salonnière Olívia da Silva Guedes Penteado was one, as was Maria Lacerda de Moura) who belonged to "the world of writings, read and produced, a territory-less purer part of [Brazil], a 'republic of letters,'" or even to "the lettered city" of São Paulo.[62] The intelligentsia's two great poles were the São Paulo Law School and the great and powerful newspapers of the state capital, although the intelligentsia as a whole encompassed all of the state's institutions of higher learning and nearly all of the publications put out throughout the state (by the 1920s, one could find at least a four-page tabloid in nearly every corner of São Paulo). The most common figures in the state's intelligentsia were the degree holder (*bacharel*), the student (*bacharelando*), and the journalist (*redator, revisor,* or reporter), who was himself often but not always the holder or pursuer of a professional degree. Their importance, in a society in which formal learning was the privilege of a minority, cannot be underestimated. Like their counterparts elsewhere, a "commitment to . . . 'modernity' defined in light of the experience of Western Europe," the United States, and, by the mid-1910s, Argentina, often put these types "at odds with their direct environment."[63] Many quickly found that a comfortable sinecure and the pleasures of private life more than made up for this tension, while others hid behind Parnassian poses or retreated into arty bohemianism, but some sought to reconcile the imported ideals of North Atlantic modernity with the realities of twentieth-century Brazil, as state builders or as would-be reformers.

2 A Republic of Layers

On 15 November 1889, Emperor of Brazil Pedro II was overthrown by military coup d'etat, ending eight decades of New World monarchical rule and setting the stage for republican government. The coup was welcomed by political leaders throughout São Paulo as republicans of long standing and erstwhile supporters of the old regime scrambled for positions and power. It was also cheered by some ordinary folks in the cities, *populares* in the state capital and some of the lower sort in Santos, who for different and even contradictory reasons saw the proclamation of the republic as something to be celebrated.[1]

The new regime displayed marked continuities with the old. For some paulistas, these holdovers were to be regretted. Like the long-standing republican Martinho da Silva Prado Júnior, who remarked that the first republican administration was "nothing more than a government of compadres," these observers soon found themselves bemoaning the new state of affairs: this was not the Republic of their dreams.[2] For others the continued commitment to order, economic growth, and social stability—clear in Bernardino de Campos's assertion that "the current regime provides the State [of São Paulo] the most ample and efficacious elements of happiness and prosperity, in full enjoyment of a splendid civilization, as long as its activity develops peacefully"—was to be lauded.[3]

In its structure and practice, the new political system was characterized by important continuities with the old. With federalism enshrined in the constitution of 1891 and civilian rule established with the inauguration of Prudente de Moraes in 1894, patronage and personalism trumped ideology in matters administrative and political.[4] The Paulista Republican Party (PRP), on even the most casual examination, came to be defined by these concerns. As one newspaperman explained, "where there are local disagreements, it is because some are 'tibiricistas' and others 'lacerdistas'[;] that is, by different paths they will all lead to

Rome."[5] On the Roman road, these pilgrims would make use of force and fraud in ways that reprised the political playacting of the empire.[6]

São Paulo's political culture was defined by ambivalence and the potential for conflict, by tensions between formal adherence to liberal, republican ideals and the continued resonance of more deeply rooted values. If republican language was used by some contenders as cover for baser motives, other political figures took these ideas very seriously; for these men, republicanism, liberalism, and their application abroad offered a vision of a Brazil as it might be. Ruy Barbosa's presidential bid of 1909–10—celebrated as the "Civilianist Campaign"—offers a window onto this political culture and its contradictions.

Structure and Practice

By the first decade of the twentieth century, one may discern the essential outlines of the republican state as it existed in São Paulo. As under the empire, clientelistic concerns and personalistic ties formed a "connecting web" that stretched from the homes of humble functionaries in the backcountry to the halls of power in the national capital of Rio de Janeiro. Social standing, employment, administrative favors, local improvements, control over land and labor, and, not least, "prestige" were the knots that gave this web its strength and coherence.[7]

But while the imperial system had its ultimate arbiter in the person of the emperor, the republican system had no single, central authority to whom all other political figures owed their allegiance, and it is at this point that the metaphor of a single, unitary web begins to unravel. To be sure, republican presidents—most notably Francisco de Paula Rodrigues Alves, an imperial counselor in a former political life—attempted to claim the prerogatives held by Pedro II, but even the most successful of these attempts lasted only a presidential term, in which the head of state had to contend with inter-regional rivalries, factionalism within the Republican Party of his home state, and ambitious military men with interests of their own. Added to these concerns were the lesser nuisances that leaders lacking a firm claim to a divine right to rule had to contend with: ridicule in the pages of an ever-growing periodical press, criticism from liberal gadflies, and the challenges posed by country folk who were by turns indifferent or openly hostile to the republican state's avowed mission of modernization, secularization, and standardization.

The state executive—who also bore the title "President," indicating the extent of federalist influence on Brazil's new political order—came closer to approximating the imperial ideal of absolute authority, within a more modest jurisdiction, but his rule was also bounded by his tenure in office and circumscribed by the competing claims of factions within his own party. He too faced critics in the press and public square. And even in São Paulo—the "model state," in the eyes of its boosters—were to be found primitive rebels: millenarians, brigands, and the odd Calabrian extortion racket.[8]

At the local level, the structure of republican politics would have been more immediately familiar to an imperial-era Rip Van Winkle. Here the most meaningful figures remained "political bosses" (*chefes políticos*), county or district or neighborhood notables who claimed the right to rule on the basis of followings near at hand and dispensations from on high.

These two figures, the sitting state president and the reigning local boss, ostensibly occupied positions in two distinct hierarchies. The president was a government executive, standing atop a formally constituted system of checks and balances. He would have identified himself as a "statesman" (*estadista*); given how low the bar has been set in other times and places, there seems little reason to begrudge him the honor. An incumbent chefe político was a party man, the local representative of and delegate to the PRP, which was in turn headed by an executive committee bringing together the most influential state-level chieftains.

These two hierarchies—of government, on the one hand, and of party, on the other—were theoretically discrete but deeply interwoven in the day-to-day practice of politics. As one observer remarked, the PRP executive committee, "in the eyes of the electorate, is the government."[9] Although not a formal member of the committee, the state president was in fact the preeminent party boss during his tenure in office, making him "the supreme administrator and the supreme chefe político."[10] At the same time, though members of the executive committee did not occupy formal positions in the state president's cabinet, each of them had a hand in the disbursement of the largesse it controlled.[11] At the county level, party and government were often even more difficult to distinguish, as local *perrepista* bosses not infrequently took the position of municipal executive (*prefeito*) for themselves.

Complicating matters further was the existence of rival claimants for power at both levels. At the topmost tier of the republican political system, there were near-constant schisms in which one group of chieftains, who in times of relative concord would themselves be contenders for positions in the executive branch of government and on the PRP executive committee, rebelled against the state president and the rump Republican Party. Even in the absence of open, avowed conflict, rivalries between state-level leaders (particularly between individual members of the executive committee) were ubiquitous: power, positions, public works—even prestige—were finite goods that in the right hands would increase one's fortune and following; in the wrong hands, they might result in the chipping away of the same to someone else's benefit.

At the local level, resources were scarcer still. In counties, districts, and neighborhoods throughout São Paulo, aspiring claimants to local power were to be found. Even as "outs," deprived of municipal office holding and of extra-municipal recognition on the part of the executive committee, they were recognized as political bosses—as chefes políticos—by their own followers and as potential challengers by incumbents; many outs also enjoyed informal ties to recognized state-level leaders. Amid a statewide schism, a particular group of local outs might be something like a shadow government, prepared to take control of their corner of São Paulo should their side end up on top. For that matter, the reigning group in a particular county might side with state-level leaders opposing the rump PRP; municipal incumbents acting in alliance with state-level outs were not as rare as one might think. Also not to be discounted was the call for municipal independence, as growing communities sought status commensurate with their size and importance, status that inevitably would mean a loss of power and resources for the reigning boss or bosses of the established county seat.

The distances—physical and otherwise—that separated contenders of purely local purview and the state-level potentates who determined government policy and distributed the party's favors were taken up by regional chieftains and official emissaries. Regional bosses might enjoy a good deal of power of their own and aspire to a seat on the PRP executive committee for themselves, while other intermediaries (most police delegates and many state legislators) were go-betweens who served at the pleasure of others.[12]

These features—layers of powerbrokers and placemen, shifting patterns of incumbency and opposition, county governments constantly increasing in number, the formal hierarchy of the executive branch of state government, all of them overlapping and intersecting with state and local party machines—defined the political system of São Paulo in the early twentieth century, bridging cities and towns, littoral and interior, centuries-old settlements and frontiers beyond the railhead.[13] It was a system that was unstable in its parts but remarkably resilient as a whole. A statesman might fall or get fed up, but there was always another eager to take his place. Particular chefes políticos might retire or get rubbed out, but each one was replaceable.

Joseph L. Love has given the most thorough accounting to date of the state-level leaders who occupied high government office and served on the PRP executive committee in the party's heyday. Amid this set was a far smaller group—an elite within an elite—containing nearly all of those leaders who had to be taken seriously in any political calculus regarding São Paulo, whether they were in or out of government.[14] Like Love's broader elite, this small group was made up of well-connected individuals who, if they were not born into the topmost reaches of paulista society, quickly found their way there.[15] Jorge Tibiriçá, a planter and magnate who bore the envied distinction of having been born and educated in Europe, was a "historic" republican (a republican under the empire). After serving as state president from 1904 to 1908, Tibiriçá enjoyed a longer continuous tenure on the PRP executive committee than any of his peers.[16] Francisco Glycerio de Cerqueira Leite was also a "historic" republican, one of the few paulistas actually in on the plotting that brought down Pedro II. His influence in counties throughout the state endured right down to his death in 1916, despite nearly constant conflicts with his fellow party chiefs and sporadic periods of ostracism in which he was deprived of a seat on the executive committee.[17] Antônio de Lacerda Franco was another chieftain of lasting influence; strongest in the eighth electoral district, but influential across the state, he sat on the executive committee for more total years than Glycerio, Tibiriçá, or anyone else.[18] Fernando Prestes de Albuquerque—the greatest party boss of the fourth electoral district—served fewer years on the executive committee, but he also served as state president once and state vice-president twice. In addition, his son Júlio served his own term as state president and would have served as national president had outside events not intervened. These were considerable accomplishments for a self-described "farmer" and self-taught country lawyer.[19]

Fernando Prestes, Lacerda Franco, Francisco Glycerio, and Jorge Tibiriçá were all "historic" or "pure" republicans (*republicanos dos tempos da propaganda* in the patriotic cant of the era), but a more checkered political past was no barrier to success in the PRP, as demonstrated by the careers of the Guaratinguetá-born brothers Francisco de Paula Rodrigues Alves and Virgílio Rodrigues Alves. Leaders of the Conserva-

·tive Party under the empire, the two men were born again under the republic, laying the way for careers that would make "rodriguesalvismo" (sometimes rendered as "alvismo") synonymous with political power in the Paraíba Valley (the second and third electoral districts) and take them and theirs to seats on the PRP executive committee and in the state and federal legislatures. Francisco was particularly successful, finding his way to the state presidency twice and the national presidency once.[20]

One of the ways in which contenders came to join this elite group of men was by establishing themselves as regional bosses. Indeed, barring upset or obstinacy, a powerful regional chieftain was bound to be invited to serve on the PRP executive committee eventually. Allying himself with his fellow *itapetininganos* in the Prestes clan, Ataliba Leonel—an odd blend of the backwoodsman and the bacharel—established himself as a regional boss in the fifth district in the early twentieth century; not long thereafter he acceded to a seat on the committee.[21] Olavo Egydio de Souza Aranha was made boss of the state capital while Manoel Joaquim de Albuquerque Lins, a friend, ally, and affinal kinsman (both men married women of the Souza Queiroz family), was state president (1908–12), earning an executive committee seat in 1916; he lost both positions in 1924–25, but his successor as citywide kingpin, Sylvio de Campos, took a seat on the executive committee a few years later.[22] The banker, planter, and coffee merchant Vicente de Paula Almeida Prado established himself in the ninth district at around the same time that Ataliba Leonel did in the fifth (one writer described Vicente as the "'tutú' da zona"); his failure to accede to the executive committee appears to have stemmed from his taking the wrong side in the statewide schism of 1923–24.[23] The greatest of regional chieftains, a force to be reckoned with in the tenth electoral district for three decades (years in which he repeatedly defied the rump PRP leadership), Joaquim da Cunha Diniz Junqueira turned down a seat on the executive committee on more than one occasion. Whether at home in Ribeirão Preto or visiting his *palacete* in the state capital, he let state-level leaders come to him.[24]

Below regional chieftains like Joaquim da Cunha stood the thousands of local bosses who manned and maintained this system from its origins under the empire through its renascence in the 1930s. These county, district, and neighborhood notables await their prosopographer, but the careers and characteristics of a few outstanding ones are worthy of mention.

In large, prosperous municipalities with suitably comfortable county seats, local bosses tended to be men of great wealth, substance, and standing. In Ribeirão Preto, Joaquim da Cunha's greatest rival was the German-born "King of Coffee" Francisco Schmidt, who from humble origins became the greatest single coffee planter in Brazil down to his death in 1924.[25] When coffee was king in Rio Claro, a pair of planters—Joaquim Augusto Salles and Marcello Schmidt (no relation)—faced off against one another there as well.[26] In nearby Araraquara, the planter Antônio Joaquim de Carvalho was dominant for much of the 1890s, years in which the national careers of his law school classmates Prudente de Moraes and Manuel Ferraz de Campos Salles were on the rise. His own career did not end as well (he was shot and killed by a political opponent in 1897), but his sons continued to make the Carvalho name an important one in local politics into the 1940s.[27]

In Presidente Prudente, on the upper Sorocabana frontier, the rustic town fathers Francisco de Paula Goulart and José Soares Marcondes (a local pioneer and a land developer, respectively) fended for local power for much of the 1920s, with each side attempting to curry favor with the state government and power brokers in the PRP. This contest between goulartistas and marcondistas reprised struggles between frontier rivals that had played out up the line in Campos Novos a dozen years earlier.[28]

Back in the center, in urbanizing, industrializing São Bernardo, power was disputed by Saladino Cardoso Franco, the son of a large local landholder, and the members of the Flaquer family, headed by the state senator and PRP founder José Luiz Flaquer, a medical doctor and investor in real estate, until his death in 1924.[29] In Osasco, similarly on the outskirts of the state capital, though within its municipal limits, rivalries between the local businessmen Delfino Siqueira and Júlio de Andrade Silva (described, respectively, as a "capitalist" and an "industrialist") defined local politics in the late 1910s and through the 1920s.[30]

Within the city itself, scores of neighborhood notables and would-be ward bosses jostled for influence. In still-proud Santa Ifigênia, the local boss and proprietor Estanislau Pereira Borges served as the public face of the PRP; he, in turn, represented the neighborhood on the city council for the greater part of the 1910s.[31] Mário do Amaral, a lawyer, ran politics in Cambuci for more than a dozen years, serving as its representative on the city council beginning in 1908; even after his election to the state legislature fourteen years later Amaral continued to dabble in neighborhood politics.[32] Bom Retiro's José Molinaro was perhaps the most infamous neighborhood boss during these years. An Italian immigrant, Molinaro started out as a coachman, later emerging as a leader among his colleagues, then a leader of the city's drivers and the president of the Centro dos Motoristas. Dispensing favors from the Centro's hall and over pasta dinners (*macarronadas*) at his home, using force and the threat of force elsewhere, by 1927 he claimed five thousand loyal voters in his home district and the power to elect his own representatives to the city council.[33]

Elsewhere, in counties forsaken by the railroads and untouched by urbanization, the scepter of command fell to less impressive types. Joaquim Augusto da Silva, a folk healer and, according to one observer, "the smartest man in [his] village," ran the county of Araçariguama for fifty years down to his death in 1921.[34] In Redenção, boss status passed from father to young son, who fresh from secondary school was given a job as a country schoolmaster in order to support himself and his family.[35] Heading the PRP in Ubatuba was a self-proclaimed *doutor* by the name of Ernesto Gomes de Oliveira. Supposedly the only local willing "to lend himself . . . to the farce," at one point he was rewarded with a paying job as "Acting Disinfector" of his coastal hometown.[36]

Even in poor counties, however, the local boss was not necessarily a country bumpkin or an unlettered hanger-on. Cunha, straddling the upcountry between the Paraíba Valley and the Rio de Janeiro coast, was led for decades by Alfredo Casemiro da Rocha, a medical doctor who had come to São Paulo from Bahia in the 1870s and established himself professionally and politically, in the latter case as an abolitionist, a republican, and an ally of Francisco Glycerio. Despite several handicaps (a base in one of the state's poorest counties, Francisco Glycerio's frequent forays into opposition, and a complexion several shades darker than most republican leaders), this cultured, urbane politician held a chair in the state legislature, first in the lower house, then in the senate, nearly continuously from 1907 to 1930, years in which he was also the recognized boss of Cunha.[37]

One's claim to "boss" status depended upon maintaining a following. For Casemiro da Rocha, this meant keeping up a clientele among the townsfolk and dirt farmers of Cunha: to key figures among the former went the county's few government jobs, to the latter went small, inexpensive favors, starting with medical attention from the good doctor when he was in the county seat.[38] At the other end of the spectrum, Ribeirão Preto's Joaquim da Cunha counted on the fealty of his plantation administrators and laborers, on the support of fellow planters in the Junqueira clan (who had their own clienteles close at hand), on the obedience of his home county's federal, state, and municipal employees, and on the cooperation of further agents, allies, and underlings: "his" representatives in municipal and state government, "his" lieutenants on the local PRP directorate, "his" journalists.[39]

In places as otherwise different as Ribeirão Preto and Cunha, family connections were crucial to establishing and extending clientage. To these connections—consanguineal and affinal—were added ties of fictive kinship, which were particularly important in areas of more recent settlement, where families were relatively smaller and less densely interconnected.[40] Frontier zones likewise saw private land-development companies and claim-jumping gangs (categories that were often difficult to distinguish from one another) play important roles in the formation of political clienteles.[41]

A key figure throughout the state was the *cabo eleitoral* (literally, "electoral corporal"), a kind of sergeant-at-arms who mediated between political bosses and rank-and-file voters. As a broker, in a very real sense, he often received a cash commission, but he might already form part of a boss's clientele in another regard (as an employee, tenant, or other dependent), in which case getting out the vote was already part of his accepted duties.[42] The cabo could also be an aspiring boss, in which case bringing friends, family members, and other followers to the polls was a way of proving one's usefulness. At the early stages of his career, José Molinaro was one of these aspiring get-out-the-vote men.[43]

The stakes for ordinary voters, for followers of men like Molinaro and their counterparts throughout the state, were fairly clear. They could be very high (a failure to come out to the polls could cost someone his livelihood) or they could be rather low (a meal, something to drink, a bit of cash).[44] Oftentimes the two types of inducement were combined: a colono, camarada, or other laborer might come out on the orders of his boss and receive a pair of shoes as his prize.[45]

The material stakes for leaders were of another order. They were seldom matters of life or death (even the most desperate local boss was not about to starve), but they could involve a great deal of money and power. Control over county government meant control over municipal employment, public works, and taxation, to say nothing of the opportunities it afforded for graft. Until 1921, in the absence of a state-appointed judge, local incumbents also enjoyed judicial power, including over the registration of land ownership, a key prize in frontier areas in particular.[46] Up to 1906, county police delegates served at the behest, and oftentimes at the expense, of the local chefe, and even after the modernizing, professionalizing reforms of that year, a well-connected boss could make sure that the police delegate (a law school graduate who was nominated and paid by the executive branch of the state government) was someone with whom he could see eye to eye.[47] Indeed, important county bosses controlled all state and federal employment in their fiefs (including the offices of state and federal tax collectors).[48] Connections further up the trough also allowed local and regional chieftains—aspiring and incumbent—to bid for state and federal public works: a school, a road, a railway spur line, each of which would bring with it local jobs, which could be distributed among family and friends or used to enlarge one's circle of followers. Roads and railways, in particular, would also boost local land values and lower the costs of bringing goods to market.[49] Until its disbandment in 1918, it was customary for a chefe of some standing to receive a patent in the National Guard, as lieutenant, captain, major, lieutenant-colonel, or colonel; along with gold braids and an honorific, the patent brought the power to shield one's followers from service in the regular army.[50]

County politics was also a springboard from which to launch a further political career. Francisco Fulano, a composite character—a town father, planter, and colonel in the National Guard, in full enjoyment of all of the perquisites of local power—might aspire to more for his son, grooming him for the formal education that he missed, capped off by a few years at the São Paulo Law School. With his degree in hand, Dr. Francisco Fulano Júnior (only those closest to him still called him "Chico" and he had opted for "Júnior" over the traditional "Filho" in his teens) might be named police delegate or state's attorney for his home county, then elected—by whatever means necessary—county councilman to start with, then picked as prefeito, then voted into the state legislature. Further climbing might yield a position in the state president's cabinet, a seat in the national legislature, or even a spot on the PRP executive committee.

At each of these levels were further stakes: favors, stipends, and sweetheart deals. Political influence afforded the sons of prominent men coveted spots in the state's most prestigious educational institutions, after which, alongside other fortunate sons, they would find their way into cushy posts in the various branches of government service.[51] Political standing brought with it administrative stipends, bank loans, government contracts, investment opportunities, and invitations to serve on the boards of utility companies and commercial, financial, and industrial concerns.[52] Municipal councilmen drew no salaries (though no one went wholly unrewarded), but their counterparts in the state and federal legislatures were well compensated.[53] Senate seats were particularly sought after: according to legislation passed in 1905, state senators served nine-year terms, during which they were expected to do little more than appear at their most august and draw prebends that were the envy of their countrymen.[54]

These stakes were contested through elections, which took a number of forms. Of the different types, regular municipal elections were the most straightforward and, in some ways, the most important: held every three years, they decided who would hold power locally and served as the starting point for further political careers.[55] All other elections complemented municipal contests; their practical outcomes (who would win the state presidency, for example) were seldom in doubt, but they did offer local and regional contenders the opportunity to demonstrate their relative strength and thus "prove" their usefulness to the state-level leaders of party and government.[56] Cases in which the actual results were decisive (in the sense of deciding which candidates "won") came during unsettled times, typically amid statewide schisms. However, even in these cases the question by election day was not whether the breakaway group or emergent faction would defeat the PRP rump outright; it was whether it would win the right to "minority representation" in the legislature.[57]

Electioneering began with the process of voter registration. In theory, the constitution of 1891 guaranteed voting rights to literate men aged twenty-one and older who were born in Brazil or had become naturalized Brazilian citizens, excluding only enlisted men, regular clergy, and the idle poor. In practice, registering to vote was no simple matter. Prospective voters began the process by presenting themselves to a board composed of the district judge, the county's four largest resident taxpayers, and three citizens elected by the sitting members of the municipal government together with an equal number of also-rans from the last municipal election. Requests had to be accompanied by proof of age and proof of at least two months' residence in the county (the latter could be provided by a judge, a police delegate, or in a document signed by "three property-holding citizens"); prospective voters were also asked to prove their literacy by inscribing their name, marital status, parentage, place of birth, age, profession, and place of residence on the electoral roll. The requirement of two months' residence was later increased to four, and beginning in 1916 prospective voters were also asked to provide proof of employment or income providing for their subsistence. If these requirements were met, petitioners could be provided a certificate of registration.[58]

This process provided ample opportunity for manipulation. The sheer difficulty of assembling the requisite documentation (at one point, proof of residence for non-homeowners entailed providing two months' worth of rental receipts, accompanied by proof that the signature on the receipts was that of the building's owner or his legal representative) alone mitigated against broad registration; the difficulty of subsequently transferring one's registration along with one's residence meant that voters often traveled to exercise the suffrage.[59] The resulting small electorate recommended itself for ease of manipulation; in Itápolis, for example, local outs accused their incumbent foes of allowing the local electorate to shrink, "supposing a smaller electorate easier to control."[60]

The electoral board itself could become an instrument by which local power-holders controlled the size and composition of the electorate. In Ribeirão Preto in the early twentieth century, attempts by county incumbents—who at that point opposed Joaquim da Cunha—to enroll voters proved unsuccessful, despite the recognition of the PRP executive committee. Joaquim da Cunha's influence over the members of the electoral board proved crucial, as they came and went in an "incessant and well-directed coming and going," depriving it of the required quorum.[61]

Elsewhere, the judges that presided over boards of registration colluded with local incumbents. Discriminating judges like these could hold up the registration of potential troublemakers and ease the way for the kind of voters local bosses could depend on.[62]

Following a registration process that could be corrupt, compromised, or prohibitively time consuming, the registered voter was prepared to vote in the next county, state, or federal election. If he chose to venture out to the polls (many did not: the number of registered voters, though low, remained far higher than the reported number of voters throughout these years),[63] it would mean taking part in a process that could be equally daunting, as well as potentially dangerous.

By law, each group of 250 voters were to have a designated polling place in a public building chosen by the municipal councilmen. In practice, it was not uncommon to have one polling place accommodate voters for an entire county or district of the peace, and to have that polling place be the home of the incumbent political boss; in one particularly telling case, Iguape's incumbents moved a polling station from the home of a party loyalist to the local jail in order to further intimidate their opponents.[64] The polling board, seated at some remove from the assembled electorate, would call out voters' names, one by one, in the order they appeared on the electoral roll. His name called, a voter would approach the table at which the board was assembled, where he would be

asked to produce his registration certificate, sign the registry of attendance, and cast his ballot.[65] Voting was to have taken place from ten
o'clock in the morning to no later than seven o'clock in the evening.
When voting ceased, the polling board was to count the ballots, note the
results in a bound volume, and post them publicly.[66]

Actually bringing out voters took a number of forms. Often, agricultural laborers were simply led to the polls by their employer or taskmas-
ter, hence the term *eleitor de cabresto* ("bridled voter").[67] Factory workers
and public functionaries were marched out in a similar fashion; the state
capital had no lack of "bridled voters."[68] Elsewhere, the spectacle of the
election itself might pass for entertainment.[69] But even in these cases,
leaders were expected to provide something in return. Meals and liba-
tions were standard fare on election days throughout the state, with
better-off bosses providing kegs of beer for their followers.[70]

There were as many ways to corrupt the process of voting as there
were to bring voters out to the polls. The methods used varied by county
and depended on the type of election (whether a special election held to
fill a single legislative seat gone vacant, which usually went uncontested,
or a hard-fought municipal contest).

The confidentiality of the vote was assured, according to the relevant
legislation, because the ballot produced by the voter (it could be hand-
written or printed and was often cut out from a newspaper) was folded
over or sealed in an envelope. In practice, however, there were countless
ways to guarantee that elections went as planned. One of the most
common and least sophisticated of these methods was for a chefe, cabo,
or member of the polling board to hand the voter a ballot and watch him
deposit it in the ballot box, following which the voter might return his
certificate of registration back to the boss who held on to it year-round.[71]
A slightly more sophisticated method was to print up visually distinctive
ballots and envelopes, so that onlookers might confirm that voters were
voting the right way.[72] Still another was to use a ballot box that was
sufficiently narrow that ballots could be removed in precisely the reverse
order in which they had been deposited and then matched with the
relevant names in the registry of attendance.[73]

Another way of rigging elections was to employ mobile voters, known
as *phosphoros* (*fósforos* in today's orthography), who used illicit certificates to vote fraudulently, often in various locations, a practice that had
existed since the empire and was used in both urban and rural areas.[74] As
a PRP executive committee member and a regional boss, Antônio de
Lacerda Franco was famed for his use of phosphoros, his henchmen

bringing "veritable levies" to his old home county of Araras in order to prevent the local opposition from taking control of town hall.[75]

Some tactics allowed chefes to dispense with ballots altogether. The simplest and most famous of these practices was known as voting *a bico de pena*, or *a Mallat*, euphemisms for the forgery of results.[76] In some cases, it was a vital means to reverse an electoral outcome that would have proven prejudicial to local power-holders and their state-level patrons.[77] In others it was adopted for its sheer simplicity and to obviate the effort and expense that an election would otherwise require. In Cosmópolis, then a submunicipal district of Campinas, Arthur Nogueira, an "intransigent perrepista chief," expressed surprise at the elaborate preparations made for elections elsewhere: "Why so much noise and so much busyness? Why doesn't Lacerda do as I do here? No ballot boxes, nor ballots, everything calm, perfect, in order." When election days came, Nogueira would send a subordinate around to gather signatures in the registry of attendance, following which he drew up the election results at home.[78] In Ribeirão Preto, Joaquim da Cunha employed a similar technique during uncontested elections to fill vacancies in the legislature, writing up the results "back at home," rather than summoning his voters.[79]

Bico de pena lent itself particularly well to the creation of the paulista equivalent of "rotten boroughs," poor, underpopulated counties that in the days following an election could be counted on to provide the requisite number of votes, once a rough estimate of that number was possible. Under this system, votes "from the live zone of the State" were thus swamped by back-country bico de pena.[80] The "forgotten counties" of Xiririca, Iporanga, Iguape, and Cananéia performed the "rotten borough" function particularly well, their "electoral colleges . . . only revealing the result of the election after the Executive Committee tells them how many votes it needs."[81] Xiririca, in particular, became "celebrated in the annals of state politics for the fraud [that] saved official candidates."[82]

When fraud was insufficient to assure a desired outcome—or was feared to be insufficient in the run-up to an election—further means might be found. Often, the suggestion of violence was enough to prevent potential spoilers from coming out to the polls, so local chefes políticos became artful rumormongers, spreading tales of police violence in order to frighten their opponents. In 1919, for example, the families of opposition figures fled São Bento de Sapucaí for Minas Gerais when faced with "promises of tumult" on election day.[83]

In cases when rumor was deemed insufficient, other means were found. The threat of military recruitment was one such means, the threat of increased taxes another.[84] In Santos in 1901, the intimidation and jailing of opposition voters in the settlements of Cubatão and Bocaina led members of the local faction to sit out municipal elections.[85] At the turn of the century—the "time in which sr. Rodrigues Alves was [state] president and sr. Lacerda Franco was boss"—one newspaper alleged that the mere "departure of a police delegate accompanied by [troops of the militarized state police], for a locale in the interior, was enough to make oppositionists return home and barricade their doors."[86] Years later, the Salesópolis chefe José Antônio Capistrano used a group of "Italian thugs" to accomplish the same end, with seventy of his opponents' voters—frightened "country folk"—staying home on election day.[87]

When valor trumped discretion or the contending sides were too closely matched, violence became a necessary part of politics. Some election cycles were relatively peaceful, others bloody by the standard of the day, but all witnessed some political violence aimed at establishing control over the polls and preventing rivals from voting.[88]

Both aims were among the calculations that led to the state's bloodiest single instance of election-day violence, a 1922 massacre in the upper Sorocabana county of Palmital stemming from a split between local perrepistas. On the one side stood José Machado, a party man who had moved to Palmital from Campos Novos, on the other the local "boss of longer standing," Cândido "Candinho" Dias Mello. By late 1922, drawing upon support from his connections in the state capital, Machado had achieved the recognition of the PRP executive committee, while Candinho's group remained in control of municipal government. It was in this context that the two factions, "both strong . . . and both with [the] lamentable ambition to rule," readied themselves for the municipal elections that would determine which side would control county government for the next three years and have the best case for support from the center. On the morning of 14 December, as voters set out for the polls across the state, the machadistas were ambushed by Candinho's hired guns. José Machado was likely the first to die; his brother Martiniano and his son João died in the street along with him; a total of six men were killed that morning and a seventh died from his wounds a few days later.[89]

The massacre at Palmital was an extreme case. Indeed, it was so extreme that it proved self-defeating, at least at the local level, in that Candinho was jailed and tried (he never returned to power in Palmital).[90] It nevertheless demonstrates the lengths to which political contenders thought that they could and indeed *should* go in the pursuit of local power. Violence was accepted—if not always acknowledged—as forming part of the standard repertoire of practices by which political power was maintained and exchanged. These practices, in turn, interacted with a complex welter of beliefs, attitudes, and symbols that political players large and small struggled to situate themselves among.

Political Culture

In elaborating a homegrown republican tradition, paulistas drew upon classical precedent, more recent but no less exotic examples from abroad, and shared understandings of progress and civilization that drew deeply from the common dreams of nineteenth-century liberals, all of which were subject to the influences of Brazil's own nineteenth-century traditions. The explicit aim of many of the leaders involved was to create a common language of republicanism and a common body of cultural symbols; the resulting political culture made for an additional sphere of conflict between patrimonial values and constitutional precepts, local privileges and cosmopolitan aspirations, personal fealty and individual independence—in short, some might argue—between order and progress.

If there is only one key to understanding political discourse in São Paulo from the nineteenth century through the mid-twentieth century, it is the term "prestige" (*prestígio*). Prestige was a word that conflated personal honor with political following and community standing with extra-municipal influence, a word that could be used in noun form or as a verb, as in *prestigiar* (to esteem, honor, or follow) or *desprestigiar* (to dishonor or otherwise discredit).

In providing a listing of local political figures, their "social position," and their "political worth," a perrepista in Guaratinguetá naturally drew on this kind of language. Heading his list was a "Capitalist" who controlled "100 to 120" voters, "one of the most prestigious chieftains of Alvismo . . . very well-connected in the neighboring towns."[91] Similarly, Vicente Prado's following in Jaú was described as "made up of the most prestigious families of the city, by the fortune, numbers and quality of their people."[92]

Prestige could also be used to denote influence in the PRP hierarchy or the state government. Thus, when a tabloid in the state capital predicted a changing of the guard in an interior county, it pointed to the "beautiful prestige in government" on the part of the leader of the out-of-power faction, who had been named state secretary of the treasury.[93]

Using the word as a verb, a paulistano journalist noted that the Santos politician Joaquim Montenegro "had been lately honored [*ultimamente prestigiado*] with a great popular demonstration."[94] For his part, having been assigned the task of effecting a reconciliation between rival groups in coffee-rich Sertãozinho, J. A. Meira Júnior sought to enforce two conditions: that his ally João de Faria not be dishonored in any way ("que não se desprestigie em caso algum o João de Faria") and that the two sides join together under the leadership of his own superior, Joaquim da Cunha.[95]

Just as prestige could be publicly conferred (as in Santos) and its opposite inflicted (as suggested by Meira Júnior), so too could it be earned. José de Barros, born into a family of artisans, became "a cabo eleitoral of the first order," then made himself "a chefe of great deservedness and real prestige in the bosom of the faction that currently directs the destinies of Sorocaba," acquiring "the highest political positions" and "a prominent place, in [its] social order" (including, by the early 1900s, a commission as colonel in the National Guard).[96] In long-settled Sorocaba, it was thus implied, hard work and knowing one's neighbors went some distance in acquiring political prestige, while in frontier Campos Novos, Indian-killing did the trick, winning Francisco Sanches de Figueiredo "fame among the backwoods folk and with [fame] great prestige," understood in charismatic terms, "to the point where this chefe congregated around himself, three quarters or more of the county's population, half-fanaticized." This support, in turn, "increased the prestige of the chefe politico in the Capital, where he came to be much esteemed for the votes he disposed of."[97]

Publicly, of course, the capital's statesmen would have had it that all prestige was well-earned or inherent. As one of their paid scribblers wrote of a fallen founder of the state's republican movement, "he soon acquired great prestige for the dedication with which he struggled in support of his ideas, and for the high-mindedness with which he spread the new creed."[98] In Fernando Prestes's case, "loyalty" to his fellow perrepistas and "character" in the form of reputed personal courage served "to explain and justify his great prestige in the bosom of the political party to which he belongs."[99]

By this point, prestige had become a familial property, a Prestes birthright, to be passed on to his son as his political career developed. It was in making a similar, clan-based claim that a representative of Itatiba's out-of-power group declared in the wake of county elections: "The prestige of the Bueno family is indisputable. Down with the oligarchy. Long live the independent electorate."[100]

The idea of "independence" introduces one of the next most crucial terms in the republican lexicon. For paulistas in the early twentieth century, as for Brazilians in general in the nineteenth century, to be "independent" was to possess the "manly liberty" that "was considered an essential requirement for . . . freedom of conscience."[101] Given Brazil's nineteenth-century history, envisioning independence's opposite required little in the way of imagination. Thus Carlos Escobar, a veteran of the abolitionist and republican movements, contrasted the behavior of the "enlightened and independent electorate" with the "most degrading slavishness" of official politics. Similarly, in attempting to turn back a potential landslide at the polls, a self-styled spokesman of "independent opinion" sought to convince public functionaries that they were "not anyone's slaves."[102]

Independence could imply a certain social standing, and thus an electoral clientele, as when a newspaperman used the words "independent persons" to refer to the "physicians, lawyers, engineers, pharmacists, agriculturalists and merchants . . . who, in turn, will bring valuable contingents to the polls."[103] But it could also be used to refer to a generic "man of independent character," who in refusing to bend before a county chief had his job taken from him, had local general stores closed to him, and was threatened and beaten.[104] Men like these were "good men, who do not depend on the money of the Treasury or the protection of coronelões," in contrast to those "subservient and wheedling men without character."[105] In the city of São Paulo, the former were addressed collectively as the "Honorable and Independent Electorate of the Capital" or referred to as the "nucleus of independent voters" who were distinguished from " 'olavista' cabos" and their followers.[106]

In addition to serving as a marker of manly liberty of action and conscience, "independence" sometimes implied impartiality, as in one journalist's contrasting "independence of character" and "political passion."[107] It was far more common, however, for independence to refer merely to one's perceived or asserted ability to act as a manly citizen, one not subject to the orders or pressures of others, without implying any lack of factional ties. Thus, three voters from Botucatu, answering the charge that they had been suborned by the opposing faction, explained that they had returned the money in question because they were "independent voters, affiliated with the cardosista republican party."[108]

But independence, like so much else in politics, was an ideal. It could be asserted in telegrams to big-city newspapers or defended in more direct fashion by the truly brave, foolhardy, or fed-up, but it rarely entered the calculations of seasoned political figures, who appreciated predictability and a certain decorum among their peers, and submission on the part of dependents. For old party hands, the appeal to independence could be answered with derision.[109]

In these circles, premiums were paid on discipline, loyalty, and hierarchy, essential ingredients in maintaining São Paulo's structure of politics. These values, like independence, could be asked for or asserted in person or in print; they could also be performed in public settings, through balloting, processions, and speeches.

Santa Ifigênia's boss Estanislau Pereira Borges, in presenting his justice-of-the-peace candidates, dispensed with the ideal of independence. Instead, as "Delegate of the party," he addressed his district electorate in the expectation that, "disciplined as it has been, [it] will vote for the aforementioned slate."[110]

A correspondent from Cravinhos, writing amid rumors that local perrepistas had backed the wrong candidate, declared that his "political chieftain"—whom he was likely parroting—had acted "with absolute loyalty to the Republican Party, never lending himself to the game of playing one side against the other."[111] Perceived disloyalty, in this context, could lead the senior PRP leadership to transfer recognition from one county faction to another, with the according transfer of local political power, control over employment, and, of course, prestige.

Accusations of disloyalty thus litter the incoming correspondence of state-level leaders as local outs sought to vaunt their loyalty and prove the perfidy of their opponents. São Luís do Paraitinga's Bernardino de Campos Republican Union, for example, accused the local "ins" of having temporarily split into two groups during a conflict between state-level leaders so that they would maintain control locally regardless of which side emerged victorious.[112] A county councilman in lower-Paulista Viradouro made similar insinuations, registering his dismay at "the attitude of those who call themselves chefes" while acting disloyally, and claimed that he and "his voters" were "incorruptible and unconditional defenders" of the government.[113]

Lesser figures might seek to stretch their avowed loyalty into a promotion, a raise, or a job. Thus Viriato Carneiro Lopes addressed Júlio Prestes "not as a [public] functionary, but as a Brazilian and a paulista," who had been congratulated for his efforts on behalf of the PRP while in law school by none other than Prestes's ally, patron, and mentor, Washington Luís. Lopes went on to outline his postgraduate career: a job as a police delegate (through the good graces of his "dear master," the law professor and well-connected perrepista Rafael Sampaio), followed by an appointment as a state's attorney. Having informed Prestes that he had held this position for "almost six years," Lopes made final mention of his support "in defense of order and of the established authorities."[114] Lauro Costa took another tack. In his first note to Prestes, he indicated that he had already registered 260 of his "friends" as PRP voters, explaining that he aimed to register as many as 500 and that he was working alone, with no assistance.[115] Two weeks later, Costa wrote that he had registered a total of 300 voters and expressed his hope that he could "count on the goodwill of Your Excellency" as a candidate for a government job in Santos.[116]

Loyalty could also be performed in public places. In Itapetininga, the coming of the republic and the extension of the franchise to non-heads of household at twenty-one brought the growing "expectation that each man of voting age considered him to whom he felt a relation of immediate dependency to be the owner of his vote, such that the number of votes that each one disposed of equaled the number of one's male dependents who were older than twenty one." This understanding was grafted onto existing patterns: "the permanent ostentation of ties of dependency and loyalty," the desire "to unite the entire social pyramid, from its base to its apex," and the "personal support of each to their immediate superior." The patriarchal basis of politics thus linked sons to heads of households, heads of households to employers, employers to local bosses in a chain of loyalties that had as its end the performance of loyalty through the system of open voting.[117]

The performance of loyalty might also consist of a public "demonstration of esteem," as in Leme following the municipal elections of 1904, or it might take the form of a banquet offered by members of a particular county's self-styled elite, a male-only event celebrating victory at the polls, commemorating the burying of the hatchet between rival groups, or feting a distinguished visitor.[118] Popular indifference and the ridicule of children aside, patriotic holidays were celebrated with uniformed tributes to the incumbents of the outlying paulistano suburb of Belenzinho in the 1910s, as "Chico" Inácio, a colonel in the National Guard and a justice of the peace, led his fellow officers and a retinue of followers (some drawn by deference, others by promises of food and drink) "through the streets of the neighborhood, passing, always, before the homes of the most influential politicians."[119] The value of loyalty was a central theme in funereal commemorations for José Molinaro in December 1928, particularly in a speech in which the state congressman Carlos

Cyrillo Júnior lauded Molinaro's "obedience to hierarchy" over the course of his years of service to the PRP.[120]

Clearly, the glorification of hierarchy, loyalty, and discipline ran counter to the also-stated commitment to manly independence, in the sense that disciplined, faithful followers exerted precious little independence of their own, but there were other ideas around which political participants large and small could rally. Chief among these was the word *progress*, emblazoned on the national flag and possessed of an ideological lineage that again puts the lie to analyses that would neatly divide Brazil's republican thinkers into "liberal" and "positivist" camps.[121]

The historic republican Manuel Ferraz de Campos Salles captured the republican zeal for progress in a state-presidential address to the legislature. In summarizing the accomplishments of his first year in office, he declared: "What is succinctly laid out here is the work of the Republic, which one could ably express in this grandiose synthesis:—prosperity in all spheres of labor, progress in all areas of activity."[122]

Progress's appeal was by no means limited to the senior PRP leadership. That it was shared by political figures throughout the state is illustrated by the profusion of newspapers entitled *O Progresso*: from the flaquista organ of São Bernardo, to its mourista analogue in São Vicente, to identically titled periodicals in Araras, Capivari, Faxina, Ibirá, Itatiba, Lins, Santa Branca, São José do Rio Pardo, Tatuí, and the state capital, to provide only a partial listing.[123]

What did progress mean? For Campos Salles, it occurred when "order is established, the public wealth expands, industries are founded, work bears fruit and attracts the competition of useful labor, the soil proves itself, youth learns, the people educate themselves, and in the center of this enormous activity, projecting to all sides the enlivening light of liberty, the Republic arises—sovereign, imperishable, inaccessible to all attacks and superior to all dangers."[124]

Humbler folks—from county bosses to local residents—shared much of what went into Campos Salles's understanding of progress. For people like these, however, progress could be measured in more immediate ways. It meant bringing the accoutrements of modern life closer to their homes, whether on the distant frontier or the forgotten towns of the littoral, in the form of railway lines, telegraph service (and later telephone service), schools, roads, paved streets, electric power, public light, clean water, promenades or other ornamental grounds, and the growth of the local economy—parish-pump claims from which even the most autocratic local boss could not completely insulate himself. Thus, when

José Cardoso de Almeida's followers in Botucatu sought to rally support they circulated a flyer declaring: "It was our Cardoso family . . . who gave our land [Running] Water, [Electric] Light, a Bishopric, a Normal School, an Elementary School, and so many other innumerable improvements; because of this, these men should take charge of the administration of the county, of our affairs; so that the land of so many illustrious Worthies moves ahead."[125] Although an opponent of the locally dominant faction, Cardoso de Almeida was able to obtain these public works because of his influence in state government.[126] Locals in the Jundiaí district of Rocinha bet that they would gain similar rewards by entrusting "their progress and improvement" to the county chieftain and state secretary of justice Eloy Chaves.[127]

County-level leaders who failed to secure these kinds of improvements were subject to censure. A republican from São José do Barreiro, angling for government funds, reported that his county's lack of a schoolhouse "has tenaciously contributed to the discredit of the incumbent Chiefs."[128] This was the kind of situation that opponents sought to exploit. Writing from Itápolis, forty-odd supporters of the municipal outs complained to the state president that the clique in power was "deadening the progress of the county" and thus neglecting its duties to their community. This neglect was clear in "the abandonment of its roads, of its buildings, the difficulty created by the lack of telephones, [and the] scarcity of [electric] illumination" in the town's streets."[129] Within three months, the same group of petitioners had founded a Popular Republican Party, "to work for the greatness and prosperity of Itapolis."[130] In the next election, their party was victorious, due at least in part to the intervention of the state government.[131]

This zeal for progress was not merely something that was put on for superiors; it also appears in the guarded correspondence of local politicians and in the public declarations of private citizens. For example, Álvaro Coelho, the boss of Presidente Venceslau, addressed José Soares Marcondes of Presidente Prudente as "the Precursor of that impetuous Cult of Work that invaded and miraculously made fruitful the Upper Sorocabana[,] transforming its ferocious jungles into a vast font of agricultural production." It was Marcondes, he continued, who "brought to that unknown zone, the bandeira of work and of progress, settling it, opening roads and founding cities."[132] Similarly, a "humble salesclerk" from Limeira wrote that his home county only began "to progress" with the "genuinely honest, genuinely limeirense" local governments that from 1897 onward "left politics on a secondary level and took care of administration first," bringing running water, a public school, a building for the local jail, and well-lighted streets.[133]

In the city of São Paulo and its environs, local residents' zeal for progress found expression in neighborhood newspapers (*jornais de bairro*) founded beginning in the 1890s for the "Defense of Neighborhood Interests." These were periodicals—Lapa's *O Progresso* was one of that neighborhood's first, while São Caetano's *O Progresso* (in São Bernardo county) was the first published outside of the state capital—that mixed local boosterism, parish-pump petitioning, and publicity for neighborhood wheeler-dealers. All three features were to be found in the pages of *O Pinheirense*, which made much of its role in bringing on the "electric, dizzying surge of our progress" in outlying Butantã, particularly in bringing the need for the paving of its main thoroughfare to the attention of the "public powers."[134]

Tied to the cult of progress was the ideal of civilization. In 1891, addressing the state constitutional convention, Américo Brasiliense made much of the fact that the transition to a republican system—"a radical change in the form of government"—had been achieved while guaranteeing "public tranquility" and without "the smallest indication of any interruption of progress." "This entirely novel occurrence," he continued, "exceptional in the existence of nations, affirms the prestige with which the Republic of the United States of Brazil will emerge from the nineteenth century, so notable for its luminous traces on the civilization of humanity."[135]

But the appeal to civilization could also be employed by those critical of the conduct of politics. One such observer, in complaining of election-day violence, called on the state government to refrain from the kind of excesses "unworthy of a civilized people," then rendered an ultimatum that, in its comparison with the backlands of Brazil's northeast, went to the heart of everything right-thinking paulistas thought they had achieved: either São Paulo was a civilized place, in which hired guns had no place on election days, "or then S. Paulo is a Canudos."[136] Comparisons could also be drawn between particular counties and references made to the "Savage's Politics" (*politica de bugre*) of certain corners of the state.[137] Or, as a big-city journalist, writing of a colleague who was run out of Rio Claro, wryly noted: "If it was in S. Carlos, in Faxina or in Santa Cruz do Rio Pardo . . . this fact would in no way surprise us. But we thought that Colonel Marcello Schmidt's fief was more civilized."[138]

A far more earnest Mário Pinto Serva, comparing his country with "all of the civilized countries," lamented through the 1910s that, in political terms, Brazil lived "in the rearguard of civilization," "on the margin of civilization," or even "on the margin of history and civilization."[139] The degree to which the signposts of civilization were borrowed from abroad could lead a steadfast liberal like Serva to some surprising intellectual alignments, as when he complained that "in Brazil there is not a socialist or laborist congressman, there is not a socialist party, just as there is not a socialist voter, something that exists among all other civilized peoples."[140]

Closely tied to the idea of civilization was the adjective *culto*, meaning "cultured" and implying a good deal more.[141] Thus a group of pro-PRP voters in the interior city of Lins—representatives "of the agricultural, commercial, industrial, liberal, and working classes"—addressed a per-repista statesman ("an austere and immaculate administrator"), making much of Brazil's striving toward "the vanguard of the most cultured peoples."[142] Culture, like civilization, was a double-edged sword, however. Newspapermen writing in support of local outs might argue that the faction they favored represented "the conscientious and cultured electorate" amid the local tyrant's "fief."[143]

Republicanism itself implied the selection of certain practices and symbols, the invention of others, and the incorporation of many of the ideas above. Paulistano republicans greeted news of the fall of the empire with a manifesto that proclaimed, "The Republic means peace, progress, civilization."[144] The republican salutation "Health and Fraternity" replaced "God save Your Excellency" in correspondence.[145] "Citizen" as a form of address enjoyed a briefer vogue—it was soon replaced by "Citizen Dr.," "Citizen Col.," and further honorifics that offered a better fit with the established hierarchies of Brazilian society—but its use never completely died out.[146] In speeches and in the columns of a growing periodical press, republican rhetoric provided a ready-made political lexicon that could be marshaled by aspiring machine politicians and by would-be reformers, and by all manner of political figures in between, as these men sought to outdo themselves in the manipulation of interests and the mastery of imported ideals.

Thus one is faced with the spectacle of São Bernardo's Saladino Cardoso Franco, then a young contender identified with a statewide schism, fulminating against his opponents: "[We] will come out to the polls, even if it means loss of life, to prove to Sr. Rodrigues Alves that the republican heart still beats. The Conservative Union of the monarchy will not govern us. . . . Long live the Republic. . . ."[147] Similarly, a spokesman for the party led by Accacio Piedade, the tyrant-to-be of lower-Sorocabana Faxina, celebrated its victory over the "local dominators" by lauding the state government for its role as "guarantor of the rights [that had been] corrupted."[148]

More convincing republican appeals were made throughout this period by Julio Mesquita, the publisher of *O Estado de S. Paulo* and a sometime politician. As a leader of the statewide schism of the turn of the century—which proclaimed itself to be the true "republican party of S. Paulo" and heir to "the beliefs of the party and of its traditions"[149]—he did more than perhaps any single figure to disseminate the kind of language that was latched onto by Saladino Cardoso Franco and the associates of Accacio Piedade. In October 1901, in an address "To the Republicans of S. Paulo," he railed against the closing of the legislative galleries to the public: "in all the countries of the civilized world, parliamentary debates are public [events], and, only here, in this falsified republic (because a republic is not this), the government fills the galleries of the parliaments with police agents and troops of the line in disguise."[150] The same theme reemerged in 1924, in a campaign in which Mesquita ended every column reaffirming that "this is not a Republic or, better yet, *the Republic is not this!*"[151] Like his idol, Ruy Barbosa, Mesquita counted himself among the "incurable idealists" who strove to set the republic aright.[152]

Republicanism itself implied at least a notional commitment to popular sovereignty that, in turn, wound its way into political discourse. Once again, the appeal to this republican tenet could be made by the cynical and committed alike, and the idea itself could take many forms.[153] For radical republicans, "to republicanize the Republic, to make it the regime promised by the Propaganda" of the 1870s and 1880s, meant "to make it the government of the people by the people."[154] For republicans of more elitist bent "the great evil of the Republic, the terrible infirmity that continues to weaken it and which will eventually kill it, if those who lead it do not take another path, is its estrangement, more evident each day, from that which one calls public opinion . . . the only element of life of all the civilized countries."[155] "Public opinion," in this context, meant the "enlightened opinion" of men of letters, as distinct from "that of the people."[156] In the context of the ostensible commitment to popular sovereignty, abstract references might even be made to "revolution . . . a right and a duty of free peoples [who are] oppressed."[157] In this case, as in most, the appeal to the right of revolution was for decorative purposes only.

At the local level, the idea of popular representation was further stretched. Thus, in the state capital, bosses Olympio Martins and Miguel Franchini, who had earlier lorded over humble Lapa, were remembered as having "lived with the people and for the people."[158] São José do Barreiro's local outs, for their part, promised to attend to "popular demands."[159] Likewise, a disgruntled perrepista from Campos Novos complained to Júlio Prestes that Leonidas do Amaral Vieira—a state congressman, the boss of nearby Santa Cruz da Rio Pardo, and a henchman of the powerful Ataliba Leonel—had imposed a leader who was "disliked by all of the people" and who, "aware of his anti-popularity," sought to smear "those who counted on the support of the electorate."[160]

However different political figures understood popular sovereignty, there was nearly universal agreement on what constituted its opposite, oligarchy. A young Altino Arantes, writing in Batatais in the 1890s, condemned the "powerful and absorbing oligarchy," equating it with "the monopolized control of public affairs, as a familial patrimony, by a group of vulgar schemers; the national will coerced by violence and electoral fraud; the constant violation of constitutional guarantees."[161] In 1901 *O Estado de S. Paulo* argued that the leaders of the rump PRP were not satisfied with simple victory at the polls: "The oligarchy does not want to win—it wants to exterminate. It is true. Always, throughout all times, since the remotest antiquity, all oligarchies were this way."[162] Speaking for themselves, the leaders of the minority faction had declared: "The Republic is the regime of light, of awakened, active and fecund [public] opinion. It is not, it should not be [a] field of shadows, sterile, abandoned and moribund: of oligarchies and dictatorships without scruples, without ideals, without aspirations."[163]

Years later, a big-city cartoonist, depicting an emaciated Hermes (the patron of commerce) bound to a stake by a top-hatted politician, declared: "Businessmen across the state should remember the commercial tax and refuse to vote for the representatives of the voracious oligarchy."[164] The Republican League of São Bernardo, in appealing to the county's "people" and its "independent electorate," denounced the flaquista faction, "this *oligarchy* . . . that is treating our dear county as if it were its own house," oppressing its residents with "exorbitant and unconstitutional taxes" and with "laws that are a veritable attack on commercial and industrial liberty, harming thirty thousand inhabitants in order to benefit one."[165]

To these writers (and to lexicographers then and now), "oligarchy" referred to the concentration of political power in a few hands or, collectively, to those few who actually held such power, while present-day historians use the term synonymously with social and especially economic power and to refer collectively to those who hold such power.[166]

Literate paulistas of the early twentieth century would have found the latter usage puzzling. Indeed, when many complained of "oligarchy" or "professional politicians," they were not bemoaning the marriage of public and private power, but rather their divorce: they found it galling that political power should be exercised (whether by state-level leaders, regional bosses, or local chefes políticos) by men who lacked the customary trappings of sociocultural status (a chair in the São Paulo Law School, refined manners and learning, a suitably distinguished ancestry) and socioeconomic success (a diversified economic portfolio and a palacete in the state capital or, for municipal-level leaders, significant local interests and a fine house in the county seat). It was in this context that one county opposition—"an independent political group"—denounced the "professional politickers," who "without a piece of land in Araras, without a cent invested in the local industries," presumed to lead.[167] In Santos in the early twentieth century, the terms "dominant oligarchy," "professional politicians," and "governismo" were used interchangeably, while the opposing faction styled itself as representing "coffee brokers," the "great contributors" to the municipal coffers.[168]

The self-styled faction of the "great contributors" was called the Santos Municipal Party, a moniker that drew upon a political tradition of long standing, municipalism (*municipalismo*). In the context of São Paulo's republican politics, municipalism described a county-level political opposition that sought—or at least claimed to seek—greater municipal autonomy and other local prerogatives, including municipal control over local revenues and the kind of local improvements demanded by progress, or a submunicipal opposition that sought outright independence as a separate county. In either case, the profession of loyalty to the sitting state and federal governments alongside opposition to local power-holders was standard municipalist practice. Like republican rhetoric, municipalist language could be employed by the sincere and cynical alike; from Araras to Ourinhos, it was common for a county's out-of-power faction to claim the honors by calling itself the "Municipal" or "Municipalist" party of its corner of the state.[169]

In other cases, municipalism served as a rallying cry for the corporate interests of one or more groups. At least in its early years, the Santos Municipal Party sought to rally and represent the port city's commercial interests.[170] Between 1916 and 1919 a paulistano analogue tried to do the same for industrial and commercial interests in the state capital.[171] Beginning in 1928, São Bernardo's Saladino Cardoso Franco faced a Municipal Party organized by the businessmen of the thriving submunicipal district of São Caetano.[172] These cases, however, were hardly representative of the municipalist norm.[173]

Another concept that figured prominently in republican discourse was *civismo*, derived from the French *civisme* and used to denote public-spiritedness. Civismo, one author explained, was vital: "A country can only progress . . . by the harmonious activity of all of its intellectual, moral, and social forces. It is necessary that everyone have a sense of his duty to the collectivity and know how to put this duty into practice." "We Brazilians should work so that," and here he went straight to the classical source for the French cognate, "with the same pride as the Romans, we can one day say: 'I am a Brazilian citizen.'"[174] In practical politics, civismo, as with so much else, was in the eye of the beholder. For Julio Mesquita's *O Estado de S. Paulo*, a locale that voted in opposition to its ostensible leader was providing "a noble lesson in civismo."[175] For Dagoberto Salles, a PRP loyalist, it was the life of the republican founding father Campos Salles that provided "a lesson in civismo."[176]

For his part, in a rare autobiographical aside, Francisco de Paula Rodrigues Alves declared: "Under the old regime I served in the ranks of the Conservative Party. I am conservative under the Republic. I believe in the republican institutions and in the labor and civismo of [my fellow] Brazilians."[177]

Brazilian republicans might also situate themselves among larger, contemporary republican traditions by connecting their own politics to those of "cultured peoples" the world over. Bastille Day was made a national holiday by the first provisional government of the republic—one of São Paulo's leading newspapers greeted the date with "an enthusiastic *viva* to the glorious country that made the great revolution of 1789"—and celebrated into the twentieth century.[178] Commemorations of 20 September not only linked paulista republicanism with another republican tradition, they also played well among Italian immigrants.[179] Much the same could be said of celebrations of the Portuguese republic.[180] At one odd historical moment, radical republicans could even find themselves commemorating 4 July, arguing that the date was not only important "for the glorious Anglo-Saxon nation," but that its "eternal principles" belonged to the entire "civilized world."[181]

It was at a similarly odd historical moment that what would become the São Paulo state flag was designed by Júlio César Ribeiro Vaughan, a Minas-born journalist, novelist, and republican. Writing a little over a year before the fall of the monarchy, Júlio Ribeiro proposed a new flag for the coming republic. Modeled on that of the United States (his father's native land), the flag consisted of thirteen horizontal stripes of black and white with a red rectangle in the upper left-hand corner, which contained a profile image of the Brazilian subcontinent within a white circle, framed by four stars. When the republic came, Júlio Ribeiro's flag flew briefly in São Paulo, until a decree of the provisional federal government established a national flag that drew heavily upon the green and yellow imperial standard.[182] However, the unofficial ornament remained in circulation and, by the early 1910s, had become the São Paulo state flag, "known and respected by all Brazilians."[183] Perrepistas adopted the symbol as their own and flew "the cloth of black stripes and red corner, recognized as 'the paulista flag,'" during official commemorations.[184]

Alongside symbols like the state flag, paulista republicans also sought to create a pantheon of the "great figures of republican propaganda," who made "heroic sacrifices, noble acts of selflessness, of true abnegation" in their struggle against the monarchy.[185] Prudente de Moraes was proclaimed to have been "the Washington of the Brazilian republic," the "patriarch of the republic," and "part of the patrimony of the nation's glory."[186] Bernardino de Campos was described similarly as "one of the most venerated traditions and one of the most faithful and loyal defenders" of the republic.[187] Radical republicans—tellingly using a fraternal rather than a patriarchal metaphor—referred to Bernardino de Campos, Prudente de Moraes, and their cohort as "brothers in the glory and ideals" of the republic.[188]

In some cases, the republican heroes literally were founding fathers, and their renown was marshaled on behalf of their living progeny and other kin. Journalists Nereu, Acylino, and Ludolpho Rangel Pestana, for example, were depicted as the "legitimate heirs of the character and mentality of the dearly departed journalist" Francisco Rangel Pestana, a historic republican, a founder of *A Província de S. Paulo* (as *O Estado* was known under the empire), and a member of the triumvirate junta that briefly governed the state after the overthrow of the monarchy.[189] Paulo de Moraes Barros, a former secretary of agriculture, was said to be descended from the "legitimate republican nobility of the State of São Paulo."[190] Carlos de Campos was remembered as the "beloved heir of the administrative abilities and fecund republican convictions of Bernardino de Campos."[191]

Given the PRP's twenty-year history of propagandizing under the empire, and the existence of an appropriately regional forefather (Diogo Antônio Feijó, who had helped lead an 1842 revolt that, with some stretching, could be framed as formative of the republican tradition), the construction of a civilian pantheon was not nearly as implausible as it seemed in Rio de Janeiro.[192] Nevertheless, it became apparent to the would-be architects of a republican imaginary that the cult of the republic's founding fathers was insufficiently heroic for the popular imagination, so the struggle for the republic was married to the campaign for the abolition of slavery.

On 13 May 1890, emancipation day was celebrated for the first time under the republic and commemorated (somewhat lamely) by the government, which declared it a holiday.[193] By the end of the decade, there was an attempt afoot to combine the two traditions, as the date, still a national holiday, was declared to have been "consecrated by the Republic to the fraternity of Brazilians."[194] With the passing of Francisco Glycerio in 1916, newspapers in his hometown of Campinas made much of his "fruitful activity in the campaigns for abolition and the proclamation of the Republic."[195]

The perceived need to create a republican *história pátria* involved a broader reimagining of the nation's past. For paulista republicans, in particular, the coming of the republic was framed as the third or fourth of their homeland's grand, progressive gifts to the nation. The first of these was the epic of the bandeiras, in which intrepid paulista adventurers roamed far from their homes and into the furthest reaches of the South American interior, thus guaranteeing the future nation's geographic greatness (that these bandeirantes left their homes in search of Indians to pillage and enslave was usually left unsaid). The second was independence, which was depicted as something that São Paulo did for the nation rather than something that a Portuguese prince did while in São Paulo (a somewhat more substantive link was made through José Bonifácio de Andrada e Silva, a Santos-born princely advisor and São Paulo's "Patriarch of Independence"). Some fifty years after the break with Portugal, the campaigns for abolition and the republic were joined, and the rest, the mythmakers wanted one to believe, was history. In this retelling of the Brazilian past runs a typical example: "All of the great national movements had their strongest impulse here. It was the same with the western colonial expansion, it was the same with Independence, with Abolitionism, with the Republic."[196]

Connections between abolition and the republic not only formed part of an attempt to create a patriot tradition, they were also suggestive of the ways in which republican citizenship was imagined. This was so even before the republic itself was a reality, with the republican movement's most important mouthpiece welcoming abolition as a "splendid victory of [public] opinion," but cautioning, "The Patria without slaves is still not the free Patria. Now begins the work of liberating the whites, estab-lishing the political constitution on broader, more secure bases for [the] happiness of the people and national glory. We should be happier today than yesterday, but know that tomorrow we will be even more so than today."[197]

Not only did the establishment of republican government ultimately loom larger than the abolition of slavery in the well-being of the Brazilian people and the standing of the nation, as far as São Paulo's leading republicans were concerned, but there was also a correlation to be made between "whites" and the future citizens of the republic and thus a corresponding, if implicit, distinction to be made between whites and blacks in terms of civic capacity. This distinction was echoed in subse-quent retellings of the coming of abolition (as something done by "whites" for "blacks") and of the establishment of the republic (as the "liberation of the whites").[198] When combined with existing understand-ings of manly independence and its opposites, and emerging ideas re-garding regional identity, this distinction made for an envisioning of republican citizenship that was nearly as explicitly racialized as it was gendered.[199]

Related to the question of republicanism was the question of liberal-ism, which, in terms of following and import, long preceded republi-canism in nineteenth-century Brazilian intellectual history, and which carried particular weight in São Paulo.[200] Thus Julio Mesquita was at-tempting to connect with a larger tradition, in which he had played no inconsiderable role, when he declared in early 1924 that the "*Estado* is a liberal newspaper and the government has come to be an odious despo-tism."[201] Three years later, his obituary read: "A liberal of a liberalism capable of all sacrifices and all devotions in the struggle against despo-tism and outrages, his intervention in the greatest democratizing cam-paigns of the Republic was made memorable."[202] As a youth, Elias Chaves Neto, born thirty-five years after Mesquita, was similarly inspired by liberalism, as an aesthetic sensibility rather than a set of ideological principles: "imbued with the French Revolution and the Napoleonic legend, intoxicated by romanticism. . . . I dreamt of journalism, the brilliant, polemical journalism of the liberal struggles of France of the previous century. It was in terms of those struggles that I interpreted Brazilian politics."[203]

Perhaps no figure in Brazilian intellectual and political life personified this tension between the dreams of nineteenth-century liberalism and the curious realities of twentieth-century Brazil better than Ruy Barbosa, the famed Bahian statesman whose disproportionately large and learned cranium, packed with constitutional theories and an enormous vocabulary, rested on narrow shoulders and a small frame. In 1909–10, the odd workings of the Brazilian federal system made him the minority opposition candidate for the national presidency. His most powerful allies in this venture were the machine politicians of São Paulo.[204]

A Campaign to Remember

The contested presidential campaign of 1909–10 emerged after months of back-room dealing on the part of Brazil's senior statesmen ended without producing the usual consensus candidate. Instead, two candidates remained in the field in August 1909: Field Marshall Hermes da Fonseca, who was supported by the federal government, the republican machines of nearly all of Brazil's individual states, and by politically active elements in the officer corps; and Ruy Barbosa, supported by his home state's machine and that of São Paulo (the PRP, having lost out in the inter-regional deal-making that made Hermes the official candidate, settled for the face-saving measures of backing a national hero and providing him with a running mate, Manoel Joaquim de Albuquerque Lins), and by like-minded liberals scattered in cities and towns throughout Brazil. Ruy and his supporters called themselves "civilianists" (*civilistas*) to distinguish themselves from their opponents, whom they dubbed "militarists." Their cause was thus *civilismo*, which had the virtuous ring of civismo.[205] In São Paulo, Ruy's campaign won the support of most of the political elite, including many politicians who had previously faced off against one another during the schism of 1901–6, while the Hermes candidacy was backed by a minority faction that included Francisco Glycerio, Pedro de Toledo, Rodolfo Miranda, and Rafael Sampaio.[206] The result, as far as São Paulo was concerned, was a six-month campaign that had as its high point Ruy's visit to the state in December 1909 and its nadir in the candidate's hotly contested defeat.

The paulista leg of Ruy's campaign began on 15 December with a slow train ride from the federal capital of Rio de Janeiro to the city of São Paulo. The first stop in São Paulo state was in Queluz, where the train was greeted by the local republican leadership and the town council as well as by "the local bar, merchants, agriculturalists, workers, teachers and students, and a great popular mass." Queluz's state's attorney, speaking on behalf of "all social classes," saluted Ruy, "exalting [his] civic qualities." He was followed on the tribune by a local student, while the county's chefe politico, José Carlos de Oliveira Garcez, offered bouquets to Ruy and his family.[207]

As the train moved on, slowly making its way to the state capital, similar scenes were enacted at stop after stop as local residents, school-children, officials, and county bosses offered flowery tributes to the candidate. Ruy responded with speeches that were no less florid, with appeals to regional pride ("Long Live the Glorious State of São Paulo!"), tributes to local rulers (Guaratinguetá was the "land that is honored with the name of Rodrigues Alves"), remembrances of fallen heroes and na-tional ideals (José Bonifácio and Brazil's "greatest liberal traditions"), and calls to rally to the cause ("the cause of honor . . . the cause of patriotism . . . the cause of the future . . . the cause of the salvation of the country's credit and its good name"). Flags waved, bands played, the national anthem was sung. Insiders were offered "a small lunch," coffee with milk, champagne, and, in Mogi das Cruzes, a five o'clock tea (served some minutes after seven). By the time their train reached the outskirts of the state capital, Ruy and his entourage had been traveling for more than twelve hours.[208]

Thousands awaited them at the station, invited by a commission of local notables, who had called on their fellow citizens, "in the name of the dynamic elements of paulista civilization," to pay homage to Ruy Barbosa, "one of the greatest figures of . . . contemporary history." Local residents were joined by political figures from throughout the state.[209] On arriving, and then as he was driven through the downtown to one of the city's most chic hotels, Ruy was applauded enthusiastically. After "the necessary repose," Ruy and twenty-nine invited guests were served an "intimate dinner," following which the "illustrious visitor" retired to his room.[210]

The following day was less hectic. After morning visits to the homes of two senior PRP leaders, Ruy and his family sequestered themselves in their hotel, receiving no visitors until mid-afternoon, when they gave a reception for around a hundred of the state's most prominent politicians and other public figures. Following the reception, Ruy dined with his family in preparation for the evening's speaking engagement.[211]

Ruy and his entourage arrived at the auditorium at eight to find it full, "all of the finest of S. Paulo's social milieu" having filtered in over the previous four hours. Bernardino de Campos—sixty-eight years old and blind in both eyes—opened the evening with a short speech, referring to the "solemn assembly" as a reflection of the "paulista soul," and to the pro-Ruy movement as "an agitation" emerging from the "popular soul."[212]

Alfredo Pujol, until recently a political opponent of Bernardino de Campos and the rump PRP, followed with a longer speech, the most daring of the evening, in which he paid tribute to "the current chief of Brazilian democracy" and "great apostle of justice and liberty," emphasizing that support for Ruy came not merely from the PRP, but also from "the people that do not have parties, the people that is above the parties, the un-submissive people, whose sovereign instinct is the incorruptible judge of public men." Pujol emphasized Ruy's contributions to Brazil's history and predicted that he would soon make equally great contributions, either as president, enacting the "great reforms that the social order demands and for the decisive support that the forces that create our progress and our riches demand," or "at the head of the liberal resistance." He then offered a laudatory overview of Ruy's public life and promised, "We, the paulistas, are here, in formation, ready for battle, with the Republic on our lips and the patria in our hearts."[213]

By comparison, Ruy's speech was rather staid. To be sure, he opened with the requisite appeals to local and regional pride (São Paulo was responsible for Brazil's "territorial greatness," its capital was "the great metropolis of progress"), but the rest of his speech was devoted to a long, drawn-out history of his candidacy, in which he emphasized his own selflessness, and to a quixotic attack on "militarism." He closed with his vision of a future, "an age of tranquility and rebirth" to be achieved through the "sincere observance of our liberal institutions."[214] His well-bred listeners, raised in a culture in which rhetorical flights of fancy were prized, no doubt found the speech thrilling (Ruy received a ten-minute-long standing ovation), but it was singularly light in content. Its airiness was in part due to the venue, to the audience, to the occasion, and to the ill-defined content of civilismo, but it was almost certainly also due to Ruy's desire to appease his hosts on the PRP executive committee, a consideration Pujol apparently gave short shrift.[215]

Although not without its moments of tension, the remainder of Ruy's visit to São Paulo was characterized by this caution. Formal wear, elaborate meals, string sextets, patriotic speeches, and, of course, champagne, were the order of the day; one evening witnessed a *marche aux flambeaux* that brought a "great mass of the people" to downtown.[216] The combination of republican rhetoric and patrician posture may bring to mind Belloc's "On a General Election," but it was impressive enough in its time; the hermista daily *São Paulo*, forced to face up to the very real enthusiasm generated by Ruy's visit, diagnosed it as a form of "mass delirium."[217]

Ruy was received as enthusiastically in Campinas and Santos, bringing together incumbents and independents, municipalists and perrepistas. In both cities, and in towns along the way, he was feted by large crowds and his accomplishments praised.[218] For all of the affected togetherness of the campaign, however, conflict and controversy could not be banished entirely. *O Estado de S. Paulo*'s correspondent, for example, distinguished between the reception that Ruy received en route to Campinas and the usual collection of the "curious and indifferent" brought together for official events. Ruy's reception in Jundiaí, he wrote, came from "the people" and the local civilianist committee, "without the encouragement of the public powers of the land"; these were people who were "not submissive to the will or favor of low-down local politicking."[219] Similarly, a speaker at one of the events in Santos went much further than many perrepistas in the audience may have liked in denouncing "politicões" and "politiqueiros" and identifying the civilianist cause with "democratic government, the government of the people by the people." Alluding to Ruy's youthful abolitionism, the same speaker argued that "yesterday's propagandist, of the liberation of the black, is today the protector of the liberty of the white."[220]

Ruy's speeches were not without bombast, to be sure. In his final speech in Santos, Ruy declared: "I do not want the government of the Nation handed out by candidacy contractors and administrative entrepreneurs. I do not want the state oligarchies centralized in one federal oligarchy. I do not want armed force replacing justice in the solution of conflicts between the Union and the States. I do not want national politics handed over to caudilhagem. I do not want Brazil reduced to the Venezuela of Cypriano de Castro or the Nicaragua of Santos Zelaya" (a set of declarations that reportedly met with a full five minutes of applause). But he closed the speech on a far different note: "We toast, with order and liberty, the government of this State . . . the exemplary administration of S. Paulo, [and] its illustrious president."[221]

Ruy returned to Rio soon thereafter, but the campaign in São Paulo did not let up at all. The war of words between "civilismo" and "militarism" was carried on in newspapers and speeches, while all manner of political operatives worked the machinery of politics in anticipation of election day.

O Estado de S. Paulo featured the "Notas civilistas," in which José Feliciano toed the civilianist line. Civilian rule, he wrote, was the mark of a country that belonged to the "civilized, western, European world" and would make for "civic culture" and "peaceful, industrial civilization," while military rule was "retrograde."[222] The civilianist cause was also backed by the PRP's *Correio Paulistano*, and by *O Tempo*, *A Propaganda*, and *O Comércio de S. Paulo*, until the latter was bought out "by the group of Francisco Glicério."[223]

Hermistas had also acquired the daily *São Paulo* and started up their own publications. The latter included *O Alarme*, *A Renascença*, *O Reporter*, *O Diário de S. Paulo*, *Zé Povo* (the latter founded after the election), and the ephemeral *O Vinte e Dois de Maio*, published by a group of mostly out-of-state students at the São Paulo Law School.[224]

As during all election cycles, the pay-to-print *secções livres* of the state capital's large newspapers were a key site for political propaganda and the settling of rhetorical scores. João Pedro da Veiga Miranda, a civilianist leader in predominantly hermista Ribeirão Preto, was accused of "treachery and disloyalty," while Joaquim da Cunha, who backed Hermes, was lauded for the "tolerance, liberty and progress" of his rule and the "running water, drainage, electric light, paving, building of gardens, planting of trees, new elementary school, high school, schools in nearly every community, new jail, [and] building for the city council" that he had brought to his home county.[225] The secções livres also published the ballots to be used on election day, with the reverse of the page left blank so that they could be folded over.[226]

The newspapers of the interior were equally caught up in the conflict. The *Correio de Salto*, for example, carried "vibrant articles and accurate news exalting Ruy Barbosa and Albuquerque Lins and condemning the unpopular and dangerous Hermes-Wenceslau candidacies," while its São Carlos counterpart depicted civilismo as a "very clear symptom of the Brazilian state of mind" and proclaimed "Long Live the Civilian Republic!"[227]

Rallies were held across the state. Lacking the support of the state's power-holders and purse masters, hermista gatherings tended to be smaller and somewhat less impressive.[228] Civilianist rallies were better attended and, it would seem, lavishly funded.[229] They often closed with tributes to local and regional chieftains as well as to the candidates. Thus, in Itapetininga, Sarapuí, and Tatuí, rallies ended with vivas for Fernando Prestes, while in Barretos the county boss Sylvestre Lima was "deliriously cheered."[230]

The same kinds of tributes could be heard in the state capital, along with other, more interesting appeals. In Brás, Della Volpe addressed his countrymen in Italian, "making them see the drawbacks of the military candidate and advising them to vote for Ruy Barbosa."[231] Across town, in Lapa, Pedro Bittencourt, identified as a "worker," gave a "vibrant speech," in which he spoke out against the "military candidate," called on "all workers" to vote for Ruy, and attacked "the military draft lottery, saying that it comes and tears sons from the home of the poor worker, at just the time in which they most need to help their families with their means of subsistence." He further argued that Hermes's defeat would be "the fall of this law." It was for this reason, "as a worker and a head of household," that Bittencourt supported Ruy Barbosa and Albuquerque Lins, "who, once elected, will guarantee the calm and tranquility of Brazilian families."[232]

As city speakers claimed their crowds and newspapers carried the conflict into the farthest reaches of the interior, the stage was set. In February, elections to the federal legislature provided a dress rehearsal for the presidential election, one in which the hermista candidates, lacking control of all but a few local governments, did as poorly as could have been predicted.[233] In the sleepy fishing hamlet of Vila Bela, hermistas, reportedly funded by a politician from Taubaté, brought out a few voters in opposition to the civilianist party headed by "prestigious chefe" Manuel de Goes Moreira.[234] In Indaiatuba, the hermistas sat out the election entirely; civilianists, as one might imagine, interpreted their abstention as a victory for the county's "proud and independent electorate," led by Alfredo Fonseca, to whom they attributed "the local progress."[235] In Jaboticabal, the "opposition chefes . . . appeared in the political arena in the guise of hermistas," dutifully voted the hermista slate, and were soundly defeated.[236] Throughout the state, the settling of accounts followed, as in Pindamonhangaba, where federal employees were fired for having voted for civilianist candidates.[237]

The threat of dismissal and other forms of official pressure continued to be employed through the presidential election. Santos, as the leading port of exit for Brazil's greatest commodity, was host to a number of federally administered agencies where senior officials imposed the Hermes candidacy on their subordinates.[238] From Ribeirão Preto, the directors of the Mogiana Railroad sent out an employee circular; Hermes was the man as well.[239]

More ominous threats were also used. In the Paraíba Valley, hermista officials toured "rural areas and the settlements of [Pindamonhangaba] in an unbridled cabal, intimidating civilianist voters with the military draft and other terrifying rumors."[240] In São Carlos, pro-Hermes *capangas* used force to try to break up a civilianist rally.[241] In Batatais, on the eve of the election, a "small group of individuals sought to disturb the peace, with the aim of alarming the electorate and spoiling the election."[242]

Meanwhile, the state's cabos made their own preparations. In Campinas, Ignacio Pellegrini Biagoni, an old hand, awaited Ruy Barbosa's assistance to swing into action, bringing with him "563 living voters[,] all country folk and ready for my call" (although, he cautioned, Ruy should only "count on 520 because there is always some illness and most principally in the rural areas"). Biagoni claimed a subordinate in each of the county's communities, each of whom would bring his voters to the county seat by railroad on the eve of the election, and he had already made preparations for "a Dinner, and a Lunch: for all."[243]

The polls opened on the morning of 1 March. In the state capital, the election went smoothly, with only the most minor disturbances; the civilianist slate was victorious throughout the city.[244] Santos witnessed a much closer race, one marked by street fighting, vote buying, and, in outlying Cubatão, the shutting down of a streetcar line in order to prevent voters from reaching the polls.[245]

In Bauru, gunplay broke out and at least one voter was gravely wounded. Civilianists claimed that the hermistas and their hired guns had provoked the conflict, while their opponents argued that the civilianists had achieved their narrow victory at the cost of "tears and blood," as hermista voters were jailed and "wounded by civilianist bullets."[246] In Lençóis, a hermista chefe, a "pharmacist, and [a] good man and [an] exemplary head of household," was killed.[247]

Elsewhere, the hermistas were victorious. Their most significant victory was in Ribeirão Preto, where Joaquim da Cunha and his allies brought out 964 voters to the civilianists' 439.[248] Although Ribeirão Preto was not the only county in which the hermista ticket won, it was by far the most impressive; hermismo's other municipal victories provided little to brag about.[249]

The election's results led to celebrations throughout the state. In the state capital, thousands of voters assembled before *O Estado de S. Paulo*'s offices as its staff posted the results from across the country as they came in during the days that followed, while a detachment of state troops stood guard in front of the offices of the hermista *São Paulo* to prevent their sack by civilianist crowds.[250] In Santos, groups of hermistas and civilianists took to the streets on the evening of 2 March. Each side had something to celebrate: the civilianists had won in Santos and across São Paulo, while the hermistas had lost locally and in their home state, but had won at the national level and lived in a city ripe with federal jobs. In their respective celebrations, the hermistas saluted the *Diário de Santos*, the *Tribuna do Povo*, and their local leader, Martim Francisco Ribeiro de Andrada, while their opponents rallied in front of the Civilianist Center, where they were treated to speeches by their own leaders. By ten that night, the celebration turned ugly as the two groups clashed on a downtown square. Order was restored only after the local police delegate called in a mixed detachment of police troops and mounted cavalry.[251]

The excitement soon passed and the business of politics resumed. The first order of business was rewarding the leaders of the hermista movement in São Paulo, who received various positions either in or through the federal government.[252] Further down the line, local hermistas received their due. In Franca, for example, the hermista boss João Antunes de Araújo Pinheiro had the federal tax collector and his assistant replaced by loyal hermistas; when pressed on the matter, Antunes explained that "his co-religionaries" wanted the posts and he could not deny them what was theirs by right.[253]

Also in the short term, civilianists and hermistas prepared for elections to be held to fill Rodolfo Miranda's seat in the federal congress, left vacant when he took the post of federal minister of agriculture. The hermistas presented Plínio de Godoy Moreira e Costa, an "illustrious republican" and the candidate "of all of the independent electorate of that district," while the PRP executive committee backed Antônio Manuel Bueno de Andrada, whose taking of the opposite side during the 1901–6 split was all but forgotten.[254]

In the longer term, there began a process of approximation between perrepistas who had backed Ruy and their ostensible enemies in the federal government. Senior leaders of the PRP rump chose as the next state president a conservative figure who had played no role in the civilianist campaign, while the party organ began to refer to the national president as "Honorable Field Marshal Hermes."[255] Parliamentary motions of support and polite telegrams were exchanged between former enemies and, in one case, a bico de pena election was fixed at Hermes's request, an event that coincided with the nomination of a paulista leader's son to a position in the federal government.[256] The ambitious up-and-comer Washington Luís—heretofore a "fervent civilianist"—became a "frank, ostentatious partisan" of a pro-Hermes politician.[257] When the PRP declined to support Ruy Barbosa's abortive presidential campaign of 1913–14, few were surprised.

3 War and the Health of the State

Facing certain defeat, Ruy backed out of what would have been the 1913–14 presidential campaign in December, leaving the field open to the Minas-born candidate of Brazil's great state machines. Although some paulista die-hards insisted on casting their votes for him on 1 March, gestures like these were soon overshadowed by events abroad, as Europe began to come apart a few months later.[1] What would come to be called the First World War, far from being a sidelight in Brazilian intellectual life, was seen as nothing short of central, absorbing the attention of Ruy and his counterparts in the paulista intelligentsia, who identified with the Entente and the civilization that they believed it represented. Intellectual discussions of the European war, in turn, overlapped with and contributed to further debates over Brazilian nationhood, out of which anxieties regarding civic readiness and citizen making came to take institutional form in patriotic groups and journals of opinion. Spilling from classrooms, newsrooms, and salons into the streets in 1917, the idea of the European war came to spark rallies and riots. Throughout São Paulo, as elsewhere, the late war years also witnessed impressive bursts of labor militancy, in 1917 and again in 1919; they also witnessed the influenza epidemic of 1918. All of these events, experienced as crises and climacterics, found their way into the formal politics of 1918–19 in important and hitherto unstudied ways.

Mobilizing Ideas

Tied to Europe by trade, tradition, and telegraph, Brazilian cities like São Paulo received news quickly and, in the mid-1910s, unquietly. Even in the smaller towns of the paulista countryside, if not the fishing villages of the littoral, the latest news came to be consumed avidly. Nelson Palma Travassos, born in Santa Rita do Passa Quatro in 1903, recalled a perfectly ordinary boyhood in a sleepy coffee county, "*Until one day . . . in the carrying out of my daily chore of going to the train station to buy the newspaper, I noted an unusual curiosity in the search for news. Everyone shocked by a front-page headline: 'European Conflagration.*' " "From that day forward," he remembered, "the world began to change, life [began] to alter its norms. The old 'gare' of the station was covered with colored signs asking everyone to produce more. New customs arrived by train. The Italians' stores filled up with maps and photographs of the king of Italy."[2]

Travassos's memories evidence some telescoping (Italy, for example, did not enter the war until nearly a year after Franz Ferdinand's assassination), but they also register something of the excitement that events in Europe generated. Indeed, after Italy joined the Allies, participation in the war went well beyond wall hangings for the hundreds of immigrants who returned to serve their mother country.[3]

For newspaper-reading natives like Travassos's father—Cesário Ferreira de Brito Travassos, a small-town physician, a civilianist in 1909–10, and an avid reader of *O Estado de S. Paulo*—and for newsmakers like Ruy Barbosa and Julio Mesquita, the war made up for in intellectual urgency what it lacked in ethnic interest.[4] Europhilia, liberal traditions, and the desire to see Brazil take its place among the great and civilized nations of the world combined to make at least symbolic Brazilian involvement in the European war a necessity in these intellectual circles.

Ruy Barbosa was the foremost national leader of the pro-Entente movement. For Ruy and his fellow founders of Rio de Janeiro's Pro-Allies League, the war's stakes were clear: on one side stood civilization and democracy, on the other barbarism and autocracy. Brazil was thus obligated to join the war on the side of the Allies.[5]

In São Paulo, Julio Mesquita adopted the same stance. From August 1914 to October 1918, he personally took responsibility for a weekly "War Bulletin," in which he summarized and interpreted the latest news from overseas.[6] While the "Bulletin" was written in a reportorial tone, Mesquita's pro-Entente sympathies were clear to all. Indeed, within six months of the war's outbreak, he felt compelled to define his newspaper's position: "*O Estado* sympathizes with the Allies, not because it dislikes Germans, but because it disagrees viscerally with the militarist and authoritarian policy that diverted it from its luminous mission and produced this hateful war"; this militarism had made Germany a "repugnant monster, which all civilization should rise up against and fight."[7] Assiduous readers of Mesquita's "Bulletin" might have also noted his periodic criticisms of political conditions at home, "in certain democracies of our personal acquaintance where [presidential] power . . . is omnipotent, because it is free to exploit the uniform and aviled submission of the electorates," a country that was not a "regime of opinion" or a "true republic," but that "strut[ted] ridiculously in beautiful, North American constitutional plumage."[8]

A Wilsonian before Woodrow Wilson, Mesquita saw the war as involving all of humanity, a war in which "a complete transformation of the world" was ultimately at stake, a "geographic transformation, political transformation, social transformation, economic transformation, moral transformation, because the soul[s] of nations and even individuals have to emerge transformed from the ashes of this vast blaze."[9] Indeed, prior to the entry of the United States into the war, Mesquita decried the "cruel indifference" of "the great and powerful North American republic" to the "moral battle that summoned the conscience . . . of the civilized world," a position that he quickly reversed as Wilson readied his country for war.[10] By this point, Mesquita had begun to argue that Brazil would be honored if, as the "United States of our continent, it could link its fate, by a fraternal alliance, to that of the United States" of North America, by joining the "most beautiful movement" of the Allies.[11]

With the break in relations between Brazil and Germany shortly thereafter, the *Revista do Brasil*—São Paulo's leading journal of opinion, which Mesquita had helped found in 1915—declared that "Brazil did its duty," if tardily and incompletely, arguing that Brazil must now declare war. In doing so, the review drew on well-established evocations of national greatness and familiar anxieties concerning the possible effects of Brazilian isolation from the currents of world opinion:

> Brazil, by its territorial extension, by its natural riches, by the number of its sons and by its position in South America, has a lofty mission to fulfill. It will never carry it out if it persists in its policy of half measures, of advances and retreats, of threats and procrastinations in which it deceived itself deplorably. Timidity and humility can be virtues in an individual; in nations, they are symptoms of incapacity or decadence. The forward march of a virile nation cannot be interrupted at every moment. . . .
>
> Either we declare war now, or tomorrow we will fall into isolation, abandonment and shame.
>
> Today we would enter the fight with head high; tomorrow perhaps this will already no longer be possible. . . . Today, we would receive the sympathy and respect of all nations that, on the side of the allies, fight for liberty and

civilization; tomorrow, we will only receive—if not something worse—a cold smile, of patronization and disdain. . . .[12]

A year later, the *Revista do Brasil* tied events abroad to domestic politics, arguing that the Allies' moral superiority was the source of their successes. Furthermore, it claimed, "Our politicians cannot remain deaf and blind to this lesson. Brazil has reached, in its political advance, a curve at which new horizons unfold before it and its feet reach a new topography. To maintain [Brazil] as it is, eyes veiled from justice and hands bound for punishment would be to betray it, to commit the most atrocious crime against it." It was time for change from above "or, soon, we will have to choose between two calamities: civil war or foreign domination."[13]

Another prominent pro-Entente member of the paulista intelligentsia, and another of the *Revista do Brasil*'s founders, was Luiz Pereira Barreto, a Rio de Janeiro-born physician, scientist, and republican of long standing who had settled in São Paulo in the 1870s.[14] A heterodox positivist, and a great admirer of Germany earlier in his life, Pereira Barreto now argued that Germany remained in the "metaphysical" stage of civilization, in which war was seen as the proper means of national aggrandizement and science was pursued for bellicose ends, a stage that England, France, and the newer nations of the Americas had already passed through on their way to the "positive stage of peaceful industry."[15] By mid-1916, in an article entitled "The Role of Youths in Social Evolution," Pereira Barreto was condemning Brazilian neutrality as well, calling on Brazil to enter the war on the side of the Allies.[16]

In appealing to youthful idealism in the context of world war, Pereira Barreto was echoing the Rio-born poet Olavo Bilac, who had opened his campaign on behalf of universal military service, public education, and civic engagement at the São Paulo Law School with a celebrated "Address to Youth" in 1915. "The present moment," Bilac had declared, was not for "empty speeches," but for "the simplicity of strong ideas," simply expressed, to provoke "hope . . . , faith and . . . heroism." Acknowledging his audience's surroundings—a "rich metropolis"—he doubted the students' ability "to conceive the chaos, the confusion and the dangers that beset all of our marvelous and inconsistent patria." Evoking the European war, Bilac argued that Brazil's crisis, a crisis of moral indifference and decay on the part of its best elements, was every bit as serious. "This is the spectacle that our cultured classes present us with," he claimed, citing the "barbarous—and mercenary" individualism amid which the "professional politicians" thrived. But even this display paled in comparison with the situation in the countryside, where "the others, the most humble popular strata, kept in the most brutish ignorance, demonstrate only inertia, apathy, superstition, [and an] absolute lack of consciousness. In the rough backlands, men are not Brazilians, nor even true men; they are beings without free or creative spirits, like the beasts, like the insects, like the trees." Bilac, however, saw a "first step toward convalescence and toward a cure" in compulsory military service, "the complete triumph of democracy; the leveling of classes; the school of order, of discipline, of cohesion; the laboratory of personal dignity . . . compulsory cleanliness, compulsory hygiene, compulsory physical and muscular regeneration." He bemoaned the fact that years after its passage—years of "sterile struggles and amoral politicking"—Brazil's draft law had not been implemented and that Brazil remained "a rich land in which many people die of hunger, a country without nationality, a patria in which patriotism is unknown," then called on the "Youths of São Paulo, Law students," to begin their "effective civic existence," turning "to public work, to social agitation, to politics," reminding them of their school's abolitionist and republican traditions and insisting on their taking a leading role in this "new campaign."[17]

Bilac's call did not go unanswered. São Paulo's well-bred youth briefly, if enthusiastically, flocked to volunteer battalions, drilling and marching in parade, sometimes even alongside ordinary conscripts.[18] More importantly, it also led to the founding of the Nationalist League by the students and professors of São Paulo's institutions of higher learning, perhaps the most important institutional manifestation of the era's intellectual ferment and calls to arms.[19]

The league's early program consisted of four items: (1) "to carry out campaigns for liberty [and] against civilian or military threats to national sovereignty"; (2) "to develop the feeling of national unity"; (3) "to obtain the efficacy of the ballot, through the civil registry [of male citizens reaching their majority], the system of electoral confidentiality, the fining of abstention or an election-day holiday, and the most efficacious penalties for fraud"; (4) "to promote the organization and development of national defense, through scouting, militia practice and military training."[20] The same measures were refined in the party's formal statutes, adopted in May 1917.[21]

The league's inclusion of proposals for electoral honesty alongside Bilackian civic measures sprung from and, in turn, contributed to a larger, ongoing debate regarding political reform. Where the war-era emphasis on military and civic readiness was informed by events in Europe, discussions of political reform were most influenced by the precocious democratization of neighboring Argentina, where President Roque Saenz Peña had instituted secret and compulsory voting with the 1912 law that bore his name.

O Combate, a São Paulo afternoon newspaper that was radical-republican in its politics and proudly "yellow-press" in style, was an early booster of the Argentine example.[22] In October 1916, after rehearsing the familiar lament that São Paulo's "progress is exclusively material, as on political grounds we are as backward as a State in which the regime of force and violence predominates," one of the newspaper's writers took Saenz Peña himself as a counterexample "because he lent his country the service of inflexibly establishing free voting and electoral honesty." The newspaper further suggested that state president Altino Arantes "could be, if he wanted, the paulista Saenz Pena" by taking similar steps "to sanitize the State's political customs."[23]

In late 1917, Abelardo Cesar, a state congressman and a member of the Nationalist League, introduced a motion calling for the introduction of the secret ballot along Argentine lines in state elections.[24] *O Estado de S. Paulo* offered its support to his effort with practical arguments in favor of secret balloting.[25] *O Combate* was more pessimistic. While its anonymous writer applauded Cesar's motion and noted that Argentines and Uruguayans already enjoyed the benefits of the secret ballot ("the only way to avoid intimidation and bribery"), he also argued, correctly, that the motion would not gain the support of the political establishment, as "the moralization of the vote would be the death of the oligarchy."[26]

This interest in and advocacy of the secret ballot, combined with invidious comparisons between the "wise and vigorous civic rebirth" of post-Saenz Peña Argentina and Brazil's "slave-quarter's regimen," lasted through the 1910s and, indeed, through the following decade as well.[27] Eventually, the Nationalist League made an explicit call for secret balloting on the Argentine model its standard.[28]

The intellectual ferment of the 1910s was not limited to the state capital. Appeals similar to those sounded by Bilac and his paulistano followers were heard in cities and towns throughout the state, in Santos, Rio Preto, Casa Branca, and elsewhere.[29] In Ribeirão Preto, Albino Camargo, a lawyer and schoolteacher, exhorted local students to join the ongoing campaign.[30] Along with likeminded professionals, Camargo founded a local review, entitled *Patria*, which served as his home county's counterpart to the state capital's *Revista do Brasil*.[31] In the second issue of *Patria*, the lawyer João Guião addressed the issues of "Compulsory Military Service and Electoral Reform" in an article that opened: "The European conflagration has been an abundant font of lessons for all nations, and happy are those that have taken advantage of the practical lessons that are being registered in contemporary history, to not become victims of their own neglect." Guião evoked Bilac, calling on his countrymen "*to nationalize* the country," arguing that the solutions to "military indiscipline and disorganization," illiteracy, electoral corruption, and administrative immorality were to be found in calls "for compulsory military service, for electoral reform, for the greater dissemination of education among the popular classes, and for rigorous administrative oversight." Effective compulsory military service was to be followed by "a well-planned electoral reform, which can guarantee [the predominance of] the national will in collective decisions, and thus we will have the country prepared to affirm [its] hegemony, in South America, at least." As proof of the efficacy of these two reforms, Guião took up the Argentine example, noting that "the Argentines had the intelligence to discretely militarize the nation, combining voter registration with surveying for compulsory military service," and he expressed his hope that Brazilian "politicians [would] adopt the same ideas."[32]

Many of the same Ribeirão Preto professionals who published *Patria* came together to found a Nationalist Center on the model of the state capital's Nationalist League. Like its paulistano analogue, Ribeirão Preto's Nationalist Center concerned itself with fostering civismo, pushing for clean elections, and promoting education and scouting.[33]

Patriotism, Pickets, and Pestilence

Appeals to national mobilization were disseminated in public speeches and, more importantly, the pages of a growing periodical press aimed at a popular audience distinct from the presumed readership of intellectual journals such as *Patria* and the *Revista do Brasil*. These publications included *O Combate*, as well as the yellow-press magazine *O Parafuso* and the evening edition of *O Estado de S. Paulo*, all three of which began publication in 1915. The *Estado*'s evening edition, nicknamed the *Estadinho*, was founded in part to capture the attention of belligerent-nation immigrants, principally Italians, and, with its enhanced sports coverage and anti-establishment vitriol, was designed to appeal to urban everymen more broadly.[34]

Reception of these mobilizing ideas was reflected in 1917 in rallies and riots as Germany stepped up its submarine campaign against Atlantic shipping and Brazil eventually entered the war. Later the same year, the outbreak of an unprecedented citywide strike, one that was echoed in industrial towns throughout the interior, brought the state's working people to the attention of the newspaper-reading public and served to illustrate the increasing importance of what was coming to be called the "social question," an experience that was repeated in 1919, with two additional waves of labor conflict. Even more paulistas were affected by the influenza epidemic of 1918, a terrifying event, the response to which revealed the increasing importance of what would come to be called "civil society" and the relative impotence of the republican state.

With the German adoption of unrestricted submarine warfare beginning 1 February 1917, the war began to assume a new immediacy, not only for Brazilian intellectuals and statesmen, but also for a broader public in São Paulo's larger cities and towns.[35] In places like the state capital, a nationalist constituency, including law students (themselves junior members of the state's intelligentsia), other students, and many middling folks, had come into being, one that had been exposed to some of the intellectual ferment of the preceding years and that apparently felt it had a stake in the European war and in defending Brazilian national dignity.

Together with newspapermen and other public figures, this constituency reacted vehemently when the Brazilian freighter *Paraná* was sunk by a German submarine in early April 1917. In the city of São Paulo, news of the *Paraná*'s sinking was greeted by rallies, demonstrations, and rioting; similar disturbances occurred in the interior town of Rio Claro.[36]

Official confirmation of the sinking of the *Paraná* arrived in Brazil on 6 April.[37] That evening, in the state capital, "numerous groups of young men" organized "a great demonstration in protest of the disrespect suffered by the Brazilian flag." The protesters marched through the downtown, bearing a flag and saluting the offices of various newspapers, while the local authorities placed police guards on German-owned businesses, the German and Austrian consulates, and the offices of the *Diário Alemão*.[38]

On the morning of 10 April, word arrived in São Paulo that the Brazilian government had broken off relations with Germany.[39] That afternoon, law students called for another demonstration protesting the sinking of the *Paraná*. Following a public meeting on the square in front of the law school, the students led marching crowds, their members now numbering in the thousands, throughout the downtown, where the "multitude" rallied in front of the U.S. consulate, the Banco Italiano, and the offices of the *Jornal do Comércio, A Gazeta, O Estado de S. Paulo,* the *Correio Paulistano,* the *Diário Popular,* and the Italian-language *Fanfulla.*[40] Patriotic speeches by Brazilians and resident foreigners coincided with riots, including an attempt at sacking the offices of the *Diário Alemão,* and culminated in an attempt at repression on the part of the police, which resulted in the death of a young man named Pedro Turbanelli Filho, identified as a Spaniard and a commercial employee.[41] A list of those injured suggests that, by the demonstration's later stages, it was composed mostly of men like Turbanelli: young, middling in social standing, and with a high proportion of immigrants and paulistas of recent immigrant stock.[42]

The next day, the city "presented the appearance of grand occasions: it was given over to the multitude, which, sometimes silent, divided into small groups, huddled in the streets, [and] sometimes bellowed and shook, the great levies, in crashing and imposing outbursts of enthusiasm." These crowds were composed of "sons of all [friendly] nationalities . . . Italians, Portuguese, Russians, French, Belgians, Syrians, etc."[43] That evening, a series of rallies and speeches gave way to a full-scale riot that culminated in the sack of the *Diário Alemão.*[44] A list of those injured in the sack again suggests a mostly young, male, middling crowd with a high proportion of immigrants or immigrants' sons.[45] The reminiscence of Paulo Nogueira Filho, then a law student, gives something of the tenor of the sack and the demonstrations that preceded it in describing it as reflecting the "lofty tone of paulista patriotism and the vigor of which it was capable in its collective reactions."[46] Similar sentiments were at work toward the end of the year, as the *Macao* was torpedoed, leading the Brazilian legislature to declare that a state of war existed between Germany and Brazil.[47] In the state capital, these events led to what another memoirist would describe, without irony, as "new street disorders that are all the best demonstrations of Brazilian patriotism," disorders seconded in towns throughout the state.[48]

In lonely opposition to the war were São Paulo's anarchist activists. Isolated and ineffectual, they were nevertheless consistent in opposing the war and nationalist identification more broadly.[49] Their isolation only came to a definitive end in mid-1917, when these activists found themselves faced with an unprecedented wave of strikes that shut down the city of São Paulo and spread into the principal urban centers of the interior.

May 1917 began with a handful of stoppages in the state capital and its environs by textile workers and stonemasons, respectively. Stagnant wage-rates amid generalized wartime inflation, increasingly intolerable working conditions, and, most importantly, the ever-increasing cost of basic foodstuffs were at the root of these strikes.[50]

One of these stoppages, that of textile workers in one section of a plant owned by the Italian-born industrialist Rodolfo Crespi, led to São Paulo's first general strike. These workers struck after two demands were not met: a wage increase and an end to the factory's practice of withdrawing "voluntary" donations to Italy's war effort from their paychecks. By the end of the month, having received partial satisfaction, the workers returned to work.[51]

Within weeks, workers in another section of the same factory walked out, taking to the streets to draw attention to their demands. This time, management responded by closing the entire factory. The strike, however, soon spread to the textile concerns of other industrialists, some of whom settled with their workers, while others remained as intransigent as Crespi. In early July, the workers of the Antarctica beverage plant joined the textile workers.

Faced with this unprecedented wave of labor stoppages, the authorities responded with force and, in an attack on a crowd of strikers and strike supporters, the state police claimed their first victim, the anarchist cobbler Antônio Martinez, who died of his wounds after being shot in the stomach. As Martinez's presence indicates, the strikes, which began without the participation of São Paulo's anarchist activists, now counted on their support and advice.

With its first martyr, the strike movement grew exponentially, becoming a general strike, and the city of São Paulo was the site of increasing conflict between strikers and the authorities. It was at this point that journalists representing the city's most important newspapers took it upon themselves to serve as intermediaries between industrialists, the state, and an anarchist-led commission representing workers. As a result of the ensuing negotiations, in which a group of the city's most important industrialists agreed, among other things, to a 20 percent wage hike and to respect the right of association, O Combate declared "The Victory of the Worker."[52]

Seen in the light of previous labor conflicts, the strike of July 1917 was undoubtedly a victory for workers. But it was a victory that came to be increasingly qualified as the bad faith of the industrialists and the state government became increasingly apparent, clear in their failure to follow through on commitments made to the strikers and in the deportations of activists.[53]

In contrast to the manifest bad faith of most industrialists and of many in the state government, the strikers of 1917 were met with sympathy on the part of newspapermen and middle-class paulistanos subject to the same rising cost of living. Indeed, apart from those affiliated with pro-government newspapers like the *Correio Paulistano* and the *Jornal do Comércio*, paulistano journalists were nearly unanimously sympathetic to the workers, though some journalists soon came to hedge on this sympathy.[54] The city's freemasons also expressed support for the strikers, and support for the latter's demands was evident among functionaries of the state Department of Labor as well.[55]

As the scope of official repression became clearer in the wake of the strike, São Paulo's independent and opposition press once again placed itself on the side of labor.[56] With the deportations of anarchist activists, the Italian-language daily *Il Piccolo* led a campaign in support of the deportees and their families.[57] Writing in *O Estado de S. Paulo*, Mário Pinto Serva challenged the constitutionality of the deportations in an article entitled "Brazilian Hospitality," while *O Combate* declared that with the deportations, "The Constitution is Revoked."[58] Among the attorneys who defended militants subject to deportation or jail were the paulistano radical Benjamin Mota, the Rio de Janeiro-based labor lawyer Evaristo de Moraes, and the maverick São Paulo city councilman José Adriano Marrey Júnior; the latter two eventually secured the release of Edgard Leuenroth, the editor of the anarchist *A Plebe*.[59]

In 1919, there were two attempts to reprise the successes of 1917.[60] The first, in May, was another partial success, with employers granting striking workers some concessions (a good number of which were unfulfilled promises from July 1917).[61] But the second attempt, which came in October, was far more important in the longer term. As political as economic in its grievances, the strike played into the hands of a state already bent on repression and alienated sectors of the population that had been sympathetic to earlier stoppages but were now increasingly fearful of labor militancy given developments abroad and closer to home.

By October 1919, much had changed since São Paulo's first general strike. Not only had the city endured more than two years of labor upheaval and repression, but the city's upper- and middle-class residents, in particular, many of whom seem to have taken the events of July 1917 in stride, now had new reason to fear "anarchists" with each news dispatch from Russia.[62]

An explosion that wracked the working-class neighborhood of Brás in the early evening of 19 October, destroying a house, further fed fear of "anarchists" in particular and social upheaval in general. The explosion apparently resulted from the accidental detonation of a bomb or bombs being built in the house, killing four known anarchist militants.[63]

According to *O Combate*, news of the explosion made a strong impression on paulistanos.[64] For its part, *O Estado de S. Paulo*, in an article published two columns over from a pair of telegraphs on "Strikes and Bolshevism in the United States," argued that the explosion of the "Infernal Bomb" was "proof that, in fact, fanatical elements are operating in the city of São Paulo, linked closely to others who are at work in Rio."[65]

A few days later, Julio Mesquita drafted an editorial on the explosion and his newspaper's attitude toward labor. Where some, including Paulo Duarte, a Mesquita family friend and protégé, would detect a reactionary attitude on the part of *O Estado de S. Paulo* during the 1919 strike, the editorial reveals a logic rooted in the nineteenth-century liberalism that was so characteristic of the newspaper.[66] Mesquita noted that when the wartime wave of strikes began, in 1917, *O Estado de S. Paulo* had criticized the heavy-handedness of the authorities "in the name of the most legitimate and most serious interests of society." Where the authorities saw labor militancy as something to be repressed, legally or illegally, Mesquita and *O Estado de S. Paulo* "understood, and understand, that in Brazil the conflict between capital and labor is a phenomenon as inevitable as in Argentina and in the United States, for example—new countries, where one's livelihood is easily secured, [even] more favorable than our own for the traditional individualistic regimen and the prosperity of the able through free competition—and, thus, we struggled and will continue to struggle for a moderate reaction (though not devoid of vigor) with rigorous respect of the existing laws, not forgetting to reform them, as the circumstances indicate and demand." While this remained *O Estado de S. Paulo*'s position, workers had become possessed by "an excessive insistence" and paulista strikes, "with rare exceptions," had ceased to reflect "reasonable economic aspirations" and had entered "the political realm, with pronounced revolutionary intentions and projects." Given this situation, Mesquita called upon the authorities to apply the existing "laws of social defense," but without excesses.[67]

Before the morning edition went to press, having received word from a commission of streetcar workers that a citywide strike was to begin in protest against the jailing of various labor militants, Mesquita appended a note to his editorial, in which he asked workers if there were not still some way to avoid the strike, reminding them of the inconvenience that the strike would cause the city's population and, worse yet, the "sad consequences" that could result "on occasions like this one." The note ended by stating that although the jailings were unjustified, the workers' response was out of proportion given the potential legal redresses at hand.[68]

Thus began the planned general strike of 1919, which was to have shut down the state capital and extended throughout the interior of the state. That morning, 23 October, the city's streets were busier than usual, with foot traffic and automobiles taking the place of the Light and Power Company's streetcars. That night, the streets were dark, the city's gas workers having joined the streetcar drivers on strike.[69] By the afternoon of 24 October, these utility and transportation workers had been joined by factory hands at some of the city's textile plants.[70] They were eventually joined by others, including railwaymen, metalworkers, construction workers, telephone workers, hatters, and barbers.[71]

It was not until 27 October, however, that the labor leadership published a formal list of demands, including the release of jailed leaders; recognition of working-class associations and of the right to organize and assemble; implementation of the eight-hour day and the ban on labor by children under the age of fourteen; a weekly break for all workers; abolition of nighttime work for minors and women; worker oversight of factory conditions and of the production of basic foodstuffs; equal pay for equal work; salaries equivalent to the real cost of living; an end to the practice of making workers provide their own tools; abolition of various fines; the lowering of rents; better hygienic conditions in working-class housing; and cheap streetcars for all "so that there are no class distinctions."[72]

By this point, goodwill on the part of non-workers had evaporated. The striking streetcar conductors were replaced by volunteers, the greatest number of them students (who had either been sympathetic to strikers or remained neutral in previous disputes), who made the *bondes* run on time until replaced by scabs from Rio de Janeiro.[73] Workers were left at the mercy of their employers, while militants were subject to arbitrary jailings and deportations.[74] By 28 October, the strike had been broken.[75]

Although the failed general strike was not the death knell for labor that some scholars have discerned (the state capital would not see another general stoppage for decades, but strikes did continue to break out through the 1920s), it did mark the beginning of the end of the unprecedented militancy of the late war years. With this shift, the months that followed the strike saw the revival of some limited support for labor on the part of non-workers, a turn to a more moderate, apolitical, and defensive stance on the part of surviving labor organizations, and a significant step toward the regimentation of management.

Relations between labor militants and non-workers had reached their nadir by the end of October. It was at this point that the offices of *A Plebe* were sacked by students, who, allegedly responding to an insult made by the newspaper's editors, acted with the tacit support of the authorities. While the sack of *A Plebe* led some journalists to express sympathy for the militants, it was not until the full scale of the government's plans for deportations was made plain that there was a significant revival of support among non-workers.[76]

The failure of the October strike and the ongoing campaign of repression by industrialists and the authorities led surviving labor organizations to emphasize their moderation. No one case better illustrates this tendency than the association representing the city's streetcar drivers, who had initiated the strike of October 1919. In late November, when a new administrative commission representing the Light and Power Company's workers reopened their union hall, its members released a manifesto inviting all to join, regardless of "political, philosophical or religious creed." Noting that "all discussions not relating to the ends of the organization are wholly forbidden in our meetings," the commission stated:

> We struggle for the harmoniousness, the fraternity, and the unity of the working-class family to which we belong, not supporting any desires except that of attaining, orderly and without outrages, our legitimate rights as free citizens. We want the eight-hour day, the abolition of unjust punishments, higher salaries and other small improvements recognized by the [Paris] Peace Conference. We are certain that we will achieve all of this, when one day the Company is convinced of our peaceful intentions and does not see in us anything more than upstanding and honorable workers who only seek what is just, rational, and humane.[77]

This moderation was abetted by the loss of the anarchist leadership to deportation (as the presence of a new administrative commission suggests) and was accompanied by backbiting among existing labor organizations, as between the Metalworkers' Union and the Workers' Federation in late December.[78]

It was also amid this second cycle of strikes that paulista textile industrialists came together to found a statewide association, the São Paulo Spinning and Textile Industrialists' Center (CIFTSP). While the CIFTSP was founded in early October, prior to the failed general strike, it was, in one historian's words, "founded largely for the purpose of controlling the workers," and the early meetings of the organization "were wholly occupied with suggestions for putting down [the] strike[s] that had broken out in sympathy with workers at the São Paulo Light Company." In the years that followed, the CIFTSP played an important role in combating labor militancy and lobbying government on behalf of the textile industry.[79]

The strikes of 1917–19 amid which the CIFTSP was founded played out in cities and towns from Santos to Rio Claro. As a result, similar patterns of sociopolitical conflict and alliances emerged throughout the state.

In Campinas, São Paulo's second city, railwaymen and other workers struck for the timely payment of better wages in July 1917. They soon faced a hostile contingent of police troops sent from the state capital. After three railwaymen were killed, a commission of local journalists, including city councilman Álvaro Ribeiro—an independent, elected without PRP support—sent a telegram of protest to the state government; one historian has read this document as indicating the "indignation and feeling of grief" of the people of Campinas.[80] Faced with the journalists' protest, the state government stood by the police, erroneously claiming that the fallen were not even workers. The municipal government, however, adopted a conciliatory stance, forming a commission that eventually negotiated an agreement under which the strikers returned to work with higher wages and the promise that no worker would be dismissed for having taken part in the movement.[81]

In May 1919, disciplined local strikers again were met with conciliation on the part of local power-holders and the active support of Ribeiro, his *Diário do Povo*, and the editor of the *Comércio de Campinas* (both journalists spoke alongside working-class leaders at a mass meeting at the city's main theater), winning the public's favor and, eventually, support for most of their demands. In the wake of the strike, there was even a movement afoot among the railwaymen of the Mogiana Railroad to form "a working-class association on a political [i.e., electoral] basis."[82] In October, the same workers gave the anarchist call for a general strike little support.[83]

In Santos, July 1917 appears to have seen little in the way of cross-class collaboration and the local labor leadership was only partially successful in rallying workers in solidarity with their paulistano counterparts.[84] But in May 1919, strikers were sheltered by the administrator of the municipal market; when the administrator was set upon by the police, city councilman Heitor de Moraes—an independent, like Campinas's Álvaro Ribeiro—issued a protest in the municipal legislature. In this strike, a relative success despite the best efforts of the city police chief, workers also counted on the support of Moraes's friend Cyrillo Freire, the editor of the *Gazeta do Povo* and a similarly self-appointed spokesman for the people.[85] Later that year, in mid-October, the workers of the City of Santos Improvement Company, which ran the city's streetcars, went on strike in the face of an increasingly threatening stand on the part of the company's management. They did so only after the city council rejected Moraes's motion, presented on the workers' behalf, charging that local firemen were training to serve as streetcar drivers.[86] During both strikes, and in the years that followed, Moraes took to the courts on behalf of workers, fighting against arbitrary imprisonment and deportation.[87]

In Piracicaba, the 1917 strike unfolded peacefully, festively even, with workers parading through the streets backed by three bands.[88] Both of the principal local newspapers, the *Gazeta de Piracicaba* (the mouthpiece of the Municipal Party, which controlled county government but did not enjoy the favor of the rump PRP leadership) and the *Jornal de Piracicaba* (ostensibly "independent" but at that point linked to the local outs, who had earned executive-committee recognition by virtue of the logic of republican politics), expressed support for the right to strike, while sniping at their political opponents. As occurred elsewhere, the strikers came to be represented by a local journalist, Pedro Krahenbuhl of the *Jornal de Piracicaba*, who eventually secured the concessions that brought the strike to an end.[89] It was in the offices of the *Jornal de Piracicaba*, which had opened its pages to working-class spokesmen at least as early as February, that a local Workers' League was founded shortly after the end of the strike.[90] In May 1919, the Workers' League called a strike for the eight-hour day, a strike that limped along, with some successes, into early June, by which point the Sorocabana Railroad was the only local interest at which workers had not yet returned to work, leaving the city isolated. The *Gazeta de Piracicaba* condemned the railroad, blaming the shutdown on the "greediness of the directors of this cursed company, who are deaf to the just request of their miserably paid subalterns, and who are doing nothing to resolve the inconvenience and loss that they cause the population."[91] The city's merchants and industrialists likewise blamed management and petitioned the state government to force the Sorocabana to reach an agreement "so that traffic is promptly reestablished before spirits become rightly exasperated and worse evils occur."[92] These calls, which came in early June, went unanswered; in early July, the striking railwaymen sought the support of the Workers' League, which called another citywide strike. With the strike spreading, the *Jornal de Piracicaba* declared: "The resistance of the [Sorocabana] directorate is useless: nothing can stop the peaceful workers."[93] It was at this point that a plot involving the strikers, anarchist activists, and the local out-of-power faction was either uncovered or manufactured by the authorities, providing a rationale for police repression.[94] When the Workers' League was subsequently closed by the police, the league's secretary, Mário Passini, was defended by João Silveira Mello, a lawyer and local opposi-tionist, much to the dismay of the state capital's anarchist activists, who complained sarcastically that he planned "to transform the League into an electoral Center, through which he will, perhaps, present himself as a candidate to governmental posts and then promulgate miraculous mea-sures for the workers."[95] While *A Plebe*'s interpretation of Mello's motives is impossible to verify, Mello was successful in his defense of Passini; working together with Jacob Diehl Neto, a fellow opposition journalist, Mello had Passini and several other workers exonerated.[96]

In other counties, information is sparser still regarding patterns of labor conflict, conciliation, and alliance, but some preliminary notes can be made. In Rio Claro, for example, a workingman's association founded by a local journalist for the purpose of electoral mobilization during the presidential campaign of April 1919 brought together two thousand workers during the following month's general strike.[97] During the state-wide strike of mid-1919, an Itapetininga city councilman, "interpreting the aspiration of the working class of Itapetininga," gave an "eloquent speech, advocating the 8-hour day and other measures," which received "unanimous approval."[98] More interesting still, and inexplicably un-studied, are the events surrounding the São Paulo Northern Railway strike of late 1919, which overlapped partially with the general strike called for in late October. In this case, a peaceful strike by railwaymen shut down traffic, thus isolating the entire northwestern portion of the state. Like their *piracicabano* counterparts, local residents responded not by turning on the strikers, but rather by blaming the company; in the new county of Catanduva, they dynamited the station in protest. Even-tually, the stoppage and the agitation surrounding it led the state govern-ment to expropriate the railroad company.[99]

Between the strikes of 1917 and 1919 another event came to intersect with the political campaigns and intellectual debates of the period, the influenza epidemic of 1918. Even more than the labor militancy of the late war years and even the war itself, the epidemic was a truly global event; it was also one over which people appeared to have even less influence or control. The epidemic and human reactions to it nevertheless had important effects on relations between state and society in São Paulo.

In early July 1918, one of the state capital's afternoon newspapers carried a story on the war in Europe bearing the whimsical headline "Atchin! . . . , atchin! . . ." (Ah-choo! . . . , ah-choo! . . .). The accompanying story informed readers that an outbreak of the flu had brought the German war effort to a standstill.[100]

Three months later, the mood in the state capital was far different. The first cases of influenza had struck Rio de Janeiro and the fear that the epidemic would soon reach São Paulo was very real.[101] By early October, suspected cases had begun to appear in neighborhoods throughout the city of São Paulo, but especially in the predominantly working-class neighborhoods east of downtown.[102] Panic set in, and many paulistanos of means fled to the interior.[103]

By mid-month, suspected cases had given way to confirmed ones, which in turn multiplied along with the terror of the population.[104] On 16 October, the city's sanitary service registered twenty-nine cases; on the following day, it registered nearly one hundred and the first two fatalities.[105] By 24 October, more than five thousand paulistanos had come to be afflicted by the virus.[106] Jacob Penteado, who survived the epidemic as a boy, remembered: "There was not a home that was not touched. In some homes, all of the residents were found dead. Entire families perished, in this sad phase of city life. . . . The cemeteries functioned day and night. One saw in the streets, at all hours of the day, mournful convoys of hearses at work."[107]

Infection rates peaked in the first week of November, morbidity rates the following week. By this point, 112,046 cases of the disease had been registered, representing roughly 20 percent of the city's population, and more than 3,000 paulistanos had died, but a decline in the strength of the epidemic could begin to be detected.[108]

By the end of the year, more than 5,000 paulistanos had succumbed to the disease. As was recognized even then, however, it could have been much worse; nearly 17,000 residents of the Federal District died of influenza during the same period.[109] Much can be attributed to the relative salubriousness of São Paulo's climate, but several sources also point to the role played by the city's civic associations—by what one could call its "civil society"—in helping to minimize the effects of the virus.[110]

As the number of new cases began to decline, *O Combate* declared:

"We did not have the horrors of Rio de Janeiro in São Paulo. For this we thank the Nationalist League, the Red Cross, the 'Estado-Fanfulla' commission, the Commercial Association, the Conference of S. Vicente de Paulo, the different immigrant associations, the scouts, all of the groups and individuals that dedicated themselves to the public good, fighting disease and hunger and avoiding the complete disorganization of the life of the city."[111] These groups solicited donations, distributed medicine, used private automobiles to get the afflicted to hospitals, and otherwise tended to the sick. The Nationalist League was particularly important, setting up hospitals throughout the city.[112] These measures were carried out without any significant official assistance; as the epidemic began to ebb, some noted that the government played no role in its decline.[113]

Such was the devastation wrought by the virus that Germany's defeat, an idea that had captured the imagination of so many in the early years of the war, passed virtually uncelebrated in early November.[114] It was not until mid-December that the city witnessed the "colossal demonstration of jubilation" in which the "paulista people affirmed, once again, its absolute estrangement from the Germanophile current, providing splendid proof of being sincerely on the side of the pioneers of Civilization, against Barbarism."[115]

Three Campaigns

The intellectual ferment and social crises of the 1910s—nationalist mobilization, labor conflict, and even the human response to epidemic disease—worked their way into the formal politics of the period. This influence was particularly clear in three electoral campaigns, two of them not regularly scheduled contests but rather special elections held to fill posts gone vacant, the third the statewide municipal elections of October 1919.

The first of these campaigns sprang directly from the urban, student-initiated patriotic campaigning of the mid-1910s. It began in May 1918, when the PRP presented José Valois de Castro, a man of the cloth and sitting federal congressman who had refused to support Brazil's joining the war against Germany, as its candidate to an empty state senate seat.[116] Valois's candidacy was deemed to be unacceptable by journalists and students in the city of São Paulo, who quickly swung into action, opposing Valois de Castro's election and putting forward the candidacy of Luiz Pereira Barreto, the pro-Allies spokesman and co-founder of the

Revista do Brasil. The result was a campaign that was largely symbolic in its appeals to youth, patriotism, civilization, and republican virtue (few dared dream that the PRP's candidate might be beaten), but that also intersected with more traditional machine politics.

The campaign against Valois began in the pages of the *Estadinho*, but leadership soon passed to the students of the state capital, chief among them the students of the São Paulo Law School, the zealous keepers of the flame of patriotism and civismo who formed the rank and file of the Nationalist League.[117] On 18 May, a commission representing "the youth of S. Paulo's superior schools" released a manifesto formally stating their opposition to Valois de Castro, whose "antinational convictions" were well known, and their intention, "conscious of [their own] patriotism," to support Pereira Barreto, entrusting his candidacy to the "Paulista People."[118]

The students were echoed by the city's journalists.[119] The *Estado de S. Paulo*'s Julio Mesquita was chief among these; he wrote a series of articles, each of which he closed with the appeal "Long Live the Brazilian Nation."[120] *O Combate* placed itself "by the side of the paulista people," seeing in Pereira Barreto's candidacy and in student activism evidence that the "Brazilian people" were "a virile race . . . a race that will regenerate itself rapidly and inevitably conquer a place among those who will exercise dominion over the world in the centuries to come."[121] The Italian-language press also expressed its support for Pereira Barreto, noting his stature as a patriot, a public figure, and a man of science.[122]

Alongside these press campaigns, Pereira Barreto's backers carried on public rallies, both in the state capital and in the cities and towns of the interior. Pereira Barreto's candidacy was formally launched in a "civic demonstration" held in downtown São Paulo on the evening of 14 May.[123] The *Diário Popular* noted the debut of "a new form of propaganda, [of the] North American method": "The students, . . . bearing 'placards,' took to the streets asking all those who were patriots to vote for Dr. Pereira Barreto. This method of propaganda was greeted by the people with [a] certain satisfaction. . . ."[124] The greatest novelty of the campaign was sending students into the cities and towns of the interior, where they gave speeches in support of Pereira Barreto's candidacy.[125]

During the three-week-long campaign, Pereira Barreto's candidacy received further support from throughout the state. The business-and-industry Municipal Party of the state capital, for example, came out publicly in favor of Pereira Barreto.[126] A group of self-described socialists, representing, in their own words, a "party of few men and little strength," did the same.[127] In Santos, Pereira Barreto received the support of the independent city councilman Heitor de Moraes and like-minded *santistas*.[128]

More importantly, ostensibly nonpolitical groups expressed support for the campaign. The state capital's liberal professionals were especially noteworthy in this regard, expressing their support in patriotic, corporate terms. The "medical class" of São Paulo, representing the city's physicians, endorsed their fellow healer in a manifesto that emphasized Pereira Barreto's qualities and their own nonpartisan status.[129] Writing to voice their own support for Pereira Barreto, a group of pharmacists emphasized their own "independence," clear in the fact that they were not "affiliated with any political party, [and] thus obeying only the dictates of our conscience."[130] Some of São Paulo's leading attorneys also published a manifesto supporting the dissident candidate.[131] Groups representing students, dentists, freemasons, and engineers did the same.[132]

Support also came from more familiar political figures. In Ribeirão Preto, for example, the Pereira Barreto candidacy not only sparked enthusiasm among the self-styled intellectuals who had founded *Patria* and the Nationalist Center, it also led Joaquim da Cunha to break with the PRP and support the opposition candidate. Not only was the candidate a friend and former resident of Ribeirão Preto, the campaign also appears to have offered an opportunity for Quinzinho to cement his local dominance and ensure the eclipse of his rival, Francisco Schmidt.[133]

On the eve of the election, *O Combate* addressed its readers, calling on them, one final time, to vote for Pereira Barreto, "illustrious sage, republican and liberal, . . . our first citizen, the paulista 'leader' of public opinion in support of our allies in the great war," predicting that "those who venerate science, those who love the Republic, those who worship the Patria, those who yearn for the victory of the 'Entente'" would vote for the opposition candidate. In a further illustration of the symbolic stakes of the election, the anonymous writer added: "The number of ballots does not matter. What matters is their meaning. Those that bear the name of Luiz Pereira Barreto indicate that their depositor is a citizen conscious of his responsibilities and the responsibilities of his Country in the international concert." "Whatever the arithmetic result of the election, its moral result is already known," as part of "the campaign for . . . civic revival" that would eventually lead to "a generalized movement" with "republicanism . . . taking hold of all classes, from the most humble to the most elevated."[134]

This deemphasis of the importance of the immediate outcome of the election, as opposed to the symbolism that Pereira Barreto's partisans chose to attach to it, must have seemed apt given the events of the following day, when many student leaders faced the obstacle of not being registered to vote.[135] Pereira Barreto supporters who were prepared to vote faced other problems. In Itararé, 230 men turned out to vote for the aged positivist, only to be met with threats of violence on the part of county power-holders.[136] In Casa Branca, supporters of Pereira Barreto who were charged with ensuring that the election was carried out fairly and honestly were turned away by local officials.[137] In Barretos, scores of local men voted for Pereira Barreto only to have their votes ignored or replaced with votes for Valois de Castro in the official tally.[138]

Alongside these familiar practices, one saw the widespread abstentionism that characterized most elections (and especially elections like this one, held on an irregular basis to fill vacated legislative posts) and the regional imbalances that were built into the republican machine. In the state capital, a mere 3,885 total votes were tallied, only 2,413 (62 percent) of which were given to the official candidate despite the "shameful compulsion" exerted by perrepista leaders. In contrast, the state's rotten boroughs provided unanimous or nearly unanimous tallies for Valois de Castro.[139]

The pro-Pereira Barreto press of the state capital was largely silent as to how the elections were conducted in Joaquim da Cunha's upper-Mogiana redoubt. Given what is known about how elections were usually carried out there, it is probably safe to assume that the results were managed, or at the very least finessed. In Ribeirão Preto itself, the official tally gave 795 votes to Pereira Barreto and only 20 to Valois de Castro. In other counties in the upper Mogiana, Pereira Barreto also won, though nowhere as overwhelmingly as in Ribeirão Preto.[140]

These upper-Mogiana tallies made up a large proportion of votes given Pereira Barreto, together with votes from the state capital and from a handful of other cities, including Campinas and Piracicaba, where he won outright, and Santos, where he lost by only a few dozen votes. Official tallies released a week after the election gave Pereira Barreto 10,152 votes to Valois's 30,295.[141]

The election itself was, in short, an anticlimax. It nevertheless serves as an illustration of how the developments of the 1910s came to work their way into republican politics, even intersecting with the work of regional chieftains such as Joaquim da Cunha. In cities and larger towns, students and journalists mounted an interesting if ineffective campaign that was self-consciously modern, one that succeeded in bringing together much of the same nationalist constituency as that mobilized during the demonstrations greeting Brazil's entry into World War I.

In the weeks following the election, journalists continued to sound off in articles that linked, either implicitly or explicitly, many of the themes present in the intellectual debates of the 1910s with the political dissidence and nationalist expression evident in the Pereira Barreto campaign. *O Estado de S. Paulo* complained that Valois had won "because the majority of the electorate is not made up of free and thinking men, but of poor automatons, and because there was very strong pressure on the part of those in power, as is notorious."[142] Julio Mesquita argued that "it is time for struggle," predicting: "Our bloodless war will probably go on slowly, as that of Europe. . . . Victory depends on perseverance. Patriotic groups can not, should not tire."[143] In an article entitled "He Who Is Not a Voter, Is Not a Good Citizen," *O Combate* proclaimed that "Patriotism is not just speaking out against the errors of those in government and enlisting oneself in the army or in militia training. It is also, and most importantly, helping the country to be well led, influencing the selection of its leaders. For this, being a voter is necessary."[144] The *Estadinho* proposed the formation of a new political party, one opposed to the "dominion" of the PRP executive committee, an idea greeted enthusiastically by the editors of *O Combate*, who proposed a minimum program that would satisfy all political "independents," including "conservatives, liberals and radicals," emphasizing freedom of conscience, adherence to the law, administrative and electoral honesty, and minority representation. As a standard around which all but anarchists could rally, *O Combate* put forward "the flag of nationalism."[145]

Meanwhile, the republican establishment regrouped and reassumed cohesion and dominance following the election, as it had in previous elections in which its candidates were challenged by perrepista outs or unaffiliated contenders. Where possible, local PRP directorates that had supported Pereira Barreto were replaced with new directorates stacked with loyalists, as in Conchas and São Joaquim. Where such settling of scores was impossible, as in Ribeirão Preto, the state-level leadership would eventually have to make peace with local power-holders.[146]

Less than a year after Pereira Barreto's defeat, Ruy Barbosa entered what would be his last presidential contest. The venerable Bahian statesman did so in a Brazil that had undergone marked changes in the decade since his 1909–1910 campaign. Added to these changes was the fact that the presidential election of 1919 was not an ordinary scheduled poll—it was called after the president-elect, Guaratinguetá's Francisco de Paula Rodrigues Alves, died on the early morning of 16 January 1919. The election to replace Rodrigues Alves was scheduled for 13 April, two weeks before elections to the São Paulo state legislature, which meant that the two contests would to a certain degree intersect, and thus at least part of the presidential campaign would involve jockeying among rival factions in the state's interior.

At the time of Rodrigues Alves's death, Ruy Barbosa was at the height of his celebrity, both as Brazil's most famous pro-war propagandist and for having recently celebrated his "Civic Jubilee."[147] To this popular acclaim, which was genuine enough, was added the interest of machine politicians from lesser Brazilian states who saw in Ruy's potential candidacy an opportunity to chip away at the hegemony of the dominant state machines. Chief among these establishment figures was Nilo Peçanha, president of the state of Rio de Janeiro.[148]

In São Paulo, Ruy's admirers scarcely waited for Rodrigues Alves to be lowered into the ground before proposing their idol's candidacy. In an editorial published three days after the president-elect's death, Julio Mesquita argued that Brazil faced a difficult conjuncture, one that demanded "an exceptional man." Fortunately, Brazil had just such a man, Ruy Barbosa, known "for his knowledge, for his talent, for his patriotism, for the high and radiant morality of his life as sage, apostle, and campaigner," honored in all languages as a "global figure." Ruy's candidacy, Mesquita argued, would offer Brazil another way, "superior to the customs of regional groupings and to oligarchical ambitions."[149]

The Revista do Brasil, ownership of which Mesquita and the other members of the magazine's founding group had recently transferred to Monteiro Lobato, then at the very outset of his own celebrity, took a similar position. In the Revista's February issue, an obituary for Rodrigues Alves was made the forum for a disquisition comparing the two statesmen, Rodrigues Alves, "the once and forever conservative," versus Ruy, the liberal under the empire, the maker of the republic, and the "eternal reformer":

> One adhere[d] to the Republic and a diluted political mentality. The other found[ed] it, but rejects the denatured republican criterion.
>
> The one . . . an administrator. The other, a statesman.
>
> The one . . . a politician. The other, a patriot.
>
> Rodrigues Alves [was] a man of his time. Ruy is one removed from the History of these nefarious days.

And, if the former [was] a great among lesser men, the latter is so among the greatest of this and other lands, in this and all times.[150]

The lead editorial of the same issue, "The Present Moment," claimed to distinguish the "apogee of the mediocratic system" in the existing political order. But its author took heart: "The National Opinion, never [before] consulted, raises its voice and from the thousand mouths of public opinion demands a Ruy presidency. . . . The submission to political incumbency unmakes itself. The collective will affirms itself. . . . The nation 'wants' Ruy Barbosa."[151]

Similar arguments were to be found at the other end of the literary spectrum, as in São Paulo's riotous, self-consciously "popular" *O Parafuso*, which announced to its "fifty or hundred thousand readers," amid scandalous reporting and material on the day-to-day problems of poor and middling folks, that Ruy was "the candidate of the People," rather than "politickers." It was, according to *O Parafuso*, "in the revolutionary character of the Ruy Barbosa candidacy that resides the reason that the People sustains it. The moment has come in which we should implant Democracy."[152]

While the presses put out more and more pro-Ruy material, ruyista groups swung into action. The first of these groups was a commission founded by law, engineering, and medical students, which called an open meeting in the state capital on 20 January.[153] Over the next few weeks, political figures big and small busied themselves with efforts on behalf of Ruy and other candidates, and committees were formed to promote Ruy's candidacy in all of São Paulo's most important centers (the state capital, Campinas, Santos, Ribeirão Preto), as well as in more out-of-the-way counties.[154]

On 25 February, a "National [Presidential] Convention" met in the federal Senate in Rio de Janeiro. Although the convention's outcome had already been arranged in meetings between representatives of Brazil's most populous states, it was still treated as a major event.[155] Grandiose speeches were the order of the day. The leader of the pro-Ruy delegates, a senator from Ceará no doubt chosen more for his rhetorical skills than his political consistency, emphasized that support for Ruy came from the "national will" rather than "political conclaves" or "party combinations"—statements that earned a vigorous challenge from the floor on the part of Álvaro de Carvalho, the ranking perrepista delegate—and made much of Ruy's role in bringing Brazil into the "campaign of civilization" that placed "Brazil among the great powers of the world, putting our homeland at the head of the destinies of America."[156] He thundered that those who opposed Ruy would widen "the chasm that is separating the political caste from national public opinion" and create "an unequalled crisis for this patria," before concluding, "the Brazilian nation acclaims . . . Ruy Barbosa as president of the Republic."[157]

Similar themes were treated in correspondence sent to the conference. The Pro-Ruy Academic Committee, writing "in the name of the students of São Paulo," made their dedication to Ruy's candidacy known in an extended appeal that placed support for Ruy in the context of the ongoing "nationalist campaign" for national defense, education, and Brazil's incipient "political regeneration." As during the Pereira Barreto campaign of the year before, the students framed their support for the "greatest of Brazilians" by emphasizing youthful idealism and their status as "an independent class par excellence" and as interpreters of the "Brazilian nationality," "popular sovereignty," and "public opinion."[158]

As the delegates revealed their ostensibly individual opinions, it was revealed that the candidacy of Epitácio Pessoa, a senator from the northeastern state of Paraíba, had secured more than enough support to claim victory. The final tally was 139 delegates for Pessoa to 42 for Ruy Barbosa. All but 2 of São Paulo's 14 delegates backed the winning candidate; only Julio Mesquita and Raphael Sampaio Vidal voted for Ruy.[159]

The adoption of Pessoa's candidacy by the republican establishments of all of the most important states (São Paulo, Minas Gerais, Rio Grande do Sul, Pernambuco, and even Ruy's home state of Bahia) made Ruy's candidacy a lost cause. However, unlike the presidential campaign of 1913–14, from which he had desisted when faced with similarly overwhelming odds, Ruy did not yield. Instead, perhaps spurred by a special enmity with Pessoa or by some inkling that this would be his last campaign, he held Nilo Peçanha to his word and, supported only by the republican machines of Pará and Rio de Janeiro, announced his plans to stand as an opposition candidate.[160]

Ruy opened his campaign on 8 March in the federal capital with a three-and-a-quarter-hour-long speech held in the great hall of the city's Commercial Association entitled "To the Propertied Classes." In his long, drawn-out address, Ruy condemned the existing political system, which he held to be the true cause of Brazilian backwardness:

> All of this Brazil, anemic, oppilated, swollen-bellied, slack-legged, cretinous, enervated, crippled, without memory, initiative, industriousness, perseverance, or courage; all this denaturation of our nationality does not come from

the black, nor from the caboclo, nor from the mestiço, nor from the Portuguese, whose vigor, insurrect and disordered, but virile, is right now reminding us of the heroic temper of the old race. It comes from the political evil, the chlorotic, enervating, defibrinating *politico*rrhea, that submits the nation to all of the physical and moral ailments of a people without hygiene of the body or of the soul.[161]

Political malfeasance was manifest in the government's indifference, incompetence, and corruption:

This evil, that our two greatest necessities in the physical and the moral order, teaching and hygiene, still do not merit the creation of a ministry of education and public health, which I have advocated for almost forty years. This evil that is cretinizing us with the proscription of merit and the consecration of incompetence. This evil that is stultifying us with the habitual spectacle of immorality in the highest councils of the Republic and the highest positions in the State. This evil that, provoking national public opinion every day by its management of our domestic affairs, still wants to challenge the public opinion of the world in its direction of our international relations.[162]

Addressing his audience directly, Ruy argued that "this evil" was able to flourish due to the "involuntary complicity of the property-owning classes, by their abstention, by their languor, by their disorganization" and called on his audience to "organize themselves" for nothing less than the political "regeneration" of Brazil.[163] Without just such a political regeneration—which would require "daring reforms" and "transcendental measures"—Brazil's "oligarchy," like its German and Russian counterparts, would "open, by [fostering] broad discontent, the doors to anarchy, to the seduction of the people by anarchy, to the dissolution of the people by anarchy."[164]

Nearly two weeks later, again in Rio de Janeiro, Ruy addressed workers in a speech entitled "The Political and Social Question."[165] Ruy opened the speech by referring to Jeca Tatú, the poor, ignorant, diseased caipira of Monteiro Lobato's *Urupês*, a figure "incapable of evolution and immune to progress." After sketching out the character for his audience, Ruy argued that Brazil's rulers thought of the Brazilian population in similar terms and that this perception was the basis for their belief that they could rule in the way they did, through corruption, intrigue, and heavy-handedness. Ruy himself took a different view:

Brazil is not [a] collective gathering of debauched creatures, over which can run, without [making] the slightest impression, the currents of the aspirations that at this time agitate all of humanity. No! Brazil is not this cold, deliquescent, cadaverized nationality that receives on its head the stamp of a gang, as the fallen woman receives on her arm the tattoo of her lover, or the galley slave, on his back, the fleur de lis of his driver. No! Brazil does not accept the grave that the exploiters of the Treasury are digging for it, the grave in which the giant armadillos of politicking have been gnawing to the bone. Nothing, none of this is Brazil.[166]

Rather, Ruy argued, the assembly before him represented Brazil:

Brazil is not "that." It is "this." Brazil, sirs, is you. Brazil is this assembly. Brazil is this immense meeting of free spirits. It is not the commensals of the budget. It is not the thieves of the Treasury. It is not the merchants of the parliament. It is not the bloodsuckers of public wealth. It is not the falsifiers of elections. It is not the buyers of newspapers [i.e., those who would suborn the press]. It is not the corruptors of the republican system. . . . . It is the active cells of national life. It is the multitude that does not flatter, does not fear, does not run, does not retreat, does not desert, does not sell itself. It is not the unconscious mass that oscillates between servitude and disorder, but rather the organic cohesion of thinking beings, the ocean of consciences, the mass of human waves where Providence stores inexhaustible reserves of heat, of power and of light for the renovation of our energies.[167]

Ruy then embarked on a long treatise on labor, social reform, and the constitution. Along the way, he endorsed the labor theory of value (though he contradicted it elsewhere), emphasized his own work on behalf of abolition in the service of Brazil's "primitive working class," and provided a brief history of social legislation in Brazil, while disparaging his foes and making his characteristic learned allusions to events overseas. He expressed his support for an effective system of accident insurance, equal pay for equal work, the regulation of child labor, the eight-hour day, maternity leave, the regulation of nighttime labor, an end to piece-work conducted in the home, and an end, where possible, to company stores. These goals could be reached through peaceful means, Ruy held, through the ballot box, constitutional revision, and class collaboration, rather than through violence.[168]

Ruy's call for social and political reform was warmly received in liberal corners in São Paulo. Julio Mesquita expressed his support—"without a doubt"—and his newspaper echoed Ruy, claiming that if Brazilians did not carry out social reform "willingly and in order, it would come by itself, forcefully and in disorder, fitfully and violently, in torment after torment, through wellsprings of blood."[169]

As suggested by Mesquita's enthusiasm, support for Ruy's candidacy came from many of the same individuals and groups that had backed Pereira Barreto against Valois de Castro the previous year. Students, professionals, and republicans of varied stripes rallied to the side of the Bahian. At the same time, March and April also witnessed working-class support, which had been scarcer in the previous year's campaign.

Students maintained the enthusiasm that they had shown from the first.[170] As the campaign went on, students increasingly found themselves speaking on behalf of the "people," as in the protest issued on behalf of the beleaguered ruyistas of Bahia by the São Paulo Law School's most important student group, "in [the] name [of the] sentiments [and] civilization [of the] Brazilian people."[171] A member of the state capital's pro-Ruy student committee also spoke in the name of the "people" against the politicians, "enriched in most cases by the hard work of the people," and decried the lack of "a representative of agriculture, a representative of commerce, a large industrialist, a man of work" among São Paulo's elected officials.[172]

This speech, published in O Estado de S. Paulo, was no doubt pleasing to members of the Municipal Party, the self-appointed political vehicle of the state capital's "propertied classes," which also gave its support to Ruy's campaign.[173] In its final call on voters to support "the candidate of democracy," the party's executive committee compared Ruy to Lloyd George, Georges Clemenceau, and Woodrow Wilson—the leaders "of our great allies"—exhorting their "fellow citizens" to work for the "victory of the national candidate."[174]

As the Municipal Party's evocation of the Allies' wartime leaders makes clear, the presidential campaign also saw the reemergence of many of the same accusations that had been so important in the Pereira Barreto campaign. Mário Pinto Serva, a member of the Nationalist League and a vocal advocate of the secret ballot, denounced Pessoa's "Monstrous Candidacy" as pro-German.[175] Julio Mesquita did the same, adding that Ruy's opponent was an "enemy of S. Paulo."[176] Another Ruy supporter, speaking to a charity event for the French war-wounded, lauded Ruy's candidacy, emphasizing, to much applause, "the prestige that the great Brazilian enjoyed among the principal nations of the 'Entente.' "[177]

In Campinas, Pedro Magalhães Júnior referred explicitly to the Pereira Barreto campaign, noting that despite government pressure the "people" had backed the previous year's dissident candidate. The government, however, was able to impose its will, "with the vilipending of the truth, with the annihilation of justice." Now, with the Ruy Barbosa campaign facing the same difficulties, Magalhães warned that if Ruy was not victorious, it would be the fault of the same people, "people feeble in protest, people incapable of reaction, people impotent to assume the responsibility of a democracy, people cowardly of a revolution."[178]

In Ribeirão Preto, Ruy's supporters also evoked the Pereira Barreto campaign, in a propaganda bulletin that declared:

> The presidential election of the 13th [of April] is not a simple conflict between two candidacies over the leadership of the nation. It is the decisive clash between "two symbols, two historical phases, two irreconcilable fundamental conceptions!"
>
> It is the old Brazil, corroded by debased oligarchies, undermined by administrative corruption, the Brazil of adulation, of the Valois, the Brazil of shady deals, of outrages, of electoral fraud, which seeks to hold back the new honest and liberal Brazil that is coming, regenerated and indomitable, prepared to reclaim a place of dignity among the great peoples of the earth.
>
> Ruy Barbosa represents the new Brazil and Epitacio Pessoa, the old.[179]

In other interior counties, speakers echoed Ruy's own words. In São Carlos, Aureliano Guimarães, a lawyer and journalist who had been an enthusiastic civilianist and a Pereira Barreto supporter, was to speak on "The Social Question and the Meaning of Ruy['s] Candidacy."[180] In Rio Claro, the law student João Fina Sobrinho, born locally to immigrant parents, spoke on "The Great Social and Political Revolution in Brazil," while the editor of Rio Claro's O Alpha, one of the interior's leading daily newspapers, helped regiment local workingmen in support of Ruy's candidacy.[181]

Particular appeals were made to urban workers in Campinas as well. In São Paulo's second city, workingmen were represented on the local pro-Ruy committee by Jorge Closel, who appealed to the "campineiro working class," comparing the two candidates: the one "supported by the will of the people" and the other "the expression of the desires of the corrupt oligarchies"; Ruy Barbosa, "whose political career . . . constitutes a testimonial of how well he understands all of our social questions," and Epitácio Pessoa, who displayed none "of the necessary qualities to lead a nationality in the critical phase that the world passes through." Ruy, Closel argued, was "the only one capable of favorably solving those questions having to do with the well-being of the working class and of the Patria in general."[182]

On the eve of the election, another pro-Ruy leader addressed the workers of Campinas, confident that they would vote for "the greatest of Brazilians" because "Brazil has two powerful supports where it will find its salvation, the proletariat and the press . . . the independent press."[183] The latter was represented in Campinas by the local office of *O Estado de S. Paulo*, by Álvaro Ribeiro's *Diário do Povo*, and by the *Comércio de Campinas*, to which was added Pedro Magalhães Júnior's *Ruy Barbosa*, published ephemerally for the campaign "for the defeat of the oligarchies, for the guarantee of liberty, for the guarantee of justice."[184] As for the "proletariat" itself, laboring men might not have supported the campaign as ostentatiously as the mostly middle-class members of the local pro-Ruy committee, but they had little love for the sitting state government, which they were not above demonstrating at the polls, and a contingent of local railwaymen was bold enough to telegraph Ruy their support.[185]

Elsewhere, support came from more traditional republican quarters. In the fifth electoral district, Gabriel Rocha, a state congressman since 1907, attempted to take advantage of popular enthusiasm for Ruy and link his independent reelection campaign to the presidential contest when faced with the PRP's endorsement of other candidates to the state legislature.[186] His bid for reelection was unsuccessful, but in true perrepista fashion, "despite having run independently for a congressman's chair and despite his fiery last-minute ruyismo," Rocha was "perfectly integrated in the P. R. P." by October's municipal elections.[187]

Ruy himself traveled to São Paulo to promote his candidacy. Arriving in the state capital by overnight train on the morning of 4 April, he was greeted at the station by a "multitude" of supporters and well-wishers, who had been invited to come out "without discrimination [on the basis] of social class, political beliefs, or nationality, excluding only the enemies of Brazil and of its allies," by a committee composed of Raphael Sampaio Vidal, Julio Mesquita, and José Carlos de Macedo Soares.[188] The enthusiasm and impressive size of the crowds that met his train and escorted the candidate and his entourage through the city center to their hotel is clear in photographs of the occasion.[189] From the hotel's second story, the crowds—the "People of S. Paulo . . . free São Paulo"—were addressed by Alfredo Pujol, a veteran of the campaign of 1909–10, and by Santos's Heitor de Moraes.[190]

After a full day of visits and tributes, Ruy addressed his supporters at the Municipal Theater. By the time he took the stage, delayed by the crush of people surrounding the building, the theater was packed.[191] Although the subject of his speech, "The International Situation," would allow him to make much of his efforts on behalf of the Allies, Ruy did not begin by talking of world affairs. Instead, he opened his speech with an idealized account of his campaign of 1909–10: "It fell to me the proud lot to contest the election in the company of this great State, the greatest of all of ours for its riches, progress and culture, but not only from the official State [i.e., the PRP and sitting state government], but also and above all, to my satisfaction and pride, from the general opinion of its people. Consubstantiated with my name and my program, the inhabitants of São Paulo and their government provided, by the unprecedented enthusiasm with which they dedicated themselves to the electoral campaign, a spectacle of rare beauty in the history of Brazilian civismo [and] elevated the prestige of the paulista name to an exceptional stature."[192]

Now, however, his candidacy was opposed by the state government. "Who changed?" Ruy asked. Answering his own question earnestly if not exactly honestly, he replied, "If anyone changed, certainly it was not me. The man of 1919 does not contradict one single point of the man of 1910. The ideals for which I struggle today are strictly the same for which I struggled nine years ago. . . . The man is the same, his convictions the same, his aim the same. If, then, I did not change, it is they who changed, they who disavow, they who renege. Renege on what? On liberty, which I advocated and you advocated with me? On the democratization of the regime, which I wanted, and which you wanted with me? On progressive reforms, which I supported, and which you supported with me?"[193]

Ruy then turned to his campaign in favor of the Allies and a Brazilian declaration of war, to which he appended a soliloquy on the intrigue surrounding his absence from the Brazilian delegation to the peace conference, emphasizing his own international fame throughout with extended quotes from foreign newspapers. He also outlined his own ideas on foreign policy, with particular emphasis on preserving the independence of weaker nations, citing Woodrow Wilson and Brazil's own Baron of Rio Branco. Ruy closed by referring to political repression in his home state of Bahia, noting that the federal government supported peace initiatives abroad while tolerating the "war" carried out against Brazil's domestic political opposition. He was applauded warmly throughout.[194]

Early the next morning, Ruy returned to Rio de Janeiro, sent off at the station with an improvised speech predicting the victory of "the dauntless champion of liberty." Campaigning did not end, however, with the "Long Live the Great [State of] São Paulo" that Ruy sounded as his train began to pull away from the platform.[195] Instead, Ruy was feted along the length of the Central do Brasil Railroad, from Mogi das Cruzes to

Queluz and into the state of Rio de Janeiro, including in such PRP strongholds as Taubaté and Guaratinguetá.[196]

In the wake of Ruy's visit, his supporters carried on the campaign. Staying behind in São Paulo was the labor lawyer Evaristo de Moraes, who had arrived with Ruy on 4 April. At rallies in Santos, Campinas, and the state capital, Moraes's blistering denunciations of São Paulo's "oligarchy" and evocations of the state's republican and abolitionist traditions, appealing to the "conscientious and independent electorate" to vote for Ruy and thus "democratize the Republic," were well-received.[197]

The PRP's efforts on behalf of Epitácio Pessoa were less impressive. While the fighting in Europe had gone on, the state's power-holders were able to use the wartime state of siege to censor the opposition press; hostilities having ceased, they were compelled to import writers—journalistic ringers—from Rio de Janeiro to bolster the beleaguered staff of the *Correio Paulistano*.[198] Perrepistas were able to organize a single pro-Pessoa rally and managed to get around two hundred paulistas to attend, including "public employees, who received insistent invitations," but their speakers were shouted down by a counterdemonstration of "paulista youth," who were in turn set upon by state troops.[199]

Paulistas went to the polls the next day. In the state capital, the usual intimidation could not avert a ruyista victory in the city proper; Pessoa only won the capital once the votes of the purlieus were tallied. In Campinas, Piracicaba, and other important counties, Ruy won outright.[200] At the day's close, surveying early returns, Julio Mesquita telegraphed Ruy: "In the capital we won the election; in the remote suburbs they gave Epitacio a slight majority of 300 votes: 3,000 against 2,700. Known total for the State: Epitacio 10,500, Ruy 8,000. There was enormous pressure and some outrages. . . . This result is from the live zone of the State. From here on the proportion [of Ruy votes to Epitácio votes] will diminish due to bico de penna, but we will still have [attained] brilliant polling."[201] The final results, as reported to the national legislature, gave Ruy more than a quarter of the state's 55,250 votes.[202]

The PRP leadership was still more satisfied than Mesquita, though for different reasons. On the day after the election, Altino Arantes, the state president, wrote Joaquim da Cunha of Ribeirão Preto by telegraph: "I was very pleased with the result of the presidential election there," where early reports gave his candidate 602 votes to Ruy's 180.[203] More to the point, Arantes was pleased that Joaquim da Cunha's return to the perrepista fold came in time for the state legislative elections to be held later that month.[204] As he wrote later the same day, raising the subject of the electoral matters at hand, the "Executive Committee adopted as its preponderant standard to place [on the ballot] in the first round the older candidates and in the second the younger ones, the latter role falling, in the 10th district, to Rafael [Corrêa de Sampaio] and Chico [Francisco da Cunha Junqueira]." He continued, "I believe that these two friends run no risk, as no rival candidates with the chance of victory exist." He then added, gingerly, "However, if my friend deems it useful for the success of the election, I can suggest to the Executive Committee the division of the district in five zones of more or less equal voting, so that all candidates receive votes in the first and second rounds."[205] Francisco Junqueira (Joaquim da Cunha's nephew) ended up receiving the greatest number of first-round votes, and the political reconciliation was complete.[206]

The last major elections of the 1910s were held in late October 1919. The unfolding of these statewide municipal elections betrays the influence of the preceding years' grand political, social, and intellectual campaigns on the county- and subcounty-level politics that formed the base of the republican system, while simultaneously illustrating the resilience of the same.

October 1919 witnessed a series of successful attempts at including workingmen in municipal-level electoral politics. In Limeira, the incumbent republican directorate reserved one spot on its electoral slate "for a representative of the working class" and then held primary elections to choose that representative. When, after some confusion, a candidate was finally chosen, Vicente Ferraz Pacheco, the official orator of the Worker's Center and a supporter of the Nationalist League, "issued an appeal to the working class to form a strong party, putting aside any resentment or animosity that might exist, and lend all their prestige to [the candidate], who in the next county council, will be the interpreter of the aspirations of the class."[207] In Jaú, it was the local opposition that included a working-class candidate on its slate, Marcellino Di Giacomo, with whom it sought to attract "the support of urban workers."[208] In the Paraíba Valley county of Lorena, local outs reserved two spots on their slate for candidates representing the liberal professions, three for commerce, two for agriculture, and one for the working class.[209] Presenting the candidacy of a fellow worker, Joaquim Coppio, Rodolpho Castro addressed a party gathering, informing the assembled that Coppio had been chosen "by real workers, men of rude labor, but who have a good understanding of their civic duties and who are not the turbulent ones who unduly agitate the working class of the large cities and fleeing through the interior of the States attempt to plant anarchistic and subversive ideas."

Unlike these agitators, stock characters in the sensationalistic news reports of the era, the working class of Lorena "seeks and will always seek to prepare and fulfill a program that has as its base the union of capital, labor and justice, these three indispensable elements for the confraternization of the Brazilian people." As town councilman, Coppio would carry on this program, "always defending the interests of the working class."[210] On 30 October, Coppio was elected, along with his counterparts in Jaú and Limeira.[211]

In still other counties, middle-class politicians who had sided with labor during the recent strikes stood for reelection. In Campinas, Álvaro Ribeiro ran another independent city council campaign against a local PRP determined to punish him for his role in the Pereira Barreto and Ruy Barbosa campaigns.[212] In Santos, councilman Heitor de Moraes found himself in a similar position, backed by fellow Ruy supporters such as Cyrillo Freire, the publisher of *Gazeta do Povo*, and Luiz Lascala, a former construction worker who apparently traded revolutionary syndicalism for dissident republicanism once established as a builder.[213] Both Moraes and Ribeiro were reelected despite their exclusion from the official slates.[214]

In the city of São Paulo, a tamer sort of independent was successful. Of a field of more than thirty candidates to the municipal council, Mário Graccho was only non-perrepista to overcome the ruling party's monopoly, due in large part to the following he had cultivated in the industrial neighborhoods east of the city center, where he practiced medicine.[215] Among the losers were all four businessmen put forward by the Municipal Party (which could have elected two councilmen but for the dilution of its votes among too many candidates) and Moacyr Piza, a young firebrand who had supported Pereira Barreto and Ruy Barbosa.[216]

Throughout much of the rest of the state, the municipal election cycle unfolded in more familiar patterns. Local bosses and their henchmen sought local power through traditional means, not the watered-down class representation seen in Jaú, Limeira, and Lorena or the independent campaigning of a Moacyr Piza, Heitor de Moraes, or Álvaro Ribeiro.

A relatively benign form of machine politics prevailed in Mogi das Cruzes. In this county just east of the state capital, on the edge of the Paraíba Valley, the physician Deodato Wertheimer (the president of a local political club since 1915 and long an aspirant to political office) counted on residents grateful for his services during the influenza epidemic; they elected him to the city council, which then named him prefeito.[217]

In upper-Paulista Araras, the local PRP faced a new challenger in a recently founded Municipal Party. When it appeared that local incumbents would resort to violence as well as fraud, a police official was ordered to keep the peace. The election itself was held peacefully, in the presence of the police delegate and with the participation of dutifully loyal voters carted in from neighboring counties; it resulted in the perrepistas electing five town councilmen and all three justices of the peace, to the municipalists' three town councilmen.[218]

No such decorum prevailed in the northern county of Barretos and, as a result, the local opposition fared more poorly. One of its leaders, himself a justice of the peace, was forced to flee, fearing for his life at the hands of the hired toughs of the local PRP chief, Antônio Olympio, who had outdone Sylvestre de Lima in bidding for recognition from the executive committee. With the justice of the peace out of the way, the olympistas set up the polls in a house belonging to Antônio Olympio himself.[219] As the elections drew closer, opposition voters were intimidated, beaten, and jailed. On the eve of the elections, opposition voters housed in the town's theater were attacked by olympista capangas and local police, who subjected the building to withering gunfire. With several of their voters dead or gravely wounded, the local opposition opted to sit out the election and the olympistas claimed victory.[220]

Elections in São Bento do Sapucaí, a relatively unimportant county in the upcountry north of the Paraíba Valley, were also held amid violence, with perrepista hired guns shooting up the home of a municipalist opponent. When another of the Municipal Party's "new folks," a then-obscure journalist named Plínio Salgado, returned fire, he was jailed. São Bento's incumbents thus retained control of county government.[221]

In the days following the municipal elections, Julio Mesquita addressed readers in two consecutive columns. He noted the higher than usual voter turnout (characteristic of municipal elections more generally) and expressed his belief "in the rebirth of civismo" among the "Brazilian people" and his hope that soon "all elections, the municipal, state, and federal elections, free themselves from the monopolizing and demoralizing control of the professional politicians." Mesquita's hope was founded on two perceptions: first, that "the election was clean, or, at least, as clean as our laws allow"; and second, that "paulista public opinion awakens, and depends only on us not to return to slumber."[222] These two beliefs were apparently influenced by the perceived need for conciliation in the face of insurgent labor and an optimistic reading of the outcomes of the Pereira Barreto and Ruy Barbosa campaigns.

Goffredo Telles—a poet, absentee planter, and *ararense* opposition leader—discerned similar forces at work. The electoral fraud and intimidation that he personally witnessed in Araras, "similar, without a doubt, to those that occur continually at points throughout the country," already appeared to him to be the "remains of a confused past," and their protagonists the embodiment of "an extinct phase of the history of our people." Brazil, Telles argued, was awakening, bringing an end to this phase and the coming of "republican honesty."[223]

In their respective prognostications, Telles and Mesquita—the former a municipalist who would return to the perrepista fold in the following decade, the latter São Paulo's most important liberal spokesman—were sorely mistaken. Telles's "republican honesty" was far from forthcoming, and, contrary to Mesquita's best hopes, Brazil's professional politicians were hardly about to give up the ghost. But in making note of changed circumstances, the two men were in the right. The preceding months and years had witnessed important developments in paulista public life alongside and, in some cases, in opposition to aspects of São Paulo's republic of layers. These developments were to endure and, indeed, to deepen over time, intersecting with the military rebellions of the Brazilian 1920s in fairly short order.

4 Knaves, Pedants, and Rebels

The years 1921–22 witnessed another contested presidential campaign, in which Rio de Janeiro's Nilo Peçanha challenged Arthur Bernardes, another Minas-born candidate of Brazil's great and powerful state machines. In his campaign, dubbed the Republican Reaction, Peçanha counted on the support of politicians from other second-tier states, jealous of the power guarded by mineiro and paulista statesmen. He also counted on dissident republicans elsewhere, including in São Paulo, and on a significant portion of the army's officer corps. As befit an old political hand, Peçanha took his loss in stride, but some of his backers did not. Military and civilian conspirators came to advocate an armed solution to the problem of a Bernardes presidency and, in an abortive first attempt, mounted a daylong uprising in Rio de Janeiro on 5 July 1922.

Romantic, heroic even, the uprising was quickly put down, to the relief of some and the disappointment of others. Two years later, however, a second anti-Bernardes rebellion, this one aimed at his overthrow where the preceding one was to have prevented his inauguration, proved much more difficult to contain. This time, conspirators chose the city of São Paulo as the site for their initial call to arms and, in short order, were able to establish control over Brazil's second-largest city and portions of the interior of its most important state, while paulista leaders were reduced to retreat and reliance on extra-regional forces to reestablish their dominance. After their withdrawal from the city of São Paulo, the rebels were able to elude capture and defeat, forming the basis for a small army that went on to campaign through the remote interior of Brazil, from Mato Grosso through Goiás and throughout the states of the northeast, skirmishing with federal troops, state policemen, and the hired guns of local chieftains.

Even as this campaign continued, veterans of the 1924 revolt, their opponents, and other eyewitnesses began to record their experiences.[1]

These firsthand accounts were eventually joined by the works of professional historians.[2] The richness of the resulting body of literature notwithstanding, some important aspects of the revolt and its aftermath
remain virtually unstudied. Too often, the revolt is viewed distinctly
from the history of its setting. During July 1924, individuals and groups
throughout São Paulo used the revolt and the chaos it produced to press
competing claims in diffuse and often contradictory ways. These men
and women represented only a tiny minority of the state's total population, to be sure, but their actions, particularly those of local political
incumbents, outs, and idealists, were significant. The response that these
traumatic events elicited from paulista intellectuals was no less significant, as was the subsequent apotheosis of the military rebels, during their
years in the wilderness and thereafter, as their leaders attained the status
of "heroes of the people" before a larger public.

A City Besieged

The month of July 1924 was an agonizing one for the population of the
state capital, marked as it was by material privation, physical danger, and
the terrifying experience of repeated artillery bombardments. Various
groups, including civic associations, social clubs, and the city's journalistic corps, stepped into the breach and attempted to maintain order and
provide assistance to the population at large. Some individuals, including
members of these groups, sought to defend legality or support the rebellion. Still others used the revolt as an occasion for mobilization on
behalf of their own visions of reform and revolution.

The outbreak of the revolt, which at first appeared to be little more
than a barracks rising, was the occasion for political figures large and
small to rally around the state government headed by Carlos de Campos,
a son of the late Bernardino de Campos and brother of Sylvio de Campos, the new boss of the state capital. Eager to offer his support, Júlio
Prestes, a rising star in the PRP, arrived at the state presidential palace in
the early morning accompanied by José Molinaro and another of the
city's neighborhood bosses. By early evening they had been joined by
around 150 other civilians, including politicians who had broken away
from the rump PRP during the party's most recent schism.[3] Even the
incumbents' political opponents of greater consistency registered their
support for the "constituted powers," confident that the government
would remain in control. Such was the case of the *Estado de S. Paulo*

group, for example, represented at that moment by Julio Mesquita's eldest son and namesake, Julio de Mesquita Filho.[4]

The president of the São Paulo Commercial Association (ACSP), José Carlos de Macedo Soares, who was traveling in the Paraíba Valley region, learned of the outbreak of the revolt via a telephone call from the industrialist Roberto Simonsen, whereupon he immediately telegraphed Carlos de Campos to offer his support.[5] Returning to São Paulo, Macedo Soares authored a public statement condemning the rebel bombardment of the state capital and, in particular, the shelling directed at the state president's residence, the seat "of a government . . . that has not yet given the least indication of impropriety, and that, on the contrary, has revealed [itself to be] a profoundly democratic government, and entirely dedicated to the interests and prosperity of the State of São Paulo." Given this "undeserved act of aggression," he called on the city's propertied classes to lend sympathy and support to the "heroic resistance" of the state government.[6]

Following the withdrawal of legalist forces on 9 July (including Carlos de Campos and the perrepistas who had joined him in the presidential palace), Macedo Soares convened a meeting of the city's leading lights, a meeting also attended by General Isidoro Dias Lopes, who headed the rebel forces. This "great meeting of industrialists and merchants" was noteworthy for its near unanimity: almost all participants supported Prefeito Firmiano Pinto's proposal to create a municipal guard for the protection of property and agreed that it was time to get back to work. (In lonely disagreement was Luiz Augusto Pereira de Queiroz, elected to the city council as an independent in 1922, only to become a vocal backer of the PRP after his nomination to a post in the executive arm of municipal government.) The meeting resulted in the publication of a manifesto calling for a return to normalcy, so that the city's industrial and commercial establishments could get back to business.[7]

When legalist forces began shelling the rebel-held city, Macedo Soares again took action, this time to protest. As ACSP president, Macedo Soares wrote General Abílio de Noronha in the hope that he would intercede and apprise President Bernardes of the situation. "The events demonstrate that one is not dealing with a simple military insurrection," he wrote. "The Revolutionary Forces are, it seems, organized for Civil War. The rebels have in their power the City of S. Paulo—the most valuable prize that they could hope for." Macedo Soares expressed little doubt that the government would eventually prevail, but he feared that this victory would be accomplished "by the leveling of S. Paulo . . . the pillage of Banks, of houses of commerce and industry . . . the massacre of its population." He implored the legalists not to permit "the economic and financial annihilation of the State of S. Paulo, the most prosperous unit of the Federation."[8]

Three days later, Macedo Soares used an emissary to send a message to Ribeirão Preto's Joaquim da Cunha. Macedo Soares lauded the powerful chieftain's defense of his upper-Mogiana redoubt, where the old boss organized his followers in a militia of sorts, adding, "It is necessary that everywhere, us, planters, merchants, and industrialists, who have [much] to lose, join together for the defense of order, which concerns all of us."[9]

On 27 July, Macedo Soares, again in his capacity as ACSP president and thus "occasional chief of the property-owning classes," made a final attempt at ending the conflict. Addressing the legalist commander, General Eduardo Socrates, in a letter he also forwarded on to state president Carlos de Campos, Macedo Soares implored the authorities to issue a forty-eight hour armistice so that peace could be negotiated between the two sides before "the State of São Paulo, and thus Brazil," fell into the "most desolate ruin." His appeal went unheeded by the legalist side but his prayers (for Macedo Soares was a man of faith as well as high finance) were answered by the rebel leaders, who evacuated their forces under cover of darkness on the night of 27–28 July.[10]

Over the course of July, the Nationalist League's position shifted more or less in tandem with that of Macedo Soares and the ACSP. The league's first public statement after the outbreak of the revolt was a protest "against the action[s] of the rebellious soldiers, who sacrifice children, women and a hard-working city."[11] When the government began to shell rebel-held areas a few days later, the league again protested: "The Nationalist League, in keeping with [its] protest against the bombardment put into effect by the revolutionary forces, now protests against the same means of combat used by the legalist forces, with [the resulting] sacrifice of the lives of women, children and persons indifferent to political struggle."[12] Throughout the rebellion, members of the league were active in the policing of the city and in providing succor to city residents.[13]

Another motion to end the shelling was drafted by Firmiano Pinto and Dom Duarte Leopoldo e Silva, the archbishop of São Paulo. It bore the signatures of incumbent politicians, lawyers, judges, educators, businessmen, and Plínio Barreto, a journalist by trade (he was a junior editor at *O Estado de S. Paulo*) then serving as the acting president of the Nationalist League.[14]

The shelling only ceased with the rebel withdrawal at the end of the month. By the time the proverbial smoke had cleared, the student body of the São Paulo Law School, from which the Nationalist League had sprung in 1916–17, was split on the subject of the rebellion. The "offspring and favorites" of the ruling clique remained stridently pro-government, sponsoring a public tribute to Carlos de Campos in mid-August. A larger group remained opposed to the revolt but no longer supported the state or federal governments, in large part in reaction to a post-revolt clampdown that included the jailing of Macedo Soares, a leading figure among law school alumni, and the closing of the Nationalist League. Finally, there were those who now "frankly supported the revolution."[15]

The law student Raul Renato Cardoso de Mello Filho had expressed his contempt for the federal government and for the legalist cause earlier, while the battle for the state capital was still joined. At mid-month he was among a group of young men who authored a statement condemning the shelling and decrying the "tyranny of dirt and blood" of Arthur Bernardes, a "ridiculous Nero."[16] Alone, Cardoso de Mello Filho went still further, calling on students, especially his fellow law students, to join the "regenerating military movement, which had sought the same welcoming and noble womb as our political emancipation," for which he was jailed by legalist troops.[17]

Clovis Botelho Vieira, a São Paulo Law School alumnus and an active campaigner for Ruy Barbosa five years earlier, issued an "open letter" calling on the Nationalist League to support the military rebels. Having read the rebels' minimal program for a provisional government (it called for instituting the secret ballot along with other mildly reformist measures, such as a ban on interstate taxation), he declared that "no independent . . . Brazilian can fight against a highly patriotic movement" that had as its aims "the most serious reforms." The centerpiece of the league's program, the secret ballot, would not be achieved through a "liberality" on the part of the "lords of the electoral machines," Botelho Vieira argued. Rather, it had "to be achieved by revolution or it will continue to be an eternal utopia in our patria." Botelho Vieira managed to escape the first post-revolt dragnet but was subsequently jailed.[18]

Belisário Penna, a mineiro in the temporary employ of the São Paulo state government, also took the side of the rebels. He justified his support, which would earn him jail time as well, on the basis of the points of agreement between his reformism and the declared aims of the military rebels, specifically educational, electoral, and judicial reform, in addition to their criticism of the Bernardes government.[19]

Leaders of São Paulo's pro–Nilo Peçanha movement of two years earlier (the Republican Reaction of 1921–22) were likewise drawn to the rebel cause. Nicolau Soares do Couto Esher, a physician and historic republican who had been president of one of São Paulo's two Republican Reaction committees, condemned *O Estado de S. Paulo* for what he saw as implicitly pro-government reporting, in particular the newspaper's failure to censure the legalist side for the deaths of noncombatants killed in its bombardments. The *Estado*'s "silence and muteness," Couto Esher argued, "demonstrate[d its] antipathy" for the ongoing "republican revolution" in São Paulo.[20] The lawyer Benjamin Mota, with Couto Esher a leader of the 1921–22 campaign, was another rebel enthusiast. Mota's support for the Republican Reaction and the July rebellion were the latest stages in a history of political opposition that took him from reformist republicanism to São Paulo's tiny, mostly Italian socialist movement of the turn of the century, on to the larger anarchist movement, and then to a new radical republicanism tinged by the mobilizing ideas of the 1910s. As a result of his support for the military rebels, Mota was imprisoned through the end of the year.[21]

Two other prominent paulistano supporters of the Republican Reaction, Mauro Machado and Pedro de Alcântara Tocci, actually joined the rebel movement, falling back with rebel forces when they withdrew from the city at the end of July. Both men were lawyers (like Benjamin Mota, Machado had struggled in the courts against the post-1919 repression of labor) and both were active in recruiting civilian support for the cause during the month of July.[22]

If an informant's testimony can be believed (Machado had made the mistake of attempting to recruit an acquaintance who had been a perrepista boss and police official in São Vicente in the 1910s), Machado's pro-rebel pitch was fairly straightforward: "Come on Assumpção, you are a young man of ideas, vigorous of speech and an optimal element for the cause of the revolutionaries, everything in this country is lost and thus I substituted this revolver for the [legal] Code and with it I will do justice by the miserably oppressed people; come on, you are my countryman and should not refuse my invitation."[23]

Tocci, for his part, had been a pro-Ruy propagandist in 1919 as well as a supporter of the Republican Reaction of 1921–22. Like Machado and Mota, Tocci was friendly toward urban labor; he had good contacts among the guttersnipe journalists of the paulistano yellow press as well. In July 1924, Tocci not only issued pro-rebel appeals in the press and in the streets, he also took to the airwaves with "subversive speeches," in what may have been the first such use of radio in Brazil.[24] The culmination of Tocci's propaganda efforts came on 23 July with a "Manifesto to the Workers from the Party of Labor":

> The contemporary world shakes and convulses, in the direction of better harmonizing labor and capital, by the victory of laborism, by the evening of the social classes, in France, in England, in Italy, in Uruguay and in Argentina, summoning the working classes to political and social representative bodies.
>
> The moment through which all of Brazil is passing, with the revolutionary forces brilliantly quartered in S. Paulo, with military and civilian elements of the greatest worth, determined that from the beginning of the Revolution the worker also lent his support, because the military problem unfolds and consolidates itself with the broad social problem. For the guarantee of proper hours, of the improvement of wages, of education, of protection to children and to women, morally and economically alleviating the life of the laborer from the high cost of living in general and from the improper pretensions of gutless, exploiting capitalism.[25]

Given this situation, the Party of Labor, "proud of the workers who already answered its appeal, those who always supported this redemptive movement,—calls and insists that the workers report to the Headquarters of the Revolutionary Forces . . . to lend them their civil and military services."[26]

Tocci and Machado were not the only paulistanos to take to the streets and rail against the legalist cause. With the Campos administration's withdrawal from the city, the "sidewalks became meeting-places," where "everyone, to a man, inveighed against Dr. Carlos de Campos" for his cowardice, even "public functionaries."[27] The federal government's attempts to dislodge the rebels, in turn, occasioned impromptu rallies protesting the "horrible crime" of the "merciless bombing," to which were invited "the propertied classes, the glorious paulista youth, the class of students[,] the value of which is never denied, the working class—living force of progress—and the people in general."[28]

Tocci's Party of Labor manifesto was not the only statement designed to appeal specifically to workers, apart from other segments of paulista society. Further appeals were made by working-class leaders, militants of the internationalist left and, eventually, by the rebel leaders themselves.

In mid-July, more than two dozen "militants of the working classes" met at the headquarters of the paulistano printers' union "to analyze the Manifesto that the Chiefs of the Revolutionary Movement published in the newspapers of this capital." The motion that this meeting produced noted that the rebel manifesto represented "all of the feeling and aspirations of those who conceived and elaborated it in the admirable aim of seeking to subdue the oppressing wave of the exploiters of the people," and that the rebels themselves seemed disposed "to carry out [the] task of regeneration of the political, social and economic customs of the Brazilian Republic—'republicanizing it'—and to restore to the people the rights of life and liberty that up to the present have not gone beyond a utopic promise existing only in the pages . . . of the Brazilian Constitution." Turning to the specific grievances of labor, the militants indicated the economic woes of working people, the de facto denial of the right to organize, the need for worker education, and the call for a shorter work day. The solution to these problems lay in a six-point program: a state-wide minimum wage, price controls on basic necessities, recognition of the right to free association, complete freedom of the press, the right to open schools for workers (previous experiments in educational self-help had been subjected to official harassment), and the eight-hour day. The workers also sought to remind rebel leaders "that they found themselves at the head of the State government, [and] that everything we have just finished proposing in the present Motion reflects not only the opinion of the paulista proletariat at the present moment through which it is passing, but also guarantees and rights that the Brazilian Constitution affords."[29]

Another statement, drafted by Afonso Schmidt, a reporter for *O Estado de S. Paulo* and an anarchist-turned-Leninist, was addressed "To the Proletariat in General" from the "Labor Committee." This manifesto invited the city's proles to a meeting at which their "moral and material support in favor of the revolution that now pushes this State on the path to a tomorrow of more liberty, justice and well-being for the oppressed classes" would be expressed.[30]

The editors of *Marreta*, heirs to the yellow-press tradition of *O Parafuso*, similarly sought to convince "The Paulista Proletariat" to show "its vibrant support for the rebellious forces." Crushed between "fat capitalists" and the "governing gang," the working class, "the manly force of all development, could not remain inactive, indifferent." Rather, workers had to support the "present movement [for the] reestablishment of justice."[31]

"To the People," read another populist appeal, "To the Oppressed poor of São Paulo." This handbill also held the "despotic and ambitious" government responsible for the lot of the common people of the state capital. The object of the military movement, so the appeal's anonymous author argued, was "to put things in their place" by ending "governmental anarchy" and regulating the prices of basic goods. It called on workers to support the revolt before tapering off into vague piety: "God bless all our deeds and deliver us from the current punishment for the reigning cruelties here that we should have expected for some time."[32]

The rebel leadership was only slowly and reluctantly convinced of the efficacy of popular mobilization, but its campaign for volunteers was relatively successful, especially among the city's immigrant communities. This campaign began on 23 July with a statement from rebel headquarters promising steady pay and good land to civilian volunteers and deserters from the legalist side.[33]

The government later estimated that the rebels were able to attract between one thousand and two thousand volunteers while they held the state capital.[34] Another account—one that noted that "initial successes, much propaganda and promises, attracted to the mutineers' ranks many citizens of São Paulo and even immigrants who had been trained in European armies during the World War"—placed the peak strength of the rebel forces at ten thousand, which would imply a far more successful recruitment effort.[35] For his part, the labor militant Everardo Dias argued that "perhaps 50 percent of those who accompanied the [rebel] forces to Bauru or to the banks of the Paraná was made up of workers and civilian sympathizers. The fields and bush of Mato Grosso are covered with the graves of workers, who died fighting there and whom no one remembers."[36]

Civilian supporters or reputed supporters who remained behind and were subject to investigation were luckier, save for the truly unfortunate few who were deported to the Amazonian north. The rebel supporters who escaped the latter death sentence included middle-class and working-class men (and one aviatrix) of various ethnicities and all manner of livelihoods, including commercial employees, schoolteachers, engineers, office workers, brewers, stonemasons, saw millers, coachmen, trash collectors, textile workers, postmen, bakers, plumbers, mechanics, housepainters, cobblers, carpenters, and railwaymen.[37]

Although attempts to rally São Paulo's working people on behalf of the 1924 revolt were tardy, relatively few, and far from effective in inciting mass popular revolt, they certainly served to raise red flags in the eyes of defenders of order and property. A pro-government chronicle of July, for example, recorded the activities of left activists with the claim that following the withdrawal of legalist forces on 9 July, "red propagandists, of anarchic and so-called libertarian ideas, shameless arrivistes . . . , contumacious drunkards and cutthroats, tolerated by the mediocre class of society, embraced one another, mutually and phrenetically, as if the revolution had been made by them and for them."[38] Macedo Soares, as the president of the ACSP, had likewise raised the specter of working-class mobilization, informing General Socrates that "the workers already agitate, and bolshevist aspirations manifest themselves openly. The subversion of the social order will surely be attempted by those without work."[39]

The most numerous group mobilized during July was composed of rioters, those almost wholly unidentified (and largely unidentifiable) men and women who took to the streets and participated in the sack of several commercial establishments on 9–10 July. The horror that these events inspired is clear in a number of published reminiscences.

Luiz Marcigaglia, the director of São Paulo's Lyceu Salesiano, observed the very beginning of the pillaging, on the morning of 9 July: "A small sacking had already begun in the house on the corner. . . . Suspicious characters, people of all colors and all ages, erupting from the nearby hovels, went on helping themselves, unceremoniously, to what little the soldiers had left there. An emaciated little mulatto carried a string of onions; a brawny black woman proudly bore a slab of salt pork; a better-off matron returned with some kitchenware."[40] As the realization grew that the city had been left completely unpoliced, "bad elements" acted "with total freedom."[41] Through the night of 9–10 July, rioting was intense as "the people, taken hold of by a fierce, barbarous and contagious instinct, robbed, destroyed, [and] burned."[42] Other evidence belies the image of the rioters as troublemakers rather than as ordinary folks, but Father Marcigaglia's depiction remains an invaluable window onto the point of view of the privileged and pious.[43]

Aureliano Leite, no less hostile than Marcigaglia to both the rebellion and the rabble, described the rioters as "rebels . . . of every type . . . blacks and whites, young and old, men and women, nationals and foreigners."[44] Antônio dos Santos Figueiredo compared the crowds to those on market days; a professed socialist, something like wishful thinking may have been at play when he argued that workers and petty functionaries did not take part in the rioting, which he claimed was dominated by luxury-minded "hoarders" rather than the "hungry people."[45] The yellow-press *A Capital*, which enjoyed a burst of popularity during the rebellion, described the rioters as populares but decried the "salient role" in the rioting that was played, according to one of its writers, by "Syrian wholesale businessmen."[46] *O Combate* noted that small businessmen—identified, in contrast, as "miserable retailers"—took advantage of the rioting to pad their stock by drawing on the holdings of large warehouses, thus profiting at the expense of their better-heeled colleagues.[47]

A *Plebe* agreed that "many people took advantage of the occasion" but argued that hunger was the prime motivation behind ordinary folks' participation in the sackings.[48] Toward the end of the month, North American arrivals to Rio de Janeiro from São Paulo reported that "one of the [Matarazzo] Company's warehouses containing mostly flour and provisions . . . was sacked by the populace on July 9th"; the sack was attributed to the fact that "the civilian population is suffering from a shortage of flour and milk" and that "prices of all foodstuffs have risen considerably."[49] The Italian consul reported that those of his country-men who pillaged alongside "other workers" were motivated by the high cost of living and a vague kind of identification with the rebel cause, and that while they rioted they inveighed against "the exploiters of the peo-ple."[50] Additional evidence suggests that in addition to obtaining needed foodstuffs, working-class rioters were acting against specific establish-ments, in particular businesses owned by their rich, factory-owning countrymen.[51] The historian Alan K. Manchester, who spent the month of July in Campinas, later wrote that the chaos of the revolt afforded the state capital's "lower classes" the opportunity to settle scores with the Matarazzo interests in particular, associated in the popular mind with war-era hording and with the state government; in Manchester's eyes, at least, the "bonfires testified to a hungry people's vengeance."[52]

As went the state capital, so went the city's satellite counties. In the São Caetano district of suburban São Bernardo, local lore—perhaps inaccu-rately—records the revolutionary enthusiasm of Arthemio Veronesi, a member of a local workingmen's association. Constantino de Moura Batista, a local physician and a friend of the paulistano politician José Adriano Marrey Júnior, is said to have been another enthusiast, and an unspecified number of workers were jailed for supporting the rebellion.[53] Saladino Cardoso Franco stuck close to Carlos de Campos's state gov-ernment, both during and after the events of July 1924, eager to have his loyalist bona fides weighed against the Campos family's ties to his fla-quista rivals.[54] Late in the century, the memory of local participation in the looting of warehouses in the paulistano neighborhood of Ipiranga lingered on in São Caetano.[55]

To the west of São Bernardo county, in similarly outlying Santo Amaro, a group of local men, including at least one former labor militant and one supporter of the Republican Reaction, took the opportunity to seize power, perhaps in cooperation with a disenchanted republican from the state capital. Obtaining the blessing of Isidoro Dias Lopes, these men took the reigns of local government but were removed from power following the rebel withdrawal from the state capital.[56]

Interior Commotions

Understanding the political jockeying of July 1924 becomes still more difficult when one moves from the state capital and its immediate environs into the state's interior counties, at least a hundred of which appear to have experienced some sort of rebel incursion or rebellion-related political mobilization. While the geographic field of analysis expands voluminously, the amount of readily available evidence contracts considerably.[57] One may nevertheless distinguish a few basic types of local experiences. The first of these experiences of the rebellion occurred in towns with large military detachments that went over to the side of the rebels. The second occurred in towns where rebel detachments passed through. The third occurred in towns where local civilians—idealists, incumbents, and outs—acted on their own initiative to defend legality, support the rebellion, or establish ostensibly apolitical local governments. In all three of these scenarios, rebel activity or rumors of rebel activity interacted with local political dynamics, which were still unsettled throughout the state in the wake of the hotly contested municipal elections of 1922 and the statewide schism of 1923–24.

In Jundiaí, the first scenario obtained as the members of the local military detachment joined their fellows in the state capital in rebellion then returned to establish rebel control over the city shortly thereafter. Although Jundiaí was a focal point for subsequent contacts with civilian sympathizers from throughout the state, local participation in the rebellion appears to have remained limited to military men; the sole civilian from Jundiaí implicated in the rebellion was the son of the local military commander.[58]

In Rio Claro, the local military detachment also went over to the side of the rebels in early July. However, rather than exert power directly, the rebels turned over power to a civilian junta, the members of which then turned over power to one of their own. In this growing city, events foreshadowed those of towns far from the revolt, where the local balance of power and the rumor of revolt combined to make for changes in local politics. Here, one can document the rebellion's engagement of persons who appear to be local outs (most members of the junta, who claimed power for the "benefit of the population") as well as by at least one ideologically motivated opponent of the regime, João Fina Sobrinho, a veteran of Ruy's 1919 campaign and the president of the local Republican Reaction committee in 1922.[59] Decades later, Fina Sobrinho would remember the "personal friendship of Ruy Barbosa" as a formative influence upon him as a law student and proudly recall his past as a "revolutionary" in 1924.[60]

Itu was another county in which a sizeable local military detachment took the side of the rebels. Here, however, rather than handing over power to local enthusiasts or members of the out-of-power faction, the ranking rebel officer took power himself and governed with the assistance of the local incumbents.[61]

In other areas, where the rebels merely passed through, outs, ins, and ideological opponents of the regime contended for power. In Ibitinga, for example, both the municipal power-holders and the local opposition attempted to take advantage of the rebel presence. As a police delegate later wrote, "The invasion of the city, at four o'clock in the morning, when the population still slept, caused a horrible panic, and the two opposing political currents took to the field, each one seeking to take advantage of the anguished situation."[62] In Avaí, both the "power-holding political party" and the "opposition party" rallied to the side of the state government, assisting in the formation of a "Patriotic Battalion" to fight against the rebels. However, with tidings of the fall of the state capital, the local political boss, Domingos Zulian, "fearful, perhaps, of losing [control of] the positions of authority," published handbills announcing "the victory of the rebels." When actual rebel troops arrived and disarmed the local police detachment, Zulian organized a civil guard to preserve order and, following some political jockeying, came out ahead of his rivals, arranging matters such that a political ally was named provisional governor.[63]

As the state's second city and a key railway center, Campinas was a prize, and, unlike Itu, Rio Claro, and Jundiaí, it was not the site of a permanent military detachment. After 9 July, it was not even patrolled by a state-appointed police delegate, as the officer on duty deserted his post. A colleague later reported that he feared an attack from rebel troops from nearby Jundiaí; one of his neighbors recorded that, "quite unpopular among the common people," the police authority "by only a few moments . . . beat the crowd which was bent on burying him in the cemetery head down and still alive."[64] Campinas's perrepista authorities likewise absented themselves and, in their absence, the ranking rebel officer in Jundiaí named the independent county councilman Álvaro Ribeiro municipal executive by telephone. Through 26 July, Ribeiro and a small group of like-minded locals kept the peace, sheltered refugees from the bombed-out state capital, and—to one memoirist's amazement—"administered the city more efficiently than in the days of normal, federal law."[65]

Piracicaba, like Campinas, was an important interior city without a permanent military detachment. Here too were local opponents of the county PRP, including some of the same men who had defended the labor militants of the late 1910s, and a local population that was, according to one account, still more hostile to their would-be rulers. The result was a rebel-recognized county government composed of local opponents of the PRP, installed on 22 July and dissolved at the end of the month with the rebel withdrawal. Despite their dutifully turning over power to the old authorities on 30 July, the members of the provisional-government faction were accused of subversion and some of their leaders were jailed, though never convicted.[66]

In Jaboticabal, in the far north of the state, conflict manifested itself when the local militia's drill instructor returned from rebel-held territory seeking to obtain arms and volunteers. He was dissuaded, but soon thereafter veterans of the dissident presidential campaigns of Ruy Barbosa and Nilo Peçanha took power and turned the town armory over to a group of rebels.[67]

In the extreme western portion of São Paulo, in Presidente Prudente, rebel forces did not figure in local political calculations until after their evacuation of the state capital, as they retreated along the Sorocabana rail line. Here, legalist mobilization had begun almost immediately after news of the rebellion arrived, with the two local political factions (marcondistas and goulartistas) joining together to form a "Patriotic Battalion" in early July.[68] At month's end, however, some locals sided with the rebels and stopped the chief of the Sorocabana's station from tearing up a stretch of railroad track, which would have delayed the rebels' flight and perhaps even prevented their regrouping.[69] Subsequently, the rebels were able to occupy the city for an entire month, a period during which these revolutionary sympathizers, as well as the goulartista opposition and disgruntled employees of local bigwigs, were able to share some power and settle scores with the marcondistas.[70]

Some counties in which the rebels failed to appear nevertheless witnessed rebellion-related political mobilization. In São Simão, for example, "civilian elements" possessed of "revolutionary ideas" obtained the blessing of the rebel command in Jundiaí and planned to form a local junta, but they ended up in jail after failing to depose the authorities.[71] A similarly abortive putsch was seen in Bebedouro, where "civilian elements . . . provoked disorders, with the aim of taking over the public positions," but were unsuccessful in attracting the rebel military presence that would have afforded them the opportunity to seize power.[72]

In Socorro, a local physician obtained the favor of the rebel leadership and ruled through the end of the month with the assistance of the journalist Alante Lorensetti, who had backed the Pereira Barreto campaign in 1918.[73] One sees an entirely different situation in Promissão, a "new and prosperous town of the Noroeste zone," where incumbent "politicians . . . fearful of losing 'the scepter of power,' hurried to adhere to the revolting movement, which appeared already triumphant to them."[74]

Events in Araras were more dramatic. In this important lower-Paulista coffee county, with its tradition of local political conflict, enthusiasm ran high for any disturbance of the political status quo. On 10 July, members of the Municipal Party seized the town hall, police station, jail, and charity hospital, then set themselves up as the local government and ruled the county through the end of the month, a period of "local disorders" with only the faintest of links to "the seditious movement" of the state capital.[75]

Information is more sparse for Ribeirão Preto, though it seems that Joaquim da Cunha was able to turn the unsettled situation to his own benefit through the appearance of magnanimity. One local recalled that "there were rebellious [civilians] here, as in all parts" of São Paulo, and that these figures (including the editors of the local A Tarde) distributed propaganda materials calling for the city government to be deposed. These local sympathizers went no further, however, and when state investigators came to Ribeirão Preto after the rebel withdrawal from the state capital, Joaquim da Cunha politely informed them that everyone in his county was a friend of the government. This gesture added to the boss's prestige and was remembered for a long time thereafter.[76]

In counties throughout the interior, railwaymen played important roles in support of the rebels' retreat. Everardo Dias argued that "the withdrawal from S. Paulo was facilitated by the organized railroad working class, which cooperated selflessly so that everything was facilitated, against the sabotage of engineers and traffic chiefs, leading later to imprisonments and investigations in which some railwaymen [who were] known as militants and leaders of their corporation suffered abuse, subsequent imprisonment, barbaric beatings and summary dismissal."[77] Although Dias glosses over the actual cooperation of "engineers and traffic chiefs," his assertion of active participation on the part of São Paulo's railwaymen is corroborated by official investigations into the rebellion, which make clear the pro-rebel activity of railway workers and some officials on the Dourado, Noroeste, and Sorocabana rail lines.[78]

In a more general sense, the revolt itself was seen as providing ordinary folks with an avenue for protest, with a way of registering their displeasure with the existing order, in the interior and in the state capital. Afonso Schmidt recalled this kind of identification fondly: "When someone felt their rights were being trampled upon, they would yell: 'Pois eu vou me queixar ao velho!' [I'm going to complain to the old man! (a reference to the rebel general Isidoro Dias Lopes)]." He added: "In the general stores, when the retailer would pad the bill, the customers would object with the explanation: 'Isidoro will return!' "[79]

Renato Jardim, who had stuck by the authorities through the month of July, witnessed similar behavior but was far less pleased: "The humble and ignorant neighborhood greengrocer topped off his complaints with the state of affairs with the picturesque invective 'It doesn't matter! Isidoro is coming!' This was also the state of mind of and the language used by the worker, the unemployed cook, and, one guesses, of the beggar. . . ."[80]

Intellectual Response

While ordinary paulistas' responses to the revolt were diffuse and contradictory, and are quite difficult for the historian to get at, the reaction that the events of July 1924 provoked among the state's intelligentsia was more coherent and is far easier to uncover. For prominent paulista intellectuals, these events were cause for deep concern. Not only had the revolt and especially the legalist reaction been violent, unmeasured, and carried out with little care for the lives of noncombatants, the revolt had broken out in the cosmopolitan capital of Brazil's most modern, dynamic, and civilized state. The city had played host to looting and some mobilization on the part of ordinary folks, and when government forces reoccupied the city, they were greeted icily. More ominously still, the revolt was interpreted as betraying a sort of national unquiet or malaise and suggested to some that Brazil might be slipping into the sort of militarized politics that had so marked the national histories of its Hispanophone neighbors.

The *Diário da Noite*, one of the state capital's leading evening newspapers, captured the general sentiment of the period well, lamenting, "Helpless, sadly helpless—this is the final lesson [of the revolt] which we desire to point out—is the pacific and industrious man in Brazil who, a stranger to political competitions, cherishes the illusion that he lives under a regime of constitutional guarantees. At the least political disturbance all the guarantees slip away from him. . . . The Brazilian citizen, thanks to the civic illiteracy of his leaders, is a slave at the mercy of the first fortunate tyrant." The *Diário*'s editorialist continued: "The revolt robbed us of our last democratic illusions. We thought that we were a Republic and it showed us that we were mistaken. We are at most simple apprentices of democracy. It is possible that we shall yet become a Republic. Under the sun everything is possible. But to reach that goal, we shall have to travel far."[81]

Monteiro Lobato took a more direct tack, writing Arthur Bernardes on 9 August, using the president's birthday as the occasion to make known his concerns, citing the "dreadful event [that] occurred in São Paulo . . . a government falls entirely, smashed into pieces, and no one comes forward to defend it," as well as the "mortal silence" with which legalist troops were met when they reoccupied the city. He confessed: "This fact terrified me. I saw the possibility of a complete subversion of order in the entire country, as happened in Russia, with the infinite retinue of suffering and horrors that revolutionary convulsions cause."[82]

This prospect led Lobato, whose time might have been more profitably spent tending to his own business interests (his eponymously named publishing house was in dire economic straits, due in part to the cessation of all business during the month of July, and would go out of business the following year), to conduct a survey of the "spiritual state" of Brazil, interviewing "hundreds of people from all social classes, rich and poor, bosses and workers, lowly folks and persons of rank." The amateur ethnographer described his fieldwork: "As most men have two opinions, one for social use and the other intimate, resulting from one's personal experience in life, I always disregarded the former, [a] simple mask, and exerted confessions of the latter." The resulting data led him to conclude:

> The spiritual state of the Brazilian people is one of open revolt. . . . I believe I am not in error in estimating that 90% of people who, when they reveal themselves openly in private, betray this state of revolt. From the spirit of

revolt to the revolutionary spirit the transition is minimal. It is enough for a military movement to break out for the change to occur and the revolted becomes a rebel. A platonic rebel, it is true, but dangerous in the extreme, as he will give the explosion the moral force of his sympathies, and material support if it is possible for him.

This extremely high percentage frightens me, and I can affirm that it has constantly grown, occurring even among public employees. It includes all social classes without exception, and above all the thinking class, the cultured part of the country.[83]

Having detected this "state of spirit," Lobato sought to discover what had inspired it. He found that it stemmed from "the complete estrangement of politics and public opinion. From all people I heard the greatest hatred of politics and of politicians—the former taken to be the art of exploiting the treasury, and the latter, to be unworthy usurpers. From whence the nation's complete disinterest in politics."[84]

This conclusion led Lobato to further questions:

Why, then, this horror that the *élite* of the nation, its best part, the rich part, the cultured part, the cerebral part, the noble part par excellence displays with such openness?

Why is the free press—that which does not receive official favors directly or indirectly—so hateful toward all governments? Why[,] spurning the press that is friendly toward government, . . . does the people give unconditional support to the opposition press?[85]

These questions, in turn, led to additional conclusions:

A mortal vice maintains ever more in force the estrangement of the government and the country's *élite*, a vice so serious that if it is not corrected in time it will bring the country to complete ruin. This vice is our electoral regime of low standing [i.e., of a low standard of voter]. The experience of peoples [elsewhere in the world] demonstrates that the representative system only provides beneficial results when the regime is one of high standing. Because [a system of] high standards is politics by the *élite* of the nation, it is respect for the natural law of all organisms, it is the cerebral part carrying out its functions of cerebrum and the muscle part (people, populace, rural folks, etc., without culture or the capacity of discernment) naturally subordinated to the cerebrum. The various elections that I have seen filled me with dread. I spoke with numerous voters[,] as a rule slavish losers, and only encountered a few who even knew the name of the candidate for whom they voted; this one came out in return for a new hat or a 50$000 bill; that one, on the order of a boss or some cabo. In none of these individuals did I note the *natural ability* to vote; they only had the *artificial ability* that the law provides. But, as the law does not provide intelligence, culture, [or] discernment to those who do not in fact possess them, this artificial ability represents a vulgar lie with terrible consequences.

. . . alongside this ignorant [and] truly beastlike multitude, I saw the *élite* of the country, the cultured part, the cerebral part, the thinking part, the noble part par excellence maintaining the most rigorous abstention. . . .

As an immediate consequence of this absurdity, we have politics, the noble art of governing, transformed into a monopoly of the politicians, that is, of those men who make politics [their] profession and livelihood.[86]

As a further result, politics was closed off "to all talents, to all new forces. No further debate is possible." The "élite" did not vote because, as a "conscious minority," it recognized the futility of struggling against "the unconscious brute mass, that is the majority." With this situation, "we have *automatically repelled from the polls precisely those men possessed of the natural capacity to vote.*"[87]

Confronted with this problem, Lobato turned to a solution that would have been familiar to São Paulo's newspaper-reading public, the secret ballot, which "works the miracle of bringing with it a high standard" for voters and, as a consequence, would keep the "brutish mass" from the polls. With the exclusion of these undesirables, the nation's "élite"—"the gentlemen, the planters, the businessmen, the *doutores*, the *letrados*, . . . who constitute the noble portion of the country"—would begin to participate in elections. Government would then be bolstered by public opinion and, were another rebellion to break out, the "people" would rally to the defense of "their" government. To buttress his argument in favor of the secret ballot, Lobato turned to now-familiar points of comparison: "All countries that have adopted the secret ballot, including Argentina and Uruguay, fell into an admirable political equilibrium, ending the phase of revolutions, because their governments became de facto direct, free, and consensual emanation[s] of the people, through the noble portion, the cerebral portion of these countries."[88]

The alternatives were clear:

There are two ways political transformations are realized. One, very painful, through revolution, as in France, as in Russia; the other, smooth, by evolution, as in England. Revolution comes when bulwarks against popular aspirations are raised from above; evolution occurs when, instead of bulwarks, governments build ramps.

Labor encountered a ramp, [and] broke against it like a wave on the beach, and England gave the world the most notable lesson in political wisdom. . . .

The wave of Russian aspirations only encountered the tremendous bulwarks of tsarism, and destroyed everything.[89]

As far as Lobato was concerned, the decision was equally clear. The secret ballot, "honestly instituted, as Saens Pena instituted it, and honestly practiced, as Victorino La Plaza practiced it," would be Brazil's "ramp."[90]

Lobato's arguments to Bernardes formed the basis for an open letter to state president Carlos de Campos signed by a group of distinguished paulista public figures, subsequently published as an eighteen-page pamphlet in at least two editions.[91] This group, headed by Lobato, included perrepistas (Spencer Vampré, João Sampaio), PRP allies (Rangel Moreira, Renato Jardim), well-bred alumni of the Nationalist League (Paulo Nogueira Filho and Joaquim Sampaio Vidal were two), educational reformers (Antônio de Sampaio Doria, Fernando de Azevedo), the agrarian advocate Manoel Lopes de Oliveira Filho, and Plínio Barreto, a junior editor of O Estado de S. Paulo.[92] These intellectuals deplored the situation Brazil found itself in, in particular "the estrangement of the government and public opinion." This situation should have been apparent to Carlos de Campos, "who in a moment of danger found himself without the support of the people." The letter continued: "It is frightening. . . . Legalism does not exist in private. Removing the mask of the public employee, the merchant, the industrialist, the academic, and even the schoolboy (reflection of his parents), we shall see their sympathy for the revolution."[93]

Once again, it was alleged that this situation could be reversed through the introduction of secret balloting, "which has already been adopted by *all cultured peoples with one single exception*."[94] With the secret ballot in place, modern men would be able to vote their consciences and fantastic changes in Brazilian society would result:

. . . the secret ballot has already instituted itself throughout the world with impressive results, and has made miracles in America.

Can we resist this universal movement and hold to an old error of utopian idealism? Can we play the part of a people that forbids the entry of a marvelous invention into its territory? Can one imagine a country that has resisted the adoption of the telephone, of the "Ford," of cinematography?

There are laggards, stragglers like our own [country], which was the last to proclaim the freedom of the black and may be the final one to free the conscience of the white. But it has to do so, as this is something imposed by the inexorable laws of evolution.

. . . . .

Instead of compulsion, which makes free men slaves, the regime of persuasion, which makes slaves free men, will emerge and naturally determine the formation of parties, indispensable to the political life of modern peoples. The undesirable voter, this pest that corrupts the polls and makes himself the sordid instrument of the parasitic politician, will keep away from the polls, not due to any law, but by order of his own mentality. Concomitantly, the noble portion of the country will replace him in the elevated mission of electing [the nation's representatives]—and we will have realized, finally, the great conquest that we so needed.[95]

Monteiro and his compatriots closed by calling on Carlos de Campos "to take charge of the great legal revolution. The path is clear as day: anticipate the movement, prevent it from coming later by force, with blood, pain, misery, what has come evolutionarily to all cultured countries, by the insight of statesmen like Saenz Peña." They appealed to regional pride, expressing their hope "that the great example would come from us," as São Paulo, which had so much to lose, would not only safeguard its wealth and status, but play its natural role as "*leader* of the Union" by pioneering the introduction of the secret ballot: "With freedom of conscience proclaimed here, inaugurating the electoral regime that we lack, soon we will see it, by contagion, dominating the entire country, and Brazil will begin, at last, to do away with this backwardness of a hundred years to which the double enslavement of the body of the black, in times past, and the conscience of the white, today, has been ignominiously condemning it."[96]

In addition to signing on to this open letter, Antônio de Sampaio Doria issued his own appeal to the national congress in an essay dated 7 September 1924 (the 102nd anniversary of the declaration of Brazilian independence). The essay, entitled "The Legal Revolution," asserted that three facts defined the political situation of Brazil: "political militarism, civilian caudilhismo, and the incitement to revolt, which rouses the people."

In discussing the first of these defining characteristics, Sampaio Doria condemned the military's participation in politics, mocking, as "dementia," the fact that the rebels, after taking up arms against the legal authorities, had issued a manifesto in which they proclaimed their loyalty to the constitution. Sampaio Doria also condemned the system of machine politics, in which the popular will went unheard, there was no separation of powers, and candidates to public office were chosen by "some caciques of the political syndicate." He argued that, given these arrangements, the "only road by which a young man can enter politics in Brazil today is by nepotism and flattery." With this system in place, "it is not surprising that the people are not content. Their tolerance is stretched to the limit. . . . The spirit of revolt that animates them can, from one moment to another, explode in the greatest of calamities."[97]

As Sampaio Doria saw it, the solution to civilian caudilhismo (the root cause of popular discontent and political militarism) was not military revolt (which would only lead to military dictatorship), but rather a twofold process of immediate political reform and education over the longer term. He framed the situation in stark terms: "There are, among our 30 million [people], 600,000 Brazilians who are intelligent, cultured, and honest. These will be the conscious nation . . . the people capable of democracy. Education, thereafter, would widen this percentage to 80, 90 or 100 percent. Until then, to the cultured minority of the country will fall the election of its governments." Electoral reform, in the form of secret and compulsory balloting on the part of this educated portion of the population, would make way for the expression of the popular will, the formation of political parties, and Brazilian national salvation.[98]

Intellectuals with ties to the PRP were equally traumatized by the events of July 1924 (as the list of supporters of Lobato's open letter to Carlos de Campos makes clear) and offered comparable diagnoses. A state functionary, Jorge Americano offered a book-length treatment in his *A lição dos factos* ("The Lesson of the Events," a work that, like Sampaio Doria's "The Legal Revolution," was dated 7 September 1924). Like Sampaio Doria, Lobato, and others, Americano reacted to the rebellion with horror, contrasting the seeming legalism of the city's population in early July with its increasing indifference and estrangement as the month went on. Americano blamed the revolt and the attitudes that it produced on a variety of perceived ills, some familiar, others novel, ranging from Brazil's racial heterogeneity to the universal pressures of "modern life."[99]

As described by Americano in his "politico-cultural essay," Brazil's regionally distinct patterns of racial intermingling contributed greatly to the lack of a common feeling of Brazilian nationality. Citing Oliveira Vianna, Americano noted that "the Indian, the black and the white did not mix with one another in equal proportions in all of the regions of the country." Over the years, this process had resulted in "the more or less distinct northern type," which was "completely different from the types of the center-south" and the "extreme south."[100]

This centuries-old process of regional differentiation was exacerbated by the regionally distinct patterns of more recent European immigration (Portuguese in Rio de Janeiro, Italian in São Paulo, German in the far south) and the tendency of immigrants to identify with their native lands. One could not expect the foreign-born to possess a feeling of Brazilian nationality; it was, Americano argued, "natural [for them] to consider [their] material interests first, and disregard the grand interests of Brazil." Their assimilation, however, was the duty of Brazilians.[101]

Regionalist sentiment on the part of Brazilians of old stock, which Americano blamed for the outbreak of the rebellion and the tenor of the legalist response, was fostered by the country's educational system. More specifically, Americano identified Brazil's two traditional law schools, in Recife and São Paulo (he was a graduate of the São Paulo academy), as "two great foci of regionalism."[102]

Americano also bemoaned the anti-national corporate identity that he called "militarism." He decried the sums of money allotted Brazil's military relative to the pittance spent on schools, arguing that only education could make the country's illiterate masses identify with "the national organism." As Americano saw it, the draft-lottery system had only exacerbated Brazilian militarism, because the training, uniforms, and even in some cases literacy bestowed upon conscripts by their superiors led "the great majority, illiterates or quasi-illiterates," to experience "the first consciousness of their own dignity" and thus "make firm their esprit de corps."[103]

Americano also pointed to a novel culprit, "modern life." "The great war put the most disparate elements of the warring nations in contact with each other, and . . . abolished many of the traditions that separated the social strata," he claimed, adding, in particularly self-aggrandizing language that "permanent contact with intellectuals allowed the worker to recognize the immense superiority of the former, but he could not fathom the profound reason for this. In his consciousness that which he already confusedly identified as iniquity came to be more clear, and he aspired to abolish it. However, in the constructive impotence of he who cannot change the profound causes, [which are] out of present-day reach, his egalitarian efforts tend to destructive leveling, through the suppression of the superior strata." As the "discovery of certain inventions and the ever-so-rapid evolution of certain others put the inferior strata in contact with the great[er] civilization, for which neither their sentiments were prepared nor their intelligence developed enough," popular resentment grew. Motion pictures, for example, made the "poor classes" aware of "the unsuspected existence of the intimate life of comfort, luxury, riches, sumptuosity and dissipation of the great homes. Thus, the comparison between this grandness and their uncomfortable [lives] naturally emerged among these classes." With each invention like the cinema, "the poor knew of new pleasures, in the exclusive reach of the rich, and anxiously aspired to them. [They] experienced the desire for satisfaction with an unhealthy violence."[104]

Economic crisis was also to blame. Americano saw this crisis as stemming from a lack of government-sponsored scientific farming techniques, the need for improved transportation, a lack of financial confidence in Brazil on the part of its creditors, and an uneven tax burden.[105]

Turning to the political crisis, Americano, like Monteiro Lobato, Sampaio Doria, and others, deplored the situation Brazil found itself in and especially the weakness of the "thinking electorate" relative to "the mass of those who act at the mercy of the electoral bosses' rulings." He also decried abstentionism: "abstention fosters, in political bosses, tranquility and the certainty that all of their decisions will be respected," when in fact such ease stemmed only from "*indifferentismo.*"[106]

To reverse these trends, Americano called for a number of reforms. Further immigration from southern Europe should be encouraged (while German and especially Asian immigration should be prohibited), but these immigrants had to be assimilated as rapidly as possible. An expansion of the educational system was also necessary; among the urban working class, in particular, U.S.-style vocational training should be encouraged. Americano also floated various proposals for financial and economic reform and called for the expansion of the railway network. On the administrative level, Americano called for the founding of a forward capital in the interior and, in politics, he saw benefits to be gained through the continued engagement of the "thinking electorate." Although this group constituted only a fraction of voters, Americano argued that "the intelligent action of superior men" might guide the "indifferent half," who would slowly become more conscientious. With each election, more and more of the formerly inactive would vote with their superiors, a general tendency that could be accelerated by the introduction of a candidacy that would bring people together. Anticipating the position of the PRP rump (which he would join as a candidate to the lower house of the state legislature in 1927), and parting ways with most other contemporary analyses, Americano did not see much use for the secret ballot.[107]

Diagnoses of Brazil's political troubles continued to be published well after the events of July 1924. In an article published on the thirty-sixth anniversary of the republic, 15 November 1925, Julio de Mesquita Filho undertook his own analysis of the current "crisis" (his article, subsequently published in book form, was entitled "The National Crisis"), which he saw epitomized in "the terrible events of July 1924," in which, "in a terrifying crescendo, we passed from the field of more or less regular elections to the field of generalized and brutal indiscipline." In his diagnosis, Mesquita drew on scientific racism, a Luso-Brazilian variant of the Hispano-American Black Legend, anti-immigrant snobbery, positivism, liberal reformism, and amateur social theory in which much of the accepted wisdom of later modernizationists was already incipient. The most striking of these ingredients, even keeping in mind that Gilberto Freyre himself never claimed to detect a lack of prejudice in São Paulo, is Mesquita's racism.[108]

Mesquita took the republic itself as the starting point for his analysis. Given the enormous material progress that had taken place since 1889 (the "improvement . . . of the ethnic conditions of the nation," the expansion of transportation and communication networks, a hundred-fold increase in the number of primary schools), Mesquita asked: How could one explain the abandonment of public life by Brazil's "intellectual elements"?[109]

Up to 1888, Mesquita discerned healthy political conflict between "two parties, which recruited their members from the homogenous mass of free citizens, most of them uncultured but endowed with enough good sense to understand the basic ideas around which the political debates of the period were joined." They were helped by Pedro II (whose "liberal and cultured spirit" minimized the population's natural tendency to autocracy, inherited from the Portuguese and reinforced by the institution of slavery) and the exclusion from politics of the "semi-barbarous fraction of the population." However, with the decree of 13 May 1888, "there came to circulate in the arterial system of our political organism the formidable and impure mass of two million negroes, suddenly given constitutional prerogatives." This "unexpected influx of toxins" led directly to a "great transformation of the national consciousness," once "full of civic ardor" but now almost instantly demonstrating "the most alarming symptoms of moral decadence."[110]

It was at this precise moment that the entire political structure of Brazil shifted, from the "authority of public opinion" that Mesquita saw as characterizing the empire to the "authority of the most prestigious families in the different regions of the republic," such that politics came to be subject to the "whims of a limited number of individuals, under whose protection anyone who sought a place in the state or federal congresses took refuge." This shift, wrote Mesquita, was the "advent of oligarchy."[111]

To the problem of the "African [sic]" was added the influx of immigrants in the late nineteenth century and the early twentieth, which also served to inhibit the "awakening of public opinion," as immigrants were motivated by personal profit rather than civic duty. However, despite the pernicious effects of Brazil's failure to assimilate European immigrants, the immigrants themselves were critical to national development as "the African toxin" was "incapable of participating in the new phase of activity" ongoing in Brazil, "The Economic Revolution" that Mesquita claimed to discern in certain regions. This "revolution" was characterized by the emergence of smallholding, as the "general mass of [rural] workers," previously the mere instruments of an "aristocratic caste of latifundists," came to own land, both from the subdivision of the latifundia in older zones and the settlement of new lands on the frontier.[112]

Moving seamlessly from ethnic to economic determinism, Mesquita argued that this "Economic Revolution" brought with it grave consequences for the "oligarchic patterns" of Brazil's "political organization." The "extraordinary development of agriculture and industry" and improvements in living standards led to a "notable modification in the spirit of the collectivity." Economic independence made for political change as numerous foreigners abandoned their roles as the illegal tools of "professional politicians" and the "masses," more broadly, began to oppose the regnant political ideas. Mesquita alleged that the five years between 1905 and 1910 were particularly noteworthy for the economic progress that they witnessed; in the political sphere, this progress was such that an event "originating in a simple political incident" (Ruy's campaign of 1909–10) unexpectedly assumed the "proportions of a veritable convulsion."[113]

"The current crisis dates from then," Mesquita argued, in the form of "irreparable conflict between the remnants of the period of transition, ensconced in power, and the popular will." Amid this conflict, the government found itself turning to measures like the anti-press legislation of the early Bernardes government and the ongoing attempt to further restrict constitutional liberties. These attempts "to reign in the independent efforts" of Brazilian "public opinion" were part of an old, familiar struggle between "the past and the present."[114]

Although Brazil as a whole was undergoing "social regeneration," the process was affecting Brazil's different regions in an uneven fashion.

Predictably, Mesquita saw São Paulo leading the way, with Rio Grande do Sul and Minas Gerais moving more slowly, and the remainder of the country tarrying in a primitive state.[115]

Mesquita's stages-of-civilization thinking was made clearer still in a comparison with the United States, in which he argued that Brazil had reached a point similar to that reached in British North America in the late eighteenth century, when "some units of the vast Anglo-Saxon dominion already showed extraordinary political capability, in contrast with the rest of the ex-British colony, which remained in an embryonic social state." São Paulo, Rio Grande do Sul, Minas Gerais, and the Federal District—areas he compared to the thirteen "Primitive states" of the North American union—had "achieved the level of maturation indispensable for . . . the democratization of the regime" through the introduction of Saenz Peña-style reforms and would be the basis of the "definitive political emancipation" of Brazil.[116]

This "democratization of the regime" would bring further changes, not least in Mesquita's home state. Given the strong presence in São Paulo of "the proletarian, . . . the force of our industry, the greatest in South America," it would not be long before an impressive socialist movement would emerge, to which would gravitate "the homogenous mass of the paulista proletariat." While at first glance this "inevitable result" of democratization would seem to threaten paulista society, its effects would be quite the opposite. A strong socialist movement would provoke the mobilization of "conservative currents rooted to the land" and thus the "definitive rebirth of civic spirit in São Paulo." As in France and the United States, the small farmer (possessor of the "instinct of *self-government*") would be the "regulating pendulum of the socio-political mechanism" as the "rural population . . . would maintain the proletariat at a respectful distance."[117]

In discussing the still-broader effects of democratization, Mesquita revealed what he thought would be the pinnacle of Brazilian political development. It would not be a democracy in which the active participation of small farmers would figure beyond the local level, except as an electoral counterweight to urban labor, nor would democratization witness the birth of an egalitarian and broadly participatory politics. Rather, Mesquita's ideal resided in the delegation of political power to intellectual elites:

A radical turnover in our political representatives would accompany this veritable revolution that the secret ballot cannot help but provoke. The intellectual élites, withdrawn in the liberal professions, in letters, in industry and agriculture since the advent of the oligarchy, would return [to public life], attracted by the purification of the political atmosphere. As in the epic saga of the Bandeiras, in the struggle for independence and the agitated times of dom Pedro II's minority, those figures representative of the community, successively incarnated in Fernão Dias, José Bonifácio and Feijó, will flourish.[118]

This profound elitism was echoed through the remainder of Mesquita's text, in which he reiterated his call for the introduction of the secret ballot, called for legislation instituting the ballot referendum, and made vaguely technocratic appeals for the expansion of higher, secondary, and primary education, reserving for the latter "the function of . . . contact between the popular mass and the thinking élites." Unintentionally calling further attention to the inconsistencies and inaccuracies in his political thought, Mesquita closed with a quote that was meant to be both pithy and apt, but in the process managed to both mangle and misattribute a passage from the Federalist papers.[119]

While Mesquita used the pages of *O Estado de S. Paulo* to publicize his diagnoses and propose remedies, his competitors and political foes at the PRP's *Correio Paulistano* reacted to the rebellion in their own way. The old newspaper's young writers—they would soon call themselves *verde-amarelistas*—published "articles in which [they] made evident to the eyes of the Nation the movement of [19]24, as an alarming symptom of a national anguish, that was worthy of study."[120] In one such article, the former São Bento municipalist Plínio Salgado took the position that there was something to be gained from the chaos, as "the aimless, disorderly and willful manifestations of Brazilian activity, expressed in revolutionary or partisan forms in recent times, far from saddening us, reveal themselves to be signs of the presence of real forces, that the new mentality of Brazil should take advantage of and steer," while his fellow verde-amarelista Cândido Motta Filho, the scion of an influential perrepista clan, warned that the time was not for self-congratulation (on the "defeat" of the rebellion with the rebel withdrawal from São Paulo), but rather for a reassessment of the republic's errors.[121]

To the reactions of the verde-amarelistas, Mesquita Filho, Jorge Americano, Sampaio Doria, and Monteiro Lobato can be added further analyses, as well as the eyewitness accounts of other paulistas who lived through the events of July 1924. Although the latter works were not intended to serve primarily as sociopolitical analyses or as prescriptions for public policy, they do offer additional insight into reactions to the rebellion on the part of the state's intelligentsia.[122]

Heroes of the People

In the years that followed the failed revolt, the veteran rebels of São Paulo, joined by another rebel column from the far south led by Luiz Carlos Prestes, formed a small army that traversed the Brazilian interior on a three-year campaign that only ended when the last rebels quit the field for exile in Bolivia once Washington Luís replaced Arthur Bernardes in the federal presidency. During the second half of the 1920s, and in particular after the lifting of the state of siege on 31 December 1926, the rebels themselves were raised to the status of "heroes of the people." Such was the case, in particular, of Prestes, Isidoro Dias Lopes, Miguel Costa (the leader of the paulista rebels in the campaigning of 1924–27), Antônio Siqueira Campos (a São Paulo-born veteran of the 1922 revolt who joined the roving campaign of 1924–27), and the Távora brothers (Joaquim, a martyr of early July, and Juarez, the younger and duller of the pair). There were multiple sites for this veneration: books by the rebels themselves, articles in various press outlets (some novel, some of long standing), and public commemorations. As part of this process, various groups attempted to link themselves to the rebels' struggle against "oligarchy."

The published reminiscences of rebel officers were one way in which the cult of the military rebels was encouraged, though probably the least important, given the relatively low runs and high prices of books published in Brazil in the 1920s. This genre included memoirs by veterans of the revolt of 1924, as well as of prior and subsequent campaigns and conspiracies. By the end of the decade, it was represented by works such as *Á guisa de depoimento*, by Juarez Távora, and *A coluna do morte*, by João Cabanas, a greatly feared and loved associate of Miguel Costa.[123]

With the lifting of the state of siege at the end of 1926, newspapers were left relatively free to comment on the events of July 1924 and the continuing march of the rebels through the Brazilian interior. As one observer remarked: "The newspapers and periodicals have been full of histories and commentaries referring to the revolt. . . . Some of the newspaper accounts have been remarkable for their frank praise and approval of the revolt and the subsequent actions of the leaders, many of whom are now outlaws in the *sertão*."[124] The same observer linked this kind of press commentary to the public mood:

The pent up indignation of the opposition Press, which has been gathering force during the years of repression under the State of Siege, has, as was probably to be expected, broken forth in a tremendous burst of torrid language. The fugitive leaders of the revolt are exalted and any bit of news about them is repeated a dozen times with verbal alterations. Already legends are growing up about these men, and their extraordinary wanderings and escapes have placed them in the popular imagination by the side of the Cid, Robin Hood, Marion, and other heroes of troubled times. Prestes, Campos, and Costa have all been promoted by the opposition Press to the grade of General while General Isidoro Dias Lopes is referred to as Marshall. All of these leaders are referred to as "liberators."[125]

In a memoir of these years, Afonso Schmidt recalled Prestes's popularity in particular. "Despite the general censorship," he wrote, "there began to appear the name of a brilliant military leader and of a feat of arms without equal not only in the history of Brazil but of the world. It was Luís Carlos Prestes, at the head of the Undefeated Column. Ever since those memorable days, the Romanesque figure of the Knight of Hope dominates the intellectual sky of Brazil. It is the incarnation of Tiradentes."[126] Another memoirist of these years remembered this campaign as "the deification of Prestes," noting that "the popular and opposition press's campaign to create a savior of the Patria was, for years, intense and uninterrupted."[127]

In São Paulo, the most assiduously pro-rebel newspaper was O Combate. Indeed, O Combate's enthusiasm for the rebel cause began in 1922, not 1924, with tributes to the "stupendous courage of the last defenders of Copacabana Fort," particularly the "Two Paulistas" who were "At the Head of 14 Heroes" in the uprising of 5 July (Siqueira Campos and Newton Prado, the latter of whom was mortally wounded that day).[128] Following the lifting of the state of siege, the afternoon newspaper printed regular contributions by João Cabanas, including, in January 1927, a manifesto calling on civilian sympathizers to unite in solidarity with the rebels, to withhold support from the government, and, not least, to "Glorify the prisoners of the Revolution" and "Glorify those who are still fighting," a task that O Combate took to heart.[129]

The newspaper became so closely identified with the rebel cause that Juarez Távora chose its press as the publisher of the first volume of his memoirs. O Combate's Nereu Rangel Pestana opened the volume with a short foreword in which he gratefully acknowledged Távora's decision to publish his memoir with O Combate, referring to the author as one "dear to all who still believe in a better future for Brazil," and dedicated the volume to Joaquim Távora, "brother, guide and master of the Author," personification of "all those who fell gloriously for the Republic in this long campaign," the "dozens, perhaps even more than a thousand," who should be venerated by "the modest worker and the aged general" alike.[130]

Other journalists followed suit. The aptly named *A Ronda* (The Patrol), another representative of the paulistano yellow press, also helped to foster the cult of the young rebels with its detailed reporting on troop movements and the progress of the column, while the director of the São Paulo offices of Assis Chateaubriand's *O Jornal* was responsible for a series of front-page articles based on interviews carried out with rebel exiles in Bolivia.[131]

Even *O Estado de S. Paulo*, usually staid in its reporting, if not in its editorial pronouncements, devoted a column to coverage of the rebel's movements, and the anonymous author of the *Estado*'s "Notas e informações" expressed admiration for the "exceptional energies" and "sacrifice" of Luiz Carlos Prestes and made much of his "legend."[132] Julio de Mesquita Filho, *O Estado de S. Paulo*'s fortunate son, later placed his own journalistic work at the center of the cult of the military rebels, recalling the "heroic days in which we, the journalists of the time, in the service of democracy, created the myth of the Knight of Hope."[133]

But it was not just in the daily newspapers of the 1920s that the rebels were lionized as they trekked through the Brazilian interior and plotted from abroad. A specialized press also came into being, one that was based around chronicles of the rebel's exploits and discussions of Brazil's need for revolution.

The first of these publications was *O Libertador*, the earliest issues of which were published in August 1924 in rebel-occupied Assis, in the upper Sorocabana, under the motto "It is necessary to republicanize the Republic." *O Libertador* featured glowing references to "the glorious memory of the 18 pioneers of the ideal of the regeneration of the regime" (the rebels of 1922) and to "São Paulo, cradle of our independence, once more rais[ing] the banner of war against the men who, forgetting the mandate that was entrusted to them, are carrying our Patria into the abyss."[134]

In the city of São Paulo, copies of *5 de Julho*, clandestinely published in the federal capital of Rio de Janeiro for two entire years, were distributed furtively but with surprising regularity among the pro-rebel faithful.[135] Afonso Schmidt also remembered the circulation of *Liberdade*, a locally produced pro-rebel *jornalzinho* that declared: "One does not ask for freedom, one takes it."[136]

Less well-remembered, but perhaps even more interesting, was *Tacape*, a cheaply produced, smaller-than-tabloid-size paulistano newspaper subtitled "Organ of Brazilian-ness" (the word *Tacape* itself referred to an indigenous weapon similar to the North American tomahawk, a further marker of its nationalist status).[137] *Tacape* was pro-rebel in a schizophrenic manner that is supremely indicative of the ideological confusion of the period and suggestive of the later fracturing of the rebel leadership into its "left" and "right" components in 1930 and after. The issue of 29 April 1928 called for the Brazilian military, led by someone like Prestes, to establish a dictatorship with the aim of educating and modernizing Brazil. The resulting dictatorship, in which the church ("suitably nationalized and called to its duty") would have its own role to play, was envisioned as creating a society organized along corporatist, paternalist, and redistributionist lines:

> The working class should be treated with paternal kindness. The rural worker, the poor Jéca Tatú, this disgraced pariah, who lives an errant life because he lacks a plot of land of his own, should be given a piece of land sufficient for his use.
>
> Brazilian landlordismo, feudal coronelismo, the multitude of claim-jumpers who took over Brazil, need to be despoiled of that which does not belong to them. Our patria is immense enough to be divided up among all Brazilians. Industrial workers need to be organized.
>
> The dictatorship should regulate labor, in our country, in an equitable way. The "blue-collar men" should themselves set the conditions that they find favorable. The proletariat is the soul of the nation. And, as such, it is just that they be given their proper role.[138]

The same issue also featured an article-length call for the secret ballot written by *Tacape*'s publisher, who scorned *bacharelismo* but was himself a student at the São Paulo Law School. A portrait of Prestes and quotes from Ruy Barbosa, who had supported the Bernardes government's establishment of a state of siege following the revolt of July 1922 (it was among the Bahian's last political pronouncements, as he had fallen ill soon thereafter and died in early 1923), offered further evidence of *Tacape*'s eclecticism.[139]

The internationalist left outdid the apparent incongruity of *Tacape*'s editorial line with an inconsistency born of pure opportunism. As the Communist Party sought to link itself to the military rebels, or at least explain their popularity, it could not dismiss them outright, but it could not grant them equal status as fellow "revolutionaries" either. From early denunciations of the "petty-bourgeois" status of the rebels through its attempt at securing Luiz Carlos Prestes as its symbolic presidential candidate in 1930, the Communist Party wavered between support and dismissal while attempting to link itself with the heroic image of the rebels.[140]

Perhaps no single group tried to portray the rebels' struggle as its own more doggedly than the opposition Democratic Party, founded in 1926. The new party did so through the public speeches of its leaders, through its hymn (written by Heitor de Moraes, Santos's long-serving independent city councilman, and dedicated to Luiz Carlos Prestes), and especially through its newspaper, the *Diário Nacional*.[141]

In a common motif, one propagandist argued that the party's founding could be traced back to the "spirited protest" of the "18 immortals" who rebelled on 5 July 1922. "Thus began the prolonged, back-and-forth, but decisive struggle, of the idealistic youths of the Army and Navy, of the visionary youths of the schools . . . against the republican mystification, out of which, within a few years, will rise the real, democratic Brazil of which our forefathers dreamed." The ancestral struggle was continued in the rebellion of 1924, "which had as its leaders Brazilians of the courage of Miguel Costa and Joaquim Tavora and of the brilliant ability of Juarez [Távora]."[142]

The *Diário Nacional* was particularly important in attempts to link the party to these idealized rebels. In March 1928, the party newspaper published a "complete account" of the march of the "Prestes Column" through the Brazilian backlands. The following month, it ran a story on "The Political Thought of Luís Carlos Prestes." On the basis of features like these, a Brazilian historian has described the *Diário* as "joining the *tenentista* line and making real the approximation of the military men in rebellion against the reigning order and [the] organized civilian political forces."[143]

A broader public took an active role in the cult of the rebel leadership through public commemorations. As far as the state of São Paulo is concerned, none were more important than the events surrounding the death and burial of native son Siqueira Campos in mid-1930.

On the early morning of 10 May 1930, Siqueira Campos drowned after the plane that was to have carried him back to clandestinity in Brazil crashed into the waters of the Río de la Plata. The next morning, the *Diário Nacional* brought the news of Siqueira Campos's death to its readers, along with a eulogy for the fallen rebel: "He was among the most capable. He was among the most competent. But, principally, the bravest. Before his valor, before his undisputed courage, the most valiant bowed, the most courageous surrendered."[144] Two days later, the *Diário* carried Paulo Nogueira Filho's "Heroic Youth," which emphasized the impact of Siqueira Campos's example on the young.[145] A week after Siqueira Campos's drowning, another *Diário Nacional* contributor contrasted the "hero of Copacabana" and "idol of the multitude" with the unpatriotic, "subservient" legislature.[146]

In Campinas, city councilmen belonging to the Democratic Party sought to lionize this "brilliant figure of the national Army," one of Brazil's "most worthy sons, not only for the courage which he always displayed, but also for his patriotism and his extraordinary qualities as a military man." In what was at once an unconvincing call for the support of the majority and an illustration of the dimensions reached by the cult of Siqueira Campos, references were made to "the notices published by the independent newspapers of the death of Siqueira Campos, showing that all are unanimous in considering this officer to be an example of bravery, of patriotism and of military skill," a figure who had always "reproached, with arms in his hands, the abuses and lack of civismo of those who hold the reigns of power." Much was made of Siqueira Campos's "having struggled with extraordinary ardor for the moralization of our political customs, degraded by fraud and the oppression of the representatives of power," and it was predicted that "his dream has to come true someday, come what may, cost what it may."[147]

In the state capital, huge ceremonies and rallies accompanied the arrival of Siqueira Campos's corpse to its final resting place. Arriving by train from the federal capital, the coffin of this "admirable paulista youth [who] dedicated the few yet tumultuous days of his existence to the service of his land and of his people" was met at the station by thousands of the city's residents, who waited through the delays caused by the demand that the train stop "in every single little way-station on the railroad, even those at which it does not usually delay, as the population of the paulista interior, unanimously," insisted on participating in the processional. Upon the train's arrival, a representative of the Democratic Party gave a speech "revisiting the life and personality of Siqueira Campos." According to the report published in *O Estado de S. Paulo*, the speech left "tears in almost all eyes," those of "old men, strong men, men accustomed to the roughest struggles, like many of those who were there."[148]

Following the speech, the crowd dispensed with the funeral carriage and carried the coffin through the streets:

> It would be difficult to describe the processional to the Carmo church, as the feelings that animated that enormous mass of the people were among the most diverse. Those people knew that it was without noise that one should proceed to a burial; but it wanted, at the same time, animated by a spirit of rebellion, to yell, to rage! And the result was that which one saw a little later: the people carried Siqueira Campos's casket through the city's downtown, disobeying orders, disobeying the prearranged itinerary, carrying it like a trophy through the streets of S. Paulo, as if to say and to affirm that, guided by him, they would be capable of great things.[149]

Following a mass, the assembled crowd retook to the streets, again parading the coffin through the downtown before moving on to a cemetery located on a bluff to the southwest of the city center. Over the course of this march, an "apotheosis rarely seen in this city," the procession attracted more participants. At the square in front of the São Paulo Law School, a student improvised a speech in which he declared the fallen soldier to have been "a martyr of the Law, battling for the moralization of our political customs and for the faithful observance of the country's laws." When the procession finally reached the cemetery, five hours after the crowd had gathered at the train station, the coffin was lowered into the ground following the speeches of two former cadets (presumably drummed out for participation in the revolt of 1922), an unnamed *popular*, and Siqueira Campos's father, who declared that "the patria had gained another hero."[150]

As of late July and early August 1924, this kind of popular enthusiasm was only in its incipience. With the rebel withdrawal from the state capital on 27–28 July, the state and federal governments (distinguishing between the two, at this moment, was particularly difficult) acted from a position of strength, jailing opponents real and imagined, closing the Nationalist League, raiding union halls, and further restricting press freedoms. It was from this position of apparent strength that the PRP rump welcomed back prodigal chieftains of the schism of 1923–24 and Olavo Egydio and Altino Arantes regained their seats on the executive committee. For a time, at least, amid the give and take of tending to followers, family, and friends, it was almost possible to pretend as if nothing at all had happened.

5 An Experiment in Democracy

Neither repression nor the reconstitution of the perrepista leadership served to restore public confidence in the existing political order. The Nationalist League remained closed, but similarly reformist groups emerged to take its place in 1924 and 1925. Municipal elections in late 1925 were the occasion for renewed infighting among the senior leaders of the PRP, and election returns confounded incumbents in several important counties. Back in the state capital, the two months following elections brought unpleasant surprises in the form of two resignations from the PRP's legislative ranks. It was in this charged political atmosphere that a varied group of political dissidents came together to found the Democratic Party of São Paulo, attracting support from throughout the state for a program of liberal, constitutionalist reform. Over the next two and a half years, the new party was able to mount a challenge to the PRP's near monopoly on political power in certain locales and among certain groups, forcing important changes in the ways formal politics were carried out throughout São Paulo.

Gathering Forces

The immediate effect of the repression that followed the 1924 revolt was to drive political dissidence underground or into ostensibly non-opposition channels. In secret, well-bred alumni of the now-banned Nationalist League, together with reform-minded artistes of the modernist avant-garde, formed what they called the "Invisible Society for Political Action," to little effect. The turn away from outright opposition was more readily apparent, if no more efficacious: efforts along these lines included Monteiro Lobato's enlistment of support from prominent perrepistas and PRP allies for his petition-producing Pro-Secret Ballot League and the founding of various associations that brought together similarly catholic ranges of intellectual opinion to puzzle out the problems of the day (the Pro-Sanitation and Education League, the Paulista Association for Social Defense and its Center for Debates, and the Brazilian Society for Economic Studies).[1]

Late 1925 saw the founding of a political party by young men of the middle, journalists and students, most of them relative outsiders or newcomers to the state capital's intellectual circles. Their manifesto to the nation combined appeals to the republican tradition in which they were raised, familiar denunciations of politics as practiced, and the usual prescriptions for reform (the secret ballot, education), with more radical proposals for social-welfare measures and "a closer approximation with the countries of Latin America." Despite a less-than-inspiring moniker and a Dylanesque criterion for membership (only men thirty-five or younger could join), the new Party of Youth did attract support from throughout the state, resulting in the founding of more than a dozen local affiliates.[2]

Youthful idealism and the enthusiasm it attracted in like-minded corners did not, however, translate into success at the polls. Only in Faxina, in the far south of the state, was a Party of Youth candidate victorious in the municipal elections of November 1925, apparently through some markedly unidealistic dealings with county incumbents.[3]

The inefficacy of the new party's opposition did not mean that local power-holders had an easy time of it in this particular election cycle. Some did, of course: Ribeirão Preto's Joaquim da Cunha added to his reputation for magnanimity by reserving one spot in the municipal legislature for the reform-minded Albino Camargo, while in scores of counties throughout the state local machines heaved on unopposed. Elsewhere, rival factions of long standing dueled for control over county government in familiar contests (marcondistas versus goulartistas in Presidente Prudente, flaquistas versus saladinocardosofranquistas in São Bernardo, camarguistas versus rodriguesalvistas in Guaratinguetá), and in a handful of key counties, local voters handed out defeats to their would-be rulers, as in Santos, Campinas, Rio Claro, and Piracicaba.[4]

Municipal elections in Santos saw the young lawyer Antônio Ezequiel Feliciano da Silva, who traveled in the same reformist, mildly pro-labor circles as Cyrillo Freire and Heitor de Moraes (he had campaigned for Ruy Barbosa alongside Moraes in 1919), and who had been involved in the student campaigning of the 1910s at the São Paulo Law School, run as an independent against the ruling party's candidates. He won, with more votes than the leading perrepista, despite splitting the non-PRP vote with two other candidates.[5]

In Campinas, local voters reelected Álvaro Ribeiro to the county board in absentia, Ribeiro having fled the country to avoid the repression that followed the events of July 1924. He received nearly twice as many votes as the leading perrepista candidate, an impressive showing that touched off an ongoing local protest attracting the support of thousands of campineiros—"lawyers, physicians, pharmacists, railwaymen"—as Ribeiro remained in exile and county power-holders declared that he would forfeit his seat by his absence.[6]

Rio Claro's perrepistas were dealt a similar defeat. Here too, a local man who had been a member of the interim county government created by the military rebels of July 1924, Eduardo de Almeida Prado, was elected to the municipal legislature as an independent with the support of long-standing enemies of the PRP.[7]

In Piracicaba, the local incumbents were routed altogether by the county's recently founded Independent Republican Party, which elected all ten councilmen. The new party, which brought together historic republicans, veteran opposition figures, local journalists, and former members of the acting county government of July 1924, presented a novel variation on the municipalist tradition: it would not oppose the state and federal governments outright, or so the claim was made, but it would not support them either. Instead, the *independentes* pledged to "struggle for local interests and campaign for the adoption of the secret ballot," earning their party the applause of newspapermen from throughout the state.[8]

In the same election, "dozens" if not "hundreds" of "independent voters" in the state capital registered their opposition to the existing system by voting for "Isidoro Dias Lopes, João Cabanas, Siqueira Campos, [Luiz Carlos] Prestes, Miguel Costa and many others" of the now-legendary rebel officers. This symbolic voting was annulled easily enough (it never appeared in the official election results).[9] Of far greater concern for PRP leaders was a pair of defections that served to highlight the degree of stress and dissension that had found its way into the Republican host.

The first of these defections came in early December 1925, when José Adriano Marrey Júnior, who had been reelected to a second term in the state legislature earlier in the year, broke with the republican establishment and resigned from the PRP. Marrey was in some ways a typical product of perrepismo—he had worked his way up in the state-capital machine under the sponsorship of Olavo Egydio—but in other ways he was unique. From his first term as a city councilman in the mid-1910s, he had cultivated an independent image, devoted himself to popular yet respectable causes, and worked to develop a following of his own among the middle- and working-class folks of the state capital independently of higher-ranking chefes and intermediary cabos. In attracting this following, he not only drew on the typical clientele-building tools of his law practice (he was a charismatic defense attorney) and his access to state patronage; he also made the most of a sharp wit and a sharper tongue that earned him admirers as he took on popular bugbears (the Canadian-owned Light and Power Company, for example) and his rivals within the PRP. And while he was never a member of the Nationalist League or the Pro-Secret Ballot League, he did establish himself as a supporter of electoral reform.[10]

Marrey announced his resignation from the PRP less than a week after the municipal elections. However, his falling out did not come about as a result of the elections themselves—if anything, Marrey had postponed breaking with the PRP until after they were over so that his announcement would make the greatest possible impact. At root was a larger conflict between the perrepista rump and the Olavo Egydio machine that went back to the inter-party schism of 1923–24, when the old boss had opposed the sitting state government and, as a result, lost the political chieftainship of the state capital and his seat on the PRP executive committee. While he regained the latter, his predominance in city politics was a thing of the past; when, in anticipation of municipal elections, he was consulted regarding possible candidates for the São Paulo city council, only two of his suggestions were heeded. Olavo Egydio took the opportunity to resign from his seat on the executive committee on 12 November, amid speculation as to whether his resignation had resulted wholly from this snub or whether it was also influenced by his declining health (he would die less than two and a half years later).[11]

Whatever the relative importance of these factors in spurring the old boss to resign, the resignation itself led to further speculation among political observers. What would Marrey's reaction be now that his most lasting link to the PRP had been sundered?[12]

The answer came nearly three weeks later, on 4 December, when Marrey and Olavo Egydio's son Alfredo resigned from their committee appointments in the state legislature. Marrey, for his part, went further, declaring, "frankly, loyally" that he disagreed with "the political direction of the Paulista Republican Party" and that, with Olavo Egydio no longer among its leaders, he was also leaving the PRP. When the house leader suggested that he should also resign from his seat in the legislature, as it was the party that had elected him, Marrey bristled, denying that the "party effort" had won him his votes, as he "would have received them anyway," and issuing the ironic challenge that his colleagues "verify if they could directly represent the popular will."[13]

Marrey did not resign. Rather, over the weeks that followed he used his seat in the legislature to hector his erstwhile allies. The day after his leaving the PRP, he revived his earlier call for the introduction of the secret ballot, bolstering his argument with an extended quote from the Republican manifesto of 1870 and noting that the desire for reform "echoes in the popular sectors" and had "invaded the scientific associations [and] the class associations and runs through every corner where there is someone who is interested in the destinies of the Patria."[14] On 11 December, he took on the *Correio Paulistano* and its lack of "authority to speak of democratic norms." In an aside, he noted that the PRP, "in the unanimous consensus of the population, was comparable to a sack full of cats," but with one key difference: "cats shut up in a sack will claw one another to get out; some Party chiefs claw one another to get back in."[15] This set of comments—"vehement and just"—reportedly caused a sensation, leading observers to fill the galleries for Marrey's next appearance, in which the "congressman of the 'left'" declared that the "party is estranged from public opinion and offends popular sentiment!" and forced a tongue-tied Oscar Rodrigues Alves to concede that his clan's followers were also subject to political persecution in the wake of the 1923–24 schism.[16]

In late December, the PRP was struck by another defection, this one by a very different kind of leader. If Marrey, as a lawyer, city councilman, and state legislator, represented something new, with his irreverent, populist style and his independent following among the humbler sort of the state capital, the state senator and law professor Reynaldo Porchat was something of a throwback, a representative of a staid, decorous, and noble-minded politics that had never really existed except as an idea in the minds of a self-deluded few. While Marrey had played machine politics and had helped invent popular politics, Porchat had been selected by state president Washington Luís to replace a previous representative of the São Paulo Law School in the paulista senate, where he sat alongside the most august and well-compensated of the state's republican leaders.[17]

All sources indicate that in his two years in the senate, Porchat comported himself with the same severe, high-minded decorum with which he so impressed his students at the São Paulo Law School. He was often critical of projects that were introduced for debate and came to deplore the legislature's role as an echo chamber for the executive. Over time, he became increasingly critical of the very ways in which paulista politics were structured and practiced, expressing his disenchantment in ways reminiscent of earlier challengers. The day before Olavo Egydio's resignation from the PRP executive committee was made public, for example, Porchat denounced the party's slate for the upcoming municipal elections: "Your excellency sees that in this great, flourishing and prosperous capital, where there is a commerce of the first order, where there is an extraordinarily advanced industry, where everything develops and prospers in a marvelous way, your excellency sees that the names put forward, except for four or five, are not representative of large commerce, nor of large industry, nor of the great planters, nor of the great proprietors, nor of the great capitalists, they are names that cannot be considered the exponents of these classes to which I am referring."[18]

If Porchat was looking for an opportunity to make a final break with the republican machine, he could not have asked for a better one than that provided by his legislative colleagues. In December, they introduced a bill that would have alienated a wide swath of public land to the city's southeast, the basis for a sweetheart deal that would have enriched insiders, including members of the legislature, many times over as the land in question was sold for a pittance for the development of a garden suburb.[19]

Porchat was said to have gotten wind of this plan and informed some of his colleagues, who expressed shock but did nothing to prevent the bill's passage.[20] On 26 December, he took to the floor and denounced the bill and the senate itself, all the while emphasizing his own tradition of independence and service. Addressing the president of the chamber directly, he declared, in his famously sonorous voice, "Sr. President, nothing remains for me to do. My dignity does not permit me to remain in this chair, when I am convinced that my work and my efforts are annulled by the submission of the Senate to the orders of the executive power." As his honorable colleagues squirmed in their seats, Porchat spoke words that would make headlines: "It was like this in Rome. And there was no remedy for Rome. . . ."[21]

Porchat, who as a professor of Roman law was something of an authority on the subject, went on to express his hope that reform would come from without, from paulista youth, guided by men "who are a title of honor for São Paulo's society"—and here he listed the names of sixteen notables, starting with Antônio Prado—because "within the Senate, and under this regime, it is impossible to accomplish anything." He then presented his formal resignation, evoking one of his own law professors, and strode out of the room, following which his colleagues, who had sat in stunned silence up to this point, hurled obscenities at his back.[22]

News of Porchat's resignation resulted in an outpouring of support. The very notables to whom Porchat had referred were particularly enthused. The grand planter, entrepreneur, and former statesman Antônio Prado quickly voiced his support for the law professor's demonstration and when some of São Paulo's most prominent public figures organized a tribute to Porchat as a gesture of their "admiration and recognition of his brilliant activity in the Paulista Senate, where with so much ardor he displayed his talent and his character, in defense of the interests of the population of the state," Prado's name headed a list of more than two hundred supporters. Among the other subscribers were many other solid men of affairs—great and powerful businessmen—alongside professionals from across the fields, intellectuals of various stripes, and would-be reformers young and old.[23]

Long-standing ideological opponents of the regime—Clovis Botelho Vieira, Nicolau Soares do Couto Esher, and Afonso Schmidt—soon seconded the motion, signing on to subsequently circulated statements of support.[24] Monteiro Lobato expressed his appreciation for Porchat's gesture by telegram.[25] Dissidents in the paulista interior were equally enthusiastic.[26] Marrey made the law professor's resignation the subject of one of his legislative harangues.[27] And the "yellow press" O Combate followed the subject with great enthusiasm.[28]

For scores of privileged young men, signing on to the Porchat tribute was a kind of political debut; some had previously taken part in student politics or attended the state capital's debating societies, but this was an event of another order, one with a far larger audience and body of participants.[29] Even perrepistas such as the newly elected city councilman Goffredo Telles and the former city councilman Heribaldo Siciliano were moved to join in the tribute.[30]

Talk of a new political party had preceded November's municipal elections and Porchat's resignation on St. Stephen's day.[31] By 28 December, reports were that Marrey Júnior was hard at work organizing a party of his own, drawing deeply on his contacts with neighborhood outs in the state capital and county-level contenders in the interior.[32] By 4 January, it was rumored that Marrey's group would call itself the Paulista Popular Republican Party.[33] A political gossip column published two days later reported, in what were presented as two unrelated stories, that Porchat's resignation had brought much "moral and material" support from upper-class paulistas to Marrey's mission of founding a party "with [the] ability to confront the P. R. P.," and that Antônio Prado was going to take to politics on his own very soon.[34] By the start of the following week, word had reached Rio de Janeiro that Prado, Porchat, and Marrey were negotiating the formation of a new party, which *O Combate* reported would be called the Popular Republican Party.[35]

Democracy in Action

After several weeks of further meeting, negotiation, and plotting, the new party's founding gathering was held, on 24 February 1926, the thirty-fifth anniversary of the promulgation of the republican constitution, in Prado's stately home. The founding brought together Prado, the titular head of the new party, and twenty-seven other men.[36]

Their political backgrounds were varied. Reynaldo Porchat and Marrey Júnior, who represented two poles of the party, scarcely require further mention, while the remaining twenty-six attendees occupied similarly heterogeneous positions on São Paulo's spectrum of respectable political opinion.

The party's honorary president, Antônio Prado, had been a Conservative Party chieftain and a counselor to Pedro II under the empire. Reconciled to the idea of a republic, or at least resigned to its inevitability, he had served as an insistently apolitical prefeito of São Paulo from 1899 to 1911. By 1913, however, he was expressing support for replacing Brazil's presidential system with a parliamentary republic. "For the paulistas the Republic is a consummated fact," he argued, but parliamentarianism would lead to "the formation of parties, with well-defined programs," in place of the existing order in which "the executive power governs almost discretionarily, whether it has the support of public opinion or not." In 1919 Prado expressed his support for Ruy Barbosa's opposition campaign and in 1921 he endorsed Nilo Peçanha's Republican Reaction. In late August 1925 he publicly endorsed the secret ballot, together with further regulation covering vote counting and confirmation of electoral outcomes, as the means by which "to guarantee the liberty of the vote, which in the current regimen should represent the sovereignty of the people," and he expressed his hope that "paulistas, sons of the land of the truly great men who contributed to the formation of the Brazilian nationality, resolve to found a real political party, based on the democratic principles of our Constitution."[37]

Prado's co-founders Francisco Morato and Luiz Augusto de Queiroz Aranha remained monarchically inclined for a good deal longer. Although the two men acknowledged that restorationism was a lost cause, as late as 1925 they continued to argue publicly that monarchy was a superior form of government and that Brazilians would be well served by aspiring toward the "liberalism and democracy" that the country had enjoyed under Pedro II.[38]

Paulo de Moraes Barros, by contrast, was raised republican, the son of a founder of São Paulo's Republican Party. With the coming of the republic, Moraes Barros became an accomplished politician in his own right, first in his hometown of Piracicaba, then at the state level (serving as São Paulo's secretary of agriculture in the early 1910s), though he often found himself opposing the PRP rump. A grand planter and industrialist with interests throughout the state, Moraes Barros took an active role in its associational life; at the time of the party's founding, he was president of the Brazilian Agricultural League.[39]

The law professor Frederico Vergueiro Steidel had been the president of the Nationalist League and a leader of the business-and-industry Municipal Party of São Paulo.[40] Luiz Barbosa da Gama Cerqueira, also a law professor, was born the son of a counselor to Pedro II but was himself a republican in his distant youth; more recently, Gama Cerqueira had been a leader of the Nationalist League as well.[41]

Of the remaining twenty founders, nearly all had taken part in the previous month's tribute to Reynaldo Porchat, ten or more had been affiliated with the Nationalist League at some point prior to its closing in 1924 (three had been founders in 1916), six had been members of the ineffectual Invisible Society for Political Action founded in the wake of the league's closing, five had been among the principal student leaders of the pro-Pereira Barreto movement in 1918, four had cosponsored Monteiro Lobato's open letter to Carlos de Campos, two had been early backers of the *Revista do Brasil*, and at least one—likely more—had supported Ruy Barbosa in 1919.[42]

At something of an odd angle to the rest of this group of twenty was the last of the party's founders, Bertho Antonino Condé, who was a relative newcomer to São Paulo, a prominent spiritist, a leading anti-fascist journalist, and generally someone "of advanced ideas," in the language of the day. He was included, one gathers, by virtue of his association with Marrey Júnior, with whom he had earlier plotted the founding of an "Evolutionist Party."[43]

Antônio Prado, a day shy of his eighty-sixth birthday, opened the meeting by reminding his guests and perhaps himself that in previous gatherings "ideas had been exchanged regarding the founding of a new political party in S. Paulo that could bring together all paulistas . . . to contribute to the ever-greater development of Brazil, deserving of a liberal politics." He noted that participants in some of the preceding discussions had argued that the post-1924 state of siege made it an inopportune time to found a new party, an argument that was quickly dispensed with by the assembled. That settled, Luiz de Queiroz Aranha (Prado's son-in-law) read a brief text that Prado had drawn up, consisting of a proposed program and a statement regarding his decision to return to party politics. The document, which has been lost, ended with the suggestion that the new group be called the Paulista Popular Party. Debates over the party's name and platform followed, after which Morato, Gama Cerqueira, and Queiroz Aranha were nominated to draw up a formal document, which would then be circulated among interested parties in advance of its public release.[44]

Within a few days, the three leaders had drawn up a proposed program for the party, at this point dubbed the "Democrat Party." Its preamble emphasized the need for political parties, their role in bringing "the various currents of opinion" to the polls in "representative democratic" countries, and their absence in Brazil, where parties "are nothing more than groupings without ideas," focused solely on securing public office (with the "possible exception of Rio Grande do Sul" and leaving aside "the recent socialist movement and the Party of Youth"). The lack of real political parties had resulted in "the discredit of the existing electoral regime" and with it the public's lack of interest in elections in general and in "the triumph of the official slates" in particular.[45]

This situation "demanded of all the sacrifice of their comforts and interests" for the sake of the public good and had led these men to found a political party with "its principal objective, to obtain for the people the free exercise of its sovereignty and the choice of its representatives." Initially, at least, the party would not take part in "electoral struggles, by virtue of the internal commotion in which the Country finds itself, as the Government itself recognizes maintaining the state of siege." Instead, "its activity will be limited to publicity for the cause it defends" until it can take part in elections "to clearly and frankly sustain the ideas of its program."[46]

These ideas were summarized in five points, the first of which read, "To defend the liberal and democratic principles consecrated in the Constitution, making the government of the people by the people a reality." The second point established that the party's defense of the constitution would involve opposition to any infringement of constitutional privileges, alluding to, but not mentioning, the Bernardes government's restriction of press freedoms, its continued recourse to state-of-siege powers, and its plans for constitutional reforms that would further expand executive power: "To oppose any constitutional revision that involves restricting individual freedoms and guarantees." Point three read: "To struggle for a reform of electoral law, in the sense of guaranteeing the veracity of the vote, demanding, for this, the secret compulsory ballot and measures securing registration, vote counting, review, and recognition." The fourth point was expressly agrarian, "To assert for agriculture the influence in the direction of public affairs to which it has a right by its importance," while the fifth was social-reformist, "To promote and defend all measures that concern the social question and, particularly, the well-being of the working classes."[47]

"Whether in the press or in public rallies," the Democrat Party would not involve itself in "personal questions." Rather, "its only object is to discuss the issues from a lofty point of view, treating exclusively to enlighten public opinion, in such a way as to make the regime constituted of the government of the people by the people a reality."[48]

Within a week of the 24 February meeting, this program had met with the approval of Antônio Prado, six of his guests, and Octaviano Alves de Lima. The last of these men, a coffee exporter, planter, and industrialist, had not been among the twenty-eight attendees of the meeting at the Prado manse, but he had circulated in some of the same reformist circles (he was a longtime advocate of a Georgist land tax) and may have been represented there by a younger relative, Sylvio Alves de Lima, perhaps because his kinsman was the holder of a law degree while his own formal education had been cut short. As Octaviano Alves de Lima's assent to the proposed program further suggests, discussions before and after 24 February involved more than the relatively tiny circle present at Prado's home and it is best to think of the members of the latter group as representatives—delegates, really—of their own groups of like-minded men.[49]

That rumors of the party's founding were finding their way into the press also indicates a larger circle of participants in these discussions. They also point to the existence of disagreement regarding the party's program.[50]

Antônio Prado, for his part, had his mind made up. Shortly after signing the draft program written by Morato, Gama Cerqueira, and

Queiroz Aranha, he returned to Rio de Janeiro, where he spent most of his time. Once there, he spoke with a reporter for a *carioca* newspaper about the new party, making special mention of agrarian interests (the *lavoura*, singled out in item four of the draft program).[51]

Back in São Paulo, the rumor was that the new party would make its public debut in a week and a half, on 15 March.[52] Apparently, however, no broader agreement had been reached on the program and the date passed without an announcement. It was not until the afternoon of 21 March that a platform was released to the public at large, along with the names of 601 supporters, as the Democratic Party of São Paulo's "Manifesto to the Nation."[53]

The platform of the new party, soon to be known as the PD, contained several changes, some apparently slight but meaningful, others of greater obvious import, and still others suggesting grammarian and stylistic bickering among the party's overschooled founders. The earlier program's hedging regarding the existence of real political parties in Rio Grande do Sul was amended: the state was an exception (and the new party's leaders would soon find allies in the southernmost state's Liberating Party). The lack of parties elsewhere resulted not only in "the discredit of the existing electoral regime," as had been argued, but in "the discredit of the regime": the problem was no longer limited to electoral practices; it extended to the government itself.[54]

The greatest number of changes came in the five points that had formed the centerpiece of the draft program, now expanded to six. Liberal-constitutionalist points 1 and 2 were combined into a new first point. Point 3 (the call for electoral reform) was reproduced as the new second point, with the stated commitment to compulsory voting edited out (it was, perhaps, thought too radical in its potential effects). Point 4 was amended to read, as the new third point: "To assert for agriculture, *for commerce, and for industry* the influence in the direction of public affairs to which they have a right by their importance," thus appealing to nonagrarian elements in São Paulo's propertied classes. The original fifth point, now the fourth, was truncated, in what appears to have been another concession to conservatives: "To promote and defend all measures that concern the social question." Finally, two new items were added as points 5 and 6: appeals for judicial and educational reforms, respectively.[55]

The 601 men who lent their names to the manifesto's initial release represented a broad sampling of the paulista upper and middle classes.[56] Although not a true cross-section of the state's population by any stretch, they were representative of a São Paulo that many of them imagined themselves as living in, or wanted to imagine themselves as living in, a well-educated, refined, and mostly comfortable society.[57] Legal professionals predominated, with 139 listing "lawyer" as their profession and 6 others "professor of law."[58] The second-largest occupational group was made up of commercial employees (80). Businessmen were the third-largest group (68). Agriculturalists constituted the fourth-largest category (59), but one of the most interesting ones, as the generic term "lavrador" was used uniformly, including for grand absentees like Antônio Prado (also a banker, coffee exporter, and industrialist) and the idle adult sons of other magnates (Paulo Nogueira Filho was one); one suspects that this verbal deflation was an agrarian-populist gesture.[59] After this heterogeneous group, the next largest groups were tellers and other bank employees (48), engineers (42), property owners (34), physicians (28), students (18), journalists (10), and industrialists (10). Among the professions that would later become more important to the PD's growth but that were represented only by tiny contingents among the original signers were lower-status liberal professionals (dentists [8], pharmacists [6], and teachers [3]) and higher-status manual workers (railwaymen [4]). The earliest adherents thus included representatives from the highest reaches of the paulista upper class through the respectable working class represented by railwaymen, with the bulk made up of liberal professionals and the middling, collar-and-tie employees of commercial houses and banks.

Alongside old paulista names like Prado and Alves de Lima were more recent additions to the regional lexicon of surnames. At least fifty of the manifesto's subscribers bore family names that did not come from Portugal or the nineteenth-century Brazilian fad of adopting a Tupi appellation. Many of these names were Italian (Faggione, Melone, Lorenzoni, for example), but others came from Spain (Lopez), Germany (Lindemberg, Bohn, Schloembach were three), and points east (Ivancko).

Scores of the particular names released along with the manifesto would have been familiar to São Paulo's newspaper-reading public, beginning with that of the former prefeito Antônio Prado. There were, of course, the names of the law professors who had helped co-found the party on 24 February (Porchat, Vergueiro Steidel, Morato, Gama Cerqueira, and Cardoso de Mello Neto), who were joined by their colleague José Ulpiano Pinto de Souza and professors from São Paulo's schools of medicine, engineering, and pharmaceutics, but there were also intellectuals of lesser venerability. Cornélio Pires, a Tietê-born humorist, folklorist, and jack-of-all-trades, was one.[60] The engineer Alexandre Ribeiro Marcondes Machado was another, beloved by paulistanos for the satirical verse he published under the pseudonym "Juo Bananére."[61] São Paulo's literary modernists had been represented at the founding meeting of 24 February by Tácito de Almeida and Antônio Couto de Barros, who were now joined among the manifesto's signatories by Argemiro Couto de Barros, Sérgio Milliet, and Mário de Andrade.[62] The watercolorist José Wasth Rodrigues also signed on, and while his aesthetic was more traditional than that of the modernist avant-garde, he was not without friends in modernist circles; years earlier, he had designed the state capital's coat of arms with Tácito de Almeida's brother Guilherme.[63] Rodrigues was one of two painters to sign the manifesto; the other was José Maria dos Reis Júnior, a Minas-born portrait and landscape artist.

Among the ten subscribers identified as journalists were Leopoldo de Freitas, a proud gaúcho long involved in dissident politics in São Paulo who had been jailed following the 1924 revolt; the Ferraz do Amaral brothers, Brenno and Pedro, born and raised in Piracicaba, but career journalists in the state capital beginning in the 1910s, as well as active members of the Party of Youth; and Armando Luiz Silveira da Motta, another career journalist, who had contributed to O Estado de S. Paulo's livelier evening edition along with Brenno Ferraz.[64] Dozens of other subscribers were active or occasional journalists, though they were identified by other callings. Clovis Ribeiro, for example, a founder of the Nationalist League, had left the editorial board of O Estado de S. Paulo for a stable job as general secretary and legal counsel to the São Paulo Commercial Association, but he continued to dabble in journalism.[65]

Ribeiro's career bore a resemblance to that of fellow signatory Octavio Pupo Nogueira, another former scribbler employed in the state capital's associational sector as the general secretary of São Paulo's textile industrialists' association.[66] Further subscribers who were prominent participants in paulista associational life included Nestor Pereira Júnior, the president of the Association of Commercial Employees; Alberto Cintra, the president of the Santos Commercial Association; and Bento Pires de Campos, a former president of the Commerce and Industry Center, which had merged with the São Paulo Commercial Association in 1917.[67]

Pires de Campos and the PD founder Vergueiro Steidel had been prominent members of the state capital's Municipal Party, founded nearly ten years earlier. The defunct commercial- and industrial-interest party was well represented among the 601 signers, with another half-dozen former municipalist leaders signing on.[68]

The Nationalist League was equally well represented. In addition to the five league founders who had participated in the gathering at Prado's home the month before were seven additional founding members, as well as other men who became active in the league subsequent to its founding, including Horácio Lafer (the scion of a Lithuanian-immigrant clan that had built a paper-industry empire in São Paulo) and the lawyer Henrique Smith Bayma, both of whom had supported the Pereira Barreto campaign as students in 1918.[69]

The Party of Youth was represented by a smaller and less representative contingent: the Ferraz do Amaral brothers and a few newly minted lawyers, one of whom had campaigned for Ruy Barbosa in 1919 as a young student. Notable by their absence were the party's scrappier leaders, less well connected than the two journalists and less polished than the lawyers, some of whom would end up joining the new party, others who would not.[70]

These young men were new opponents of the reigning political order, but veteran opposition figures also figured among the manifesto's subscribers. The Rio-born medical professor Rubião Meira was among the most persistent: he had supported Pereira Barreto and Ruy Barbosa in 1918 and 1919, helped lead the Republican Reaction in São Paulo in 1921–22, taken part in an early military conspiracy in 1922 (although this was not public knowledge at the time), and run his own independent protest candidacies in various elections.[71]

In 1918, Meira had been joined in his support for Pereira Barreto by Alberto Seabra, another of São Paulo's most distinguished physicians and a co-signatory of the PD manifesto. With the partial exceptions of the Pereira Barreto campaign and a protest candidacy of his own in 1924, Seabra had been more of an intellectual than an activist up to this point. A hygienist, a supporter of the introduction of the secret ballot, an advocate of a Georgist tax on land, and a believer in Latin American solidarity, he had been a founder of the *Revista do Brasil* and the Pro-Sanitation and Education League, and an early enthusiast of the Paulista Social Defense Society and its Center for Debates.[72]

Still other signatories were relative unknowns but bore storied names. João Mendes de Almeida Neto, whose small role in the Pereira Barreto campaign had undoubtedly already been forgotten, was the direct descendant of one of Antônio Prado's great rivals in the Conservative Party. Theodoro Sampaio Filho's namesake was a famed engineer, city planner, and historian whose work in São Paulo and Santos had focused on sanitation. Francisco Mesquita was the second son of Julio Mesquita, the publisher of *O Estado de S. Paulo*; he was not the only member of the *Estado* family to sign on to the PD manifesto, but he was the most important (Armando de Salles Oliveira, an in-law, also subscribed, but he took no further role in party activity). All three young men—Almeida Neto, Sampaio Filho, and Mesquita—were graduates of the São Paulo Law School.[73]

The formal unveiling of the manifesto to which these men lent their names was a public meeting held in the great hall of the Associação Auxiliadora das Classes Laboriosas, one of São Paulo's oldest mutualist groups. Antônio Prado, who presided, was joined on the dais by twenty of the men he had hosted on 24 February, as well as by Antônio Cândido Rodrigues, a fellow grand planter and industrialist, as well as a sitting state senator of similarly advanced age who had taken the losing side in the schism of 1923–24, and by Luiz de Queiroz Lacerda, a lawyer who had participated in the Nationalist League's campaign for the secret ballot and the recent tribute to Reynaldo Porchat.[74]

Prado opened the meeting with a speech in which he acknowledged that the party's manifesto was brief, but went on to argue that it demonstrated "that in the State of S. Paulo there is a part of the population made up of men notable for their talent, enlightenment and social distinction, capable of forming a political party with set ideas about the governing of the country." The PD, as Prado saw it, did not aim for "the conquest of power"; rather, it sought "to receive it directly from the people to whom it has the duty to enlighten about their political importance": "It is necessary that the people know . . . that sovereignty is in their hands and that it is they that temporarily delegate their powers to the country's government. Only then will we have real government of the people by the people."[75]

Following the reading of an account of the meeting of 24 February, it was Marrey Júnior's turn to speak. He did not disappoint, declaring, amid "frenetic applause": "The needs of the country called for this association of a handful of men, self-sacrificing and devoted to public affairs." None of these men, he argued, "from the first steps [in the founding of the new party] to this consecration, have any [ties of] dependency that render suspicious their initiative and activity." Their motivation—their "guiding star," in his words—was "the well-being of Brazil," now suffering under a "pseudo-democracy" in which "the government of the people by the people has been pure mockery," regardless of what a "cohort of Pontius Pilates" might assert. Marrey raised the now-familiar example of Argentina, then the no-less-familiar comparison with

Brazil: "Here indifference, manifest in all aspects of national life, has been one of the greatest Brazilian evils. There is no 'control' by public opinion. Almost all contestants in national elections are political clients. Parties are lacking, the secret ballot is lacking, the expression of an electoral mass in the choice of leaders is lacking." Despite this dire situation, Brazilian leaders (and here he alluded to Washington Luís, a former state president and national president-to-be) continued to assert "that the reigning electoral process is very good," while "the men of power in our State ... flee from the secret ballot like Satan flees from the Cross" and were mere "defenders of their own personal interests," supporting the PRP "to fill public posts and make ... [a] livelihood from the positions they occupy." In this situation, in which "well-intentioned men are always left aside," the new party would become a "school of civismo," a "school of sacrifice" that would transcend the oligarchic, nepotistic, clientelist politics of the present and place Brazil among "the great democracies ... in each of which the government maintains itself according to the popular will."

Marrey then proposed that the new party's provisional directorate be made up of Prado, Gama Cerqueira, Morato, Cardoso de Mello Neto, Waldemar Ferreira, Paulo de Moraes Barros, Luiz de Queiroz Aranha, Antônio Cajado de Lemos, Paulo Nogueira Filho, and Prudente de Moraes Neto, all of whom had been among those present at the Prado mansion on 24 February. All ten names were acclaimed by the audience, which further played its appointed role by insisting that Marrey too serve on the directorate.

Moraes Barros spoke next, providing a far more staid speech than Marrey's, one that was "listened to with all attention and applauded various times." He began by evoking the republican movement of the 1870s, noting that within twenty years of its emergence, "twenty rapid instants in the existence of a nation ... the Republic was already proclaimed." This example, Moraes Barros argued, should serve "to demonstrate to the unbelievers, so numerous today, that the ground in which we will sow is not [one] of essential barrenness." His agrarian metaphor established, Moraes Barros further argued, "Our aspirations are much more limited and modest than those of the well-intentioned patriots of 1870. We do not aim to transform by the root the institutions that rule us." Instead, Moraes Barros called for a renewal of participation in public life. Such a renewal of civismo, he claimed, was the means by which to reverse "this ... abstention, in the middle of which the [state and federal] governments administer the precious patrimony of our material and moral goods as they see fit, as irresponsible sovereigns." It would be a long road, he held, one fraught with obstacles, but one on which the keepers of Brazil's "glorious traditions" were bound to soldier on.

A reading of the party's Manifesto to the Nation followed, then a speech by Queiroz Aranha, who began by referring to the British party system, then argued, on the basis of Brazil's nineteenth-century history, that "party government is also a Brazilian tradition," a tradition that had come to an end, despite the "stupendous episode of democracy" represented by the presidential campaign of 1909–10. The current lack of parties in Brazil was reflected in the "enervating stagnation" of public life, though Queiroz Aranha held out hope that "the political crisis has now completed its cycle." He paid tribute to the party's patriarch, Antônio Prado (with his tradition "of authority, of distinction" making him the "necessary man" in the current "troubled times"), then tried his hand at populist appeals, some successful if somewhat stuffy ("Our mission is to take from Caesar that which is not Caesar's and to render unto the people what is of the people . . ."), others clumsy ("The party manifesto is a political letter addressed to the Brazilian people, to be read among the cultivated classes and also deciphered by our more humble and uncultured compatriots").

Brenno Ferraz spoke next, reading a statement from the Party of Youth welcoming the PD's founding and pledging its cooperation, then making his own case for the new party to join with his party in its dedication "to problems of the social magnitude of agricultural and popular credit," an "objective that will carry our people to the integral fulfillment of their economic, political and social destinies." The PD founder Fábio de Camargo Aranha responded with thanks for the Party of Youth's support, then Reynaldo Porchat complied with the hall's repeated requests for him to speak, making much of the party's place among "those who are guided by rectitude" and its aim "to teach the Brazilian [man] not to fear his responsibilities."

Speeches from the floor and the galleries followed. Inadvertently illustrating the breadth of opinion represented on the dais, one "young man of the people, anonymous among the anonymous applauders," decried the presence of so many former monarchists among the founders of what was supposed be a democratic party, a point of view that was reportedly shared by Bertho Condé, who kept his concerns to himself.[76]

The broader response to the meeting was enthusiastic, with the party receiving a hearty welcome in the independent and opposition press, from the state capital's great dailies to its yellow press through the smaller newspapers of the interior.[77] *O Estado de S. Paulo* dubbed the gathering of 21 March "The Public Consecration of an Ideal."[78] The *Diário da Noite* applauded the PD as a "beautiful movement of opinion," which stood in stark contrast to São Paulo's "ferocious oligarchy": "The new party introduces itself with the best credentials. At its front one finds names of great significance, some nobly representative figures and a respectable mass of citizens whom by their social position constitute [men of] great worth. All of the professions have a contingent that has joined the party and, with three or four exceptions, the men that enlisted in its ranks are not militant politicians. It is a political party that recruits [its members] from outside of politics, with patriotic rather than partisan objectives."[79]

O Combate similarly lauded the PD's founding by "people belonging to all of S. Paulo's social classes" as "A Great Event in National Politics."[80] *O Sacy*, a yellow-press magazine founded by Cornélio Pires two months earlier, likewise welcomed the new party, an unsurprising development given Pires's personal support for the PD.[81]

In the interior, Jaboticabal's *Gazeta Liberal*, published by supporters of Ruy Barbosa's 1919 campaign who had been implicated in the revolt of 1924, was an early backer of the PD. Indeed, the editors of the *Gazeta Liberal* had expressed their support for the party when its founding was only a rumor, making special mention of their regard for Marrey Júnior.[82]

O Popular, published in the lower-Mogiana town of Vargem Grande, made the case that "all free and thinking men with the rights to this title in the zoological series" were rallying around Antônio Prado and the new party.[83] In central-zone Laranjal, the editor-proprietor of *A Tarde* and other critics of republican practice took satisfaction in noting among the PD's founders "a pleiad of most competent men, of great rigor and sublime ideals," making specific mention of Prado, Porchat, Marrey, Prudente de Moraes Neto, Rubião Meira, and Paulo Nogueira Filho, the last of whom had passed through Laranjal while campaigning for Luiz Pereira Barreto eight years earlier.[84]

If these descriptions scan as more than a little fawning, they nevertheless provide an accurate reflection of how the party was received. Support for the party, expressed in a patriotic, republican idiom familiar to São Paulo's newspaper-reading public, came from throughout the state, from all reaches of what was understood to be paulista society, from large planters, merchants, and industrialists, through the professions and on to smaller-scale agriculturalists, small businessmen, and collar-and-tie employees before reaching the literate and respectable upper reaches of the working class.

Beginning the very day of the PD's public debut, the state capital's self-described "men of goodwill" wrote to express their support. Armando Pinto Ferreira, a lawyer, wrote Marrey "as a Brazilian and a patriot" of the opinion that "the oligarchy and the retention of [constitutional] powers" would destroy the republic unless a "party of honorable, patriotic, free people of sound principles" like the PD's founders opposed such an outcome.[85] Antônio Ferraz Napoles of outlying Penha, a seventy-five-year-old historic republican, joined with his sons, "hoping for the political regeneration" outlined in the "program of the new party," while Hermes Victorino Chinaglia, a businessman in Vila Mariana, adhered "with immense jubilation . . . to the Democratic Party, which emerges led by men of real Brazilian sentiment."[86]

Similar letters poured in from throughout the state over the course of the weeks and months that followed. Throughout this correspondence were additional appeals to these and further aspects of São Paulo's patriotic, republican tradition, leavened with references to the mobilizing ideas of the 1910s and to the events of the 1920s.

João Gastão Duchein, a resident of "our historic district of Ipiranga" and apparently a victim of the police roundup that followed July 1924, wrote Marrey to request "the inclusion of my name on the list of adhering Brazilian citizens."[87] A dozen men, "representing a handful of independent voters from the neighborhoods of Pary and Canindé," were among the first in the state capital to start their own subscription list of local supporters, "in agreement with the noble ideals contained in the brilliant manifesto directed to the nation and read yesterday at the memorable meeting of investiture of the Party, these ideals that represent the true sentiment of all good, patriotic *Brazilians*," thus fulfilling "a great civic duty . . . the duty that all must struggle and care for the greatness and ennoblement of the beloved Patria."[88] Joaquim de Azevedo, a merchant in upper-Sorocabana Ourinhos, made special mention of his hope that the PD would "put an end to the false!" (elections and other political arrangements); he too went to work gathering local supporters, distributing handbills inviting "all independent citizens" to join him in supporting the new party.[89]

Writing from Ribeirão Preto, Thomaz Duffles, a thirty-four-year-old pharmacist, offered his "humble services" to the PD, as a "son of S. Paulo" who had abandoned politics after Ruy Barbosa's defeat in 1919, "completely disillusioned with our Country's electoral machine."[90] Francisco Carneiro Ribeiro Santiago, born in Minas Gerais in 1860, but a resident of São João da Boa Vista, expressed his desire to join the party, "whose goal . . . is to sanitize the republican regime." He was "not a militant politician, but a voter and a practicing physician [identified elsewhere as a capitalist as well], without any obligation, at any time, to the higher-ups in politics of a government of oligarchs and autocrats."[91] Benjamin Ferraz da Cunha, a businessman of sorts, active in industry and agriculture in rough-and-tumble Palmital, wrote as a survivor of his home county's infamous massacre of 1922, hoping to see "in this dear Brazil an exemplary government, a government of the people for the people" such that "this our dear and Rich Brazil" would be "no longer enslaved by the government of Oligarchy, this government that humiliates us, this government that doesn't support agriculture, doesn't support industry, doesn't support commerce, this government that only draws up and passes laws for taxes on top of taxes[,] heavy taxes[,] taxes that are poorly applied [and still] there is nothing that can satisfy it, still it turns to loans from foreign countries, in the end we have no guarantees at all, the voter has no guarantee, he's turned away by gunshot. . . ."[92]

Oscar de Souza, a forty-year-old bookkeeper whose father may have been a supporter of Ruy's 1919 campaign and the Republican Reaction of 1921–22, but himself a political novice, wrote of the feeling of "patriotic resurgence" that came over him while watching the PD's investiture on 21 March. The assembly, he claimed, made him see "that in our land independence still exists and that in this chaos in which we live men are still coming forward capable of offering better days to the Patria we love, days in which the veils of hypocrisy and despotism having fallen together, we can live openly, days in which is given to us the happiness of knowing in what way the product of our honest work is consumed and the certainty that our prerogatives as citizens will be respected."[93]

Another early correspondent, a commercial employee who had already visited the party's headquarters in person the day before and added his "humble name to the list of combatants for the *white* 13th of May," wrote with an idea. As the new party's campaign was nothing less "than a true abolitionist campaign, destined to restore the liberty of all Brazilians," the PD should take up voluntary contributions, as had occurred during the campaign for the abolition of black slavery. Such a campaign would represent a truly republican way to fund the new party, in contrast to the "pseudo parties that exploit power [and] dispose of the coffers of the public treasury for their own expenses."[94]

Adherents opining on what the party's specific policies should be were by no means rare. Clovis Botelho Vieira joined enthusiastically, in "this dark hour of the nationality," but lamented that the party manifesto had not more forcefully denounced "the permanent state of siege, which has become a kind of plague upon the Republic," becoming "a formidable weapon of unpopular governments, strangulating public liberties, and creating for the presidents of the States and the Republic a situation of absolute irresponsibility." "We are a country that has a permanently suspended Constitution," he argued, "an absolutist regime."[95]

Writing from upper-Mogiana Cravinhos on 13 May, a local business-man eagerly joined the PD's campaign "to introduce real Democracy . . . dealing a death blow to the oligarchies," and thus carrying out the "urgent and patriotic work of moral sanitation," making special mention of the federal government's infringement of the freedom of the press, its state of siege, and its campaign for constitutional revision.[96] Similar concern for "the defense of the Brazilian Constitution" was expressed by an ex-sergeant, mustered out of the state's militarized police for taking part in the revolt of 1924, who likewise hoped that the new party and its program "will be the advance sentinel of the Patria," while a civilian supporter of the 1924 movement, a stonemason in São Carlos, offered his support for "all of the acts and deliberations of the *Democrat Party*."[97]

In the speeches of 21 March (subsequently published in nearly all of the state's leading newspapers) appeals to paulista regionalism had been relatively muted. As with the dropping of the draft program's "perhaps" regarding the existence of real political parties in Rio Grande do Sul, this was done with an eye toward alliances outside of São Paulo. As Luiz de Queiroz Aranha had explained, "Our partisan activity begins in S. Paulo without us having in mind the slightest glimmer of regionalism"; rather, it was up to "us, the Brazilians, to carry out this program of free men, high-minded and conscious of our duties to the Patria."[98] To a great degree, the party's early adherents followed this precedent, but regional patriotism was never wholly suppressed. Ribeirão Preto's Thomaz Duf-fles, for example, had made special mention of his status as a "son of S. Paulo," while João Gastão Duchein referenced "*nossa pauliceia*"—"our São Paulo."[99] Expressions of support like these came from throughout the state, with locals identifying themselves "as Paulistas and Brazilians" and their leaders as "other paulistas [of] pure blood and character."[100] Al-tinópolis's Simplício Ferreira took an entirely opposite approach to that counseled by Queiroz Aranha, expressing his belief that the PD "will soon be the crucible of national politics, especially that of [this] State, in which we are most interested."[101] The cinematographer Flamínio de Campos Gatti, who had co-produced one of Brazil's first documentary films with Cornélio Pires, denounced politics as practiced, fondly recalled the late, great Ruy Barbosa, and identified the rebels of 1924 as "brave bandeirantes," thereby linking them with São Paulo's proudest regional tradition.[102]

These early supporters of the PD clamored for publication of their names in the press, writing to correct misspellings and omissions.[103] In Queiroz Aranha's words, by having their names published, such men were in effect voting "in the crystalline ballot box of the press against all of the candidates of the oligarchy."[104] Or, as a columnist for *O Combate* had put it first, in commenting on the "lists of expressions of support arriv[ing] at the party's seat filled with the names of people from all social classes": "The Party is putting a paradox into effect. It struggles for the secret ballot, but it is practicing a veritable open plebiscite."[105] For many of these aspiring PD members—soon to be called *democráticos*—having one's name printed on party rolls was a form of participation in and of itself as well as a marker of their status as independent citizens, even those for whom the ideal of independence was just that, an ideal.

For citizens like these, clientage remained a reality, a strategy for individual advancement and a determinant of political activity. Ulysses de Campos Mello, a cashiered officer of the state police force, signed the PD manifesto and offered his services to the new party, as clerk, assistant, "or even doorman, or in any other service" as his pension was insufficient.[106] Similarly, in late 1926, when an employee of the Companhia Paulista de Estradas de Ferro wrote to declare his solidarity with the PD, "of which is President and founder my esteemed Chief the Most Excellent Counselor Antonio Prado" (also president and founder of the Companhia Paulista) and added that he had served the company for sixteen years, something other than enthusiasm for the party's program seems to have been at play.[107]

Clientelist concerns were not, however, paramount in all cases in which they were present. Jundiaí's railwaymen may have been drawn to the PD by the presence of Antônio Prado at its head, or by the adherence of the Companhia Paulista's engineer, Francisco Paes Leme de Monlevade (which itself may have been determined by clientelist calculus), but they remained enthusiastic supporters of the party after Prado retired as the president of the Companhia Paulista in January 1928 (and after Prado died in 1929) and were often more active than Monlevade in organizing local party activity.[108]

In other cases, expressions of support came with an explicit cohort of clients. For example, Consolação's José Menotti Chiarugi put "180 votes of *my friends* at the disposal" of the party's leaders, referring once again to "my 180 votes" in the run-up to the PD's first experiment in electoral politics. This was language that would have been immediately familiar to perrepista ward bosses.[109]

The elitist underpinnings of republican political culture, in particular the understanding that a certain sort (men of property possessed of prestige) would lead while others would follow, were similarly inseparable from the PD's early growth. Indeed, given the earlier careers and family histories of many of the PD's leaders, there is a temptation to see these understandings as encoded in the party's DNA. However, there were also deliberate, pragmatic reasons for following precedent. A particular county's largest planter could be a patron in the traditional sense—he could be a PD chefe—but an absentee planter's name at the head of a local party's rolls could also provide the necessary cover for townsfolk with interests and ideas of their own. A local merchant, José Ribeiro de Faria took this tack in coffee-rich Cravinhos, in the heart of Joaquim da Cunha's upper-Mogiana stronghold, running the county PD on his own but making sure that state-level leaders interceded with "the county's principal planters" on his behalf.[110]

As the PD attracted support from across the state, the party's makeup shifted rapidly. While lawyers had represented the largest single occupational grouping among the PD manifesto's original 601 subscribers, followed by commercial employees, businessmen, and agriculturalists, the composition of the rank and file changed considerably as the party grew. A month after the party's founding, the five largest groups of adherents were commercial employees (2,071), businessmen (763), workers (720), bank employees (661), and railwaymen (473). This broadening at the party's base continued as the PD grew.[111]

This increase in the number of middle-class and working-class supporters, both in absolute terms and relative to the numbers present among the party's first 601 supporters, was accompanied by a similar increase in the party's members who were Brazilian-born children of immigrants, naturalized immigrants, or immigrants seeking naturalization. Indeed, in a society like early-twentieth-century São Paulo's what might appear to posterity to be two processes was actually one. So, for example, in capital-zone Guarulhos, an early party groupuscule was led by José Ciampetti, an engineer, whose lieutenants included Raphael Rocco, Antônio Brancaleone, and Paschoalino Camisotti; in Caconde, in the lower Mogiana, Antônio Antonini, an accountant, was among the earliest party officers, as was Alfredo Bauer, a lawyer in Araraquarense-zone Jaú.[112]

Representatives of one hundred of these local affiliates took part in the party's first congress, convened in December 1926. Addressing the assembly, Paulo Nogueira Filho outlined the year's developments: the outfitting of the PD's secretariat in the state capital, which had processed the adhesions of more than 45,000 men from throughout São Paulo; Piracicaba's Independent Republican Party's pledge to support the new party; the founding of affiliates throughout the state; and ongoing efforts at voter registration. Nogueira Filho also discussed the organization of a 120-member consultative council, representing "all of the social classes." The as-yet-unrealized idea was for the council to serve as an advisory board that would draw on its members' fields of expertise and interest, sorting out the kind of technical problems that had previously occupied non-opposition groups like the Association for Social Defense's Center for Debates and the Brazilian Society for Economic Studies.[113]

The congress was also the occasion for debates over the formalization of the party's bylaws. Bertho Condé proposed three amendments to the platform released to the public on 21 March: that the platform's first item be rewritten to reflect the fact that Brazil had a constitution and that the PD would work "to *reestablish* the liberal principles *that were consecrated in the Constitution of 1891*"; that labor be granted consideration in item three ("To assert for agriculture, commerce and industry *and its workforce* the influence to which it has a right"); and that a seventh item calling for the overhaul of Brazil's bureaucracy be added. Mário de Souza Queiroz, a planter in Limeira, proposed, "Considering that our wealth and well-being depend on agricultural production," that the platform include a plank indicating the PD's intention: "To promote and defend all measures that relate to agricultural production, such as: Training, organization of agricultural cooperatives and Syndicates." Other matters for debate included whether the party should endorse expanding university-level education specifically or education in general, and whether the party should advocate free trade or protectionism. In both of the latter two cases, the argument that the party should set aside "secondary questions of organization" in order to appeal to the widest possible public won the day. Souza Queiroz's proposed amendment was also rejected, as were all but the first of Condé's. Delegates also voted by secret ballot for members of the PD's Central Directorate (the members of the provisional directorate were confirmed in their posts, joined by Reynaldo Porchat, with the co-founders Joaquim de Sampaio Vidal and Condé to serve as substitutes) and its consultative council (the slate presented by the PD leadership won, through not unanimously), to which Condé submitted a further set of "considerations about public education, the working-class question, [and] the political and administrative regimen."[114]

The congress's main order of business was the decision to participate in federal legislative elections to be held in February, then the election of candidates, also by secret ballot. The winners were Gama Cerqueira, Marrey Júnior, Francisco Morato, Paulo de Moraes Barros, and Luiz de Queiroz Aranha. Gama Cerqueira was to run for the senate in a state-wide election, a race widely recognized as unwinnable, while the remaining four candidates would run for seats in the lower house. Marrey was to run for the lower house in the first federal district, which covered the state capital and much of the western half of the state. Morato would run for a seat representing most of the central and northwestern areas of the state, including Campinas, his hometown of Piracicaba, and Rio Preto, the gateway to the far northwestern frontier. Moraes Barros would run in the third district, which covered the coffee-rich Mogiana zone and its regional capital, Ribeirão Preto. Queiroz Aranha pulled the short straw and was elected to run in the fourth federal district, which covered the older, eastern portion of the state made up of the Paraiba Valley and its environs, where the PD had faced its greatest challenges. Each of these four lower-house candidates would run in open elections against five or six perrepistas.[115]

Leading up to the election, the party began to publish the *Folha do Partido Democrático* as a broadside in sympathetic newspapers. Propaganda materials, some of them designed by Wasth Rodrigues, were circulated in the capital and the interior: buttons and flags emblazoned with the Phrygian bonnet ("the cashew" was the popular nickname), posters and leaflets calling on conscientious and independent citizens to vote for the candidates of the opposition party.[116] Politicking was also carried out by less pacific means: in one paulistano neighborhood, pro-government toughs attacked a PD member whom they found putting up posters. A running gun battle ensued in which the democrático killed one perrepista, wounded four others, and was himself wounded.[117]

The election itself was held under widely varied conditions. In the state capital, the election was carried out in a generally orderly fashion, with a handful of exceptions (a pointed threat in Jardim América, a scuffle in Lapa, some rounds fired off in Bom Retiro), such that local democráticos were able to take advantage of the assurances of the city police chief and vote their consciences, or at least the consciences of their cabos. Election day was generally orderly in the larger cities of the interior as well.[118]

That these elections were for the most part orderly did not mean that they were clean. In the state capital and throughout the state, there were all manner of irregularities: polling places were never opened, lists of voters vanished, election monitors were turned away, and the hallowed bico de pena technique was widely used. In the more isolated and backward parts of the state, elections were held with still less decorum, in certain cases, as in Itararé, amid serious violence.[119]

Early results were propitious for the PD. It quickly became apparent that the party had elected three of its four candidates: Morato, Marrey, and Moraes Barros. On the afternoon of the election, O Combate could report that Marrey led the field in the first district, Morato in the second, and Moraes Barros in the third. (In the fourth district, it was already clear that Queiroz Aranha could not win, with only 2,389 votes to 6,621 for the least successful PRP candidate, while Gama Cerqueira's loss had been a foregone conclusion.) As the days passed and bico de pena reports came in from rotten boroughs throughout the state, perrepista tallies increased but the election of these three candidates could not be reversed.[120]

Taking their seats in the federal legislature soon thereafter, the new congressmen were lauded in the press: "three names representing three programs. Marrey Junior, idol of the masses, paladin of the people's interests. . . . Although less popular, both [of the other two PD congressmen] are of elevated moral, civic, and political position. Dr. Francisco Morato, venerated master of law," and "Dr. Paulo de Moraes Barros, militant politician of old stock, ex-secretary of Agriculture."[121]

The work of party building continued in the wake of the election and through the PD's second congress, held in May 1927. Formal policy proposals were few at this gathering, although the case was made for an amnesty that would allow Brazil's military rebels to return from exile. The main item on the agenda was the decision whether to take part in the upcoming state presidential election or to let the PRP's Júlio Prestes run unopposed. It was a matter of intense debate, ultimately decided by a narrow vote (195 in favor of abstention, 177 opposed), the winning rationale being that an outright defeat in a head-to-head election would result in a general slackening of enthusiasm for the new party.[122]

Júlio Prestes was duly elected, running all but unopposed (by way of a protest candidacy, the Party of Youth instructed its members to vote for Rubião Meira, to the satisfaction of João Cabanas and the editors of O Combate).[123] Prestes's inauguration, however, was the date picked by party leaders for a set of events designed to steal any thunder that his swearing-in ceremony might conjure up. On 14 July, after mass rallies in the state capital, the party sent propaganda troupes, or "caravans," out to spread the word. Dubbed a "lesson in nationalism" by an enthusiastic journalist and the "vanguard of Bolshevism" by a hostile one, twenty-nine caravans reached nearly every county in São Paulo over the next few days, holding rallies, distributing propaganda, and pressing flesh with actual and potential local leaders.[124] July also saw the PD begin publishing its own newspaper, the *Diário Nacional,* the circulation of which grew by leaps and bounds over the next year and a half, making it, for a time, the state capital's second most widely circulating newspaper.[125]

In December, the party convened its largest congress to date. As in the two prior congresses, policy matters were discussed, including proposals that the PD endorse compulsory voting, women's suffrage, and replacement of the draft lottery system with universal military service. These relatively radical proposals were laid aside fairly quickly in favor of the congress's chief order of business, the selection of candidates for state legislative elections to be held 24 February 1928, a process that proved far more contentious than that of a year earlier.[126]

For a full two months before the congress would-be candidates and their supporters had jockeyed for position while political columnists laid bets on winners and losers. Bertho Condé, backed by Marrey Júnior and many of the state capital's neighborhood organizations, was an early favorite, but his candidacy was less than pleasing to other key segments of the PD, who sought to steer the party "to its highest exponents, its choicest names, the most eminent figures of its organization." The resulting conflict became a broader struggle between currents, one of which was dubbed "popular" and the other avowedly more representative of patrician segments of the party leadership. The popular current included some young men with credible claims to "popular" backgrounds (Condé and the lapsed seminarian Lázaro Maria da Silva, who had worked his way through law school as a teacher, stenographer, and journalist), established political figures who represented "popular" causes (Marrey and the Santos city councilman Antônio Feliciano), and at least one democrático whose "popular" bona fides rested entirely on his personal relationship with Marrey (Vicente Dias Pinheiro, who came from a family of planters and political outs in São José do Rio Pardo). Battling openly on behalf of the "aristocratic," "official," or "university" slate were a dozen or more "Young Turks," including the party founders Fábio de Camargo Aranha, Prudente de Moraes Neto, and Tácito de Almeida, and members of the *Estado de S. Paulo* group, whose guiding light, the elder Julio

Mesquita, had passed away earlier in the year. These men, if not made of money themselves, came from old families and had "good relations"; such was the case of Paulo Duarte, an *Estado* staffer whose portfolio impressed less than his full name, Paulo Alfeu Junqueira de Monteiro Duarte. The disdain with which the Young Turks viewed the aspiring populists was all but tangible, as in Duarte's description a few years later: "some unquiet elements, without ideals, ambitionists"; "blabbermouths, of a lack of judgment that only ignorance provides"; "that group of political mountebanks—the Party's slum."[127]

In the end, Condé removed his name from consideration (he was elected a full member of the PD's directorate instead) and popular and aristocratic candidates were elected for a complete ticket of Antônio Feliciano, Gama Cerqueira, Henrique Bayma, Augusto Ferreira de Castilho, Amadeu Amaral, Cardoso de Mello Neto, Luiz de Queiroz Aranha, Vicente Pinheiro, João Silveira Mello, Orizombo Loureiro, and Zoroastro Gouveia. The congress also elected candidates to the upper house, but as with Queiroz Aranha's candidacy to the federal senate earlier in the year, these were protest candidacies with no hope of victory.[128]

No one current was entirely pleased with the outcome. At least one young man of means tendered his resignation.[129] Lázaro Maria da Silva complained that he had been betrayed by Nogueira Filho, and locals in déclassé neighborhoods like Belenzinho and Penha griped over Condé's capitulation.[130] Seeing an opportunity, would-be populists in the PRP sought to exploit this dissatisfaction. Bom Retiro's José Molinaro declared that the PD had not chosen Condé as a candidate because he was a "poor man," while the perrepista city councilman Diogenes de Lima said that the attempted imposition of the aristocratic slate of candidates demonstrated, "They read from the old Franciscan primer: do as I say not as I do."[131]

In the elections themselves, fraud was again widespread, but the PD was able to elect six of its eleven candidates to the lower house: Gama Cerqueira and Antônio Feliciano in the first district, Queiroz Aranha in the sixth, Vicente Pinheiro in the seventh, Zoroastro Gouveia in the tenth, and, in the eighth, Pedro Krahenbuhl, who had been picked in an impromptu primary to stand for office in place of João Silveira Mello, who as a sitting justice of the peace (elected by Piracicaba's Independent Republican Party) was ineligible to serve in the state legislature.[132] In the capital, the PD claimed victory in Ipiranga, Lapa, and Penha, where its candidates received more votes than any single PRP candidate. The PD also "won" in Santos and Campinas.[133] The self-consciously urban, refined, and even perhaps progressive character of these victories was summed up in snobbish form by a leader in northwestern Novo Horizonte: "In the towns where people read, where there is electric light and one bathes . . . we were victorious . . . S. Paulo, Campinas, Piracicaba, S. José do Rio Pardo, Botucatu, Catanduva and others."[134] The PD's candidates were beaten outright in the second and third districts (the Paraíba Valley zone), as well as in the fourth district (the fiefdom of the Prestes family), the fifth (Ataliba Leonel's bailiwick, where Cardoso de Mello Neto claimed that fraud and intimidation had robbed him of votes that would have easily put him above the inflated totals of his perrepista rivals), and the ninth (where Orizombo Loureiro may have been similarly robbed of a victory).[135]

The February elections over, the work of building and sustaining local organizations—to say nothing of local enthusiasm—continued, even as Júlio Prestes's government used intimidation and selective cooptation to bolster its standing. There were also municipal elections to be held in October, the first complement of county elections to be held since the party's founding.[136]

On 31 August representatives from each of the state capital's twenty submunicipal districts voted in a primary for candidates to the city council and for prefeito, in what may have been the first use of an Australian-style ballot in Brazil. Marrey Júnior was the party's overwhelming choice for prefeito, while the winning city-council candidates were Francisco Emygdio da Fonseca Telles, Waldemar Ferreira, Carlos de Moraes Andrade, Bertho Condé, Manfredo Costa, Nicolau Moraes Barros, Plínio Queiroz, Rubião Meira, Henrique de Souza Queiroz, and Prudente de Moraes Neto. Similar primaries were held throughout the state.[137]

Shortly before the municipal elections, a polemic in the pages of the São Paulo press came to intersect with party politics, student mobilization, and conflict between pro- and anti-fascist Italians, making for four days of rioting in the state capital, not unlike that seen the decade before in response to German attacks on Brazilian shipping. The conflict, ostensibly over insults to Brazilian national dignity in the Italian-language newspaper *Il Piccolo*, led to an upsurge in the popularity of the Democratic Party, the *Diário Nacional*, and the opposition press more broadly.[138] The effects of the PD's wrapping itself in the national flag, however, may have been undone by a slip committed by Marrey Júnior at roughly the same time, when he suggested, in deliberately provocative terms, that the federal government should intervene in São Paulo to prevent the PRP from making the position of prefeito of the city of São Paulo an appointed rather than an elected office, prompting perrepistas to accuse him of regional disloyalty.[139]

Perrepista harping on Marrey's "wholly asinine insult to the *amour propre* of the Paulistas" was complemented by intimidation, fraud, and violence as the election cycle went on.[140] In Piracicaba, where the PD had counted on winning, locals remained at home on election day, fearing violence.[141] Elsewhere, the opposition came out, but fraud was the rule. In hardscrabble Brás, PD leaders waxed indignant over the lack of transparency in vote tallying and further fraud and intimidation.[142] These middling and working-class paulistanos would have been truly offended by practices elsewhere: an election-day shootout in nearby Cambuci, democráticos being prevented from voting by armed thugs in historic Itu, and numbers-game bookies buying votes for the PRP in Santos.[143]

The PD had expected to elect at least three city councilmen in the state capital. As it turned out, none of its candidates were recognized. The PRP's success was so complete, amid such blatant fraud, that the not unreasonable rumor was floated that perrepista leaders had overestimated the degree of chicanery they would need to win a city-council majority and had thus not even allowed for the now-customary recognition of one or two democráticos. That the PD's justice of the peace candidates won in a couple of neighborhoods was small consolation to the party faithful.[144]

Elsewhere, the PD's city council candidates were able to claim victory. In Vicente Pinheiro's São José do Rio Pardo, the party won an outright majority.[145] In Campinas, comparatively clean elections led to the victory of four PD candidates; one was to drop dead from an attack of uremia a week after the election.[146] Despite the best efforts of the city's bookmakers, the PD elected three candidates to Santos's municipal legislature, including the veteran local oppositionist Heitor de Moraes.[147] In other counties, local affiliates were able to claim one or two town-council seats, but these local victories were overshadowed by the PD's utter defeat in the city of São Paulo, the true center of the state, home to the party's most important leaders and the greatest number of its followers.[148]

This defeat was demoralizing for the party leadership and rank and file alike. Legal political mobilization seemed fruitless to many, a perception that fostered apathy. Among some leaders, the situation seemed to indicate that reform could only be achieved through force of arms, which led to further neglect of party building. At the same time, there were growing tensions within the party, as the loose coalition that had been brought together over the course of the preceding three years came under increasing strain.

The Democratic Host

If they had wanted to, the PRP's leaders could have taken much of the credit for the sorry state of the opposition as 1928 drew to a close. The democráticos' early successes, by contrast, were due to the breadth of existing political dissatisfaction in São Paulo and the willingness of a widely varied range of contenders to band together under a reformist program. Among the PD's most active founding members and most influential leaders were intellectuals, agrarians, outs, upper-class youths, and populists. To varying degrees these and still further types can be identified among the party's lesser lights (its local leaders and rank and file) as well as in the wider reformist milieu in which the PD acted.

In the broadest sense, nearly all of the PD's senior leaders were intellectuals. As holders of advanced degrees and contributors to newspapers and journals of opinion, they were all part of the state capital's intelligentsia. But within this cohort was a narrower, self-selected group of men of learning and letters—letrados, ilustrados—centered around the São Paulo Law School. The letrado exemplar was the professor of law, someone like Francisco Morato, Reynaldo Porchat, Vergueiro Steidel, Cardoso de Mello Neto, or Gama Cerqueira at the time of the party's founding, joined shortly thereafter by Waldemar Ferreira, but a published author with a law degree (someone like the party founder and secret-ballot enthusiast Mário Pinto Serva) might also qualify, if only just. The letrado of the 1920s, like his nineteenth-century predecessors, based his claim to rule on the mastery of imported liberal ideals. Younger letrados had no personal experience of anything other than republicanism and presidentialism, but among the older ones there was more than a little nostalgia for the nineteenth century's liberal monarchism and its British-styled parliamentary system, as was clearly the case for Francisco Morato.[149]

Agrarians formed a much smaller group among the party's founders and senior leaders. Large landholders and prominent figures in São Paulo's agricultural associations, the agrarians saw themselves as fit to rule by virtue of the economic importance of agriculture in general and coffee in particular. The former state secretary of agriculture Paulo de Moraes Barros—one wag dubbed him São Paulo's "essentially agricultural parliamentarian"—embodied this tendency; in 1928, he was joined on the party's Central Directorate by Henrique de Souza Queiroz, another prominent planter leader. As PD propagandists and in their extra-partisan politicking Moraes Barros and Queiroz Aranha were tireless defenders of coffee, cotton, and agricultural interests more broadly (although both men also held investments in industry). While their insistence on the importance of agriculture was widely shared, the agrarians' prescriptions were neither uniform nor unanimous. Letrado leaders sometimes appealed to Brazil's agricultural past, present, and presumed future, but these appeals were often framed in liberal, neophysiocratic terms. The PD's captains of agriculture, by contrast, had little time for laissez faire and actively sought state support in the form of credit, subsidized immigrant labor, cheap transportation, technical training, tax relief, and overseas publicity, while sometimes disagreeing among themselves about the relative efficacy of particular measures.[150]

The PD leadership also included men who joined the opposition after failure or frustration in a traditional political career. Some letrados were themselves outs (Gama Cerqueira was one) and the agrarians Souza Queiroz and Moraes Barros both qualified as well, but in these cases political opportunism was outweighed by other concerns. Among the party's state-level leaders the purest example of a political out was Vicente Dias Pinheiro, whose family of large planters enjoyed a great deal of power in their home county of São José do Rio Pardo, but relatively scant influence further up in the PRP hierarchy.[151]

Upper-class youths are relatively easier to identify among the party's founders and principal leaders: Paulo Nogueira Filho was one, Joaquim de Sampaio Vidal another. Like his professors at the São Paulo Law School, the upper-class youth thought of himself as a modern, cosmopolitan liberal. Indeed, his law degree made him an honorary member of the state's intelligentsia, regardless of any ceiling on his intellectual aspirations or abilities. Unlike many of the letrados, however, family wealth meant that these young men did not have to lecture at the law school or build their own practices. Instead, young men like Sampaio Vidal and especially Nogueira Filho could give themselves over entirely to the plotting and speechifying that had so enchanted them as law students while their classmates petitioned for jobs in government or settled into private practice.[152]

The final type of party leader was the populist, who worked to broaden the party's base beyond the disaffected patricians and upper reaches of the middle class represented by the party's founders, and who anticipated more significant changes in society and politics, stylistic and structural, than the party's other leaders were willing to consider. The most prominent PD populists were Marrey Júnior and Bertho Condé. Marrey, though his interest in reform as an end rather than a means was limited, did see the efficacy of creating a personal clientele among lower-middling paulistanos and the literate upper reaches of the working class. He did so in part through his use of language, on the stump and in the legislature, that was distinct from the learned treatises offered up by letrados, agrarians, and upper-class youths in its simplicity, sarcasm, and popular appeal, as well as through his support for some social-reformist measures.[153] Condé, for his part, was an outspoken advocate of social reform and a defender of labor, as a party leader and in his private practice. He was the sole member of the senior leadership to reach out to workers as a class, which he did in public speeches on "The Working Class and Politics," and through his proposals to PD congresses.[154]

Many leaders fell between these broad types. Fábio de Camargo Aranha—young, a member of the state capital's toniest clubs, and well-connected in paulistano intellectual circles—was also an advocate for agrarian interests. The poet Tácito de Almeida certainly thought of himself as the equal of any letrado his age and was the holder of a law degree, but he traveled in the party's most foppishly aristocratic circles. Even many of those leaders identified primarily as letrados, agrarians, outs, upper-class youths, or populists can be shown to have represented more than one general tendency. Vicente Pinheiro, for example, may have been the quintessential PD out, but he was also a coffee planter and was associated with the party's popular wing on the basis of his friendship with Marrey, who as a recovering olavista was something of an out himself.

At the local level, in the neighborhoods of the state capital and the cities and towns of the interior and the littoral, party affiliates were manned by similar sorts of contenders. Street-corner populists and local magnates, neighborhood intellectuals and small-town newspapermen, municipal outsiders and fresh-faced county notables were to be found in varying combinations in local organizations throughout the state, in configurations that regularly shifted as members joined, moved, quit, and were voted in and out of positions of authority by the rank and file.

In working-class Bom Retiro, where the PD had its single largest concentration of voters, the party was led in its early years by Estevão Montebello, who came from a political family in the district. Montebello, something of a rabble-rouser in his own right, was a faithful follower of

Marrey Júnior, who saw to it that he was rewarded with a job as an advertising commissions agent for the *Diário Nacional* despite the fact that the newspaper's well-bred writers and funders despised him and his kind.[155]

The PD's next largest group of paulistano voters was in upscale Santa Cecília, where a handful of well-off professionals were the most active leaders, advised by a consultative council that included Alberto Seabra and Bento Pires de Campos.[156] As befit a group as privileged as this one, the Santa Cecília organization contracted a district secretary, a teacher (whether by training, trade, or both is unclear) who lived with his family in the rear of the local headquarters and who was often more active than district officers in keeping up with party affairs.[157]

In neighboring Consolação, the party was led in its early years by a group that included Nicolau Soares do Couto Esher, Luiz Pinto de Queiroz, José Menotti Chiarugi, and José Paulino Nogueira.[158] Couto Esher, a physician, had been a historic republican but was a longtime opponent of the PRP. He also wrote for *O Combate* under the pseudonym "Dr. Lauresto."[159] Pinto de Queiroz, who like Couto Esher had been born in Rio de Janeiro, was a self-made man, a grand industrialist who had co-founded the São Paulo Municipal Party. In late 1928 he was elected second justice of the peace, not in Consolação, but in Sé, where his main office was located.[160] Chiarugi was an old journalist and the manager of the yellow-press *A Ronda*.[161] José Paulino Nogueira was the younger brother of the political dilettante Paulo Nogueira Filho; his own interests appear to have leaned more toward business and travel than politics.[162]

In Agua Branca and Lapa, on what were then the western outskirts of the city, the PD's directorate was made up of a lawyer, a pharmacist, a railwayman, a builder, a small merchant, a glazier, two accountants, two mechanics, and two commissions agents. Heading the list was João Wagner Wey, an ambitious pharmacist whom the PRP, fearing defeat, wooed to its side in advance of the municipal elections of October 1928; among those who remained in opposition were Antenor de Campos Moura, a lawyer who had traveled in Santos's opposition circles, and Roberto Zimberger, about thirty at the time of the party's founding, who had earned a normal-school degree before going into business and who had been an enthusiast of the Nationalist League's educational efforts.[163]

The democráticos of Penha, just as far from the city center as Lapa, but to the east rather than the west, were led by the physician Armando Marcondes Machado; among his lieutenants was the district's third substitute justice of the peace, an out if there ever was one.[164] The PD's affiliate in the district of Butantã, similarly on the city's edge but to the southwest, was run by local professionals and businessmen, including the publishers of the neighborhood-interest *O Pinheirense*.[165]

Just to the south of Pinheiros, in Santo Amaro county, the party relied on Lucas Masculo, a former labor activist who was all but ruined after having taken part in the county's rebel-appointed government in 1924; the local PD, unsurprisingly, struggled.[166] In similarly suburban São Bernardo, the party was more fortunate. Its local leaders included João Amazonas, a lawyer who had moved to the area from Santos, where he was included in the local Republican Reaction organization; the Setti family, industrialists who for some time had been pursuing political power commensurate with their economic importance; the Italian-born builder Arthemio Veronesi, who may have been a former syndicalist and who brought with him friends, family, and further followers; at least two young men from the premiere graduating class of the county's first secondary school; and various outs from the county's flaquista faction, which had been all but vanquished in 1925. Through these men and the party's state-level leaders, the PD also had links to a municipalist faction that sought to make the São Bernardo subdistrict of São Caetano an independent county.[167]

The PD's leadership in Campinas was similarly heterogenous, though the notables at its very top were older and more settled than José Amazonas. The president of the local organization through the party's early years was Antônio Alves da Costa Carvalho, a historic republican who had practiced law in Campinas since receiving his degree from the São Paulo Law School in the 1880s. Carvalho had served in the state and municipal legislatures in earlier years but neglected to cash in on his political connections, to the bemusement of Francisco Glycerio, a former comrade-in-arms.[168] Francisco de Araujo Mascarenhas, like Carvalho, was an old republican, a medical doctor who had volunteered to practice in the field during the Federalist Revolt of the 1890s. Like Carvalho, he had served in various official posts since then, but he had also been involved in opposition politics consistently through the preceding decade, from endorsing Pereira Barreto in 1918 to backing the breakaway minority faction of the PRP in early 1924.[169] The remaining members of the PD's earliest local directorate were similarly distinguished professionals and prominent businessmen, but they were soon joined by younger men: a junior member of the local pro-Ruy committee of 1919, a son of the retired paulistano chieftain Olavo Egydio de Souza Aranha, and the Rio-born physician Waldemar Rangel Belfort de Mattos, for whom the PD was the beginning of a far longer political journey.[170]

Campinas's Álvaro Ribeiro had kind words for the party from exile but was less than completely enthusiastic upon his return; he did not give any intention of wanting to join the PD until shortly before his death in August 1929, despite close relationships with many of its local leaders (Francisco Mascarenhas, for example, assisted in his campaign to found a clinic for Campinas's poor children).[171] Ribeiro's protégé and collaborator Pedro Magalhães Júnior, whose brother Tasso had been active in the early rallying of local supporters, did join the party, running on its slate in the municipal elections of October 1928 and winning a seat on the city council along with Belfort de Mattos.[172]

Álvaro Ribeiro's santista counterparts—the former councilman Heitor de Moraes and the sitting councilman Antônio Feliciano—were quicker to rally around the new party. The two port-city populists were joined by four other lawyers: Antônio's older brother, Lincoln, himself no stranger to opposition politics; Waldemar Leão, a graduate of the Recife Law School who had been a leader of Santos's pro-Ruy movement of 1919; Antônio Bruno Barbosa, like Leão a northeastern-born admirer of the Bahian statesman, as well as a supporter of the Republican Reaction of 1921–22; and the native son Francisco Malta Cardoso, a former member of the Nationalist League and the Invisible Society for Political Action who had campaigned for Pereira Barreto in 1918. These mostly young lawyers were joined by a customs agent, a medical doctor, and a clutch of local businessmen, nearly all of them coffee brokers. This last group included Antônio Teixeira de Assumpção Neto, a former president of the Santos Commercial Association, and, for a time, Alberto Cintra, the sitting president of the association, who was brought to his senses in mid-1927 when Júlio Prestes promised him a place in Santos's perrepista leadership and a seat in the state legislature.[173]

The PD's leadership on the upper-Sorocabana frontier was not all that different from that in coastal Santos, central-zone Campinas, or the capital zone. Indeed, taking the county of Presidente Prudente as an example, it was very similar to that of capital-zone São Bernardo in that it was headed by a law school graduate who was known in Santos's opposition circles and rounded out by a group of mostly middle-class men, including political novices and unlucky outs. The party's president, Tito Lívio Brasil, had been a friend of Monteiro Lobato's from childhood, was a journalist as well as a lawyer, and seemed to be drawn to opposition politics as a vocation. He was a hermista when most of São Paulo was for Ruy and was in contact with labor-left activists at around the same time; he ran for (and won) a seat on the Santos city council at the head of an anti-machine Democratic League in 1916; in Presidente Prudente, he worked with the municipalist opposition in the absence of a purer alternative and, when examples of the latter appeared, in the revolt of 1924 and with the founding of the PD two years later, he was more than at home. The remaining members of the party's early leadership were not as well-connected as Tito Lívio Brasil, but nearly all were likewise men of the town rather than the agricultural districts: professionals, entrepreneurs, or both (one of the latter, the owner-operator of Presidente Prudente's first pharmacy, led local protests against the Sacco and Vanzetti executions). The city's more traditional political figures remained aloof from the movement until late 1927, when face ("prestige") demanded a bold gesture on the part of the hitherto-municipalist Progressive Republican Party; this out-of-power group's support for the PD lasted just long enough to make the point.[174]

In Piracicaba, the leaders of the Independent Republican Party, still smarting from their treatment following the events of July 1924, went over to the PD en masse. Their support was no small thing, as it meant that the PD could count on around three thousand votes and a friendly local government in one of the state's most important counties.[175]

The situation in Piracicaba was not the norm, nor was it long lasting (in 1927, Júlio Prestes succeeded in splitting the Independent Republican Party). In the state's remaining counties, local leaders were either ideologically motivated or out of power and wanting in, a fact that was recognized by foe and founder alike. Menotti Del Picchia, a perrepista state legislator, divided municipal-level democráticos into two categories, young idealists like the pharmacist he had met in Capão Bonito, and faceless malcontents, while Paulo Nogueira Filho emphasized idealism but acknowledged contacts with traditional outs, referred to euphemistically as "some existing municipal political organizations."[176]

At the level of the rank and file, of voters, poll watchers, petitioners, and crowd participants, the party's makeup was no less varied. It included a good number of men of means like most of the party's founders—gentleman "physicians, engineers and law-degree holders"—but this comfortable few was outnumbered by a larger mass of middle-class and working-class men, who on election days were joined by the PD's own eleitores de cabresto.[177]

Writing of solidly middle-class and working-class enthusiasm, as opposed to the support of the local "élite," democrático leaders in Ribeirão Preto—most of them law-degree holders, some with interests in coffee—expressed surprise: "We can verify that the best voter, during propaganda work and later on election day, the one with the most ardent and enlightened civic consciousness, the most independent and courageous one, is not, as is generally supposed, the presumed voter of high standing, the capitalist, the planter, the law-degree holder, etc., but the worker, the commercial employee, the tailors, cobblers, dentists, pharmacists, physicians, in sum all those who live from their day-to-day work."[178] These were the men, middle-class and some working-class, who monitored polling places and distributed propaganda, and who formed the largest contingent of PD supporters in urban centers such as Ribeirão Preto and the state capital, where the PD was strongest, as even its enemies recognized.[179]

The term "middle class" itself was only beginning to be used in São Paulo during these years, but it was nevertheless applied to actual and prospective party supporters along with other categories suggestive of middling standing. In Campinas, when a PD propagandist condemned the incumbents' plans to subsidize a luxury hotel and suggested that his party would spend such funds on affordable housing "for people of the middle classes," his comments met with acclaim on the part of the "great popular mass."[180] A correspondent in the state capital's Vila Mariana neighborhood explained the "certain sluggishness" that had overtaken voter registration efforts by pointing out that his district's PD supporters were mostly of "the middle class, all devoted to the work that occupies the day."[181]

The demands of work and the attractions of private life, to which were added the risks presented by political activism, were real enough, but in a certain sense men who were of the humanistic or collar-and-tie middle had less to lose than their capitalist counterparts, provided that they lived in one of the state's more civilized cities or towns. As one early supporter wrote, "planters, merchants and industrialists" might be slower to join the PD "by virtue of the still-prevailing *Fear* that all have of seeing their interests damaged by local *Bosses*."[182] Most of the men thus described were not of the paulista upper class but of the entrepreneurial middle; a good number nevertheless took a role in party politics. If they did, they faced potential difficulties that their professional and salaried counterparts did not have to worry about. In both cases, prospective PD voters could do as sympathetic public employees did, disguising opposition ballots with "envelopes of the *celeberrimous*" (the PRP).[183] However achieved, the aspiration was for ruled and ruler to be "a citizen with a clear conscience . . . like any bourgeois."[184]

As far as working-class support for the PD is concerned, the most important group was the state's railwaymen, from whom had already come support for Ruy Barbosa's last campaign and the military rebels of

1924. Within two weeks of the PD's public debut, railwaymen represented the fifth or sixth largest group of the "free men who have the courage to publicly assume responsibility for their opinions," despite their relative underrepresentation among the first 601 subscribers of the party manifesto.[185] This support came from railroading centers throughout the state, from all of the lines operating in São Paulo. In Campinas, for example, the local party secretary wrote of voter registration efforts: "Progress has exceeded our expectations, especially the large number of Railwaymen who have appeared at our Site daily, including those of the [state-owned] Sorocabana."[186] Back in the state capital, one of the PD's key assets in reaching out to railwaymen as a class was Marcos Mélega, a founder of the Party of Youth who had worked for the São Paulo Railway for sixteen years, at the tail end of which he had represented the company's workers on a council set up to oversee their pension fund. Denouncing the misappropriation of funds earned him the ire of company management but lasting respect on the part of employees. The support that paulista railwaymen gave Mélega's new party was acknowledged even in usually critical circles.[187]

Railwaymen were the most important group of working-class democráticos, but they were not the only ones. In industrial Vila Prudente, the PD sub-directorate was a good deal more active than its relatively privileged superiors in Ipiranga in the run-up to the municipal elections of 1928; the following year, local democráticos took up collections to support striking printers.[188] In the city of São Paulo as a whole, a "minimum" of forty-five thousand workers were registered voters during these years.[189] Many abstained from voting, but enough laboring men cast their ballots for the PD to give their self-appointed leaders fits. As the mouthpiece of the Communist Party-organized Worker and Peasant Bloc proclaimed, amid specific appeals to hatters, printers, cobblers, tailors, drivers, construction workers, and textile operatives, as well as railwaymen: "The support of São Paulo's workers for the Democratic Party, shortly after its founding, was up to a certain point admissible, for two principal reasons: 1) because in opposing the perrepista incumbents, it proposed to continue the political work of the revolutionary movement of 1924; 2) because at that point there did not exist a genuine workers' party, that is, one that would confront the exploiting bourgeoisie with workers' politics, the proletariat could not waver between the conservative bourgeoisie that oppresses it and the 'liberal' bourgeoisie that claimed 'to liberate the people.'"[190]

This anonymous editorialist, writing in October 1928, went on to argue that the situation he had described no longer held and that work-ers should no longer "esteem a bourgeois party . . . opposed to the most vital interests of the proletariat."[191] Left unacknowledged was that the Worker and Peasant Bloc had thrown its support to the democrático Antônio Feliciano in elections to the state legislature earlier that year, giving up on its own candidate, Nestor Pereira Júnior, the president of the Association of Commercial Employees (himself one of the original 601 subscribers of the PD manifesto), and that its denunciation of cross-class voting was part of a larger reaction against the "simply absurd, inconsequential and incomprehensible support of workers for bourgeois candidates" that had set in soon after the earlier elections.[192] Despite six months of this kind of browbeating, at least one local Worker and Peas-ant Bloc organization was prepared to throw its support to the PD as late as September 1928.[193]

To independent working-class and middling support were added the ballots of more familiar figures. PD "bridled voters," for example, were seen and herded on election days, if in far smaller numbers than their perrepista counterparts.[194] Elsewhere, PD leaders with few or no depen-dents of their own enquired if their home county's absentees (in cases where they were known to be party members) might be impressed upon to have their administrators make sure that the help voted the right way.[195] Absentees' claims, however, did not always go uncontested. In Campinas's Arraial dos Souzas district in early 1928, the administrator of extensive properties belonging to a "rich planter" walked off the job when the absentee owner sought to impose his political will. When the colonos joined the administrator, a democrático, in his walk-off, the planter had to relent and give all of his employees free reign in matters political; good agricultural labor was simply too scarce.[196] All of these cases would have fallen into the category of "voluminous contingents of voters, principally in the interior," belonging to "adherents that bring with them [further] groupings of . . . voters."[197]

Changes Democratic

Beyond the PD's leaders, its rank and file, and the bridled voters claimed by both categories of party faithful were still further sources of support. Indeed, party activity unfolded in a broader reformist milieu that was dissident and often sympathetic if not always formally democrático, one that included public health and educational reformers such as Belisário

Penna and Antônio de Sampaio Doria, writers like Paulo Prado and Raul Bopp, and journalists from the publishers of *O Estado de S. Paulo* to the amateur scribblers of the state capital's neighborhood tabloids.[198] The party also drew support from outside of São Paulo, from Rio de Janeiro's Maurício de Lacerda, who had anointed himself Luiz Carlos Prestes's representative in Brazil and who campaigned hard for the PD, to some of the rebel exiles themselves, who wrote approvingly of the party for paulista audiences.[199] The breadth of this coalition made for the party's early successes, even as it guaranteed that the PD would be a fractious host. This fractiousness, in turn, meant that the changes effected by the PD would be diffuse and largely unintended.

From its founding, and particularly after the lifting of the state of siege at the close of 1926, the PD contributed mightily to the cult of the rebel exiles. That its role in this myth-making process has since been forgotten has a great deal more to do with subsequent politics than it does with actual history.[200] Amid the apotheoses of Luiz Carlos Prestes, Miguel Costa, and other rebel leaders, PD members also were active in the campaign for amnesty, a campaign that combined symbolic and practical politics, while leaders from Morato to Marrey represented rebel exiles before the courts.[201]

Amnesty was not the only political issue embraced by the PD that combined the practical and the symbolic. The secret ballot itself was no doubt viewed as an instrument that, once introduced, would deliver power to democrático leaders and deliver Brazil from its political woes, but in campaigning for its introduction, the PD also linked itself to an existing political tradition and all that went with it. A thirty-two-page pamphlet of one of Marrey Júnior's legislative speeches also reprinted selections from Monteiro Lobato's open letter to Arthur Bernardes of 1924: "The secret ballot works the miracle of bringing with it a high standard [for voters]. . . . repelling the venal or unconscientious voter and attracting the free and conscious vote of the country's *élite*." The former's "interest was entirely subaltern, it was not civic interest, due to his natural incapacity for civismo. And we will have thus repelled the slavish muscle from the farce of acting the part of the cerebrum."[202] Late that same year, the PD carried out the national distribution of a book-length compendium of arguments for the introduction of the secret ballot, one containing page after page of similar claims that the secret ballot would end the election-day participation of the unfit (often depicted in racially loaded language) and make politics an honorable activity for independent, upstanding paulista citizens.[203]

The PD also exercised a preeminent role in the deepening and diffusion of São Paulo's peculiar regionalist-cum-nationalist tradition. Although the party's leaders had initially attempted to downplay this aspect of paulista political culture, particularly at the party's debut on 21 March 1926, it soon revealed itself as a central theme in the party's propaganda and as a mobilizing tool for party leaders. In late April 1926, for example, speaking at the investiture of the PD's provisional directorate in Jaú, Waldemar Ferreira argued that "the principal obligation of all Brazilians" was to form a "grand party, with a well-defined program," adding that "São Paulo was fated to be the crystallization point of this great political task, because, as Cincinato Braga said: 'it is in the paulista's very blood the tireless drive to belong to a patria that makes itself known to the world for the amplitude of its territory, for the value of its riches, for the intellectual and moral brilliance of its sons.' But not only for this. Principally because São Paulo's responsibility for the territorial and political integration of Brazil, from bandeirismo to the proclamation of the Republic, places upon it the obligation to strive toward its historic purpose."[204]

Similar allusions to destiny-defining past glories were sounded at the first party congress, in evocations of the colony's initial "three small and vigorous nucleuses of strong men, laboring at the gigantic fundaments of the History of S. Paulo" and São Paulo's place "in the august sun of the seventh of September," when the colony's bid for independence began.[205] Not only was this kind of regionalist trumpetry taken up by the party faithful, it was also bugled back to them by allies from out of state. Maurício de Lacerda, for example, following an eight-day tour of São Paulo campaigning on behalf of the PD, declared: "It was from S. Paulo that came Independence, it was from S. Paulo that came abolition and it was even from São Paulo that the Republic came. All of the great impulses for the progress of Brazil, in the various stages of its political evolution, came from S. Paulo. And it is from São Paulo that the redemption of the patria will still come."[206]

That party events saw the paulista flag fly alongside the national standard and the PD banner designed by Wasth Rodrigues went without saying.[207] Iconographic propaganda drew on regional identification as well, as in one poster depicting São Paulo as a very white bandeirante wielding a sword labeled "Democratic Party" against "the Assault of the Pygmies," depicted, in miniature, as an Afro-Brazilian eleitor de cabresto, a ragtag "foreign" voter, and a phosphoro peering out from behind a gravestone (presumably one bearing the same name as one of his voter-registration certificates).[208] The connection between capable citizenship, manly independence, and racially coded identity was made only slightly more subtly in slides displayed in paulista cinemas: "The Democratic Party Will End this Slavery," proclaimed one caption, alongside a rendering of a manacled hand casting a ballot.[209]

The use of the silver screen for political propaganda was a novelty, as were the PD's propaganda tours of distant interior towns, the grand "caravans" of 1926–28. Locals summoned by fireworks marveled at the spectacle of visitors, parades, and speeches, and townies who had only heard of these happenings clamored for visits to their out-of-the-way burgs.[210]

Given this enthusiasm, the PRP's leaders were forced to follow suit. In July 1926, Alexandre Marcondes Filho—an up-and-coming figure in state-capital perrepismo—denounced the inactivity of his fellows, arguing that traditional ways of carrying on politics were no longer viable: "In truth . . . the [Republican] Party, through the Commission [i.e., the PRP executive committee], uses the machine it built [thirty years earlier], but does not adapt it to new ends, does not perfect it, does not modernize it." Facing this apparent obsolescence, Marcondes Filho called for modern propaganda and recruitment "à americana," the purchase, subsidization, or founding of a new pro-PRP newspaper, and other modernizing measures.[211]

Results were decidedly mixed. Speaking in Jaú two weeks after Waldemar Ferreira, Marcondes Filho received a tepid reception from a gathering of fellow out-of-towners, a handful of local families, and agricultural laborers trucked in from the county's plantations.[212] In Rio Preto, a similar mission was found even less convincing. Floriano de Leme, a pro-government newspaperman, reported that the city's professionals, all originally from outside of the county, "bring political ideas that are not easy to overcome" and were left unconvinced by the PRP's propagandists.[213] Perrepistas were more successful in print, as the state capital's new boss, Sylvio de Campos, bought the *S. Paulo-Jornal* and men of his confidence transformed the newspaper into a pro-government analogue of the opposition-friendly *Folhas*.[214]

In print and in person, perrepistas were also obliged to counter the opposition's linking of the PD with São Paulo's regionalist traditions. Marcondes Filho, for example, rejected the identification of the PD with *paulistinidade* and argued against the importation of the secret ballot on the grounds that Brazilians should not abandon their traditions, "the bedrock of the nationality."[215] In the run-up to the municipal elections of October 1928, the state capital's perrepistas accused the PD's candidate for prefeito (their former compatriot Marrey Júnior) of neglecting "traditions of independence and love for Republican institutions" and of lacking "paulista sentiment," and they called on the population of "the State of São Paulo"—"the greatest, the most cultured of the Brazilian Federation"—to "raise its voice loudly, vibrantly and in unison" against him.[216]

At the same time that the PD's activity forced the perrepista leadership to spend more time, treasure, and effort before the public than they were accustomed, it also presented local and regional contenders with opportunities to impugn the loyalty of their rivals or otherwise question their right to rule. In late 1927, for example, the incumbents of upland Salesópolis informed state president Júlio Prestes that a rival had hosted strangers who had taken to the streets drunk, "giving *morras* to local politicians and the P.R.P. and *vivas* to the Democratic Party and its people."[217] Writing from Araraquarense-zone Matão, a dissatisfied politician declared that he and his—who were, to a man, "loyal soldiers of the Paulista Republican Party"—had been wronged by Lacerda Franco and by the powerful chieftain's local followers. The lacerdistas, he further charged, were carrying out "even more disastrous political activity, in which they don't respect their adversaries' most ordinary rights." These trespasses "had provoked a wave of discontent that resulted in, among other things, the breaking away to the Democratic Party of part of the electorate, until now cohesive with respect to the government, despite local divergences, which explains the votes that the candidate of this party had in the last elections." He added, of course, that he was addressing Júlio Prestes not only on the basis of what was right, but most of all for the good of the PRP.[218]

That this kind of intra-party jockeying for power met with indulgence on the part of the state president illustrates the position of strength enjoyed by the ruling party. Indeed, the familiar division of most municipal polities into factions vying for the support of the PRP leadership was as much an asset to the party as it was a liability, as was clear at the time.[219] Out-of-power groups might flirt with the PD, and some of the disenchanted would even join the new party, but the political goods that they longed for were in the hands of the PRP's leaders. From the perspective of early 1929 they seemed destined to remain there, despite the various changes in the practice of politics witnessed over the course of the previous three years.

6 Moments and Truths

From the perspective of early 1929, it appeared that the opposition was foundering and the PRP leadership was regaining the political momentum. One could speculate that, in the absence of intervening events, the democrático coalition might have come apart sooner rather than later, some of its members returning to the Republican fold, others remaining in opposition (perhaps even in a more radicalized opposition), and still others returning to private life.[1]

But these events did come, and in rapid succession, during a period of less than year and a half between July 1929 and October 1930: the decision by Washington Luís to impose Júlio Prestes as his successor in the national presidency rather than reach a compromise with his counterparts at the controls of Minas Gerais's political machine; the emergence of Getúlio Vargas's opposition candidacy; the collapse of coffee prices in late 1929; the murder of the defeated vice-presidential candidate João Pessoa; and the overthrow of Washington Luís and his replacement by Vargas in what has come to be called the "Revolution of 1930." Each of these events served to further roil the waters of paulista politics.

Pre-Presidential Politics

By mid-1929 it was evident that Brazil would witness its first contested presidential election in eight years, as the official machines of Minas Gerais and Rio Grande do Sul, on the one hand, and São Paulo, on the other, lined up behind the candidacies of the gaúcho state president Getúlio Vargas and the paulista state president Júlio Prestes, respectively. However, the PD's adoption of Vargas's opposition candidacy was not accomplished without conflict or compromise.[2] In late July, newspaper columns were thick with rumor. The *Jornal do Brasil*, published in Rio de

Janeiro, noted that the "impression in the [federal legislature was] that a paulista name, like that of Sr. Julio Prestes," could not fail to impress PD "coffee planters, convinced of the expedience of supporting a candidate [who is] perfectly identified with the interests of coffee agriculture." In examining the PD delegation, the same article reported that Paulo de Moraes Barros and Marrey Júnior were showing themselves to be favorable to Prestes's candidacy, while the letrado leader Francisco Morato favored throwing the party's support to Vargas.[3] In São Paulo, the *Folha da Manhã's* "Juca Pato" discussed similar scenarios and claimed that rumors regarding the position to be taken by the PD in the presidential campaign were vying with talk of *futebol* for attention in the streets of the state capital.[4]

Behind the scenes, Júlio Prestes—not yet the official candidate—sounded out the press and other politicians on behalf of Washington Luís. On 24 July, he reported that the federal congressmen Eloy Chaves, Álvaro de Carvalho, and Altino Arantes (former members of the break-away faction of 1923–24 one and all) appeared to be "solidly on [the] side" of the PRP rump and that *O Estado de S. Paulo* was coming around, with a "majority in the editorial offices and [of the] publishers" leaning toward supporting the PRP (he mentioned Armando de Salles Oliveira and Carolino da Motta e Silva by name). The only major holdout was Julio de Mesquita Filho, who "appears to have [a] commitment to Assis Brasil [a gaúcho oppositionist] and also demands [a] liberal program and ideas."[5] Four days later, Prestes informed the federal president, *O Estado de S. Paulo* "will be on our side, but also does not want compensations except for one or two seats" in the federal legislature. Prestes would look into the matter, but he made no commitment.[6]

In a manifesto dated 30 July, the state's great industrialists, long linked to the prestista wing of the PRP, made known their support for Júlio Prestes's candidacy. Through their corporate association (the São Paulo State Center of Industries, or CIESP, founded in 1928 in part as a result of conflict between pro-PRP and anti-PRP factions of the São Paulo Commercial Association), these grandees called for manufacturers throughout the state to mobilize in support of the perrepista candidate and, in particular, to add as many of their employees as possible to the rolls of paulista voters.[7]

In early August, local democráticos in the São Paulo neighborhood of Bela Vista (including the PD populists Clovis Botelho Vieira and Lázaro Maria da Silva) sent their support for Vargas's campaign against the "backwoods fascism" of the PRP, as did their counterparts in the downtown neighborhood of Sé.[8] Meanwhile, the youth wing of the PD promoted demonstrations in the city center in support of Vargas's candidacy.[9]

Prominent paulista intellectuals also weighed in. Mário Pinto Serva reported that it was "The Duty of the Democrats" to adopt Vargas's candidacy as a means to combat *caciquismo*.[10] Taking an opposing view, contributors to the party newspaper, the *Diário Nacional*, continued to push for support for Júlio Prestes.[11] The veteran opposition figure Rubião Meira opposed the PD's supporting Vargas, as did Cornélio Pires, who decried the two machine candidates and declared his intention to vote for the exiled military rebel Luiz Carlos Prestes by way of protest, "in accordance with the ideals of the Democratic Party . . . in accordance with [his] own ideals."[12]

Representatives of PD organizations from across the state met in São Paulo at the end of August to formally adopt a position on the presidential election. By the time the congress opened, it was clear that Francisco Morato had convinced his fellow party leaders of the efficacy of supporting Vargas and that the party would adopt the opposition candidacy as its own.[13] The motion to support Vargas passed overwhelmingly with 341 votes in favor and only 3 against: 2 from the delegation representing Júlio Prestes's hometown of Itapetininga, where local democráticos perhaps thought they might be better served by a native son in the presidential palace, and 1 from the delegation representing São Joaquim. Two other attendees spoke in favor of the PD running its own candidate, but one was not the representative of a local directorate, so had no vote, and the other may not have had the full support of his own directorate.[14]

Some democráticos were put off by the party's decision to back Vargas. Renato Paes de Barros, who had joined the PD after backing the losing side in the PRP's schism of 1923–24, left the party in "absolute disagreement" with its support of Vargas.[15] Other resignations followed, including that of Antônio de Queirós Telles, a leading figure in the Brazilian Agricultural League.[16] One young democrático—jailed the year before in a police crackdown on a pro-PD rally—claimed to discern a "vendetta against S. Paulo" in the gaúcho-led Liberal Alliance (as the pro-Vargas coalition was dubbed); as "a paulista loving of his native land," he quit the Democratic Party and pledged his support for Júlio Prestes.[17]

Never a democrático, Monteiro Lobato wrote Prestes from New York to express his support for the official candidate. The commercial attaché— with characteristic colorfulness he referred to himself as "an exiled paulista"—justified his support: "first) because at issue is Júlio Prestes;

second) because your polic[ies] in the presidency would mean that which Brazil most needs: administrative continuity; third) because it is time for the supreme post to be occupied by a young man." There was a fourth and final reason as well. As Lobato explained, using regionalist metonyms to represent Minas Gerais and Rio Grande do Sul, "it is not with cheese, or cured beef that the grave problems facing Brazil will be resolved. It is with coffee, audacity, vision, initiative and the other Yankee qualities that characterize the paulista."[18]

The PRP's support for Prestes was a foregone conclusion (though individual leaders might flirt with the *aliancista* cause),[19] but it was not formalized until 12 September at the National Republican Convention held in the federal capital. There, together with the representatives of the incumbent machines of seventeen other Brazilian states, the federal senator Antônio Padua Salles, the federal congressman Manuel Pedro Villaboim, and São Paulo's prefeito, José Pires do Rio, made official what had long been decided by Washington Luís.[20]

Coffee's Contentious Collapse

Coffee's preeminent position in the Brazilian national economy made it impossible to insulate coffee policy from partisan politics. That the two happened to sometimes intersect in public debate, however, does not imply that party politics was ever the exclusive reflection of coffee interests, even at moments like the economic crisis of 1929–30. The PD had its agrarian representatives, but these figures agreed on little more than their mutual desire to establish the political preeminence of planters; their proposed solutions to problems of overproduction, transportation, and (perceived) labor shortage were rarely in agreement. Some favored a continuation of the maintenance of artificial price supports through the withholding of coffee from the world market (the program of "valorization" in place, in various forms, since 1906); others had opposed the program from the start. Likewise, the Republican Party had its own agrarians: large-scale planters who served alongside men like Paulo de Moraes Barros in the various trade associations.[21] Indeed, in campaigning for the presidency in late 1929, Júlio Prestes himself proudly proclaimed coffee to be the "basis of [Brazilian] wealth" and the coffee planter to be "the type most representative of the nationality."[22]

At less exalted levels, the relationship between coffee and party politics becomes even more complicated. Moments of crisis might lead to expressions of militant political opposition among some members of the lavoura, but they might also encourage other planters to attempt to curry favor with incumbents. Disunity and fickleness were the lavoura's two most prominent characteristics when it came to politics, as is clear in its members' response to what is now recognized as the beginnings of the twentieth century's Great Depression.

The collapse of Brazilian coffee prices preceded the U.S. stock market crash of October 1929. Increasing overproduction augured the demise of the already overburdened system of valorization. By September, the prospect of the third bumper crop in three years made catastrophe imminent; rumor set the crash in motion early the following month. Thus, in the Brazilian case, the world economic slump that began in 1929–30 exacerbated a preexisting pattern of overproduction by depriving the country of the ready credit and expanding markets that would allow it to maintain the valorization binge and to continue to sell its coffee abroad at the volume of the late 1920s, even at much-reduced prices.[23]

Just as the collapse of Brazilian coffee prices preceded the crash of October 1929, so too did partisan conflict regarding coffee policy. Paulo de Moraes Barros, the PD's self-appointed defender of agriculture, took to the floor of the federal legislature to condemn government coffee policy on 19 July and 29 August, arguing that artificially high coffee prices— maintained at inflated rates, he alleged, to bolster support for the PRP's candidate in the coming campaign for the federal presidency—were benefiting Brazil's competitors.[24] In attempting to refute his arguments, perrepistas dubbed Moraes Barros one of "The Enemies of Coffee."[25]

By mid-October, with coffee futures half of what they had been in late September, a bewildering array of responses to the coming crisis was already evident. Mid-month found the rump São Paulo delegation to the federal legislature locked in debate with a congressman from Rio de Janeiro who favored taking on a loan abroad to support the coffee industry. Back in São Paulo, the newest member of the paulistano yellow press denounced "The Crisis of the Rubiacea."[26]

On 16 October, with colonos unpaid, the commerce of the interior suspended, and industry paralyzed, the presidents of the Brazilian Rural Society, Brazilian Agricultural League, and Paulista Agriculture Society—perrepistas one and all—were received by Júlio Prestes at the state-presidential palace. All four men expressed their confidence that the crisis would soon be resolved.[27]

At the end of the month, by which time full-fledged panic had set in among businessmen in Santos, a similar delegation met with a different reception at the national presidential palace in Rio de Janeiro. Faced with the supplication of planters and coffee brokers desirous of government assistance in the form of the emission of additional paper money or a moratorium on planter debt, Washington Luís listened politely, then explained that rather than providing solutions, these measures would only lead to further economic problems, adding that the Banco do Brasil was prepared to aid the "planters of São Paulo." His polite but firm response was soon rendered in the press as a brusque "Every man for himself!"[28]

It was at this point that rumors spread regarding a split in Santos's PRP.[29] O Combate predicted that the entire state soon would be up in arms.[30] Even some of the "planter-congressmen" of the PRP's delegation to the state legislature voiced their unease, discussing "the situation of coffee with true indignation."[31]

At the same time, in a seeming reversal, the "democratic delegation" to the state legislature proclaimed itself to be "on the side of the government for the solution of the current financial crisis."[32] Speaking for the PD's delegation to the federal legislature, Francisco Morato affirmed that the situation was improving, as the panic had ended and the measures enacted by the Banco do Brasil were yielding fruit. He did, however, express his hope that the memory of the crisis would not soon pass and thus serve as a cautionary example well into the future.[33]

Morato could not have been more wrong. The economic crisis was only just beginning, although conciliation tended to remain the order of the day in both legislatures. As coffee futures continued to drop, Hilário Freire, a perrepista, lauded the PD's support for the government while blaming bankers for the ongoing crisis.[34]

Moving from the state capital to the interior, conflict replaced conciliation, if only temporarily. In Colina, in the far north of the state, a commission of planters drafted a written protest "against the ruinous activity of the Coffee Institute," informing Júlio Prestes that they intended to sit out the presidential election in protest and calling on their fellow planters to do the same.[35] On the very same day, a meeting of planters in Campinas displayed no such unanimity, with some condemning the government and others, albeit a minority, expressing their support for it.[36]

North of Campinas, in Descalvado, a meeting of planters followed the lead of their countrymen in Colina, writing Prestes to inform him that they would not give him their "electoral support" in March "as a sign of protest against the lack of support of coffee." Two members of the local PRP directorate, one of them a sitting town councilman, made the meeting the occasion for their resignations from the party.[37]

The planters of Colina also found admirers closer to home, in the Mogiana region. In São João da Boa Vista, planters signed on to a motion of solidarity with the planters of Colina, reportedly at the instigation of local democráticos.[38] In Cravinhos, planters meeting to lay down ground rules on how best to stiff their colonos also heard at least one of their colleagues express his solidarity with the *colinenses'* protest "against the indifference of the government to the current situation of coffee agriculture."[39] A group of planters in the regional center of Ribeirão Preto also censured Júlio Prestes, while another local commission expressed its support, but the much-vaunted break between local coffee growers and the state and federal governments never amounted to much.[40]

As the case of Cravinhos indicates, the real victims of the collapse of coffee prices were the colonos and camaradas of São Paulo, who were the first to lose out as profits dried up. As rural folks increasingly came to take matters into their own hands, social dissolution joined economic collapse on the list of planters' fears.[41]   •

The intersection of coffee policy and politics—of both the partisan and the associational variety—reached its peak the following month, with a Congresso de Lavradores that, tough talk aside, accomplished little. Held in the state capital on 2–4 December, the coffee-growers' congress was sponsored by the Brazilian Agricultural League (LAB) and attended by representatives of the Brazilian Rural Society (SRB) and—despite some initial reluctance on the part of its senior leadership—the Paulista Agriculture Society (SPA). Its aim, initially at least, was to present a common front on the ongoing crisis.[42]

Corporate unity, however, was not very much in evidence either at the gathering itself or in subsequent reporting on it. The meeting was most important as a forum for anti-government recrimination, despite the promise made by its organizers to Arthur Diederichsen, the president of the SPA, that the congress would forbid "any and all political discussion."[43]

This promise was laid aside in short order. On the opening day, Aphrodisio Sampaio Coelho—a conference organizer, the son-in-law of the late PRP chieftain Jorge Tibiriçá, and a tibiriçista contender in the Noroeste zone in his own right in the 1910s—took a rather simple view of the coffee situation: "Its collapse . . . is solely the fault of the government."[44] Another orator proclaimed, "The government can decree laws as it pleases, until it wishes to destroy the lavoura. If this were to occur, the alert lavoura would not leave such a government standing."⁴⁵

João Pedro da Veiga Miranda's mild defense of the government—he declared proudly, "Our government is not a Russian autocracy"—was widely heckled, though it appears that his proposals for ending state protection of the coffee-bag industry and for lowering export taxes were heard out. Oswald de Andrade, a staff writer at the *Correio Paulistano*, was shouted down when he attempted a similar defense, calling on the assembly to "Be Paulistas!" and adapt themselves to new economic realities.⁴⁶

Oddly enough, given the group's stated reluctance to get involved in political debates, it was a representative of the SPA that uttered the most infamous of the many statements made at the meeting. Addressing the congress on its very first day, Alfredo Pujol declared: "The motto is, today, the planters with the government. And, if we are not heeded, tomorrow it will be the planters without the government. And then, the planters against the government."⁴⁷

Reactions to the congress were indicative of the confusion of the period. *O Combate*—which had welcomed the congress as a "decisive gesture of Agriculture"—was generally supportive, though it suggested that the assembly could have better represented agriculture by including more modest agriculturalists and by excluding planters who had lost their holdings (*fazendeiros fallidos*).⁴⁸ The anti-opposition *Folha da Manhã*, by contrast, argued that the "Failed Congress" had not represented large coffee planters and that Veiga Miranda, though he was booed, was one of the "few [real] planters" in attendance.⁴⁹

Strong language aside, the end product of the gathering was the election of still another committee, to which was entrusted the task of presenting the conference's resolutions to Júlio Prestes. The latter task was accomplished dutifully and politely.⁵⁰ By mid-month, the *Diário da Noite* was already noting the committee's "excessive prudence" and suggesting that "the members of the Commission who are in touch with the state president" may have "been deluded by the fascinating promises that politicians know how to make on the eve of elections," while the "noble agricultural class" that the committee was supposed to represent was succumbing to dissension and the entreaties of the powerful.⁵¹

Needless to say, the mass mobilization of the state's coffee growers never came to pass. Pujol's "planters against the government" was part wishful thinking, part empty threat. Rather, in examining the Liberal Alliance campaign, the plotting of the post-electoral period, and the upheaval of October 1930, one finds some planters with the government, some planters without the government, some planters against the government, many moving between these three positions as it suited them, and—an alternative left unconsidered by Pujol and most historians of the period—the largest portion of planters on the sidelines, simple observers of the grand events of 1929–30, like the vast majority of their countrymen.

A Liberal Alliance?

The Liberal Alliance of 1929–30, which brought together the political machines of Minas Gerais, Rio Grande do Sul, and Paraíba and dissident political figures in São Paulo, Rio de Janeiro, and elsewhere in the federation, is often paired with the Civilianist Campaign of 1909–10.[52] For the state of São Paulo, at least, a more apt comparison is the Republican Reaction: once again inter-regional political competition took on an ostensibly ideological guise and attracted the support of local dissidents in opposition to state-level power-holders. Conditions in São Paulo had changed markedly, however, in the eight years since Nilo Peçanha's presidential bid. Armed rebellion had become part of the repertoire of political dissent, a statewide opposition party had been organized and was now attempting to recover from its defeat in the municipal elections of October 1928, and coffee prices had collapsed. To which must be added candidate Getúlio Vargas's decision to campaign in São Paulo, while Peçanha had declined, a decision that has been attributed to motives ranging from a willingness to hew close to the rules of inter-regional conflict, to friendships with prominent members of the PRP hierarchy, to threats from members of the same political machine.

Apparently, Vargas was at least as reluctant to campaign in São Paulo as Peçanha had been, due in part, it seems, to an incipient gentlemen's agreement with Washington Luís, but perhaps also due to some of the same motives that had led Peçanha to decline—ever sphinx-like, he left little indication of his reasoning. Convincing him to visit São Paulo fell to democrático leaders and members of the Macedo Soares family.[53]

In mid-December 1929, it was still up in the air whether or not Vargas would visit São Paulo, a fact that led to fretting among the PD's leaders.[54] At the end of the month, when Vargas received a triumphant reception in Rio de Janeiro, the PD agrarian Paulo de Moraes Barros described it in glowing terms—"it was formidable, it was something never seen before

roamed the streets," shouting vivas for the opposition and demanding speeches from aliancista propagandists.[63]

On 6 January, Vargas and his running mate, accompanied by their wives, a handful of PD leaders, and a few other prominent supporters, were to travel to Santos, from which Vargas and his wife would return to Rio Grande do Sul. They opted to travel to the port city by automobile, stopping in the industrializing suburb of São Bernardo, where a handful of democráticos spoke before an assembled crowd. Similar celebrations took place at the base of the Serra do Mar, in Cubatão.[64]

Once in Santos the convoy made its way to the downtown's Praça Ruy Barbosa, where one of the PD's city councilmen, Antônio Bruno Barbosa, welcomed Vargas, celebrating his embrace by the "paulista spirit." Barbosa then decried the existing political system in a blistering speech before the open-air crowd, following which party leaders, the candidates, and their guests retired to party headquarters, a move that inspired some resentment among non-PD getulistas.[65]

Inside the hall, Antônio Feliciano spoke first, providing a brief history of the PD and its campaign "to regenerate the political customs of the country," from its origins in the "warm coals of the revolution" of 1924 through its support for the Liberal Alliance. He was followed by João Pessoa and by the carioca oppositionist Adolpho Bergamini. Despite calls for the presidential candidate to speak, Vargas desisted, with Bruno Barbosa explaining for him that he was too tired.[66]

Vargas may have been saving himself for his speech at the banquet that followed, held at the chic Parque Balneário Hotel. He was introduced by Waldemar Leão (another PD city councilman), who closed his speech with a toast "for the victory of Brazilian democracy, represented by the famed candidates of the Liberal Alliance." Vargas's speech was brief and relatively curt by comparison; a supportive journalist described it as "short and incisive." He opened with a nod to Santos and its impressive progress before moving on to "coffee, symbol of the power of S. Paulo." In what was the afternoon's only mention of coffee policy, he decried the government's position and stated his support for the coffee trade before speaking briefly of the need for clean elections and an amnesty for the military rebels. The next morning Vargas and his wife set off for Rio Grande do Sul by seaplane.[67]

Vargas's reception in São Paulo was judged to be a great victory for the PD. Indeed, one PD populist claimed that the "triumphal reception" demonstrated that "the only force that exists in a Republic is the force of the popular will" and that it augured the "white revolution" that would come on election day.[68] In some corners, however, apprehension was already beginning to be expressed. Despite the popular response, it was "incontestable that sr. Getulio Vargas maintained a discretion that did not please the militant politicians . . . in São Paulo." A journalist quoted an unnamed PD leader as saying: "This man is made of ice. . . . He greets one well, smiling to everyone. He has the same smile for all. And that's as far as it goes. He doesn't speak about the platform, about the events of the day, about the balance of forces [or] the coming election. He smiles and nothing more." The anonymous journalist, however, concluded that Vargas's guardedness did not matter: "What matters to the people is that sr. Getulio Vargas is today the representation of the nation's demands, the incarnation of our protest."[69]

But even the aliancista campaign could not completely mask existing conflicts within the PD. Shortly before the opening of another party congress, Zoroastro Gouveia and Paulo Duarte, an editor of the *Diário Nacional*, were said to have had a "serious incident." This public conflict, ostensibly sparked by the newspaper's sloppy treatment of Gouveia's speeches, became the occasion for renewed conflict between Gouveia's allies and Duarte's aristocratic cohort.[70]

Two days later, in the speech that opened the PD congress, the letrado Gama Cerqueira predicted a peaceful transition to democratic government: "Just as we achieved, without social lacerations, without fratricidal struggles, without bloodletting, the most important social reforms, like the abolition of slavery and the proclamation of the republican regime, so the evolution to the true implantation of the Republic in the liberal and democratic forms of our Constitution is following in the same path."[71]

The congress also saw PD agrarians make another bid for the support of coffee growers, as Moraes Barros declared that the time had come for "an alliance between agriculture and the Democratic Party." He then presented a motion coauthored with Henrique de Souza Queiroz and Vicente Pinheiro calling on the PD to "demonstrate its complete solidarity with paulista agriculture in the anguished situation that it suffers through, and guarantee its support for the solution of the grave problems that so affect the economy of the state of São Paulo."[72]

As campaigning began in earnest, several novelties were apparent. The most notable of these was the use of radio, a first in presidential politics. Prestistas were the first to use radio, most notably on Rádio Educadora Paulista, but in late February, the PD's most famed speakers took to the airwaves as well, drumming up support for the aliancista cause.[73]

Increasingly pinched, democrático leaders also took the unprecedented step of taking up public subscriptions to fund the campaign. Throughout the state, local PD organizations were called upon to remit funds to defray "its great costs." Many answered the call, thus contributing, in one correspondent's words, to "the prosperity and greatness of our Party." In the city of São Paulo, a PD Women's Committee took to the streets to collect donations. Although their efforts were made light of by the anti-aliancista press—*O Combate*, under lease to pro-PRP journalists, pilloried the "brutes of democracy" who "exploited" the "prestige of women" and called it "regeneration"—the campaign itself was taken very seriously by state power-holders, who had the political police compile lists of contributors.[74]

The senior leadership of the PRP also took preparations for the presidential election very seriously. While their party's victory in São Paulo was assured, an impressive turnout would be necessary to balance out the blocs of votes that the state machines of Minas Gerais and Rio Grande do Sul would produce for Vargas. The enrollment of new voters, the suborning of newspapers and wire services, the intimidation of opposition voters, and outright fraud would be the means by which to guarantee this result.

Voter registration was made a high priority by the state government, which made it known to local PRP directorates that it would like to see the size of their electorates doubled in the run-up to the presidential election.[75] Privately, Júlio Prestes informed Washington Luís that he expected that the number of registered voters in São Paulo would rise to six hundred thousand by the end of the year.[76]

Padding the rolls took many forms. In the state capital, minors were said to be enrolling en masse on behalf of PRP cabos.[77] Neighboring Santo Amaro, which lacked the PD presence of the state capital, was a convenient place for the registration of ineligible voters who would later vote in São Paulo.[78] In notorious Palmital, 354 new voters, including foreigners, minors, and illiterates, were put on the rolls in only six weeks in late 1929.[79]

In enrolling new voters, the PRP machine could count on the collaboration of São Paulo's great industrialists. Octavio Pupo Nogueira, the secretary-general of the CIESP and the CIFTSP, a cousin of Paulo Nogueira Filho, and a former democrático, made the case to the two groups' members:

> As You Sirs saw from the publication that I sent you yesterday, the great associations of the paulista industrial class, in their totality, are going to promote the electoral enrollment of the industries of the State of São Paulo.

At the same time, as You Sirs have also already seen, they will also lend their entire solidarity to Dr. Julio Prestes de Albuquerque, who is nominated for the Presidency of the Republic by 18 of the 21 States of the Federation.

We should point out to You Sirs that Dr. Julio Prestes[,] in addition to being paulista, is also an enthusiast of industrial enterprise; every time that it was possible for him to attend to the just revindications of [industry], he did so with sincerity and pleasure; he showed himself to be, in S. Paulo, a foresighted administrator; he knows our needs and never remained deaf to our well-founded grievances; he considers that [industry] is an admirable factor in the country's progress and, thus, that its promotion should be the object of careful attention [on the part of] public authorities.

The exercise of the post of President of the Republic will not modify the sentiments that the illustrious statesman has for the national industries and, thus, our great class associations close ranks around his name.[80]

The campaign of 1929–30 also saw the PRP and its allies devote an unprecedented amount of attention to print propaganda. Between August 1929 and February 1930, hundreds of thousands of pieces of propaganda supporting Júlio Prestes's candidacy—handbills, pamphlets, books, and posters—were distributed throughout Brazil. Mário Guastini, a pro-Prestes journalist, published hundreds of articles in São Paulo alone.[81] This prestista propaganda included clericalist hysterics, as in a handbill that made the claim that all Catholics should vote for the "militant Catholic" Júlio Prestes rather than Vargas, whose gaúcho upbringing was equated with positivist anti-Catholicism, as well as more soberminded, even statesmanlike claims. A poster of "The National Candidate" was an example of the latter, promising that as president "Sr. Julio Prestes . . . will continue the patriotic activity that he carried out in S. Paulo, promising to Brazil: administrative continuity; [the] defense of production; order, peace, and work; [the] greatness and unity of the Patria; respect for the will of the electorate and the results of the polls; [and] liberty within the law."[82] Further signs of the times took an ultra-modernist cast, in four-color posters bearing idealized images of skyscrapers and airplanes and text proclaiming Prestes to be "the *Force* of our *Idealism*, which conquers for *Civilization* the *Barbarous Land* and *Projects* on the *Firmament* the *Audacious Profiles* of *Modern Cities*."[83]

Propagandizing proceeded alongside attempts at intimidating the opposition. In early February 1930, Sylvio de Campos's state-capital cabos attempted to carry out the sack of the *Diário Nacional*. Two hundred democráticos, reportedly armed to the teeth, served as an effective deterrent, however, and the newspaper's offices remained under armed guard for the rest of the year.[84]

No such discretion was necessary in many interior counties. In Mogi das Cruzes, Mário Murta, a democrático journalist, was jailed.[85] Further east in the Paraíba Valley, in Cruzeiro, the local police delegate forbid supporters of the Liberal Alliance from holding a rally.[86] In Itu, a reinforced detachment of state troops was used to intimidate PD voters.[87] Meanwhile, in Tietê, a police delegate by the name of Menêmio Lobato set about harassing the opposition, as he had in the run-up to the last elections. Small farmers, "in general descendants of Italians[,] and very good Brazilians . . . , at the head of whom is Snr. Pedro Luiz Giovanetti, an honorable and hardworking man," were singled out for particularly poor treatment, "for the simple fact that these folks belong to the democratic party."[88]

The elections themselves were held under widely varied conditions. In the state capital, for example, election monitors complained of phosphoros and other illegal voters in Liberdade, but held up conditions in Moóca as exemplary.[89] In Bauru, seventy-one democráticos claimed to have voted for the aliancista ticket only to have their votes given to the candidates of the PRP.[90] In the underpopulated Porto Feliz district of Boituva, the election was carried out a bico de pena, tallying up more votes than in the county seat.[91]

Throughout the election cycle, perrepistas helped themselves by suborning the press, which they found could be managed, if not as completely as the election results (the most popular newspapers remained independent), then at least in a neater fashion. Payments to newspapers and wire services in Rio de Janeiro, Minas Gerais, and throughout the state of São Paulo guaranteed that the official story could be found in outlets other than the *Correio Paulistano* and the *S. Paulo-Jornal*.[92]

Even without pliant newspapermen and local fraud, intimidation, and violence (which, on election day at least, may have been practiced still more widely in contests between local factions loyal to the PRP executive committee and the state government than in locales where there were aliancistas active),[93] the results would have not been significantly different. Júlio Prestes had won soundly, with final tallies giving him 57.7 percent of the vote nationwide.[94] And not only had the Liberal Alliance's candidates lost, but the PD's candidates for the federal legislature had all been defeated as well, depriving the party of a voice in national politics.[95]

Conspiracies, Coincidences, and Cooptation

The election results were maddeningly disappointing for the PD leadership. The PRP was able to maintain itself in power, even in the face of economic collapse and inter-regional conflict. The *Diário Nacional*'s publisher, Joaquim Sampaio Vidal, summed up much of this disappointment in a retrospective look at the political history of his home state:

> When the Democratic Party of São Paulo was founded in 1926, it did not encounter support among the productive or property-owning classes, although there were items [that should have been] of interest to these classes in its program. Recently, at the height of the financial crisis of coffee, in the Congresso da Lavoura, a vibrant meeting with the appearance of an assembly of [just] demands, the motto-challenge was issued: "Today[,] the planters with the government. If we are not heeded, tomorrow it will be the planters without the government and then the planters against the government." Only ninety days have passed and what remains of that volcano? Only an echo . . . and the ironic smile that remains on the lips of our professional politicians. . . . We cannot expect anything from our property-owning classes. They did not react in 1893. They did not respond to Rui's appeals in 1909 and 1919. Facing the formidable crisis they did not struggle in 1929. It is in the people that our hope lies. Once the anonymous masses manage to establish electoral honesty, then I believe that the property-owning classes will come out to dispute positions [in government]. For now, they are a dead weight, unconsciously favoring the professionals of politics.[96]

These disappointments aired, the hopeful attitude toward the people dissipated and earlier patterns repeated themselves. Some important defections from the Republican Party were registered, but on the whole the PD lost more supporters than it gained.[97] The financial situation of the party and its local affiliates became even more difficult.[98] At the leadership level, interest in armed rebellion again surged, and plotting with rebel exiles and former participants in the Liberal Alliance began anew.[99]

An earlier plot, involving rebel veterans, journalists, and democráticos in the state capital and the interior had been found out in January 1930 when agents of São Paulo's secret police (the DOPS) attempted to arrest

Siqueira Campos, then living incognito in a house in the paulistano neighborhood of Cambuci. Siqueira Campos shot his two would-be jailors and fled to the offices of *O Estado de S. Paulo*, where he was sheltered by Julio de Mesquita Filho. Thereafter, the *Estado*'s Maurício Goulart set him up in a new apartment, for which they took the reasonable precaution of hiring a Barbadian maid who spoke no Portuguese, and plotting continued.[100]

In May 1930, the senior rebel leadership, including Siqueira Campos, gathered in Buenos Aires for a meeting that put the storied leader in the wrong place at the wrong time: it was on 9 May that a storm sent his return flight to Santos crashing into the ocean. Awaiting him in the port city were a group of aspiring revolutionaries headed by Maurício Goulart. Ricardo Hall, another veteran of the campaign of 1924–27, replaced Siqueira Campos at the head of the paulista conspiracy, but he was soon found out and fled to Buenos Aires.[101]

While the drowning of Siqueira Campos hurt the cause, another coincidence, the murder of the defeated vice-presidential candidate, João Pessoa, on 26 July 1930, was a boon to the opposition. Although it is now commonly accepted that Pessoa's killing had nothing to do with national politics, at the time the opposition used the event to bolster its sagging fortunes.

On 28 July, the PD's topmost leaders met to discuss what the appropriate reaction to Pessoa's murder should be. Marrey, whom one acquaintance would later remember as having a special "horror" of armed politics, counseled "patience" and "calm" and asked that his colleagues wait for the judiciary to act. Other speakers were far more vehement. In the end, party leaders resolved to commemorate Pessoa's passing by flying the party flag at half-mast, dressing in mourning, sending emissaries to his funeral and condolences to his family, celebrating a mass, and dedicating a portrait of the deceased. They also resolved to call a public meeting for the following evening.[102]

The meeting was held at the party's headquarters. Some of the PD's most renowned speakers, including Marrey, Zoroastro Gouveia, and Carlos de Moraes Andrade (brother of the poet), made much of "the incontestable merits of Dr. João Pessoa." In his speech, Gouveia proposed the founding of a João Pessoa Patriotic Society to achieve "true democracy" in Brazil through "resistance to the outrages of the bad governments, forcing the fulfillment of the country's Constitution and laws." A "very orderly" march of "all that mass of people" that had turned out for the meeting then paraded through the downtown. They were met on the Praça João Mendes, facing the building that housed the state legislature, by a squad of police agents led by Laudelino de Abreu, the DOPS's chief inspector, who fired over the marcher's heads. The crowd did not disperse, however, until addressed by the PD congressman Antônio Feliciano, who gave a brief speech from a balcony of the state legislative building, lauding João Pessoa and asking that the crowd disperse peacefully.[103]

The peaceful dispersal of the crowd was achieved, but the mobilization sparked by Pessoa's murder was not over. On 1 August, when classes at the São Paulo Law School resumed after winter break, students and professors, including democráticos, perrepistas, and independents, paid tribute to the fallen politician.[104] Members of the leading student association also called for a gathering to decide what the group's response should be; when Antônio Januário Pinto Ferraz, the director of the law school and a longtime PRP state senator, forbade the use of school facilities for such a meeting, they met at the great hall of the Associação Auxiliadora das Classes Laboriosas, where they denounced Washington Luís, holding him, as Brazil's president, responsible for Pessoa's murder.[105]

Law students, among them a good many members of the PD's youth wing, also held a public rally on 7 August. According to an agreement worked out with Laudelino de Abreu, the rally was to be limited to the square in front of the law school, but matters soon got out of hand. As speaker after speaker took to the square, denouncing the government, lauding its foes, and calling for revolution, the crowd of onlookers grew. When it looked as if the demonstration was reaching a natural end, a democrático student, José Augusto Costa, climbed atop the square's statue of José Bonifácio with a Brazilian flag given to him by Ruy Fogaça de Almeida—one of many non-student democráticos in attendance—and called for the crowd to march through the downtown. Police agents sought to prevent the march, first by seizing the standard, then by firing over the heads of the crowd, and the demonstration turned riotous, with students breaking into the law school's armory and returning to the square bearing rifles, bayonets, and sabers. Some students fired (with blanks, it was later learned) at the police agents, who had been reinforced by state troops, while still more students and populares took to the square, singing the national anthem and calling for the return of their standard. It was at this point that Pinto Ferraz, in his capacity as director of the law school, brokered what was believed to be an acceptable compromise. Summoning a detachment of regular army troops, he called on the students to surrender their arms to the latter group; in return, he promised, Laudelino de Abreu would return the flag. The students gave up at least some of their arms (reports vary), but the flag was not returned, and the hostile truce was broken when the federal and state forces exchanged fire and the students and populares engaged the police and state cavalry in hand-to-hand combat. By the time a commission of perrepista law professors managed to cross the barricades and negotiate an end to the standoff, more than a dozen policemen, troops, students, and other rioters had been wounded; one state soldier would later die of a gunshot wound sustained during the conflict.[106]

As commemorations and protests spread throughout the state, plotting continued.[107] Zoroastro Gouveia, Aureliano Leite, and other participants in the protests and rioting of early August were active in the far north of the state, as was Djalma Dutra, a veteran of the rebel campaign of 1924–27. An uprising was to have taken place in late August, in coordination with groups across the Minas state line, with the aim of seizing the city of Ribeirão Preto, but it was delayed, as were similar plots in the Paraíba Valley and on the Paraná state line.[108]

Throughout, these and other plots—real, imagined, and invented—were monitored, to a greater or lesser degree, by those in power. DOPS agents, ordinary policemen, and informers formed a network that operated in counties throughout the state.[109]

While these spies and snitches went about their work, the ordinary give-and-take of perrepista politics continued at all levels. The biggest prize, the state presidency, was available with Prestes's coming accession to the federal presidency, and rumors circulated of possible contenders, chief among them Ataliba Leonel, "the patriarch of the 5th district," whose "electoral prestige is indisputable."[110]

Meanwhile, politics in Ribeirão Preto were increasingly embattled. The county's long-standing chieftain, Joaquim da Cunha, had retired after the presidential election, citing his age and expressing his support for Washington Luís and Júlio Prestes. His retirement, however, set off a larger struggle among his former lieutenants, which was only settled after the old boss reassumed power in June 1930, a month after his seventieth birthday.[111]

The situation in the state capital was little different. Here, in the key districts of Brás and Ipiranga, and elsewhere throughout the city, local perrepistas struggled among themselves for positions and prestige on the very eve of what would come to be called the "Revolution of 1930" and continued to do so as mineiro and gaúcho troops advanced on São Paulo.[112]

Alongside the ubiquitous, clientelistic conflicts that occurred within loyalist ranks, the cooptation of elements from the Democratic Party was undertaken by PRP leaders. In the paulistano neighborhood of Penha, for example, the PD leadership was welcomed to the Republican Party in the wake of the March elections, with the former democráticos citing the futility of continued struggle and the need for local improvements obtainable through traditional political means. The local PD president, Armando Marcondes Machado, was also rumored to have been promised one of the state's "lucrative jobs."[113] In Campinas, the democráticos of Arraial dos Souzas joined together with their opponents, similarly citing the "benefits to the collectivity" to be had by making common cause with their former foes.[114] The PD also lost one of its state congressmen, Pedro Krahenbuhl, who—apparently oblivious to the plotting going on around him—defected to the ruling party a few days before the outbreak of the October 1930 rebellion.[115]

Still other democráticos quietly turned away from party activism without taking the formal step of renouncing their membership in the PD. As October approached, they returned "to their professional duties, to their law practices, to their medical offices, to their factories and their commercial establishments."[116]

Rumor, Evasion, and Riot

When the rebellion came, the PD's Aureliano Leite attempted to liaison with rebel forces in Minas Gerais (he was a mineiro by birth) but was jailed en route to Poços de Caldas. He was sent back to São Paulo and, on 22 October, jailed again, joining Carlos de Moraes Andrade and several other plotters in prison. Paulo Duarte joined them the following day. Meanwhile, having departed São Paulo well in advance of the actual uprising, Paulo Nogueira Filho accompanied rebel forces northward from Rio Grande do Sul.[117]

Deprived of their leadership (Siqueira Campos's absence was the most notable in this regard), paulista plotters were left unprepared for the rebellion of October 1930. Their opponents in the PRP maintained control of the state through the morning of 24 October, with loyal troops controlling the high ground at Itararé on the Paraná state line and DOPS agents on stakeout in front of the offices of the *Diário Nacional* and the homes of prominent oppositionists.[118] Still other opposition figures affirmed their support for the government in the face of armed rebellion;

such was the case of Francisco Paes Leme de Monlevade, who had been elected to the Jundiaí city council in October 1928.[119]

Its newspapers censored, the state of São Paulo was awash in rumor as the month of October 1930 went on.[120] As one reporter remembered, the "*Diário Nacional*, subject to censorship, did not state what it knew and what it stated was not believed."[121] Shortwave radio became the most reliable source of news, even as passing on such news was criminalized.[122]

Amid this uncertainty, with the state government calling up reservists and "recruiting" vagrants as volunteers, many young men did all they could to avoid service.[123] To be sure, some of the state's fortunate sons— Fernando Prestes Neto and Sylvio de Campos Filho were two—dutifully donned reservists' uniforms or joined volunteer battalions, but they received suitably safe assignments.[124] Ordinary folks shunned the call-up; one middle-class paulistano would later recount his plans to flee if confronted by recruiters.[125]

It was only after news of Washington Luís's imprisonment arrived from Rio de Janeiro that the state capital's would-be revolutionaries took to the streets, bearing banners celebrating his ouster. Casa Arbrust, an arms dealership, was broken into and its stock was sacked. Now armed, crowds of "malcontents and idealists, revolutionaries and troublemakers," set out to settle scores. Among them were many younger and more radical democráticos, who released their own manifesto calling on the "Paulista People" to take to the streets. By six o'clock in the evening, "promiscuous shooting" between rioters and police troops had resulted in "several civilians shot," as well as the sack of "three Government newspaper offices."[126]

By the time order was reestablished on 26 October, a total of nine newspapers had had their offices or printing plants destroyed by groups of rioters, in successive waves that betrayed some amount of coordination. *A Gazeta* and the *Correio Paulistano* had been first, following which the editor of Sylvio de Campos's *S. Paulo-Jornal* watched as the crowds swarmed across the Praça da Sé toward his office. "It was my newspaper's turn," he later observed. The *Folha da Manhã* and the *Folha da Noite* were also sacked, as were *O Combate*, *Il 430*, *Fanfulla*, and *Il Piccolo* (among the rioters were Italian anti-fascist exiles). Rádio Educadora Paulista only survived due to the timely transfer of its ownership.[127]

After the first attacks on the newspapers came the assault on the seat of the PRP executive committee and the hall of the Republican Club. Each was sacked and, much to the consternation of future historians, all of their contents were burned in the streets.[128]

The offices and homes of prominent perrepistas were also targeted. Crowds broke into the office of the state congressman Cyrillo Júnior, on one of the upper floors of the Martinelli skyscraper, and launched its contents into the streets below, where they were burned. The law offices of other perrepistas—Alexandre Marcondes Filho and Júlio Prestes among them—were also sacked; concentrated as they were in a few city blocks, they made easy targets.[129] Sylvio de Campos's house was successfully defended, but the homes of Laudelino de Abreu and José Maria do Valle—the DOPS chief and a prison warden, respectively, two of São Paulo's most hated and feared government figures—were pillaged and put to the torch.[130]

Businesses linked to the regime were also set upon. Casa Rodovalho, an undertaker's firm with a state-established monopoly, was among the first to be hit; in tearing the place apart, rioters were said to have found thousands of voter registration certificates.[131] The city's Fiat showroom was also attacked, the company having donated two airplanes to pro-government forces in mid-October.[132]

There were also targets that were economic rather than political. Hungry paulistanos took advantage of the confusion to sack warehouses and seize foodstuffs, just as "a multitude of 150 famished persons" had done in the county of Pitangueiras two months earlier.[133]

José Maria do Valle's Cambuci prison—the "Bastille of Cambuci"— also fell to rioters, who stormed the building, freed its prisoners, then set it alight at the urging of unnamed speakers. Another of the city's jails almost fell into the hands of general-population prisoners led by a former PRP cabo; in the end it was the political prisoners who, at the warden's request, reestablished order.[134]

The city's gambling dens, where ordinary folks bet on the numbers game known as the *jogo do bicho*, were also set upon. The dens were not only thought to hold cash, they were also a longtime target of the middle-class moralizers of the PD and the yellow press. Hélio Silva, then a young reporter in the paulista capital, also records that the gambling dens were believed to be linked to the PRP machine, a claim seconded by another anti-aliancista reporter and by still other observers.[135]

Amid total damages estimated at one million U.S. dollars, the crowds also made small gestures at reconstruction. The Praça do Patriarcha was renamed "Praça João Pessoa." Avenida Carlos de Campos became "Avenida Siqueira Campos" and Rua Direita became "Rua Juarez Távora," in temporary tribute to two of the heroes of the people. Similar rechristenings occurred at street corners throughout the city.[136]

In Santos, order was maintained until the morning of 24 October, with newspapers reporting that the government remained in full control. Pro-government newspapers also reported that volunteers were flocking to defend the regime, but it was an open secret that the Santista Legion's ranks were being filled by the "unemployed of any nationality, and a few beachcombers."[137]

Throughout the month, santistas kept abreast of what was actually occurring through rumor and shortwave radio, which on the morning of 24 October brought the news that Washington Luís had been overthrown. His overthrow was confirmed mid-afternoon and a "short while after, crowds of the younger element (mostly of the lower class) began to parade the streets with Brazilian and in some cases red flags, singing and shouting 'Viva a Revolução.' "[138] As in the state capital, the rioters first turned on pro-government newspapers, sacking the offices of *A Tribuna*, the *Gazeta do Povo*, and the *Folha de Santos*. Only the latter was not completely destroyed.[139]

Then came the homes of local perrepistas. The home of João Carvalhal Filho, a federal senator, was sacked and then "burned . . . to the ground, because he was, it is said, the chief organizer of the Legionarios, and had received large amounts of money for this end." The homes of the city councilman Adelson Barreto and the police delegate Carlos Hummel were also sacked, and the houses of "several other people," including Ismael de Souza (the director of the concessionary company that controlled the waterfront and another organizer of pro-government "volunteers"), "were . . . threatened" by crowds.[140]

The rioters "also tore down several street name plates substituting them for [sic] names of popular revolutionary leaders." It was not long thereafter, however, that the provisional military government sent in troops to reestablish order and close the city's bars, as "the mob, because of the communists, who were taking advantage of the situation, presented a certain amount of danger."[141]

Similar outbreaks were witnessed elsewhere in the state as news of Washington Luís's ouster spread. Passing through Pindamonhangaba en route to the state capital on 24 October, Jorge Americano came upon a scene he described in bacchanalian terms: "wine-soused individuals, with idiotic grins," circling about a bonfire of the belongings of Antônio Dino da Costa Bueno, a state senator and a member of the PRP executive committee.[142] The following day, in São Bernardo, following a series of "patriotic demonstrations," locals sacked the pro-government *Folha do Povo*.[143]

In Rio Claro, according to the correspondent of the *Diário da Noite*, news of Washington Luís's overthrow caused "intense joy" among local residents. Taking to the streets on 25 October, locals were only dissuaded from sacking the pro-government *Diário de Rio Claro* by the "timely intervention" of two PD leaders, João Fina Sobrinho and Benedito Pires Joly. As in Santos, local streets were renamed, one after Siqueira Campos, the county's late, lamented native son, and another after João Pessoa.[144]

In Ribeirão Preto, despite Joaquim da Cunha's return to politics, the incumbents had been unable to rally a volunteer battalion, as they had in 1924. At month's end, the fall of Washington Luís led to riots like those seen elsewhere in the state: "Multitudes took to the streets, sacked the offices of the newspaper *A Cidade*, took over the city hall and declared a provisional government." The rioters left Joaquim da Cunha himself unmolested, but they were not so cowed that they did not attempt at least a symbolic settling of scores with some of his henchmen.[145]

In the wake of the rioting of 24–25 October, democráticos, their allies, and other well-wishers greeted the victorious revolutionaries as they passed through São Paulo on their way to Rio de Janeiro. Miguel Costa, arriving in the state capital on 28 October, was greeted by masses of paulistas delighted at seeing "the figure of the man who lived for seven years in exile, for the crime of desiring a free and better patria." A commission of supporters, including João Fina Sobrinho and Bertho Condé, presented him with a bouquet, following which he was cheered as he made his way through the downtown streets on horseback.[146] Vargas himself received a similar demonstration the following day, amid banners bearing his name and the names of his paulista allies, with the "lower classes" demonstrating "tremendous enthusiasm."[147]

The sounds of cheering crowds summoned by newspapermen settled nothing, any more than the anti-PRP fury of 24 and 25 October had. But taken together they did signify a great deal, issuing forth, as both did, from aspects of paulista political culture that had come to be over the preceding years and which were far from spent.

Conclusion and Epilogue
Politics, Culture, and Class in the History
of Twentieth-Century Brazil

The political development of the people is markedly different.
Many causes: streams of immigrants; European dictatorships and
revolutions; newspapers; population growth, which corresponds to
an increase in the numbers of ambitious men of letters and discon-
tented illiterates. Diverse, variable, complex, subtle and innumerable causes.

There are latent yet indestructible forces that will explode at the
first opportunity: Freemasonry (Marrey Junior); capitalism (Commercial Association of Santos); agriculture (*vide* Instituto [do]
Café); [the] working class (reduction of work days and working
hours); public functionaries (class associations), etc. etc.
—Alexandre Marcondes Filho to Sylvio de Campos,
São Paulo, July 1926

We have come to a point at which all have become revolutionaries,
via various paths. Sr. Isidoro Dias Lopes, Sr. Arthur Bernardes, Sr.
Assis Brasil, Sr. Washington Luiz, Sr. Luiz Carlos Prestes and Sr.
Julio Prestes, in this way and in that way, each display their own
conviction that it is necessary to set Brazil aright. Some call themselves regenerators, others rebels. At bottom, all are agents, con-
sciously or unconsciously, of a shared state of mind, of the idea that
this cannot continue as it is.—*Diário da Noite*, 22 Sept. 1927

In this drought, a single spark from a passing train will set the
entire cornfield alight . . .
—Nhôzinho Rato, chefe político, Una, circa Oct.–Dec. 1929

A young perrepista, aspiring to statesmanship, an anonymous writer for a mildly anti-government newspaper, and a rustic, plain-speaking local boss offered three very different but not uncomplementary political analyses, from their own distinct vantage points and at particular historical moments. Marcondes Filho, a graduate of the São Paulo Law School and a protégé of the reigning state-capital chieftain, wrote his mentor a few months after the founding of the Democratic Party, by which time the party's early, unprecedented growth was impossible to deny, and tied the party's emergence to broader currents of socioeconomic change: "Diverse, variable, complex, subtle and innumerable causes" that did not exclude the demonstration effect of events abroad or the local circulation of ideas, which occurred predominantly through the periodical press but nevertheless reached those who could not themselves read. The *Diário da Noite's* nameless staffer, writing on the occasion of a meeting of the minds between PD leaders and opposition figures from elsewhere in Brazil, did not shrink from offering an equally ambitious analysis, echoing Monteiro Lobato—perhaps unknowingly—and detecting a shared sense of unease on the part of rebellious military officers, heavy-handed men of government, and one of the PD's gaúcho allies, the neophysiocratic liberal Joaquim Francisco de Assis Brasil. In late 1929, with a contested presidential election looming and coffee prices crashing, Nhôzinho Rato did not write, he spoke, and his words more than captured the feeling of impending catastrophe held by establishment power-holders, with the apt image of the "cornfield" applied to his clique's control over the machinery of government.[1]

The three positions defy simple categorization—as good political analysis, like good history, tends to do—but it would not be too unfair to refer to them as reflecting sociological, personificative, and metaphorical perspectives, respectively. Marcondes Filho placed a recent challenge to the PRP in a broader context than many of his fellow perrepistas, seeing it and related conflicts as stemming from and intersecting with developments—provincial, national, and international—that went back decades and were themselves ongoing. The *Diário da Noite's* writer made the political personal, linking particular public figures with a generalized sense that Brazilian politics had to change; the individuals behind these names, of course, had been shaped by developments that were no less real for having unfolded outside the margins of the particular newspaper columns in question, and their own biographies were far from finished. Nhôzinho Rato's metaphor of the cornfield returns posterity's attention to features of São Paulo's political structure—in particular, its proprietary and personalistic aspects—that were so deeply ingrained as to often escape mention. That the ability of Nhôzinho Rato and his patrons to maintain power seemed perilously uncertain from the perspective of late 1929 (it would appear more secure a few months later, if only for a time), does not mean that these aspects of politics were not to endure.

The challenge for the historian is to take account of these multiple levels at which politics played out in São Paulo. It is not a challenge that has been particularly well met. Indeed, the case could be made that the contemporary analyses made by Nhôzinho Rato, Marcondes Filho, and the *Diário da Noite* offer a far more sophisticated window onto the political conflicts of the 1920s than is found in much of the existing historiography, in which pat, deterministic, and often monocausal hypotheses regarding neatly bounded events prevail: a rising middle class (in the nineteenth-century European sense, the twentieth-century New World sense, or a muddle of both), coffee-planter reaction, inter-regional brinkmanship, the institutional interests of the army officer corps, or a supposedly novel "nationalism" are pointed to as producing the "Crisis of the 1920s" and the "Revolution of 1930."[2] Amid these momentous events, to quote one of the least serious interpretations of the 1920s, "Brazilian Brazil, obscure Brazil, unknown Brazil, authentic Brazil emerged. We became conscious of ourselves."[3]

Motives and Meanings

Brazilian Brazil may or may not have been in evidence in the 1920s, but historical history and political politics certainly were, just as they had been in the 1910s and would be in the 1930s. The motives and meanings of these politics are to be found in ideas, interests, and institutions (some old, some of more recent vintage) that elude easy explication, in part because they were themselves in the making, and that continued to exert their influence on Brazilian politics in the 1930s and after, together with those individuals who survived and themselves soldiered on.

Power and Class

Power and class—political eminence and socioeconomic standing—were not coterminous in São Paulo. When paulista journalists, even radical journalists, wrote of the "oligarchy," they were not referring to the state's great bankers, industrialists, merchants, and planters, but to "professional politicians," and when they wrote of São Paulo's "conservative classes," they were not referring to conservatism as a political philosophy, but to property owners, those who had an economic stake to preserve, however modest (the category thus included family farmers, petty entrepreneurs, and small urban proprietors). To be sure, the state's most prominent incumbents were themselves wealthy, though many were not born rich, and political standing within the PRP was on offer to pedigreed men of money, but translating wealth into political power demanded deal-making, no less than the reverse; it was not a given.

Between 1926 and 1930, the PD's challenge to the PRP intersected with a host of other conflicts, including the established pattern of municipal-level struggle between local notables, anti-government armed movements and conspiracies, and the regionally based, intra-elite conflict of the decade's close. Class conflict, however, was of nearly negligible importance in the emergence of the PD and its subsequent confrontation with the PRP; above all, this was a political confrontation, in which considerations regarding power, ideology, and political tradition drove conflict.

To pretend otherwise would be to overlook the similar social profile of the two parties' senior leaderships, made up of "old and new politicians, whose disagreements . . . never represented structural differences, men who belonged to the same classes and often frequented the same social circles or were linked by business and familial ties."[4] In typological terms, similarities between the two sets of leaders were just as marked: Raphael Sampaio Vidal was no less of an agrarian than Paulo de Moraes Barros; Alcântara Machado was the letrado equal of Reynaldo Porchat; and Alexandre Marcondes Filho was a match for Paulo Nogueira Filho in his youthful political ambition (though his apparent willingness to apply himself to remunerative work distinguished him from his democrático doppelganger). By definition, there were no outs in the PRP leadership, but on pondering the discomfort of those in the opposing camp, more than one perrepista must have thought to himself, "There but for the grace of Júlio Prestes go I. . . ." At one remove from its topmost tier, the PRP even had populists of its own: José Molinaro was nothing if not of the people, and he claimed to be for them as well.[5]

As the example of José Molinaro suggests, the PRP displayed the pragmatism characteristic of political machines the world over (the Gilded Age United States, for example), gladly suffering ward and county bosses of ruder, more plebian stock—even unnaturalized immigrants—who could be counted on to bring out the vote in exchange for jobs, favors, and the other small perquisites of state-party patronage.[6]

The PRP also depended upon public functionaries to a greater extent than the opposition, but it otherwise drew supporters from the same strata of society, from the patriciate through respectable workingmen (as regards the latter group, it is difficult to believe that the state's overtures toward railwaymen during the 1920s were not reactions, however tardy, to their apparent receptiveness to opposition politics).

In bringing out urban voters, all available evidence indicates that perrepistas showed less compunction than the moralistic democráticos in the use of force and favors to recruit from what were seen as the dregs of society. In the countryside, leaders of both parties took it as a given that the resident employees of a particular planter owed it to their patron or patroness to vote the way he or she desired.

There are only two social groups for which differences of any significance emerge in comparing the two parties. The first, hardly a "class" by any reasonable definition, was the state's liberal professionals, who were overrepresented in the PD vis-à-vis the PRP at all levels. This overrepresentation almost certainly had more to do with the party's program than its ostensible class interests—it is hardly surprising that an ideologically inspired party attracted greater numbers of intellectuals (law professors, journalists, other humanistic professionals) than a patronage-driven machine.[7] The second group was the grand capitalists who controlled the CIESP, the industrial-interest association founded in part as a result of conflict between anti-PRP and pro-PRP factions within the São Paulo Commercial Association. These great industrialists sided with the PRP as a rule and were particularly enthusiastic in their support for Júlio Prestes.[8]

Patrons and Clients

The example of the CIESP's support for the PRP—what some scholars term "corporate clientelism"[9]—raises the larger issue of clientage. In the context of municipal polities divided into two or more factions of local notables vying for recognition from government and party brokers on high, political conflict unfolded in largely predictable ways, with the relative amount of fraud or violence varying according to the intensity of conflict, the relative size of the contending factions, and the particular personalities involved, as well as by subregion within the state. However, at moments of broader political dissidence, when open conflicts between state- or national-level leaders emerged or a wholesale changing of the guard appeared imminent, this structure made what might otherwise be a matter of interest only to capital-based politicians a matter of pressing political import in counties throughout the state as local political figures engaged in an often-precise calculus of the relative political forces at stake, which side they should back (or whether they should sit out a particular contest), what they stood to gain, and what they stood to lose.

Particularly compelling evidence of this kind of political calculus surfaces in the documentation generated by investigations of the military revolt of July 1924. Indeed, such documentation presents an especially interesting case because it shows how an event occurring outside of the bounds of party politics became the occasion for intense politicking among ordinary local leaders. In Espírito Santo do Pinhal, for example, one municipal out advocated seizing control of county government as soon as possible, "because the incumbents could adhere to the rebels in São Paulo and they would be left not knowing what to do and without the support of General Isidoro."[10] In São João do Bocaina, a rebel detachment named a local government consisting of sitting town councilmen; the latter, "partisans of legality, only pretended to accept, not committing any [revolutionary] act."[11] Avaí's prefeito was bolder, publishing a pro-rebel handbill in late July, when news arrived of the fall of the state capital. An investigator later concluded that he was "wary, perhaps, of losing the positions of authority."[12] In Barretos, local outs initially adopted a position of careful neutrality, loyal to their patron on the PRP executive committee but neither pro-government nor pro-rebel: "by the directorate it was resolved that in view of [the fact that they] obey the political orientation of Dr. Altino Arantes[,] who already telegraphed Dr. Carlos de Campos declaring his solidarity [in] a telegram that was transcribed in the newspaper O Popular[,] the official newspaper of the party[,] it could not nor should it assume any position contrary to the orientation of Dr. Altino Arantes and that it should not attack the government or support the revolution in any way."[13] This position cost the party's leaders in the short term, as they were accused of supporting the rebellion, but the accusation failed to stick: in January 1926 they took control of county government.[14]

Generations and Institutions

Something very much like the personalistic and clientelistic calculations of civilian political figures may also have been at work in the officer corps of the Brazilian army during this period, as the successful outcome of an armed rebellion would have presented young officers with the opportunity to vault their way up the chain of command. But this kind of motivation is impossible to isolate and was complemented by shared generational experiences.[15]

In an interview conducted in 1978, an aged Luiz Carlos Prestes empha-sized youth itself as a factor in the making of revolt. Acknowledging his cohort's "audacity," Prestes explained: "It is that the mean age of the column was lower than 30 . . . some men of more advanced age, old revolutionaries from the civil wars of Rio Grande do Sul, but the major-ity were young." He returned to the same theme later in the interview: "Before all else it is interesting to restate that the column was a move-ment made by young men and that it had a very adventuring character while also revealing the qualities of character of its components like audacity, the desire to keep up the fight and the march."[16]

Accounts from São Paulo—contemporary and retrospective—are rife with similar emphases on the role of youth. Antônio dos Santos Fi-gueiredo, a reporter for *O Estado de S. Paulo* but himself a self-proclaimed socialist, commented of the military rebellions of the 1920s: "This re-sistance represented a state of mind, the new spirit of youth, that dawns in Brazil. If it wore the uniform of the army it was out of mere chance. . . . The revolution of S. Paulo was made by this youth."[17] The *Estado's* Julio de Mesquita Filho likewise noted the prevalence of "men who had not yet reached the age of forty": "In the Army, lieutenants and captains; out here, journalists and young men looking for new political spaces in which the regimentation of the forces in the field would be possible."[18] The relatively youthfulness of the political opposition was also commented upon by the perrepista sympathizer Renato Jardim, the embittered PD populist José Augusto Costa, the military rebel Nelson Tabajara de Oliveira, the labor militant Everardo Dias, and the former democrático legislative candidate Augusto Ferreira de Castilho.[19]

As these writers suggest, youth itself was a factor in civilian dissent as well as military rebellion. One of the first organized challenges to the PRP to emerge following the rebellion of 1924 was the appropriately—if uninspiringly—named Party of Youth, which had among its founders the journalist Paulo Gonçalves, born in Santos in 1897 and educated at a local school maintained by working-class mutualists. The Party of Youth's program combined appeals to patriotic duty and evocations of the once-glorious republican tradition in which its founders had been raised with calls for reforming politics and enacting social-welfare mea-sures (the latter, perhaps, reflecting Gonçalves's firsthand experiences of privation and working-class self-help).[20]

Early 1926 saw the founding of the Democratic Party of São Paulo, which called for reform along similarly patriotic, republican lines, though with a marked emphasis on the narrowly political over the broadly social.

The relative youth of the PD's topmost leadership in comparison with that of the PRP has been noted: Joseph L. Love found that "the PRP group's median year of birth was 1875; the PD group's was 1890. Coming to maturity after 1910, the typical PD leader missed both the initial coffee boom and the first industrial surge, as well as the opportunity to invest in railroads."[21] This generational cohort also grew up under the republic (rather than the empire), its members were educated in the republic's schools, and their formative years were marked by World War I and the mobilizing ideas of the 1910s, details that were not lost on contemporaries.[22]

Suggestive evidence indicates that the PD presented a younger profile than the PRP at all levels. Young rank-and-file democráticos—aristocratic tyros and aspiring rabble-rousers alike—played key roles in politically inspired rioting in September 1928, August 1930, and October 1930; among the participants in the latter two rounds of mobbing would have been members of what was the São Paulo Law School's largest entering class to date.[23]

For his part, the PD populist Clovis Botelho Vieira, in an autobiographical reading of the party's emergence, claimed that his party was born of the "generous impulse of Brazilian youth." He and his cohort, as he described it, had cut their collective teeth on the patriotic liberalism of Ruy Barbosa, Olavo Bilac, and Julio Mesquita, and turned against "a politics without ideal[s] and without patriotism, rooted in the illiteracy of the great mass[es] and the indifference of the more cultured classes."[24]

Culture and Cosmopolitanism

When Botelho Vieira referred to the "more cultured classes," he was summoning up a bundle of sociocultural attributes that his audiences (his words were delivered in a speech in São Carlos in September 1928, then published in newspaper, pamphlet, and book form)[25] would already have had in mind. To be cultured was to be literate, respectable, and modernly cosmopolitan, but while literacy was more or less measurable, the other attributes were subject to interpretation and debate.

The idea of the "cultured" had come up again and again in the preceding years in campaigns for the introduction of the secret ballot, a rallying cry of the Nationalist League, the military rebels of July 1924, the Party of Youth, and the PD. Botelho Vieira himself noted that the measure had been "adopted in all of the cultured countries," in Argentina, the dominions of the British Empire, and the United States, where it had redeemed a corrupt politics not unlike that practiced by Brazil's "troglodytic," "retrograde" politicians.[26]

Mário Pinto Serva had made a similar case the decade before in his *O voto secreto* ("The Secret Ballot"): "Classic types of the primitive phase of South American history, a phase already left behind by Argentina and Uruguay, still figure in our political gallery. We have not yet reached the definitive stage in which the stable and secure path of the *cultured* nations begins to appear clearly."[27]

Another enthusiast of "The Argentine Lesson"—one who called the secret ballot the "gold standard of democracy in the Latin-American republics"—observed: "The truth, visible even by the blind, is that from open voting comes, aside from corruption, systematic popular alienation from the polls. . . . A majority of *men of culture* abstain from coming out to the polls 'because it isn't worth it' . . . and even, oftentimes, out of a certain moral repugnance. . . . The inveterate habit is fraud. To get involved in it . . . is to lower oneself."[28]

In the context of these and further debates, the secret ballot, and with it the elimination of various forms of electoral fraud, from vote buying to rank intimidation, was envisioned as a means to make voting an honorable and decent activity for cultured, mostly upper- and middle-class citizens conscious of their civic rights and duties. Oftentimes, this ideal voter was imagined as white; whether or not this formulation was made expressly, the emphasis was on the fitness of the future electorate. For these cultured cosmopolitans, the making of a Brazilian democracy like those admired abroad would demand the "formation of an electorate solely of the capable," as Antônio de Sampaio Doria insisted in an August 1930 address.[29]

Manliness and Civismo

That this active citizenry of the capable would be male almost went without saying. In São Paulo, in the absence of an organization like that led by Bertha Lutz in Rio de Janeiro, women's suffrage was very nearly a nonissue. The state's leading feminist, an iconoclast closest intellectually to the anarchist movement, was hostile to electoral politics in general. Relatively radical reformists like Bertho Condé might endorse the extension of the suffrage, but responses to the idea of women voting were far from enthusiastic, even among men who saw eye to eye with Condé on most matters political.[30]

The political realities of the 1920s, however, were probably less important in the engenderment of citizenship than nineteenth-century understandings of masculine independence that had been assimilated into paulista republicanism from the beginning. The gulf separating this civic ideal and republican practice was emphasized by a journalist from Faxina, who seconded the opposition's summons "to independent men of good will to the work [of] rebuilding the nation, robbed since [18]89."[31] Writing from Jaú, a supporter of the PD called on those "men whose feet don't drag shackles and whose hands don't carry chains," "those who put the interests of the Patria and the Republic above individual interests," to join with the party faithful.[32]

Condé himself put a primer in the hands of prospective voters: "He who persecutes subalterns and he who submits himself to vote in disagreement with his own conscience, is no more than the shadow of a man"; "The Democratic Party only seeks the votes of free, capable, conscientious men"; "He who falsifies elections has no honor, [and] is unworthy of any consideration."[33] Condé's commandments closely matched a run of Nationalist League propaganda that had been distributed years earlier, though he almost certainly was unaware of this fact.[34]

The overlap between understandings of masculine honor and civic standing could lend political insult a powerful charge. In São Bernardo in June 1928, for example, a PD rally ended in the exchange of gunfire after a visiting speaker declared that those who had voted with his party had proven their manhood, while whoever had voted against it was "half a man."[35]

The civic, masculine ideal could be used laudingly as well as insultingly. With Marrey Júnior running for reelection to the federal legislature in 1930, the *Praça de Santos* described the "intrepid popular congressman" as the "brave representative" of the "free electorate": this "manly figure [and] conductor of men" was "a modern chefe," in contrast to the political "mummies," stealthy and corrupt, who tried to run politics behind the scenes.[36] The same sorts of attributes were applied liberally to the military rebels of the mid-1920s: Luiz Carlos Prestes was a "virile figure" and Miguel Costa, the "fearless rebel of 1924," was a "brave countryman" who, although far from home, "in exile, only thinks of the greatness of his Patria and the puri[fication] of republican practice."[37]

Nationalism and Regionalism

Another great iconic, masculine symbol was the bandeirante, borrowed from regional lore and put to various political uses during these years. It was a symbol that, in addition to conjuring up images of regional greatness, could be seen as national in a foundational sense and, as such, could be grasped on to by those otherwise critical of regionalist displays.

A writer for the *Diário da Noite*, for example, claimed to deplore the flying of the paulista flag, calling it "an imposition of regionalism upon the anonymous mass," but nevertheless argued: "The cult of the bandeirantes . . . should be encouraged so that everyone, from the Amazon to the Prata, definitively recognizes that the greatest treasure that our forebears left us was this enormous Patria, unified and cohesive."[38]

Both kinds of mythmaking and mobilizing ideas, regionalist and nationalist, were ubiquitous in political campaigning. São Paulo's Nationalist League took up the symbol of the bandeirante in its campaign to register new voters; democráticos enlisted him in their struggle against the PRP, while also attempting to link themselves with the defense of the Brazilian nation, as in the events surrounding the rioting of September 1928.[39] Counterattacking, PRP stalwarts accused their opponents of "sãopaulophobia" and dubbed Júlio Prestes the "National Candidate" in the election of 1930, but in celebrating his victory supporters attributed it to the "fecund activity of the paulistas, heirs of the glorious traditions of the bandeirantes," and to their "civilizing impulse," which they contrasted with the useless demagoguery of "bad patriots."[40] Throughout these years, contenders from elsewhere in Brazil, from Ruy Barbosa and Evaristo de Moraes to Maurício de Lacerda and Getúlio Vargas, could be counted upon to make the requisite appeals to symbols like the bandeirante and to São Paulo's preeminent place in the Brazilian past, present, and presumed future.[41]

Both nationalist and regionalist appeals were evident in discussions of electoral reform, from the 1910s into the 1930s. Eliminating election-day corruption, as well as serving as a means by which to make politics a decent activity for upstanding, civic-minded men, the secret ballot was paired with education and military service as a nation-building device. It was in this context, shortly after Washington Luís's overthrow, that São Paulo's most persistent advocate of its introduction borrowed the Italian statesman Massimo D'Azeglio's nineteenth-century saw, declaring, "Brazil is made; now we must make Brazilians."[42] But again, it was generally understood that São Paulo would take a leading role in this process. As the "*leader* of the Union" it would thus fulfill the "secular mission" that had been its since the time of the bandeirantes.[43]

Readers and Rioters

The ideological currents of this period—from advocacy of the secret ballot to the elaboration of São Paulo's distinct regionalist-cum-nationalist tradition—were spread primarily through print and, in particular, through newspapers. As one journalist asserted not long after the failure of São Paulo's first real experiment in commercial publishing (the Editora Monteiro Lobato), "In Brazil, those who know how to read, as a general rule, do not read books; they read newspapers. And this is true, above all, in relation to the popular classes."[44]

São Paulo, due in large part to its law school, had long possessed a vibrant press. Shortly after the turn of the twentieth century, one visitor observed, "The state of São Paulo is the region of Brazil where the press has most widely developed. There are few municipes [sic] without a newspaper. Fourteen daily morning and evening papers with the best international telegraph service and provided with a good information office may be found in the city of São Paulo." By this point, the state was home to nearly two hundred Portuguese-language newspapers and more than a dozen foreign-language papers published for and by immigrants and expatriates.[45]

In the years that followed, the number of newspapers and their circulations continued to grow. To take one example of the latter, in 1910, the circulation of O Estado de S. Paulo stood at about twenty thousand copies per day; by 1915, the circulation had doubled, with one observer guessing that these forty thousand copies reached around one hundred thousand readers; by 1928, the printed circulation had doubled again.[46] Meanwhile, and with increasing frequency in the 1920s, new newspapers and other periodicals appeared, including daily newspapers with relatively large circulations (Folha da Noite, A Ronda, Folha da Manhã, Diário Nacional, S. Paulo-Jornal, Diário da Noite, and Diário de S. Paulo, all of which were founded between 1921 and 1929), pro-rebel tabloids (Tacape, Rio's 5 de Julho), the scandal sheets of the so-called yellow press (O Sacy, A Encrenca), associational organs (A Federação, O Comerciário), and a growing number of newspapers catering to the middle-class and working-class folks of particular neighborhoods (the jornais de bairro).[47]

A yellow-press journalist seconded the observer of O Estado de S. Paulo in noting that these publications reached a larger public as particular copies traded hands: "A newspaper doesn't have just one reader; whoever bought it lends it to someone who didn't, and you can calculate an average of three readers for each issue of any publication."[48] These exchanges took place in private homes, places of business, and public spaces; in "the drugstores, the barbershops, the cafés, the cultural and recreational associations and clubs," periodicals were kept on hand for clients and members, while juicier bits of news-printed material "were repeated in salons, in cafés, on streetcars, on street corners, everywhere."[49]

It is at this point that the question of class returns. The old arguments that the PD or the military rebels of the 1920s represented a "rising middle class" are all but moribund, and rightfully so, but it is clear that the formation of a significant opposition party and the very real cult of the rebel officers depended on the emergence of a mass public that was heavily middle class in composition and orientation. Newspapers such as *O Estado de S. Paulo, A Ronda,* and the *Folha da Manhã*—to name only three—hardly presented a united front on the events of the day (although all registered dissatisfaction with the status quo), but they did form one of the bases of a broader and more participatory politics that was coming into being at least as early as the 1910s.[50]

If print culture was one pole of this new politics, the public square was another, one that was not entirely unrelated. With newspapers' posting of up-to-the-minute news at their editorial offices, the streets and squares in front of these offices became gathering places. Excitement—political or otherwise—would call for impromptu speeches to be delivered from the upper floors of these solid city structures down to the crowds gathered below, the members of which might appoint their own representatives to respond.[51]

Street corners could also be used for speeches, and streets for rallies and processions, for this cause or against that one. In exceptional circumstances, city streets and public squares were taken over by riotous crowds, as they were most notably in April 1917, September 1928, and October 1930; in all three of these cases, mobs made up of mostly young and middling men targeted newspapers' offices.

To 1932

The festival atmosphere of October 1930, with its rioting, rallies, processions, and parades, was not to last, though it did stretch into November, prolonged by the continuing passage through São Paulo of victorious leaders from the south and by the efforts of local political figures to find their way to the winning side. Nhôzinho Rato was not alone among old county bosses in fastening a red bandana around his neck and welcoming the inevitable: it was, he said, "Our last effort to prevent our counties from falling into the hands of ambitious folks who don't understand anything about local politics. And also we want to protect our friends from political persecution!"[52]

Along with the support of the likes of Nhôzinho Rato, victory brought with it the problem of governance, which in turn brought further problems, but after some initial grappling about, a provisional state government was established. The new government included democráticos and non-democráticos at the ministerial level, with the Pernambuco-born military man João Alberto Lins de Barros serving first as the federal government's military representative, then as its *interventor*, or acting governor.[53]

Miguel Costa, who enjoyed a great deal more power in the provisional government than his early title indicated (he was named "special inspector" of São Paulo's militarized police, formal command over which was given to a less-distinguished officer), was a leading figure in efforts to regiment local support for what was already being called a "revolution." Costa's Revolutionary Legion, founded in mid-November, initially supported João Alberto (who appeared, for a time, to be a co-founder) and recruited among fellow military men and civilian supporters of the new order, including democráticos. The group's purpose, it was avowed, was to carry on the process of "national regeneration" and secure the "continuity of revolutionary action." Protestations of revolutionary purism and impersonalism aside, the legion recruited promiscuously in perrepista circles as well and would soon find itself at loggerheads with João Alberto and the PD.[54]

The miguelistas of the Revolutionary Legion were not the only contenders to seek out supporters among stalwarts of the old regime; the PD took the same tack, eagerly welcoming new members of questionable credentials.[55] PD leaders showed less political savvy, however, in the settling of scores within their own ranks. When an unnamed democrático brusquely informed Clovis Botelho Vieira that "revolutions are not made without the fanatical, [but] the expulsion of these bad elements is the first task of the revolutionaries after the phase of struggle is over," he only made the legionnaires' poaching of PD populists easier.[56]

These and further conflicts, characterized by all sides' chasing after jobs and punctuated by continual recourse to the provisional federal government headed by Getúlio Vargas, found their most immediate result in near-constant administrative turnover. In early December, João Alberto's democrático allies quit their ministerial-level posts, citing a dustup over the nomination of police delegates; four months later, the PD as a whole broke with his provisional state government. Miguel Costa took a less direct approach, but he also came to oppose João Alberto's remaining in office; his back-channel efforts paid off, if not in full, with João Alberto's replacement in July 1931 by Laudo Ferreira de Camargo, an Amparo-born judge. In November, Laudo de Camargo resigned; he was replaced by a military man from out of state, Manuel Rabelo, whose two cabinets lasted fewer than four months combined.[57]

Rabelo's time in office was marked by the formation of a Paulista United Front (FUP) by the PD and the PRP, now joined in opposition to the federal government headed by Getúlio Vargas, and by mass rallies in which thousands of paulistas took to the streets of the state capital to demand a new governor, one who was "Civilian and Paulista," in the rallying cry of the day. These demonstrations and much behind-the-scenes negotiation led to the naming of another interventor in early March: civilian and paulista Pedro de Toledo, who had abandoned his home state's politics for the Brazilian diplomatic corps twenty years earlier. It was at this point that Miguel Costa transformed the Revolutionary Legion into a formal political party, the Paulista Popular Party, in anticipation of a return to constitutional government.[58]

The politics of the street, however, had not played themselves out. Two months into Pedro de Toledo's government, mass demonstrations in the state capital forced his acceptance of a United Front cabinet. That afternoon and evening, crowds sacked the miguelista *Correio da Tarde* and the anti-FUP *A Razão*; when they attempted to assault the headquarters of the Paulista Popular Party, the crowds gave what would be called "The Paulista Cause" its first martyrs, including four young men whose initials were adopted by a group that was part secret society, part United Front paramilitary, the MMDC.[59]

From the uprising of 22–23 May, it was a short step to outright rebellion against the federal government. On 9 July, this too came to pass, with the outbreak of a three-month-long conflict in which volunteers "embracing the blue blood of São Paulo's planters and aristocracy, as well as farmers, laborers, business men, and all classes of society" joined up "against what they consider to be humiliations imposed over a period of 20 months by a coterie of adventurers." The rebellion was the bloodiest single conflict of Brazil's twentieth century: small beer by the standards of the civilized world (Brazilian patriots might take some comfort from this fact), but extraordinarily important in the continued elaboration of São Paulo's distinct traditions and in the unfolding of subsequent Brazilian history.[60]

The overwhelming tendency has been to view the events of 1932 (the demonstrations of February, the mass mobilization of late May, and the rebellion of July-October) as purely conjunctural—as reactionary splashing about that aimed at reversing the grand parting of the waters of

October 1930: thus the rendering of the revolt as a "counterrevolution." The latter caricature (not altogether inaccurate, though far from the whole picture) becomes unintentionally funny in references to 1932 as "Brazil's Thermidor" and, more importantly, obscures the very real continuities between the events of 1932 and the developments of the preceding decades, in organization, political culture, and personnel.[61]

In organizational terms, it is difficult to imagine the regionalist revolt enjoying the success that it did in rallying the state's population against the federal government, outfitting volunteers, and sustaining the cause for eighty-odd days without the experience, expertise, and cadres of at least two of the groups that emerged from the political struggles of the 1910s and 1920s. The PD may have been unsuccessful in beating the PRP outright at the rigged game of electioneering between 1926 and 1930, but its local and state-level organizations were vital in the regimentation of volunteers in São Paulo's cities and towns in 1932.[62] Similarly, the CIESP—born, in part, of the politicking of the late 1920s—played a key role in sustaining the paulista cause.[63]

At the level of political practice, the experience of the preceding decades was vital as well. The mass rallies of February and May 1932 clearly harked back to existing traditions, as did the riots that followed. Indeed, one perrepista sympathizer insinuated that the "sacking of Brazilian newspapers" was a recent innovation on the part of the PRP's foes; one need not accept his insistence on the absolute novelty of the practice to acknowledge that the 1910s and 1920s witnessed its broader diffusion and that the kinds of demonstrations from which these riots sprang were instrumental in the rallying of support for the rebellion of 1932.[64] Pamphleteering and still further kinds of mass propaganda put to widespread use in the run-up to the 1932 revolt, from exhortatory four-color posters to blustery radio broadcasts, were likewise borrowed from the campaigns of the 1910s and 1920s. Even women's participation, an oft-noted aspect of the events of 1932, was anticipated by the PD women's auxiliaries of the 1920s and the welcoming committees of October and early November 1930.[65]

That the political practices pioneered by the PD in the 1920s were borrowed by the miguelistas after 1930 offers additional evidence of their perceived efficacy. The PD's propaganda caravans, in particular, were seen as so effective that the technique was adopted by the leaders of the Revolutionary Legion in their own attempts to rally support in 1931.[66]

At the level of political culture, the regionalist rebels of 1932 drew deeply on themes that had been rehearsed over and over again during the previous decades. The idea of São Paulo-as-Brazil, the exaltation of paulista civilization and its identification with whiteness, the denigration of other regions and particularly of the northeast, and the manly figure of the enterprising, patriotic bandeirante—his civismo beyond doubt—had all found a place in the political imaginary of the preceding decades.[67]

Regionalist identification was not, however, the sole province of the FUP. São Paulo's "revolutionary" legionnaires were no less eager to identify themselves with their home state's invented traditions. In this context, miguelistas declared that their man had a "paulista heart," that he was the "paulista revolutionary hero"; they too believed that the redemption of Brazil had to come from São Paulo and marched under the banner of "São Paulo for the Paulistas." There were even attempts on the part of miguelistas to link the rebel mythmaking of the 1920s with the bandeirante tradition and to portray Miguel Costa as the legitimate heir of the late Siqueira Campos and a "paulista bandeirante."[68]

After Regionalist Revolt

The miguelistas' attempts to link their party and its leader with the kind of regionalist identification that fueled the 1932 revolt were even less successful than the revolt itself. Indeed, in a certain sense, the miguelistas were the biggest losers of 1932: their Paulista Popular Party all but disappeared, while the PRP emerged from the obscurity to which its defeat in 1930 had seemed to condemn it as a more credible if also less cohesive political force. The PD, for its part, limped along in the wake of the defeat of a cause that it was identified with more than any other group.

Defeat did little to dispel the appeal of paulista regionalism. If anything, it acquired a greater emotional charge, as the aura of youthful sacrifice was added to the old tropes of paulista superiority. Separatism, a minor ideological presence in São Paulo (as opposed to the propaganda of the federal government) during the rebellion, became respectable in the wake of its defeat. As a Bahian-born veteran of the paulista cause wrote, "The lost Revolution touched the paulista soul deeply. An emotional hostility set hearts aflame, separatist tendencies burst forth, regional pride grew, expressing itself in gestures, in bitter silences, and in books and studies of the revolution, history, glories and progress of the State."[69] With paulista claims that the calling of a constitutional assembly in 1933 was a response to their state's efforts the year before, constitutionalism itself came to be wrapped up in memories of the revolt as the

"Paulista Cause" became a "Constitutionalist Revolution." The emotional appeal of these markers of regional identity was such that unlikelier contenders than the miguelistas would attempt to link themselves with the tradition over the next two decades, from the spokesmen of Brazil's Moscow-aligned Communist Party to Getúlio Vargas and his paulista allies, with the former group issuing cynical appeals to São Paulo's struggle for "liberty" and "democracy" and the latter grasping after emblems of the region's antiquity and its high modernity.[70]

Other aspects of São Paulo's distinct tradition—its most regionally chauvinist features—were left in the willing hands of fewer and fewer men and women. The members of this circle also tended to be the paulistas most committed to celebration of the heroes of provincial lore: the republic's civilian pantheon (Prudente de Moraes, Campos Salles, Bernardino de Campos, and the honorary paulista Ruy Barbosa, a group now joined by latecomers such as Francisco de Paula Rodrigues Alves and Antônio Prado), the forerunner Diogo Antônio Feijó, and São Paulo's independence-era hero, José Bonifácio de Andrada e Silva. This group strove hardest of all to control the memory of São Paulo's colonial past, as *bandeirologistas*, but the icon itself, the bandeirante, ultimately came to belong to all claimants and to mean less and less as a result.

The cult of the military rebels of the 1920s was long lived as well. The movement of the 1920s and the hero worship that went with it acquired the name *tenentismo*, and attempts to capture its banner of youthful sacrifice on behalf of particular political causes were made again and again over the course of the following years. For better and for worse, tenentismo, unlike bandeirantismo, remained indelibly linked to particular living men and the named dead, and its meaning could only be stretched so far; it would have been difficult for a generic *tenente* to figure as the trademark of a commercial television station or the code name of a government operation involving the summary detention, torture, and murder of political opponents. By the close of the 1960s, the nameless bandeirante had no such luck.

This is not to say that the tenente emerged with his hands unbloodied. Luiz Carlos Prestes, picked by his brothers-in-arms to serve as their greatest exemplar during the campaigning of the 1920s so that the attention of their newspaper-reading countrymen could be more acutely focused, broke with his comrades while in Argentine exile. Prestes now saw them as insufficiently radical, naive at best, cynical at worst. In either case, they failed to see which way History was moving. Prestes believed that he did, and so the image of the Knight of Hope became inextricably linked to the Brazilian Communist Party and the defense of the Soviet Union.

Other rebel veterans drew on the tenentista mythos for less murderous causes. Miguel Costa, whose star had faded as Prestes's rose over the course of the march (Prestes was chosen over Costa as the movement's public face at least in part, one gathers, because Costa was not a native-born Brazilian), lent his influence and appeal to the São Paulo chapter of the popular-frontist National Liberating Alliance (ANL), as did João Cabanas. In July 1935, the ANL was banned, just a few months after its founding, after Prestes, the honorary president of the national organiza-tion, issued a stupid, self-destructive call for its members to rise in arms against the Brazilian government. The radical-democratic promise that the ANL represented was snuffed out, not to be rekindled, at least not in São Paulo.

Of the other great surviving heroes of the rebellions of the 1920s, most resumed military careers following the changing of the guard of October 1930, which is not to say that they were unaware of their public standing or political influence. In 1945, Eduardo Gomes—a veteran of the revolts of 1922 and 1924—stood for the Brazilian presidency. In São Paulo, his most important supporters were the *Estado de S. Paulo* group and other patrician liberals who had backed the PD in the 1920s. Their institutional vehicle was the National Democratic Union (UDN), and while the *udenista* leadership was thick with storied names, the rank and file was small and getting smaller.

Surviving perrepistas, at all levels, tended to get behind Gomes's oppo-nent, the fellow military man Eurico Gaspar Dutra, a timeserver who had backed the Bernardes and Washington Luís governments in the 1920s, Vargas's provisional government in the early 1930s, and the coup d'etat of November 1937 that transformed Vargas's short-lived constitutional gov-ernment (brought into being by a constitutional assembly held in 1933–34) into a dictatorial New State modeled on Salazarist Portugal, among other European regimes of the interwar years. The New State had brought to an end the perrepistas' seven years in the wilderness: although the PRP itself was banned, along with all other political parties, its men were favored over former democráticos in the staffing of the new regime throughout the state. The informal party of government that they were thus able to create became the São Paulo chapter of a de jure party in the waning days of the New State, the Social Democratic Party (PSD). Hardly a party in the ideological sense, never mind a social-democratic one, the PSD machine was successful in electing Dutra to the presidency in 1945.

Dutra also benefited from the support of another new party, the Brazilian Labor Party (PTB), which had Getúlio Vargas as its "president of honor" and its roots in the corporatist structures of the New State's Ministry of Labor, headed by the one-time perrepista modernizer Alexandre Marcondes Filho from 1941 to 1945. In São Paulo, the PTB was an unstable, ever-weakening host. Many of its most important leaders were new to party politics, but some younger perrepistas and a few PD populists passed through its ranks as well.

The most radical PD populists—and a few of the party's intellectuals—had been miguelistas in 1930–32, members of the various radical-democratic "socialist" parties founded from November 1932 onward, and supporters of the ANL in 1935, as had many of their civilian and military allies. In the postwar period surviving members of these groups were to be found in the Communist Party, in left-opposition groups (Trotskyist, Luxemburgist), and in left-nationalist and democratic-socialist circles, with most of the democratic socialists joining the Brazilian Socialist Party founded in 1947.

These various groups were important intellectually, but with the exception of the Communist Party they were of little lasting electoral influence. In their electoral insignificance they resembled other postwar parties in which older contenders resurfaced: the Christian Democratic Party, the similarly faith-based Party of Popular Representation, and many others.

Ultimately, political parties were less important than personalities during these years. São Paulo's most important were Adhemar de Barros and Jânio Quadros. Both men were born too late to have had much in the way of political careers before the 1930s, but they were not without their links to older political traditions.

Adhemar, raised a perrepista, had taken part in the regionalist revolt of 1932 (a fact that figured in his campaign propaganda) and served as Vargas's man in São Paulo from 1938 to 1941. He had an easy manner, an eye for the big chance, and a humorously foul mouth, among other attributes that brought to mind the late José Molinaro, and was equally at home among businessmen, farmhands, urban workers, and fellow political hacks. Drawing on his own talents and clientele, and exploiting the weaknesses of also-rans, by 1950 he had built his Social Progressive Party (PSP) into the state's most impressive machine, displacing the PSD and the PTB as São Paulo's party of government and of lunchbox-lugging men of labor. Electoral success and popular adoration came to adhemarismo despite the fact that the most substantive evidence of the PSP's "progressivism" was Adhemar's personal commitment to dedicating new public works. Along the way, he got richer and richer. "*Rouba mas faz*," they said, "He steals, but he gets things done." His was a perrepismo for the age of the common man.[71]

Jânio had been born out of state, moving to the city of São Paulo as a teenager. He was thus one of the first great São Paulo-based politicians not to claim to have participated in the 1932 revolt, which became less and less of a liability (and, perhaps, more and more of an asset) as the state was increasingly peopled by migrants from elsewhere in Brazil. Rumpled suits, emotional speeches, and boundless energy made Jânio the populist equal of Adhemar, though unlike Adhemar he never built a party of his own and he put forward the image of a self-denying moralist rather than a salty-tongued bon vivant. It is not widely known that Jânio's first lessons in politics included a brief apprenticeship with Marrey Júnior, but on reflection the connection to the greatest of PD populists is not a matter of antiquarian interest alone. Emphatic appeals to direct connections between leader and led, attention to the state capital's outlying districts, unstated but unsubtle alliances with the press, penny-pinching moralism, the defense of urban consumers more generally—even their leaders' out-of-state origins—were threads running through democrático populism and janismo. Common too were the derisive responses of upper-crust counterparts and competitors: Jânio Quadros "could be a great man," remarked a udenista state legislator, the much-younger brother of a democrático Young Turk, "if he took a bath." If adhemarismo was perrepismo for the people, Jânio represented liberalism for the little guy.[72]

In the mid-1950s—heady, historic times—janismo and adhemarismo were the two strongest political forces in São Paulo and one or both of their leaders seemed destined for great success at the national level, particularly after Vargas took his leave from active politicking with his self-inflicted coup de grâce of 24 August 1954. But these were historically important years in less immediate ways as well. The year 1954 also saw the celebration of the four hundredth anniversary of the founding of São Paulo (to the delight of bandeirologistas and ordinary paulistas alike), while the twenty-fifth anniversary of the regionalist revolt of 1932 came three years later. Each of these two anniversaries occasioned an outpouring of historical retrospectives, as did the fact that by the 1950s even the most precocious of the political contenders of the first third of the twentieth century had reached late middle age and were beginning to look back at the struggles of their youth, many with pen in hand.

In June 1957, Waldemar Ferreira—a founder of the Nationalist League, the Democratic Party, and the UDN—gave an address at São Paulo's leading antiquarian society entitled "The Law School in the Uprising of July 9, 1932." In it, he traced the "high-minded spirit of the Law School" from its founding in the early nineteenth century, to the campaigns of the 1910s and 1920s, and on to the regionalist revolt of 1932. Along the way, Ferreira could not resist commenting on the present: Bilac's call to arms of 1915 still rang true, he argued, as "the country of today" remained "mercenary and barbarous."[73]

In 1954, *O Estado de S. Paulo*'s Julio de Mesquita Filho recalled his turn against João Alberto's "revolutionary" government, a government that his conspiring had helped bring to power:

> The democráticos and us, the paulistas of the so-called "Estado" group, who then agreed to participate in the revolutionary movement, did so in the belief that we were carrying out a mission that had been left to us by our forebears. . . . We were certain that, once the splendid movement was victorious, we would see that for which all of the great ones of São Paulo had struggled, the Andradas, Feijó and Prudente, the great benefits of democracy, extend throughout all of Brazil. We were wrong when we assumed that the Andradas, Feijó, Prudente and Brazil were one and the same, when, in reality, [Brazil] was much closer to Getúlio Vargas and his kind.[74]

As far as Mesquita Filho and his own kind were concerned, Vargas's "kind" was epitomized, in São Paulo, by Adhemar de Barros, but it was a category that in the eyes of many paulista aristocrats (and Mesquita Filho, unlike his namesake, was nothing if not an aristocrat) also included Jânio Quadros. When it came to Adhemar, this was a deep, abiding contempt. In Quadros's case, aristocratic udenistas—men like Mesquita Filho and Waldemar Ferreira—could hold their noses and support Jânio against Vargas's heirs, as they would in 1959–60, but it was clear that this was not the Democracy of their dreams.[75]

Clovis Botelho Vieira would likely have attributed these grudges to what he described, in 1959, as the "traditions of intransigence of the directors of [*O Estado de S. Paulo*]" and their allies. For Botelho Vieira, the "Brazilian Revolution, which had begun with Civilismo and the Republican Reaction . . . and, after the 2 fifths of July, came to spill over in the movement of 1930[,] is still not finished"; it was ongoing, despite "regressions, [such as] the New State."[76] Mário Maia Coutinho, a student leader of the Republican Reaction in 1921–22 and a labor lawyer in the 1930s, who ran an independent, "nationalist, popular and progressive" campaign for the federal legislature in 1958, would have agreed: much remained to be done despite the "two serious armed movements," the "two revolutions, that of [19]30 and that of [19]32" that were made "so as to obtain the secret ballot and convoke a constitutional assembly"; he also deplored the missteps made along the way.[77] Aristides Lobo, who had been drummed out of the Communist Party in 1929 after a series of conflicts with its Rio-based leadership that began with São Paulo's Worker and Peasant Bloc throwing its support to the PD in the elections of February 1928, had reached a few conclusions of his own by the late 1950s: on observing the Soviet experience, "that liberty is more important than bread"; in looking at contemporary Brazil, that "although Jânio is a demagogue, he is a democrat, as he showed when he was governor," and that a demagogue was certainly to be preferred to "a general who shouldn't be in politics anyway."[78] The latter-day letrados of São Paulo's UDN, for all their book learning, did not reach the last of Lobo's conclusions until it was far too late.

It was during these same years—the years of janismo and adhemarismo, of quadricentennial jubilees and quarter-century commemorations—that a group of São Paulo-based intellectuals came together to found a new journal of opinion and debate. This group included a fair number of contemporaries of Lobo, Maia Coutinho, and Botelho Vieira, men who had also witnessed firsthand and even taken part in the political happenings of the earlier twentieth century. Among them were Afonso Schmidt, a rabble-rouser of 1924 who had recently published a memoir on the occasion of the paulistano quadricentennial; Sérgio Milliet, an ex-democrático of the party's anti-popular wing and a supporter of the paulista cause of 1932 who had once written of his despair over Brazil in ways reminiscent of Julio de Mesquita Filho, but who had since acquired a social conscience, shed most of his racism and some of his snobbery, and been among the founders of the postwar Brazilian Socialist Party; Caio Prado Júnior, of the old, moneyed clan (Antônio Prado was his great-uncle), who over the course of 1931 had quit the PD and joined the Communist Party, where he remained and where his cash contributions, if not his ideas, were always welcome; and Elias Chaves Neto, another well-born paulista, who as a young man in the 1910s had been "imbued with the French Revolution" and "dreamt of journalism, the brilliant, polemical journalism of the liberal struggles of France of the previous century," who had published one of the first book-length responses to the military revolt of 1924, and who now, as the new journal's editor, puzzled over the problems of democracy and progress in a Brazil in which he saw the developments of the 1910s, and especially the military revolts of the 1920s, as having begun "a succession of revolutions that have not, perhaps, yet reached their end. . . ."[79]

The new journal was called the *Revista Brasiliense*, a title chosen in part to evoke the *Revista do Brasil* of the 1910s and 1920s. The first issue opened with a statement professing fidelity to the "tradition of culture" of the late Monteiro Lobato and defining the journal's appointed role as bringing together writers "interested in examining and debating our economic, social, and political problems." The *Revista Brasiliense*'s self-conscious links with that tradition, and with the Lobato-era *Revista do Brasil* in particular, were further indicated by the subject of the journal's first article, "Monteiro Lobato and the *Revista do Brasil*."[80]

In the same issue, Everardo Dias, who had been the president of São Paulo's Worker and Peasant Bloc and its candidate in the paulistano municipal elections of 1928, as well as a conspirator in 1924 and 1930, wrote fondly of Monteiro Lobato, Marrey Júnior, Tito Lívio Brasil, and their cohort, "a splendid youth, beautiful minds that spread culture, civismo, optimism, liberty, abnegation, personal disinterest," "young men who later would figure in all of the country's movements of a political and democratic character."[81] Another early issue brought news of the premature death, at age fifty-nine, of Waldemar Belfort de Mattos, the Rio-born physician who, "belonging to a generation that took its first steps on the path of labor to the sound of the trumpets of the end of the first world war," had started out in politics as a democrático, then quit the PD in 1932 rather than submit to its alliance with the PRP and, soon thereafter, had taken a leading role in São Paulo's socialist movement alongside his former colleague on Campinas's city council, Pedro Magalhães Júnior, the able understudy of the great campineiro independent Álvaro Ribeiro.[82] Two years after Belfort de Mattos's passing, the *Revista Brasiliense* eulogized Miguel Costa, "one of the greatest figures of the Brazilian revolutionary struggles that began with the rising of Copacabana Fort in 1922, defeated the Old Republic in 1930; and then, went on forging, although through profound contradictions and not rarely, of marked retreats, the new Brazil of our days."[83]

Although Monteiro Lobato was the *Revista Brasiliense*'s totem figure, its writers and publishers were also carrying forward the tradition of the *Revista do Brasil*'s founders, the men who had handed over control of the review to Lobato in 1918. While working through their own profound contradictions and seeking to undo the marked retreats of the previous decades, some members of the *Brasiliense* group might have been made to recognize a kindred experience in the life of one of the *Revista do Brasil*'s founding editors, who in struggling to realize the Republic of his dreams had declared, "The destiny of peoples who want to live free is that of Sisyphus. . . . One shouldn't lament the sweat that one spills on this labor." Squinting, they might even have discerned "heroism, sacrifice," and "the ideals and the art forms . . . of great historic tragedy."[84]

Glossary of Portuguese Terms

ararense adj.: of the county of Araras; n.: someone from the county of Araras.

bacharel n.: holder of an advanced degree (usually a law degree, but in some cases used to refer to holders of medical and engineering degrees); pl.: bacharéis.

bacharelando n.: pursuer of an advanced degree (usually a law degree, but in some cases used to refer to pursuers of medical and engineering degrees).

bandeira n.: banner, flag; in a historical context, may refer to sixteenth- and seventeenth-century slave-hunting expeditions.

bandeirante n.: sixteenth- and seventeenth-century slave-hunting explorer from the central area of today's São Paulo.

bico de pena (bico de penna) adj./n.: literally "tip of a pen," but more aptly translated as "stroke of a pen," as in "by the stroke of a pen"; refers to the forgery of election results.

bonde n.: streetcar; term coined in nineteenth-century Rio de Janeiro on the basis of the early, bond-backed development of the national capital's public-transportation system, a usage later extended to cities elsewhere in Brazil.

cabo (cabo eleitoral) n.: literally "electoral corporal"; a figure responsible for "getting out the vote" of friends, followers, and fellow underlings on election day.

cachaça n.: strong, white liquor distilled from the first pressing of harvested sugar cane.

caipira n.: semi-peasant rural folk of southeastern Brazil; figuratively a hick, hayseed, or country bumpkin.

camarada n.: hired farm- or ranch-hand.

campineiro adj.: of the county of Campinas; n.: someone from the county of Campinas.

capanga n.: slang term for a hired gun; thus thug, ruffian, roughneck.

carcamano n.: a peddler; pejorative slang for an Italian immigrant involved in petty commerce.

carioca adj.: of the city of Rio de Janeiro; n.: someone from the city of Rio de Janeiro.

chefe n.: chief, chieftain.

colono n.: a resident coffee-plantation laborer, usually an immigrant; responsible for tending a set number of trees in return for a small wage and access to land, colono families also were responsible for the harvest, at which time they would receive additional pay or part of the harvest.

democrático adj.: of the Democratic Party of São Paulo; n.: a member or adherent of the Democratic Party of São Paulo.

doutor n.: literally "doctor"; used to refer to a holder of an advanced degree in law or engineering, as well as in medicine.

eleitor de cabresto n.: literally "bridled voter"; an individual who voted on someone else's orders, often after being led to the polls.

fluminense adj.: of the state of Rio de Janeiro (but not the city); n.: someone from the state of Rio de Janeiro (but not the city).

gaúcho adj.: of the state of Rio Grande do Sul; n.: someone from the state of Rio Grande do Sul.

ilustrado adj.: enlightened, learned, illustrious; n.: someone said to possess these qualities.

itapetiningano adj.: of the county of Itapetininga; n.: someone from the county of Itapetininga.

lavoura n.: agriculture, or agriculturalists as a group; in São Paulo, often used to refer to coffee agriculture or to coffee planters as a group.

letrado adj.: literally "lettered," but suggestive of great formal learning, usually, but not always, in matters juridical; n.: someone said to possess these qualities.

mineiro adj.: of the state of Minas Gerais; n.: someone from the state of Minas Gerais.

nortista adj.: literally "northern," meaning of northern Brazil; n.: someone from northern Brazil. Contemporary usage distinguishes between "the North" (Rondônia, Acre, Amazonas, Roraima, Pará, Amapá, and Tocantins states) and "the Northeast" (Maranhão, Piauí, Ceará, Rio Grande do Norte, Paraíba, Pernambuco, Alagoas, Sergipe, and Bahia states), with the newer term *nordestino* used adjectivally to refer to the latter region and in noun form to refer to its inhabitants, but this distinction was only beginning to be made during the early twentieth century.

palacete n.: literally "little palace"; members of São Paulo's upper class referred to their mansions as palacetes.

paulista adj.: of the state of São Paulo; n.: someone from the state of São Paulo.

paulistano adj.: of the city of São Paulo; n.: someone from the city of São Paulo.

perrepista adj.: of the Paulista Republican Party (PRP); n.: a member or adherent of the PRP.

phosphoro (fósforo) n.: someone who voted illegally at more than one polling place.

piracicabano adj.: of the county of Piracicaba; n.: someone from the county of Piracicaba.

prefeito n.: municipal executive, a position anaologous to that of mayor.

santista adj.: of the city of Santos; n.: someone from the city of Santos.

Notes

Abbreviations

AAA Arquivo Altino Arantes

AAL Arquivo Aureliano Leite

AEL Arquivo Edgard Leuenroth

AESP Arquivo do Estado de São Paulo

AGV Arquivo Getúlio Vargas

AIHGSP Arquivo do Instituto Histórico e Geográfico de São Paulo

AJCDJ Arquivo Joaquim da Cunha Diniz Junqueira

AJCMS Arquivo José Carlos de Macedo Soares

AJPA Arquivo Júlio Prestes de Albuquerque

ALN Arquivo Liga Nacionalista

AMF Arquivo Alexandre Marcondes Filho

ANP Arquivo Nilo Peçanha

APD Arquivo Partido Democrático

ARB Arquivo de Rui Barbosa

AR1924 Arquivo Revolução de 1924 em São Paulo

CEDAE Centro de Documentação Cultural Alexandre Eulalio

CIESP Centro das Industrias do Estado de São Paulo (São Paulo State Center of Industries)

CIFTSP Centro dos Industriaes de Fiação e Tecelagem de São Paulo (São Paulo Spinning and Textile Industrialists' Center)

CML Coleçaõ Maurício de Lacerda

CPDOC Centro de Pesquisa e Documentação de História Contemporânea do Brasil

CRB Casa de Rui Barbosa

DC Directorio Central / Diretório Central (PD Executive Committee)

DOPS Delegacia de Ordem Politica e Social (São Paulo State Secret Police)

FMC Fundo Miguel Costa

FPD Fundo Paulo Duarte

MR Museu da República

PD Partido Democratico de São Paulo (Democratic Party of São Paulo)

PHO   Programa de História Oral
PRP   Partido Republicano Paulista (Paulista Republican Party)
RG59   Record Group 59, General Records of the Department of State
RG84   Record Group 84, Records of the Foreign Service Posts of the
    Department of State
USNARA   United States National Archives and Records Administration

Introduction

1. A. M. Gibson, "Brazil and Her Destiny," *New York Times*, 23 Dec. 1889, p. 1; A. M. G. [A. M. Gibson], "Brazil Past and Present," *New York Times*, 24 Aug. 1890, p. 17; "Yankee City of Brazil," *New York Times*, 23 Dec. 1900, p. 7; "Reyes in Sao Paulo, Among 'The Yankees of Brazil,'" *New York Times*, 3 Aug. 1913, p. 2 (of magazine section); Rudyard Kipling, *Brazilian Sketches* (New York: Doubleday, Doran & Co., 1940 [1927]), 66, 68; Paul Vanorden Shaw, "Forces Behind the Revolution in Brazil," *New York Times*, 12 Oct. 1930, sec. 9, p. 1; Stefan Zweig, *Brazil: Land of the Future*, trans. Andrew St. James (New York: Viking Press, 1941), 214; Sylvester Baxter, "A Continent of Republics," *Outlook* (New York), 8 Dec. 1906, unpag.

2. Examples of out-of-state celebrations of things paulista, some of which bear more than passing resemblance to those quoted in the paragraph above, include: A. [Antonio] Carneiro Leão, *S. Paulo em 1920* (Rio de Janeiro: Annuario Americano, 1920); Belisario Penna, *Saude e trabalho* (São Paulo: n.p., 1924), esp. 28–29; Arthur Neiva, *Daqui e de longe . . . Chronicas nacionaes e de viagem* (São Paulo: Comp. Melhoramentos de S. Paulo, 1927), esp. 126–38; Gilberto Freyre, *New World in the Tropics: The Culture of Modern Brazil* (New York: Alfred A. Knopf, 1959), 106. See also Javier Bueno, *Mi viaje a América* (Paris: Casa Editorial Garnier Hermanos, 1913), 75.

3. E.g., Maria Beatriz Bianchini Bilac, *As elites políticas de Rio Claro: Recrutamento e trajetória* (Campinas: Ed. da Universidade Estadual de Campinas, 2001).

4. The quote is from Alan Knight, *The Mexican Revolution*, 2 vols. (Cambridge: Cambridge University Press, 1986), x.

5. At least in the first of these two realizations, I was not alone. No less an authority than Boris Fausto had recently written, "We do not know in detail the mechanisms of oligarchic politics in the capital of São Paulo." See his "Imigração e participação política na primeira república: O caso de São Paulo," in Fausto et al., *Imigração e política em São Paulo* (São Paulo: Sumaré, 1995), 11.

6. On the latter, see my "Coronelismo in Theory and Practice: Evidence, Analysis, and Argument from São Paulo," *Luso-Brazilian Review* 42, no. 1 (2005): 99–117.

7. A forceful case for state-level studies was made by a generation of histo-

rians of Brazil beginning in the late 1960s. The point man was Joseph L. Love. See his *Rio Grande do Sul and Brazilian Regionalism, 1882–1930* (Stanford: Stanford University Press, 1971) and *São Paulo in the Brazilian Federation, 1889–1937* (Stanford: Stanford University Press, 1980). See also: John D. Wirth, *Minas Gerais in the Brazilian Federation, 1889–1937* (Stanford: Stanford University Press, 1977); Robert M. Levine, *Pernambuco in the Brazilian Federation, 1889–1937* (Stanford: Stanford University Press, 1978); Eul-Soo Pang, *Bahia in the First Brazilian Republic: Coronelismo and Oligarchies, 1889–1934* (Gainesville: University of Florida Press, 1979); Linda Lewin, *Politics and Parentela in Paraíba: A Case Study of Family-Based Oligarchy in Brazil* (Princeton: Princeton University Press, 1987). Barbara Weinstein, "Brazilian Regionalism," *Latin American Research Review* 17, no. 2 (1982): 262–76, discusses the first four of these works, abbreviated (and, in three of four cases, preliminary) versions of which were published in 1975 as Joseph Love, John Wirth, and Robert Levine, "O poder dos estados: Análise regional," in *História geral da civilização brasileira*, part 3, *O Brasil republicano*, vol. 8, *Estrutura de poder e economia, 1889–1930*, 6th ed., ed. Boris Fausto (Rio de Janeiro: Bertrand Brasil, 1997 [1975]), 51–151. On the army, see Peter M. Beattie, *The Tribute of Blood: Army, Honor, Race, and Nation in Brazil, 1864–1945* (Durham: Duke University Press, 2001).

8. The surviving files of the Democratic Party of São Paulo contain a good bit of evidence for this point (AIHGSP, APD, esp. *pacote* 48), which is also attested to by a handful of scholarly works. See, in particular, Paulo F. Vizentini, *Os liberais e a crise da república velha* (São Paulo: Brasiliense, 1983); Vizentini, *A crise dos anos 20: Conflitos e transição*, 2nd ed. (Porto Alegre: Ed. da Universidade Federal do Rio Grande do Sul, 1998 [1992]); Vizentini, ed., *O Rio Grande do Sul e a política nacional: As oposições civis na crise dos anos 20 e na revolução de 30*, 2nd ed. (Porto Alegre: Martins, 1985 [1982]), pp. 13–73 of which present a fine interpretive essay by the editor.

9. John Womack, Jr., *Zapata and the Mexican Revolution* (New York: Alfred A. Knopf, 1969), 54–55; Knight, *The Mexican Revolution*, 1:78; Alan Knight, "Latin America," in *The Oxford History of the Twentieth Century*, ed. Michael Howard and Wm. Roger Louis (Oxford: Oxford University Press, 1998), 280.

10. Florencia Mallon, *Peasant and Nation: The Making of Postcolonial Mexico and Peru* (Berkeley: University of California Press, 1995).

11. Richard Graham, *Patronage and Politics in Nineteenth-Century Brazil* (Stanford: Stanford University Press, 1990); Lewis Namier, *The Structure of Politics at the Accession of George III*, 2nd ed. (London: MacMillan and Co., 1957 [1929]). This seems an appropriate place to add that Graham's *Patronage and Politics* is one of very few works on nineteenth-century Brazilian history purporting to be "national" in scope that actually deliver on the claim, making it a key exception to the general rule regarding the elusiveness of national history (above).

12. The classics include Love, *São Paulo in the Brazilian Federation*; José Ênio

Casalecchi, *O Partido Republicano Paulista: Política e poder, 1889–1926* (São Paulo: Brasiliense, 1987); Edgard Carone and Maria Sílvia Arantes Junqueira, "Atas do Partido Republicano Paulista," *Estudos Históricos* 11 (1972): 135–230. Municipal-level studies, including works by professional historians and by local chroniclers, were extremely useful in examining the structure of republican politics. See esp. chap. 2.

13. John Charles Chasteen, *Heroes on Horseback: A Life and Times of the Last Gaucho Caudillos* (Albuquerque: University of New Mexico Press, 1995); Judy Bieber, *Power, Patronage, and Political Violence: State-Building on a Brazilian Frontier, 1822–1889* (Lincoln: University of Nebraska Press, 1999); Roger Kittleson, "'Ideas Triumph Only after Great Contests of Sorrows': Popular Classes and Political Ideas in Porto Alegre, Brazil, 1889–1893," in *Liberals, Politics, and Power: State Formation in Nineteenth-Century Latin America*, ed. Vicent C. Peloso and Barbara A. Tenenbaum (Athens: University of Georgia Press, 1996), 235–58; Kittleson, *The Practice of Politics in Postcolonial Brazil: Porto Alegre, 1845–1895* (Pittsburgh: University of Pittsburgh Press, 2006); Angela Maria de Castro Gomes, *A invenção do trabalhismo*, 3rd ed. (Rio de Janeiro: Ed. da Fundação Getúlio Vargas, 2005 [1988]). José Murilo de Carvalho's *A formação das almas: O imaginário da república no Brasil* (São Paulo: Companhia das Letras, 1990) is only a partial exception: it examines selected aspects of republican political culture but does so almost exclusively in the context of Brazil's national capital.

14. Hilda Sabato, "Citizenship, Political Participation and the Formation of the Public Sphere in Buenos Aires, 1850s–1880s," *Past and Present* 136 (Aug. 1992): 139–63; Sabato, *The Many and the Few: Political Participation in Republican Buenos Aires* (Stanford: Stanford University Press, 2001), quote on p. 10.

15. Sabato, *The Many and the Few*, 2.

16. Ibid., 2–3, 188 n. 2.

17. The government-party of the state machine was exceptional in certain important regards.

18. Cf. Sabato, *The Many and the Few*, chap. 8.

19. Dain Borges, for one, sees Rio de Janeiro's "40% male literacy" of the late nineteenth century as having "laid the foundation for something approaching a public sphere in an illiterate, agrarian nation." See his "Intellectuals and the Forgetting of Slavery in Brazil," *Annals of Scholarship* 11, nos. 1–2 (1996): 38.

20. Sabato, "Citizenship, Political Participation, and the Formation of the Public Sphere," quotes on pp. 150, 158; Sabato, *The Many and the Few*, quote on p. 181. The juxtaposition of these quotes tempts one to add, "All that is solid melts into air," but Sabato does not make the argument that the allusion would require.

21. In addition to Sabato's "Citizenship, Political Participation, and the Formation of the Public Sphere" and *The Many and the Few*, see her "On Political Citizenship in Nineteenth-Century Latin America," *American Historical Review*

106, no. 4 (Oct. 2001): 1290–1315. These comments on Sabato's work are not intended as criticism or censure. Rather, they are intended to illustrate some of the particularities of this project by reference to a well-known, generally respected body of original scholarship.

22. Emilia Viotti da Costa, *The Brazilian Empire: Myths and Histories*, rev. ed. (Chapel Hill: University of North Carolina Press, 2000 [1985]), quotes on p. xix.

23. Recently, Viotti da Costa has called for "a synthesis that will avoid all forms of reductionism and reification (whether economic, cultural, or linguistic), that will not lose sight of the articulation between the micro- and macrophysics of power, that will recognize that human subjectivity is at the same time constituted by and constitutive of social realities." See her "New Publics, New Politics, New Histories: From Economic Reductionism to Cultural Reductionism—in Search of Dialectics," in *Reclaiming the Political in Latin American History: Essays from the North*, ed. Gilbert M. Joseph (Durham: Duke University Press, 2001), 29. Terminological disarticulation aside, it might be added that the relative consonance of this description of the historian's craft and that contained in the quotes from *The Brazilian Empire* above suggest one ongoing project rather than two distinctly different ones. It is also suggestive of Viotti da Costa's skepticism regarding the novelty (to say nothing of the utility) of much of what lies behind the label of the " 'new political/cultural history' of Latin America." For a discussion of the latter, see Gilbert M. Joseph, "Reclaiming 'the Political' at the Turn of the Millennium," in Joseph, *Reclaiming the Political in Latin American History*, 3–16 (quote on p. 11).

1. São Paulo as a Developing Society

1. Thomas H. Holloway, *Immigrants on the Land: Coffee and Society in São Paulo, 1886–1934* (Chapel Hill: University of North Carolina Press, 1980), 13.

2. The Paraíba Valley makes up the greatest part of the "Cone Leste Paulista," but the latter also includes such counties (*municípios*) as Atibaia, Bragança, and Nazaré, which are on the easternmost edge of the central plateau.

3. In Brazil, these scholars have included Eden Gonçalves de Oliveira, José Francisco de Camargo, and Sérgio Milliet, the last of whom will reappear briefly in the pages that follow. Pierre Monbeig and Pierre Deffontaines, both Frenchmen, have also contributed to the debate, as has Howard L. Gauthier, a North American geographer. Love, *São Paulo in the Brazilian Federation*, 23–25, 315 nn. 83–85. See also Holloway, *Immigrants on the Land*, 185 n. 17.

4. Love, *São Paulo in the Brazilian Federation*, 25; maps 1–4 in this book. In adopting the Love-Camargo model, I have made some changes so that it might better reflect municipal and other geographic boundaries as they existed or were understood to have existed up to the early 1930s.

5. Stuart B. Schwartz, "Plantations and Peripheries, c. 1580–1750," in *Colonial Brazil*, ed. Leslie Bethell (Cambridge: Cambridge University Press, 1987), 111–17.

6. On the sociocultural importance of the law schools, see Andrew J. Kirkendall, *Class Mates: Male Student Culture and the Making of a Political Class in Nineteenth-Century Brazil* (Lincoln: University of Nebraska Press, 2002).

7. Love, *São Paulo in the Brazilian Federation*, 25–26.

8. Ibid., 26; Holloway, *Immigrants on the Land*, 15; quote from Cândido Motta Filho, *Contagem regressiva* (Rio de Janeiro: José Olympio, 1972), 246.

9. Instituto Brasileiro de Geografia e Estatística figures from Love, *São Paulo in the Brazilian Federation*, 26.

10. Love, *São Paulo in the Brazilian Federation*, 26; Eugenio Egas, ed., *Os municipios paulistas*, 2 vols. (São Paulo: Secção de Obras d' *O Estado de S. Paulo*, 1925), 2:1699, 1786.

11. Love, *São Paulo in the Brazilian Federation*, 26–27; Holloway, *Immigrants on the Land*, 15, 18.

12. Holloway, *Immigrants on the Land*, 15, 18; Love, *São Paulo in the Brazilian Federation*, 26–27. Stanley J. Stein, *Vassouras: A Brazilian Coffee County, 1850–1890* (Cambridge: Harvard University Press, 1957), chaps. 9–11, is a classic account of similar processes of decline as they occurred in a *fluminense* county further east in the Paraíba Valley.

13. Monteiro Lobato, *Cidades mortas* (various editions [1919]). For a brief biography, see Luís Correia de Melo, *Dicionário de autores paulistas* (São Paulo: n.p., 1954), 212–315.

14. On economic diversification in the Paraíba Valley, see, for example: Egas, *Os municipios paulistas*, 1:356–57, 365, 579, 722–23, 958–59, 1084–85, 1129–30, 2:1860–61, and 2078–80, which notes, among other things, that "local industry is well-developed" in Jacareí and Mogi das Cruzes.

15. Love, *São Paulo in the Brazilian Federation*, 27–28; Holloway, *Immigrants on the Land*, 15, 18–19.

16. Holloway, *Immigrants on the Land*, 18–19; Love, *São Paulo in the Brazilian Federation*, 27–28.

17. Love, *São Paulo in the Brazilian Federation*, 28; Egas, *Os municipios paulistas*, 1:403, 1014, 2:1409, 2018, 2206; " 'O Combate' na Lapa," *O Combate*, 19 April 1916, p. 2.

18. By 1931–32, the populations of the counties of Campinas and Jundiaí were evenly split between city and town. In Sorocaba, more than 60 percent of the population lived in the county seat. In Piracicaba, with its 110 workshops, factories, and other manufacturing establishments (*fábricas*), nearly 40 percent of the population lived in the city. Secretaria da Agricultura, Industria e Commercio de São Paulo, *Os municipios do estado de São Paulo* (São Paulo: n.p., 1933), 91–94, 238–39, 326–29, 448–50. The urban-rural breakdown of Itu's population is not published in this source. Ibid., 221.

19. Love, *São Paulo in the Brazilian Federation*, 28–29; Holloway, *Immigrants on the Land*, 19.

20. Holloway, *Immigrants on the Land*, 19–20; Love, *São Paulo in the Braizilian Federation*, 28–29.

21. Love, *São Paulo in the Braizilian Federation*, 29–30, 56; Holloway, *Immigrants on the Land*, 20–21.

22. Love, *São Paulo in the Brazilian Federation*, 30–31; Holloway, *Immigrants on the Land*, 21; Egas, *Os municipios paulistas*, 2:1579–80.

23. Love, *São Paulo in the Brazilian Federation*, 31; Holloway, *Immigrants on the Land*, 21–22; Darcy Siciliano Bandeira de Mello, *Entre índios e revoluções: Pelos sertões de São Paulo, Mato Grosso e Goiás de 1911 a 1941* (São Paulo: Soma, 1982), 20–32, 48–77.

24. Love, *São Paulo in the Brazilian Federation*, 31; Holloway, *Immigrants on the Land*, 22–23; Amador Nogueira Cobra, *Em um recanto do sertão paulista* (São Paulo: Typ. Hennies [&] Irmãos, 1923). For a model county-level study, see Diores Santos Abreu, *Formação histórica de uma cidade pioneira paulista: Presidente Prudente* (Presidente Prudente: Faculdade de Filosofia, Ciência e Letras de Presidente Prudente, 1972).

25. Love, *São Paulo in the Brazilian Federation*, 32; Holloway, *Immigrants on the Land*, 24; the date for the arrival of the lower Sorocabana railway is taken from Ralph Mennucci Giesbrecht's website, http://www.estacoesferroviarias .com.br/, which has served me well as a general reference work on São Paulo's railway network.

26. Instituto Astronomico e Geographico de São Paulo, *Carta geral do estado de São Paulo, 1933* (a map).

27. H. B. Johnson, "Portuguese Settlement, 1500–1580," in Bethell, *Colonial Brazil*, 12.

28. Love, *São Paulo in the Brazilian Federation*, 32–33; Holloway, *Immigrants on the Land*, 24–25.

29. Egas, *Os municipios paulistas*, 1:795–800, 2:1722–1741.

30. Repartição de Estatistica e Archivo de São Paulo, *Divisão judiciaria e administrativa e districtos eleitoraes do estado de São Paulo em 1926* (São Paulo: Officina do *Diario Official*, 1927), 47.

31. Ibid., 46, 47.

32. Ibid., 47; below, chap. 2.

33. Repartição de Estatistica e Archivo, *Divisão judiciaria*, 47–48.

34. Ibid., 48.

35. Ibid.; Ganymédes José Santos de Oliveira, *Uma vez, Casa Branca . . .* (São Paulo: São Paulo Editora, 1973), 113, 116–17.

36. Repartição de Estatistica e Archivo, *Divisão judiciaria*, 48; Eliana Tadeu Terci, "A cidade na primeira república: Imprensa, política e poder em Piracicaba" (tese de doutorado, Universidade de São Paulo, 1997), 7.

37. Repartição de Estatistica e Archivo, *Divisão judiciaria*, 48.

38. Ibid.

39. The turn of phrase belongs to Alfredo Ellis Júnior, an amateur historian who played a bit part in the politics of the 1920s and 1930s. See his *Raça de gigantes* (São Paulo: Helios, 1926). Much of this general view survived well into the development of historical study as a professional discipline in Brazil, most notably in the work of his daughter, Myriam Ellis, who belongs to the first generation of historians trained at the University of São Paulo. See her "As bandeiras na expansão geográfica do Brasil," in *História geral da civilização brasileira*, vol. 1, *Do descobrimento à expansão territorial*, ed. Sérgio Buarque de Holanda (São Paulo: Difel, 1960), 273–96. Antonio Celso Ferreira, *A epopéia bandeirante: Letrados, instituições, invenção histórica, 1870–1940* (São Paulo: Ed. da Universidade Estadual Paulista, 2002), is a recent monograph on the invention of this particular tradition.

40. Schwartz, "Plantations and Peripheries, c. 1580–1750," 110–18.

41. James Lockhart and Stuart B. Schwartz, *Early Latin America* (Cambridge: Cambridge University Press, 1983), 373, 381; Schwartz, "Plantations and Peripheries, c. 1580–1750," 117.

42. Thomas W. Walker, "Ribeirão Preto, 1910–1960," trans. Mariana Carla Magri, in Walker and Agnaldo de Sousa Barbosa, *Dos coronéis à metrópole: Fios e tramas da sociedade e da política em Ribeirão Preto no século XX* (Ribeirão Preto: Palavra Mágica, 2000), 39–40; D. Abreu, *Formação histórica de uma cicade pioneira paulista*; Cobra, *Em um recanto do sertão paulista*, chap. 1. In his history of the Prado family, Darrell E. Levi records the mutual hostility that initially prevailed between mineiro pastoralists and coffee-mad outsiders when the two groups first encountered each other in the upper Mogiana. See *The Prados of São Paulo, Brazil: An Elite Family and Social Change, 1840–1930* (Athens: University of Georgia Press, 1987), 71.

43. Love, *São Paulo in the Brazilian Federation*, 154, 159; Kirkendall, *Class Mates*.

44. Renato Jardim, *Reminiscências: De Resende, estado do Rio, às plagas paulistas, S. Simão, Batatais, Altinópolis e Ribeirão Preto* (Rio de Janeiro: José Olympio, 1946), 145–47, 157–58.

45. George Reid Andrews, *Blacks and Whites in São Paulo, Brazil, 1888–1988* (Madison: University of Wisconsin Press, 1991), chaps. 2–3; Warren Dean, *Rio Claro: A Brazilian Plantation System, 1820–1920* (Stanford: Stanford University Press, 1976), 152–53, 191–92; Holloway, *Immigrants on the Land*, 172–73; Carlos José Ferreira dos Santos, *Nem tudo era italiano: São Paulo e a pobreza, 1890–1915* (São Paulo: Annablume, 1998).

46. Holloway, *Immigrants on the Land*.

47. Boris Fausto, *Trabalho urbano e conflito social*, 4th ed. (São Paulo: Difel, 1986 [1976]), chap. 2; Joel Wolfe, *Working Women, Working Men: São Paulo and the Rise of Brazil's Industrial Working Class, 1900–1955* (Durham: Duke University Press, 1993), chap. 1.

48. See Sônia Dias, "Francisco Matarazzo," in Alzira Alves de Abreu et al., eds., *Dicionário histórico-biográfico brasileiro*, 2nd ed. (Rio de Janeiro: Ed. da Fundação Getúlio Vargas, 2001 [1984]), 3:3630–31.

49. As suggested by Jardim, *Reminiscências*.

50. Egas, *Os municipios paulistas*, 1:800; Eduardo Carlos Pereira and Elizabeth Filippini, *Cem anos de imigração italiana em Jundiaí* (São Paulo: Estudio RO, 1988).

51. On the classes conservadoras: untitled note, *O Combate*, 14 Dec. 1927, p. 1; José Carlos de Macedo Soares to Rodrigo Monteiro Diniz Junqueira, São Paulo, 19 July 1924, AESP, AJCMS, caixa AP153, pacote 3; Valentim Gentil et al. to Julio Prestes de Albuquerque, Itapolis, 28 July 1928, AESP, AJPA, caixa AP07; Odilon Negrão et al., to Julio Prestes de Albuquerque, Itapolis, 9 Oct. 1928, AESP, AJPA, caixa AP07; Luis Amaral, *A hora da expiação: O momento brasileiro, em synthese* (São Paulo: n.p., 1930), 5. On the classes liberaes: "O Partido Democratico" (newspaper clipping labeled *O Sãomanuelense*, 17 June 1926), AIHGSP, APD, album I; Valentim Gentil et al. to Julio Prestes de Albuquerque, Itapolis, 28 July 1928, AESP, AJPA, caixa AP07; Odilon Negrão et al. to Julio Prestes de Albuquerque, Itapolis, 9 Oct. 1928, AESP, AJPA, caixa AP07; Comitê Operário e Camponês Pró-Constituinte, "Trabalhadores," *A Plateia*, 14 July 1932, reprinted (in modernized orthography) in Emilia Viotti da Costa, ed., *1932: Imagens contraditórias* (São Paulo: Arquivo do Estado, 1982), 20–21, and in Jeziel De Paula, *1932: Imagens construindo a história* (Campinas: Ed. da Universidade Estadual de Campinas, 1998), 118–19; Renato Jardim, *A aventura de outubro e a invasão de São Paulo*, 2nd ed. (Rio de Janeiro: Civilização Brasileira, 1932), 124 (the "chamada [so-called] classe liberal"). That the term "classes conservadoras" did not imply any kind of ideational conservatism beyond that demanded by the material stake in society that property represented is indicated by the fact that clergy, even high clergy, were not considered members. *Classes preservadoras* would not have the same alliterative ring to it, but it would maintain the term's most vital part, that deriving from the Latin *servare*, and thus have the same basic meaning. By the same token, it goes without saying that attorneys, to take one particular professional cohort as an example, were not assumed to be Gladstonians; they practiced a liberal profession but could be as hidebound in their politics as anyone else.

52. On the tension(s) surrounding the adoption of this model, see Brian P. Owensby, *Intimate Ironies: Modernity and the Making of Middle-Class Lives in Brazil* (Stanford: Stanford University Press, 1999).

53. For example: Gilberto Freyre, *Order and Progress: Brazil from Monarchy to Republic*, trans. Rod W. Horton (New York: Alfred A. Knopf, 1970); Dean, *Rio Claro*; Dean, *The Industrialization of São Paulo, 1880–1945* (Austin: University of Texas Press, 1969).

54. Obviously, my understanding of the paulista upper class as it existed during this period owes a great deal to Joseph Love's work on political elites in

São Paulo. See his *São Paulo in the Brazilian Federation*; also Love and Bert J. Barickman, "Rulers and Owners: A Brazilian Case Study in Comparative Perspective," *Hispanic American Historical Review* 66, no. 4 (Nov. 1986): 743–65. The two groups were not coterminous; however, most of Love's population (it is not a sample, he reminds us) would have been born into or joined the upper ranks of paulista society.

55. Quoted in Fausto, *Trabalho urbano e conflito social, 1890–1920*, 129.

56. Ibid.

57. Jacob Penteado, *Memórias de um postalista* (São Paulo: Martins, 1963), 13, 23–24.

58. Fausto, *Trabalho urbano e conflito social, 1890–1920*, chap. 2; Wolfe, *Working Women*, chap. 1.

59. Fausto, *Trabalho urbano e conflito social, 1890–1920*, 129.

60. The single most important work in this regard has been Holloway, *Immigrants on the Land*.

61. C. Santos, *Nem tudo era italiano*.

62. Teodor Shanin, *Russia as a "Developing Society"* (New Haven: Yale University Press, 1985), 204; Angel Rama, *The Lettered City*, trans. John Charles Chasteen (Durham: Duke University Press, 1996). The allusion to *The Lettered City* should be read cautiously, as São Paulo differed significantly from the cities that were Rama's main models (Mexico City, Lima, and even Rio de Janeiro). It was a second city rather than a colonial capital, and its importance as a population center was more recent and was due to a significant extent to local entrepreneurialism.

63. Quotes from Shanin, *Russia as a "Developing Society,"* 204. It might be noted that the ideals of modernity and rationality noted by Shanin were not without their own tensions and contradictions, even in the societies in which they are or were said to have flourished.

2. A Republic of Layers

1. Afonso Arinos de Melo Franco, *Rodrigues Alves: Apogeu e declínio do presidencialismo*, 2 vols. (Rio de Janeiro: José Olympio, 1973), 1:83; [Cândido] Motta Filho, *Uma grande vida* (São Paulo: Edições de *Política*, 1931), 64; Maria Lucia Caira Gitahy, "The Port Workers of Santos, 1889–1914,": Labor Movement in an Early 20th Century City" (Ph.D. diss., University of Colorado, 1991), 84, 196–97, 332; Gitahy, *Ventos do mar: Trabalhadores do porto, movimento operário e cultura urbana* (São Paulo: Ed. da Universidade Estadual Paulista, 1992), 34–37, 126–27, 144–45 (n. 39); Francisco Martins dos Santos, *História de Santos, 1532–1936*, 2 vols. (São Paulo: Empreza Graphica da *Revista dos Tribunaes*, 1937), 1:313, 2:65–82.

2. Martinho da Silva Prado Júnior, quoted in Levi, *The Prados of São Paulo,*

Brazil, 164; J. M. de Carvalho, *A formação das almas*, 52. See also Barbara Weinstein, "Not the Republic of Their Dreams": Historical Obstacles to Political and Social Democracy in Brazil," *Latin American Research Review* 29, no. 2 (1994): 262–73.

3. Presidente de São Paulo, *Mensagem apresentado ao congresso de S. Paulo, a 7 de abril de 1893, pelo dr. Bernardino de Campos, presidente do estado* (n.p., 1893), 20.

4. The abolition of slavery, with federalism one of the nineteenth century's two great issues, had been settled for the republicans a year and a half before the overthrow of Pedro II, on 13 May 1888.

5. "As eleições de hoje," *O Combate*, 30 Oct. 1919, p. 1. For the sake of consistency and coherence, I use the term "Paulista Republican Party" and its abbreviation PRP to refer to the state's ruling party, although the terms were not used consistently throughout this period. The party was sometimes known as the Partido Republicano do Estado de São Paulo, sometimes simply as the Partido Republicano, and, for a brief period, as the Partido Republicano Federal. I have also found the party referred to as the Partido Republicano Governista. See Carone and Junqueira, "Atas do Partido Republicano Paulista," 140; "A [single word, probably "scisão," redacted by censor] no P. R. G.," *O Combate*, 22 May 1918, p. 1.

6. See Graham, *Patronage and Politics in Nineteenth-Century Brazil*.

7. The phrase "connecting web" is Richard Graham's. See ibid., 1. It was in the first decade of the twentieth century that the system of state electoral districts outlined in chap. 1 was adopted. Assembléia Legislativa de São Paulo, *Legislativo paulista: Parlamentares, 1835–1999*, ed. Auro Augusto Caliman (São Paulo: Imprensa Oficial, 1999), 69, 71.

8. See, for example, Cobra, *Em um recanto do sertão paulista*, 108–14; Antônio de Almeida Prado, *Crônica de outrora* (São Paulo: Brasiliense, 1963), 112–24; Karl Monsma, Oswaldo Truzzi, ande Silvano da Conceição, "Solidariedade étnica, poder local e banditismo: Uma quadrilha calabresa no oeste paulista, 1895–1898," *Revista Brasileira de Ciências Sociais* 53 (Oct. 2003): 71–96.

9. A., "No dia 30," *O Estado de S. Paulo*, 4 Nov. 1904, p. 1.

10. " 'O Combate' ouve a respeito o senador Rodolpho Miranda," *O Combate*, 12 Jan. 1921, p. 1 (emphasis added). See also Menotti Del Picchia, *A longa viagem*, 2 vols. (São Paulo: Martins, 1970–1972), 2:168–71, 183; Cândido Motta Filho, *Dias lidos e vividos* (Rio de Janeiro: José Olympio, 1977), 135.

11. A., "No dia 30," *O Estado de S. Paulo*, 4 Nov. 1904, p. 1. Although they did not occupy formal positions in the executive branch, sitting members of the PRP executive committee could, and often did, serve in the state and federal legislatures. For some examples, see Love, *São Paulo in the Brazilian Federation*, 295–96, 300.

12. On legislators and police delegates, see, for example, Del Picchia, *A longa viagem*, 2:243–50; Paes Leme Junior (pseud. Júlio da Silveira Sudário [Melo,

Dicionário de autores paulistas, 626]), *Breve notícias históricas sobre Itápolis* (São Paulo: n.p., 1938), 172–74.

13. The city of São Paulo was exceptional in only two regards. First, movements for municipal independence on the part of its constituent parts were unknown in these years (though movements for the establishment of new submunicipal districts were not: e.g., "O bairro do Ypiranga," *O Combate,* 24 Nov. 1915, p. 4). Second, the reigning chefe of the state capital enjoyed power and standing comparable to that of the greatest regional chieftains of the interior (below, this chap.).

14. Love coded the careers of 263 individuals, 56 of whom served on the PRP executive committee during its 41-year incumbency. If one discounts the victims of the purge and counterpurge of 1891–92 and those who served on the committee for a year or less and adds the two elected state presidents who would otherwise not be included (Washington Luís and Júlio Prestes), one is left with a total of 32 men. On the basis of a catholic reading of records from the era and of subsequent histories, and given that not all of these men were active at the same time, and keeping in mind that some important figures are excluded altogether from the group of 32 (Álvaro da Costa Carvalho, who was part of Love's original population; Joaquim da Cunha Diniz Junqueira, who was not), one might still hazard a guess that the members of the republican "elite within an elite" never numbered more than one to two dozen men at any one time.

15. My "elite within an elite" was slightly less well-educated as an aggregate than Love's larger group, as it includes a number of prominent republicans who lacked university degrees (including Antônio de Lacerda Franco, Fernando Prestes de Albuquerque, and Francisco Glycerio de Cerqueira Leite, the latter two of whom were self-trained practicing lawyers early in their careers), while excluding scores of men who were educated at the São Paulo Law School but never came to exert comparable influence.

16. "Jorge Tibiriçá," *O Estado de S. Paulo,* 30 Sept. 1928, p. 8; Love, *São Paulo in the Brazilian Federation,* 168–70, 295–296. Here and elsewhere I have also drawn on a chart illustrating service on the PRP executive committee, by member, which Professor Love drew up on the basis of information from the *Correio Paulistano* for the years 1889–1930 and was kind enough to share with me (henceforth Love, "The Party in Power").

17. Altino Arantes, *Passos do meu caminho* (Rio de Janeiro: José Olympio, 1958), 306–14; Clovis Glycerio Gracie de Freitas, *Jornada republicana: Francisco Glycerio* (São Paulo: Plexus, 2000); José Sebastião Witter and Francisco de Assis Barbosa, "Francisco Glicério, um republicano pragmático," in *Idéias políticas de Francisco Glicério,* ed. José Sebastião Witter (Rio de Janeiro: Casa de Rui Barbosa, 1982), 23–63; Love, *São Paulo in the Brazilian Federation,* 106–108, 110–115, 171, 178, 187–188; Love, "The Party in Power"; "A morte do senador Glycerio," *O Estado de S. Paulo,* 13 April 1916, p. 3.

18. Love, *São Paulo in the Brazilian Federation*, 296; Love, "The Party in Power"; "A politica," *O Combate*, 15 March 1916, p. 1; "Quem sáe da Commissão Directora?," *O Combate*, 28 April 1919, p. 1; "Coronel Lacerda Franco," *O Estado de S. Paulo*, 20 May 1936, p. 4; *Album de Araras: Documentário histórico, geográfico, ilustrativo do município de Araras* (Araras: n.p., 1948), unpag.; copy of letter, [Fábio Barreto] to Washington Luis, Ribeirão Preto, 5 April 1927, AESP, AJCDJ, caixa AP174, pasta 6.

19. D. Abreu, *Formação histórica de uma cidade pioneira paulista*, 210–11; Célio Debes, *Júlio Prestes e a primeira república* (São Paulo: Arquivo do Estado, 1982), see esp. 17–19 on Fernando Prestes's early life and career; Love, *São Paulo in the Brazilian Federation*, 130, 172, 288–89, 296; Love, "The Party in Power"; Mário Guastini, *Tempos idos e vividos* (São Paulo: Universitária, 1944), 186–88; Motta Filho, *Dias lidos e vividos*, 184–88; Oracy Nogueira, "Os movimentos e partidos políticos em Itapetininga," *Revista Brasileira de Estudos Políticos* 11 (June 1961): 238–43; "Coronel Fernando Prestes de Albuquerque," *O Estado de S. Paulo*, 26 Oct. 1937, p. 3.

20. He was elected to the national presidency for a second, nonconsecutive term but was too sick to take office, dying shortly after what would have been his second inaugural. I discuss the careers of the Rodrigues Alves brothers at greater length in my "Coronelismo in Theory and Practice," 102–4. Other former monarchists who made good on their conversions included João Alvares Rubião Júnior, Manoel Pessoa de Siqueira Campos, Antônio Dino da Costa Bueno, Manoel Joaquim de Albuquerque Lins, and Olavo Egydio de Souza Aranha. Love, "The Party in Power."

21. "Reorganização da comissão diretora do Partido Republicano. Ata da convenção dos diretórios municipais realizada no dia 22 de novembro de 1913" and "Ata da eleição da comissão diretora do Partido Republicano" (10 July 1920), both of which are published in Carone and Junqueira, "Atas do Partido Republicano Paulista," 194, 204; "Ser opposicionista em Pirajú é ser heróe," *O Combate*, 8 Jan. 1916, p. 1; "A politica" and "Politica de bugre," *O Combate*, 27 April 1916, p. 1; "A politica," *O Combate*, 1 March 1916, p. 1; "A politica," *O Combate*, 17 Oct. 1919, p. 1; "O papel da comissão directora na comarca de Santa Cruz do Rio Pardo," *O Combate*, 19 April 1921, reprinted in secção livre of *O Estado de S. Paulo*, 23 April 1921, p. 8; "As occorencias de Palmital," *Correio Paulistano*, 17 Oct. 1923, reprinted in secção livre of *O Estado de S. Paulo*, 18 Oct. 1923, p. 10; José Carlomagno to Secretario do PD, Santa Cruz do Rio Pardo, 25 May 1926, AIHGSP, APD, pacote 34; José Soares Marcondes, "Presidente Prudente," in secção livre of *O Estado de S. Paulo*, 4 Jan. 1927, p. 10; D. Abreu, *Formação histórica de uma cidade pioneira paulista*, 87, 90, 210–11, 217–18; J. C. [José Custódio] Alves de Lima, *Recordações de homens e cousas do meu tempo* (Rio de Janeiro: Leite Ribeiro, Freitas Bastos, Spicer & Cia., 1926), 263; Arantes, *Passos do meu caminho*, 301–6; Jefferson Del Rios, *Ourinhos: Memórias de uma cidade paulista* (Ourinhos: Prefeitura Municipal, 1992), 18,

33, 213–14; Paulo Duarte, *Memórias*, 10 vols. (São Paulo: Hucitec, 1974–1980 [vol. 10 published in Rio de Janeiro by Paz e Terra]), 8:207–8; Jayme Leonel et al., *O último dos coronéis: Homenagem dos autores ao grande brasileiro, General Ataliba Leonel, no primeiro centenário do seu nascimento* (São Paulo: n.p., 1975); Love, *São Paulo in the Brazilian Federation*, 130, 172–73; Motta Filho, *Contagem regressiva*, 195–97; Assembléia Legislativa, *Legislativo paulista*, 87–89, 91–94, 103–4; "Ataliba Leonel," in A. Abreu et al., *Dicionário histórico-biográfico brasileiro*, 3:3096.

22. Love, *São Paulo in the Brazilian Federation*, 114, 296; "Ata da posse da Comissão Diretiva do Partido Republicano, eleita para funcionar durante quatro anos, a contar desta data," São Paulo, 5 June 1916, in Carone and Junqueira, "Atas do Partido Republicano Paulista," 199–200; *A Tribuna* (São Paulo), 27 Sept. 1913, in secção livre of *O Estado de S. Paulo*, 15 Oct. 1913, p. 9; "Chapa de vereadores," in secção livre, *O Estado de S. Paulo*, 15 Oct. 1913, p. 8; "O dr. José Piedade não é candidato," *O Combate*, 25 June 1915, p. 1; "Triumpha a Mallat," *O Combate*, 3 Aug. 1915, p. 4; "A Politica," *O Combate*, 30 May 1916, p. 1; "A politica," *O Combate*, 24 Nov. 1916, p. 1; "Um logar de escripturario dá origem a um caso politico," *O Combate*, 17 Jan. 1917, p. 1; "A politica," *O Combate*, 18 Oct., 1918, p. 1; "A politica," *O Combate*, 29 April 1919, p. 1; "A politica," *O Combate*, 1 Oct. 1919, p. 1; Olavo Egydio de Souza Aranha to *Correio Paulistano*, São Paulo, n.d., published as "Politica da capital," in secção livre, *O Estado de S. Paulo*, 23 April 1922, p. 11; "Noticias diversas," *O Estado de S. Paulo*, 30 Jan. 1924, p. 4; Themis, "Politicando," *O Pinheirense*, 30 March 1924, p. 1; "Dr. Olavo Egydio," *O Estado de S. Paulo*, 7 March 1928, p. 4; "Fallecimentos" (on Albuquerque Lins), *O Estado de S. Paulo*, 8 Jan. 1926, p. 2; P. Duarte, *Memórias*, 7:297; Renato Jardim, *Um libello a sustentar: Additamento ao livro "A aventura de outubro e a invasão de São Paulo"* (Rio de Janeiro: Civilização Brasileira, 1933), 49; "Politica da capital," *O Combate*, 14 Nov. 1925, p. 1; "Politica da capital," *O Combate*, 17 Nov. 1925, p. 1; "Sílvio de Campos," in A. Abreu et al., *Dicionário histórico-biográfico brasileiro*, 1:1035–36. Today's cliché, "São Paulo é um país!" ([the city of] São Paulo is its own country!), may not have rung true in the first third of the twentieth century, but the state capital was already a "region" in political terms.

23. *O Estado de S. Paulo*, 16 Dec. 1909, p. 5; "O caso da cadeia de Barra Bonita," *O Combate*, 21 Dec. 1918, p. 1; "Ao eleitorado paulista," 2 Feb. 1924, in secção livre of *O Estado de S. Paulo*, 9 Feb. 1924, p. 9; "A politica pelo interior," *O Combate*, 28 Sept. 1925, p. 1; "Vicente de Almeida Prado," *O Estado de S. Paulo*, 6 Jan. 1956, p. 5; "Vicente de Paula de Almeida Prado," in A. Abreu et al., *Dicionário histórico-biográfico brasileiro*, 4:4763–64; Assembléia Legislativa, *Legislativo paulista*, 89–92, 104; Maria Apparecida Franco Pereira, "O comércio cafeeiro na praça de Santos: O comissário de café, 1870–1920," in Pereira et al., *Santos: Café e história* (Santos: Leopoldianum, 1995), 29. The quote is from "A politica," *O Combate*, 21 Jan. 1916, p. 1.

24. Alexandre Carolo, "Quinzinho da Cunha" in *Os desbravadores*, ed. Galeno Amorim (Ribeirão Preto: Palavra Mágica, 2001), 59–64; Rubem Cione, *História de Ribeirão Preto*, 3rd ed. (Ribeirão Preto: IMAG, 1990), 240–45; Frederick Vincent Gifun, "Ribeirão Prêto, 1880–1914: The Rise of a Coffee County" (Ph.D. diss., University of Florida, 1972), 135–36; Jardim, *Reminiscências*, 200; Walker, "Ribeirão Preto, 1910–1960," 63–74; untitled notice, *O Combate*, 5 April 1918, p. 1; "A politica," *O Combate*, 8 April 1918, p. 1; "A politica," *O Combate*, 8 June 1918, p. 1; "A politica," *O Combate*, 27 June 1918, p. 1; "A politica," *O Combate*, 2 July 1918, p. 1; "A politica," *O Combate*, 6 Sept. 1918, p. 3; "Politicando . . . ," *A Capital*, 6 April 1926 [misprinted as "6 March 1926"], p. 1; "Falecimentos," *O Estado de S. Paulo*, 15 Sept. 1932, p. 3; telegram, Altino Arantes to Joaquim da Cunha, São Paulo, 4 April 1919, AESP, AAA, caixa AP86; telegram, Altino Arantes to Carlos de Campos, São Paulo, 4 April 1919, AESP, AAA, caixa AP86; telegram, Altino Arantes to Joaquim da Cunha, São Paulo, 14 April 1919 (two of this date), AESP, AAA, caixa, AP86; Washington Luiz to Joaquim da Cunha, Rio de Janeiro, 11 Jan. 1927, AESP, AJCDJ, caixa AP174, pasta 3; "Um homem de grande valor," *O Trabalho* (Espírito Santo do Pinhal), 4 Nov. 1924, p. 1, AESP, AJCDJ, caixa AP175, envelope 2.

25. Nelson Carrer, "Francisco Schmidt," in Amorim, *Os desbravadores*, 65–69; Cione, *História de Ribeirão Preto*, 245–48; Gifun, "Ribeirão Prêto, 1880–1914," 94–95, 133, 134, 161, 184–85; Jardim, *Reminiscências*, 210–12; Walker, "Ribeirão Preto, 1910–1960," 62–70.

26. Bilac, *As elites políticas de Rio Claro*, 56–58; Ana Maria Penha Mena Pagnocca, *Crônica dos prefeitos de Rio Claro, 1908–1983* (Rio Claro: Arquivo Público e Histórico, 1983), 17.

27. Rodolpho Telarolli, *Poder local na república velha* (São Paulo: Nacional, 1977), esp. 29–37, 165–68, 205–8; "Os assasinatos politicos recomeçaram no interior," *O Combate*, 13 Oct. 1916, p. 1; Heloisa Helena Michetti and M. Antonieta de A. G. Parahyba, "O jôgo das fôrças políticas da vida de Araraquara," *Revista de Ciência Política* 2, no. 3 (July-Sept. 1968): 62–67.

28. D. Abreu, *Formação histórica de uma cidade pioneira paulista*, esp. 45n.–47n., 82–90; P. Duarte, *Memórias*, 8:204–6; P. Duarte, unpublished manuscript (presumably a draft of unpublished volume[s] of his *Memórias*), p. 14, CEDAE, FPD, pasta PI.16; José Soares Marcondes, "Presidente Prudente," in secção livre of *O Estado de S. Paulo*, 4 Jan. 1927, p. 10; Tito Livio Brasil to Directorio Central, Presidente Prudente, n.d. [Feb. 1927], AIHGSP, APD, pacote 36; impresso, "Manifesto aos nossos amigos e correligionarios: A atitude do Partido Progressista," Presidente Prudente, 10 Nov. 1927, AIHGSP, APD, pacote 36; unsigned note [probably written by the state president's secretary, Lazary Guedes], n.d., with attachment: José Soares Marcondes to Julio Prestes de Albuquerque, Presidente Prudente, 30 Sept. 1929, AESP, AJPA, caixa AP11. On Campos Novos, see Cobra, *Em um recanto do sertão paulista*.

29. John D. French, "Industrial Workers and the Origin of Populist Politics

in the ABC Region of Greater São Paulo, 1900–1950" (Ph.D. diss., Yale University, 1985), 72–85; Octaviano A. Gaiarsa, *Santo André: Ontem, hoje, amanhã* (Santo André: Prefeitura Municipal, 1991), 96–99, 191; Itamir Lello Orsi and Eddy C. Paiva, *Famílias ilustres e tradicionais de Santo André* (n.p., 1991), 1:9; Wanderley dos Santos, *Antecedentes históricos do ABC paulista, 1550–1892* (São Bernardo: Prefeitura do Município, 1992), 230, 237–38; Assembléia Legislativa, *Legislativo paulista*, 83, 87–89, 102–3.

30. "As eleições," *O Combate*, 30 Oct. 1919, p. 3; "As eleições," *O Combate*, 31 Oct. 1919, p. 3; "A victoria esmagadora do coronel Julio de Andrade Silva," *O Combate*, 15 Dec. 1919, p. 1; "Grave conflicto em Osasco," *O Combate*, 8 Jan. 1920, p. 3; "Foram alveijadas a tiros o coronel Andrade Silva e dois de seus filhos," *O Combate*, 9 Jan. 1920, p. 1; "José Maia Filho foi apenas o braço executor do plano assassino," *O Combate*, 14 Jan. 1920, p. 1; "A politica," *O Combate*, 15 May 1920, p. 1; "O pleito de Osasco," *O Combate*, 15 May 1920, p. 3; "Politica de Osasco," *O Combate*, 1 June 1920, p. 1; "Politica da capital," *O Combate*, 23 June 1921, p. 3; "Politica e politicos," *O Combate*, 28 Oct. 1921, p. 3; "Politica e politicos," *O Combate*, 2 Jan. 1922, p. 1; "Intrigando . . . ," *O Combate*, 21 Nov. 1925, p. 4; "Intrigando . . . ," *O Combate*, 20 Dec. 1927, p. 6; "Intrigando . . . ," *O Combate*, 11 Jan. 1928, p. 6; "Intrigando . . . ," *O Combate*, 16 Jan. 1928, p. 2.

31. "Notas e informações," *O Estado de S. Paulo*, 24 Oct. 1913, p. 3; "Noticias diversas," *O Estado de S. Paulo*, 26 Oct. 1913, p. 7; Estanislau Pereira Borges, "Districto de Santa Ephigenia," 29 Oct. 1913, in secção livre, *O Estado de S. Paulo*, 30 Oct. 1913, p. 11; "Um vereador quer ser administrador de cemiterio," *O Combate*, 30 May 1916, p. 1; "Camara municipal," *O Combate*, 14 Jan. 1918, p. 1; "Ata da eleição da comissão diretora do Partido Republicano" (10 July 1920), in Carone and Junqueira, "Atas do Partido Republicano Paulista," 203; Estanislau Borges, "Santa Ephigenia," in secção livre, *O Estado de S. Paulo*, 19 Feb. 1921, p. 8.

32. *Twentieth Century Impressions of Brazil* (London: Lloyd's Greater Britain Publishing, 1913), 664; British Chamber of Commerce of São Paulo and Southern Brazil, *Personalidades no Brasil / Men of Affairs in Brazil* (São Paulo: [printed by São Paulo Editora], n.d.), 49; "Moradores do Cambucy . . . ," *O Combate*, 24 Dec. 1915, p. 1; "Camara municipal," *O Combate*, 14 Jan. 1918, p. 1; "Ata da eleição da comissão diretora do Partido Republicano" (10 July 1920), in Carone and Junqueira, "Atas do Partido Republicano Paulista," 203; "Coisas politicas," *O Combate*, 13 Dec. 1922, p. 1; "O pleito municipal de hontem na capital correu animadissimo," *O Combate*, 15 Dec. 1922, p. 1; Assembléia Legislativa, *Legislativo paulista*, 94.

33. Del Picchia, *A longa viagem*, 2:257; Zeila de Brito Fabri Demartini, "O coronelismo e a educação na 1.ª república," *Educação & Sociedade* 34 (Dec. 1989): 72; P. Duarte, *Memórias*, 7:297; Love, *São Paulo in the Brazilian Federation*, 131; "Vida social," *O Combate*, 5 Dec. 1922, p. 1; "O pleito municipal de hontem na capital correu animadissimo," *O Combate*, 15 Dec. 1922, p. 1; "Intri-

gando . . . ," *O Combate*, 17 Nov. 1925, p. 4; "Nas vesperas do pleito federal," *Diario da Noite*, 23 Feb. 1927, p. 3; Partido Democratico, *As fraudes de vereadores na capital de S. Paulo* (São Paulo: Empreza Graphica da *Revista dos Tribunaes*, 1929), 12–19, AIHGSP, APD, pacote 15, item 1. The kind of power wielded by neighborhood bosses like Molinaro, councilmen like Mário do Amaral, and citywide chieftains like Olavo Egydio was enough of a prize that influential leaders from elsewhere in the state also kept a hand in the capital's neighborhood, legislative, and public-sector politics. "A politica," *O Combate*, 29 Sept. 1916, p. 1; "A politica," *O Combate*, 14 Oct. 1919, p. 1; José Soares Marcondes to Julio Prestes de Albuquerque, São Paulo, 12 Nov. 1929, AESP, AJPA, caixa AP13 (including attachments, one of which [Marcondes to Prestes, São Paulo, 26 Nov. 1929] is a distinct document that must have been misfiled at some point in the process of organizing Prestes's papers); José Soares Marcondes to Julio Prestes de Albuquerque, São Paulo, 17 Jan. 1930, AESP, AJPA, caixa AP14; Penteado, *Memórias de um postalista*, 147.

34. Carlos Escobar, "Araçariguama," *O Combate*, 15 Aug. 1921, p. 1; Casalecchi, *O Partido Republicano Paulista*, 293; "Reorganização da comissão diretora do Partido Republicano, Ata da convenção dos diretórios municipais realizada no dia 22 de novembro de 1913," in Carone and Junqueira, "Atas do Partido Republicano Paulista," 301.

35. Casalecchi, *O Partido Republicano Paulista*, 291; "A politica," *O Combate*, 29 March 1919, p. 1; "O sr. Oscar faz tambem a sua politica," *O Combate*, 27 May 1919, p. 1.

36. "A politica," *O Combate*, 27 June 1917, p. 1; "Politica de Ubatuba," *O Combate*, 14 Jan. 1918, p. 2; "Ata da eleição da comissão diretora do Partido Republicano" (10 July 1920), in Carone and Junqueira, "Atas do Partido Republicano Paulista," 205; Ernesto de Oliveira et al. to Julio Prestes de Albuquerque, Ubatuba, 20 Dec. 1927, AESP, AJPA, caixa AP06. The quotes are from "O sr. Oscar faz tambem a sua politica," *O Combate*, 27 May 1919, p. 1.

37. See Oracy Nogueira's *Negro político, político negro* (São Paulo: Ed. da Universidade de São Paulo, 1992), the great Cunha-born social scientist's last book, a semi-fictionalized biography of Casemiro da Rocha; also Assembléia Legislativa, *Legislativo paulista*, 84, 88, 90–94, 104; "Reorganização da comissão diretora do Partido Republicano, Ata da convenção dos diretórios municipais realizada no dia 22 de novembro de 1913" and "Ata da eleição da comissão diretora do Partido Republicano" (10 July 1920), both of which are published in Carone and Junqueira, "Atas do Partido Republicano Paulista," 194, 203; Robert W. Shirley, *The End of a Tradition: Culture Change and Development in the Município of Cunha, São Paulo, Brazil* (New York: Columbia University Press, 1971), 80–83, 97, 103, 209, 215. Shirley, an anthropologist, used the pseudonym "Thales de Salvador" to refer to Casemiro da Rocha.

38. O. Nogueira, *Negro político, político negro*; Shirley, *The End of a Tradition*, 80–83, 97.

39. Gifun, "Ribeirão Prêto, 1880–1914," 135–36, 142 n. 18, 161, 185; Walker, "Ribeirão Preto, 1910–1960," 55, 58–64; Jardim, *Reminiscências*, 200–1; "Em Ribeirão Preto," *O Combate*, 5 Jan. 1918, p. 3; Carlos Escobar, "O pennacho," *O Combate*, 13 May 1920, p. 1; Leite Lopes to Paulo Nogueira Filho, Ribeirão Preto, 27 Jan. 1927, AIHGSP, APD, pacote 36.

40. Cobra, *Em um recanto do sertão paulista*, 148; Motta Filho, *Contagem regressiva*, 195–96; D. Abreu, *Formação histórica de uma cidade pioneira paulista*, 208, 216; Brenno Ferraz [do Amaral], *Cidades vivas* (São Paulo: Monteiro Lobato, 1924), 123–24.

41. D. Abreu, *Formação histórica de uma cidade pioneira paulista*, passim (see esp. p. 216); C. [Carlos] Castilho Cabral, *Batalhões patrioticos na revolução de 1924* (São Paulo: Livraria Liberdade, 1927), 14–15; P. Duarte, *Memórias*, 8:204–6; P. Duarte, unpublished manuscript, p. 14, CEDAE, FPD, pasta PI.16; Pierre Monbeig, *Pioneiros e fazendeiros de São Paulo*, trans. Ary França and Raul de Andrade e Silva (São Paulo: Hucitec, 1984), 143–45, 202–3; "Os successos em Pennapolis," *O Combate*, 3 July 1918, p. 4; "A politica," *O Combate*, 28 Aug. 1918, p. 1.

42. "Como os olympistas venceram em Cajobi," *O Combate*, 11 Nov. 1916, p. 1; "O conselheiro obteve em Itapetininga 1.024 votos!," *O Combate*, 25 Nov. 1916, p. 1; French, "Industrial Workers and the Origin of Populist Politics in the ABC Region of Greater São Paulo, 1900–1950," 24–25; Motta Filho, *Contagem regressiva*, 172; Penteado, *Memórias de um postalista*, 147–48; Walker, "Ribeirão Preto, 1910–1960," 77 n. 39.

43. José Molinaro, "Eleição municipal," in secção livre of *O Estado de S. Paulo*, 26 Oct. 1913, p. 12; Molinaro, "Bom Retiro," in secção livre of *O Estado de S. Paulo*, 29 Oct. 1913, p. 11; Molinaro, "Eleição municipal," in secção livre of *O Estado de S. Paulo*, 30 Oct. 1913, p. 11; "As manobras de um cabo eleitoral estrangeiro," *O Combate*, 27 Oct. 1920, p. 3.

44. "Eleições," *O Estado de S. Paulo*, 18 Dec. 1901, p. 1; Veiga Miranda, "A eleições municipaes em S. Paulo," *O Imparcial* (Rio de Janeiro), mid-Oct. 1913, in secção livre of *O Estado de S. Paulo*, 19 Oct. 1913, p. 12; "A reforma eleitoral," *O Combate*, 5 Aug. 1916, p. 1; "Quem não é eleitor, não é bom cidadão," *O Combate*, 4 June 1918, p. 1; "Porque votou com o Partido Municipal de Itapetininga, foi demittido!," *O Combate*, 2 Dec. 1919, p. 1; "Votar contra seus superiores é um acto de indisciplina!," *O Combate*, 10 Dec. 1919, p. 1; Casemiro de Carvalho Paulista to Directorio Central do PD, São Carlos, 2 March 1927, AIHGSP, APD, pacote 37; Casemiro de Carvalho Paulista to Directorio Central do PD, São Carlos, 29 Aug. 1927, AIHGSP, APD, pacote 37; Basilio Batalha to Directores do PD, Mogy das Cruzes, 25 Nov. 1927, AIHGSP, APD, pacote 36; "Pela politica" (newspaper clipping labeled *Folha da Noite*, 1 March 1928), AIHGSP, APD, album X; Orizombo Loureiro to Directorio Central do PD, Jahú, 8 Feb. 1929, AIHGSP, APD, pacote 9; José Borges to Julio Prestes de Albuquerque, São Paulo, 12 Aug. 1929, AESP, AJPA, caixa AP09; *A camara e a*

prefeitura de Guaratinguetá perante as commissões de syndicancia estadual e municipal: Assombrosos documentos encontrados no archivo da extincta camara ([Guaratinguetá?]: Typ. Ferreira, 1931), CEDAE, FPD, pasta DET.139; D. Abreu, *Formação histórica de uma cidade pioneira paulista*, 216–17; Del Rios, *Ourinhos*, 38–39, 164; French, "Industrial Workers and the Origin of Populist Politics in the ABC Region of Greater São Paulo, 1900–1950," 78; Oracy Nogueira, *Família e comunidade: Um estudo sociológico de Itapetininga* (Rio de Janeiro: Centro Brasileiro de Pesquisas Educacionais, 1962), 534–35; Penteado, *Memórias de um postalista*, 44, 148. Receipts from electoral expenses ranging from beer to lunches to payments to cabos responsible for voter registration make up a large part of the "Documentação Pessoal" series of Joaquim da Cunha's papers. AESP, AJCDJ, caixa AP175.

45. Interview with Paulo Duarte by Lúcio Lahmeyer Lobo and Rodrigo Belingrodt Marques Coelho, São Paulo, 16 Mar. 1977, CPDOC, PHO; Mario de Andrade, "Osvaldo de Andrade," *Revista do Brasil*, Sept. 1924, p. 33; Benedito Carlos Marcondes Coelho, *O processo político da comunidade guaratinguetaense* (Santos: Secretaria de Estado da Cultura, 1982), 21; O. Nogueira, "Os movimentos e partidos políticos em Itapetininga," 241; Eduardo Maffei, *A greve: Romance* (Rio de Janeiro: Paz e Terra, 1978), 33. Maffei's *A greve* is the first volume of a tetralogy, marketed as historical fiction but also including nonfictionalized "Contrapuntos" and even in some of its purely novelistic passages containing factual material drawing on the author's own experiences and his research on early-twentieth-century Brazilian history.

46. "Um appello ao sr. Coronel Fernando Prestes," *O Combate*, 28 June 1915, p. 1; "A politica," *O Combate*, 25 Sept. 1916, p. 1; "A regeneração das finanças de São Carlos," *O Combate*, 7 Nov. 1916, p. 1; "Os gastos excessivos da prefeitura," *O Combate*, 29 Dec. 1916, p. 1; "Os successos de Santos," *O Combate*, 13 Jan. 1917, p. 1; "A isenção de impostos ao Instituto Paulista" and "Como são dispendidas as rendas de Baurú," *O Combate*, 7 Mar. 1917, p. 3; "A politica," *O Combate*, 12 Nov. 1918, p. 1; "A desgraçada situação de Palmeiras," *O Combate*, 16 Dec. 1918, p. 3; Carlos Escobar, "O pennacho," *O Combate*, 13 May 1920, p. 1; *Progress in South America: The Remarkable Growth of the City and State of Sao Paulo* (London: Office of *The Sphere*, n.d.), 8; D. Abreu, *Formação histórica de uma cidade pioneira paulista*, 155–57, 301–3; Roberto Capri, *O estado de São Paulo e seus municipios*, 3 vols. in 1 (São Paulo: n.p., 1913) 2:8; Coelho, *O processo político da comunidade guaratinguetaense*, 45–46, 48–49; Del Rios, *Ourinhos*, 24–27, 75–77; Teresinha Paiva de Faria et al., *Decadência do café numa comunidade vale-paraibana* (Guaratinguetá: n.p., 1973), 59–63; French, "Industrial Workers and the Origin of Populist Politics in the ABC Region of Greater São Paulo, 1900–1950," 82–84; Gifun, "Ribeirão Prêto, 1880–1914," 116, 144 n. 25; Love, *São Paulo in the Brazilian Federation*, 126, 131, 259; Cunha Mendes, *A psychologia do eleitorado brasileiro* (Rio de Janeiro: Leite Ribeiro, 1926), 220–26; O. Nogueira, "Os movimentos e partidos políticos em Itape-

tininga," 239, 241; Paulo Nogueira Filho, *Ideais e lutas de um burguês prog-ressista: O Partido Democrático de São Paulo e a revolução de 1930*, 2 vols. (São Paulo: Anhambi, 1958), 1:169; Osorio Rocha, *Barretos de outrora* (São Paulo: n.p., 1954), 293; Walker, "Ribeirão Preto, 1910–1960," 55–58; "É preciso deixar o povo falar" (interview with Caio Prado Júnior by Lourenço Dantas Mota, Oliveiros S. Ferreira, and Carlos Estevam Martins, 11 June 1978), in *A história vivida*, 3 vols., ed. Lourenço Dantas Mota (São Paulo: *O Estado de São Paulo*, 1981–1982), 1:303.

47. "É preciso deixar . . .," in L. Mota, *A história vivida*, 1:311; D. Abreu, *Formação histórica de uma cidade pioneira paulista*, 210, 218; Coelho, *O processo político da comunidade guaratinguetaense*, 37; Del Picchia, *A longa viagem*, 2:83–85; French, "Industrial Workers and the Origin of Populist Politics in the ABC Region of Greater São Paulo, 1900–1950," 83–84; Leão, *S. Paulo em 1920*, 116–18; Aureliano Leite, *Subsídios para a história da civilização paulista* (São Paulo: Saraiva, 1954), 267; Love, *São Paulo in the Brazilian Federation*, 129; Fabio Barreto to Joaquim da Cunha Diniz Junqueira, Ribeirão Preto, 28 Jan. 1926 [*sic*], AESP, AJCDJ, caixa AP174, pasta 3; Fabio Barreto to Joaquim da Cunha Diniz Junqueira, Ribeirão Preto, 10 Feb. 1927, AESP, AJCDJ, caixa AP174, pasta 3; Saladino Cardoso Franco to Julio Prestes de Albuquerque, São Bernardo, 27 June 1928 (with marginalia [by Julio Prestes or Lazary Guedes?]), AESP, AJPA, caixa AP07; Waldomiro Borges Canto to José Soares Marcondes, Presidente Wenceslau, 2 May 1929, AESP, AJPA, caixa AP08.

48. "Ata da reunião de 8 de abril [de 1892]," in Carone and Junqueira, "Atas do Partido Republicano Paulista," 143; "Ata da reunião de 9 de abril [de 1892]," in ibid., 144; "Ata da reunião de 1.º de maio [de 1892]," in ibid., 145; Saladino Cardoso Franco to Julio Prestes de Albuquerque, São Bernardo, 27 June 1928 (with marginalia [by Julio Prestes]), AESP, AJPA, caixa AP07; D. Abreu, *Formação histórica de uma cidade pioneira paulista*, 211; Coelho, *O processo político da comunidade guaratinguetaense*, 26, 28, 30, 33–35, 37; Del Rios, *Ourinhos*, 38–39; Demartini, "O coronelismo e a educação *na 1.ª república*," 56–57, 62, 64–66; P. Duarte, *Memórias*, 8:208; Faria et al., *Decadência do café numa comunidade vale-paraibana*, 54–55.

49. Ivan Subiroff (pseud., Nereu Rangel Pestana), "Os 1.000 alqueires do padrinho," *O Combate*, 9 June 1920, p. 1; D. Abreu, *Formação histórica de uma cidade pioneira paulista*, 183–84, 187; Del Rios, *Ourinhos*, 19, 26, 166; Demartini, "O coronelismo e a educação *na 1.ª república*," 48–49, 54–55; P. Duarte, *Memórias*, 8:208; Love, *São Paulo in the Brazilian Federation*, 330 n. 53; Alves Motta Sobrinho, *Gama Rodrigues: Humanista e médico, 1.º deputado municipalista brasileiro* (São Paulo: Sala Euclides da Cunha, 1962), 34; O. Nogueira, *Família e comunidade*, 189, 192–93, 533–37; Antonio da Gama Rodrigues, *Gens lorenensis: Do sertão de Guayparé à formosa cidade de Lorena, 1646–1946* (n.p., 1956), 125–126, 131, 133, 138; Walker, "Ribeirão Preto, 1910–1960," 59. The lion's share of these projects were state works rather than federal public works. As

Love notes, federal public works were relatively unimportant in São Paulo as a whole (*São Paulo in the Brazilian Federation*, 198–99).

50. "A Guarda Nacional foi dissolvida," *O Combate*, 30 May 1918, p. 1; Beattie, *The Tribute of Blood*, 32, 103–4, 210, 272; Cione, *História de Ribeirão Preto*, 253; Jacob Penteado, *Belenzinho, 1910: Retrato de uma época* (São Paulo: Martins, 1962), 196–99; A. Prado, *Crônica de outrora*, 64; Rocha, *Barretos de outrora*, 221; A. Rodrigues, *Gens lorenensis*, 123–24; Nelson Palma Travassos, *Quando eu era menino . . .* (São Paulo: EdArt, 1960), 34; P. P. (pseud., Paulo Rangel Pestana), "A vida nacional," *O Estado de S. Paulo*, 9 Jan. 1908, p. 1. Paulo Rangel Pestana is identified as "P. P." in Eugenio Egas, *Galeria dos presidentes de São Paulo*, 3 vols. (São Paulo: Secção de Obras d' *O Estado de S. Paulo*, 1926–1927), 2:10.

51. As suggested in Antônio de Alcântara Machado's *crônicas* "Notas biográficas do novo deputado" and "Nacionalidade," in *Brás, Bexiga e Barra Funda*, repr. ed. (Belo Horizonte: Vila Rica Editores, n.d. [first published 1927], pp. 57–62, 69–76); also, Carlos Castilho Cabral, *Tempos de Jânio e outros tempos* (Rio de Janeiro: Civilização Brasileira, 1962), 5; Coelho, *O processo político da comunidade guaratinguetaense*, 34–35; Paulo Duarte, *Agora nós* (São Paulo: n.p., 1927), 298–99; Jayme Leonel et al., *O último dos coronéis*, 13; Wladimir Toledo Piza, *Por quem morreu Getúlio Vargas* (Rio de Janeiro: Ampersand, 1998), 48; "Écos e factos," *O Combate*, 24 April 1915, p. 1; "O caso da gratificação ao proprio filho," *O Combate*, 21 March 1917, p. 1; " 'O Combate' em Campinas," *O Combate*, 14 March 1921, p. 3; P. Duarte, unpublished manuscript, pp. 248–49, CEDAE, FPD, pasta PI.17.

52. Francisco Glycerio and Washington Luis Pereira de Sousa, "Aos paulistas e aos brasileiros," São Paulo, 8 Jan. 1900, reprinted in Assis Cintra, *Os escandalos da 1.ª república* (São Paulo: J. Fagundes, 1936), 139–45 (see p. 142); Carlos Escobar, "O pennacho," *O Combate*, 13 May 1920, p. 1; Ivan Subiroff (pseud., Nereu Rangel Pestana), "Os 1.000 alqueires do padrinho," *O Combate*, 9 June 1920, p. 1; "Tudo se harmonisará," *O Combate*, 28 Oct. 1922, p. 1; M. Carlos, "A moderação e virtude nas chefias," *A Propaganda*, July 1925, unpag.; D. Abreu, *Formação histórica de uma cidade pioneira paulista*, 68–69; Dean, *The Industrialization of São Paulo, 1880–1945*, 44–45, 101–2; Dean, "The Planter as Entrepreneur": The Case of São Paulo," *Hispanic American Historical Review* 46, no. 2 (May 1966): 147; Del Rios, *Ourinhos*, 25–26, 166, 206; Faria et al., *Decadência do café numa comunidade vale-paraibana*, 55; French, "Industrial Workers and the Origin of Populist Politics in the ABC Region of Greater São Paulo, 1900–1950," 82–83; Love, *São Paulo in the Brazilian Federation*, esp. chaps. 2 and 5.

53. "Eleições municipaes," *O Estado de S. Paulo*, 30 Oct. 1919, p. 4; "Intrigando . . . ," *O Combate*, 5 Oct. 1927, p. 6; W. Piza, *Por quem morreu Getúlio Vargas*, 48; Alvaro Ribeiro, *Falsa democracia / A revolução em São Paulo em 1924* (Rio de Janeiro: F. de Piro & Cia., 1927), 78n.–79n.

54. Assembléia Legislativa, *Legislativo paulista*, 70; "A politica," *O Combate*,

10 April 1919, p. 1; Lauresto E. (pseud., Nicolau Soares do Couto Esher), "Uma comedia no senado," *O Combate*, 31 Dec. 1925, p. 8.

55. "Eleições municipaes," *O Estado de S. Paulo*, 30 Oct. 1919, p. 4; Rosa Fátima de Souza, *O direito à educação: Lutas populares pela escola em Campinas* (Campinas: Ed. da Universidade Estadual de Campinas, 1998), 120n.

56. João Xavier Dias da Costa to Nilo Peçanha, Jundiahy, 4 March 1922, MR, ANP, caixa 27, pasta 1; P. Duarte, *Memórias*, 8:332–33.

57. In São Paulo, the much discussed "right" to minority representation ultimately depended on the whim of the sitting state president; there was nothing comparable to the guaranteed one-third of all state and federal legislative posts provided for in Rio Grande do Sul. Assembléia Legislativa, *Legislativo paulista*, 77; Love, *Rio Grande do Sul*, 87–88.

58. Estado de São Paulo, *Lei e regulamento sobre a qualificação eleitoral do estado de São Paulo* (São Paulo: Typographia do *Diario Official*, 1900); Assembléia Legislativa, *Legislativo paulista*, 73–74; Victor Nunes Leal, *Coronelismo: The Municipality and Representative Government in Brazil*, trans. June Henfrey (Cambridge: Cambridge University Press, 1977 [1949]), 121–24; Joseph L. Love, "Political Participation in Brazil, 1881–1969," *Luso-Brazilian Review* 7, no. 2 (Dec. 1970): 7; Maria Lígia Coelho Prado, *A democracia ilustrada: O Partido Democrático de São Paulo, 1926–1934* (São Paulo: Ática, 1986), 59–60; Rodolpho Telarolli, *Eleições e fraudes eleitorais na república velha* (São Paulo: Brasiliense, 1982), 9–10, 13–16, 21, 23–26.

59. Assembléia Legislativa, *Legislativo paulista*, 73–74; "Notas e informações," *O Estado de S. Paulo*, 28 Feb. 1910, p. 1; "Noticias do interior," *O Estado de S. Paulo*, 23 Oct. 1913, p. 2; "Noticias do interior e do litoral do estado," *O Estado de S. Paulo*, 2 Nov. 1913, p. 5; Goffredo T. da Silva Telles, "Politica," *O Estado de S. Paulo*, 5 Nov. 1919, p. 3; Paulo Aguiar Souza to José Adriano Marrey Junior, Araraquara, 19 Feb. 1927, AIHGSP, APD, pacote 35.

60. Valentim Gentil et al. to Julio Prestes de Albuquerque, Itapolis, 28 July 1928, AESP, AJPA, caixa AP07.

61. Jardim, *Reminscências*, 208–9.

62. "Questionario" filled out by Persio de Queiroz, São Paulo, 16 Dec. 1926, AIHGSP, APD, pacote 34; "Questionario" filled out by Arthur Cruz Galvão do Rio Apa, São Paulo, 27 Dec. 1926, AIHGSP, APD, pacote 33; Camillo Lellis to Direcção do PD, Itapetininga, 17 Feb. 1927, AIHGSP, APD, pacote 33 (misfiled document); João Luiz da Costa to "Amigo Dr. Jayme," Salto Grande, 20 Aug. 1929, AESP, AJPA, caixa AP10; Alvaro A. Coelho to Julio Prestes de Albuquerque, Presidente Wenceslau, 8 Oct. 1929, AESP, AJPA, caixa AP20.

63. For example, in 1902 the state's electoral rolls contained 105,534 names, but only 42,077 votes were tallied in state presidential elections held that year, while 53,908 votes were tallied in federal presidential elections held the same year. Twenty years later, the state claimed 164,234 voters; in the semicompetitive national presidential election held that year, 99,355 paulistas

were said to have voted. In 1930, 516,651 names appeared on voter rolls, but only 365,600 votes were tallied. Love, *São Paulo in the Brazilian Federation*, 143, 335.

64. Assembléia Legislativa, *Legislativo paulista*, 74–75; Telarolli, *Eleições e fraudes eleitorais na república velha*, 34–38; "A politica," *O Combate*, 24 Nov. 1916, p. 1; "As eleições do dia 30," *O Combate*, 28 Oct. 1919, p. 1; "As eleições," *O Combate*, 31 Oct. 1919, p. 3; "Aos republicanos de S. Paulo," *O Estado de S. Paulo*, 13 Dec. 1901, p. 1; "Eleições," *O Estado de S. Paulo*, 17 Dec. 1901, pp. 1–2.

65. Assembléia Legislativa, *Legislativo paulista*, 74–75. The degree to which the practice of open voting reinforced the structure of politics outlined above was emphasized by Mário Pinto Serva: "There is no electoral liberty. . . . The public functionary is afraid of the government, the colono or rural worker is afraid of the planter, the planter is afraid of the chefe politico, the chefe politico is afraid of the Executive Committee, the worker is afraid of the factory owner, the debtor is afraid of the creditor, the congressman is afraid of the president. . . ." Serva, "A mascara da republica," in his *O voto secreto, ou a organisação de partidos nacionaes* (São Paulo: Imprensa Methodista, n.d.), 51.

66. Assembléia Legislativa, *Legislativo paulista*, 74–78; Telarolli, *Eleições e fraudes eleitorais na república velha*, 40, 49–50. Even the provision that the polling board and ballot box be set up at some distance from the assembled voters was flouted, as in Iguape in 1901. "Aos republicanos de S. Paulo," *O Estado de S. Paulo*, 19 Dec. 1901, p. 2.

67. "Quem não é eleitor, não é bom cidadão," *O Combate*, 4 June 1918, p. 1; D. Abreu, *Formação histórica de uma cidade pioneira paulista*, 217; O. Nogueira, "Os movimentos e partidos políticos em Itapetininga," 240–41; Assembléia Legislativa, *Legislativo paulista*, 74.

68. Benjamin Mota, "O direito do voto," *O Combate*, 14 Dec. 1915, p. 1; "A machina de fazer senadores e deputados funccionou admiravelmente," *O Combate*, 3 Feb. 1916, p. 1; "Os operarios da Limpeza Publica não têm liberdade de voto?," *O Combate*, 11 Oct. 1922, p. 1; A. Paulino, "Em torno das eleições municipaes," *O Combate*, 8 Nov. 1928, p. 6.

69. Bilac, *As elites políticas de Rio Claro*, 57; Telarolli, *Eleições e fraudes eleitorais na república velha*, 78. It should be added that in still other cases, the prospect of political violence made the approach of election days something that rural folks greatly feared.

70. "Documentação Pessoal" series, AESP, AJCDJ, caixa AP175; *A camara e a prefeitura de Guaratinguetá perante as commissões de syndicancia estadual e municipal: Assombrosos documentos encontrados no archivo da extincta camara* ([Guaratinguetá?]: Typ. Ferreira, 1931), CEDAE, FPD, pasta DET.139; D. Abreu, *Formação histórica de uma cidade pioneira paulista*, 217; Del Rios, *Ourinhos*, 164; French, "Industrial Workers and the Origin of Populist Politics in the ABC Region of Greater São Paulo, 1900–1950," 78; Jardim, *Reminiscências*, 199; O. Nogueira, *Família e comunidade*, 535; Penteado, *Memórias de um postalista*, 148.

71. "Eleições," *O Estado de S. Paulo*, 17 Dec. 1901, p. 2; "Uma eleição de vereador disputada," *O Combate*, 5 Jan. 1918, p. 3; "Um appello que tambem serve para S. Paulo," *O Combate*, 23 Feb. 1918, p. 3; P., "Coisas da cidade," *O Estado de S. Paulo*, 1 Nov. 1919, p. 5; D. Abreu, *Formação histórica de uma cidade pioneira paulista*, 217; French, "Industrial Workers and the Origin of Populist Politics in the ABC Region of Greater São Paulo, 1900–1950," 78; Assembléia Legislativa, *Legislativo paulista*, 75; Travassos, *Quando eu era menino . . .*, 105–7.

72. Assembléia Legislativa, *Legislativo paulista*, 76; French, "Industrial Workers and the Origin of Populist Politics in the ABC Region of Greater São Paulo, 1900–1950," 78.

73. See Assembléia Legislativa, *Legislativo paulista*, 75; Telarolli, *Eleições e fraudes eleitorais na república velha*, 87.

74. Felix Guimarães Junior, "Bom Retiro," in secção livre of *O Estado de S. Paulo*, 28 Oct. 1913, p. 10; Leopoldo Amaral, "Reminiscencias," *O Estado de S. Paulo*, 29 Oct. 1913, p. 3 (which refers to the use of phosphoros under the empire); Telarolli, *Eleições e fraudes eleitorais na república velha*, 87–88; Penteado, *Memórias de um postalista*, 147–48.

75. "A politica," *O Combate*, 17 Sept. 1919, p. 1. See also Nogueira Filho, *Ideais e lutas de um burguês progressista*, 1:50–51; "A acção do Partido Municipal Ararense," *O Municipal* (Araras), 11 Jan. 1920, in secção livre of *O Estado de S. Paulo*, 13 Jan. 1920, p. 8; "Eleições municipaes," *O Estado de S. Paulo*, 17 Dec. 1922, p. 4.

76. "A bico de pena" translates as "by the tip of a pen," while "a Mallat" refers to a brand of pen imported from France. Sebastião Teixeira, *O Jahú em 1900: Repositorio de dados, informações e documentos para a historia do Jahú* (Jahú: Correio do Jahú, 1900), 89–90, uses the two terms interchangeably, as does "Triumpha a Mallat," *O Combate*, 3 Aug. 1915, p. 4.

77. "Eleições," *O Estado de S. Paulo*, 17 Dec. 1901, p. 1; "O pleito de sabbado," *O Combate*, 28 April 1919, p. 1.

78. Nogueira Filho, *Ideais e lutas de um burguês progressista*, 1:50–51 (quote on p. 51).

79. P. Duarte, untitled manuscript, page labeled both 262a and 264, CEDAE, FPD, pasta PI.17.

80. The quote is from a telegram, Julio Mesquita [to Ruy Barbosa], [São Paulo], 13 [April 1919], CRB, ARB, CR.E 25/20, doc. 976. See also Travassos, *Quando eu era menino . . .*, 107–9.

81. Antonio Feliciano to "Prezado Paulo," Santos, 28 Jan. 1927, AIHGSP, APD, pacote 37.

82. "A politica," *O Combate*, 10 Nov. 1916, p. 1.

83. "Politica de bugre e liberdade de voto," *O Combate*, 15 Dec. 1919, p. 1.

84. Letter [to *O Estado de S. Paulo*], Mococa, n.d., printed in *O Estado de S. Paulo*, 22 Dec. 1901, p. 2; "Eleições," *O Estado de S. Paulo*, 18 Dec. 1901, p. 1; "Os municipios," *O Estado de S. Paulo*, 26 Feb. 1910, p. 3.

85. Telegram [to *O Estado de S. Paulo*], Santos, 15 Dec. 1901, printed in *O Estado de S. Paulo*, 16 Dec. 1901, p. 1.

86. "As eleições de hoje," *O Combate*, 30 Oct. 1916, p. 1.

87. Claudio José de Souza to Julio Prestes de Albuquerque, Sallesopolis, 3 March 1930, AESP, AJPA, caixa AP15.

88. Political violence could, and did, occur independently of electoral politics. For an interesting micro-historical study of one such case, see Telarolli, *Poder local na república velha*.

89. "Eleições municipaes," *O Estado de S. Paulo*, 17 Dec. 1922, p. 4; "Eleições municipaes," *O Estado de S. Paulo*, 21 Dec. 1922, p. 4; "Eleições municipaes," *O Estado de S. Paulo*, 24 Dec. 1922, p. 4; "A tragedia de Palmital," in secção livre of *O Estado de S. Paulo*, 21 Sept. 1923, p. 8; P. Duarte, *Memórias*, 8:333; A. Leite, *Subsídios para a história da civilização paulista*, 297–99.

90. Candinho's patron, Ataliba Leonel, was implicated as well, though never convicted. "Ataliba Leonel," in A. Abreu et al., *Dicionário histórico-biográfico brasileiro*, 3:3096.

91. Antonio Paixão, "Relatorio," Guaratinguetá, 20 Sept. 1929: enclosure "Relatorio das pessoas, que, nesta cidade passaram a apoir a Alliança," AESP, AJPA, caixa AP29, pasta 71.

92. Orizombo Loureiro to Directorio Central, Jahú, 8 Feb. 1929, AIHGSP, APD, pacote 9.

93. "A politica," *O Combate*, 27 March 1916, p. 1.

94. "A scisão no Partido Municipal," *O Combate*, 15 Jan. 1919, p. 1.

95. J. A. Meira Junior to Joaquim da Cunha Diniz Junqueira, Ribeirão Preto, 30 Oct. 1925, AESP, AJCDJ, caixa AP174, pasta 3.

96. Zulmiro de Campos, *Vultos de Sorocaba* (São Paulo: Sociedade Editora Olegario Ribeiro, 1921), 105–7; *O Estado de S. Paulo*, 16 Dec. 1909, p. 5.

97. Cobra, *Em um recanto do sertão paulista*, quotes on pp. 147, 179.

98. Egas, *Galeria dos presidentes de São Paulo*, 2:5.

99. Ibid., 115–16.

100. "Eleições," *O Estado de S. Paulo*, 18 Dec. 1901, p. 1.

101. Quotes from Beattie, *The Tribute of Blood*, 175. See also Graham, *Patronage and Politics in Nineteenth-Century Brazil*, 17–18; O. Nogueira, *Família e comunidade*, 529, 534.

102. Carlos Escobar, "As adhesões," *O Combate*, 20 Jan. 1922, p. 1; Melo, *Dicionário de autores paulistas*, 201; "Aos republicanos de S. Paulo," *O Estado de S. Paulo*, 13 Dec. 1901, p. 1. The racialization of citizenship implied in references to "slaves" and "slavishness" is the subject of further discussion below, this chap.

103. "Noticias de Bebedouro" (newspaper clipping, labeled *Diario da Noite*, 5 June 1926), AIHGSP, APD, album II.

104. "O assassinato do coronel Accacio Piedade," *O Parafuso*, 3 Nov. 1917, unpag.

105. "Quantos eleitores independentes ha no 1.º districto?," *O Parafuso,* 25 March 1917, unpag.

106. José Brasil Paulista Piedade, "Ao digno e independente eleitorado da capital," in secção livre of *O Estado de S. Paulo,* 15 Oct. 1913, p. 9; "O sr. Marrey Junior contra o sr. Alcantara Machado?," *O Combate,* 7 Oct. 1919, p. 1.

107. Telegram from *Correio de Botucatu* [to *O Estado de S. Paulo*], 28 Oct. 1904, in *O Estado de S. Paulo,* 29 Oct. 1904, p. 1.

108. "Eleições," *O Estado de S. Paulo,* 1 Nov. 1904, p. 1.

109. Motta Filho, *Contagem regressiva,* 128.

110. Estanislau Pereira Borges, "Districto de Santa Ephigenia," São Paulo, 29 Oct. 1913, in secção livre, *O Estado de S. Paulo,* 30 Oct. 1913, p. 11.

111. "A politica," *O Combate,* 5 March 1919, p. 1.

112. Hydelbrando C. Paranhos to Julio Prestes de Albuquerque, S. Luis de Parahytinga, 28 Aug. 1927, AESP, AJPA, caixa AP06; Hydelbrando C. Paranhos to Washington Luiz, S. Luis do Parahytinga, 20 April 1928, AESP, AJPA, caixa AP07.

113. Manuel Vaz to Julio Prestes de Albuquerque, Viradouro, n.d., AESP, AJPA, caixa AP21.

114. Viriato Carneiro Lopes to Julio Prestes de Albuquerque, Sta. Cruz do Rio Pardo, 25 July 1929, AESP, AJPA, caixa AP09. On Rafael Sampaio, see P. Duarte, *Memórias,* 3:352–53; Assembléia Legislativa, *Legislativo paulista,* 93–95, 97, 104; untitled note, *O Combate,* 10 Feb. 1919, p. 1; "Tonico Lista está na rua!," *O Combate,* 5 Nov. 1921, p. 1.

115. Lauro Costa to Julio Prestes de Albuquerque, São Paulo, 30 Sept. 1929, AESP, AJPA, caixa AP11.

116. Lauro Costa to Julio Prestes de Albuquerque, São Paulo, 15 Oct. 1929, AESP, AJPA, caixa AP12.

117. O. Nogueira, *Família e comunidade,* 534.

118. "Eleições," *O Estado de S. Paulo,* 31 Oct. 1904, p. 1; Travassos, *Quando eu era menino . . . ,* 223.

119. Penteado, *Belenzinho, 1910,* 199–200.

120. Fausto, "Imigração e participação política na primeira república," 12 (citing *Correio Paulistano,* 28–29 Dec. 1928); quote from Love, *São Paulo in the Brazilian Federation,* 131.

121. Cf., for example, J. M. de Carvalho, *A formação das almas.*

122. Presidente de São Paulo, *Mensagem enviada ao congresso legislativo, a 7 de abril de 1897, por Campos Salles, presidente do estado* (n.p., 1897), 104.

123. "Os municipios," *O Estado de S. Paulo,* 18 Dec. 1909, p. 4; "De S. Vicente," *O Combate,* 19 Aug. 1916, p. 1; "A politica," *O Combate,* 12 March 1919, p. 1; "Noticias diversas," *O Estado de S. Paulo,* 12 Feb. 1924, p. 4; *O Progresso* (Santa Branca), 6 March 1927 (in AIHGSP, APD, album V); *O Progresso* (Faxina), 19 Feb. 1927 and 12 March 1927 (in AIHGSP, APD, album V); Antonio

Elias Barbosa to Nilo Peçanha, Ibirá, 3 March 1922, MR, ANP, caixa 26; B. Amaral, *Cidades vivas*, 85; French, "Industrial Workers and the Origin of Populist Politics in the ABC Region of Greater São Paulo, 1900–1950," 77; Maria Elisa Vercesi de Albuquerque, *Os jornais de bairro na cidade de São Paulo* (São Paulo: Imprensa Oficial do Estado, 1985), 21; Freitas Nobre, *História da imprensa de São Paulo* (São Paulo: Edições Leia, 1950), 156, 227.

124. Presidente de São Paulo, *Mensagem enviada ao congresso legislativo, a 7 de abril de 1897, por Campos Salles, presidente do estado*, 104.

125. "É hora!," Botucatu, n.d., quoted in "A politica," *O Combate*, 27 March 1916, p. 1.

126. On the founding of the elementary school, see Marco Alexandre de Aguiar, *Botucatu: Imprensa e ferrovia* (São Paulo: Arte e Ciência, 2001), 43–44. Between the 1890s and the 1910s, Cardoso de Almeida held a number of key posts in the state executive branch: secretary of justice, chief of police, secretary of the interior, secretary of agriculture, and secretary of the treasury. On the federal level, he also served briefly as president of the Banco do Brasil and as the leader of the São Paulo delegation to the lower house of the national legislature. See Love, *São Paulo in the Brazilian Federation*, 289–91, 293, 299–300.

127. "Noticias do interior," *O Estado de S. Paulo*, 20 Oct. 1913, p. 2.

128. Reynaldo Maia Santo to Julio Prestes de Albuquerque, São José do Barreiro, 18 Aug. 1927, AESP, AJPA, caixa AP06, a report corroborated by Antonio Soares Lara, "Politica de Barreiro," *O Regional* (Caçapava), 19 April 1925, unpag.

129. Valentim Gentil et al. to Julio Prestes de Albuquerque, Itapolis, 28 July 1928, AESP, AJPA, caixa AP07.

130. Odilon Negrão et al. to Julio Prestes de Albuquerque, Itapolis, 7 Oct. 1928, AESP, AJPA, caixa AP07.

131. Bento Ribeiro da Luz to Julio Prestes de Albuquerque, Itapolis, 16 Oct. 1928, AESP, AJPA, caixa AP07; telegram, [Bento] Ribeiro da Luz to Julio Prestes de Albuquerque, Itapolis, 26 Oct. 1928, AESP, AJPA, caixa AP22; telegram, Odilon Negrão and Valentim Gentil to Julio Prestes de Albuquerque, 28 Oct. 1928, AESP, AJPA, caixa AP22; Odilon Negrão to Julio Prestes de Albuquerque, Itapolis, 4 Nov. 1928, AESP, AJPA, caixa AP07; Odilon Negrão to Julio Prestes de Albuquerque, Itapolis, 25 Jan. 1929, AESP, AJPA, caixa AP08; Paes Leme Junior, *Breves notícias históricas sobre Itápolis*, unpag. section (p. 165 by my count); "Manifesto do Partido Republicano Popular lançado a 11 de agosto de 1928 e redigido pelo sr. Odilon Negrão" and "Discurso do sr. Odilon Negrão após a victória do seu partido," in ibid., 224–37.

132. Alvaro Coelho to Cel. Marcondes, Santos, 10 May 1929, AESP, AJPA, caixa AP08. Coelho is identified as the prefeito of Presidente Venceslau in Alvaro A. Carvalho to Julio Prestes de Albuquerque, 8 Oct. 1929, AESP, AJPA, caixa AP21.

133. Um caixeiro, "Limeira," in secção livre of *O Estado de S. Paulo*, 25 Oct. 1913, p. 10.

134. M. Albuquerque, *Os jornais de bairro na cidade de São Paulo*, provides an introduction (see p. 21 on Lapa's *O Progresso*); Ademir Medici, *Migração e urbanização: A presença de São Caetano na região do* ABC (São Paulo: Hucitec, 1993), 52–54; "Pinheiros ha dois annos," *O Pinheirense*, 7 July 1929, p. 1 ("electric, dizzying . . ." —a sign of the modernist times); "Pinheiros-Butantan," *O Pinheirense*, 9 Dec. 1923, p. 1.

135. Presidente de São Paulo, *Fala dirigida ao congresso constituinte de S. Paulo pelo governador do estado, Dr. Americo Braziliense de Almeida Mello, no dia 8 de junho de 1891* (n.p., 1891), 8–9.

136. "Correrão em ordem os trabalhos eleitoraes?," *O Combate*, 22 Oct. 1919, p. 1.

137. For example, "O papel da commissão directora na comarca de Santa Cruz do Rio Pardo," in secção livre of *O Estado de S. Paulo*, 23 April 1921, p. 8.

138. "Como se entende em S. Paulo a liberdade de imprensa," *O Parafuso*, 29 Sept. 1917, unpag.

139. Serva, *O voto secreto, ou a organisação de partidos nacionaes*, passim (quotes on pp. 255, 288, 290); Serva, "Na rectaguarda da civilização," *Revista do Brasil*, July 1920, pp. 208–11.

140. Serva, *O voto secreto, ou a organisação de partidos nacionaes*, 353–54 (quote on p. 353). Serva's lament was far from unprecedented: Partido Republicano de S. Paulo, *A scisão, 1901* (São Paulo: Typographia da Industrial de S. Paulo, 1901), 6; *O Tempo*, 3 Jan. 1903 and 15 Jan. 1903, quoted in Silvia Levi-Moreira, "Liberalismo e democracia na dissidência republicana paulista: Estudo sobre o Partido Republicano Dissidente de São Paulo, 1901–1906" (tese de doutorado, Universidade de São Paulo, 1991), 68–69.

141. On "The Importance of Being Culto" in the context of middle-class identity, see Owensby, *Intimate Ironies*, 58–62.

142. João Sampaio Leite and Francisco Santos Piragibe to Julio Prestes de Albuquerque, Lins, 19 Sept. 1929, AESP, AJPA, caixa AP11. Note the division of society into the "agricultural, commercial, [and] industrial" classes (the *classes conservadoras*), the liberal classes, and the working classes. The latter signifier came to be included in republican discourse well after the signified's contributions to paulista society.

143. "Politica de Araras," *O Combate*, 11 Sept. 1919, p. 1.

144. *A Provincia de São Paulo*, 16 Nov. 1889, p. 2.

145. J. M. de Carvalho, *A formação das almas*, 13.

146. Ibid. "Noticias do interior," *O Estado de S. Paulo*, 30 Oct. 1913, p. 2, includes a rather late use of the address "Citizen voter."

147. Saladino Cardoso Franco [to *O Estado de S. Paulo*], São Bernardo, 14 Dec. 1901, in *O Estado de S. Paulo*, 15 Dec. 1901, p. 1.

148. Queiroz [to *O Estado de S. Paulo*], Faxina, 31 Oct. 1904, in *O Estado de S.*

Paulo, 1 Nov. 1904, p. 1. On Faxina and Accacio Piedade: "Ser opposicionista em Pirajú é ser heróe," *O Combate*, 8 Jan. 1916, p. 1; "A politica," *O Combate*, 3 Feb. 1916, p. 1; "Os assassinatos politicos," *O Combate*, 13 Oct. 1916, p. 1; "Como se entende em S. Paulo a liberdade de imprensa," *O Parafuso*, 29 Sept. 1917, unpag.; "O assassinio do deputado Accacio Piedade," *O Combate*, 26 Oct. 1917, p. 1; "O assassinato do coronel Accacio Piedade," *O Parafuso*, 3 Nov. 1917, unpag.

149. Prudente de Moraes et al., "Aos republicanos de S. Paulo," 7 Sept. 1901, in Levi-Moreira, "Liberalismo e democracia na dissidência republicana paulista," 172–77 (quotes on p. 176).

150. "Aos republicanos de S. Paulo," *O Estado de S. Paulo*, 29 Oct. 1901, p. 1.

151. For example (the emphasis is *not* added): "Notas e informações," *O Estado de S. Paulo*, 5 Feb. 1924, p. 3; "Notas e informações," *O Estado de S. Paulo*, 6 Feb. 1924, p. 3; "Notas e informações," *O Estado de S. Paulo*, 9 Feb. 1924, p. 3; "Notas e informações," *O Estado de S. Paulo*, 13 Feb. 1924, p. 3. See also Paulo Duarte, *Júlio Mesquita* (São Paulo: Hucitec, 1977), 151–54.

152. "Notas e informações," *O Estado de S. Paulo*, 19 Feb. 1924, p. 3.

153. A debate on the subject is summarized in "Centro de Debates," *O Estado de S. Paulo*, 22 Oct. 1925, p. 8.

154. "A candidatura do sr. Altino Arantes traz irreparavel vicio de origem," *O Combate*, 6 Nov. 1915, p. 1.

155. *O Estado de S. Paulo*, 4 Sept. 1901, quoted in Maurício Goulart, "Júlio Mesquita," in Aureliano Leite et al., *Homens de São Paulo* (São Paulo: Martins, 1954), 364.

156. Nestor Rangel Pestana to Julio Mesquita, São Paulo, 6 Aug. 1913, in P. Duarte, *Júlio Mesquita*, 66–68 (quote on p. 68).

157. Julio Mesquita (speech of 30 Aug. 1902 to the lower house of the state legislature), quoted in P. Duarte, *Júlio Mesquita*, 37.

158. Osvaldo S. Lima, untitled article, *Commercio da Lapa*, 9 Feb. 1928, p. 1.

159. "Nos bastidores da politica" (newspaper clipping, labeled *Diario da Noite*, 27 Nov. 1925), AESP, AJCDJ, caixa AP174, pasta 2.

160. Aristides Vicente de [illegible] to Julio Prestes de Albuquerque, Campos Novos, 12 Feb. 1930, AESP, AJPA, caixa AP14; "Os municipos," *O Estado de S. Paulo*, 19 Jan. 1926, p. 5; José Carlomagno to Secretario do PD, Santa Cruz do Rio Pardo, 25 May 1926, AIHGSP, APD, pacote 34; "Santa Cruz do Rio Pardo," unsigned, undated sheet, with attachment, AIHGSP, APD, pacote 8; Casalecchi, *O Partido Republicano Paulista*, 309.

161. In *A Lei* (Batatais), quoted in Arantes, *Passos do meu caminho*, 374–75.

162. "Aos republicanos de S. Paulo," *O Estado de S. Paulo*, 15 Dec. 1901, p. 1.

163. Prudente de Moraes et al., "Aos republicanos de S. Paulo," 7 Sept. 1901, in Levi-Moreira, "Liberalismo e democracia na dissidência republicana paulista," 172–77 (quote on p. 177).

164. "Chegou a hora da vingança!," *O Combate*, 1 March 1918, p. 1.

165. "Ao eleitorado independente do municipio de São Bernardo," in secção livre of *O Estado de S. Paulo*, 24 Oct. 1913, p. 7 (original emphases).

166. Thus we are faced with terms that approach oxymoronism, the most often used of which is "dissident oligarchs," which refers not to what a lexicographer might guess (those few who hold political power who dissent from those few who hold political power?), but rather, one infers, to selected members of a small, *economically* powerful group who oppose those other members of the same small, economically powerful group who hold *political* power.

167. Quotes from "A acção do Partido Municipal Ararense," *O Municipal* (Araras), 11 Jan. 1920, in secção livre of *O Estado de S. Paulo*, 13 Jan. 1920, p. 8, and "Politica de Araras," *O Municipal* (Araras), n.d., in secção livre of *O Estado de S. Paulo*, 29 March 1920, p. 8. The relative holdings of the leaders of the two local factions (in terms of coffee trees, other agricultural and pastoral interests, local industry, and rural and urban real estate) are listed in "Politica de Araras," in secção livre of *O Estado de S. Paulo*, 8 Jan. 1920, p. 8, and "Politica de Araras," *O Municipal* (Araras), 25 April 1920, in secção livre of *O Estado de S. Paulo*, 28 April 1920, p. 7.

168. "O Partido Municipal de Santos," *O Combate*, 23 Nov. 1915, p. 1.

169. Oracy Nogueira's "Contribuição à história do municipalismo no Brasil," *Revista de Administração* 7, nos. 25–28 (1953): 38–72, represents the best introduction to paulista municipalism that I am aware of, though it is not without its faults. Nogueira's focus on the county of Itapetininga (founded in 1770, long after the glory days of municipal independence characteristic of the earlier colonial period) in the context of the late nineteenth century leads him to undervalue the colonial precedents for municipally based localism and to credit North Atlantic political literatures with inspiring what they may have merely served to substantiate. Aspects of these colonial precedents are touched upon in Caio Prado Junior, *The Colonial Background of Modern Brazil*, trans. Suzette Macedo (Berkeley: University of California Press, 1967), 366–73, 490 (nn. 24, 25).

170. *Twentieth Century Impressions of Brazil*, 706; João F. Wright et al., "Eleição municipal," Santos, 26 Oct. 1910, in secção livre, *O Estado de S. Paulo*, 29 Oct. 1910, p. 7; "O Partido Municipal de Santos," *O Combate*, 23 Nov. 1915, p. 1; "A politica," *O Combate*, 25 Nov. 1916, p. 1; Gitahy, "The Port Workers of Santos, 1889–1914," 169.

171. "O partido municipal," *O Combate*, 24 Nov. 1916, p. 1; "Notas e informações," *O Estado de S. Paulo*, 24 Nov. 1916, p. 4; "A politica," *O Combate*, 12 Nov. 1919, p. 1.

172. Telegram, Armando de Arruda et al. to Julio Prestes de Albuquerque, São Caetano, 2 June 1928, AESP, AJPA, caixa AP22; "Partido Municipal de São Caetano," *S. Caetano Jornal*, 3 June 1928 [possibly 8 June 1928], reprinted in secção livre of *O Estado de S. Paulo*, 12 June 1928, p. 17; Armando de Arruda Pereira et al. to Julio Prestes de Albuquerque, São Caetano, 3 April 1929, AESP,

AJPA, caixa APO8; José de Souza Martins, *Suburbio: Vida cotidiana e história no suburbio da cidade de São Paulo; São Caetano, do fim do império ao fim da república velha* (São Paulo: Hucitec, 1992), 213–14; Medici, *Migração e urbanização*, 37–39, 378, 391; Valdenizio Petrolli, "História da imprensa no ABC paulista" (tese de mestrado, Instituto Metodista de Ensino Superior, 1983), 1:21–23.

173. That cases of municipalist opposition on the part of distinct socioeconomic interest groups were relatively rare is due in large part to the fact that traditional associational activity—petitioning, propagandizing, and pressing flesh—and associational clientelism (using a distinct group to leverage power within the PRP, as José Molinaro did as the leader of the state capital's drivers) were generally more successful avenues to achieving corporate goals. Indeed, that interest-group municipalism emerged at all is an interesting question that begs further study.

174. Mario Pinto Serva, "O civismo no Brasil," in his *O voto secreto, ou a organisação de partidos nacionaes*, 40–44 (quotes on pp. 40, 41).

175. "A eleição," *O Estado de S. Paulo*, 3 March 1910, p. 7.

176. Dagoberto Salles, *A vida de um brasileiro, que é uma lição de civismo: Campos Salles* (São Carlos: Typ. Artistica, 1917); British Chamber of Commerce of São Paulo and Southern Brazil, *Personalidades no Brasil / Men of Affairs in Brazil*, 654.

177. Quoted in Arantes, *Passos do meu caminho*, 334.

178. *O Estado de S. Paulo*, 14 July 1890, quoted in P. Duarte, *Júlio Mesquita*, 13; "A grande revolução," *O Combate*, 14 July 1915, p. 1.

179. *Gazeta de Santa Rita*, 28 Sept. 1903, reprinted in Travassos, *Quando eu era menino . . .* , 268–72; "XX de setembro," *O Combate*, 20 Sept. 1915, p. 1.

180. For example, "A brilhante commemoração da data de amanhã," *O Combate*, 4 Oct. 1919, p. 1.

181. "A independencia dos Estados Unidos," *O Combate*, 4 July 1919, p. 1.

182. Hilton Federici, *Símbolos paulistas: Estudo histórico-heráldico* (São Paulo: Secretaria da Cultura, Comissão de Geografia e História, 1981), 20–25; *A Provincia de São Paulo*, 16 Nov. 1889, p. 2; "A Republica," *A Provincia de São Paulo*, 17 Nov. 1889, p. 1. See J. M. de Carvalho, *A formação das almas*, chap. 5, on the adoption of the new national flag.

183. Federici, *Símbolos paulistas*, 22–23, 25 (quote on p. 25).

184. J. Canuto, "Campanha em pról da unidade nacional," clipping from *Diario da Noite* (dated 11 Sept. 1929), AIHGSP, APD, pacote 59; "A morte do senador Glycerio," *O Estado de S. Paulo*, 14 April 1916, p. 5. The funeral tributes described in the latter article were sponsored by the state government. *O Estado de S. Paulo*, 13 April 1916, p. 3.

185. "A morte do senador Glycerio," *O Estado de S. Paulo*, 13 April 1916, p. 3.

186. Quotes (Duarte de Azevedo and Paulo Egydio) from "A morte do Dr. Prudente," *O Estado de S. Paulo*, 4 Dec. 1902, p. 2.

187. "Bernardino de Campos," *O Estado de S. Paulo*, 19 Jan. 1915, p. 3.

188. "Campos Salles," *O Combate*, 28 June 1915, p. 1.

189. "'O Combate,' " *O Combate*, 6 Dec. 1922, p. 1.

190. "Notas e informações," *O Estado de S. Paulo*, 20 Feb. 1924, p. 3.

191. Presidente de São Paulo, *Mensagem apresentada ao congresso legislativo, em 14 de julho de 1927, pelo Dr. Dino da Costa Bueno, presidente do estado de São Paulo* (n.p., 1927), 8.

192. See J. M. de Carvalho, *A formação das almas*, chaps. 2–3.

193. "13 de Maio," *O Estado de S. Paulo*, 14 May 1890, p. 1.

194. "Notas e informações," *O Estado de S. Paulo*, 13 May 1899, p. 1.

195. "Em Campinas," *O Estado de S. Paulo*, 14 April 1916, p. 5.

196. "Onde estão os defensores da republica?," *O Combate*, 19 Nov. 1915, p. 1. See also Júlio Prestes's comments on the centennial of Brazilian independence, quoted in Marly Silva da Motta, *A nação faz cem anos: A questão nacional no centenário da independência* (Rio de Janeiro: Ed. da Fundação Getúlio Vargas, 1992), 106; and Maria Lígia Coelho Prado, "O pensamento conservador paulista: O regionalismo de Cincinato Braga," *Anais do Museu Paulista* 31 (1982): 235–45 (see esp. p. 238).

197. "A patria livre," *A Provincia de S. Paulo*, 15 May 1888, p. 1.

198. For two examples, see Francolino Camêu, *Politicos e estadistas contemporaneos* (Rio de Janeiro: Officinas Graphicas d'*O Globo*, 1928), 229; F. Santos, *História de Santos, 1532–1936*, chap. 23.

199. For the 1920s and after, see below, esp. chaps. 4 and 5; also, Barbara Weinstein, "Racializing Regional Difference: São Paulo vs. Brazil, 1932," in *Race and Nation in Modern Latin America*, ed. Nancy P. Applebaum, Anne S. Macpherson, and Karin Alejandra Rosemblatt (Chapel Hill: University of North Carolina Press, 2003), 237–62; James P. Woodard, "Regionalismo paulista e política partidária nos anos vinte," *Revista de História* 150 (2004): 44, 52–53.

200. Emilia Viotti da Costa's *The Brazilian Empire* can be read as a meditation on, or an indictment of, liberalism in nineteenth-century Brazil (see esp., but not exclusively, pp. 53–77, "Liberalism: Theory and Practice"); whether taken as one or the other (or as both), it remains a critical starting point. See also her "Liberalismo e democracia," *Anais de História* 7 (1975): 9–30. On paulistas' attachment to "liberal constitutionalism" and "juridical liberalism" in the early decades of the twentieth century (the two terms are treated more or less synonymously), see Thomas E. Skidmore, *Politics in Brazil, 1930–1964: An Experiment in Democracy* (Oxford: Oxford University Press, 1967), 9, 333 n. 13; Skidmore, *Black into White: Race and Nationality in Brazilian Thought*, 2nd ed. (Durham: Duke University Press, 1993 [1974]), 158–59. For the argument that São Paulo was "born" liberal in a broader sense and within a broader time frame, see Simon Schwartzman, *São Paulo e o estado nacional* (São Paulo: Difel, 1975).

201. *O Estado de S. Paulo*, 30 Jan. 1924, quoted in P. Duarte, *Júlio Mesquita*, 150.

202. Amadeu Amaral, in *O Estado de S. Paulo*, 16 March 1927, quoted in P. Duarte, *Júlio Mesquita*, 166; see also Antônio Figueiredo, *Memórias de um jornalista* (São Paulo: Unitas, 1933), 215–33.

203. Elias Chaves Neto, *Minha vida e as lutas de meu tempo* (São Paulo: Alfa-Omega, 1978), 27.

204. Not incidentally, the cult of Ruy Barbosa was the most successful of the various attempts at apotheosizing a civilian, republican hero. Devotion to Ruy Barbosa took off, however, not on the basis of any of his domestic accomplishments, but rather following his participation in the Hague conference of 1907, in which he "gave Brazil the glory of a cultured country," as one writer remarked, apparently unironically, more than seventy years later. P. Duarte, *Júlio Mesquita*, 41. See also João Felipe Gonçalves, *Rui Barbosa: Pondo as idéias no lugar* (Rio de Janeiro: Ed. da Fundação Getúlio Vargas, 2000), 115–22.

205. João Mangabeira, *Rui: O estadista da república* (Rio de Janeiro: José Olympio, 1943), 106–39. For a brief account of the Civilianist Campaign, see J. Gonçalves, *Rui Barbosa*, 123–37.

206. Jorge Americano, *São Paulo naquele tempo, 1895–1915* (São Paulo: Saraiva, 1957), 476; Guastini, *Tempos idos e vividos*, 183–184, 187–88, 191; Aureliano Leite, *Páginas de uma longa vida* (São Paulo: Martins, 1966), 34–35; Aureliano Leite, *História da civilização paulista* (São Paulo: Martins, 1946), 167; Love, *São Paulo in the Brazilian Federation*, 114.

207. "Ruy Barbosa," *O Estado de S. Paulo*, 16 Dec. 1909, p. 4; *Brazil Magazine* (Rio de Janeiro), Dec. 1909, unpag.; Ruy Barbosa, *Excursão eleitoral ao estado de S. Paulo* (São Paulo: Casa Garraux, 1909), 8–9. José Carlos de Oliveira Garcez is identified as a local boss in *Correio Paulistano*, 30 Sept. 1906, reprinted in Casalecchi, *O Partido Republicano Paulista*, 291; and "Eleições municipaes," *O Estado de S. Paulo*, 1 Nov. 1913, p. 4.

208. "Ruy Barbosa," *O Estado de S. Paulo*, 16 Dec. 1909, p. 4; *Brazil Magazine* (Rio de Janeiro), Dec. 1909, unpag.; Barbosa, *Excursão eleitoral ao estado de S. Paulo*, 9–30; Isaac Grínberg, *História de Mogi das Cruzes: Do começo até 1954* (São Paulo: n.p., 1961), 117.

209. *Brazil Magazine* (Rio de Janeiro), Dec. 1909, unpag.; "Ao povo," *O Estado de S. Paulo*, 14 Dec. 1909, p. 12; "Ruy Barbosa," *O Estado de S. Paulo*, 16 Dec. 1909, p. 5; Barbosa, *Excursão eleitoral ao estado de S. Paulo*, 30–31; Paulo de Almeida Nogueira, *Minha vida: Diário de 1893 a 1951* (São Paulo: Emprêsa Gráfica *Revista dos Tribunais*, 1955), 172.

210. *Brazil Magazine* (Rio de Janeiro), Dec. 1909, unpag.; "Ruy Barbosa," *O Estado de S. Paulo*, 16 Dec. 1909, pp. 4–5; Paulo de Almeida Nogueira, *Minha vida*, 172.

211. "Ruy Barbosa," *O Estado de S. Paulo*, 17 Dec. 1909, p. 7.

212. Ibid.; Barbosa, *Excursão eleitoral ao estado de S. Paulo*, 33–35; Guastini, *Tempos idos e vividos*, 183.

213. Pujol's speech was published in full in *O Estado de S. Paulo*, 17 Dec. 1909, p. 3, and Barbosa, *Excursão eleitoral ao estado de S. Paulo*, 35–42. On Pujol's recent opposition to the PRP rump, see Levi-Moreira, "Liberalismo e democracia na dissidência republicana paulista," 39, 41, 55, 177–78.

214. Slightly different versions of Ruy's speech were published in *O Estado de S. Paulo*, 17 Dec. 1909, pp. 1–3, and *Brazil Magazine* (Rio de Janeiro), Dec. 1909, unpag. My quotations are drawn from the latter.

215. Barbosa, *Excursão eleitoral ao estado de S. Paulo*, 95; "Ruy Barbosa," *O Estado de S. Paulo*, 17 Dec. 1909, p. 7; Paulo de Almeida Nogueira, *Minha vida*, 172. On the devotion to learned speech, see, for example, Freyre, *Order and Progress*, 81–82, 84–86, 125–26.

216. "Ruy Barbosa," *O Estado de S. Paulo*, 17 Dec. 1909, p. 7; "Ruy Barbosa," *O Estado de S. Paulo*, 18 Dec. 1909, pp. 4–5; "Ruy Barbosa," *O Estado de S. Paulo*, 19 Dec. 1909, pp. 4–5; Barbosa, *Excursão eleitoral ao estado de S. Paulo*, 95–151; Paulo de Almeida Nogueira, *Minha vida*, 172.

217. Ruy contested the diagnosis on the stump in Santos. "Ruy Barbosa," *O Estado de S. Paulo*, 22 Dec. 1909, p. 4; Barbosa, *Excursão eleitoral ao estado de S. Paulo*, 263.

218. *O Estado de S. Paulo*, 20 Dec. 1909, pp. 6–7; *O Estado de S. Paulo*, 21 Dec. 1909, p. 4; *O Estado de S. Paulo*, 22 Dec. 1909, p. 4; *O Estado de S. Paulo*, 23 Dec. 1909, p. 7; *O Estado de S. Paulo*, 24 Dec. 1909, p. 3; Barbosa, *Excursão eleitoral ao estado de S. Paulo*, 152–269.

219. "Ruy Barbosa," *O Estado de S. Paulo*, 20 Dec. 1909, p. 6. Cf. the account from the PRP's *Correio Paulistano* reprinted in Barbosa, *Excursão eleitoral ao estado de S. Paulo*, 151–57.

220. "Ruy Barbosa," *O Estado de S. Paulo*, 23 Dec. 1909, p. 7. Like Alfredo Pujol, the speaker in question, Francisco Salles Braga, had recently opposed the rump PRP in the schism of 1901–6: Levi-Moreira, "Liberalismo e democracia na dissidência republicana paulista," 186.

221. "Ruy Barbosa," *O Estado de S. Paulo*, 27 Dec. 1909, p. 4; Barbosa, *Excursão eleitoral ao estado de S. Paulo*, 266–69.

222. José Feliciano, "Notas civilistas," in *O Estado de S. Paulo*, 22 Feb. 1910, p. 1, 23 Feb. 1910, p. 1, and 25 Feb. 1910, p. 3.

223. Ana Luiza Martins, *Revistas em revista: Imprensa e práticas culturais em tempos de república; São Paulo, 1890–1922* (São Paulo: Ed. da Universidade de São Paulo, 2001), 256; Affonso A. de Freitas, *A imprensa periodica de São Paulo desde seus primordios até 1914* (São Paulo: Typ. do *Diario Official*, 1915), 737, 743–44; Paulo Duarte, *História da imprensa em São Paulo* (São Paulo: Escola de Comunicações e Artes, Universidade de São Paulo, 1972), 23.

224. P. Duarte, *História da imprensa em São Paulo*, 28, 29; Freitas, *A imprensa periodica de São Paulo desde seus primordios até 1914*, 737, 739–41, 745–46; Nobre, *História da imprensa de São Paulo*, 209–11, 215; A. Martins, *Revistas em revista*, 256; A. Leite, *Páginas de uma longa vida*, 33.

225. "Caso virgem" and "Ribeirão Preto," in secção livre of *O Estado de S. Paulo*, 1 March 1910, p. 7.

226. For example, the secções livres of *O Estado de S. Paulo* for 23 Feb. 1910 and 1 March 1910 (each on p. 7).

227. "Os municipios," *O Estado de S. Paulo*, 26 Feb. 1910, p. 3; *Correio de S. Carlos* article reprinted in "Movimento civilista," *O Estado de S. Paulo*, 26 Feb. 1910, p. 6.

228. "Telegrammas," *O Estado de S. Paulo*, 18 Feb. 1910, p. 5; "Notas e informações," *O Estado de S. Paulo*, 25 Feb. 1910, p. 3; "Movimento civilista," *O Estado de S. Paulo*, 1 March 1910, p. 4; "A candidatura Lins será uma affronta," *O Combate*, 22 Oct. 1915, p. 1; A. Leite, *Páginas de uma longa vida*, 34–35.

229. "A candidatura Lins será uma affronta," *O Combate*, 22 Oct. 1915, p. 1; "A cruzada do civismo," *O Combate*, 25 May 1918, p. 1.

230. "Telegrammas," *O Estado de S. Paulo*, 24 Feb. 1910, p. 4; "Telegrammas," *O Estado de S. Paulo*, 1 March 1910, p. 2.

231. "Movimento civilista," *O Estado de S. Paulo*, 28 Feb. 1910, p. 4.

232. Ibid. There were other moments at which workers or those claiming to represent them spoke in support of the civilianist cause, including in Santos ("Telegrammas," *O Estado de S. Paulo*, 27 Feb. 1910, p. 2), Taubaté (telegram, Operarios [da] fabrica [de] tecidos to Ruy Barbosa, Taubaté, 28 Feb. 1910, CRB, ARB, CR.E 20/18, doc. 853), and Jacareí ("Ruy Barbosa," *O Estado de S. Paulo*, 29 Dec. 1909, p. 7). Working-class involvement in republican politics is a subject that, like interest-group municipalism, I am only able to scratch the surface of in this work. It too is deserving of further study.

233. Election results in *O Estado de S. Paulo*, 23 Feb. 1910, p. 2; *O Estado de S. Paulo*, 24 Feb. 1910, p. 4; *O Estado de S. Paulo*, 28 Feb. 1910, p. 3.

234. "Os municipios," *O Estado de S. Paulo*, 15 Feb. 1910, p. 3.

235. Ibid.

236. "Os municipios," *O Estado de S. Paulo*, 23 Feb. 1910, p. 4.

237. "Telegrammas," *O Estado de S. Paulo*, 18 Feb. 1910, p. 5.

238. "Telegrammas," *O Estado de S. Paulo*, 16 Feb. 1910, p. 4; "Telegrammas," *O Estado de S. Paulo*, 18 Feb. 1910, p. 5; "Telegrammas," *O Estado de S. Paulo*, 21 Feb. 1910, p. 4; "Telegrammas," *O Estado de S. Paulo*, 26 Feb. 1910, p. 4; "Telegrammas," *O Estado de S. Paulo*, 1 March 1910, p. 2. For a partial list of these federal agencies, see Gilbert Last, *Facts about the State of São Paulo* (São Paulo: British Chamber of Commerce of São Paulo and Southern Brazil, 1926), 47.

239. "Telegrammas," *O Estado de S. Paulo*, 1 March 1910, p. 2.

240. "Os municipios," *O Estado de S. Paulo*, 26 Feb. 1910, p. 3.

241. "Telegrammas," *O Estado de S. Paulo*, 25 Feb. 1910, p. 4.

242. "Telegrammas," *O Estado de S. Paulo*, 1 March 1910, p. 2.

243. Ignacio Pellegrini Biagoni to Ruy Barbosa, Campinas, 3 Feb. 1910, CRB, ARB, CR.E 20/13, doc. 647.

244. "A eleição de hontem," *O Estado de S. Paulo*, 2 March 1910, p. 1; "A eleição," *O Estado de S. Paulo*, 2 March 1910, p. 3.

245. "A eleição de hontem," *O Estado de S. Paulo*, 2 March 1910, p. 1; "Telegrammas," *O Estado de S. Paulo*, 2 March 1910, p. 2; "A eleição," *O Estado de S. Paulo*, 2 March 1910, p. 3; "A eleição," *O Estado de S. Paulo*, 4 March 1910, p. 6.

246. "Telegrammas," *O Estado de S. Paulo*, 2 March 1910, p. 2; "A eleição," *O Estado de S. Paulo*, 2 March 1910, p. 4; "A eleição," *O Estado de S. Paulo*, 3 March 1910, p. 7; Azarias Ferreira Leite to Ruy Barbosa, Baurú, 22 May 1910, CRB, ARB, CR.E 20/23, doc. 1093. The final tally for the county of Bauru was 139 votes for Ruy-Lins to 135 for Hermes-Wenceslau. *O Estado de S. Paulo*, 4 March 1910, p. 1.

247. Azarias Ferreira Leite to Ruy Barbosa, Baurú, 22 May 1910, CRB, ARB, CR.E 20/23, doc. 1093.

248. "A eleição de 1 de março," *O Estado de S. Paulo*, 4 March 1910, p. 1; Walker, "Ribeirão Preto, 1910–1960," 66.

249. *O Estado de S. Paulo*, 5 March 1910, p. 1. Cf. Walker, "Ribeirão Preto, 1910–1960," 66.

250. Telegram, "Commissão Directora" to Ruy Barbosa, São Paulo, 1 March 1910, CRB, ARB, CR.E 20/19, doc. 925; "A eleição," *O Estado de S. Paulo*, 2 March 1910, p. 3; photograph in *O Estado de S. Paulo*, 3 March 1910, p. 3; "A eleição," *O Estado de S. Paulo*, 3 March 1910, p. 7; "A eleição," *O Estado de S. Paulo*, 4 March 1910, p. 6.

251. "Telegrammas," *O Estado de S. Paulo*, 3 March 1910, p. 4.

252. Americano, *São Paulo naquele tempo, 1895–1915*, 477.

253. P. Duarte, *Memórias*, 1:212–13. See also A. Leite, *Histora da civilização paulista*, 167; A. Leite, *Páginas de uma longa vida*, 37.

254. Pedro de Toledo et al., "Junta republicana," in secção livre of *O Estado de S. Paulo*, 9 March 1910, p. 9; "Notas e informações," *O Estado de S. Paulo*, 13 March 1910, p. 4; Levi-Moreira, "Liberalismo e democracia na dissidência republicana paulista," 178.

255. Casalecchi, *O Partido Republicano Paulista*, 140–41; "O 'Jornal do Commercio,' o sr. Rodrigues Alves e a liberal politica paulista," *O Combate*, 29 Nov. 1916, p. 1; *Correio Paulistano* quoted in Francisco Nunes de Oliveira, "Hontem e hoje," in secção livre, *O Alpha* (Rio Claro), 28 Oct. 1911, p. 2.

256. Nestor Rangel Pestana to Julio Mesquita, São Paulo, 31 July 1913, in P. Duarte, *Júlio Mesquita*, 59. See also A. Leite, *Páginas de uma longa vida*, 37.

257. P. Duarte, *Júlio Mesquita*, 63.

3. War and the Health of the State

1. Telegram, "Comité Civilista" to Ruy Barbosa, Jundiaí, 1 March 1914, CRB, ARB, CR.E 22/5, doc. 234; telegram, "Amigo dedicado" to Ruy Barbosa, São

Simão, 1 March 1914, CRB, ARB, CR.E 22/5, doc. 236; telegram, Elipidio Bastos to Ruy Barbosa, Guariba, 1 March 1914, CRB, ARB, CR.E 22/5, doc. 238; telegram, Luiz Medeiros to Ruy Barbosa, São Paulo, 1 March 1914, CRB, ARB, CR.E 22/5, doc. 239; A. Leite, *Subsídios para a história da civilização paulista*, 282.

2. Travassos, *Quando eu era menino . . .*, 262–63 (original emphasis).

3. A. Leite, *Subsídios para a história da civilização paulista*, 284.

4. Travassos, *Quando eu era menino . . .*, 4, 261–63; "Ruy Barbosa," *O Estado de S. Paulo*, 16 Dec. 1909, p. 5; "Telegramas," *O Estado de S. Paulo*, 23 Feb. 1910, p. 2.

5. Mangabeira, *Rui*, 247–51, 254–58. A selection of Ruy's speeches from the period were collected in the posthumously published *A grande guerra*, ed. Fernando Nery (Rio de Janeiro: Guanabara, 1932). On the Pro-Allies League, see Skidmore, *Black into White*, 149–50. Ruy Barbosa's incoming correspondence as president of the league is housed at the CRB, ARB, CR.E 23/1–2.

6. Julio Mesquita, *A guerra, 1914–1918*, 4 vols. (São Paulo: Terceiro Nome, 2002), collects a complete run of *O Estado de S. Paulo*'s "Boletim da guerra."

7. "Boletim da guerra," 21 Dec. 1914, in ibid., 1:129.

8. Quotes from the Boletins for 6 Nov. 1916 and 25 Dec. 1916 in ibid., 3:504 and 540.

9. "Boletim da guerra," 23 Nov. 1914, in ibid., 1:118.

10. The quote is from "Boletim da guerra," 4 Dec. 1916, in ibid., 3:522. For Mesquita's subsequent volte-face, see, for example, "Boletim da guerra," 9 April 1917, in ibid., 3:596.

11. "Notas e informações," *O Estado de S. Paulo*, 6 April 1917, p. 3.

12. "Brasil-Allemanha," *Revista do Brasil*, April 1917, p. 502. On the *Revista do Brasil* more broadly, see Tania Regina de Luca, *A "Revista do Brasil:" Um diagnóstico para a (n)ação* (São Paulo: Ed. da Universidade Estadual Paulista, 1998).

13. "A politica brasileira," *Revista do Brasil*, April 1918, 386.

14. Roque Spencer Maciel de Barros, *A evolução do pensamento de Pereira Barreto* (São Paulo: Grijalbo, 1967); Eduardo Batista, "Luiz Pereira Barreto," in Amorim, *Os desbravadores*, 47–58; de Luca, *A "Revista do Brasil,"* 46; Gifun, "Ribeirão Prêto, 1880–1914," 85–86.

15. Pereira Barreto, "Pró-Belgica" (1914), quoted in R. Barros, *A evolução do pensamento de Pereira Barreto*, 246; see also A. Leite, *Subsídios para a história da civilização paulista*, 283.

16. R. Barros, *A evolução do pensamento de Pereira Barreto*, 247, citing "O papel dos moços na evolução social" (1916).

17. Olavo Bilac, "Oração aos moços," is reprinted in Nogueira Filho, *Ideais e lutas de um burguês progressista*, 2:626–29, from which the quotes above are taken. First-person accounts of Bilac's visit to São Paulo include P. Duarte, *Memórias*, 3:315–16; Nogueira Filho, *Ideais e lutas de um burguês progressista*,

1:54–55. See also Skidmore, *Black into White*, 153–54; and Beattie, *The Tribute of Blood*, 228–33.

18. P. Duarte, *Memórias*, 3:338; Nogueira Filho, *Ideais e lutas de um burguês progressista*, 1:55–57.

19. "Liga Nacionalista," *Revista do Brasil*, Dec. 1916, 408; "Notas e informações," *O Estado de S. Paulo*, 16 Dec. 1916, p. 5; Silvia Levi-Moreira, "Ideologia e atuação da Liga Nacionalista de São Paulo, 1917–1924," *Revista de História* 116 (1984): 67–74; Levi-Moreira, "A luta pelo voto secreto no programa da Liga Nacionalista de São Paulo, 1916–1924," *Revista Brasileira de História* 7 (Mar. 1984): 72–80; Paul Manor, "The Liga Nacionalista de São Paulo: A Political Reformist Group in Paulista Academic of Yore, 1917–1924," *Jahrbuch für Geschichte von Staat, Wirtschaft und Gesellschaft Lateinamerikas* 17 (1980): 317–353; Jorge Americano, *São Paulo nesse tempo, 1915–1935* (São Paulo: Melhoramentos, 1962), 355–56; P. Duarte, *Memórias*, 3:345; A. Leite, *Subsídios para a história da civilização paulista*, 287; Pelágio Lôbo, *Recordações das arcadas* (São Paulo: Reitoria de Universidade de São Paulo, 1953), 79–81; Nogueira Filho, *Ideais e lutas de um burguês progressista*, 1:73–77; Skidmore, *Black into White*, 157–59.

20. "Notas e informações," *O Estado de S. Paulo*, 16 Dec. 1916, p. 5.

21. The statutes are reprinted in Manor, "The Liga Nacionalista de São Paulo," 335.

22. "As lições do Prata," *O Combate*, 3 March 1916, p. 1; "Écos e factos," *O Combate*, 8 March 1916, p. 1; "Na Argentina," *O Combate*, 30 March 1916, p. 1; "Écos e factos," *O Combate*, 3 April 1916, p. 1. The newspaper's publishers embraced the "yellow-press" slur in its inaugural issue: "Écos e factos," *O Combate*, 24 April 1915, p. 2.

23. "O que são e o que deviam ser as eleições," *O Combate*, 16 Oct. 1916, p. 1 (emphasis added).

24. The motion was published in "Congresso legislativo," *O Estado de S. Paulo*, 20 Oct. 1917, p. 4. Cesar did not explicitly mention Argentina in his motion, but his description of how the secret ballot was to be enacted matched contemporary Argentine practice rather than the better-remembered "Australian ballot." On Cesar and the League, see Levi-Moreira, "A luta pelo voto secreto no programa da Liga Nacionalista de São Paulo, 1916–1924," 73n.; Manor, "The Liga Nacionalista de São Paulo," 339; Nogueira Filho, *Ideais e lutas de um burguês progressista*, 1:78.

25. "Noticias diversas," *O Estado de S. Paulo*, 21 Oct. 1917, p. 7.

26. "O voto secreto," *O Combate*, 20 Oct. 1917, p. 1. Given the structure of paulista politics, an initiative like this one would have to come from the executive (as in Argentina) rather than a member of the legislature.

27. The quotes are from Mario Pinto Serva, "Na rectaguarda da civilização," *Revista do Brasil*, July 1920, p. 209; see also below, chaps. 4, 5.

28. F. Vergueiro Steidel to Ruy Barbosa, São Paulo, 26 July 1919, CRB, ARB,

CR 1601/1; José Carlos de Macedo Soares et al., "Ao eleitorado paulista," São Paulo, 20 April 1922, *O Estado de S. Paulo*, 21 April 1922, p. 3; João Sampaio, *O voto secreto* (São Paulo: n.p., 1922); Levi-Moreira, "A luta pelo voto secreto no programa da Liga Nacionalista de São Paulo, 1916–1924," 74.

29. Heitor de Moraes, *Patria rediviva: De Pires Ferreira a Martim Francisco* (São Paulo: Secção de Obras d'*O Estado de S. Paulo*, n.d. [1918]); Clovis Botelho Vieira, *A grande guerra e as tradições liberaes do Brasil* (São Paulo: Livraria e Officinas Magalhães, 1918); Francisco Azzi, *Educação civica* (São Paulo: Weiszflog [&] Irmãos, 1916). See also Nogueira Filho, *Ideais e lutas de um burguês progressista*, 1:90.

30. Albino Camargo, "A missão da mocidade," *Revista do Brasil*, Jan. 1917, 98–100; Francisco Ribeiro Sampaio, *Renembranças* (Campinas: Academia Campinense de Letras, 1975), 123–24; Alaor Barbosa, *Um cenáculo na paulicéia: Um estudo sobre Monteiro Lobato, Godofredo Rangel, José Antônio Nogueira, Ricardo Gonçalves, Raul de Freitas e Albino de Camargo* (Brasília: Projeto Editorial, 2002).

31. The inside cover of the first issue lists the review's founders. *Patria* (Ribeirão Preto), Jan. 1916.

32. João Guião, "O serviço militar obrigatorio e a reforma eleitoral," *Patria* (Ribeirão Preto), Feb. 1916, 50–54. The inside cover of the same issue lists a "Dr. João Rodrigues Guião," who is in turn identified as a lawyer in Joaquim da Cunha Diniz Junqueira et al. to "Illmo Correligionario e Amigo," Ribeirão Preto, 1 Aug. 1930, AESP, AJCDJ, caixa AP 174, pasta 1.

33. Laudo Ferreira de Camargo and Albino Camargo Netto, "Relatorio do Centro Nacionalista de Ribeirão Preto," Ribeirão Preto, 18 May 1918, AIHGSP, ALN, pacote 2, item 1; "Sete de setembro," *O Combate*, 5 Sept. 1917, p. 1; "Bibliographia," *O Estado de S. Paulo*, 19 Oct. 1919, p. 3.

34. On the evening edition of *O Estado de S. Paulo*, see P. Duarte, *Júlio Mesquita*, 78–80; P. Duarte, *Memórias*, 3:310, 319, 345; Figueiredo, *Memórias de um jornalista*, 146–51, 156; " 'O Estadinho,' " *O Combate*, 26 May 1919, p. 1. *O Parafuso* is the subject of an excellent monograph, Brás Ciro Gallotta, "*O Parafuso*: Humor e crítica na imprensa paulistana, 1915–1921" (tese de mestrado, Pontifícia Universidade Católica de São Paulo, 1997); see also Oswald de Andrade, *Um homem sem profissão: Memórias e confissões* (Rio de Janeiro: José Olympio, 1954), 99, 131–32; P. Duarte, *Memórias*, 7:267, 8:215–18; Nobre, *História da imprensa de São Paulo*, 222; Penteado, *Belenzinho, 1910*, 198. For information on *O Combate*, I have relied heavily upon the newspaper itself as a source in the absence of scholarly monographs or contemporary chronicles on the subject, though Paulo Duarte ventures a brief and only partially inaccurate synopsis in his *História da imprensa em São Paulo* (see p. 30).

35. On the German turn to unrestricted submarine war, see Frederick C. Luebke, *Germans in Brazil: A Comparative Study of Cultural Conflict During World War I* (Baton Rouge: Louisiana State University Press, 1987), 119–20.

36. A. Leite, *Subsídios para a história da civilização paulista*, 287.

37. Luebke, *Germans in Brazil*, 126.

38. "Em S. Paulo," *O Combate*, 7 April 1917, p. 1.

39. "O rompimento de relações," *O Combate*, 10 April 1917, p. 1; "Noticias diversas," *O Estado de S. Paulo*, 11 April 1917, p. 5.

40. "O attentado allemão," *O Combate*, 10 April 1917, p. 1; "Noticias diversas," *O Estado de S. Paulo*, 11 April 1917, pp. 5–6; Charles L. Hoover to Alexander Benson, São Paulo, 11 April 1917, USNARA, RG84, Consular Posts, São Paulo, Brazil, vol. 19, 800. *O Estado de S. Paulo* estimated that the "multitude" numbered some four to five thousand, while Consul Hoover, perhaps a bit hysterically, detected "at least 15,000."

41. "O Brasil e a guerra," *O Combate*, 11 April 1917, p. 4; "Noticias diversas," *O Estado de S. Paulo*, 11 April 1917, p. 6; P. Duarte, *Memórias*, 3:345; Charles L. Hoover to Alexander Benson, São Paulo, 11 April 1917, USNARA, RG84, Consular Posts, São Paulo, Brazil, vol. 19, 800.

42. *O Estado de S. Paulo* listed ten men who received medical treatment from the city's service: João José Dias da Costa (identified as a sixty-two-year-old laborer), Emilio Fragale (a twenty-three-year-old barber), José Silveira (identified only as a "youth"), Abib Nastre (a forty-three-year-old confectioner), Armindo de Araujo (a nineteen-year-old butler or scullion [*copeiro*]), Domingo Curci (a twenty-year-old joiner), Romeu Pacheco (a student), João Inne (a fifty-year-old "Syrian,"), Jacob And (another "Syrian," from the interior town of Itapira), and Cesarino Jorge (a twenty-one-year-old clerk). "Noticias diversas," *O Estado de S. Paulo*, 11 April 1917, p. 6.

43. "Noticias diversas," *O Estado de S. Paulo*, 12 April 1917, p. 5.

44. Ibid., 5–6; "O Brasil e a guerra," *O Combate*, 12 April 1917, p. 1; A. Leite, *Subsídios para a história da civilização paulista*, 287.

45. *O Estado de S. Paulo* lists six civilians (non-policemen) who received medical treatment from the city's "Assistencia": José Narciso (a seventeen-year-old seller of greengroceries), Juvenal Guerra (twenty), Sylvio Maracini (a worker), Angelo Novelli (a stoker), Constantino Trota (a tailor), and Arthur Miranda (a clerk). "Noticias diversas," *O Estado de S. Paulo*, 12 April 1917, p. 6.

46. Nogueira Filho, *Ideais e lutas de um burguês progressista*, 1:59. Nogueira Filho claims to have participated in the law student protest of 10 April and the succeeding demonstrations, but he is silent as to his participation or non-participation in the sack of the *Diário Alemão* (ibid., 1:58–59).

47. The resolution was approved by the legislature on 26 October 1917. See Luebke, *Germans in Brazil*, 160.

48. P. Duarte, *Memórias*, 4:359; "O Brasil na guerra," *O Combate*, 30 Oct. 1917, p. 1; "O Brasil na guerra," *O Combate*, 31 Oct. 1917, p. 1; "O aspecto da cidade, hontem a noite," *O Combate*, 1 Nov. 1917, p. 1; "A chacina do povo em Santos," *O Combate*, 5 Nov. 1917, p. 1; "O congresso vae decretar o estado de sitio," *O Combate*, 6 Nov. 1917, p. 1; Luebke, *Germans in Brazil*, 167–68; Fer-

nando Teixeira da Silva, *Operários sem patrões: Os trabalhadores da cidade de Santos no entreguerras* (Campinas: Ed. da Universidade Estadual de Campinas, 2003), 102, 310.

49. "Pelo proletariado," *O Combate*, 24 April 1915, p. 2; "Pelo proletariado," *O Combate*, 27 April 1915, p. 2; "Manifesto contra a guerra," *O Combate*, 19 April 1917, p. 3; "A Alliança Anarchista ao povo," *A Plebe*, 23 June 1917, p. 3; Joel Wolfe, "Anarchist Ideology, Worker Practice: The 1917 General Strike and the Formation of São Paulo's Working Class," *Hispanic American Historical Review* 71, no. 4 (Nov. 1991): 809; Wolfe, *Working Women, Working Men*, 14–15.

50. The following discussion of the strike of 1917 draws heavily on Fausto, *Trabalho urbano e conflito social, 1890–1920*; Christina Roquette Lopreato, *O espírito da revolta: A greve geral anarquista de 1917* (São Paulo: Annablume, 2000); and the relevant issues of *O Combate*.

51. The assembled workers had also spoken out against the use of child labor. See Lopreato, *O espírito da revolta*, 104.

52. "A victoria do operario," *O Combate*, 16 July 1917, p. 1.

53. Fausto, *Trabalho urbano e conflito social, 1890–1920*, chap. 7; Lopreato, *O espírito da revolta*, chap. 5; P. Duarte, *Memórias*, 4:350.

54. "A miseria em revolta," *O Combate*, 13 July 1917, p. 1; "A victoria do operariado," *O Combate*, 16 July 1917, p. 1; P. Duarte *Júlio Mesquita*, 101; P. Duarte, *Memórias*, 4:349–50; Lopreato, *O espírito da revolta*, 202–8.

55. "O movimento grevista," *O Combate*, 14 July 1917, p. 3; Wolfe, *Working Women, Working Men*, 21, 22–23.

56. Lopreato, *O espírito da revolta*, 159–61; P. Duarte, *Júlio Mesquita*, 101–2.

57. Lopreato, *O espírito da revolta*, 169.

58. Quoted in Lopreato, *O espírito da revolta*, 170.

59. Lopreato, *O espírito da revolta*, 174–97; Edgar Rodrigues, *Nacionalismo e cultura social, 1913–1922* (Rio de Janeiro: Laemmert, 1972), 164.

60. Far less is known about the two attempted general strikes of 1919 than the general stoppage of 1917. While entire works have been dedicated to the strike of 1917 (Boris Fausto, "Conflito social na república oligárquica: A greve de 1917," *Estudos Cebrap* 10 [1974]: 79–109; Iara Aun Khoury, ed., *As greves de 1917 em São Paulo e o processo de organização proletária* [São Paulo: Cortez, 1981]; Lopreato, *O espírito da revolta*; Wolfe, "Anarchist Ideology, Worker Practice"), the events of 1919 have typically been skimmed over (see, for example, Fausto's *Trabalho urbano e conflito social, 1890–1920* and Wolfe's *Working Women, Working Men*, which cover the strike of 1917 in far greater detail than the two strikes of 1919). As a result, there seems to be some confusion, especially surrounding the causes of the abortive general strike of October 1919, which is generally attributed to economic grievances but on the basis of available evidence seems to have been sparked by the arrests of anarchist activists.

61. P. Duarte, *Memórias*, 5:321ff.; "O movimento grevista," *O Combate*, 6 May

1919, p. 1; "O movimento grevista," *O Combate*, 7 May 1919, p. 1; "O movimento grevista," *O Combate*, 8 May 1919, p. 1; "O movimento grevista," *O Combate*, 9 May 1919, p. 1; "O movimento grevista," *O Combate*, 10 May 1919, p. 1; "O movimento grevista," *O Combate*, 12 May 1919, p. 1; "O movimento grevista," *O Combate*, 14 May 1919, p. 1; "O movimento grevista," *O Combate*, 15 May 1919, p. 1; "O movimento grevista," *O Combate*, 16 May 1919, p. 1; "O movimento grevista," *O Combate*, 17 May 1919, p. 1.

62. In his memoirs, Duarte recalled that "the strike [of October 1919] became unpopular not only due to the inconveniences imposed on all of the city['s population], but also due to the mass executions in Russia and other cruelties practiced there, which terrified conservatives and reactionaries, especially the latter." P. Duarte, *Memórias*, 5:330, also 4:364, 5:327. Also see P. Duarte, *Júlio Mesquita*, 126; Andrade, *Um homem sem profissão*, 210.

63. "Bomba infernal," *O Estado de S. Paulo*, 20 Oct. 1919, p. 2; "Uma fabrica de bombas na rua João Boemer," *O Combate*, 20 Oct. 1919, p. 1; "A horrivel catastrophe da rua João Boemer," *O Combate*, 21 Oct. 1919, p. 1; P. Duarte, *Memórias*, 5:327–29. Paulo Duarte recorded that years later Altino Arantes, who was state president in 1919, told him that the bombs were being made for an attempt on his life, which was to have taken place during festivities celebrating the thirtieth anniversary of the republic, on 15 November 1919. P. Duarte, *Memórias*, 5:328.

64. "A horrivel catastrophe da rua João Boemer," *O Combate*, 21 Oct. 1919, p. 1.

65. "Bomba infernal," *O Estado de S. Paulo*, 20 Oct. 1919, p. 2.

66. See P. Duarte, *Memórias*, 5:329.

67. "Notas e informações," *O Estado de S. Paulo*, 23 Oct. 1919, p. 3.

68. Ibid. Although *O Estado de S. Paulo* opposed the strike, it did not spare the republican establishment, ridiculing the *Correio Paulistano*'s suggestion that workers should resort to the (corrupt) ballot box rather than work stoppages to better their lot: "Notas e informações," *O Estado de S. Paulo*, 29 Oct. 1919, p. 3; P. Duarte, *Memórias*, 5:330–31.

69. "Noticias diversas," *O Estado de S. Paulo*, 24 Oct. 1919, p. 4.

70. "O movimento operario," *O Combate*, 24 Oct. 1919, p. 3. In at least one case, the "general strike" coincided with a strike based on grievances that were exclusive to one particular factory. "Na fabrica Mellilo," *O Combate*, 25 Oct. 1919, p. 3.

71. "O movimento operario," *O Combate*, 27 Oct. 1919, p. 1.

72. The worker's demands are reprinted in P. Duarte, *Memórias*, 5:330.

73. "Vae se normalisando o serviço de bondes . . . ," *O Combate*, 24 Oct. 1919, p. 1; "A greve geral condemnada a um fracasso," *O Combate*, 25 Oct. 1919, p. 1; "Noticias diversas," *O Estado de S. Paulo*, 24 Oct. 1919, p. 4; "Noticias diversas," *O Estado de S. Paulo*, 28 Oct. 1919, p. 2; P. Duarte, *Memórias*, 5:330; Fausto, *Trabalho urbano e conflito social, 1890–1920*, 237.

74. "Como seu deu a prisão do sr. Damiani," *O Combate*, 22 Oct. 1919, p. 3; "Vae se normalisando o serviço de bondes . . . ," *O Combate*, 24 Oct. 1919, p. 1; "A greve geral condemnada a um fracasso," *O Combate*, 25 Oct. 1919, p. 1; "Telegrammas," *O Combate*, 29 Oct. 1919, p. 3; "Uma desintelligencia entre o consul hespanol e a policia do Rio," *O Combate*, 31 Oct. 1919, p. 1; "Movimento operario," *O Combate*, 7 Nov. 1919, p. 3; "Movimento operario," *O Combate*, 11 Nov. 1919, p. 3; "Uma carta de Alexandre Zanella," *O Combate*, 10 Dec. 1919, p. 1; "A policia paulista embarcou hontem tres operarios," *O Combate*, 17 Dec. 1919, p. 1. *A Plebe*'s issues of 22 and 29 Nov. 1919 present the activists' own perspective on their persecution by the authorities.

75. "O movimento operario," *O Combate*, 27 Oct. 1919, p. 1; "O movimento operario," *O Combate*, 28 Oct. 1919, p. 1; "Noticias diversas," *O Estado de S. Paulo*, 28 Oct. 1919, p. 3.

76. "'Autos da fé' em plena rua Quinze!," *O Combate*, 3 Nov. 1919, p. 1; *O Parafuso*, 4 Nov. 1919 and 11 Nov. 1919, the former of which bore the cover story "A gréve e os estudantes"; Fausto, *Trabalho urbano e conflito social, 1890–1920*, 237, 239–40.

77. "Movimento operario," *O Combate*, 29 Nov. 1919, p. 1.

78. "Movimento operario," *O Combate*, 23 Dec. 1919, p. 1. The October strike itself also saw some disagreement among groups claiming to represent workers, but some of this confusion might be attributable to dirty tricks on the part of the authorities or management. "A greve geral condemnada a um fracasso," *O Combate*, 25 Oct. 1919, p. 1; "O movimento operario," *O Combate*, 28 Oct. 1919, p. 1.

79. Dean, *The Industrialization of São Paulo, 1880–1945*, 162–66 (quotes on p. 162). Dean writes that the "first meeting [of the CIFTSP] convened only a few weeks after a generalized strike movement in which the employers had acceded to the workers' demands for an eight-hour day," but he cites the *Atas* of a meeting for 1 October 1919 on the same page. Ibid., 162, 162n. Dean was most likely referring to the strikes of May, a few *months* earlier, but at least one subsequent monograph, perhaps on the basis of Dean's work, suggests that the industrialists founded the CIFTSP "in the midst of a strong strike movement that once again shook the city of São Paulo" (Lopreato, *O espírito da revolta*, 201). Fausto and Wolfe attribute the group's founding to the generalized labor militancy of the period (Fausto, *Trabalho urbano e conflito social, 1890–1920*, 188; and Wolfe, *Working Women, Working Men*, 25). Terezinha Ferrari has contributed a monograph tracing the CIFTSP's activities from its founding through its conversion into a state-linked syndicate. See her "Ensaio de classe: O Centro dos Industriais de Fiação e Tecelagem de São Paulo, 1919–1931; Estudo sobre a organização do empresariado têxtil durante os anos vinte" (tese de mestrado, Pontifícia Universidade Católica de São Paulo, 1988).

80. Lopreato, *O espírito da revolta*, 130–31 (quote on p. 131); Souza, *O direito à educação*, 105; "O movimento grevista," *O Combate*, 14 July 1917, p. 3; Tere-

sinha Aparecida Del Fiorentino, "O operariado campineiro de 1930 a 1945," *Revista da SBPH* 1 (1983): 18–19; Ribeiro, *Falsa democracia*, 107–11. On Álvaro Ribeiro, see also: Mário Pires, *Campinas: Sementeira de ideais* (Limeira: Edição "Letras de Província," n.d.), 41–43; Júlio Mariano, "História da imprensa em Campinas," in *Monografia histórica do município de Campinas* (Rio de Janeiro: Instituto Brasileiro de Geografia e Estatística, 1952), 310; Souza, *O direito à educação*, 119.

81. Lopreato, *O espírito da revolta*, 132–33; Ribeiro, *Falsa democracia*, 110. The commission was made up of Campinas's prefeito, Heitor Penteado, the city councilman Omar Simões Magro, the lawyer Pedro Magalhães, and a delegation of five workers (Ribeiro, *Falsa democracia*, 132n.). Magalhães was a self-made man (his legal training was self-inflicted), a historic republican, and an associate of Álvaro Ribeiro's: Pelágio Lôbo, "O fôro de Campinas do império e na república," in *Monografia histórica do município de Campinas*, 332; Paulo de Castro Pupo Nogueira, "O fôro de Campinas, 1918–1950," in ibid., 353; Raul Soares de Moura et al. to Ruy Barbosa, Campinas, 27 June 1909, CRB, ARB, CR.E 20/1, doc. 20; " 'O Combate' em Campinas," *O Combate*, 7 Dec. 1922, p. 2; " 'O Combate' em Campinas," *O Combate*, 9 Dec. 1922, p. 2.

82. "A gréve," *O Combate*, 8 May 1919, p. 3; "O movimento grevista," *O Combate*, 9 May 1919, p. 1; "O movimento grevista," *O Combate*, 10 May 1919, p. 1; "O movimento grevista," *O Combate*, 12 May 1919, p. 1; "O movimento grevista," *O Combate*, 15 May 1919, p. 1; "A gréve," *O Combate*, 16 May 1919, p. 3; Del Fiorentino, "O operariado campineiro de 1930 a 1945," 19–20. The quote is from Um grupo de operarios, "De Campinas," *A Plebe*, 14 June 1919, p. 3.

83. Everardo Dias claims that on 23 October the "working-class organizations of Campinas and Sorocaba sent delegations to São Paulo, with motions of solidarity with the workers on strike [in the capital], and declared that they would go on a solidarity strike," and that the following day some sort of repression took place in Campinas. See Dias, *História das lutas sociais no Brasil* (São Paulo: Alfa-Omega, 1977), 306. However, the newspaper *O Combate*, usually sympathetic to the claims of labor activists, reported on 27 October: "The workers of Campinas, despite the appeals made by the Federação Operaria of this capital, up until now have not shown the slightest desire to stop working" (p. 1). In providing background for her discussion of Campinas's post-1930 working-class history, Del Fiorentino discusses the strikes of July 1917 and May 1919 but makes no mention at all of October 1919; see her "O operariado campineiro de 1930 a 1945," 18–20.

84. Maria Valéria Barbosa, Nelson Santos Dias, and Rita Márcia Martins Cerqueira, *Santos na formação do Brasil: 500 anos de história* (Santos: Prefeitura Municipal, 2000), 48; Lopreato, *O espírito da revolta*, 136–38; F. Silva, *Operários sem patrões*, 97–99, 233–35; "O movimento grevista," *O Combate*, 14 July 1917, p. 3.

85. "A gréve," *O Combate*, 6 May 1919, p. 3; "O movimento grevista," *O*

Combate, 7 May 1919, p. 1; "A gréve," *O Combate,* 8 May 1919, p. 3; "O movimento grevista," *O Combate,* 9 May 1919, p. 1; "O movimento grevista," *O Combate,* 10 May 1919, p. 1; "O movimento grevista," *O Combate,* 12 May 1919, p. 1; "O movimento grevista," *O Combate,* 15 May 1919, p. 1; F. Silva, *Operários sem patrões,* 259–62, 282–86, 310–11.

86. "Noticias diversas," *O Estado de S. Paulo,* 17 Oct. 1919, p. 5; Heitor de Moraes, "Manifesto," in secção livre of *O Estado de S. Paulo,* 20 Oct. 1919, p. 6; "Noticias diversas," *O Estado de S. Paulo,* 21 Oct. 1919, p. 4; "Noticias diversas," *O Estado de S. Paulo,* 22 Oct. 1919, p. 4; "Noticias diversas," *O Estado de S. Paulo,* 23 Oct. 1919, p. 5; "Noticias diversas," *O Estado de S. Paulo,* 24 Oct. 1919, p. 4; "O movimento operario," *O Combate,* 17 Oct. 1919, p. 1; "Sensacionaes declarações do gerente da City," *O Combate,* 21 Oct. 1919, p. 3; F. Silva, *Operários sem patrões,* 297–301, 305–6. In the same city council meeting in which he issued his motion on behalf of the Sociedade dos Empregados da Companhia City, Moraes also issued a proposal to improve municipal education, emphasizing the degree to which the "crisis" faced by the working classes was due to the "ignorance of the children of the proletariat," itself due to the deficiency of the educational system. Both motions were published in "Noticias do interior," *O Estado de S. Paulo,* 17 Oct. 1919, p. 4.

87. Edgar Rodrigues, *Os companheiros,* 5 vols. (Rio de Janeiro: vjr, 1994–1998 [vols. 3–5 published in Florianópolis by Editora Insular]), 4:120, 5:135, 5:186–87; F. Silva, *Operários sem patrões,* 247, 286, 291, 293, 305–6, 310–11; "Movimento operario," *O Combate,* 27 May 1919, p. 1; "O movimento operario," *O Combate,* 17 Oct. 1919, p. 1; "Sensacionaes declarações do gerente da City," *O Combate,* 21 Oct. 1919, p. 3; "Noticias diversas," *O Estado de S. Paulo,* 22 Oct. 1919, p. 4; "Noticias diversas," *O Estado de S. Paulo,* 24 Oct. 1919, p. 4; "Prisão de dois operarios de Santos," *O Combate,* 27 Oct. 1919, p. 3; "As violencias policiaes em Santos," in secção livre, *O Estado de S. Paulo,* 31 Oct. 1919, p. 6; "E não estava preso!," *O Combate,* 20 Jan. 1920, p. 1; "A greve nas Docas de Santos," *O Combate,* 11 Dec. 1920, p. 1; "A greve nas Docas de Santos," *O Combate,* 14 Dec. 1920, p. 1; "A greve nas Docas de Santos," *O Combate,* 15 Dec. 1920, p. 1; "Habeus corpus em favor dos operarios . . . ," *O Combate,* 21 Jan. 1921, p. 1; "A policia de S. Paulo mais uma vez derrotada," *O Combate,* 18 May 1921, p. 1. In the mid-1920s, the paulistano socialist Antônio dos Santos Figueiredo would refer approvingly to Moraes's leadership. See his *A evolução do estado no Brasil* (Porto: n.p., 1926), 177.

88. Lopreato, *O espírito da revolta,* 135–36; Terci, "A cidade na primeira república," 155–56, 162–66, 170–71.

89. Terci, "A cidade na primeira república," 156–69.

90. Ibid., 171–74.

91. "O movimento grevista," *O Combate,* 15 May 1919, p. 1; Terci, "A cidade na primeira república," 173–81 (quote on p. 181).

92. Ibid., 181.

93. Ibid., 182.

94. Ibid., 182–91. Terci, while discounting the possibility that there were plans for a full-fledged insurrection, accepts that some sort of plot for anarchist-inspired "direct action" existed (see esp. pp. 183–84) and takes at face value the assertion that the local outs were involved in the conspiracy (p. 186). Given that those tried for conspiracy were subsequently exonerated, I am somewhat more skeptical.

95. "As innominaveis violencias de que foi victima o operariado," *A Plebe*, 19 July 1919, p. 3. *A Plebe* refers to Passini's lawyer only as a director of *A Tarde*. On the basis of Terci's "A cidade na primeira república" (p. 186) and the state capital's *O Combate* (4 Sept. 1919, p. 1), I identify João Silveira Mello as Passini's lawyer.

96. "Os accusados foram absolvidos por unanimidade," *O Combate*, 4 Sept. 1919, p. 1; Terci, "A cidade na primeira república," 186.

97. "O movimento grevista," *O Combate*, 10 May 1919, p. 1; "Organisação de um partido operario," *O Combate*, 2 April 1919, p. 1; "As 'previas' para a reno-vação da camara estadual," *O Combate*, 5 April 1919, p. 1.

98. "Em pról do operariado," *O Combate*, 6 June 1919, p. 1.

99. "A estação de Catanduva destruida a dynamite," *O Combate*, 13 Oct. 1919, p. 1; "Um appello de Rio Preto a 'O Combate,'" *O Combate*, 14 Oct. 1919, p. 1; "Para alguma coisa serve protestar," *O Combate*, 15 Oct. 1919, p. 1; "O movi-mento operario," *O Combate*, 27 Oct. 1919, p. 1; "Rio Preto," *O Combate*, 4 Nov. 1919, p. 1; "Noticias diversas," *O Estado de S. Paulo*, 15 Oct. 1919, p. 4.

100. "Atchin! . . . , atchin! . . . ," *O Combate*, 2 July 1918, p. 1.

101. "A 'influenza hespanhola,'" *O Combate*, 23 Sept. 1918, p. 1; "A 'hespan-hola,'" *O Combate*, 24 Sept. 1918, p. 1; "A 'hespanhola' já chegou ao Brasil," *O Combate*, 27 Sept. 1918, p. 1.

102. "A 'hespanhola' em S. Paulo," *O Combate*, 10 Oct. 1918, p. 1; Claudio Bertolli Filho, "A gripe espanhola em São Paulo," *Ciência Hoje* 58 (Oct. 1989): 31.

103. P. Duarte, *Memórias*, 4:418; Paulo de Almeida Nogueira, *Minha vida*, 297; Nogueira Filho, *Ideais e lutas de um burguês progressista*, 1:91.

104. P. Duarte, *Memórias*, 4:420.

105. "A pandemia da 'hespanhola,'" *O Combate*, 30 Oct. 1918, p. 1.

106. "A 'influenza hespanhola' em S. Paulo,'" *O Combate*, 25 Oct. 1918, p. 1.

107. Penteado, *Belenzinho, 1910*, 281–82. See also Figueiredo, *Memórias de um jornalista*, 174–78.

108. "A 'hespanhola,'" *O Combate*, 14 Nov. 1918, p. 1.

109. "A hecatombe da 'hespanhola,'" *O Combate*, 30 Dec. 1918, p. 1; Bertolli Filho, "A gripe espanhola em Sâo Paulo," 31.

110. "A 'hespanhola,'" *O Combate*, 14 Nov. 1918, p. 1; P. Duarte, *Memórias*, 4:420–21; A. Leite, *Subsídios para a história da civilização paulista*, 288–89; Penteado, *Belenzinho, 1910*, 282.

111. "A 'hespanhola,'" *O Combate*, 14 Nov. 1918, p. 1.

112. "A 'influenza hespanhola' em S. Paulo," *O Combate*, 24 Oct. 1918, p. 1; "A 'influenza hespanhola' em S. Paulo," *O Combate*, 25 Oct. 1918, p. 1; "A 'hespanhola,'" *O Combate*, 26 Oct. 1918, p. 1; "A pandemia da 'hespanhola,'" *O Combate*, 30 Oct. 1918, p. 1; "Noticias diversas," *O Estado de S. Paulo*, 19 Oct. 1919, p. 4; "Livro de recortes e actas" (bound volume), n.d., AIHGSP, ALN, pacote 1; P. Duarte, *Memórias*, 4:422; A. Leite, *Subsídios para a história da civilização paulista*, 288–89; Lôbo, *Recordações das arcadas*, 80; Nogueira Filho, *Ideais e lutas de um burguês progressista*, 1:91–92; Penteado, *Belenzinho, 1910*, 282.

113. "A 'hespanhola,'" *O Combate*, 14 Nov. 1918, p. 1.

114. "A Allemanha capitulou incondicionalmente," *O Combate*, 8 Nov. 1918, p. 1.

115. "A victoria dos alliados," *O Combate*, 16 Dec. 1918, p. 1.

116. In late October 1917, when President Wenceslau Braz and his cabinet asked the national Congress and Senate to recognize that a state of war existed between Brazil and the German Empire, he received nearly unanimous support in both houses. One of only a handful of exceptions, however, came from São Paulo's delegation, Congressman José Valois de Castro, who had also publicly demonstrated his support for the *Diário Alemão* after its sack in April. "A declaração de guerra," *O Combate*, 27 Oct. 1917, p. 1; P. Duarte, *Memórias*, 4:394; Guastini, *Tempos idos e vividos*, 45–46; A. Leite, *Subsídios para a história da civilização paulista*, 287; Nogueira Filho, *Ideais e lutas de um burguês progressista*, 1:82.

117. P. Duarte, *Memórias*, 4:394; Nogueira Filho, *Ideais e lutas de um burguês progressista*, 1:82–83; "O dr. Pereira Barreto glorificado pela mocidade paulista," *O Combate*, 14 May 1918, p. 3.

118. Affonso Paes de Barros et al., "Ao povo paulista," São Paulo, 18 May 1918, AIHGSP, ALN, pacote 2, item 2. The manifesto is reprinted in Nogueira Filho, *Ideais e lutas de um burguês progressista*, 2:633–34.

119. P. Duarte, *Memórias*, 4:395.

120. Quoted in Nogueira Filho, *Ideais e lutas de um burguês progressista*, 1:83.

121. "A candidatura Pereira Barreto," *O Combate*, 15 May 1918, p. 1.

122. *Fanfulla* and *Il Piccolo* are quoted in "A imprensa italiana," *O Combate*, 15 May 1918, p. 3.

123. "O dr. Pereira Barreto glorificado pela mocidade paulista," *O Combate*, 14 May 1918, p. 3; "A candidatura Pereira Barreto," *O Combate*, 15 May 1918, p. 1.

124. Quoted in Nogueira Filho, *Ideais e lutas de um burguês progressista*, 1:84.

125. "A propaganda no interior," *O Combate*, 20 May 1918, p. 3; "A propaganda," *O Combate*, 29 May 1918, p. 3; Nogueira Filho, *Ideais e lutas de um burguês progressista*, 1:85–86.

126. "A adhesão do Partido Municipal," *O Combate*, 28 May 1918, p. 3. The party's manifesto is reprinted in Nogueira Filho, *Ideais e lutas de um burguês progressista*, 2:634.

127. "Os socialistas," *O Combate*, 31 May 1918, p. 3; "Aos operarios," in secção livre of *O Estado de S. Paulo*, 1 June 1918, p. 9. This group of professed "socialists" likely included Benjamin Mota, who had co-authored, with Pereira Barreto, a statement of support for dissident candidates in elections to the federal legislature held earlier in the year. Luiz Pereira Barreto and Benjamin Mota, "Drs. Martim Francisco e Carlos Botelho," *O Combate*, 28 Feb. 1918, p. 1. Another appeal, this one to urban workers, noted Valois de Castro's praise for the killing of the freethinking educator Francisco Ferrer in 1909. "Operarios eleitores!" in secção livre of *O Estado de S. Paulo*, 1 June 1918, p. 9.

128. "A candidatura Pereira Barreto," *O Combate*, 18 May 1918, p. 3; untitled note, *O Combate*, 28 May 1918, p. 1.

129. A. C. de Camargo et al., "Manifesto da classe medica ao povo," São Paulo, 19 May 1918, AIHGSP, ALN, pacote 2, item 2; "A classe medica paulista adopta a candidatura Barreto," *O Combate*, 20 May 1918, p. 3.

130. J. A. Pinto Coelho et al., "Eleição senatorial," São Paulo, 24 May 1918, AIHGSP, ALN, pacote 2, item 2.

131. "O manifesto dos advogados," *O Combate*, 25 May 1918, p. 1.

132. Elias Machado de Almeida et al. to Comité de Propaganda da Candidatura Pereira Barreto, São Paulo, 25 May 1918; Amador Cintra do Prado et al., São Paulo, n.d. (untitled declaration of support from 148 students of the Escola Politécnica); João Nascimento da Silveira et al. to Commissão Academica, São Paulo, 30 May 1918; Trajano Martins et al., "Ao brioso e independente eleitorado do Estado de São Paulo," São Paulo, 27 May 1918; Costabile Comenale et al. to Commissão de Propaganda da Candidatura do Dr. Luiz Pereira Barreto; Juvenal Lacerda to Mocidade Academica, São Paulo, 22 May 1918; Arthur Guimarães to Commissão Pro Candidatura Dr. Luiz Pereira Barreto, São Paulo, 25 May 1918; Alfredo Rubino et al., "Moção dos alumnos da Faculdade de Direito de S. Paulo á Commissão de Propaganda da Candidatura do Dr. Luiz Pereira Barreto," n.d.; "Aos engenheiros de São Paulo," n.d.; Flaminio Favero to Paulo Nogueira Filho, São Paulo, 23 May 1918 (these documents are filed in AIHGSP, ALN, pacote 2, item 2).

133. "Em Ribeirão Preto," *O Combate*, 16 May 1918, p. 1; "A candidatura Pereira Barreto," *O Combate*, 18 May 1918, p. 1; "Em Ribeirão Preto," *O Combate*, 18 May 1918, p. 3; "A [one word, likely "scisão," censored] no P. R. G.," *O Combate*, 22 May 1918, p. 1; "Ribeirão Preto, unanime, contra a candidatura Valois," *O Combate*, 24 May 1918, p. 3; "A politica," *O Combate*, 25 May 1918, p. 1; untitled article, *O Combate*, 25 May 1918, p. 1; "O dr. Francisco da Cunha Junqueira, por ser contrario . . . ," *O Combate*, 27 May 1918, p. 1; "A candidatura Barreto," *O Combate*, 28 May 1918, p. 1; "A attitude do candidato Junqueira," *O Combate*, 30 May 1918, p. 3; "Manifestação aos drs. Francisco Junqueira e Veiga Miranda," *O Combate*, 31 May 1918, p. 1; P. Duarte, *Memórias*, 4:395; Walker, "Ribeirão Preto, 1910–1960," 70.

134. *O Combate*, 31 May 1918, p. 1.

135. Nogueira Filho, *Ideais e lutas de um burguês progressista*, 1:86–87.

136. "O 'bochismo' em funcção em Itararé," *O Combate*, 1 June 1918, p. 1.

137. "As eleições de hontem," *O Estado de S. Paulo*, 2 June 1918, p. 5.

138. Ibid.; "A fraude campeou," *O Combate*, 3 June 1918, p. 1; "As eleições," *O Estado de S. Paulo*, 3 June 1918, p. 4; "As eleições," *O Estado de S. Paulo*, 8 June 1918, p. 5; "Noticias diversas," *O Estado de S. Paulo*, 28 Oct. 1919, p. 2; P. Duarte, *Memórias*, 4:398.

139. "A fraude campeou," *O Combate*, 3 June 1918, p. 1; "As eleições," *O Combate*, 3 June 1918, p. 3; "As eleições," *O Estado de S. Paulo*, 4 June 1918, p. 4; "As eleições," *O Estado de S. Paulo*, 5 June 1918, p. 3; "As eleições," *O Estado de S. Paulo*, 6 June 1918, p. 4.

140. "As eleições de hontem," *O Estado de S. Paulo*, 2 June 1918, p. 5. *O Estado de S. Paulo* reported that Pereira Barreto won in Cravinhos (378 to 118), São Simão (254 to 83), São Joaquim (186 to 20), and Viradouro (70 to 49). In neighboring Sertãozinho, where Francisco Schmidt (who backed Valois de Castro) had extensive holdings, Pereira Barreto lost (58 to 105).

141. Nogueira Filho, *Ideais e lutas de um burguês progressista*, 1:87; "As eleições de hontem," *O Estado de S. Paulo*, 2 June 1918, p. 5; "As eleições," *O Estado de S. Paulo*, 8 June 1918, p. 5.

142. "As eleições de hontem," *O Estado de S. Paulo*, 2 June 1918, p. 5.

143. "Notas e informações," *O Estado de S. Paulo*, 4 June 1918, p. 3.

144. "Quem não é eleitor, não é bom cidadão," *O Combate*, 4 June 1918, p. 1. Referring to the Pereira Barreto campaign, the anonymous writer added: "Newspaper articles, manifestos, speeches, rallies, all are fruitless," if the intended audience was not made up of voters.

145. "Para republicanizar a Republica, organize-se o partido da opposição," *O Combate*, 5 June 1918, p. 1.

146. "O castigo," *O Combate*, 7 June 1918, p. 1; "A politica," *O Combate*, 9 July 1918, p. 1. *O Estado de S. Paulo* had reported that the local electorate in Conchas had split between Pereira Barreto and Valois de Castro (with 161 to 163 votes), while in São Joaquim, Pereira Barreto had won, with 186 votes to Valois de Castro's 20. "As eleições de hontem," *O Estado de S. Paulo*, 2 June 1918, p. 5.

147. J. Gonçalves, *Rui Barbosa*, 146–48; also J. Gonçalves, "'As imponentes festas do sol': O jubileu cívico-literário de Rui Barbosa," in Isabel Lustosa et al., *Estudos históricos sobre Rui Barbosa* (Rio de Janeiro: Casa de Rui Barbosa, 2000), 151–204.

148. J. Gonçalves, *Rui Barbosa*, 154–55; "Os ministros, escolhidos pelo sr. Rodrigues Alves, pedem demissão," *O Combate*, 17 Jan. 1919, p. 1; "Foi marcado o dia da eleição presidencial," *O Combate*, 18 Jan. 1919, p. 1; "A candidatura Ruy Barbosa," *O Combate*, 20 Jan. 1919, p. 1; P. Duarte, *Memórias*, 5:297.

149. "Notas e informações," *O Estado de S. Paulo*, 19 Jan. 1919, p. 3.

150. "Conselheiro Rodrigues Alves," *Revista do Brasil*, February 1919, pp. 233–34.

151. " . . . A nação 'quer' Ruy Barbosa": "O momento," *Revista do Brasil*, February 1919, pp. 133–34.

152. *O Parafuso*, 25 February 1919, passim. The quote on *O Parafuso*'s readership is from B. A. [the magazine's publisher, Benedicto de Andrade], "A ignomia de São Paulo," in the same unpag. issue.

153. "A candidatura Ruy Barbosa," *O Combate*, 20 Jan. 1919, p. 1.

154. "Os politicos em actividade," *O Combate*, 21 Jan. 1919, p. 1; "A victoria da candidatura Ruy parece assegurada," *O Combate*, 30 Jan. 1919, p. 1; "A politica," *O Combate*, 1 Feb. 1919, p. 1; "Apresentação de uma candidatura opposta à de Ruy Barbosa" and "A visita do sr. Lauro Muller ao ministro inglez," *O Combate*, 10 Feb. 1919, p. 1; "Os candidatos em fóco," *O Combate*, 12 Feb. 1919, p. 1; P. Duarte, *Memórias*, 5:297–99, 309; telegram, Miguel Nogueira et al. to Ruy Barbosa, Rio Preto, 28 Jan. 1919, CRB, ARB, CR.E 25/3, doc. 112; telegram, Helenio Miranda Moura to Ruy Barbosa, Santos, 1 Feb. 1919, CRB, ARB, CR.E 25/4, doc. 163; Francisco Corrêa, Attilio Velloso, and Clovomiro Lacerda to Ruy Barbosa, Casa Branca, 3 Feb. 1919, CRB, ARB, CR.E 25/4, doc. 199; Adolpho Marcondes do Amaral et al. to Ruy Barbosa, São Bento do Sapucahy, 8 Feb. 1919, CRB, ARB, CR.E 25/6, doc. 282; telegram, Leonel Orsolini, Heitor Bittencourt, and Fabio Lopes to Ruy Barbosa, Ribeirão Preto, 9 Feb. 1919, CRB, ARB, CR.E 25/7, doc. 301; telegram, Pedro Penteado to Ruy Barbosa, Amparo, 9 Feb. 1919, CRB, ARB, CR.E 25/7, doc. 303; telegram, Paes de Barros to Ruy Barbosa, São João da Bôa Vista, 13 Feb. 1919, CRB, ARB, CR.E 25/7, doc. 340; telegram, Marcondes to Ruy Barbosa, São Paulo (Belemzinho), 15 Feb. 1919, CRB, ARB, CR.E 25/8, doc. 360; telegram, Rocha Bastos, Cesario Travassos, and Pedro Doria to Ruy Barbosa, Jaboticabal, 22 Feb. 1919, CRB, ARB, CR.E 25/9, doc. 402; telegram, "Commissão Academica Pro Ruy" to Ruy Barbosa, São Paulo, 22 Feb. 1919, CRB, ARB, CR.E 25/9, doc. 412; telegram, Penido Burnier, Alvaro Ribeiro, and Felix da Cunha to Ruy Barbosa, Campinas, 23 Feb. 1919, CRB, ARB, CR.E 25/9, doc. 414; "A candidatura Ruy Barbosa," *O Estado de S. Paulo*, 24 Feb. 1919, p. 3. In the state capital, Italian residents founded their own Comitato Popolare Italiano Pró Ruy Barbosa: Mario Delanti and [one illegible name] to Ruy Barbosa, São Paulo, 4 Feb. 1919, CRB, ARB, CR.E 25/5, doc. 209.

155. "Apresentação de uma candidatura opposta à de Ruy Barbosa," *O Combate*, 10 Feb. 1919, p. 1; "Na reunião dos 'leaders,' hontem, os amigos do sr. Ruy propõem o sr. Lins," *O Combate*, 21 Feb. 1919, p. 1; "Uma entrevista com o deputado sr. Macedo Soares," *O Estado de S. Paulo*, 8 March 1919, p. 3; "A candidatura Ruy Barbosa," *O Estado de S. Paulo*, 13 March 1919, p. 3; "Notas e informações," *O Estado de S. Paulo*, 9 April 1919, p. 3; "A convenção de 25 de Fevereiro," *Correio da Manhã* (Rio de Janeiro), 26 Feb. 1919, reprinted in Ruy Barbosa, *Campanha presidencial, 1919* (Bahia: Livraria Catalina, 1919), 23–47; P. Duarte, *Memórias*, 5:300, 309; Afranio de Carvalho, *Raul Soares, um líder da república velha* (Rio de Janeiro: Forense, 1978), chap. 5.

156. The speech is reprinted in R. Barbosa, *Campanha presidencial, 1919*, 26–35 (quotes on pp. 29, 33).

157. Ibid., 35.

158. Ibid., 24–25.

159. Ibid., 39–44.

160. "No pleito de 13 de Abril serão suffragados dois candidatos," *O Combate*, 3 March 1919; "A candidatura Ruy Barbosa," *O Estado de S. Paulo*, 14 March 1919, p. 3; J. Gonçalves, *Rui Barbosa*, 136, 156.

161. "Ás classes conservadoras," in R. Barbosa, *Campanha presidencial, 1919*, 53–104 (quote on p. 63, emphasis added). In São Paulo, Ruy's speech was published in full in São Paulo's *Revista do Brasil* (March 1919, pp. 255–88) and in *O Estado de S. Paulo* ("O discurso do sr. Ruy Barbosa ás classes conservadoras," 10 March 1919, pp. 3–4).

162. "Ás classes conservadoras," in R. Barbosa, *Campanha presidencial, 1919*, 64.

163. Ibid.

164. Ibid., 100–2 (quotes on p. 102).

165. "A questão social e politica no Brasil," in R. Barbosa, *Campanha presidencial, 1919*, 107–69. Once again, Ruy's speech was republished in São Paulo as "A questão social e politica no Brasil" (*Revista do Brasil*, April 1919, pp. 381–421) and "A questão social no Brasil" (*O Estado de S. Paulo*, 22 March 1919, pp. 3–5). The source of Ruy's newfound appreciation for the problems faced by working people is unclear. Paulo Duarte, quoting a letter dated 6 March 1919 from Julio Mesquita to Nestor Rangel Pestana, a staffer at *O Estado de S. Paulo*, seems to attribute it to Mesquita; the letter read, in part: "Saturday I plan to speak with Ruy. I want to see if he will take on the social question, and, with his liberal and tolerant spirit, save us from the abyss into which the violent ones drive us." P. Duarte, *Júlio Mesquita*, 119 (original orthography restored). Wolfe, citing a Foreign Office report, claims that in late 1918 Ruy already "believed [that] only social legislation could prevent the outbreak of a revolution." Wolfe, *Working Women, Working Men*, 213 n. 87. June E. Hahner, on the basis of a short recollection by Evaristo de Moraes Filho, claims that the inspiration came later and was due to the influence of the labor lawyer Evaristo de Moraes and two of his associates. Hahner, *Poverty and Politics: The Urban Poor in Brazil, 1870–1920* (Albuquerque: University of New Mexico Press, 1987), 284, 370 n. 82.

166. "A questão social e politica no Brasil," in R. Barbosa, *Campanha presidencial, 1919*, 112.

167. Ibid.

168. Ibid., 115–69.

169. "A candidatura Ruy Barbosa," *O Estado de S. Paulo*, 23 March 1919, p. 4. In contrast, São Paulo's anarchist activists subjected Ruy's overture to blistering criticism that lasted long past the April election (see *A Plebe*, 29 March

1919, 5 April 1919, 12 April 1919, 19 April 1919, 26 April 1919, 14 June 1919, 5 July 1919), the vehemence of which leads one to believe that the republican statesman had made some impact among these militants' presumed constituency.

170. "A candidatura Rui Barbosa," *O Combate*, 20 Jan. 1919, p. 1; "O movimento a favor da candidatura Ruy Barbosa," *O Combate*, 28 Jan. 1919, p. 1.

171. Telegram, Antonio Carlos de Abreu Sodré to Delfim Moreira, São Paulo, 28 March 1919, printed in "A candidatura Ruy Barbosa," *O Estado de S. Paulo*, 29 March 1919, p. 4.

172. "A candidatura Ruy Barbosa," *O Estado de S. Paulo*, 27 Feb. 1919, p. 4.

173. "A candidatura Ruy Barbosa," *O Estado de S. Paulo*, 25 March 1919, p. 3; "Senador Ruy Barbosa," in secção livre of *O Estado de S. Paulo*, 3 April 1919, p. 9. Ruy also received the support of the Associação União Commercial of Espírito Santo do Pinhal. "A candidatura Ruy Barbosa," *O Estado de S. Paulo*, 13 March 1919, p. 3; "A candidatura Ruy Barbosa," *O Estado de S. Paulo*, 16 March 1919, p. 3.

174. "Partido Municipal" (propaganda item), in *O Estado de S. Paulo*, 11 April 1919, p. 3.

175. Mario Pinto Serva, "Candidatura monstrengo," *O Estado de S. Paulo*, 2 April 1919, p. 4; also Serva, *O voto secreto, ou a organisação de partidas nacionaes*, passim, and "Organização putrefacta," *O Estado de S. Paulo*, 1 March 1919, p. 3.

176. "Notas e informações," *O Estado de S. Paulo*, 9 April 1919, p. 3.

177. "A candidatura Ruy Barbosa," *O Estado de S. Paulo*, 16 March 1919, p. 3.

178. "A candidatura Ruy Barbosa," *O Estado de S. Paulo*, 26 Feb. 1919, p. 5.

179. "A candidatura Ruy Barbosa," *O Estado de S. Paulo*, 13 April 1919, p. 4.

180. "A candidatura Ruy Barbosa," *O Estado de S. Paulo*, 28 March 1919, p. 4; telegram, Aureliano Guimarães et al. to Ruy Barbosa, São Carlos, 15 Dec. 1909, CRB, ARB, CR.E 20/9, doc. 419; "Movimento civico," *O Combate*, 20 May 1918, p. 3; untitled note, *O Combate*, 12 July 1918, p. 1.

181. Lícia Capri Pignataro, *Imigrantes italianos em Rio Claro e seus descendentes* (Rio Claro: Arquivo Público e Histórico, 1982), 2:62–64; "A candidatura Ruy Barbosa," *O Estado de S. Paulo*, 25 March 1919, p. 3 (in which Fina is misidentified as João *Faria* Sobrinho); "Organisação de um partido operario," *O Combate*, 2 April 1919, p. 1; "As 'previas' para a renovação da camara estadual," *O Combate*, 5 April 1919, p. 1; Aloysio Pereira et al., *Rio Claro sesquicentenária* (Rio Claro: Museu Histórico e Pedagógico Amador Bueno da Veiga, 1978), 210–11. In February, Acacio de Azeredo wrote Ruy Barbosa, informing the candidate that he had spoken at a rally in Rio Claro that brought together more than eight hundred members of the "working classes," in addition to students and the "city's other classes." Among the other speakers were a worker and a law student, whose names Azeredo neglected to mention. Acacio de Azeredo to Ruy Barbosa, Araraquara, 9 Feb. 1919, CRB, ARB, CR.E 25/7, doc. 304; telegram, "Redacção Alpha" to Ruy Barbosa, Rio Claro, 8 Feb. 1919, CRB, ARB, CR.E 25/6, doc. 278.

182. "A candidatura Ruy Barbosa," *O Estado de S. Paulo,* 24 Feb. 1919, p. 3; "A candidatura Ruy Barbosa," *O Estado de S. Paulo,* 13 April 1919, p. 4. Closel (sometimes spelled Clozel) is identified only as a worker (*operario*) in the latter source. He is identified as the chief of the woodworking section of the Mogiana Railroad's Campinas workshop in "A politica," *O Combate,* 9 Oct. 1919, p. 1.

183. "A candidatura Ruy Barbosa, *O Estado de S. Paulo,* 13 April 1919, p. 4.

184. Ibid.; "A candidatura Ruy Barbosa," *O Estado de S. Paulo,* 16 March 1919, p. 3.

185. "Notas e informações," *O Combate,* 1 April 1919, p. 3; telegram, Augusto Bertolini et al. to Ruy Barbosa, Campinas, 11 April 1919, CRB, ARB, CR.E 25/16, doc. 760. On the makeup of the local pro-Ruy committee: "A candidatura Ruy Barbosa," *O Combate,* 4 April 1919, p. 4.

186. "A candidatura Ruy Barbosa," *O Estado de S. Paulo,* 5 April 1919, p. 6; Assembléia Legislativa, *Legislativo paulista,* 88–92.

187. "O pleito de sabbado," *O Combate,* 28 April 1919, p. 1; "A politica," *O Combate,* 14 Oct. 1919, p. 1 (emphasis added).

188. "A candidatura Ruy Barbosa," *O Estado de S. Paulo,* 5 April 1919, p. 6; "Ruy Barbosa," *O Combate,* 4 April 1919, p. 1; "Ao povo," *O Combate,* 3 April 1919, p. 1; P. Duarte, *Memórias,* 5:318; Ernesto Leme, *Rui e São Paulo* (Rio de Janeiro: Casa de Rui Barbosa, 1949), 27.

189. Photographs published in *O Combate,* 4 April 1919, p. 3; *O Estado de S. Paulo,* 5 April 1919, p. 6; *O Estado de S. Paulo,* 6 April 1919, p. 3; *O Parafuso,* 22 April 1919, unpag. See also Leme, *Rui e São Paulo,* 27.

190. "A candidatura Ruy Barbosa," *O Estado de S. Paulo,* 5 April 1919, p. 6.

191. "A candidatura Ruy Barbosa," *O Estado de S. Paulo,* 5 April 1919, p. 6; "Ruy Barbosa," *O Combate,* 5 April 1919, p. 1; P. Duarte, *Memórias,* 5:318; Leme, *Rui e São Paulo,* 27.

192. "O caso internacional," in R. Barbosa, *Campanha presidencial, 1919,* 199–285 (quote on pp. 199–200). The speech was also published in *O Estado de S. Paulo,* 5 April 1919, pp. 3–5, and the *Revista do Brasil,* June 1919, pp. 99–130 (in the latter case with an introduction lauding the speech and bemoaning Brazil's political situation).

193. "O caso internacional," in R. Barbosa, *Campanha presidencial, 1919,* 201–2.

194. Ibid., 205–85; "A candidatura Ruy Barbosa," *O Estado de S. Paulo,* 5 April 1919, p. 6.

195. "A candidatura Ruy Barbosa," *O Estado de S. Paulo,* 6 April 1919, p. 5.

196. "A candidatura Ruy Barbosa," *O Estado de S. Paulo,* 7 April 1919, p. 4; "O voto secreto," *O Combate,* 7 April 1919, p. 1.

197. "A candidatura Ruy Barbosa," *O Estado de S. Paulo,* 7 April 1919, p. 4; "A candidatura Ruy Barbosa," *O Estado de S. Paulo,* 8 April 1919, p. 4; "A candidatura Ruy Barbosa," *O Estado de S. Paulo,* 9 April 1919, p. 3; "Candidatura Ruy Barbosa," *O Combate,* 9 April 1919, p. 3.

198. On the use of wartime censorship for political ends: Nereu Rangel Pestana, "O Combate," S. Paulo, 11 March 1919, in *O Combate*, 12 March 1919, p. 1; Nereu Rangel Pestana, "O estado de sitio e a censura á imprensa," S. Paulo, 17 March 1918, in *O Combate*, 18 March 1918, p. 1; "O Combate," *O Combate*, 24 April 1925, p. 1; P. Duarte, *Memórias*, 4:363–64; Jorge Caldeira, "Julio Mesquita, fundador do jornalismo moderno no Brasil," in Mesquita, *A guerra*, 1:32. On importing journalists from Rio de Janeiro: P. Duarte, *Memórias*, 5:320.

199. Telegram, "Mocidade Paulista" to Ruy Barbosa, São Paulo, 12 April 1919, CRB, ARB, CR.E 25/17, doc. 806; "A candidatura Ruy Barbosa," *O Estado de S. Paulo*, 13 April 1919, p. 4.

200. "A eleição presidencial," *O Estado de S. Paulo*, 14 April 1919, p. 3; "Ruy Barbosa obteve uma esplendida votação," *O Combate*, 14 April 1919, p. 1.

201. Transcription of incoming telegram from Julio Mesquita to Ruy Barbosa, São Paulo, 13 [April] 1919, CRB, ARB, CR.E 25/20, doc. 976.

202. Electoral results from Love, *São Paulo in the Brazilian Federation*, 143.

203. Telegram, Altino Arantes to Joaquim da Cunha, São Paulo, 14 April 1919, in bound volume labeled "Presidencia Altino Arantes, Telegrammas, 1919–1920," AESP, AAA, caixa AP86. *O Estado de S. Paulo* reported that in Ribeirão Preto, Epitácio had beaten Ruy by 602 to 180 votes. "A eleição presidencial," *O Estado de S. Paulo*, 14 April 1919, p. 3.

204. Telegram, Altino Arantes to Carlos de Campos, 4 April 1919, in bound volume labeled "Presidencia Altino Arantes, Telegrammas, 1919–1920," AESP, AAA, caixa AP86; "Ribeirão Preto," *O Combate*, 9 April 1919, p. 1; "Será constituido o directorio de Ribeirão Preto?," *O Combate*, 13 Jan. 1919, p. 1.

205. Telegram, Altino Arantes to Joaquim da Cunha Junqueira, 14 April 1919, in bound volume labeled "Presidencia Altino Arantes, Telegrammas, 1919–1920," AESP, AAA, caixa AP86.

206. Election results in "O pleito de sabbado," *O Combate*, 28 April 1919, p. 1; Assembléia Legislativa, *Legislativo paulista*, 94; also, telegram, Altino Arantes to Julio Cardoso, São Paulo, 16 April 1919, in bound volume labeled "Presidencia Altino Arantes, Telegrammas, 1919–1920," AESP, AAA, caixa AP86.

207. "A politica," *O Combate*, 13 Sept. 1919, p. 1; "A politica," *O Combate*, 19 Sept. 1919, p. 1; "A politica," *O Combate*, 7 Oct. 1919, p. 1; "A politica," *O Combate*, 9 Oct. 1919, p. 1; Vicente Ferraz Pacheco to Vergueiro Steidel, Limeira, 13 Aug. 1920, AIHGSP, ALN, pacote 2, item 1.

208. "A politica," *O Combate*, 20 Oct. 1919, p. 1.

209. "A politica," *O Combate*, 13 Oct. 1919, p. 1.

210. "Os operarios e as eleições municipaes," *O Combate*, 14 Oct. 1919, p. 1. Elsewhere in the state, there were similar efforts to include workingmen in formal politics. In Itapetininga, the opposition Municipal Republican Party included in its directorate "a representative of the working class." In Campinas, the pro-Ruy campaigner Jorge Closel was put forward as the candidate of the

working class in October's municipal elections, although he appears to have dropped out of the race. "A politica," *O Combate*, 28 March 1919, p. 1; "A politica," *O Combate*, 9 Oct. 1919, p. 1; "A politica," *O Combate*, 16 Oct. 1919, p. 1; "Eleições municipaes," *O Estado de S. Paulo*, 30 Oct. 1919, p. 4.

211. "As violencias e 'trucs' do 'arnolphismo,'" *O Combate*, 31 Oct. 1919, pp. 1–2; "Ainda as fraudes e violencias do 'arnolphismo,'" *O Combate*, 3 Nov. 1919, p. 1; "Eleições municipaes," *O Estado de S. Paulo*, 31 Oct. 1919, p. 4; "Eleições municipaes," *O Estado de S. Paulo*, 2 Nov. 1919, p. 4.

212. "A politica," *O Combate*, 16 Oct. 1919, p. 1; "Campinas," reprinted from Campinas's *Diario do Povo*, 18 Oct. 1919, in the secção livre of *O Estado de S. Paulo*, 19 Oct. 1919, p. 7.

213. "Eleições municipaes," *O Estado de S. Paulo*, 30 Oct. 1919, p. 4; F. Silva, *Operários sem patrões*, 112, 239–40, 246–47, 310–12; "A candidatura Ruy Barbosa," *O Estado de S. Paulo*, 26 Feb. 1919, p. 5; "A candidatura Ruy Barbosa," *O Estado de S. Paulo*, 13 March 1919, p. 3; "A candidatura Ruy Barbosa," *O Estado de S. Paulo*, 23 March 1919, p. 4; "A candidatura Ruy Barbosa," *O Estado de S. Paulo*, 13 April 1919, p. 4; E. Rodrigues, *Os companheiros*, 4:38–39. Spellings of Luiz Lascala's surname varied; these variations include La Scala and Lascalas.

214. "Eleições municipaes," *O Estado de S. Paulo*, 31 Oct. 1919, pp. 3–4; "Eleições municipaes," *O Estado de S. Paulo*, 1 Nov. 1919, p. 2.

215. "O pleito de hoje," in secção livre of *O Estado de S. Paulo*, 30 Oct. 1919, p. 8; "Candidatos em penca," *O Combate*, 30 Oct. 1919, p. 1; "Eleições municipaes," *O Estado de S. Paulo*, 31 Oct. 1919, p. 3; "Eleições municipaes," *O Estado de S. Paulo*, 1 Nov. 1919, p. 2; P. (pseud., Pinheiro Jr.), "Coisas da cidade," *O Estado de S. Paulo*, 1 Nov. 1919, p. 5; P. Duarte, *Memórias*, 5:333; Graccho's practice is mentioned in Penteado, *Belenzinho, 1910*, 280.

216. "Eleições municipaes," *O Estado de S. Paulo*, 31 Oct. 1919, p. 3; "As eleições de hontem," *O Combate*, 31 Oct. 1919, p. 1; "As eleições municipaes," *O Parafuso*, 11 Nov. 1919, unpag. Moacyr Piza's role in the Pereira Barreto and Ruy Barbosa campaigns is mentioned in P. Duarte, *Memórias*, 9:300, and in scores of contemporary newspaper reports. See also Piza's own *Tres campanhas* (São Paulo: Secção de Obras d'*O Estado de S. Paulo*, 1922), pts. 1 and 2 of which deal with the Pereira Barreto campaign and his own municipal-council run, respectively. Neither Piza nor the business-and-industry Municipal Party of São Paulo was long for this world. The Municipal Party disbanded within the year, while Piza killed himself in 1923. "A politica," *O Combate*, 12 Nov. 1919, p. 1; "Desfralda a bandeira do voto secreto e a abandona no campo!," *O Combate*, 3 Dec. 1919, p. 1; P. Duarte, *Memórias*, 9:302–3.

217. Grínberg, *História de Mogi das Cruzes*, 145, 146, 164–65, 169–70; "Noticias diversas," *O Estado de S. Paulo*, 4 Nov. 1919, p. 5.

218. "A politica," *O Combate*, 17 Sept. 1919, p. 1; "Eleições municipaes," *O Estado de S. Paulo*, 31 Oct. 1919, p. 4; "As eleições," *O Combate*, p. 3; "Eleições municipaes," *O Estado de S. Paulo*, 1 Nov. 1919, p. 2.

219. "Noticias diversas," *O Estado de S. Paulo*, 28 Oct. 1919, p. 2; "As eleições do dia 30," *O Combate*, 28 Oct. 1919, p. 1.

220. "Eleições municipaes," *O Estado de S. Paulo*, 31 Oct. 1919, p. 4; "As eleições," *O Combate*, 31 Oct. 1919, p. 3; "Eleições municipaes," *O Estado de S. Paulo*, 1 Nov. 1919, p. 2; "Os acontecimentos de Barretos," *O Combate*, 3 Nov. 1919, p. 1.

221. "Em S. Bento do Sapucahy," *O Combate*, 27 Oct. 1919, p. 1; "Politica de bugre e liberdade de voto," *O Combate*, 10 Nov. 1919, pp. 1–2; "Politica de bugre e liberdade de voto," *O Combate*, 15 Dec. 1919, pp. 1–2.

222. "Notas e informações," *O Estado de S. Paulo*, 1 Nov. 1919, p. 3; "Notas e informações," *O Estado de S. Paulo*, 2 Nov. 1919, p. 3.

223. "Politica," *O Estado de S. Paulo*, 17 Nov. 1919, p. 3.

4. Knaves, Pedants, and Rebels

1. Representative works include: João Cabanas, *A columna do morte* (Asunción: Kraus, 1926); Joaquim Nunes de Carvalho, *A revolução no Brasil, 1924–1925: Apontamentos para a história*, 2nd ed. (Rio de Janeiro: Typ. São Benedicto, 1930); Cyro Costa and Eurico de Goes, *Sob a metralha: Historico da revólta em São Paulo, de 5 de julho de 1924* (São Paulo: Monteiro Lobato, 1924); Paulo Duarte, *Agora nós* (São Paulo: n.p., 1927); Antonio dos Santos Figueiredo, *1924: Episodios da revolução de S. Paulo* (Porto: n.p., 1924); Aureliano Leite, *Dias de pavor: Figuras e scenas da revolta de S. Paulo* (São Paulo: Monteiro Lobato, 1924); Luiz Marcigaglia, *Férias de julho: Aspectos da revolução militar de 1924 ao redor do Lyceu Salesiano de S. Paulo*, 2nd ed. (São Paulo: Escolas Profissionaes do Lyceu Coração de Jesus, 1927 [1924]); Abilio de Noronha, *Narrando a verdade* (São Paulo: Monteiro Lobato, 1924); Nelson Tabajara de Oliveira, *1924: A revolução de Isidoro* (São Paulo: Nacional, 1956); Ribeiro, *Falsa democracia*; Amilcar Salgado dos Santos, *A brigada Potyguara* (n.p., 1925); José Carlos de Macedo Soares, *Justiça: A revolta militar em São Paulo* (Paris: n.p., 1925); Juarez Tavora, *Á guisa de depoimento sobre a revolução brasileira de 1924* (São Paulo: Ed. O Combate, 1927).

2. Three decades on, Anna Maria Martinez Corrêa's *A rebelião de 1924 em São Paulo* (São Paulo: Hucitec, 1976) remains by far the best such work.

3. Júlio Prestes de Albuquerque, *1924: Um depoimento*, ed. Célio Debes (São Paulo: Arquivo do Estado, 1981), 22–25. An anti-PRP journalist, Antônio dos Santos Figueiredo, likewise noted that the members of the "last [breakaway faction] were the first to lend their services to the federal government." See his *1924*, 116.

4. Figueiredo, *1924*, 45–46. Julio Mesquita (Pai) was by this point in semi-retirement, spending much of his time at the family's farm in Louveira (in Jundiaí county) or waxing nostalgic with old friends in Campinas, where he

had grown up and gotten his start in politics and journalism. He had long suffered from what family and friends referred to as "pulmonary problems" (tuberculosis, one gathers) and would die in March 1927. See Esther Mesquita, *Um livro de memórias sem importância,* trans. Lucia de Salles Oliveira (São Paulo: Livraria Duas Cidades, 1982).

5. Soares, *Justiça,* 25–26; Vilma Keller, "José Carlos de Macedo Soares," in A. Abreu et al., *Dicionário histórico-biográfico brasileiro,* 5:5521; René Thiollier, *O homem da galeria: Echos de uma epoca* (São Paulo: Depositaria Livraria Teixeira, n.d.), 26–27.

6. José Carlos de Macedo Soares, "Associação Commercial de S. Paulo," *O Estado de S. Paulo,* 8 July 1924, p. 3; idem, *Justiça,* 27–28; Thiollier, *O homem da galeria,* 28–30.

7. Pereira de Queiroz's account of the meeting is reproduced in Costa and Goes, *Sob a metralha,* 83–85. See also Procurador Criminal da Republica, *Successos subversivos de São Paulo: Denuncia apresentada ao exmo. sr. dr. juiz federal da 1ª vara de São Paulo* (Rio de Janeiro: Imprensa Nacional, 1925), 69–70; A. Leite, *Dias de pavor,* 74–87; A. Leite, *Páginas de uma longa vida,* 41; Soares, *Justiça,* chap. 1; Corrêa, *A rebelião de 1924 em São Paulo,* 132–40. Earlier in the year, Pereira de Queiroz had explained his decision to enlist in the PRP in a speech in the municipal legislature. Its publication in *O Estado de S. Paulo*'s pay-to-print section was an occasion for some levity on the part of the newspaper's typesetters: S. A. Pereira de Queiroz, "A situação politica," São Paulo, 9 Feb. 1924, in secção livre, *O Estado de S. Paulo,* 10 Feb. 1924, p. 14.

8. José Carlos de Macedo Soares to Abilio de Noronha, São Paulo, 16 July 1924, reprinted in Costa and Goes, *Sob a metralha,* 139–40; Corrêa, *A rebelião de 1924 em São Paulo,* 143n.–44n.; and Soares, *Justiça,* 78–79.

9. José Carlos de Macedo Soares to Rodrigo Monteiro Diniz Junqueira, São Paulo, 19 July 1924, AESP, AJCMS, caixa AP153, pacote 3. The letter is reprinted, in slightly different form, in Corrêa, *A rebelião de 1924 em São Paulo,* 157n. On Ribeirão Preto during July 1924, see Corrêa, *A rebelião de 1924 em São Paulo,* 176; Walker, "Ribeirão Preto, 1910–1960," 72.

10. The letter to Socrates, and the cover letter transmitting a copy to Carlos de Campos, are published in Corrêa, *A rebelião de 1924 em São Paulo,* 149n. (see also pp. 150–51 on the rebel withdrawal); Costa and Goes, *Sob a metralha,* 248–49; and Soares, *Justiça,* 124–25. On Macedo Soares, see British Chamber of Commerce of São Paulo and Southern Brazil, *Personalidades no Brasil,* 432; Wanor R. Godinho and Oswaldo S. Andrade, *Constituintes brasileiros de 1934* (Rio de Janeiro: n.p., 1934), 195–96; Melo, *Dicionário de autores paulistas,* 607–8; Vilma Keller, "José Carlos de Macedo Soares," in A. Abreu et al., *Dicionário histórico-biográfico brasileiro,* 5:5520–27; Mônica Kornis, "Liga Eleitoral Católica," in ibid., 3:3119; Marieta de Morais Ferreira and Dora Flaksman, "Partido Democrata Cristão (1945–1965)," in ibid., 4:4297.

11. Quoted in Costa and Goes, *Sob a metralha,* 40.

12. Quoted in ibid., 93.

13. "Liga Nacionalista," *O Estado de S. Paulo*, 15 July 1924, p. 1; "Os abrigos da 'Liga Nacionalista,'" *O Combate*, 25 July 1924, p. 1; Figueiredo, *1924*, 115; Marcigaglia, *Férias de julho*, 202, 204; Corrêa, *A rebelião de 1924 em São Paulo*, 157.

14. The petition is reprinted in Costa and Goes, *Sob a metralha*, 144–46; P. Duarte, *Agora nós*, 114–15; and Marcigaglia, *Férias de julho*, 186–87.

15. P. Duarte, *Agora nós*, 293–95, 298–99.

16. Quoted in Corrêa, *A rebelião de 1924 em São Paulo*, 142–43.

17. Raul Renato Cardoso de Mello Filho, "Aos academicos de S. Paulo," São Paulo, 19 July 1924, in *A Capital*, 22 July 1924, p. 2; P. Duarte, *Agora nós*, 292.

18. "Carta aberta," *A Capital*, 20 July 1924, p. 1; Corrêa, *A rebelião de 1924 em São Paulo*, 157n.; British Chamber of Commerce of São Paulo and Southern Brazil, *Personalidades no Brasil*, 744–45; Melo, *Dicionário de autores paulistas*, 28; telegram, Clovis Botelho Vieira to Ruy Barbosa, Rio Preto, 8 Feb. 1919, CRB, ARB, CR.E 25/6, doc. 275; transcription of telegram, Clovis Botelho Vieira to Ruy Barbosa, São Paulo, 21 [March] 1919, CRB, ARB, CR.E 25/20, doc. 976; "A candidatura Ruy Barbosa," *O Estado de S. Paulo*, 4 April 1919, p. 4; "A candidatura Ruy Barbosa," *O Estado de S. Paulo*, 9 April 1919, p. 3; "A candidatura Ruy Barbosa," *O Estado de S. Paulo*, 11 April 1919, p. 4; "A candidatura Ruy Barbosa," *O Estado de S. Paulo*, 14 April 1919, p. 3; Clovis Botelho Vieira, *O general Ataliba Leonel* (São Paulo: n.p., 1959), 3–4. Antônio dos Santos Figueiredo agreed with Botelho Vieira that the league had had an obligation to support the revolution. See his *1924*, 210–11. The rebels' minimum program, "Condições da junta revolucionaria para depor as armas," published in various paulistano newspapers on 18 July, is reprinted in Costa and Goes, *Sob a metralha*, 143–44.

19. Figueiredo, *1924*, 249–51; Corrêa, *A rebelião de 1924 em São Paulo*, 158n.; Belisario Penna, "Manifesto á nação," Limeira, 22 July 1924, in *A Capital*, 27 July 1924, p. 2; Belisario Penna [to his children], Limeira, 22 July 1924, AIHGSP, AR1924, caixa 7; Joaquim Carvalho, *A revolução no Brasil, 1924–1925*, unpag. front matter and pp. 51–52; Helena Faria, "Belisário Pena," in A. Abreu et al., *Dicionário histórico-biográfico brasileiro*, 4:4524.

20. Couto Esher, "Uma observação," *A Capital*, 14 July 1924, p. 2; "Notas para um archivo," *O Combate*, 22 Feb. 1928, p. 6.

21. *O Combate*, 4 Aug. 1924, p. 1; *O Combate*, 31 Jan. 1925, p. 4; Dias, *História das lutas sociais no Brasil*, 317; John W. F. Dulles, *Anarchists and Communists in Brazil, 1900–1935* (Austin: University of Texas Press, 1973), 8, 243, 256; Melo, *Dicionário de autores paulistas*, 405–6; E. Rodrigues, *Nacionalismo e cultura social, 1913–1922*, 35, 65–66, 210–13, 437, 438, 444; Edilene Toledo, *Travessias revolucionárias: idéias e militantes sindicalistas em São Paulo e na Itália, 1890–1945* (Campinas: Ed. da Universidade Estadual de Campinas, 2004), 186, 274, 377 n. 30; "Mais um manifesto pró Nilo-Seabra," *O Combate*, 29 July 1921, p. 1; "A successão presidencial da republica," *O Combate*, 30 July 1921, p. 1; "A

successão presidencial da republica," *O Combate*, 1 Aug. 1921, p. 1; "O regresso do dr. Seabra ao Rio," *O Combate*, 3 Aug. 1921, p. 1; "Pró Nilo-Seabra," *O Combate*, 3 Oct. 1921, p. 3; "Em S. Paulo," *O Combate*, 10 Oct. 1921, p. 1; "Em S. Paulo," *O Combate*, 24 Oct. 1921, p. 1; Benjamin Mota, "A reacção republicana e a formação de um partido nacional," *O Combate*, 14 Feb. 1922, pp. 1, 3; Serafim Leme da Silva et al., "Ao eleitorado independente de São Paulo," São Paulo, 3 April 1922, in secção livre, *O Combate*, 27 April 1922, p. 2.

22. Dulles, *Anarchists and Communists in Brazil, 1900–1935*, 140; "As informações do sr. Thyrso Martins ao juizo federal," *O Combate*, 7 Jan. 1920, p. 1.

23. Procurador Criminal da Republica, *Successos subversivos de São Paulo*, 217; Policia de São Paulo, *Movimento subversivo de julho*, 50; Corrêa, *A rebelião de 1924 em São Paulo*, 158n. (Mauro Machado quote, orthography restored); Nicolau Soares do Couto Esher to Nilo Peçanha, São Paulo, 12 Feb. 1922, MR, ANP, caixa 48; "Mais um manifesto pró Nilo-Seabra," *O Combate*, 29 July 1921, p. 1; "A successão presidencial da republica," *O Combate*, 30 July 1921, p. 1; "A successão presidencial da republica," *O Combate*, 1 Aug. 1921, p. 1; "O regresso do dr. Seabra ao Rio," *O Combate*, 3 Aug. 1921, p. 1; "Em S. Paulo," *O Combate*, 24 Oct. 1921, p. 1; Serafim Leme da Silva et al., "Ao eleitorado independente de São Paulo," São Paulo, 3 April 1922, in secção livre, *O Combate*, 27 April 1922, p. 2; "A politica," *O Combate*, 2 Dec. 1916, p. 1.

24. Procurador Criminal da Republica, *Successos subversivos de São Paulo*, 79, 111; Duarte, untitled manuscript, p. 232, CEDAE, FPD, PI.16; Figueiredo, *1924*, 199; "A candidatura Ruy Barbosa," *O Estado de S. Paulo*, 5 April 1919, p. 6; "A candidatura Ruy Barbosa," *O Estado de S. Paulo*, 9 April 1919, p. 3; "A candidatura Ruy Barbosa," *O Estado de S. Paulo*, 10 April 1919, p. 3; "A successão presidencial da republica," *O Combate*, 1 Aug. 1921, p. 1; "O regresso do dr. Seabra ao Rio," *O Combate*, 3 Aug. 1921, p. 1; "A reacção republicana," *O Combate*, 19 Jan. 1922, p. 1; "O nosso anniversario," *O Combate*, 26 April 1922, p. 1; Laura Christina Mello de Aquino, *Os "tenentes" estrangeiros: A participação de batalhões estrangeiros na rebelião de 1924 em São Paulo* (João Pessoa: Ed. da Universidade Federal de Paraíba, 1998), 54; Eduardo Maffei, *Vidas sem norte: Romance do tenentismo* (São Paulo: Brasiliense, 1980), 23–24, 82, 91, 93 (pp. 23–24 are from the narrative, novelistic portion of Maffei's book and refer to a character, a popular lawyer named "Tucci"; the remaining pages cited are from his factual "Contrapunto" and refer by name to Tocci, whom Maffei claims to have known personally). A figure apparently based on Tocci makes a fleeting appearance in Menotti Del Picchia's novel *Tormenta* (São Paulo: Nacional, 1932), 147.

25. "Manifesto aos operarios do Partido do Trabalho," São Paulo, 23 July 1924, AIHGSP, AR1924, caixa 7.

26. Ibid.

27. Figueiredo, *1924*, 100.

28. Quote from Corrêa, *A rebelião de 1924 em São Paulo*, 142; "Comicio," *A Capital*, 14 July 1924, p. 1.

29. The motion is published in Edgar Rodrigues, ed., *Alvorada operária: Os congressos operários no Brasil* (Rio de Janeiro: Mundo Livre, 1979), 331–34. See also Figueiredo, *1924*, 211–12; Corrêa, *A rebelião de 1924 em São Paulo*, 164–65; Dulles, *Anarchists and Communists in Brazil, 1900–1935*, 241–42; French, "Industrial Workers and the Origin of Populist Politics in the ABC Region of Greater São Paulo, 1900–1950," 99–101.

30. Figueiredo, *1924*, 235–36; *O Estado de S. Paulo*, 26 July 1924, quoted in Corrêa, *A revolução de 1924 em São Paulo*, 161n. On Schmidt, who had also, briefly, been among the fervent supporters of the First World War to end all wars, see his "A encruzilada," in *Testamento de uma geração*, ed. Edgard Cavalheiro (Porto Alegre: Livraria do Globo, 1944), 53–58; Melo, *Dicionário de autores paulistas*, 565–66.

31. "O proletariado paulista," *Marreta*, 27 July 1924 (from CEDAE, FPD, pasta DET.158); P. Duarte, *Memórias*, 8:220–21.

32. "Ao povo," n.d., CEDAE, FPD, pasta DET.157; Corrêa, *A revolução de 1924 em São Paulo*, 162–63.

33. The statement issued by the Quartel General das Forças Revolucionarias em São Paulo may be found in Costa and Goes, *Sob a metralha*, 177–78. It is discussed in Figueiredo, *1924*, 238.

34. The official report on the rebellion estimates that the rebels initially numbered around two thousand men, but their numbers reached more than five thousand by 9 July and that "over the course of the occupation, with the adhesions received and the incorporation of civilians and foreign battalions," the number of men under rebel command rose to around seven thousand, then dipped to "little more than three thousand men" under Isidoro's command during the retreat. Policia de São Paulo, *Movimento subversivo de julho*, 79. According to Juarez Távora, when the bulk of the rebel army regrouped in Bauru after its withdrawal from the state capital—including "soldiers from the Army, from the [Força Pública] of São Paulo and civilian volunteers," but not including detachments that were sent on diversionary maneuvers—it numbered three thousand. See his *Uma vida e muitas lutas*, 3 vols. (Rio de Janeiro: José Olympio, 1973–76), 1:145.

35. C. R. Cameron, Political Report No. 7, "Echoes of the São Paulo Revolt of July, 1924," 31 Jan. 1927, 4, USNARA, RG59, 832.00/616. On immigrant volunteers, see also Policia de São Paulo, *Movimento subversivo de julho*, 61–77; "As lições da revolta," *O Combate*, 12 Aug. 1924, p. 1; A. Leite, *Dias de pavor*, 133–34; N. Oliveira, *1924*, 101–2; Corrêa, *A rebelião de 1924 em São Paulo*, 161–62; Angelo Trento, *Do outro lado do Atlântico: Um século de imigração italiana no Brasil*, trans. Mariarosaria Fabris and Luiz Eduardo de Lima Brandão (São Paulo: Nobel, 1988), 390; Aquino, *Os "tenentes" estrangeiros*.

36. Dias, *História das lutas sociais no Brasil*, 140.

37. Corrêa, *A rebelião de 1924 em São Paulo*, 158–62; Procurador Criminal da Republica, *Successos subversivos de São Paulo*, 79–85, 216–21; Policia de São

Paulo, *Movimento subversivo de julho*, 47–51, 55–57, 61–77; Ralph Mennucci Giesbrecht, *Sud Mennucci: Memórias de Piracicaba, Porto Ferreira, São Paulo...* (São Paulo: Imprensa Oficial, 1997), 35.

38. Costa and Goes, *Sob a metralha*, 46.

39. José Carlos de Macedo Soares to Eduardo Socrates, São Paulo, 27 July 1924, reprinted in Costa and Goes, *Sob a metralha*, 249.

40. Marcigaglia, *Férias de julho*, 73. See also A. Leite, *Dias de pavor*, 20–21.

41. Marcigaglia, *Férias de julho*, 86–88.

42. Ibid., 102–3.

43. In the preface of his memoir of July 1924, Marcigaglia expressed his opinion that if violent revolution had to be made in Brazil, it should be carried out by "the process of Mussolini or Primo de Rivera." Ibid., 23.

44. A. Leite, *Dias de pavor*, 73–74.

45. Figueiredo, *1924*, 99, 106.

46. "O mercado da rua 25 de março foi saqueado por grande numero de populares," *A Capital*, 9 July 1924, p. 1; "O saque," *A Capital*, 9 July 1924, p. 2; "Syrio não é povo!," *A Capital*, 9 July 1924, p. 2; Figueiredo, *1924*, 149.

47. "A 'vida apertada' de certos negociantes," *O Combate*, 21 July 1924, p. 1; "Saques," *O Combate*, 21 July 1924, p. 1; "Tem que devolver," *O Combate*, 21 July 1924, p. 1. The quote is from "Applique-se a lei!," *O Combate*, 22 July 1924, p. 1. Laura Christina Mello de Aquino quotes similar statements from the *Jornal do Comércio*. See her *Os "tenentes" estrangeiros*, 28, 47 n. 16.

48. Quoted in Dulles, *Anarchists and Communists in Brazil, 1900–1935*, 239.

49. Memorandum, "Military Revolt at São Paulo," A. Gualin to State Department, Rio de Janeiro, 24 July 1924, USNARA, RG59, 832.00/405.

50. Quoted in Trento, *Do outro lado do Atlântico*, 388. Jorge Americano, in an equally hostile account, contended that the rebels gave the ransacked foodstuffs and beverages "to the workers, as a means of attracting them to the cause of revolt. In those days, in which everything belonged to everyone, fine wines and foreign delicacies were not wanting on working-class tables." See his *A lição dos factos: Revolta de 5 de julho de 1924* (São Paulo: Saraiva, 1924), 139.

51. Trento, *Do outro lado do Atlântico*, 388. Joel Wolfe has argued that "workers sacked food warehouses in Brás, Mooca, and other neighborhoods in riots carefully targeted against the holdings of industrialists, especially Francisco Matarazzo and Pinotti Gamba." Wolfe, *Working Women, Working Men*, 37. Drawing on British consular documentation unconsulted by the author, Wolfe went on to argue that "workers stole and destroyed machinery in some factories and burned down certain flour mills they blamed for the high prices of foodstuffs." Ibid., 37, 220 n. 144. In this scenario, working-class men and women would have had in mind grievances and targets similar to those of the petty retail merchants described in *O Combate*. In another scenario, sketched by Angelo Trento, "stores and businesses" owned by the "Italian elite" were

targeted because of the latter's links to the PRP leadership. See his *Do outro lado do Atlântico*, 387.

52. Alan K. Manchester, "Reminiscences of a Latin American Revolution," *South Atlantic Quarterly* 32, no. 1 (Jan. 1933): 78–79 (quote on p. 79); also, "A verdadeira causa da alta do feijão," *O Combate*, 18 May 1917, p. 1.

53. J. Martins, *Subúrbio*, 214, 268–69, 273–74. See also, among the plates following p. 225, the photograph of a 75mm shell that Veronesi evidently held on to as a keepsake of the rebellion. Martins further identifies Veronesi as an anarchist. Given recent work on labor-left ideas in Italo-Brazilian circles during these years, and his subsequent involvement in electoral politics (below, chap. 5), it seems at least as likely that he was a syndicalist. For a very fine examination of the trans-Atlantic syndicalist tradition, see Toledo, *Travessias revolucionárias*.

54. French, "Industrial Workers and the Origin of Populist Politics in the ABC Region of Greater São Paulo, 1900–1950," 70–71; "Intrigando . . . ," *O Combate*, 21 Oct. 1925, p. 4; "Intrigando . . . ," *O Combate*, 6 Nov. 1925, p. 4; "Intrigando . . . ," *O Combate*, 14 Nov. 1925, p. 4.

55. J. Martins, *Subúrbio*, 268. The relative meaninglessness of this sort of mobilization for the vast majority of the population is expressed elegantly if perhaps excessively by José de Souza Martins: "Historical documentation speaks of incidents that occurred in [São Caetano], but does not indicate that the local population had participated in them as a protagonist. I have attempted to pass on to the reader . . . the same [impression] that [the documentation] gave me, a history of mute and immobile silhouettes. Those who moved and spoke were passing through the locale and had nothing to do with it and its people. At the same time that the Revolution played itself out, the workers would have been looking for work." Ibid., 20.

56. The new local government consisted of Lúcio Damaso de Carvalho, Lucas Masculo, and Cícero Costa. Policia de São Paulo, *Movimento subversivo de julho*, 102; Maria Helena Petrillo Berardi, *Santo Amaro* (São Paulo: Prefeitura Municipal, Secretária de Educação e Cultura, 1969), 99–100; telegram, Cicero Costa and Franco Ferreira to Nilo Peçanha, São Paulo, 27 June 1921, in bound vol., *Correspondencia recebida dos estados de São Paulo . . .* , MR, ANP, caixa 55; "A successão presidencial da republica," *O Combate*, 1 Aug. 1921, p. 1; "A successão presidencial," *O Combate*, 11 Aug. 1921, p. 1; Hermínio Linhares, *Contribuição à história das lutas operárias no Brasil*, 2nd ed. (São Paulo: Alfa-Omega, 1977 [1955]), 56; Toledo, *Travessias revolucionárias*, 324, 334 n. 146. The legal prefeito, Isaias Branco de Araújo, who may have abandoned his office, suggested that Marrey Júnior attempted to install a local government aligned with the anti-rump schism of 1923–24, but as his testimony is the only mention of like activity that I have come across, I am reluctant to lend it too much credence. Araújo is quoted in Corrêa, *A rebelião de 1924 em São Paulo*, 170n.

57. The accounts that follow draw heavily on Policia de São Paulo, *Movimento subversivo de julho* (pp. 81–262 of which deal with the interior of the state). This source is far from pristine; indeed, as Paulo Duarte argued at the time: "The investigations from the interior are full of persecutions of political adversaries who were never revolutionaries" as police officials sought to punish "the opponents of the Republican Party." P. Duarte, *Agora nós*, 18. However, the report was based on a wealth of documentation gathered by government investigators, documentation that Anna Maria Martinez Corrêa had direct access to in researching her *A rebelião de 1924 em São Paulo*. Although the problem of multiple, independent attestation remains for a third of the cases that I discuss in the paragraphs that follow, I take some solace in the fact that on the basis of the published report and my own research on longer term political alignments in scores of individual counties I have reached many of the same overall conclusions reached by Corrêa.

58. Policia de São Paulo, *Movimento subversivo de julho*, 83–91.

59. Ibid., 128–35; João Fina Sobrinho to Nilo Peçanha, Rio Claro, 9 March 1922, MR, ANP, caixa 27, pasta 1; A. Pereira et al., *Rio Claro sesquicentenária*, 212; on Fina Sobrinho's involvement in Ruy's campaign of 1919, see chap. 3, above. The junta member Eduardo de Almeida Prado, to whom power was turned over as the revolutionary prefeito, was a more conventional out (he was a local planter and had been a perrepista and president of the town council in 1921–22). See Pagnocca, *Crônica dos prefeitos de Rio Claro, 1908–1983*, 47.

60. Pignataro, *Imigrantes italianos em Rio Claro e seus descendentes*, 2:62–64 (quotes on p. 63, original orthography restored). Additional evidence indicates that Fina Sobrinho was incarcerated with other rebels in 1924 and may have been involved in pre-revolutionary plotting involving the local military detachment in Rio Claro. João Fina Sobrinho et al. to J. F. Assis Brasil, no location, n.d. [likely late 1924], in Vizentini, *O Rio Grande do Sul e a política nacional*, 126–29; João Fina Sobrinho to Nilo Peçanha, Rio Claro, 10 March 1922, MR, ANP, caixa 27, pasta 1. According to the rebel veteran Nelson Tabajara de Oliveira, Fina Sobrinho and his brother Manoel took part in the "Coluna Paulista" in 1924. See his *1924*, 185.

61. Policia de São Paulo, *Movimento subversivo de julho*, 98–101; Costa and Goes, *Sob a metralha*, 316–18.

62. Policia de São Paulo, *Movimento subversivo de julho*, 161–62. This situation was not uncommon. One junior officer described the resulting difficulty of organizing local governments to Antônio dos Santos Figueiredo: "He returned, that day, from an excursion through the interior. Izidoro Dias Lopes had charged him with organizing local governments, preferably calling upon members of the oppositions for administrative posts. He could not carry out his orders as the incumbents, fearing the loss of their places, offered to lend their services to the revolutionaries, alleging that the program of the latter was

the same one that they had always adopted in their long political career[s]! . . ."
Figueiredo, *1924*, 166.

63. Policia de São Paulo, *Movimento subversivo de julho*, 194–95.

64. Ibid., 91; Manchester, "Reminiscences of a Latin American Revolution," 77.

65. Policia de São Paulo, *Movimento subversivo de julho*, 91–94; Ribeiro, *Falsa democracia*, 275–413; Manchester, "Reminiscences of a Latin American Revolution," 79–80 (quote on p. 80).

66. Gustavo Jacques Dias Alvim, *"O Diário": A saga de um jornal de causas* (Piracicaba: Ed. da Universidade Metodista de Piracicaba, 1998), 32; Corrêa, *A rebelião de 1924 em São Paulo*, 172n., 174n.; Cecílio Elias Netto, *Memorial de Piracicaba: Século XX* (Piracicaba: Instituto Histórico e Geográfico de Piracicaba, 2000), 172; Giesbrecht, *Sud Mennucci*, 35; Policia de São Paulo, *Movimento subversivo de julho*, 163–65; Terci, "A cidade na primeira republica," 226–48, 250–51.

67. Policia de São Paulo, *Movimento subversivo de julho*, 145–49; Costa and Goes, *Sob a metralha*, 359–61; telegram, Rocha Barros et al. to Ruy Barbosa, 4 Feb. 1919, CRB, ARB, CR.E 25/5; telegram, Rocha Barros et al. to Ruy Barbosa, Jaboticabal, 22 Feb. 1919, CRB, ARB, CR.E 25/9; telegram, *Democrata* to Nilo Peçanha, Jaboticabal, 20 [June?] 1921, in bound volume, Reacção Republicana, *Correspondencia recebida dos Estados de São Paulo, Paraná, S. Catharina, Rio Grande do Sul, Minas Gerais, Matto Grosso e Goyaz no periodo de junho a setembro de 1921*, MR, ANP, caixa 55; Cantidio Brêtas to Nilo Peçanha, Jaboticabal, 6 March 1922, MR, ANP, caixa 37. The lawyer Cantidio Brêtas [Cantídio Bretas], who was nominated military governor of Jaboticabal by the military rebels, is identified by Everardo Dias as one of the "first socialist and syndicalist propagators, organizers and militants in Brazil" in his *História das lutas sociais no Brasil*, 317.

68. Cabral, *Batalhões patrioticos na revolução de 1924*, 13–25.

69. Policia de São Paulo, *Movimento subversivo de julho*, 245; D. Abreu, *Formação histórica de uma cidade pioneira paulista*, 239, 239n.–40n.

70. Policia de São Paulo, *Movimento subversivo de julho*, 245; Cabral, *Batalhões patrioticos na revolução de 1924*, 165–71.

71. Policia de São Paulo, *Movimento subversivo de julho*, 109–11. One of the would-be junta members reemerges in the documentation years later as the secretary of the local PRP directory. Telegram, Ribeiro do Valle and Annubes Velloso to Julio Prestes de Albuquerque, São Simão, 12 March 1929, AESP, AJPA, caixa AP22.

72. Policia de São Paulo, *Movimento subversivo de julho*, 150; Leaflet, "Ao povo brasileiro," Bebedouro, 15 July 1924, AIHGSP, AR1924, caixa 7.

73. Policia de São Paulo, *Movimento subversivo de julho*, 169–70; Alante Lorensetti and José Ribeiro Pereira to "Commissão de Estudantes encarregada

da propaganda da candidatura do sabio e patriota dr. Luiz Pereira Barreto," Soccorro, 18 May 1918, AIHGSP, ALN, pacote 2, item 2.

74. Policia de São Paulo, *Movimento subversivo de julho*, 199–200 (quotes on p. 199).

75. Ibid., 114–21; *Album de Araras: Documentário histórico, geográfico, ilustrativo do município de Araras* (Araras: n.p., 1948), unpag.

76. "Nos bastidores da politica" (newspaper clipping labeled *Diario da Noite*, 27 Nov. 1925), AESP, AJCDJ, caixa AP174, pasta 2; Walker, "Ribeirão Preto, 1910–1960," 72.

77. Dias, *História das lutas sociais no Brasil*, 140. See also Dulles, *Anarchists and Communists in Brazil, 1900–1935*, 243.

78. Procurador Criminal da Republica, *Successos subversivos de São Paulo*, 182; Policia de São Paulo, *Movimento subversivo de julho*, 177–85, 240–85; "Foi preso o chefe do trafego da Douradense," *O Combate*, 12 Aug. 1924, p. 1; N. Oliveira, *1924*, 50. A handful of São Paulo-based railwaymen of the Central do Brasil line were also implicated in the rebellion. See Corrêa, *A rebelião de 1924 em São Paulo*, 159n.

79. Afonso Schmidt, *Bom tempo* (São Paulo: Brasiliense, 1958), 317. Everardo Dias makes observations similar to Schmidt's and reprints popular songs from the 1920s that commemorated and incited revolt in "O 5 de julho de 24 e sua repercussão popular no país," *Revista Brasiliense*, May-June 1962, pp. 158–59, 161.

80. Jardim, *A aventura de outubro e a invasão de São Paulo*, 14–15; "O dr. Washington Luis chega a S. Paulo," *O Combate*, 30 July 1924, p. 1. An anonymous contributor to *O Pinheirense* likewise linked the truculence of two workers, one of them a Hungarian, to the military rebellions of the 1920s. "Dentro da noite," *O Pinheirense*, 4 Aug. 1929, p. 1.

81. Quoted, in English translation, in C. R. Cameron, Political Report No. 7, "Echoes of the São Paulo Revolt of July, 1924," 31 Jan. 1927, 14, USNARA, RG59, 832.00/616.C.

82. Monteiro Lobato to Arthur Bernardes, São Paulo, 9 Aug. 1924, AIHGSP, AAL, pacote 12, item 1.

83. Ibid.

84. Ibid.

85. Ibid. (original emphasis).

86. Ibid. (original emphases).

87. Ibid. (original emphasis).

88. Ibid. (emphases added).

89. Ibid.

90. Ibid. (the spelling of Saenz Peña's name is Lobato's own). Bernardes responded a month later: "I am in complete agreement with your judicious

opinion regarding the adoption of a high standard for . . . the electorate." He also noted that a study of constitutional reform was underway and took issue, in part, with Lobato's assertion that rampant disaffection among paulistas was the root cause of the unsettled times: "With regard to the attitude of the paulista people in the face of the uprising of July 5, I recognize that the lack of a more prompt civic reaction was in part due to the reasons indicated in your worthy letter but I believe that th[is] lamentable occurrence was also due to the influence of the foreign element" in the city of São Paulo. Arthur Bernardes to Monteiro Lobato, Rio de Janeiro, 6 Sept. 1924, AIHGSP, AAL, pacote 12, item 1.

91. Lobato et al., *O voto secreto: Carta aberta ao exmo. snr. dr. Carlos de Campos* (São Paulo: n.p., 1924); "O voto secreto," *O Combate*, 19 Oct. 1925, p. 3; Marcia Mascarenhas Camargos and Vladmir Sacchetta, "Procura-se Peter Pan . . . ," in *Minorias silenciadas: História da censura no Brasil*, ed. Maria Luiza Tucci Carneiro (São Paulo: Imprensa Oficial, 2002), 212–15.

92. The other signatories were Alcibiades Piza, Antônio Carlos de Assumpção, Renato Maia, Erasmo de Assumpção, Ayres Neto, Mário Pinto Serva (the most persistent advocate of the secret ballot), Joaquim Cândido de Azevedo, Agenor de Camargo, Schmidt Sarmento, Ovídio Pires de Campos, Brenno Ferraz do Amaral, Prudente de Moraes Neto, and Christiano Altenfelder Silva. See Lobato et al., *O voto secreto*, 17–18.

93. Ibid., 11–12, 14.

94. Ibid., 12 (original emphasis).

95. Ibid., 12–15.

96. Ibid. (original emphasis). The presence of regionalist motifs like "*leader of the union*" in contemporary accounts is considered in Cássia Chrispiano Adduci, "Nação brasileira e 'mística paulista': Uma análise dos memorialistas da rebelião militar de 1924 em São Paulo," *Lutas Sociais* 5 (1998): 7–24.

97. "A revolução legal," published in his *O espirito das democracias* (São Paulo: Monteiro Lobato, 1924), 133–75 (quotes on pp. 134–35, 138–39, 142).

98. Ibid., 144–75 (quote on p. 148).

99. Americano, *A lição dos factos*; Melo, *Dicionário de autores paulistas*, 47.

100. Americano, *A lição dos factos*, 1, 33.

101. Ibid., quote on p. 43.

102. Ibid., 34.

103. Ibid., chap. 3 (quotes on pp. 63, 64).

104. Ibid., 135–40 (quotes on pp. 135–36).

105. Ibid., 147–69.

106. Ibid., 186 (emphasis added).

107. Ibid., chaps. 3–9. "Jorge Americano," in A. Abreu et al., *Dicionário histórico-biográfico brasileiro*, 1:211.

108. Julio de Mesquita Filho, "A crise nacional," *O Estado de S. Paulo*, 15 Nov. 1925, p. 2; Mesquita Filho, *A crise nacional: Reflexões em torno de uma data* (São

Paulo: Secção de Obras d' *O Estado de S. Paulo*, 1925), quote on pp. 66–67; Freyre, *Order and Progress*, chap. 6 (esp. pp. 203, 207–9).

109. Mesquita Filho, *A crise nacional*, 4.

110. Ibid., 7–9, 11. This repugnant assertion was a familiar refrain for Mesquita, who elsewhere blamed the decline of "civic sentiment" in Brazil on "contact with the African [*sic*]" and wrote of the "mental chaos in which the influx of Africans [*sic*] submerged us." Ibid., 13, 18. Mesquita's racism did not go wholly unchallenged. In *O Commentario*, a journal edited by João Pedro da Veiga Miranda under the inspiration of Alberto Torres (the journal led with the epigraph "The first duty of the modern State is to form the national man," from Torres's *A organização nacional*), an anonymous author quoted from Ruy Barbosa by way of rebuttal: "This denaturation of our nationality does not come from the black, nor the caboclo, nor the mestiço . . . It comes from the political evil . . . that submits the nation to all of the physical and moral ailments of a people without hygiene of the body or the soul." *O Commentario*, 15 April 1926, pp. 57–63 (quote on p. 63).

111. Mesquita Filho, *A crise nacional*, 15–16.

112. Ibid., 21–26. Mesquita estimated that 45 percent of the "paulista agricultural zone" was now in the hands of small farmers.

113. Ibid., 27–29.

114. Ibid., 31–33.

115. Ibid., 35–39.

116. Ibid., 41–52 (quotes on pp. 41, 51, 52); see also pp. 65–68.

117. Ibid., 55–62 (quotes on pp. 55 [emphasis indicating Mesquita's use of English], 58, 59, 60, 61–62).

118. Ibid., 62.

119. Ibid., 65–92 (quote on p. 84).

120. Plinio Salgado, untitled preface to Candido Motta Filho, *Alberto Torres e o thema da nossa geração* (São Paulo: Schmidt, n.d. [between 1931 and 1933]), v.

121. Ibid. (including Salgado citing Motta Filho), v–vi (quote on v).

122. See, for example, Elias Chaves Neto, *A revolta de 1924* (São Paulo: Officinas Graphicas Olegario de Almeida Filho & Comp., 1924); A. Leite, *Dias de pavor*; Macedo Soares, *Justiça*; Ribeiro, *Falsa democracia*. Both Macedo Soares's and Ribeiro's accounts were written primarily as the means by which they would attempt to clear their respective names after having been accused of collaborating with the rebels, but they did contain some policy prescriptions. Macedo Soares revealed what he thought would be the solution to Brazil's "disorders," writing that the "synthetic formula for the viability of the Republic in Brazil" consisted of a "real vote" (to be obtained through the secret ballot), popular education (to create an "enlightened electorate"), and the "good money" obtainable through sound financial policies (*Justiça*, 6–9). Álvaro Ribeiro, for his part, declared his devotion to "the basic principles of

democracy: *administrative morality—electoral sovereignty and minority represen-*
tation" (*Falsa democracia,* vii [original emphasis]).

123. See note 1, above, this chap.

124. C. R. Cameron, Political Report No. 7, "Echoes of the São Paulo Revolt of July, 1924," 31 Jan. 1927, 3 (original emphasis), USNARA, RG59, 832.00/616.

125. Ibid., 11.

126. Schmidt, *Bom tempo,* 317–19.

127. Davino Francisco dos Santos, *A coluna Miguel Costa e não coluna Prestes* (São Paulo: Edicon, 1994), 39.

128. The quotes are from "A revolução no Rio," *O Combate,* 8 July 1922, p. 1.

129. The manifesto is quoted and discussed in C. R. Cameron, Political Report No. 7, "Echoes of the São Paulo Revolt of July, 1924," 31 Jan. 1927, 11–12, USNARA, RG59, 832.00/616.

130. "Ao leitor," in Tavora, *Á guisa de depoimento sobre a revolução brasileira de 1924,* 5. Another rebel memoir, Joaquim Nunes de Carvalho's *A revolução no Brasil, 1924–1925,* noted the participation of Nereu's brother Acylino in the "patriotic . . . campaign" of the "independent press" (p. 51). See also Távora, *Uma vida e muitas lutas,* 1:216, 1:226–27, where the author notes his commit- ment to Nereu Rangel Pestana as well as the fact that brisk sales of *Á guisa de depoimento* provided him with enough money for the day-to-day expenses of exile and some savings.

131. On *A Ronda,* see, for example, the 8 Feb. 1927 and 24 Feb. 1927 covers of this "Morning Newspaper of the Popular Classes." On *O Jornal* (Rio de Ja- neiro), see Dulles, *Anarchists and Communists in Brazil, 1900–1935,* 330–31 (quote on p. 330).

132. Quotes from "Notas e informações," *O Estado de S. Paulo,* 11 Feb. 1927, p. 3.

133. Júlio de Mesquita Filho, "Os ideais democráticos na revolução bra- sileira," in his *Política e cultura* (São Paulo: Martins, 1969), 95.

134. *O Libertador* (Assis), 5 Aug. 1924, pp. 1–2, 4; Reis Perdigão, "Marco 20," in *5 de Julho, 1922–1924* (Rio de Janeiro: Henrique Velho, n.d. [1944]), 105; *O Libertador* in *5 de Julho, 1922–1924,* 128ff; clippings in CEDAE, FPD, pasta DET.157; José Augusto Drummond, *A coluna Prestes: Rebeldes errantes* (São Paulo: Brasiliense, 1985), 61; Nelson Werneck Sodré, *História da imprensa no Brasil,* 4th ed. (Rio de Janeiro: Mauad, 1999 [1966]), 363.

135. Dias, *História das lutas sociais no Brasil,* 187–89; Rodolfo Mota Lima, "Sintese histórica," in *5 de Julho, 1922–1924* (Rio de Janeiro: Henrique Velho, n.d. [1944]), 143; Schmidt, *Bom tempo,* 318; Sodré, *História da imprensa no Brasil,* 363; clippings in CEDAE, FPD, pasta DET.157.

136. Schmidt, *Bom tempo,* 318.

137. "Orgam de brasilidade" in the original orthography.

138. "O nosso credo," *Tacape,* 28 April 1928, p. 4.

139. *Tacape,* 28 April 1928; Melo, *Dicionário de autores paulistas,* 383; J. Gon- çalves, *Rui Barbosa,* 165–67.

140. See, for example, Dulles, *Anarchists and Communists in Brazil, 1900–1935,* 344–45, 375, 393–94, 398–99, 410–11, 413–14, 419, 428–35, 485; "Opportunismo democratico," *Folha do Bloco Operario e Camponez,* published in *O Combate,* 29 Oct. 1928, p. 5.

141. Sheet music of "Clarinada," AIHGSP, APD, pacote 12, item 1. The Democratic Party is the subject of chap. 5.

142. Clovis Botelho Vieira, *Os grandes ideaes do Partido Democratico* (São Paulo: Rossetti, 1928), 15–16.

143. Sodré, *História da imprensa no Brasil,* 366, 370 (emphasis added). *Tenentismo* was the word that came to be used for the rebel military movement of the 1920s and the rebels' subsequent activity in and out of government from October 1930 onward.

144. Quoted in Nogueira Filho, *Ideais e lutas de um burguês progressista,* 2:458.

145. Nogueira Filho, *Ideais e lutas de um burguês progressista,* 2:459.

146. Clovis Botelho Vieira, "O Congresso subserviente e o heróe de Copacabana," *Diario Nacional,* 17 May 1930, reprinted in his *Na imprensa,* 91–94.

147. "A morte do tenente Siqueira Campos," *O Estado de S. Paulo,* 15 May 1930, p. 2.

148. "Os funeraes de Siqueira Campos," *O Estado de S. Paulo,* 6 June 1930, p. 4; "Chegou o cadaver de Siqueira Campos, o heróe que commandou a epopéa de Copacabana," *O Combate,* 5 June 1930, p. 1; Nogueira Filho, *Ideais e lutas de um burguês progressista,* 2:459.

149. "Os funeraes de Siqueira Campos," *O Estado de S. Paulo,* 6 June 1930, p. 4.

150. Ibid.; "Chegou o cadaver de Siqueira Campos, o heróe que commandou a epopéa de Copacabana," *O Combate,* 5 June 1930, p. 1.

5. An Experiment in Democracy

1. Ernesto Leme, *A casa de Bragança: Memórias* (São Paulo: Parma, 1981), 118; Rangel Moreira, *Em face da revolução* (São Paulo: n.p., 1930), 38–39, 201 n. 14; Nogueira Filho, *Ideais e lutas de um burguês progressista,* 1:138–44, 145–46, 150; Lobato et al., *O voto secreto;* "Fundação da Liga pró Saneamento e Instrucção," *O Combate,* 23 July 1925, p. 4; "Uma grande obra meritoria," *O Combate,* 27 July 1925, p. 1; "Associação Paulista de Defesa Social," *O Estado de S. Paulo,* 11 Aug. 1925, p. 6; "Noticias diversas," *O Estado de S. Paulo,* 15 Aug. 1925, p. 5; "Defesa social," *O Estado de S. Paulo,* 16 Sept. 1925, p. 5; "Defesa social," *O Estado de S. Paulo,* 17 Sept. 1925, p. 4; "O Centro de Debates," *O Estado de S. Paulo,* 12 Oct. 1925, p. 3; "Associação Paulista de Defesa Social," *O Estado de S. Paulo,* 15 Oct. 1925, p. 5; "Sociedade Brasileira de Estudos Economicos," *O Estado de S. Paulo,* 18 Oct. 1925, p. 6; "Noticias diversas," *O Estado de S. Paulo,*

22 Oct. 1925, p. 8; "Dr. Firmiano Pinto," *O Estado de S. Paulo*, 6 Dec. 1925, p. 6; "Sociedade Brasileira de Estudos Economicos," *O Estado de S. Paulo*, 18 Nov. 1925, p. 7; "Sociedade Brasileira de Estudos Economicos," *O Estado de S. Paulo*, 24 Nov. 1925, p. 6; "Noticias diversas," *O Estado de S. Paulo*, 4 Dec. 1925, p. 6; "Noticias diversas," *O Estado de S. Paulo*, 13 Dec. 1925, p. 4; Paulo Duarte, unpublished manuscript, pp. 573–578, CEDAE, FPD, pasta PI.17.

2. "Partido da Mocidade," *O Estado de S. Paulo*, 12 Oct. 1925, p. 7; "Noticias diversas," *O Estado de S. Paulo*, 13 Oct. 1925, p. 4; "Partido da Mocidade," *O Estado de S. Paulo*, 16 Oct. 1925, p. 6; "Partido da Mocidade," *O Estado de S. Paulo*, 20 Oct. 1925, p. 6; "Caixa do 'O Trabalhador Graphico,'" *O Trabalhador Graphico*, 24 Oct. 1925, p. 4; "Partido da Mocidade," *O Estado de S. Paulo*, 28 Oct. 1925, p. 7; "Partido da Mocidade," *O Estado de S. Paulo*, 30 Oct. 1925, p. 7; "Noticias diversas," *O Estado de S. Paulo*, 12 Nov. 1925, p. 6; "Partido da Mocidade," *O Estado de S. Paulo*, 15 Nov. 1925, p. 9; "Partido da Mocidade," *O Estado de S. Paulo*, 19 Nov. 1925, p. 5; "Noticias diversas," *O Estado de S. Paulo*, 20 Nov. 1925, p. 6; "Partido da Mocidade," *O Estado de S. Paulo*, 24 Nov. 1925, p. 6; "Partido da Mocidade," *O Estado de S. Paulo*, 28 Nov. 1925, p. 6; "As eleições de hontem," *O Estado de S. Paulo*, 30 Nov. 1925, p. 2; "Partido da Mocidade," *O Estado de S. Paulo*, 14 Jan. 1926, p. 5; "A successão presidencial," *O Combate*, 2 Feb. 1926, p. 1; Francisco Gurgel Pismel, José [illegible middle name] Castilho, and Alexandre [illegible surname] to Directorio Provisorio, Itaporanga, 25 March 1926, AIHGSP, APD, pacote 33; A. Fleury to "Presidente e D. Membros do 'Partido Democratico,'" Itararé, 30 March 1926, AIHGSP, APD, pacote 33; "Partido da Mocidade," *O Combate*, 1 April 1926, p. 4; Commissão Executiva da Colligação Operária, "Razões principaes porque combatemos o partido da mocidade," *O Solidario* (Santos), 5 April 1926, p. 2; "'O Combate' em Campinas," *O Combate*, 22 May 1926, p. 4; Roberto Santamaria Filho to Antonio Prado, São João da Bôa Vista, 21 Dec. 1926, AIHGSP, APD, pacote 34; "Nas vesperas do pleito eleitoral, *Diario da Noite*, 18 Feb. 1927, p. 1; "Partido da Mocidade," *O Estado de S. Paulo*, 20 May 1927, p. 6; "Partido da Mocidade," *O Estado de S. Paulo*, 21 May 1927, p. 6; "Partido Democratico," newspaper clipping from *O Pinheirense* (dated 5 June 1927), AIHGSP, APD, album VII; Eurico Branco Ribeiro to J. F. Saldanha Sobrinho, São Paulo, 30 June 1927, transcribed in "Chefe do serviço eleitoral do Butantan" [illegible] to Arlindo A. Amaral, São Paulo, 4 July 1927, AIHGSP, APD, pacote 15, item 4; "Notas e noticias," *O Pinheirense*, 1 Jan. 1928, p. 1; "Pinheiros ha dois annos," *O Pinheirense*, 7 July 1929, p. 1; Dulles, *Anarchists and Communists in Brazil, 1900–1935*, 290–91; Afonso Schmidt, "Paulo Gonçalves," *Revista da Academia Paulista de Letras* 48 (Dec. 1949): 39–40. The party's founding manifesto is reprinted in Casalecchi, *O Partido Republicano Paulista*, 285–87.

3. "Intrigando . . . ," *O Combate*, 24 Nov. 1925, p. 4; "As eleições de hontem," *O Estado de S. Paulo*, 30 Nov. 1925, p. 2; "As 'eleições' de hontem," *O Combate*, 30 Nov. 1925, pp. 1, 4; "Partido da Mocidade," *Folha da Manhã*, 1 Dec. 1925,

reprinted in secção livre, *O Estado de S. Paulo*, 3 Dec. 1925, p. 10; "Eleições municipaes," *O Estado de S. Paulo*, 3 Dec. 1925, p. 2; "O Partido da Mocidade em Faxina," *O Combate*, 22 Dec. 1925, p. 4; Commissão Executiva da Colligação Operária, "Razões principaes porque combatemos o partido da mocidade," *O Solidario* (Santos), 5 April 1926, p. 2.

4. "Nos bastidores da politica" (newspaper clipping labeled *Diario da Noite*, 27 Nov. 1925), AESP, AJCDJ, caixa AP174, pasta 2; Coelho, *O processo político da comunidade guaratinguetaense*, 62–64; D. Abreu, *Formação histórica de uma cidade pioneira paulista*, 216–18; French, "Industrial Workers and the Origin of Populist Politics in the ABC Region of Greater São Paulo, 1900–1950," 80–81; "Intrigando . . . ," *O Combate*, 11 Nov. 1925, p. 4; "Intrigando . . . ," *O Combate*, 14 Nov. p. 4; "Intrigando . . . ," *O Combate*, 25 Nov. 1925, p. 4; "Politica de S. Bernardo," *O Combate*, 27 Nov. 1925, p. 5; "Intrigando . . . ," *O Combate*, 27 Nov. 1925, p. 6; "As eleições de hontem," *O Estado de S. Paulo*, 30 Nov. 1925, p. 2; "Eleições municipaes," *O Estado de S. Paulo*, 1 Dec. 1925, p. 5; "Eleições municipaes," *O Estado de S. Paulo*, 3 Dec. 1925, p. 2; "Eleições municipaes," *O Estado de S. Paulo*, 4 Dec. 1925, p. 4; "Intrigando . . ." and "Rio Claro não quiz ficar atraz," *O Combate*, 5 Dec. 1925, p. 1; "Intrigando . . . ," *O Combate*, 10 Dec. 1925, p. 4.

5. "Intrigando . . . ," *O Combate*, 19 Nov. 1925, p. 4; "As eleições de hontem," *O Estado de S. Paulo*, 30 Nov. 1925, p. 2; F. Santos, *História de Santos, 1532–1936*, 1:421; "A candidatura Ruy Barbosa," *O Estado de S. Paulo*, 20 March 1919, p. 3; Waldemar Ferreira, "A Faculdade de Direito na arrancada de 9 de julho de 1932," *Revista da Faculdade de Direito* 55 (1960): 421; F. Silva, *Operários sem patrões*, 286, 312–13; "Antônio Feliciano da Silva," in A. Abreu et al., *Dicionário histórico-biográfico brasileiro*, 5:5388; British Chamber of Commerce of São Paulo and Southern Brazil, *Personalidades no Brasil*, 267.

6. "Intrigando . . . ," *O Combate*, 14 Nov. 1925, p. 4; "Noticias do interior," *O Estado de S. Paulo*, 20 Nov. 1925, p. 6; "As eleições de hontem," *O Estado de S. Paulo*, 30 Nov. 1925, p. 2; "As 'eleições' de hontem," *O Combate*, 30 Nov. 1925, p. 4; "O caso do vereador Alvaro Ribeiro," *O Combate*, 8 May 1926, p. 4; "O caso do vereador Alvaro Ribeiro," *O Combate*, 12 May 1926, p. 4; Ribeiro, *Falsa democracia*, v, 412–14, 463–508. The quote is from "Depois de elegel-o, Campinas quer Alvaro Ribeiro em seu seio," *O Combate*, 19 Jan. 1926, p. 1.

7. "Intrigando . . . ," *O Combate*, 14 Nov. 1925, p. 4; "Rio Claro não quiz ficar atraz," *O Combate*, 5 Dec. 1925, p. 1; "Intrigando . . . ," *O Combate*, 9 Dec. 1925, p. 4; "Intrigando . . . ," *O Combate*, 4 Jan. 1926, p. 4; Pagnocca, *Crônica dos prefeitos de Rio Claro, 1908–1983*, 43, 47.

8. "Intrigando . . . ," *O Combate*, 12 Nov. 1925, p. 6; "As eleições de hontem," *O Estado de S. Paulo*, 30 Nov. 1925, p. 2; "Noticias do interior," *O Estado de S. Paulo*, 12 Dec. 1925, p. 5; "Intrigando . . . ," *O Combate*, 15 Dec. 1925, p. 6; Alvim, "O Diário," 32; Elias Netto, *Memorial de Piracicaba*, 172; Terci, "A cidade na primeira república," 251–57 (quote on p. 252).

9. "As 'eleições' de hontem," *O Combate*, 30 Nov. 1925, pp. 1, 4.

10. Aureliano Leite, "Marrey Júnior" (unpublished notes), AIHGSP, AAL, pacote 13; Marrey Júnior to Miguel Costa, São Paulo, 18 April 1945, AEL, FMC, pasta 34; Luiz Tenorio de Brito, *Memórias de um ajudante de ordens* (São Paulo: Nacional, 1951), 137; "As vagas de vereador," *O Combate*, 29 June 1915, p. 4; "Foi adiada a manifestação de apreço ao dr. Marrey," *O Combate*, 14 Oct. 1916, p. 1; "Politica da capital," 27 Oct. 1922, p. 1; "O voto secreto," *O Combate*, 26 Sept. 1925, p. 4; "O voto secreto em S. Paulo," *O Combate*, 30 Sept. 1925, p. 1; "O voto secreto em S. Paulo," *O Combate*, 1 Oct. 1925, p. 1; "Mexericos . . . ," *A Capital*, 9 Nov. 1926, p. 6. Marrey was also a prominent figure in paulista freemasonry.

11. "Politica da capital," *O Combate*, 14 Nov. 1925, p. 1; "Politica da capital," *O Combate*, 17 Nov. 1925, p. 1; "Dr. Olavo Egydio," *O Estado de S. Paulo*, 7 March 1928, p. 4. In 1924, Marrey had sided with Olavo Egydio against the rump PRP. A. (Antonio) Candido Rodrigues et al., "Ao eleitorado paulista," São Paulo, 2 Feb. 1924, in secção livre, *O Estado de S. Paulo*, 9 Feb. 1924, p. 9; "Noticias diversas," *O Estado de S. Paulo*, 12 Feb. 1924, p. 4.

12. "Politica da capital," *O Combate*, 14 Nov. 1925, p. 1.

13. "Congresso do estado," *O Estado de S. Paulo*, 5 Dec. 1925, p. 2; "Politica da capital," *O Combate*, 5 Dec. 1925, p. 1; "Congresso do Estado," *O Estado de S. Paulo*, 6 Dec. 1925, p. 5. Alfredo Egydio did not resign from the PRP until the following meeting of the state legislature.

14. "Congresso do Estado," *O Estado de S. Paulo*, 6 Dec. 1925, p. 5.

15. "Congresso do Estado," *O Estado de S. Paulo*, 12 Dec. 1925, p. 4. Marrey also made much of the votes he had received "from oppositionists and from voters who seldom go out to the polls" and that he had always lived off of his earnings as a practicing lawyer rather than from an administrative post.

16. "Intrigando . . . ," *O Combate*, 12 Dec. 1925, p. 4; "Na camara dos deputados," *O Combate*, 15 Dec. 1925, p. 6. Dubbing Marrey, once in opposition, the "congressman of the 'left'" followed the precedent of the federal capital. See, for example, "Intrigando . . . ," *O Combate*, 15 Jan. 1926, p. 4.

17. Figueiredo, *Memórias de um jornalista*, 123–25; Leme, *A casa de Bragança*, 117; Lôbo, *Recordações das arcadas*, 268–76, 284; Nogueira Filho, *Ideais e lutas de um burguês progressista*, 1:147; Francisco Pati, *O espírito das arcadas* (São Paulo: n.p., 1950), 42–43, 53–56; F. Santos, *História de Santos, 1532–1936*, 2:390–96; Porchat resignation speech, 26 Dec. 1925 (from *Jornal do Comércio* [São Paulo], 27 Dec. 1925), reprinted as "Discurso do prof. Reynaldo Porchat, renunciando a sua cadeira no senado do estado de S. Paulo—26–12–1925," in Nogueira Filho, *Ideais e lutas de um burguês progressista*, 2:635–38.

18. Quoted in "Intrigando . . . ," *O Combate*, 14 Nov. 1925, p. 4.

19. Paulo Duarte, unpublished manuscript, pp. 76–78, CEDAE, FPD, pasta PI.16; Paulo Duarte, unpublished manuscript, pp. 600, 601 (latter out of place), CEDAE, FPD, pasta PI.17; Nogueira Filho, *Ideais e lutas de um burguês progressista*, 1:147–48.

20. Paulo Duarte, unpublished manuscript, pp. 76–78, CEDAE, FPD, pasta

PI.16; Paulo Duarte, unpublished manuscript, pp. 600, 601 (latter out of place), CEDAE, FPD, pasta PI.17.

21. Porchat resignation speech, 26 Dec. 1925 (from *Jornal do Comércio* [São Paulo], 27 Dec. 1925), reprinted as "Discurso do prof. Reynaldo Porchat, renunciando a sua cadeira no senado do estado de S. Paulo—26–12–1925," in Nogueira Filho, *Ideais e lutas de um burguês progressista*, 2:635–38; " 'Assim foi em Roma: E Roma não teve remedio!,'" *O Combate*, 28 Dec. 1925, p. 1. See Lôbo, *Recordações das arcadas*, 272, 273; Pati, *O espírito das arcadas*, 53–56, 105–6, 109, for descriptions of Porchat's public speaking.

22. Porchat resignation speech, 26 Dec. 1925 (from *Jornal do Comércio* [São Paulo], 27 Dec. 1925), reprinted as "Discurso do prof. Reynaldo Porchat, renunciando a sua cadeira no senado do estado de S. Paulo—26–12–1925," in Nogueira Filho, *Ideais e lutas de um burguês progressista*, 2:635–38; Leme, *A casa de Bragança*, 117–18; Pati, *O espírito das arcadas*, 54; " 'Assim foi em Roma: E Roma não teve remedio!,'" *O Combate*, 28 Dec. 1925, p. 1; "Intrigando . . . ," *O Combate*, 29 Dec. 1925, p. 4; Lauresto E., "Uma comedia no senado," *O Combate*, 31 Dec. 1925, p. 8; Paulo Duarte, unpublished manuscript, pp. 76–78, CEDAE, FPD, pasta PI.16; Paulo Duarte, unpublished manuscript, pp. 600, 601 (latter out of place), CEDAE, FPD, pasta PI.17; Nogueira Filho, *Ideais e lutas de um burguês progressista*, 1:148, 150.

23. "Intrigando . . . ," *O Combate*, 30 Dec. 1925, p. 4; " 'Assim foi em Roma: E Roma não teve remedio!,'" *O Combate*, 28 Dec. 1925, p. 1; Paulo Duarte, unpublished manuscript, pp. 76–78, CEDAE, FPD, pasta PI.16; Paulo Duarte, unpublished manuscript, pp. 600, 601 (latter out of place), CEDAE, FPD, pasta PI.17; Nogueira Filho, *Ideais e lutas de um burguês progressista*, 1:148–50. The commission's invitation was printed as "Ao povo paulista," *O Estado de S. Paulo*, 1 Jan. 1926, p. 4, from which the quotes in the text are taken.

24. "Mensagem ao Dr. Reynaldo Porchat," *O Estado de S. Paulo*, 12 Jan. 1926, p. 5.

25. "Noticias diversas," *O Estado de S. Paulo*, 6 Jan. 1926, p. 6; Raimundo de Menezes, *História pitoresca de quarenta cadeiras: Anedotário da Academia Paulista de Letras* (São Paulo: Hucitec, 1976), 170.

26. "Noticias diversas," *O Estado de S. Paulo*, 6 Jan. 1926, p. 6; "Mensagem ao Dr. Reynaldo Porchat," *O Estado de S. Paulo*, 12 Jan. 1926, p. 5.

27. "Intrigando . . . ," *O Combate*, 31 Dec. 1925, p. 1.

28. " 'Assim foi em Roma': E Roma não teve remedio!," *O Combate*, 28 Dec. 1925, p. 1; "Intrigando" and "Ainda a renuncia do Dr. Porchat," *O Combate*, 29 Dec. 1925, p. 4; Lauresto E., "Uma comedia no senado," *O Combate*, 31 Dec. 1925, p. 8.

29. Compare, by way of illustration, the relevant entries in British Chamber of Commerce of São Paulo and Southern Brazil, *Personalidades no Brasil*, and Melo, *Dicionário de autores paulistas*, with the lists of names in "Ao povo paulista," *O Estado de S. Paulo*, 1 Jan. 1926, p. 4; "Noticias diversas," *O Estado de*

S. *Paulo*, 5 Jan. 1926, p. 6; "Noticias diversas," *O Estado de S. Paulo*, 6 Jan. 1926, p. 6; "Mensagem ao Dr. Reynaldo Porchat," *O Estado de S. Paulo*, 12 Jan. 1926, p. 5.

30. "Intrigando . . . ," *O Combate*, 7 Jan. 1926, p. 4.

31. Nogueira Filho, *Ideais e lutas de um burguês progressista*, 1:151; E., "Partido paulista," *O Combate*, 9 Jan. 1925, p. 1; Velho Paulista, "Partido paulista," *O Combate*, 23 Jan. 1925, p. 1; Antonio Prado, "O voto secreto," Rio de Janeiro, 30 Aug. 1925, printed in *O Estado de S. Paulo*, 1 Sept. 1925, p. 3 (also published in *Correio da Manhã* [Rio de Janeiro] and reprinted in Nazareth Prado, ed., *Antonio Prado no imperio e na republica*, [Rio de Janeiro: F. Briguet, 1929], 432–34); "O conselheiro Antonio Prado vae fundar um partido em São Paulo," *O Combate*, 25 Sept. 1925, p. 1; Velho Paulista, "A evolução dos partidos politicos," *O Combate*, 22 Dec. 1925, p. 1.

32. "Intrigando . . . ," *O Combate*, 28 Dec. 1925, p. 4; also, "Politica paulista," *O Combate*, 31 Dec. 1925, p. 8.

33. "Intrigando . . . ," *O Combate*, 4 Jan. 1926, p. 4.

34. "Intrigando . . . ," *O Combate*, 6 Jan. 1926, p. 4.

35. "O partido opposicionista de S. Paulo," *Correio da Manhã* (Rio de Janeiro), 13 Jan. 1926, reprinted in *O Combate*, 13 Jan. 1926, p. 4; "Intrigando . . . ," *O Combate*, 11 Jan. 1926, p. 4.

36. Nogueira Filho, *Ideais e lutas de um burguês progressista*, 1:154–55; N. Prado, *Antonio Prado no imperio e na republica*, 409–11. The twenty-seven others were Porchat, Marrey, Frederico Vergueiro Steidel, Francisco Morato, Luiz Augusto de Queiroz Aranha, Luiz Barbosa da Gama Cerqueira, José Joaquim Cardoso de Mello Neto, Waldemar Martins Ferreira, Paulo de Moraes Barros, Abrahão Ribeiro, Mário Pinto Serva, Samuel Augusto de Toledo, Paulo Nogueira Filho, Tácito de Almeida, Antônio Cajado de Lemos, Antônio Carlos Couto de Barros, José Mariano de Camargo Aranha, Henrique Neves Lefevre, Joaquim de Abreu Sampaio Vidal, Prudente de Moraes Neto, Moacyr Eyck Alvaro, Adhemar de Souza Queiroz, Sylvio Alves de Lima, Fábio de Camargo Aranha, Paulo Vicente de Azevedo, Euzebio de Queiroz Mattoso, and Bertho Antonino Condé. Also present, as invited guests rather than founding members of the party, were Bias Bueno and Paulo Gonçalves, representing the Party of Youth.

37. Rubens do Amaral, "Antônio Prado," in Leite et al., *Homens de São Paulo*, 237–51; Levi, *The Prados of São Paulo, Brazil*, 47, 91–93, 99, 175–77; "Uma face interessante e nova da questão parlamentarista" (newspaper clipping from *Gazeta das Noticias* [Rio de Janeiro], n.d. [April 1913]) and "O sr. conselheiro Antonio Prado concede-nos mais uma entrevista" (*Gazeta das Noticias* [Rio de Janeiro], dated 30 April 1913), Oliveira Lima Library, Oliveira Lima clipping collection, volume 34; "A palavra de dois grandes velhos paulistas," *O Combate*, 14 Dec. 1921, p. 1; Antonio Prado, "O voto secreto," Rio de Janeiro, 30 Aug. 1925, reprinted in *O Estado de S. Paulo*, 1 Sept. 1925, p. 3.

38. "Noticias diversas," *O Estado de S. Paulo*, 4 Dec. 1925, p. 6. See also Nogueira Filho, *Ideais e lutas de um burguês progressista*, 2:492; M. Prado, *A democracia ilustrada*, 16; Jorge Miguel Mayer, "Francisco Morato," in A. Abreu et al., *Dicionário histórico-biográfico brasileiro*, 4:3896–98; Terci, "A cidade na primeira república," 260–61.

39. Regina Hipólito, "Paulo de Morais Barros," in A. Abreu et al., *Dicionário histórico-biográfico brasileiro*, 1:564–65; British Chamber of Commerce of São Paulo and Southern Brazil, *Personalidades no Brasil*, 499–500; José Claudio Barriguelli, ed., *O pensamento político da classe dominante paulista, 1873–1928* (São Carlos: Arquivo de História Contemporânea, 1986), 13; Love, *São Paulo in the Brazilian Federation*, 291. On Moraes Barros's role in São Paulo's agricultural associations, see Renato Monseff Perissinotto, "Estado, capital cafeeiro e crise política na década de 1920 em São Paulo, Brasil," *Hispanic American Historical Review* 80, no. 2 (May 2000): esp. 306n., 307n., 308n.

40. "Notas e informações," *O Estado de S. Paulo*, 16 Dec. 1916, p. 5; "O Partido Municipal," *O Combate*, 5 Feb. 1917, p. 1.

41. Jorge Miguel Mayer, "Gama Cerqueira," in A. Abreu et al., *Dicionário histórico-biográfico brasileiro*, 2:1321.

42. Antonio Prado et al., "Ao povo paulista," *O Estado de S. Paulo*, 1 Jan. 1926, p. 4; "Noticias diversas," *O Estado de S. Paulo*, 5 Jan. 1926, p. 6; "Noticias diversas," *O Estado de S. Paulo*, 6 Jan. 1926; pp. 5–6; "Mensagem ao dr. Reynaldo Porchat," *O Estado de S. Paulo*, 12 Jan. 1926, p. 5; "Notas e informações," *O Estado de S. Paulo*, 16 Dec. 1916, p. 5; "Ao eleitorado paulista," *O Estado de S. Paulo*, 21 April 1922, pp. 3–4; "Na Liga Nacionalista," *O Estado de S. Paulo*, 13 July 1924, p. 1; Jorge Miguel Mayer, "Cardoso de Melo Neto" and "Paulo Nogueira Filho," in A. Abreu et al., *Dicionário histórico-biográfico brasileiro*, 4:3744, 4:4102; Melo, *Dicionário de autores paulistas*, 37; Nogueira Filho, *Ideais e lutas de um burguês progressista*, 1:140; "Manifesto da commissão acadêmica," São Paulo, 18 May 1918, in ibid., 2:633–34; Lobato et al., *O voto secreto*; Nestor Rangel Pestana to Oliveira Lima, São Paulo, n.d., and attachment, "Prospecto, *Revista do Brasil*," Oliveira Lima Library, Oliveira Lima correspondence collection; "A candidatura Ruy Barbosa," *O Estado de S. Paulo*, 8 April 1919, p. 4 (on Ruy Barbosa's campaign of 1919, see also Nogueira Filho, *Ideais e lutas de um burguês progressista*, 1:104–105).

43. [José Correia] Pedroso Júnior and Nicolau Tuma, *Homenagem postuma* [ao] *constituinte Bertho Condé* (Brasília: Departamento de Imprensa Nacional, 1966); Penteado, *Memórias de um postalista*, 14–16; "Berto Condé," in A. Abreu et al., *Dicionário histórico-biográfico brasileiro*, 2:1490–91; Bertho Condé, *Ensaios de politica espiritualista* (São Paulo: Ed. O Pensamento, 1927); Nogueira Filho, *Ideais e lutas de um burguês progressista*, 1:151; "Como se fundou o Partido Democratico," *A Platea*, 4 Nov. 1930, pp. 1–2. On Condé's activity as an antifáscist journalist, see João Fábio Bertonha, *Sob a sombra de Mussolini: Os italianos de São Paulo e a luta contra o fascismo, 1919–1945* (São Paulo: FAPESP /

Annablume, 1999), 221–22. A selection of his articles was gathered by the anti-fascist leader Antonio Piccarolo and remain in Piccarolo's papers at the Istituto Italiano di Cultura di São Paulo (pasta 16). Condé was something of an odd man out in other regards. Not because he had been born out of state (Euzebio de Queiroz Mattoso and Gama Cerqueira were fellow fluminenses, while Marrey Júnior was a mineiro), but by virtue of other elements of his background. The son of a postal functionary, he completed his education at the second-tier Faculdade de Ciências Jurídicas e Sociais do Rio de Janeiro and made his living as a journalist and a practicing lawyer. By contrast, Queiroz Mattoso, Gama Cerqueira, and Marrey all held degrees from the more prestigious São Paulo Law School; Queiroz Mattoso and Marrey were married into well-established paulista families (Queiroz Mattoso, for example, was the son-in-law of Reynaldo Porchat); and while Condé's friend Marrey also made his living as a trial attorney, Gama Cerqueira held a chair at the São Paulo Law School and Queiroz Mattoso was a businessman's lawyer, with interests of his own in industry and banking. Jorge Miguel Mayer, "Gama Cerqueira" and "José Adriano Marrey Júnior" in A. Abreu et al., *Dicionário histórico-biográfico brasileiro*, 2:1321, 3:3603; British Chamber of Commerce of São Paulo and Southern Brazil, *Personalidades no Brasil*, 309, 468, 599–600; Nogueira Filho, *Ideais e lutas de um burguês progressista*, 1:332, 2:431.

44. Nogueira Filho, *Ideais e lutas de um burguês progressista*, 1:154–55; N. Prado, *Antonio Prado no imperio e na republica*, 409–11.

45. "Manifesto do Partido Democrata," São Paulo, 27 Feb. 1926, published in Nogueira Filho, *Ideais e lutas de um burguês progressista*, 2:641–42 (quotes on p. 641).

46. Ibid.

47. Ibid., 2:642.

48. Ibid.

49. Ibid., 2:641–42; British Chamber of Commerce of São Paulo and Southern Brazil, *Personalidades no Brasil*, 44; Melo, *Dicionário de autores paulistas*, 310; Octaviano Alves de Lima, *Revolução econômico-social*, 2nd ed. (São Paulo: Brasiliense, 1947 [1931]); J. Lima, *Recordações de homens e cousas do meu tempo*, 42–43; "Associação Paulista de Defesa Social," *O Estado de S. Paulo*, 15 Oct. 1925, p. 5; "Sociedade Brasileira de Estudos Economicos," *O Estado de S. Paulo*, 24 Nov. 1925, p. 6; "Ao povo paulista," *O Estado de S. Paulo*, 1 Jan. 1926, p. 4. Ongoing discussions among these additional circles of supporters would explain why Aureliano Leite recalled participating in the party's founding, despite his apparent absence from the meeting held on 24 February. A. Leite, *Páginas de uma longa vida*, 44. See also Leme, *A casa de Bragança*, 118.

50. "Intrigando . . . ," *O Combate*, 25 Feb. 1926, p. 1; "Politicando . . . ," *A Capital*, 1 March 1926, p. 1; "Partido Liberal," *O Combate*, 1 March 1926, p. 4; "Politicando . . . ," *A Capital*, 4 March 1926, p. 1; "Um novo partido politico em S. Paulo," *O Combate*, 6 March 1926, p. 1; Carlos Escobar, "Partido Liberal," *O*

Combate, 9 March 1926, p. 1; Carlos Escobar, "Ainda o Partido Liberal," *O Combate*, 19 March 1926, p. 1; "Como se fundou o Partido Democratico," *A Platea*, 4 Nov. 1930, pp. 1–2.

51. "O novo partido paulista," *O Combate*, 5 March 1926, p. 1. Cf. Motta Filho, *Contagem regressiva*, 60, which quotes Prado as having said in 1926 that because Brazil had "entered the industrial epoch, when man, before the machine, acquires consciousness of his value," the oligarchic politics characteristic of "rural civilization" should come to an end "as they are counterfeiting the designs of the Republic."

52. "Um novo partido politico em S. Paulo," *O Combate*, 6 March 1926, p. 1.

53. "Partido Democratico," *O Estado de S. Paulo*, 21 March 1926, p. 6; "Installação do Partido Democratico" and "Manifesto á Nação," *O Estado de S. Paulo*, 22 March 1926, pp. 2, 3, respectively; "Um grande acontecimento na politica nacional," *O Combate*, 22 March 1926, p. 1.

54. "Manifesto á Nação," *O Estado de S. Paulo*, 22 March 1926, p. 3.

55. Ibid. (emphasis added).

56. Ibid. The listing of subscribers' names and professions is reprinted, with only a few typographical errors, in N. Prado, *Antonio Prado no imperio e na republica*, 392–408. A brief statistical analysis is found in Levi, *The Prados of São Paulo, Brazil*, 203–4, which I draw upon through the following paragraphs.

57. One thinks here of Ruy Barbosa's spirited but myopic rebuttal of Monteiro Lobato, in which he argued that he and his comfortable, cultured, and cosmopolitan audience represented the "real Brazil" rather than Lobato's miserable, ignorant, and hopeless Jeca Tatú. Above, chap. 3.

58. Even these tallies understate the importance of law-school graduates in the formation of the party, as many founders who had attended the São Paulo Law School listed their primary occupation as something other than the law: Antônio Prado, Luiz de Queiroz Aranha, Paulo Nogueira Filho, Joaquim Sampaio Vidal, for example. In addition, many, if not most, of the eighteen men listed as students were students of law, as was at least one of the lower-status professionals, the schoolteacher Lázaro Maria da Silva.

59. Richard Cobb used the phrase "verbal deflation" to characterize "a certain inverted snobbery [that] caused many people to 'democratize' their occupations." See his "The Revolutionary Mentality in France," in *A Second Identity: Essays on France and French History* (London: Oxford University Press, 1969), 126.

60. British Chamber of Commerce of São Paulo and Southern Brazil, *Personalidades no Brasil*, 209; Melo, *Dicionário de autores paulistas*, 481–82.

61. Mario Carelli, *Carcamanos e comendadores: Os italianos de São Paulo da realidade à ficção, 1919–1930*, trans. Ligia Maria Pondé Vassallo (São Paulo: Ática, 1985), 103–21; Melo, *Dicionário de autores paulistas*, 327–28; P. Duarte, *História da imprensa em São Paulo*, 29; A. Martins, *Revistas em revista*, 439–40.

62. Melo, *Dicionário de autores paulistas*, 37, 56–58, 86, 591–92; P. Duarte, *História da imprensa em São Paulo*, 31. See also Lisbeth Rebollo Gonçalves, *Sérgio Milliet: Crítico de arte* (São Paulo: Ed. da Universidade de São Paulo 1992), 23–24, 34–36, 56.

63. L. Gonçalves, *Sérgio Milliet*, 56; Melo, *Dicionário de autores paulistas*, 30–31, 537.

64. On Leopoldo de Freitas: British Chamber of Commerce of São Paulo and Southern Brazil, *Personalidades no Brasil*, 405; untitled notices, *O Estado de S. Paulo*, 29 Oct. 1901, p. 1; "A prisão do director do 'Estado' e outros," *O Combate*, 4 Aug. 1924, p. 1. On the brothers Ferraz do Amaral: Melo, *Dicionário de autores paulistas*, 43, 45–56; Pedro Ferraz do Amaral, "Introdução," in Brenno Ferraz do Amaral, *A literatura em São Paulo em 1922*, ed. Pedro Ferraz do Amaral (São Paulo: Conselho Estadual de Cultura, 1973), 9–20; Aureliano Leite, "Apresentação," in Pedro Ferraz do Amaral, *Celso Garcia* (São Paulo: Martins, 1973), 9–12; "Partido politico da mocidade," *O Estado de S. Paulo*, 13 Oct. 1925, p. 4; "Partido da Mocidade," *O Estado de S. Paulo*, 19 Nov. 1925, p. 5; "Partido da Mocidade," *O Estado de S. Paulo*, 12 Jan. 1926, p. 4. On Silveira da Motta and the *Estadinho*: Melo, *Dicionário de autores paulistas*, 405 (on Brenno Ferraz, see p. 43).

65. Melo, *Dicionário de autores paulistas*, 523; Vivaldo Coaracy, *Encontros com a vida: Memórias* (Rio de Janeiro: José Olympio, 1962), 224–26; Julio de Mesquita Filho, "Clovis Ribeiro," *O Estado de S. Paulo*, 25 Jan. 1946, p. 6.

66. British Chamber of Commerce of São Paulo and Southern Brazil, *Personalidades no Brasil*, 610; Melo, *Dicionário de autores paulistas*, 424; P. Duarte, *História da imprensa em São Paulo*, 29; A. Martins, *Revistas em revista*, 252.

67. On Pereira Júnior: "Movimento associativo," *O Estado de S. Paulo*, 20 March 1926, p. 2; Nestor Pereira Junior, "Politica de approximação," *A Federação*, 30 Sept. 1926, p. 1 (see also p. 4); Directorio Provisorio to Nestor Pereira, São Paulo, 7 Aug. 1926, AIHGSP, APD, pacote 54; A. Sender Junior to Directores do PD, São Paulo, 22 Aug. 1926, AIHGSP, APD, pacote 45. On Cintra: Alberto Cintra to Presidente e Mais Directores do PD, Santos, 11 Aug. 1927, AIHGSP, APD, pacote 37; "O dissidio," *O Combate*, 26 Aug. 1927, p. 1. On Pires de Campos, the Commerce and Industry Center, and the São Paulo Commercial Association: "O dr. Marrey foi eleito e o commercio paulista se arregimenta," *O Combate*, 5 July 1915, p. 4; Ilka Stern Cohen, "Em nome das classes conservadoras: Associação Comercial de São Paulo, 1917–1928" (tese de mestrado, Pontifícia Universidade de São Paulo, 1986); Sérgio Lamarão and André Faria, "Associação Comercial de São Paulo," in A. Abreu et al., *Dicionário histórico-biográfico brasileiro*, 1:400.

68. "O Partido Municipal installou-se hontem," *O Combate*, 5 Feb. 1917, p. 1.

69. "Notas e informações," *O Estado de S. Paulo*, 16 Dec. 1916, p. 5; "Na Liga Nacionalista," *O Estado de S. Paulo*, 13 July 1924, p. 1; Jorge Miguel Mayer, "Horácio Lafer" and "Henrique Bayma" in A. Abreu et al., *Dicionário histórico-*

biográfico brasileiro, 3:2998, 1:599, respectively; "Manifesto da commissão acadêmica," São Paulo, 18 May 1918, reprinted in Nogueira Filho, *Ideais e lutas de um burguês progressista,* 2:633–34.

70. "Partido da Mocidade," *O Estado de S. Paulo,* 12 Oct. 1925, p. 7; "Partido politico da mocidade," *O Estado de S. Paulo,* 13 Oct. 1925, p. 4; "Partido da Mocidade," *O Estado de S. Paulo,* 19 Nov. 1925, p. 5; "Partido da Mocidade," *O Estado de S. Paulo,* 27 Nov. 1925, p. 6; "Partido da Mocidade," *O Estado de S. Paulo,* 12 Jan. 1926, p. 4; "A successão presidencial," *O Combate,* 2 Feb. 1926, p. 1; Nogueira Filho, *Ideais e lutas de um burguês progressista,* 1:155; "A candidatura Ruy Barbosa," *O Estado de S. Paulo,* 8 April 1919, p. 4. Clovis Vieira de Moraes, a pharmacy student when he helped found the Party of Youth, was not among the subscribers of the manifesto of 21 March, but he did eventually join the party, while his fellow founder Francisco de Paula Gonçalves (Paulo Gonçalves), a poet, playwright, journalist, and the great-grandson of freed slaves, never did. "Partido politico da mocidade," *O Estado de S. Paulo,* 13 Oct. 1925, p. 4; Clovis de Moraes to Marrey Junior, São Paulo, 13 April 1929, AIHGSP, APD, pacote 46; Melo, *Dicionário de autores paulistas,* 261; Silva Sobrinho, *Santos noutros tempos,* 83–88; Figueiredo, *Memórias de um jornalista,* 201; F. Santos, *História de Santos, 1532–1936,* 2:441–42; Schmidt, "Paulo Gonçalves," 33–42; "Paulo Gonçalves," *O Estado de S. Paulo,* 9 April 1927, p. 2.

71. British Chamber of Commerce of São Paulo and Southern Brazil, *Personalidades no Brasil,* 647; Duílio Crispim Farina, *Medicina no planalto de Piratininga* (São Paulo: n.p., 1981), 188; A. C. de Camargo et al., "Candidatura Luiz Pereira Barreto: Manifesto da classe medica ao povo," São Paulo, 19 May 1918, AIHGSP, ALN, pacote 2, item 2; "Movimento civico," *O Combate,* 20 May 1918, p. 3; transcription of telegram, Baeta Neves et al. to Ruy Barbosa, São Paulo, 24 [Jan.?] 1919, CRB, ARB, CR.E 25/20, doc. 976; "O pleito de hoje," *O Combate,* 26 April 1919, p. 1; Carlos Escobar, "Dr. Rubião Meira," *O Combate,* 26 Jan. 1921, p. 1; "A Reacção Republicana," *O Combate,* 20 Jan. 1922, p. 1; telegram, Rubião Meira to Nilo Peçanha, São Paulo, 27 Feb. 1922, MR, ANP, caixa 26; Rubião Meira to Nilo Peçanha, São Paulo, 2 March 1922, MR, ANP, caixa 26; Rubião Meira, "Ao eleitorado independente do 1.º e 3.º districtos estaduaes e aos correligionarios da Reacção Republicana de São Paulo," São Paulo, 20 April 1922, in secção livre, *O Estado de S. Paulo,* 22 April 1922, p. 8; Rubião Meira, "Eleições municipaes," in secção livre, *O Estado de S. Paulo,* 19 Nov. 1925, p. 10; A. Leite, *Páginas de uma longa vida,* 42n.

72. British Chamber of Commerce of São Paulo and Southern Brazil, *Personalidades no Brasil,* 669–70; Melo, *Dicionário de autores paulistas,* 567–68; A. C. de Camargo et al., "Candidatura Luiz Pereira Barreto: Manifesto da classe medica ao povo," São Paulo, 19 May 1918, AIHGSP, ALN, pacote 2, item 2; "Movimento civico," *O Combate,* 20 May 1918, p. 3; Alberto Seabra, "Justiça e conflictos sociaes," *O Estado de S. Paulo,* 12 Feb. 1924, p. 4; Alberto Seabra, *Problemas sul-americanos* (São Paulo: Monteiro Lobato, 1923); Nestor Rangel

Pestana to Oliveira Lima, São Paulo, n.d., and attachment, "Prospecto, *Revista do Brasil*," Oliveira Lima Library, Oliveira Lima correspondence collection; "Fundação da Liga pró Saneamento e Instrucção," *O Combate*, 23 July 1925, p. 4; "Associação Paulista de Defesa Social," *O Estado de S. Paulo*, 11 Aug. 1925, p. 6; "Noticias diversas," *O Estado de S. Paulo*, 2 Jan. 1926, p. 5.

73. "Manifesto da commissão acadêmica," São Paulo, 18 May 1918, reprinted in Nogueira Filho, *Ideais e lutas de um burguês progressista*, 2:633–34; Levi, *The Prados of São Paulo, Brazil*, 96–97; Luiz Augusto Maia Costa, "O ideário urbano paulista na virada do século: O engenheiro Theodoro Sampaio e as questões territoriais e urbanas modernas, 1886–1903" (tese de mestrado, Universidade de São Paulo, 2001), chap. 1; J. Romão da Silva, "Teodoro Sampaio: A vida, a obra, a figura humana," and Teodoro Sampaio, "Teodoro Sampaio por ele mesmo," 30 Nov. 1913, in Teodoro Sampaio, *São Paulo no século XIX e outros ciclos históricos*, ed. Hildon Rocha (Petrópolis: Vozes, 1978), 42–57; E. Mesquita, *Um livro de memórias sem importância*, 82–83.

74. "Installação do Partido Democratico," *O Estado de S. Paulo*, 22 March 1926, p. 2. *O Estado de S. Paulo*'s account is reprinted, in slightly rearranged form, in N. Prado, *Antonio Prado no imperio e na republica*, 389–90, 408–26. On paulista mutualism, see Tânia Regina de Luca, *O sonho do futuro assegurado: O mutualismo em São Paulo* (São Paulo: Contexto, 1990). On Cândido Rodrigues: Carlos Escobar, "O Pennacho," *O Combate*, 13 May 1920, p. 1; A. Salgado, "Manifesto Democrático," *A Capital*, 24 March 1926, p. 1; Assembléia Legislativa, *Legislativo paulista*, 100–3; A. Candido Rodrigues et al., "Ao eleitorado paulista," São Paulo, 2 Feb. 1924, in secção livre, *O Estado de S. Paulo*, 9 Feb. 1924, p. 9. On Queiroz Lacerda: N. Prado, *Antonio Prado no imperio e na republica*, 402; "Ao eleitorado paulista," *O Estado de S. Paulo*, 21 April 1922, pp. 3–4; "Ao povo paulista," *O Estado de S. Paulo*, 1 Jan. 1926, p. 4.

75. This paragraph and the following five paragraphs draw most heavily on "Installação do Partido Democratico," *O Estado de S. Paulo*, 22 March 1926, p. 2; "Um grande acontecimento na politica nacional," *O Combate*, 22 March 1926, p. 1.

76. "Installação do Partido Democratico," *O Estado de S. Paulo*, 22 March 1926, p. 2; "Um grande acontecimento na politica nacional," *O Combate*, 22 March 1926, p. 1; untitled article by "O.," *Braz-Jornal*, 28 March 1926, pp. 1–2; O., "Partido Democratico," *Braz-Jornal*, 4 April 1926, p. 1.

77. Clippings from *O Combate, Diario da Noite, A Platea, S. Paulo-Jornal, Folha da Manhã*, all of which were published in the state capital, as well as from the interior newspapers *Gazeta Liberal* (Jaboticabal), *O Popular* (Vargem Grande), and *A Tarde de Laranjal*, in AIHGSP, APD, album I.

78. "Installação do Partido Democratico," *O Estado de S. Paulo*, 22 March 1926, p. 2.

79. "O Partido Democratico" (newspaper clipping labeled *Diario da Noite*, 22 March 1926), AIHGSP, APD, album I.

80. "Um grande acontecimento na politica nacional," *O Combate*, 22 March 1926, p. 1.

81. "Partido Democratico," *O Sacy*, 26 March 1926, p. 21; P. Duarte, *História da imprensa em São Paulo*, 32.

82. Clippings from *Gazeta Liberal*, 1 April 1926, AIHGSP, APD, album I; "Intrigando . . . ," *O Combate*, 1 Feb. 1926, p. 1; "Intrigando . . . ," *O Combate*, 13 Feb. 1926, p. 1; Policia de São Paulo, *Movimento subversivo de julho*, 145–49; Costa and Goes, *Sob a metralha*, 359–61; telegram, Rocha Barros et al. to Ruy Barbosa, 4 Feb. 1919, CRB, ARB, CR.E 25/5; telegram, Rocha Barros et al. to Ruy Barbosa, Jaboticabal, 22 Feb. 1919, CRB, ARB, CR.E 25/9; telegram, *Democrata* to Nilo Peçanha, Jaboticabal, 20 [June?] 1921, in bound volume, Reacção Republicana, *Correspondencia recebida dos Estados de São Paulo, Paraná, S. Catharina, Rio Grande do Sul, Minas Gerais, Matto Grosso e Goyaz no periodo de junho a setembro de 1921*, MR, ANP, caixa 55; Cantidio Brêtas to Nilo Peçanha, Jaboticabal, 6 March 1922, MR, ANP, caixa 37.

83. Moacyr Fortunio, "Partido Democratico," *O Popular* (Vargem Grande), 4 April 1926, pp. 1–2, in AIHGSP, APD, album I.

84. Marcello Longhi to Paulo Nogueira Filho, Laranjal, 23 May 1926, AIHGSP, APD, pacote 33; Henrique Longhi, "Partido Democratico" (newspaper clipping labeled *A Tarde de Laranjal*, 13 May 1926), AIHGSP, APD, album I; Gustavo Martins, "Para frente!" (newspaper clipping labeled *A Tarde de Laranjal*, 13 May 1926), AIHGSP, APD, album I; Nogueira Filho, *Ideais e lutas de um burguês progressista*, 1:86.

85. Armando P. Ferreira to "Illustre Amigo Dr. Marrey," São Paulo, 21 March 1926, AIHGSP, APD, pacote 45; Armando Pinto Ferreira to PD president et al., São Paulo, 20 Aug. 1927, and attachments, AIHGSP, APD, pacote 45.

86. Antonio Ferraz Napoles, Sebastião Ferraz Napoles, and Ubaldo Ferraz Napoles to "Exmos Snrs. Fundadores do Partido Democrata," São Paulo, 21 March 1926, AIHGSP, APD, pacote 45; Hermes Victorino Chinaglia to "O Illm. Snr. do 'Partido Democratico,'" São Paulo, 21 March 1926, AIHGSP, APD, pacote 45.

87. João Gastão Duchein to Marrey Júnior, São Paulo, 22 March 1926, AIHGSP, APD, pacote 45.

88. João Iorio et al. to DC, São Paulo, 22 March 1926 (original emphasis), AIHGSP, APD, pacote 45.

89. Joaquim de Azevedo to Waldemar Ferreira, Ourinhos, 24 March 1926, AIHGSP, APD, pacote 33; Joaquim de Azevedo to Directores, Ourinhos, 4 April 1926, and attachment (Joaquim de Azevedo, "Partido Democratico," Ourinhos, 30 March 1926), AIHGSP, APD, pacote 33.

90. Thomaz Duffles to Presidente do PD, Ribeirão Preto, 22 March 1926, AIHGSP, APD, pacote 34.

91. Francisco C. Ribeiro Santiago to DC, n.d., AIHGSP, APD, pacote 47; British Chamber of Commerce of São Paulo and Southern Brazil, *Personali-*

dades no Brasil, 660; José Alexandre de Almeida to "Exmos. Snrs.," São João da Boa Vista, n.d. [1926], AIHGSP, APD, pacote 34.

92. Benjamin Ferraz da Cunha to Commissão do PD, Ourinhos, 11 April 1926, AIHGSP, APD, pacote 34.

93. Oscar de Souza to Directorio Provisorio do PD, São Paulo, 23 March 1926, AIHGSP, APD, pacote 45; Oscar de Souza to Directores do PD, 30 March 1926, AIHGSP, APD, pacote 45; Ludgero de Souza to Ruy Barbosa, São Paulo, 28 Jan. 1919, CRB, ARB, CR.E 25/2, doc. 91; Ludgero de Sousa to Nilo Peçanha, São Paulo, 5 March 1922, MR, ANP, caixa 27, pasta 1.

94. Antonio Monteiro da Cruz to Directores do PD, São Paulo, 27 March 1926 (emphasis added), AIHGSP, APD, pacote 45; "Partido Democratico," *O Estado de S. Paulo,* 5 April 1926, p. 4.

95. Clovis Botelho Vieira to Antonio Prado, São Paulo, 22 March 1926, AIHGSP, APD, pacote 45.

96. José Ribeiro de Faria to DC, Cravinhos, 13 May 1926, AIHGSP, APD, pacote 33.

97. Waldemar da Silva Braga to Directores do PD, São Paulo, 30 March 1926, AIHGSP, APD, pacote 45; Procurador Criminal da Republica, *Successos subversivos de São Paulo,* 216; José Munerato [to PD], São Carlos, 3 April 1926 (original emphasis), AIHGSP, APD, pacote 34; José Munerato to Waldemar Ferreira and Paulo Nogueira Filho, São Carlos, 12 April 1926, AIHGSP, APD, pacote 34; Policia de São Paulo, *Movimento subversivo de julho,* 138 (where his surname is spelled "Numerato").

98. Quoted in "Installação do Partido Democratico," *O Estado de S. Paulo,* 22 March 1926, p. 2; also, Directorio Provisorio, "Partido Democratico," *O Estado de S. Paulo,* 28 March 1926, p. 3.

99. Thomaz Duffles to Presidente do PD, Ribeirão Preto, 22 March 1926, AIHGSP, APD, pacote 34; João Gastão Duchein to Marrey Júnior, São Paulo, 22 March 1926, AIHGSP, APD, pacote 45.

100. Benedicto Cursino Santos to Presidente e Demais Membros do Partido Democrata do E. de São Paulo, Redempção, 14 April 1926, AIHGSP, APD, pacote 34; Osorio de Oliveira e Souza to Directorio do PD, Ribeirão Preto, 11 April 1926, AIHGSP, APD, pacote 34; Gustavo Porto to Directores do PD, São Carlos, 22 March 1926, AIHGSP, APD, pacote 34; Cnêo de Almeida Sampaio to Secretario do PD, Chavantes, 6 July 1926, AIHGSP, APD, pacote 33.

101. Simplicio Ferreira to Antonio Prado, Altinopolis, 24 May 1926, AIHGSP, APD, pacote 33.

102. Flaminio de Campos Gatti to Marrey Junior, São Paulo, 29 March 1926, and F. C. Gatti to PD, São Paulo, 7 April 1926, AIHGSP, APD, pacote 45.

103. Joaquim S. Barbeiro to Presidente e Demais Membros do Partido Democratico, Barretos, AIHGSP, APD, pacote 33; Ivo Martins to PD, Batataes, AIHGSP, APD, pacote 33; Joaquim Custodio de Oliveira to Marrey Junior, Bury, 10 Aug. 1926, AIHGSP, APD, pacote 33; Silvino Mendes da Oliveira to

Marrey Junior, Campinas, 30 March 1926, AIHGSP, APD, pacote 33; Cnêo de Almeida Sampaio to Secretario do PD, Chavantes, 6 July 1926, AIHGSP, APD, pacote 33; José Toledo Arruda to Membros do Conselho do PD, Guarantan, AIHGSP, APD, pacote 33; Alceu Geribello to PD, Itu, 26 March 1926, AIHGSP, APD, pacote 33; Marinho Junior to Directores do PD, 8 May 1926, AIHGSP, APD, pacote 33; José Floriano de Siqueira to Directorio Provisorio do PD, Jacarehy, 5 May 1926, AIHGSP, APD, pacote 33; Cesar Maretti to Directorio do PD, Mogy Mirim, 30 March 1926, AIHGSP, APD, pacote 33; Augusto Silva to Paulo de Moraes Barros, Santos, AIHGSP, APD, pacote 34; Mucio de Barros Aguiar to Chefes do PD, Santos, 24 March 1926, AIHGSP, APD, pacote 34; Alvaro Galvão to PD, São Paulo, AIHGSP, APD, pacote 45; Rufino Tavares to PD, São Paulo, 23 March 1926, AIHGSP, APD, pacote 45; Marciliano Gonçalves da Silva [to PD], São Paulo, [no day] March 1926, AIHGSP, APD, pacote 45; Wenefledo Toledo to Director do PD, São Paulo, 26 March 1926, AIHGSP, APD, pacote 45; Oscar de Souza to Directores do PD, São Paulo, 5 April 1926, AIHGSP, APD, pacote 45.

104. Queiroz Aranha speech of 7 Sept. 1926, quoted in "Partido Democratico," *O Estado de S. Paulo*, 27 Dec. 1926, p. 4; see also Nogueira Filho, *Ideais e lutas de um burguês progressista*, 1:174.

105. "Intrigando . . . ," *O Combate*, 7 April 1926, p. 4.

106. Ulysses de Campos Mello to Directores do PD, São Paulo, 31 March 1926, AIHGSP, APD, pacote 45.

107. Synesio Barreto to Directorio, Brasilea, 15 Dec. 1926, AIHGSP, APD, pacote 45. Angling for a transfer from Brasília (a tiny way-station not far from the railhead on the upper-Paulista frontier, not to be confused with Brazil's current capital) seems Barreto's likeliest reason for writing.

108. José Antonio Braga et al. to Directores do Partido Democratico, Jundiahy, n.d. [1926], AIHGSP, APD, pacote 33; "Partido Democratico" (newspaper clipping labeled *Folha de Jundiahy*, 11 April 1926), AIHGSP, APD, album I; "O pleito de 24" (newspaper clipping labeled *O Povo*, 20 Feb. 1927), AIHGSP, APD, album V; Brazilio Silveira Martins to Directorio Central, Jundiahy, 9 Sept. 1928, AIHGSP, APD, pacote 38; Brazilio Silveira Martins, "Resposta do questionario," n.d., AIHGSP, APD, pacote 21; N. Prado, *Antonio Prado no imperio e na republica*, 355ff.

109. José Menotti Chiarugi to Berto Condé, São Paulo, 16 Aug. 1926 (emphasis added), and José Menotti Chiarugi to DC, São Paulo, 17 Jan. 1927, AIHGSP, APD, pacote 45.

110. José Ribeiro de Faria to Commissão Directora do PD, Cravinhos, 13 May 1926, AIHGSP, APD, pacote 33; José Ribeiro de Faria to Paulo Nogueira Filho, Cravinhos, 28 June 1926, AIHGSP, APD, pacote 33; Directorio Provisorio to Octacilio D. Martins, São Paulo, 14 Aug. 1926, AIHGSP, APD, pacote 54; José Ribeiro de Faria, "Questionario," Cravinhos, 14 Nov. 1926, AIHGSP, APD, pacote 33; José Ribeiro de Faria, "Questionario," Cravinhos, 26 Dec. 1926,

AIHGSP, APD, pacote 33; Paulo de Moraes Barros to "Paulito," Ribeirão Preto, 5 Feb. 1927, AIHGSP, APD, pacote 36; [outgoing mail, PD headquarters] to Octacilio D. Martins, 31 May 1927, AIHGSP, APD, pacote 54; [outgoing mail, PD headquarters] to Morato, São Paulo, 31 May 1927, AIHGSP, APD, pacote 54. Athos Ribeiro, a lawyer, adopted a similar strategy in frontier Pirajuí, guiding the local party as its secretary while leaving the provisional presidency in the hands of a grand coffee planter: "Partido Democratico," *O Estado de S. Paulo*, 22 April 1926, p. 6; Secretaria da Agricultura, Industria e Commercio, *Os municipios do estado de São Paulo*, 333; Athos Ribeiro et al. to Directores do PD, Pirajuhy, 24 March 1926, AIHGSP, APD, pacote 34; Athos Ribeiro to Director de Semana do Directorio Provisorio, Pirajuhy, n.d., AIHGSP, APD, pacote 34; Athos Ribeiro, "Manifesto aos delegados do 5.° districto ao Congresso do Partido Democratico," Pirajuhy, 28 Nov. 1927, in *O Combate*, 3 Dec. 1927, p. 3; "Intrigando . . . ," *O Combate*, 3 Dec. 1927, p. 8.

111. Levi, *The Prados of São Paulo, Brazil*, 203–4; "Nos bastidores da politica" (newspaper clipping labeled *Diario da Noite*, 25 March 1926), AIHGSP, APD, album I; "Partido Democratico" (newspaper clipping labeled *S. Paulo-Jornal*, 26 March 1926), AIHGSP, APD, album I; "As adhesões recebidas pelo Partido Democratico" (newspaper clipping labeled *S. Paulo-Jornal*, 4 April 1926), AIHGSP, APD, album I; Directorio Provisorio [do Partido Democratico], "Ao povo" (newspaper clipping labeled *S. Paulo-Jornal*, 24 April 1926), AIHGSP, APD, album I. In her examination of party lists published in *O Estado de S. Paulo* during November and December 1926, representing just over 3 percent of total adherents by that point, Maria Cecília Spina Forjaz found the four largest occupational groups to be commercial employees (329), agriculturalists (217), workers (97), and railwaymen (91). She only found five who identified themselves as lawyers. See her *Tenentismo e Aliança Liberal, 1927–1930* (São Paulo: Polis, 1978), 40–42.

112. Raphael Rocco to DC, Guarulhos, n.d. [late June/early July 1926], AIHGSP, APD, pacote 33; Antonio Antonini to Membros do Conselho Central do PD, Caconde, 31 May 1926, AIHGSP, APD, pacote 33; Orozimbo Augusto de Almeida Loureiro to Directorio Provisorio do PD, Jahu, 8 April 1926, AIHGSP, APD, pacote 33; "Partido Democratico," *O Estado de S. Paulo*, 27 April 1926, p. 6.

113. Nogueira Filho, *Ideais e lutas de um burguês progressista*, 1:175–77; "Partido Democratico," *O Estado de S. Paulo*, 27 Dec. 1926, p. 4; "Congresso do Partido Democratico," *O Combate*, 27 Dec. 1926, p. 4; "Partido Democratico" (newspaper clipping labeled *Diario da Noite*, 22 Dec. 1926), AIHGSP, APD, album IV. On the eventual workings of the PD consultative council's technical committees: Nogueira Filho, *Ideais e lutas de um burguês progressista*, 1:253–54; "Intrigando . . . ," *O Combate*, 17 Dec. 1927, p. 6.

114. Francisco Oliva and José O. Carvalho, *Projecto de regulamentação da escolha de candidatos do Partido* (São Paulo: Typ. Rio Branco, 1926), and José

Bennaton Prado, *Proposta para o 1º Congresso* (São Paulo: Typ. Rio Branco, 1926), both in AIHGSP, APD, pacote 20, item 1; "Segunda sessão do primeiro congresso do Partido Democratico," n.d., AIHGSP, APD, pacote 20, item 1; Mario de Souza Queiroz, "Indicação para lei organica do Partido Democratico," 27 Dec. 1926, AIHGSP, APD, pacote 20, item 1; "Sessão solemne de encerramento do primeiro congresso do Partido Democratico," n.d., AIHGSP, APD, pacote 20, item 2; "Partido Democratico," *O Estado de S. Paulo*, 27 Dec. 1926, p. 4; "Congresso do Partido Democratico," *O Combate*, 27 Dec. 1926, p. 4; "Partido Democratico," *O Combate*, 29 Dec. 1926, p. 6. On Mário de Souza Queiroz: Celma da Silva Lago Baptistella, "Evolução dos viveiros de citros no Brasil," *Informações Econômicas* 35, no. 4 (April 2005): 76; British Chamber of Commerce of São Paulo and Southern Brazil, *Personalidades no Brasil*, 701; L. Corrêa da Silva et al. to Presidente e demais membros do PD, Limeira, 15 June 1927, AIHGSP, APD, pacote 36.

115. "Partido Democratico," *O Estado de S. Paulo*, 27 Dec. 1926, p. 4; "Intrigando . . . ," *O Combate*, 27 Dec. 1926, p. 1; "Congresso do Partido Democratico," *O Combate*, 27 Dec. 1926, p. 4; "Partido Democratico," *O Combate*, 29 Dec. 1926, p. 6; "Intrigando . . . ," *O Combate*, 30 Dec. 1926, p. 6; Nogueira Filho, *Ideais e lutas de um burguês progressista*, 1:175–77; M. Prado, *A democracia ilustrada*, 61.

116. A representative sample of newspapers and leaflets may be found in AIHGSP, APD, albums IV and V. Pacote 13 of the same archive contains larger propaganda posters from the period; while pacote 2 (second series) contains a handful of party buttons like those worn by the faithful. A PD flag from the era is on display at the museum maintained by the Instituto Histórico e Geográfico de São Paulo. On Wasth Rodrigues's role in designing "símbolos partidários," see Nogueira Filho, *Ideais e lutas de um burguês progressista*, 1:178.

117. "No ardor das paixões politicas," *Folha da Manhã*, 15 Feb. 1927, p. 8; "Politica de capangas e violencias," *O Povo*, 16 Feb. 1927, p. 1.

118. "Está travada, em todo o Estado, a grande batalha politica," *Diario da Noite*, 24 Feb. 1927, p. 1; "São Paulo poz á prova o seu brio," *O Combate*, 25 Feb. 1927, p. 1.

119. "São Paulo poz á prova o seu brio," *O Combate*, 25 Feb. 1927, p. 1; "Ainda o pleito de ante-hontem," *O Combate*, 26 Feb. 1927, p. 1; *O Sul de S. Paulo* (Itararé), 27 Feb. 1927, in AIHGSP, APD, album V.

120. Election data from *O Combate* issues of 25 Feb. 1927, p. 1; 26 Feb. 1927, p. 1; 2 March 1927, p. 1.

121. Abel Castilho, "Nova Bandeira" (newspaper clipping labeled *A Voz do Povo* [Presidente Prudente], 9 June 1927), AIHGSP, APD, album VII. In the state capital, the *Diario Popular* had kind words for the newly elected opposition congressmen (A. R., "Diariamente" [newspaper clipping labeled *Diario Popular*, 9 June 1927], AIHGSP, APD, album VII).

122. Nogueira Filho, *Ideais e lutas de um burguês progressista*, 1:184–85; Clovis

Botelho Vieira, "Proposta ao congresso do Partido Democratico," 5 May 1927, AIHGSP, APD, pacote 20, item 5; "Partido Democratico," *O Estado de S. Paulo*, 8 May 1927, p. 4; "O congresso extraordinario do Partido Democratico e o banquete aos seus candidatos," *O Combate*, 9 May 1927, pp. 1, 4; Antonio da Silva Prado et al., "Ao povo paulista," São Paulo, 25 May 1927, published in *O Estado de S. Paulo*, 27 May 1927, p. 3.

123. "O Partido da Mocidade," *O Combate*, 14 May 1927, p. 6; "Cabanas, apreciando o movimento civico do Partido da Mocidade," *O Combate*, 4 June 1927, p. 6; "As eleições de hontem," *O Combate*, 6 June 1927, p. 6.

124. "Lição de nacionalismo" (newspaper clipping labeled *Diario da Noite*, 12 July 1927) and Gregorio do Matto, "A guarda avançada do Bolshevismo" (newspaper clipping, labeled *Correio Paulistano*, 26 July 1927), both in AIHGSP, APD, album VII. The caravans, their members, and destinations are listed in the appendix of Nogueira Filho, *Ideais e lutas de um burguês progressista*, 2:645–48.

125. The information on newspaper circulation is from M. Prado, *A democracia ilustrada*, 39; C. R. Cameron, Report 151, "São Paulo Press on the Kellogg Pact," 4 Sept. 1928, and C. R. Cameron, Report 167, "Fascism in São Paulo," 29 Oct. 1928, both in USNARA, RG84, Consular Posts, São Paulo, Brazil, volume 90, 800 series.

126. "Aspectos e impressões do grande Congresso para a escolha dos candidatos democraticos," *O Combate*, 6 Dec. 1927, p. 1; Barriguelli, *O pensamento político da classe dominante paulista, 1873–1928*, 105–9; Nogueira Filho, *Ideais e lutas de um burguês progressista*, 1:197–202, 2:651–56. The policy proposals were forwarded to the PD's Central Directorate and to the directorate of the newly formed National Democratic Party, where they languished.

127. Joaquim Sampaio Vidal ran his own campaign, ostensibly aloof from both factions but possibly as a pro-aristocratic spoiler, while Paulo Nogueira Filho sought to have it both ways but ultimately sided with his fellows against Lázaro Maria da Silva's candidacy. "Intrigando . . . ," *O Combate*, 5 Oct. 1927, p. 6; "Intrigando . . . ," *O Combate*, 7 Oct. 1927, p. 6; "Intrigando . . . ," *O Combate*, 11 Oct. 1927, p. 6; "Intrigando . . . ," *O Combate*, 15 Oct. 1927, p. 6; "Intrigando . . . ," *O Combate*, 17 Oct. 1927, p. 2; "Intrigando . . . ," *O Combate*, 18 Oct. 1927, p. 6; "Intrigando . . . ," *O Combate*, 20 Oct. 1927, p. 6; "Intrigando . . . ," *O Combate*, 22 Oct. 1927, p. 6; "Intrigando . . . ," *O Combate*, 25 Oct. 1927, p. 6; "Intrigando . . . ," *O Combate*, 1 Nov. 1927, p. 6; "Intrigando . . . ," *O Combate*, 17 Nov. 1927, p. 2; Abrahão Ribeiro et al., "Manifesto aos delegados ao terceiro congresso," São Paulo, 22 Nov. 1927, published in secção livre, *O Estado de S. Paulo*, 25 Nov. 1927, p. 10 (also in *O Combate*, 26 Nov. 1927, p. 3); "A chapa democratica," *Diario da Noite*, 22 Nov. 1927, reprinted in secção livre, *O Estado de S. Paulo*, 25 Nov. 1927, p. 10; Waldemar Fleury, "Politica paulista," *O Combate*, 22 Nov. 1927, p. 2; "Intrigando . . . ," *O Combate*, 24 Nov. 1927, p. 6; "Intrigando . . . ," *O Combate*, 25 Nov. 1927, p. 1; "Intrigando . . . ," *O Combate*, 26 Nov. 1927, p. 3;

Joaquim A. Sampaio Vidal, "Partido Democratico," in secção livre, *O Combate*, 28 Nov. 1927, p. 6; "Intrigando . . . ," *O Combate*, 28 Nov. 1927, p. 6; "Intrigando . . . ," *O Combate*, 30 Nov. 1927, p. 6; "Mauricio de Lacerda vem a S. Paulo," *Diario da Noite*, 29 Nov. 1927, reprinted in secção livre, *O Estado de S. Paulo*, 3 Dec. 1927, p. 13; "Candidaturas democraticas," *O Combate*, 1 Dec. 1927, p. 1; "Intrigando . . . ," *O Combate*, 1 Dec. 1927, p. 6; M. Costa, "Uma candidatura indispensavel," in secção livre, *O Estado de S. Paulo*, 2 Dec. 1927, p. 11; "Notas e informações," *O Estado de S. Paulo*, 3 Dec. 1927, p. 3; Athos Ribeiro, "Manifesto aos delegados do 5.º districto ao Congresso do Partido Democratico," in secção livre, *O Combate*, 3 Dec. 1927, p. 3; "Intrigando . . . ," *O Combate*, 3 Dec. 1927, p. 8; untitled note, *O Combate*, 3 Dec. 1927, p. 8; "Intrigando . . . ," *O Combate*, 5 Dec. 1927, p. 1; "A orientação do Partido Democratico no III Congresso" (newspaper clipping labeled *O Diario* [Jahu], 7 Dec. 1927), AIHGSP, APD, album IX; Nogueira Filho, *Ideais e lutas de um burguês progressista*, 1:197–98, 201–3. The quote "to its highest . . ." is from "A proxima assemblea democratica," *Diario da Noite*, 20 Nov. 1927, reprinted in secção livre, *O Estado de S. Paulo*, 25 Nov. 1927, p. 10; for Paulo Duarte's quote, see his *Que é que ha? Pequena historia de uma grande pirataria* (São Paulo: n.p., 1931), 147–49. On Condé, Marrey, and Antônio Feliciano, see above, this chap.; on Vicente Pinheiro, see below, this chap. On Lázaro Maria da Silva: telegram, Directorio Central to Lazaro Maria da Silva, São Paulo, n.d., AIHGSP, APD, pacote 54; "Candidatos do povo," *Hoje*, 23 Nov. 1945, p. 6; Leme, *A casa de Bragança*, 95.

128. "Aspectos e impressões do grande Congresso para a escolha dos candidatos democraticos," *O Combate*, 6 Dec. 1927, p. 1; Nogueira Filho, *Ideais e lutas de um burguês progressista*, 1:198–202.

129. Antonio Cajado de Lemos to Directores, São Paulo, 5 Dec. 1927, AIHGSP, APD, pacote 45; "Intrigando . . . ," *O Combate*, 8 Dec. 1927, p. 6.

130. "Intrigando . . . ," *O Combate*, 5 Dec. 1927, p. 1.

131. "Intrigando . . . ," *O Combate*, 6 Dec. 1927, p. 6; "Intrigando . . . ," *O Combate*, 7 Dec. 1927, p. 6; "Pelos bastidores da politica," *O Combate*, 8 Dec. 1927, p. 1; "A politica da capital," *O Combate*, 9 Dec. 1927, p. 1.

132. A. Leite, *História da civilização paulista*, 182; Nogueira Filho, *Ideais e lutas de um burguês progressista*, 1:202, 210–16; "Intrigando . . . ," *O Combate*, 3 Jan. 1928, p. 2; "Intrigando . . . ," *O Combate*, 13 Jan. 1928, p. 6; "Intrigando . . . ," *O Combate*, 24 Jan. 1928, p. 6.

133. Other municipalities in which the PD's candidates won more votes than the leading perrepista candidate included Piracicaba, São José do Rio Pardo, Catanduva, Brodowski, and Cachoeira. Its candidates reportedly ran as close seconds in Jaú, Penápolis, Bauru, Dois Córregos, "and innumerous [other] cities." See "Echos das eleições do dia 24" (newspaper clipping dated 3 March 1928), AIHGSP, APD, album X.

134. S. Castilho Pereira, "Badaladas!" (newspaper clipping labeled *A Comarca de Novo Horizonte*, 12 May 1928), AIHGSP, APD, album X.

135. "O pleito no 5.º districto" (newspaper clipping labeled *O Democratico* [Botucatu], 29 March 1928), AIHGSP, APD, album X; Nogueira Filho, *Ideais e lutas de um burguês progressista*, 1:215.

136. Nogueira Filho, *Ideais e lutas de um burguês progressista*, 1:247–54.

137. Incoming nominations, AIHGSP, APD, pacote 12, item 2; José Joaquim Cardoso de Mello Netto et al., "Acta da reunião dos Directorios Districtaes da Capital," São Paulo, 30 Aug. 1928, AIHGSP, APD, pacote 12, item 3; Nogueira Filho, *Ideais e lutas de um burguês progressista*, 1:289–91; "A previa democratica," *O Combate*, 31 Aug. 1928, p. 6; "Actas das previas realizadas no interior, 1928," AIHGSP, APD, pacote 13, item 2; "Intrigando . . . ," *O Combate*, 2 Oct. 1928, p. 2; "Em Casa Branca," *Diario Nacional*, 6 Oct. 1928, p. 3; "O Partido Democratico em actividade," *Diario Nacional*, 9 Oct. 1928, p. 6.

138. C. R. Cameron, Report 167, "Fascism in São Paulo," 29 Oct. 1928, USNARA, RG84, Consular Posts, São Paulo, Brazil, volume 90, 800 series; Nogueira Filho, *Ideais e lutas de um burguês progressista*, 1:306–10.

139. C. R. Cameron, Report 167, "Fascism in São Paulo," 29 Oct. 1928, USNARA, RG84, Consular Posts, São Paulo, Brazil, volume 90, 800 series; A. Leite, *História da civilização paulista*, 184; Nogueira Filho, *Ideais e lutas de um burguês progressista*, 1:305–6, 310–12; telegram, Alvaro Corrêa Campos to Julio Prestes de Albuquerque, São Paulo, 8 Oct. 1928, AESP, AJPA, caixa AP22; telegram, José Izaias to Julio Prestes de Albuquerque, Sertãozinho, 11 Oct. 1928, AESP, AJPA, caixa AP22; Levinio de Souza e Silva et al. to DC, São Paulo, 5 Oct. 1928, AIHGSP, APD, pacote 46.

140. Quote from C. R. Cameron, Report 167, "Fascism in São Paulo," 29 Oct. 1928, USNARA, RG84, Consular Posts, São Paulo, Brazil, volume 90, 800 series; A. Leite, *História da civilização paulista*, 183; Nogueira Filho, *Ideais e lutas de um burguês progressista*, 1:303, 317–24.

141. Chart, "8º Districto," n.d. [1928], AIHGSP, APD, pacote 13; "Piracicaba sob o regimen do terror," *O Combate*, 30 Oct. 1928, p. 5; *Como se fazem eleições no Estado de São Paulo* (São Paulo: n.p., 1928), AIHGSP, APD, pacote 6, item 2.

142. PD, Directorio Districtal do Braz to DC, São Paulo, 5 Nov. 1928, AIHGSP, APD, pacote 45 (this document is misfiled with material from Nov. 1926).

143. "Como estão correndo as eleições," *O Combate*, 30 Oct. 1928, p. 6; Marinho Junior to Directorio Central, Ytú, 6 Nov. 1928, AIHGSP, APD, pacote 38; "O pleito em Santos," *O Combate*, 3 Nov. 1928, p. 2; *Como se fazem eleições no Estado de São Paulo* (São Paulo: n.p., 1928), AIHGSP, APD, pacote 6, item 2.

144. "Saibam todos," *O Combate*, 5 Nov. 1928, p. 6; PD-Santa Cecília, "Questionario," São Paulo, 13 Dec. 1928, and PD-Sé, "Questionario," São Paulo, n.d., AIHGSP, APD, pacote 21, item 1.

145. Alipio Luis Dias, "Questionario," S. José do Rio Pardo, 2 Dec. 1928, AIHGSP, APD, pacote 21, item 1.

146. "Em Campinas," *O Combate*, 1 Nov. 1928, p. 2; "Fallece, em Campinas, um vereador eleito pelo Partido Democratico," *O Combate*, 8 Nov. 1928, p. 5.

147. PD-Santos, "Questionario," 8 Dec. 1928, AIHGSP, APD, pacote 21; "O pleito em Santos," *O Combate*, 3 Nov. 1928, p. 2.

148. Brazilio Silveira Martins, "Resposta do questionario," n.d., AIHGSP, APD, pacote 21, item 1; "Questionario," Rio Claro, n.d., AIHGSP, APD, pacote 21, item 1; Nogueira Filho, *Ideais e lutas de um burguês progressista*, 1:324; M. Prado, *A democracia ilustrada*, 75. Even in Santos and Campinas, the party elected fewer councilmen than it had anticipated: charts for "1º Districto" and "6º Districto," n.d., AIHGSP, APD, pacote 13, item 4.

149. Ana Luiza Martins and Heloisa Barbuy, *Arcadas: História da Faculdade de Direito do Largo de São Francisco* (São Paulo: Melhoramentos, 1999), offers an introduction to the letrados' habitat; Kirkendall, *Class Mates*, explores some of the older letrados' habits of mind as students; M. Prado, *A democracia ilustrada*, notes Morato's monarchism (see p. 16), as does Terci, "A cidade na primeira república," 260–61.

150. Regina Hipólito, "Paulo de Morais Barros" and "Henrique de Sousa Queirós," in A. Abreu et al., *Dicionário histórico-biográfico brasileiro*, 1:564–65, 4:4835–36; British Chamber of Commerce of São Paulo and Southern Brazil, *Personalidades no Brasil*, 499–500, 700; Earl Richard Downes, "The Seeds of Influence: Brazil's 'Essentially Agricultural' Old Republic and the United States, 1910–1930" (Ph.D. diss., University of Texas, 1986), 502; Love, *São Paulo in the Brazilian Federation*, 297; Perissinotto, "Estado, capital cafeeiro e crise política na década de 1920 em São Paulo, Brasil," passim; M. Prado, *A democracia ilustrada*, 17–19; "Intrigando . . . ," *O Combate*, 4 May 1926, p. 1; "Intrigando . . . ," *O Combate*, 19 Aug. 1926, p. 8; "A lucta na capital," *O Combate*, 30 Oct. 1928, p. 1. The quote is from "A madraçaria da 'esquerda'" (newspaper clipping labeled *Folha da Manhã*, 6 Sept. 1927), AIHGSP, APD, album VIII.

151. "O Partido Democratico em S. José do Rio Pardo" (newspaper clipping labeled *Diario da Noite*, 10 Oct. 1927), AIHGSP, APD, album IX; "Notas para um archivo," *O Combate*, 17 Feb. 1928, p. 3.

152. Nogueira Filho, *Ideais e lutas de um burguês progressista*; Jorge Miguel Mayer, "Paulo Nogueira Filho" and "Joaquim Sampaio Vidal," in A. Abreu et al., *Dicionário histórico-biográfico brasileiro*, 4:4102–5, 5:6056–57.

153. See above, this chap.; "As eleições federaes," *Folha do Partido Democratico*, in *O Combate*, 21 Jan. 1927, p. 5; A. Fleury, "Ao eleitorado independente," *O Sul de S. Paulo* (Itararé), 6 Feb. 1927, p. 1; "Nas vesperas do pleito eleitoral," *Diario da Noite*, 18 Feb. 1927, p. 1; "O 'caso Marrey' e a limitação das responsabilidades," *Folha da Manhã*, 6 Oct. 1928, p. 1.

154. Bertho Condé, "A saude e a . . . politica" (newspaper clipping labeled *Folha da Manhã*, 8 July 1926), AIHGSP, APD, album II; handbill, Partido Democratico, "Convite ao Povo," n.d. (late 1926 or early 1927), AIHGSP, APD, album IV; PD propaganda leaflet, "Conferencia do Dr. Bertho Condé," n.d., AIHGSP, APD, album V; "As eleições de 24" (newspaper clipping labeled *O Povo*, 18 Feb. 1927), AIHGSP, APD, album V; "Movimento operario," *O Combate*,

27 Sept. 1928, p. 2; "Cinco dias na 'gaveta' do Cambucy," *Folha da Manhã*, 29 Sept. 1928, p. 5; "No regimen burguez é assim . . . ," *O Trabalhador Graphico*, 2 April 1929, p. 1; "O proletariado accusa!," *O Trabalhador Graphico*, 4 April 1929, p. 2; "Solidariedade," *O Trabalhador Graphico*, 19 April 1929, p. 1; "A U. T. G. e as violencias policiaes," *O Trabalhador Graphico*, 4 May 1929, p. 2. Condé was also the only member of the senior PD leadership to advocate extending the vote to women. "Aspectos e impressões do grande Congresso para a escolha dos candidatos democraticos," *O Combate*, 6 Dec. 1927, p. 1.

155. "Nas vesperas do pleito federal," *Diario da Noite*, 23 Feb. 1927, p. 3; "Intrigando . . . ," *O Combate*, 11 Oct. 1927, p. 6; "Intrigando . . . ," *O Combate*, 31 Oct. 1927, p. 6; "Intrigando . . . ," *O Combate*, 12 Jan. 1928, p. 1; "Intrigando . . . ," *O Combate*, 17 Jan. 1928, p. 6; Victor Zaramella to secretaria central, São Paulo, 21 Dec. 1926, AIHGSP, APD, pacote 45; Estevão Montebello, "Questionario," São Paulo, 27 Dec. 1926 [1 of 2], AIHGSP, APD, pacote 45; Estevão Montebello, "Questionario," São Paulo, 27 Dec. 1926 [2 of 2], AIHGSP, APD, pacote 45; Estevam Montebello to "presado correligionario," São Paulo, 1 April 1927, AIHGSP, APD, pacote 45; Estevam Montebello to PD secretary, São Paulo, 1 April 1927, AIHGSP, APD, pacote 45; telegram, Montebello to PD, São Paulo, 21 May 1927, AIHGSP, APD, pacote 45; "Os incorporadores" of S. A. *Diario Nacional* to Estevam Montebello, São Paulo, 17 June 1927, AIHGSP, APD, pacote 54; "A situação politica actual" (newspaper clipping labeled *O Combate*, 24 Nov. 1927), AIHGSP, APD, album IX; P. Duarte, *Que é que ha?*, 147–49; Sergio Milliet, *Roberto* (São Paulo: L. Niccolini & Cia., 1935), 149, 151; Nogueira Filho, *Ideais e lutas de um burguês progressista*, 1:289. Another member of the Montebello clan was employed by the PD secretariat: Adelardo Soares Caiuby to Thezoureiro do PD, São Paulo, 29 Oct. 1926, AIHGSP, APD, pacote 45.

156. Nogueira Filho, *Ideais e lutas de um burguês progressista*, 1:289, 2:652, 676; Odon Lima Cardoso to PD, São Paulo, 29 March 1927, AIHGSP, APD, pacote 45; Directorio de Sta. Cecilia to "presado amigo e correligionario," São Paulo, 4 April 1927, AIHGSP, APD, pacote 45; Manfredo Costa and Odon Lima Cardoso to DC, São Paulo, 9 April 1927, AIHGSP, APD, pacote 45; Manfredo Costa, Odon Lima Cardoso, and José de Camargo Calazans to DC, São Paulo, 21 May 1927; Carlos de Moraes Andrade to DC, São Paulo, 8 Aug. 1927, AIHGSP, APD, pacote 45; Manfredo Antonio da Costa and Carlos de Morais Andrade to DC, São Paulo, 22 Nov. 1927, AIHGSP, APD, pacote 45; "Intrigando . . . ," *O Combate*, 24 Jan. 1928, p. 6.

157. "1° Districto[:] Correspondentes," n.d. [May 1927], AIHGSP, APD, pacote 20, item 6; Manfredo A. Costa to DC, São Paulo, 23 Dec. 1927, AIHGSP, APD, pacote 45.

158. Nicolau Soares do Couto Esher and Brasilio Leal to PD president, São Paulo, 13 Dec. 1926, AIHGSP, APD, pacote 45; "Partido Democratico," *O Estado de S. Paulo*, 14 Dec. 1926, p. 6; Nicolau Soares do Couto Esher to DC, São

Paulo, 5 April 1927, AIHGSP, APD, pacote 45; [illegible (two signatures)] to director, São Paulo, 19 April 1927, AIHGSP, APD, pacote 45; Affonso Henrique Mendes to DC, São Paulo, 25 April 1927, AIHGSP, APD, pacote 45; "1° Districto[:] Correspondentes," n.d. [May 1927], AIHGSP, APD, pacote 20, item 6; Nogueira Filho, *Ideais e lutas de um burguês progressista*, 2:653.

159. "Notas para um archivo," *O Combate*, 22 Feb. 1928, p. 6; his nom de plume (the final syllables of each of his names, except the patronym: Nico*lau* Soa*res* do Cou*to*) is explained in Robert Leonard McIntire, *Portrait of Half a Century: Fifty Years of Presbyterianism in Brazil, 1859–1910* (Cuernavaca: Centro Intercultural de Documentación, 1969), chap. 9, p. 19.

160. "A Sociedade L. Queiroz," *O Combate*, 7 Feb. 1917, p. 1; "O Partido Municipal," *O Combate*, 5 Feb. 1917, p. 1; PD-Sé, "Questionario," São Paulo, n.d., AIHGSP, APD, pacote 21, item 1.

161. José Menotti Chiarugi to Berto Condé, São Paulo, 16 Aug. 1926, AIHGSP, APD, pacote 45; "Nas vesperas do pleito federal," *Diario da Noite*, 23 Feb. 1927, p. 3. Chiarugi was also manager and part owner of the yellow-press magazine *O Sacy* for at least a couple of months: Cornelio Pires, "O Sacy," *O Sacy*, 31 Dec. 1926, unpag.; masthead information from *O Sacy*, 7 Jan. 1927, 21 Jan. 1927, and 18 Feb. 1927.

162. Nogueira Filho, *Ideais e lutas de um burguês progressista*, passim; British Chamber of Commerce of São Paulo and Southern Brazil, *Personalidades no Brasil*, 529.

163. Untitled list of directorate members from Lapa, n.d., AIHGSP, APD, pacote 6; [illegible] to PD secretary, São Paulo, 28 Jan. 1927, AIHGSP, APD, pacote 45; João Wagner Wey to Marrey Junior, São Paulo, 14 Feb. 1927, AIHGSP, APD, pacote 45; João Wagner Wey et al. to Paulo Nogueira Filho, São Paulo, 14 Feb. 1927, AIHGSP, APD, pacote 45; Lycurgo Lopes da Cruz to DC, São Paulo, 18 April 1927, AIHGSP, APD, pacote 45; Lycurgo L. da Cruz to DC, São Paulo, 6 May 1927, AIHGSP, APD, pacote 45; "1° Districto[:] Correspondentes," n.d. [May 1927], AIHGSP, APD, pacote 20, item 6; Lycurgo Lopes da Cruz to DC, São Paulo, 18 Jan. 1928, AIHGSP, APD, pacote 46; Roberto Zimberger to DC, São Paulo, 29 Aug. 1928 [1 of 2], AIHGSP, APD, pacote 46; Roberto Zimberger to DC, São Paulo, 29 Aug. 1928 [2 of 2], AIHGSP, APD, pacote 46; João Wagner Wey et al., "Ao eleitorado democratico da Lapa," in secção livre, *Commercio da Lapa*, 30 Aug. 1928, p. 2; "Intrigando . . . ," *O Combate*, 26 Oct. 1928, p. 2; Leonidas Pereira de Almeida, "Partido Democratico," *Commercio da Lapa*, 29 Oct. 1928, p. 1; "Politica da Lapa," in secção livre, *Commercio da Lapa*, 29 Oct. 1928, p. 3; "Questões politicas," in secção livre, *Commercio da Lapa*, 17 Nov. 1928, p. 3; Nogueira Filho, *Ideais e lutas de um burguês progressista*, 2:656, 676; Heitor de Moraes et al., "Ao eleitorado do 1.° districto," Santos, 5 Feb. 1918, published in *O Combate*, 9 Feb. 1918, p. 1; Roberto Zimberger to Directoria da Liga Nacionalista, São Paulo, 17 Sept. 1920, AIHGSP, ALN, pacote 2. The peak of Wey's political career came in the

postwar period, when he was briefly appointed prefeito of Sorocaba. Vicente Caputti Sobrinho, *Minha terra, minha gente* (Sorocaba: Fundação Ubaldino do Amaral, 1995), 109.

164. Armando Marcondes Machado et al. to PD president, São Paulo, 29 May 1926, AIHGSP, APD, pacote 45; Manoel Egydio dos Santos to Directores, São Paulo, 5 June 1926, AIHGSP, APD, pacote 45; Manoel Egydio dos Santos to Directores do PD, São Paulo, 26 Jan. 1927, AIHGSP, APD, pacote 54 (misfiled); M. E. dos Santos to directores, São Paulo, 2 April 1927, AIHGSP, APD, pacote 45; M. E. dos Santos to Directores, São Paulo, 18 April 1927, AIHGSP, APD, pacote 45; M. E. dos Santos to Directores, São Paulo, 3 May 1927, AIHGSP, APD, pacote 45; Armando Marcondes Machado to directores, São Paulo, 11 June 1927, AIHGSP, APD, pacote 45; M. E. dos Santos, "Relação dos Juizes de Paz e Supplentes deste Districto da Penha de França," São Paulo, 28 Oct. 1927, AIHGSP, APD, pacote 15, item 5; M. E. dos Santos to Directores, São Paulo, 21 Nov. 1927, AIHGSP, APD, pacote 45; M. E. dos Santos to DC, São Paulo, 16 Dec. 1927, AIHGSP, APD, pacote 45; Armando Marcondes Machado to Directores, São Paulo, 16 Feb. 1928, AIHGSP, APD, pacote 46; M. E. dos Santos, "Acta da reunião para tomar conhecimento situação financeira do directorio" (copy), 10 March 1928, AIHGSP, APD, pacote 46; Armando Marcondes Machado to Directores, São Paulo, 16 March 1928, AIHGSP, APD, pacote 46; Glycerio Rodrigues to DC, São Paulo, 27 June 1928, AIHGSP, APD, pacote 46; Armando Marcondes Machado to DC, São Paulo, 13 April 1929, AIHGSP, APD, pacote 46; Nogueira Filho, *Ideais e lutas de um burguês progressista*, 2:652, 676.

165. "Acta de Reunião Preparatoria para Formação do Directorio Provisorio do Districto de Butantan," n.d., AIHGSP, APD, pacote 1; "Directorio Provisorio de Butantan," n.d., AIHGSP, APD, pacote 6; "Butantan," unsigned, undated sheet, AIHGSP, APD, pacote 8; José Tucunduva Sobrinho to PD, São Paulo, 25 Feb. 1927, AIHGSP, APD, pacote 45; "Ao povo de Butantan," São Paulo, 17 May 1927, AIHGSP, APD, pacote 45; J. F. Saldanha Sobrinho to PD Secretary, São Paulo, 21 May 1927, AIHGSP, APD, pacote 45; J. F. Saldanha Sobrinho to "Presidente e Mais Membros do Directorio do Partido Democratico de Cotia," São Paulo, 24 May 1927, AIHGSP, APD, pacote 15, item 3; Albertino Iasi to Secretario Geral, São Paulo, 28 May 1927, AIHGSP, APD, pacote 45; Albertino Iasi to DC, São Paulo, 3 July 1927, AIHGSP, APD, pacote 45; Alberto Cardozo de Mello Filho and Armando Pinto to Directores do PD, São Paulo, 2 Aug. 1927, AIHGSP, APD, pacote 45; José J. F. Saldanha Sobrinho to Secretario Geral, 23 Nov. 1927, AIHGSP, APD, pacote 45; Saldanha Sobrinho to Arlindo Amaral, São Paulo, 24 Jan. 1928, AIHGSP, APD, pacote 46; "Saibam todos," *O Combate*, 30 March 1928, p. 2; "Á guiza de apresentação," *O Pinheirense* (2nd series), Jan. 1926, p. 2; Francisco Iasi, "Pinheiros-Butantan," *O Pinheirense* (1st series), 9 Dec. 1923, p. 1.

166. "Santo Amaro," unsigned, undated sheet, AIHGSP, APD, pacote 8; "1º

Districto[:] Correspondentes," n.d. [May 1927], AIHGSP, APD, pacote 20, item 6; Lucas Másculo, "Questionario," Santo Amaro, n.d., AIHGSP, APD, pacote 21, item 1; Augusto Jorge Maluf to Centro Democratico, Santo Amaro, 21 Oct. 1927, AIHGSP, APD, pacote 37; Lucas Masculo to DC, Santo Amaro, 8 Nov. 1927, AIHGSP, APD, pacote 37; Lucas Masculo to DC, 7 Dec. 1927, AIHGSP, APD, pacote 37; Lucas Másculo to Secretario da Commissão Central, Santo Amaro, 2 March 1928, AIHGSP, APD, pacote 38; Nogueira Filho, *Ideais e lutas de um burguês progressista*, 2:653; Policia de São Paulo, *Movimento subversivo de julho*, 102; Linhares, *Contribuição à história das lutas operárias no Brasil*, 56; Toledo, *Travessias revolucionárias*, 324, 334 n. 146.

167. "Acta da sessão de installação da Commissão Districtal de São Cae-tano," n.d. [Feb. 1927], AIHGSP, APD, pacote 15, item 2; "1º Districto[:] Corre-spondentes," n.d. [May 1927], AIHGSP, APD, pacote 20, item 6; "Acta da posse do Directorio Definitivo do Partido Democratico de São Bernardo," 20 Nov. 1927, AIHGSP, APD, pacote 1, item 2; Sylvio Magaldi and José Amazonas to DC, São Bernardo, 31 July 1927, AIHGSP, APD, pacote 37; Sylvio Magaldi to DC, São Bernardo, 17 Nov. 1927, AIHGSP, APD, pacote 37; Sylvio Magaldi to DC, São Bernardo, 24 Nov. 1927, AIHGSP, APD, pacote 37; Saldino Cardoso Franco to Julio Prestes de Albuquerque, São Bernardo, 27 June 1928, AESP, AJPA, caixa AP07; "Acta de eleição do sub-directorio definitivo de São Caetano, do muni-cipio de São Bernardo," 16 Aug. 1928, AIHGSP, APD, pacote 1, item 2; Carmello Crispini, "Acta da posse do sub directorio definitivo do Partido Democratico de São Caetano," 12 Sept. 1928, AIHGSP, APD, pacote 38; "Acta da eleição para a formação do Directorio Definitivo do Partido Democratico do Districto de Santo André," 22 Sept. 1928, AIHGSP, APD, pacote 1, item 2; Agostinho Silva, "Acta da eleição para candidatos a juizes de paz do Districto de Santo André e um vereador á Camara Municipal de São Bernardo," n.d. [late Sept.-early Oct. 1928], AIHGSP, APD, pacote 13, item 2; "Intrigando . . . ," *O Combate*, 2 Oct. 1928, p. 2; "As fraudes em S. Bernardo," *O Combate*, 3 Nov. 1928, p. 3; "Relatorio apresentado pelo Dr. José Amazonas," São Bernardo, 4 Nov. 1928, AIHGSP, APD, pacote 38; "São Bernardo," n.d., AIHGSP, APD, pacote 8; Nogueira Filho, *Ideais e lutas de um burguês progressista*, 2:656, 677; José Antonio de Almeida Amazonas to "Dr. Juiz de Direito da 1ª Vara Civil da Capital," São Paulo, 26 Sept. 1927, AIHGSP, APD, pacote 37 (filed under Santos); "O dr. J. J. Seabra passou por Santos," *O Combate*, 17 Jan. 1922, p. 1; "Os Veronesi em São Caetano do Sul," *Jornal de São Caetano*, 28 July 1988, p. 7b; Antonio Barile to Marrey, São Caetano, n.d. [February 1927] (document fragment), AIHGSP, APD, pacote 47 (misfiled); telegram, Armando de Arruda et al. to Julio Prestes de Albuquerque, São Caetano, 2 June 1928, AESP, AJPA, caixa AP22; "Partido Municipal de São Caetano," *S. Caetano Jornal*, 3 June 1928 [perhaps 8 June 1928], reprinted in secção livre of *O Estado de S. Paulo*, 12 June 1928, p. 17; "Pela politica," *Folha da Noite*, 3 Aug. 1928, reprinted in secção livre of *O Estado de S. Paulo*, 5 Aug. 1928, p. 17; Armando de Arruda Pereira et al. to Julio Prestes de

Albuquerque, São Caetano, 3 April 1929, AESP, AJPA, caixa AP08; French, "Industrial Workers and the Origin of Populist Politics in the ABC Region of Greater São Paulo, 1900–1950," 80–81, 87, 91n.; Gaiarsa, *Santo André*, 178; José de Souza Martins, *São Caetano do Sul em quatro séculos de história* (São Caetano do Sul: Saraiva, 1957), 125–26; J. Martins, *Subúrbio*, 213–14, 269, 273–74, and plates following p. 225; Medici, *Migração e urbanização*, 37–38; N. Prado, *Antonio Prado no imperio e na republica*, 406.

168. "O Partido Democratico," *O Combate*, 5 July 1926, p. 1; untitled newspaper clipping (labeled *Folha da Noite*, 3 April 1927), AIHGSP, APD, pacote VI; "Campinas," unsigned, undated sheet, AIHGSP, APD, pacote 9; *O Pharol* (Campinas), marginalia indicates issue of 25 July 1928, AIHGSP, APD, pacote XI; Pelágio Lôbo, "O fôro de Campinas do império e na república," in *Monografia histórica do município de Campinas* (Rio de Janeiro: Instituto Brasileiro de Geografia e Estatística, 1952), 331–32; "Eleições," *O Estado de S. Paulo*, 31 Oct. 1904, p. 1; "Os municipios," *O Estado de S. Paulo*, 1 Nov. 1904, p. 2; "Eleições municipaes," *O Estado de S. Paulo*, 31 Oct. 1910, p. 4; Assembléia Legislativa, *Legislativo paulista*, 83–84; Ribeiro, *Falsa democracia*, 15–17.

169. "O Partido Democratico," *O Combate*, 5 July 1926, p. 1; "A politica," *O Combate*, 3 Feb. 1919, p. 1; George Lloyd, "Coisas de Campinas," *O Combate*, 17 May 1926, p. 3; "Eleições," *O Estado de S. Paulo*, 31 Oct. 1904, p. 1; "Os municipios," *O Estado de S. Paulo*, 1 Nov. 1904, p. 2; "Eleições municipaes," *O Estado de S. Paulo*, 31 Oct. 1910, p. 4; "Eleições municipaes," 31 Oct. 1913, p. 4; "A candidatura Pereira Barreto," *O Combate*, 23 May 1918, p. 1; "'O Combate' em Campinas," *O Combate*, 12 April 1921, p. 2; "'O Combate' em Campinas," *O Combate*, 17 April 1922, p. 3; "'O Combate' em Campinas," *O Combate*, 28 April 1922, p. 3; "Eleições estaduaes," *O Combate*, 2 May 1922, p. 3; "'O Combate' em Campinas," *O Combate*, 23 Oct. 1922, p. 2; "A politica em Campinas," *O Combate*, 6 Dec. 1922, p. 1; "'O Combate' em Campinas," *O Combate*, 6 Dec. 1922, p. 3; "'O Combate' em Campinas," *O Combate*, 7 Dec. 1922, p. 2; "'O Combate' em Campinas," *O Combate*, 9 Dec. 1922, p. 2; "Noticias diversas," *O Estado de S. Paulo*, 12 Feb. 1924, p. 4.

170. "O Partido Democratico," *O Combate*, 5 July 1926, p. 1; Leopoldo Amaral, *Campinas actual* (n.p., n.d.), 128; Brito, *Memórias de um ajudante de ordens*, 110; "A lei do arrocho," *O Combate*, 28 Jan. 1916, p. 1; "'O Combate' em Campinas," *O Combate*, 9 Dec. 1922, p. 2; George Lloyd, "Coisas de Campinas," *O Combate*, 17 May 1926, p. 3; "'O Combate' em Campinas," *O Combate*, 22 May 1926, p. 4; "Coisas de Campinas," *O Combate*, 26 June 1926, p. 2; untitled newspaper clipping (labeled *Folha da Noite*, 3 April 1927), AIHGSP, APD, pacote VI; Souza, *O direito à educação*, 124n.; "Campinas," unsigned, undated sheet, AIHGSP, APD, pacote 9; *O Pharol* (Campinas), marginalia indicates issue of 25 July 1928, AIHGSP, APD, pacote XI; "A candidatura Ruy Barbosa," *O Estado de S. Paulo*, 4 April 1919, p. 4; "Fallece, em Campinas, um vereador eleito pelo Partido Democratico," *O Combate*, 8 Nov. 1928, p. 5; Melo,

Dicionário de autores paulistas, 60–61; British Chamber of Commerce of São Paulo and Southern Brazil, *Personalidades no Brasil*, 111–12; "Waldemar Belfort de Mattos," *Revista Brasiliense*, Jan.-Feb. 1957, pp. 124–25.

171. Ribeiro, *Falsa democracia*, 63n.; "Alvaro Ribeiro em Campinas," *O Combate*, 17 June 1927, p. 6; "A concentração democratica no 6.º districto," *O Combate*, 23 March 1929, p. 8; "De Campinas," *O Combate*, 15 Aug. 1929, p. 7; Carlos F. de Paula, "Assistência pública," in *Monografia histórica do município de Campinas* (Rio de Janeiro: Instituto Brasileiro de Geografia e Estatística, 1952), 485.

172. Nogueira Filho, *Ideais e lutas de um burguês progressista*, 2:678; Tasso de Magalhães to Marrey Junior, Campinas, 5 April 1926, AIHGSP, APD, pacote 33; Tasso de Magalhães to Marrey Junior, Campinas, 12 April 1926, AIHGSP, APD, pacote 33; "Partido Democratico," *O Estado de S. Paulo*, 14 April 1926, p. 5; "Alvaro Ribeiro voltará para o 'Diario do Povo,'" *O Combate*, 6 June 1927, p. 1; "Absolvidos!," *O Combate*, 14 June 1927, p. 1; "Em Campinas," *O Combate*, 1 Nov. 1928, p. 2.

173. Antonio E. Feliciano da Silva to Conselho Provisorio do PD, Santos, 15 Dec. 1926, AIHGSP, APD, pacote 34; Leopoldo Figueiredo and Antonio E. Feliciano da Silva to Paulo Nogueira Filho, Santos, 23 Dec. 1926, AIHGSP, APD, pacote 34; Antonio de Lima, "Resultado das eleições para mesarios em 25 de janeiro de 1927," Santos, 26 Jan. 1927, AIHGSP, APD, pacote 37; "1º Districto[:] Correspondentes," n.d. [May 1927], AIHGSP, APD, pacote 20, item 6; "Santos," n.d., AIHGSP, APD, pacote 8; "Em Santos," *O Combate*, 24 April 1928, p. 2; "A festa civica do Partido Democratico em Santos," *Diario Nacional*, 2 Oct. 1928, p. 12 (my count, pages of AESP's copy torn); "Eleição municipal em Santos," *O Combate*, 27 Oct. 1928, p. 6; Nogueira Filho, *Ideais e lutas de um burguês progressista*, 1:138–40, 2:656, 676; unsigned entries, "Antônio Feliciano da Silva" and "Lincoln Feliciano da Silva," in A. Abreu et al., *Dicionário histórico-biográfico brasileiro*, 5:5388, 5428–29; British Chamber of Commerce of São Paulo and Southern Brazil, *Personalidades no Brasil*, 75, 139, 267, 396; Melo, *Dicionário de autores paulistas*, 130, 158, 395–96; N. Prado, *Antonio Prado no imperio e na republica*, 394, 397; Heitor de Moraes et al., "Ao eleitorado do 1.º districto," Santos, 5 Feb. 1918, published in *O Combate*, 9 Feb. 1918, p. 1; transcription of telegram, Julio Conceição et al. to Ruy Barbosa, Santos, 31 [Jan.?] 1919, CRB, ARB, CR.E 25/20, doc. 976; telegram, Waldemar Leão to Ruy Barbosa, Santos, 29 Jan. 1919, CRB, ARB, CR.E 25/3, doc. 109; "A candidatura Ruy Barbosa," *O Estado de S. Paulo*, 26 Feb. 1919, p. 5; "Santos," *O Combate*, 2 Aug. 1921, p. 3; "O dr. J. J. Seabra passou por Santos," *O Combate*, 17 Jan. 1922, p. 1; "Santos," *O Combate*, 21 Jan. 1922, p. 3; "Ao eleitorado paulista," *O Estado de S. Paulo*, 21 April 1922, pp. 3–4; "Em Santos," *O Combate*, 20 April 1928, p. 6; "O Partido Democratico e as proximas eleições municipaes," *Diario Nacional*, 5 Oct. 1928, p. 2; "A campanha eleitoral do Partido Democratico," *Diario Nacional*, 6 Oct. 1928, p. 2; Bruno Barbosa, "Ruy Barbosa," *Revista do Brasil*, May 1923, pp. 71–74; Francisco Malta Cardoso to

Vergueiro Steidel, Santos, 13 Oct. 1920, AIHGSP, ALN, pacote 2; "Movimento cívico," *O Combate*, 20 May 1918, p. 3; M. Pereira, "O comércio cafeeiro na praça de Santos," 11; Alberto Cintra to Presidente e Mais Directores do PD, Santos, 11 Aug. 1927, AIHGSP, APD, pacote 37; "O dissidio," *O Combate*, 26 Aug. 1927, p. 1; untitled note, *O Combate*, 27 Aug. 1927, p. 6; Carlos Escobar," "Uma apostasia," *O Combate*, 10 Sept. 1927, p. 6.

174. D. Abreu, *Formação histórica de uma cidade pioneira paulista*, 180–82, 196, 218, 221–24, 330, 239–47, 253; Antonio Correa de Almeida to DC, Presidente Prudente, 14 May 1926 (two items, telegram and letter), AIHGSP, APD, pacote 34; Tito Livio Brasil and Antonio Correa de Almeida to DC, Presidente Prudente, 29 June 1926, AIHGSP, APD, pacote 34; Eliseu Prestes Cesar and Felix Ribeiro da Silva Junior, "Manifesto aos nossos amigos e correligionarios: A attitude do Partido Progressista," Presidente Prudente, 10 Nov. 1927, AIHGSP, APD, pacote 37; Tito Livio Brasil to DC, Presidente Prudente, n.d. [early 1927], AIHGSP, APD, pacote 37; "Presidente Prudente," unsigned, undated sheet, AIHGSP, APD, pacote 8; "Noticias do interior e do litoral do estado," *O Estado de S. Paulo*, 20 Oct. 1913, p. 3; "A politica," *O Combate*, 11 Oct. 1916, p. 1; "A politica," *O Combate*, 16 Oct. 1916, p. 1; "A politica," *O Combate*, 30 Oct. 1916, p. 1; "As eleições municipaes," *O Combate*, 31 Oct. 1916, p. 1; "Noticias diversas," *O Estado de S. Paulo*, 9 Feb. 1924, p. 3; "Em Presidente Prudente," *O Combate*, 7 July 1927, p. 1; "O caso Sacco-Vanzetti," *O Combate*, 9 Aug. 1927, p. 5; "Intrigando . . . ," *O Combate*, 12 Nov. 1927, p. 6; "Intrigando . . . ," *O Combate*, 18 May 1929, p. 5; José Alvarenga, *E o sertão acabou* (Osvaldo Cruz, São Paulo: by the author, 1998), 232; Barbosa, *Um cenáculo na paulicéia*, 23, 83–84, 89, 103, 125, 131; Clóvis Moura, *Sacco e Vanzetti: O protesto brasileiro* (São Paulo: Brasil Debates, 1979), 38; Nogueira Filho, *Ideais e lutas de um burguês progressista*, 2:655, 678; Edgar Rodrigues, *Socialismo e sindicalismo no Brasil, 1675–1913* (Rio de Janeiro: Laemmert, 1969), 257; Policia de São Paulo, *Movimento subversivo de julho*, 245; F. Santos, *História de Santos, 1532–1936*, 1:419.

175. "Partido Democratico," *O Estado de S. Paulo*, 27 Dec. 1926, p. 4; Terci, "A cidade na primeira república," 258–61. The figure of three thousand votes was based on the Independent Republican Party's performance in the municipal elections of 1925; according to Terci, slightly more than two thousand voters actually came out and voted for the PD slate in February 1927.

176. Terci, "A cidade na primeira república," 264; clipping of newspaper article by J. B. de Sousa Amaral (labeled *Diario da Noite*, 1 Sept. 1927), AIHGSP, APD, album VIII; Del Picchia, *A longa viagem*, 2:244–45; Nogueira Filho, *Ideais e lutas de um burguês progressista*, 1:166. A foreign observer expressed a similar view: "It was organized by, and includes among its members, many advanced political thinkers and idealists, but is largely composed of 'outs.'" Agnes S. Waddell, "The Revolution in Brazil," *Foreign Policy Association Information Service* 6, no. 26 (4 Mar. 1931): 492.

177. The quote is from "O momento politico," *O Combate*, 24 Oct. 1928, p. 3.

178. J. F. Salles Pupo et al., "As eleições de 24 de Fevereiro em Ribeirão Preto," 14 March 1927, AIHGSP, APD, pacote 15, item 8.

179. Percival de Oliveira, "As eleições da Capital," *Diario de S. Paulo*, 24 Aug. 1929, reprinted in Oliveira, *O ponto de vista do P. R. P.* (São Paulo: São Paulo Editora, 1930), 17.

180. "Comicio democratico em Campinas," *O Combate*, 27 Oct. 1928, p. 2.

181. "Questionario" for Villa Marianna, 23 Dec. 1926, AIHGSP, APD, pacote 45.

182. [Illegible] to "Meu Caro Moacyr" [Moacyr Alvaro], Araraquara, 23 March 1926 (original emphasis), AIHGSP, APD, pacote 33; also, Francisco Wohters to Waldemar Ferreira, Joanopolis, 12 Nov. 1926, AIHGSP, APD, pacote 33; Mathias Pires de Campos to DC, Laranjal, 26 May 1927, AIHGSP, APD, pacote 36; "Adhesões ao Partido Democratico de São Paulo," Monte Azul, n.d. [filed with 1927 materials], AIHGSP, APD, pacote 36. On the middle class in politics in general and in the PD in particular, see Owensby, *Intimate Ironies*, esp. chap. 9; M. Prado, *A democracia ilustrada*, 34–36.

183. João [illeg.] to Paulo Nogueira Filho, São Paulo, 22 Feb. 1927, AIHGSP, APD, pacote 45.

184. "Commentarios" (newspaper clipping labeled *Voz do Povo* [Presidente Prudente? Ourinhos? Jacareí?], 17 June 1926, AIHGSP, APD, album II. As suggested by the word "citizen," the anonymous writer was using the Portuguese cognate for "bourgeois" in its pre-Marxian sense.

185. "As adhesões recebidas pelo Partido Democratico" (newspaper clipping labeled *S. Paulo-Jornal*, 4 April 1926), AIHGSP, APD, album I.

186. Adrião de Almeida Monteiro to Sergio M. da Costa e Silva, Campinas, 2 May 1927, AIHGSP, APD, pacote 35.

187. P. Duarte, *Memórias*, 8:250; P. Duarte, unpublished manuscript, pp. 545–49, CEDAE, FPD, pasta PI.17; "Partido politico da mocidade," *O Estado de S. Paulo*, 13 Oct. 1925, p. 4; "Pelos ferroviarios," *O Combate*, 29 April 1925, p. 1; "'O Combate' em Campinas," *O Combate*, 5 Feb. 1926, p. 3; João Wagner Wey to Marcos Melega, São Paulo, 14 Feb. 1927, AIHGSP, APD, pacote 45; Marcos Del Roio, *A classe operária na revolução burguesa: A política de alianças do PCB, 1928–1935* (Belo Horizonte: Oficina de Livros, 1990), 65.

188. "Intrigando . . . ," *O Combate*, 1 Feb. 1928, p. 2; "Os democraticos de Villa Prudente e a greve," *O Trabalhador Graphico*, 30 March 1929, p. 2; "No regimen burguez é assim . . . ," *O Trabalhador Graphico*, 2 April 1929, p. 1; "O proletariado accusa!," *O Trabalhador Graphico*, 4 April 1929, p. 2; "Solidariedade," *O Trabalhador Graphico*, 19 April 1929, p. 1; "A U. T. G. e as violencias policiaes," *O Trabalhador Graphico*, 4 May 1929, p. 2; Partido Democratico, "Ao povo," São Paulo, n.d. (handbill, late 1926 or early 1927), AIHGSP, APD, album IV.

189. The estimate is Everardo Dias's: "As proximas eleições municipaes e o proletariado" (an interview), *O Combate*, 29 Oct. 1928, p. 3.

190. "Opportunismo democratico," *Folha do Bloco Operario e Camponez,* published as a broadside in *O Combate,* 29 Oct. 1928, p. 5.

191. Ibid.

192. "[Traba]lhadores da Paulicéa não podem ser votados!," unlabeled newspaper clipping (text includes Worker and Peasant Bloc of São Paulo manifesto of 20 Feb. 1928), on microfilm, AEL, CML, rolo 2; "A frente unica nas eleições de amanhã [*sic*]," *O Combate,* 22 Feb. 1928, p. 6; "O B. O. C. e as eleições paulistas de 24 de fevereiro," *O Combate,* 23 March 1928, p. 6; Tangapema [pseud.], "Bloco Operario e Camponez," *O Combate,* 18 April 1928, p. 4; Francisco José da Silveira, "Bloco Operario e Camponez," *O Combate,* 20 April 1928, p. 6; Nogueira Filho, *Ideais e lutas de um burguês progressista,* 1:207–8. See also Del Roio, *A classe operária na revolução burguesa,* 63–65.

193. Alberoni de Cabral to DC, Sertãozinho, [day missing] Sept. 1928, AIHGSP, APD, pacote 38.

194. Maria Lígia Prado places strong emphasis on the PD's use of eleitores de cabresto. See her *A democracia ilustrada,* 26–28, and "O Partido Democrático de São Paulo: adesões e aliciamento de eleitores, 1926–1934," *Revista de História* 117 (1984): 71–85.

195. José Ribeiro de Faria to Paulo Nogueira Filho, Cravinhos, 28 June 1926, AIHGSP, APD, pacote 33; Simplicio Ferreira to Director do PD, Altinopolis, 20 Jan. 1927, AIHGSP, APD, pacote 35; João Silveira Mello to Paulo [likely Paulo de Moraes Barros], Piracicaba, 19 Dec. 1927, AIHGSP, APD, pacote 36; Paulo de Moraes Barros to Paulo Nogueira Filho, Ribeirão Preto, 5 Feb. 1927, AIHGSP, APD, pacote 36; Paulo de Moraes Barros to Paulo Nogueira Filho, Ribeirão Preto, 15 Feb. 1927, AIHGSP, APD, pacote 36.

196. "Intrigando . . . ," *O Combate,* 28 Jan. 1928, p. 2.

197. "As adhesões recebidas pelo Partido Democratico" (newspaper clipping labeled *S. Paulo-Jornal,* 4 April 1926), AIHGSP, APD, album I.

198. G. de Paula Santos to PD, São Paulo, 23 Oct. 1926, AIHGSP, APD, pacote 45; Waldemar Fleury (on Belisário Penna), in *O Povo,* 26 Oct. 1926, p. 6; "Julio Mesquita," *O Estado de S. Paulo,* 27 April 1927, p. 3; Nogueira Filho, *Ideais e lutas de um burguês progressista,* 1:243; Itagyba Canabrava, "A reforma parcial da constituição paulista," and A. Albuquerque, untitled article, both in *Commercio da Lapa,* 29 Oct. 1928, p. 1.

199. Assorted newspaper clippings (Rio de Janeiro, Santos, São Paulo, 1928) on microfilm, AEL, CML, rolo 2 (fotos. 52a–56a, 58–60, 60b–61b, 64–65a, 66–69, 70a–73, 75, 76a, 79a, 83–85b, 88b, 93); João Cabanas, "Ao povo de S. Paulo," *O Combate,* 8 Feb. 1928, p. 1.

200. See above, chap. 4.

201. "Como decorreu o primeiro dia do julgamento . . . ," *O Combate,* 21 May 1927, p. 1; "A conferencia de Mauricio de Lacerda," *O Combate,* 17 June 1927, p. 1; Francisco Morato, *A desnacionalização do Major Miguel Costa e a irrevogabilidade da naturalização* (São Paulo: n.d., 1928). The latter work

is a pamphlet, a copy of which is in the AEL library at the University of Campinas.

202. J. A. Marrey Junior, *O Partido Democratico no Congresso Federal* (São Paulo: Secção de Obras d' *O Estado de S. Paulo*, 1927), original emphasis. The endpages of the pamphlet (a copy of the pamphlet forms part of the library collection of the AEL at the University of Campinas) attribute this quote to Ruy Barbosa. While the possibility exists that Monteiro Lobato lifted the passage from the Bahian statesman, I have found no evidence along these lines and believe it to be rather unlikely. Someone (Mário Pinto Serva, for example) would absolutely have found him out had this been a case of plagiarism. It seems more likely that Lobato's words were attributed to Ruy to give them still-greater authority.

203. Partido Democratico, *O voto secreto: Collectanea de opiniões, discursos e documentos sobre o assumpto*[, ed. Mario Pinto Serva] (São Paulo: Livraria Liberdade, 1927); Mario Pinto Serva to Sergio Milliet, São Paulo, 15 June 1927, AIHGSP, APD, pacote 45; Mario Pinto Serva to DC, São Paulo, 11 Oct. 1927, AIHGSP, APD, pacote 45; "O voto secreto," *O Combate*, 17 Nov. 1927, p. 2; "Clovis Ribeiro," *O Estado de S. Paulo*, 29 Jan. 1946, p. 4.

204. "Partido Democratico," *O Estado de S. Paulo*, 27 April 1926, p. 6.

205. "Partido Democratico," *O Combate*, 29 Dec. 1926, p. 6.

206. "As impressões que Mauricio de Lacerda colheu," *O Combate*, 24 Feb. 1928, p. 1.

207. "Intrigando . . . ," *O Combate*, 24 Jan. 1928, p. 6; J. Canuto, "Campanha em prol da unidade nacional" (newspaper clipping labeled *Diario da Noite*, 11 Sept. 1929), AIHGSP, APD, pacote 59.

208. Propaganda poster, "De pé S. Paulo!," AIHGSP, APD, pacote 13, item 8. This poster is reprinted in Assembléia Legislativa, *Legislativo paulista*, 71.

209. A copy of the slide may be found in AIHGSP, AAL, pacote 1.

210. "Democratico Roxo" to "Snrs. do Conselho provizorio do Partido Democrata," Barretos, 16 May 1926, AIHGSP, APD, pacote 33; Ariovaldo C. de Carvalho to Paulo Nogueira Filho, Fartura, 26 Jan. 1926, AIHGSP, APD, pacote 33; M. F. Pinto Pereira to Paulo Nogueira Filho, Franca, 3 June 1926, AIHGSP, APD, pacote 33; Gustavo Martins to Paulo Nogueira Filho, Laranjal, 30 Jan. 1927, AIHGSP, APD, pacote 36; Gentil Ferreira da Silva to DC, Mocóca, 27 Dec. 1927, AIHGSP, APD, pacote 36; "A hora extraordinaria do civismo," *O Combate*, 15 July 1927, p. 1; "Os comicios democraticos," *O Combate*, 6 Feb. 1928, p. 6.

211. Alexandre Marcondes Filho to Sylvio de Campos, São Paulo, July 1926, in CPDOC, AMF, doc. 1926.07.00. This letter is transcribed in *A revolução de 30: textos e documentos*, 2 vols., ed. Manoel Luiz Lima Salgado Guimarães et al. (Brasília: Ed. da Universidade de Brasília, 1982), 1:40–52. See also P. Duarte, *Que é que ha?*, 51.

212. Telegram, Alfredo Bauer to Partido Democratico, Jahú, 16 May 1926, AIHGSP, APD, pacote 33; "Propaganda politica," *S. Paulo-Jornal*, 20 May 1926,

pp. 7–8; Marcondes Filho, "Conferencia politica realisada na cidade de Jahú, por occasião do primeiro commicio de propaganda do Partido Republicano Paulista, reproduzido de accordo com as notas tachygraphicas, em 1926," CPDOC, AMF, doc. Pi 1926.00.00; P. Duarte, *Que é que ha?*, 51.

213. Floriano de Leme to Julio Prestes de Albuquerque, 15 Oct. 1929, AESP, AJPA, caixa AP11.

214. The *Folha da Noite* had been founded in 1921 by former staffers of the evening edition of *O Estado de S. Paulo*. It was enough of a success to demand a morning counterpart, the *Folha da Manhã*, by mid-1925. P. Duarte, *História da imprensa*, 31–32; Carlos Guilherme Mota and Maria Helena Capelato, *História da "Folha de São Paulo," 1921–1981* (São Paulo: Impres, 1980), chap. 1; Nobre, *História da imprensa de São Paulo*, 229; Sodré, *História da imprensa no Brasil*, 356–65.

215. Alexandre Marcondes Filho, "Conferencia politica realisada na cidade de Jahú, por occasião do primeiro commicio [sic] de propaganda do Partido Republicano Paulista, reproduzido de accordo com as notas tachygraphicas, em 1926," in CPDOC, AMF, doc. pi 1926.00.00.

216. Quoted in Célio Debes, *Washington Luís*, 2 vols. to date (São Paulo: Imprensa Oficial do Estado, 1994–), 2:190–91.

217. Antonio Citrangulo to Julio Prestes de Albuquerque, Sallesopolis, n.d., with attachment, João Gomes de Vasconcellos et al. to Julio Prestes de Albuquerque, Sallespolis, 27 Nov. 1927, AESP, AJPA, caixa AP06.

218. Ytalo Ferreira to Julio Prestes de Albuquerque, Mattão, 27 March 1928, AESP, AJPA, caixa AP07.

219. Simplicio Ferreira to Secretario do PD, Altinopolis, 25 Aug. 1926, AIHGSP, APD, pacote 33; José Umbelino Lopes to Marrey Junior, Caconde, 11 June 1926, AIHGSP, APD, pacote 33; Valentin Gentil to Marrey Junior, Itapolis, 1 Dec. 1926, AIHGSP, APD, pacote 33; Benjamin Ferraz da Cunha to Directorio do PD, Palmital, 10 Dec. 1926, AIHGSP, APD, pacote 34; Leopoldo Amaral Meira to Membros do Directorio Provisorio, Taquaritinga, 29 April 1926, AIHGSP, APD, pacote 35; Spinola e Castro to DC, Barretos, 12 Feb. 1927, AIHGSP, APD, pacote 35; Basilio Batalha to Directores do PD, Mogy das Cruzes, 25 Nov. 1927, AIHGSP, APD, pacote 36; João Alcides de Avellar to Paulo Nogueira Filho, Olympia, 18 Nov. 1927, AIHGSP, APD, pacote 36.

6. Moments and Truths

1. As suggested by "Partido Democratico," *O Estado de S. Paulo*, 6 Feb. 1929, p. 6; "Notas e informações," *O Estado de S. Paulo*, 7 Feb. 1929, p. 3.

2. Although supported by the political machines of Rio Grande do Sul and Minas Gerais, Vargas's candidacy was an opposition candidacy at the federal level, as the PRP's Washington Luís maintained control of the national presidency.

3. Untitled newspaper clipping (labeled *Jornal do Brasil* [Rio de Janeiro], 21 July 1929), AIHGSP, APD, pacote 1 (2nd series).

4. Newspaper clipping of untitled Juca Pato column (labeled *Folha da Manhã* [São Paulo], 31 July 1929), AIHGSP, APD, pacote 1 (2nd series).

5. Júlio Prestes de Albuquerque to Washington Luís, São Paulo, 24 July 1929, in Debes, *Júlio Prestes e a primeira república*, 83–84 (quotes on p. 84); A. (Antonio) Candido Rodrigues et al., "Ao eleitorado paulista," São Paulo, 2 Feb. 1924, in secção livre, *O Estado de S. Paulo*, 9 Feb. 1924, p. 9.

6. Júlio Prestes de Albuquerque to Washington Luís, São Paulo, 28 July 1929, in Debes, *Júlio Prestes e a primeira república*, 84–85 (quotes on p. 85). The situation of the Rio press (with the notable exception of the Chateaubriand newspapers) was already well defined: "The newspapers are taken care of, not entirely at our disposal, as I had wanted, but sympathetic to our cause and on our side, against the others." It should be added that *O Estado de S. Paulo* ended up supporting Vargas, but talks between members of the *Estado* group and Júlio Prestes continued. After the latter's victory at the polls, members of the *Estado* group sought to convince him to come out in favor of electoral reform as the national president-elect. See Maria Helena Capelato and Maria Lígia Coelho Prado, *O bravo matutino: Imprensa e ideologia no jornal "O Estado de S. Paulo"* (São Paulo: Alfa-Omega, 1980), 34–37; "Getúlio Vargas queria dobrar São Paulo" (interview with Antonio Pereira Lima by Lourenço Dantas Mota and Frederico Branco, 24 Sept. 1978), in L. Mota, *A história vivida*, 2:164.

7. Their manifesto, "Aos industriaes paulistas," was published in the *Correio Paulistano*, 3 Aug. 1929, and is quoted in Debes, *Júlio Prestes e a primeira república*, 85. See also Vera Calicchio, "Centro das Indústrias do Estado de São Paulo," in A. Abreu et al., *Dicionário histórico-biográfico brasileiro*, 2:1309; below, this chap.

8. Clovis Botelho Vieira et al. to Directorio Central, São Paulo, 2 Aug. 1929, AIHGSP, APD, pacote 46; Oscar Machado de Almeida et al. to Directorio Central, São Paulo, 5 Aug. 1929, AIHGSP, APD, pacote 46. Clovis Botelho Vieira had already registered his disagreement with the position of the *Diário Nacional* and had made plain his intention to support Getúlio Vargas regardless of which candidate the PD decided to back. Clovis Botelho Vieira to DC, São Paulo, 1 Aug. 1929, AIHGSP, APD, pacote 46.

9. "Grandes manifestações da mocidade democratica de S. Paulo em propaganda das candidaturas liberaes" (newspaper clipping labeled *Diario Carioca* [Rio de Janeiro], 11 Aug. 1929), AIHGSP, APD, pacote 58; "Propaganda eleitoral" (newspaper clipping labeled *Praça de Santos*, 8 Sept. 1929), AIHGSP, APD, pacote 59.

10. Mario Pinto Serva, "O dever dos democraticos" (newspaper clipping labeled *Diario da Noite* [São Paulo], 31 July 1929), AIHGSP, APD, pacote 1 (2nd series).

11. R. G. Galvão to Directorio Central, São Paulo, 2 Aug. 1929, AIHGSP, APD, pacote 46.

12. "A 'Alliança Liberal' e o Partido Democrático" (newspaper clipping from *Folha da Manhã*, 28 Aug. 1929), AIHGSP, APD, pacote 58; Cornelio Pires, "Com toda a franqueza e lealdade" (newspaper clipping from *A Ordem* [Rio de Janeiro], 18 Aug. 1929), AIHGSP, APD, pacote 58.

13. M. Prado, *A democracia ilustrada*, 85.

14. "Acta da sessão plenaria do quinto congresso (extraordinario) do Partido Democratico de São Paulo, effectuada em 31 de agosto de 1929," AIHGSP, APD, livro I; "A successão presidencial," *O Estado de S. Paulo*, 1 Sept. 1929, p. 6; A. Leite, *Páginas de uma longa vida*, 47–48; Nogueira Filho, *Ideais e lutas de um burguês progressista*, 1:374–76.

15. Renato Paes de Barros to Directorio Central, São Paulo, 3 Sept. 1929, AIHGSP, APD, pacote 46; "Noticias diversas," *O Estado de S. Paulo*, 12 Feb. 1924, p. 4.

16. Luis de Sampaio Freire to Luis Barbosa da Gama Cerqueira, São Paulo, 6 Sept. 1929, AIHGSP, APD, pacote 46; José da Cunha Freire to Directores do PD, São Paulo, 6 Sept. 1929, AIHGSP, APD, pacote 46; [illegible first name] Mello to Presidente do PD, São Paulo, 13 Sept. 1929, AIHGSP, APD, pacote 46; Manoel Francisco Pinto Pereira to Directorio Central, 16 Sept. 1929, AIHGSP, APD, pacote 46; calling card, Antonio de Queirós Telles to Directores do PD, 25 Sept. 1929, AIHGSP, APD, pacote 46. Queirós Telles is identified as a leader of the Brazilian Agricultural League in Perissinotto, "Estado, capital cafeeiro e crise política na década de 1920 em São Paulo, Brasil," 307n.; M. Prado, *A democracia ilustrada*, 144, 146n.

17. Antonio Amaral Mello to Julio Prestes de Albuquerque, São Paulo, 22 Sept. 1929, AESP, AJPA, caixa AP11; "Consequencias das eleições municipaes," *O Estado de S. Paulo*, 8 Nov. 1928, p. 7; "A policia a serviço do P. R. P.," *O Combate*, 8 Nov. 1928, p. 2.

18. Monteiro Lobato to Júlio Prestes de Albuquerque, New York, 28 Aug. 1929, in Debes, *Júlio Prestes e a primeira república*, 96.

19. Telegram, João Neves da Fontoura to Getulio Vargas, [Rio de Janeiro?], 1 Sept. 1929, CPDOC, AGV, GV29.09.01/4.

20. Debes, *Júlio Prestes e a primeira república*, 86.

21. For example, Alberto Cintra and Bento de Abreu Sampaio Vidal. "O bysantinismo da 'Sociedade Rural,' " *O Combate*, 12 June 1930, p. 1.

22. "Plataforma de governo de Julio Prestes de Albuquerque, candidato á presidencia da republica para o quatriennio de 1930–1934," Rio de Janeiro, 17 Dec. 1929, reprinted in Debes, *Júlio Prestes e a primeira república*, 181–200 (quotes on p. 186).

23. A brief account is provided by Love, *São Paulo in the Brazilian Federation*, 48–49.

24. Paulo de Moraes Barros, *Politica do café* (Rio de Janeiro: Imprensa Nacional, 1930), 3–49.

25. "Os inimigos do café," *Correio Paulistano*, 31 Aug. 1929, reprinted in *O Combate*, 6 Sept. 1929.

26. Coffee futures from "A derrocada do café," *O Combate*, 17 Oct. 1929, p. 1; "A crise do café," *O Combate*, 16 Oct. 1929, p. 6; "A crise da rubiacea," *A Encrenca*, 18 Oct. 1929, unpag.

27. Representing the three groups were Bento de Abreu Sampaio Vidal, Vicente de Almeida Prado, and Arthur Diederichsen, respectively. "A derrocada do café," *O Combate*, 17 Oct. 1929, p. 1.

28. Octaviano José de Mello to Laudelino de Abreu, São Paulo, n.d., CEDAE, FPD, DET.61; "O esforço para uma solução," *O Combate*, 30 Oct. 1929, p. 1; "A beira do abysmo economico," *O Combate*, 31 Oct. 1929, p. 1; Moreira, *Em face da revolução*, 44–46, 202–5 (but cf. the same author's *Fragoa brasileira* [São Paulo: F. Fragale & Cia., 1926], passim). It would not be the first time that the press attributed a callous yet apocryphal comment to Washington Luís. "The social question is a matter for the police," is the better known of the two cases. See Debes, *Washington Luís*, vol. 1, chap. 15.

29. "O P. R. P. de Santos scinde-se," *O Combate*, 30 Oct. 1929, p. 1; "Intrigando . . . ," *O Combate*, 1 Nov. 1929, p. 8.

30. "O esforço para uma solução," *O Combate*, 30 Oct. 1929, p. 1.

31. "É terrivel a crise de numerario," *O Combate*, 30 Oct. 1929, p. 1.

32. "Intrigando . . . ," *O Combate*, 1 Nov. 1929, p. 8; "Saibam todos," *O Combate*, 4 Nov. 1929, p. 2.

33. "O que fala o sr. Morato sobre o café," *O Combate*, 5 Nov. 1929, p. 6. A few days earlier, Morato had confided to Gama Cerqueira that he agreed with Washington Luís's decision not to concede an emission of paper currency or a moratorium on planter debt. DOPS record of conversation between Francisco Morato (Rio de Janeiro) and Gama Cerqueira (São Paulo), 3 Nov. 1929, CEDAE, FPD, pasta DET.61. The extra-regional members of the Liberal Alliance also expressed their support for coffee agriculture. "A crise por que atravessa o café," *O Combate*, 15 Oct. 1929, p. 1; "A Alliança Liberal defende o café," *O Combate*, 31 Oct. 1929, p. 1.

34. "A derrocada do café," *O Combate*, 7 Nov. 1929, p. 1.

35. "O café e o cambio em continua baixa," *O Combate*, 18 Nov. 1929, p. 1.

36. "Numerosos lavradores reuniram-se ante-hontem em Campinas," *O Combate*, 18 Nov. 1929, p. 1.

37. "A crise cafeeira," *O Combate*, 23 Nov. 1929, p. 1.

38. Geraldo Cyriaco Rodrigues de Andrade to Laudelino de Abreu, São João da Boa Vista, n.d., CEDAE, FPD, pasta DET.62.

39. "A crise cafeeira," *O Combate*, 23 Nov. 1929, p. 1.

40. "A crise do café ameaça-nos com surpresas amargas," *O Combate*,

22 Nov. 1929, p. 1; "Intrigando . . . ," *O Combate,* 20 Nov. 1929, p. 8; "A lavoura de Ribeirão Preto rompe com os governos da União e do Estado," *O Combate,* 25 Nov. 1929, p. 1; "Os mystificadores e os gritadores" (newspaper clipping labeled *Folha da Manhã,* 27 Nov. 1929), AIHGSP, APD, pacote 59.

41. "Os apuros das finanças paulistas," *O Combate,* 1 Nov. 1929, p. 1; "A formidavel crise que assalta S. Paulo," *O Combate,* 18 Nov. 1929, p. 1; "A crise do café ameaça-nos com surpresas amargas," *O Combate,* 22 Nov. 1929, p. 1.

42. Love, *São Paulo in the Brazilian Federation,* 226–27; M. Prado, *A democracia ilustrada,* 144, 145–46.

43. "Congresso dos lavradores," *O Combate,* 26 Nov. 1929, p. 4.

44. Quoted as a banner headline in *O Combate,* 3 Dec. 1929, p. 1; also, Love, *São Paulo in the Brazilian Federation,* 226. On aphrodisismo in the Noroeste: "Em Pennapolis," *O Combate,* 27 May 1918, p. 1; "Da Noroeste," *O Combate,* 5 Sept. 1918, p. 1; "A politica," *O Combate,* 9 Sept. 1918, p. 3; "A politica," *O Combate,* 11 Sept. 1918, p. 1; "Os partidarios do sr. Aphrodisio promovem nova mashorca," *O Combate,* 17 Jan. 1919, p. 3; "A politica," *O Combate,* 8 March 1919, p. 1; "A politica," *O Combate,* 12 March 1919, p. 1.

45. "A hora historica da lavoura," *O Combate,* 4 Dec. 1929, p. 1.

46. Ibid.; "Uma voz da lavoura," in secção livre, *O Estado de S. Paulo,* 5 Dec. 1929, p. 16; P. Duarte, *Que é que ha?,* 42.

47. Quoted in Boris Fausto, *A revolução de 1930: Historiografia e história,* 16th ed. (São Paulo: Companhia das Letras, 1997 [1970]), 130; "Congresso dos lavradores," *O Combate,* 26 Nov. 1929, p. 4.

48. "A reivindicações da lavoura," *O Combate,* 5 Dec. 1929, p. 1.

49. "Congresso fracassado," *Folha da Manhã,* 4 Dec. 1929, in secção livre, *O Estado de S. Paulo,* 5 Dec. 1929, p. 18.

50. "Notas e informações," *O Estado de S. Paulo,* 7 Dec. 1929, p. 4.

51. "O congresso da lavoura e a commissão dos quinze," *Diario da Noite,* 17 Dec. 1929, in secção livre, *O Estado de S. Paulo,* 18 Dec. 1929, p. 14.

52. For example, Quélia Holandina Quaresma, "Electoral Mobilization and the Construction of a Civic Culture in Brazil, 1909–1930" (Ph.D. diss., University of Miami, 1998).

53. A. Leite, *Páginas de uma longa vida,* 48–49; Nogueira Filho, *Ideais e lutas de um burguês progressista,* 2:401–4; Percival de Oliveira, "Outras causas," *Diario de S. Paulo,* 14 Jan. 1930, reprinted in the same author's *O ponto de vista do P. R. P.,* 231–32; Hélio Silva, *1930: A revolução traída* (Rio de Janeiro: Civilização Brasileira, 1966), 36–37.

54. DOPS transcript of telephone conversation between Paulo Nogueira Filho (São Paulo) and Francisco Morato (Rio de Janeiro), 15 [Dec. 1929], CEDAE, FPD, pasta DET.61.

55. DOPS transcript of telephone conversation between Paulo Nogueira Filho (São Paulo) and Paulo de Moraes Barros (Rio de Janeiro), 30 [Dec. 1929], CEDAE, FPD, pasta DET.61.

56. DOPS transcript of telephone conversation between José Carlos de Macedo Soares (São Paulo) and José Eduardo de Macedo Soares (Rio de Janeiro), 1 Jan. [1930], CEDAE, FPD, pasta DET.61; Nogueira Filho, *Ideais e lutas de um burguês progressista*, 2:403–4. See also P. Duarte, *Que é que ha?*, 226–27; A. Leite, *Páginas de uma longa vida*, 48–49.

57. Nogueira Filho, *Ideais e lutas de um burguês progressista*, 2:404; *O Combate*, 3 Jan. 1930, p. 6; DOPS transcript of telephone conversation between Paulo de Moraes Barros (Rio de Janeiro) and Paulo Nogueira Filho (São Paulo), 2 [Jan. 1929], CEDAE, FPD, pasta DET.61.

58. *Diario Nacional*, 5 Jan. 1930, p. 2; A. Leite, *Páginas de uma longa vida*, 50; "Uma excursão triumphante da causa liberal" (newspaper clipping labeled *O Globo* [Rio de Janeiro], 7 Jan. 1930), AIHGSP, APD, pacote 2 (2nd series).

59. *Diario Nacional*, 5 Jan. 1930, p. 2; Antonio Paixão, "Relatorio," Guaratinguetá, 20 Sept. 1929: enclosure "Relatorio das pessoas, que, nesta cidade passaram a apoir a Alliança," AESP, AJPA, caixa AP29, pasta 71; Brito Broca, *Memórias* (Rio de Janeiro: José Olympio, 1968), 170, 215.

60. "Como foram recebidos os candidatos liberaes," *O Estado de S. Paulo*, 5 Jan. 1930, p. 6; "Mais de trezentos mil pessoas applaudiram os candidatos da Aliança Liberal," *Diario Nacional*, 5 Jan. 1930, pp. 1, 4; "Estão em São Paulo os presidentes do Rio Grande do Sul e da Parahyba" (newspaper clipping labeled *Folha da Manhã*, 5 Jan. 1930), AIHGSP, APD, pacote 2 (2nd series); "Impressões do dr. Gama Cerqueira sobre as formidaveis manifestações em São Paulo ao dr. Getulio Vargas por occasião da sua chegada" (newspaper clipping labeled *Diario Carioca* [Rio de Janeiro], 5 Jan. 1930), AIHGSP, APD, pacote 2 (2nd series); "Foi uma apotheose" and "Saibam todos," *O Combate*, 6 Jan. 1930, p. 6 ; "Uma palestra com o notavel criminalista dr. Evaristo de Moraes," *Diario Nacional*, 7 Jan. 1930, p. 1; "O regresso da comitiva liberal" (newspaper clipping labeled *Diario da Noite* [Rio de Janeiro], 7 Jan. 1930), AIHGSP, APD, pacote 2 (2nd series); A. Leite, *Páginas de uma longa vida*, 50–51; Nogueira Filho, *Ideais e lutas de um burguês progressista*, 2:404–9; Aurino Moraes, *Minas na Aliança Liberal e na revolução*, 2nd ed. (Belo Horizonte: Pindorama, 1933), 146; Leven Vampré, *São Paulo, terra conquistada* (São Paulo: Sociedade Impressora Paulista, 1932), 38; Cleide Lopes, "Em cima do acontecimento: A revolução de 30 e a imprensa paulista" (tese de mestrado, Pontifícia Universidade Católica de São Paulo, 1988), chap 2.

61. "Como foram recebidos os candidatos liberaes," *O Estado de S. Paulo*, 5 Jan. 1930, p. 6. In his private correspondence and public utterances, Vargas had already shown himself to be well aware of the appeal of this kind of regionalist imagery, and as early as August, he was quoted in Porto Alegre's *Diário de Noticias* as having said, "To be in favor of the defense of coffee, one need not be paulista, it is enough to be Brazilian," a turn of phrase picked up by Paulo de Moraes Barros, the quintessential PD agrarian. [Getúlio Vargas] to João Neves da Fontoura, Porto Alegre, 9 Sept. 1929, CPDOC, AGV, GV29.09.09/6; [Getúlio

Vargas] to João Neves da Fontoura, Porto Alegre, 20 Nov. 1929, CPDOC, AGV, GV29.11.20/2; "A successão presidencial," *O Estado de S. Paulo*, 1 Sept. 1929, p. 6.

62. "Como foram recebidos os candidatos liberaes," *O Estado de S. Paulo*, 5 Jan. 1930, p. 6.

63. Ibid.; "Foi uma apotheose" and "Saibam todos," *O Combate*, 6 Jan. 1930, p. 6 ; "A successão presidencial" (newspaper clipping labeled *Jornal do Commercio* [Rio de Janeiro], 7 Jan. 1930), AIHGSP, APD, pacote 2 (2nd series); "O regresso da comitiva liberal" (newspaper clipping labeled *Diario da Noite* [Rio de Janeiro], 7 Jan. 1930), AIHGSP, APD, pacote 2 (2nd series); A. Leite, *Páginas de uma longa vida*, 50–51; Nogueira Filho, *Ideais e lutas de um burguês progressista*, 2:404–9.

64. "Successão presidencial," *O Estado de S. Paulo*, 7 Jan. 1930, p. 5; "A successão presidencial" (newspaper clipping labeled *Jornal do Commercio* [Rio de Janeiro], 7 Jan. 1930), AIHGSP, APD, pacote 2 (2nd series); "A hora de fé republicana," *O Combate*, 7 Jan. 1930, p. 1.

65. "Successão presidencial," *O Estado de S. Paulo*, 7 Jan. 1930, p. 5; "Um archiduque na democracia" (newspaper clipping labeled *Jornal da Noite* [Santos], 7 Jan. 1930), AIHGSP, APD, pacote 2 (2nd series); "A hora de fé republicana," *O Combate*, 7 Jan. 1930, p. 1.

66. "Successão presidencial," *O Estado de S. Paulo*, 7 Jan. 1930, p. 5.

67. Ibid.; "A chegada do inimigo do café" (newspaper clipping labeled *Folha da Manhã*, 5 Jan. 1930), AIHGSP, APD, pacote 2 (2nd series); "A hora de fé republicana," *O Combate*, 7 Jan. 1930, p. 1; A. Moraes, *Minas na Aliança Liberal e na revolução*, 147.

68. Lazaro Maria da Silva, "O significado da apotheose," *O Combate*, 9 Jan. 1930, p. 3; also, Nogueira Filho, *Ideais e lutas de um burguês progressista*, 2:412.

69. X, "A pequena nota" (newspaper clipping labeled *Diario do Povo*, 8 Jan. 1930), AIHGSP, APD, pacote 2 (2nd series).

70. "Intrigando . . . ," *O Combate*, 10 Jan. 1930, p. 6; "Partido Democratico," *O Combate*, 11 Jan. 1930, p. 1.

71. "Está reunido o sexto congresso do Partido Democratico," *O Estado de S. Paulo*, 11 Jan. 1930, p. 5; "Partido Democratico," *O Combate*, 11 Jan. 1930, p. 1; H. Silva, *1930*, 36; Nogueira Filho, *Ideais e lutas de um burguês progressista*, 2:414.

72. Paulo de Moraes Barros, Henrique de Souza Queiroz, and Vicente Prado, untitled proposal, São Paulo, 11 Jan. 1930, AIHGSP, APD, pacote 21, item 5; "Encerrou-se hontem o sexto congresso do Partido Democrático," *O Estado de S. Paulo*, 12 Jan. 1930, p. 2.

73. Moreira, *Em face da revolução*, 49–55; "Os democraticos e o radio" (newspaper clipping labeled *A Capital*, 19 Feb. 1930), AIHGSP, APD, pacote 60.

74. PD correspondence from contributors, AIHGSP, APD, pacote 13, item 6 and item 7 (single pasta—quotes from Miguel Spinelli to Thomaz Lessa, Antonio Soares Lara, and Octavio de Lima e Castro, Olympia, 29 Jan. 1930, and Israel de Arruda to Prudente de Moraes Netto, São Paulo, 12 April 1930); DOPS

lists of contributors, CEDAE, FPD, pasta DET.61. The header of *O Combate*, 13 Feb. 1930, p. 3, proclaimed: "O 'Diario Nacional' informa, sem pudor, que continua na cavação dos nickeis o comité feminino, ignolbilmente [*sic*] explorado pelos marmanjões da democracia. —É a primeira vez, no Brasil, que os politicos se servem do prestigio das mulheres. —Chama-se a isso: regeneração. . . ." On the lease of *O Combate*, see P. Duarte, *História da imprensa em São Paulo*, 30; *O Combate*, 21 Jan. 1930, pp. 1–2; *O Combate*, 21 July 1930, p. 1.

75. Telegram, Elias Camargo Salles to Julio Prestes de Albuquerque, São Carlos, 30 July 1929, AESP, AJPA, caixa AP22; telegram, Antonio Ferreira to Julio Prestes de Albuquerque, Ribeirão Preto, 31 July 1929, AESP, AJPA, caixa AP22; telegram, Horacio Rudge et al. to Julio Prestes de Albuquerque, São Paulo, 6 Aug. 1929, AESP, AJPA, caixa AP23; João Luiz da Costa to "Amigo Dr. Jayme" [Jayme Leonel?], Salto Grande, 20 Aug. 1929, AESP, AJPA, caixa AP10; Francisco Pinto da Cunha to Julio Prestes de Albuquerque, Serra Negra, 21 Sept. 1929, AESP, AJPA, caixa AP10; "O alistamento eleitoral está sendo intensificado tanto na capital como no interior" (newspaper clipping labeled *Diario de S. Paulo*, 7 Aug. 1929), AIHGSP, APD, pacote 58; Júlio Prestes de Albuquerque to Washington Luís, São Paulo, 24 July 1929, in Debes, *Júlio Prestes e a primeira república*, 83–84.

76. Júlio Prestes de Albuquerque to Washington Luís, São Paulo, 24 July 1929, in Debes, *Júlio Prestes e a primeira república*, 83–84. This assurance notwithstanding, the number of registered voters in São Paulo state by election day was 516,651. Love, *São Paulo in the Brazilian Federation*, 335. Throughout this period, Júlio Prestes's office kept close watch on voter registration, drawing up tables and other documents to illustrate the expansion of the paulista electorate. Table, "Alistamento Eleitoral no Estado de São Paulo—Por Municipios," n.d., AESP, AJPA, caixa AP30; Table, "Alistamento Eleitoral no Estado de São Paulo[:] Estatistica por Comarcas," n.d., AESP, AJPA, caixa AP30; Mesquita Junior to "Exmo. Sr. Secretario," São Paulo, 26 Oct. 1929, AESP, AJPA, caixa AP30 (includes attachment: "Movimento da Qualificação Eleitoral do Estado de São Paulo, Boletim Quinzenal"); Mesquita Junior to "Exmo. Sr. Secretario," São Paulo, 13 Nov. 1929, AESP, AJPA, caixa AP30 (includes attachment: "Movimento da Qualificação Eleitoral do Estado de São Paulo, Boletim Quinzenal"); Mesquita Junior to "Exmo. Sr. Secretario," São Paulo, 26 Nov. 1929, AESP, AJPA, caixa AP30 (includes attachment: "Movimento da Qualificação Eleitoral do Estado de São Paulo, Boletim Quinzenal"); Mesquita Junior to "Exmo. Sr. Secretario," São Paulo, 10 Dec. 1929, AESP, AJPA, caixa AP30 (includes attachment: "Movimento da Qualificação Eleitoral do Estado de São Paulo, Boletim Quinzenal"); Mesquita Junior to "Exmo. Sr. Secretario," São Paulo, 23 Dec. 1929, AESP, AJPA, caixa AP30 (includes attachment: "Movimento da Qualificação Eleitoral do Estado de São Paulo, Boletim Quinzenal"); Mesquita Junior to "Exmo. Sr. Secretario," São Paulo, 11 Jan. 1930, AESP, AJPA, caixa AP30 (includes attachment: "Movimento da Qualificação

Eleitoral do Estado de São Paulo, Boletim Quinzenal"); "Estatistica Eleitoral Referente Ao Mez de Outubro do Corrente Anno," n.d., AESP, AJPA, caixa AP30; "População e alistamento eleitoral do Estado de São Paulo em 31 de Dezembro de 1929," AESP, AJPA, caixa AP30; "Graphico Demonstrativo do Alistamento," n.d., AESP, AJPA, caixa AP30; "Mappa demonstrativo da qualificação eleitoral no Estado de São Paulo, durante o anno de 1929," n.d., AESP, AJPA, caixa AP30; "Quadro comparativo do eleitorado e da população de Minas, São Paulo, Rio Grande do Sul, e Districto Federal: Anno de 1929," AESP, AJPA, caixa AP30; "Relação elaborada pela Secção de Estatística Eleitoral da Secretaria da Justiça e Segurança Publica," n.d., AESP, AJPA, caixa AP31; "Districtos Estadoes," 1 Feb. 1930, AESP, AJPA, caixa AP31; Gabinete da Presidencia do Estado de São Paulo, *Quadro das secções eleitoraes do Estado de São Paulo, organisado para as eleições federaes de 1.º de março de 1930* (1930), AESP, AJPA, caixa AP31.

77. J. S. P. to Paulo Nogueira Filho, São Paulo, 7 Feb. 1930, AIHGSP, APD, pacote 46; "Um Democrata" to José Adriano Marrey Junior, São Paulo, 19 Feb. 1930, AIHGSP, APD, pacote 46.

78. Director da Secção Legal to DC, São Paulo, 30 Nov. 1929, AIHGSP, APD, pacote 54.

79. Firmo Braga and Octavio Pinto Ferraz to DC, Palmital, 19 Dec. 1929, AIHGSP, APD, pacote 39.

80. O. Pupo Nogueira to "Presados Srs." (CIFTSP Circular no. 57), São Paulo, 1 Aug. 1929, CEDAE, FPD, pasta DET.139; also, Pupo Nogueira to Julio Prestes de Albuquerque, São Paulo, 17 Aug. 1929, AESP, AJPA, caixa AP09; Trento, *Do outro lado do Atlântico*, 390. The manifesto to which he refers is quoted above, this chap. "Octavio" to "Meu caro Paulito" [Paulo Nogueira Filho], São Paulo, 20 Oct. 1928, AIHGSP, APD, pacote 46, is his letter of resignation from the party.

81. Mario Guastini to Lazary Guedes, São Paulo, 8 May 1930, AESP, AJPA, caixa AP15.

82. Handbill, "Catholicos!," AESP, AJPA, caixa AP32; "O Candidato Nacional," reprinted in *O Combate*, 1 March 1930, p. 3.

83. Original emphasis. The poster is reproduced, in black and white, in Hélio Silva and Maria Cecília Ribas Carneiro, *História da república brasileira*, vol. 7, *Fim da 1ª república* (São Paulo: Três, 1975), 26.

84. A. Leite, *História da civilização paulista*, 185; A. Leite, *Páginas de uma longa vida*, 51–52; Nogueira Filho, *Ideais e lutas de um burguês progressista*, 2:420–23. At the end of the month, PRP cabos also sought to break up PD-Liberal Alliance rallies in the state capital. "Attentado contra a vida do deputado democratico Marrey Junior" (newspaper clipping labeled *O Povo*, 24 Feb. 1930), AIHGSP, APD, pacote 60; "O que houve em verdade, em Vila Guilherme, provocado pelos jagunços do P. R. P." (newspaper clipping labeled *O Povo*, 24 Feb. 1930), AIHGSP, APD, pacote 60; "Desordeiros tentam matar o

deputado Marrey Junior" (newspaper clipping labeled *Diario da Noite*, 24 Feb. 1930), AIHGSP, APD, pacote 60; "Na vigilia do pleito presidencial" (newspaper clipping labeled *Diario de S. Paulo*, 25 Feb. 1930), AIHGSP, APD, pacote 60.

85. Nogueira Filho, *Ideais e lutas de um burguês progressista*, 2:418.

86. Telegram, Antonio Feliciano to "Exmo. Snr. Presidente do Estado de São Paulo," São Paulo, n.d. [1930], AIHGSP, APD, pacote 54.

87. "Os desmandos da autoridade policial de Itú" (newspaper clipping labeled *Diario da Noite*, 26 Feb. 1930), AIHGSP, APD, pacote 60.

88. Roque de Matteo to Heitor Penteado, São Paulo, 3 Feb. 1930, CEDAE, FPD, pasta DET.61; Nogueira Filho, *Ideais e lutas de um burguês progressista*, 2:284, 317–18.

89. Carlos Mendes Leite, "Districto de Liberdade: Relatorio do pleito de 1 de março," São Paulo, n.d., AIHGSP, APD, pacote 16, item 2; Celso Leme to DC, São Paulo, 15 March 1930, AIHGSP, APD, pacote 16, item 2. See also A. Leite, *História da civilização paulista*, 185; A. Leite, *Páginas de uma longa vida*, 51 (see esp. 51n.); Vieira, *Na imprensa*, 104–6.

90. Antonio Gonçalves Fraga et al. to "Exmo Snr Dr Juiz Federal," Tibiriça [a district of the peace in Bauru], 2 March 1930, AIHGSP, APD, pacote 16.

91. Gustavo Martins to Paulo Nogueira Filho, Laranjal, 7 March 1930, AIHGSP, APD, pacote 16, item 2.

92. "Inquerito efetuado na Secretaria do Interior a respeito dos pagamentos feitos pela verba 'socorros publicos' no periodo entre 22 de outubro de 1929 e 26 de setembro de 1930," CEDAE, FPD, pasta DET.139. The mix of old and new orthography in the title of this document suggests one of two possibilities: it is a forgery or a hasty transcription. I tend toward the latter explanation. In any case, the payment of PRP kickbacks to newspapers is multiply attested by independent sources: "A verba soccorros publicos de São Paulo" (newspaper clipping labeled *Correio do Povo* [Porto Alegre], 15 Nov. 1930), AESP, AJCMS, caixa AP152, pacote 3; "Inquiry in Brazil Shows Wide Graft," *New York Times*, 15 Nov. 1930, p. 9. Fábio de Sá Barreto later admitted to diverting public funds to the Prestes campaign while serving as state secretary of the interior; Walker, "Ribeirão Preto, 1910–1960," 74.

93. Telegram, Benevenuto Costa e Silva, Aristedes Vicente de Mayo, and Claudino José Bernardo to Julio Prestes de Albuquerque, Pau d'Alho, 20 Feb. 1930, AESP, AJPA, caixa AP24; telegram, Antonio Paulino Miranda to Julio Prestes de Albuquerque, Sallesopolis, 25 Feb. 1930, AESP, AJPA, caixa AP24; telegram, Claudio José de Souza to Julio Prestes de Albuquerque, Sallesopolis, 27 Feb. 1930, AESP, AJPA, caixa AP24; Claudio José de Souza et al. to Julio Prestes de Albuquerque, Sallesopolis, 3 March 1930, AESP, AJPA, caixa AP15; João Sabino Machado et al. to Julio Prestes de Albuquerque, Sallesopolis, 15 March 1930, AESP, AJPA, caixa AP15.

94. Alzira Alves de Abreu, "Aliança Liberal," in A. Abreu et al., *Dicionário histórico-biográfico brasileiro*, 1:106.

95. "Notas e informações," *O Estado de S. Paulo*, 6 March 1930, p. 3.

96. Joaquim Sampaio Vidal, in *Diario Nacional*, 18 March 1930, quoted in Fausto, *A revolução de 1930*, 130–31. The ellipses and the modernization of the orthography are Fausto's.

97. Sorocabano revoltado, "O que nos veio de Sorocaba," *O Povo* (newspaper clipping dated 17 March 1930), AIHGSP, APD, pacote 61; Cyro Tassara de Padua to "Snr. Secretario," São Paulo, 20 May 1930, AIHGSP, APD, pacote 54; Luiz de Barros Vianna to DC, São Paulo, 16 May 1930, AIHGSP, APD, pacote 46; Sergio da Costa e Silva [Sergio Milliet] to presidente do PD, São Paulo, 5 June 1930, AIHGSP, APD, pacote 46. In Tietê, the much-abused local democráticos, complaining of neglect, declared their independence from the PD's Central Directorate. Firmiano Alves Lima et al. to DC, Tiete, 18 April 1930, AIHGSP, APD, pacote 40; "Crise no P. D.," *Diario de S. Paulo* (newspaper clipping dated 24 April 1930), AIHGSP, APD, pacote 61; "Os restos de um partido" (newspaper clipping labeled *Folha da Noite*, 29 May 1930), AIHGSP, APD, pacote 61.

98. J. F. de Oliveira Moraes to DC, São Paulo, 16 May 1930, AIHGSP, APD, pacote 46; M. L. Martins to presidente do PD, São Paulo, 4 June 1930, AIHGSP, APD, pacote 46; Mario Masagão to "Membros da Commissão para Angrariar Donativos para a Campanha Eleitoral," São Paulo, 25 July 1930, AIHGSP, APD, pacote 46.

99. A caustic take on the PD's turn to plotting may be found in Sérgio Milliet's fictionalized *Roberto*, 152–53. In the autobiographical novel, "José Joaquim" and the "Partido Social Paulista" are thinly veiled depictions of Paulo Nogueira Filho and the PD, respectively.

100. Mesquita Filho, "Os ideais democráticos na revolução brasileira," 97–98; Nogueira Filho, *Ideais e lutas de um burguês progressista*, 2:396–98, 411, 451–56; N. Oliveira, *1924*, 185–89; H. Silva, *1930*, 27–30, 137; interview with Jorge Duque Estrada, by Israel Beloch, Rio de Janeiro, 21 June 1977, CPDOC, PHO. Surviving documentation reveals that the DOPS relied on domestic servants to obtain information: Juventino Paulo do Amaral to Lincoln de Albuquerque, São Paulo, 10 Jan. 1930, CEDAE, FPD, pasta DET.62.

101. Miguel Costa to Cunha Cruz, Buenos Aires, 10 May 1930, AEL, FMC, pasta 14; Miguel Costa to Francisco Orcy, Buenos Aires, 9 June 1930, AEL, FMC, pasta 14; Nogueira Filho, *Ideais e lutas de um burguês progressista*, 2:456–62; N. Oliveira, *1924*, 189–93; H. Silva, *1930*, 121–30; Távora, *Uma vida e muitas lutas*, 1:267. In his memoirs, Juarez Távora noted that Siqueira Campos's death was one of the major reasons that there was no uprising in São Paulo in October 1930. See ibid., 2:74. João Alberto is quoted to the effect that there would have been an uprising in São Paulo in mid-1930 were it not for Siqueira Campos's death in Dias, *História das lutas sociais no Brasil*, 170.

102. "O Partido Democratico e a morte do presidente João Pessoa," *O Combate*, 28 July 1930, p. 6; Aureliano Leite, "Marrey Júnior" (unpublished notes), AIHGSP, AAL, pacote 13.

103. Henrique Souza Queiroz et al., "Ao povo paulista," São Paulo, 28 July 1930, in *O Estado de S. Paulo*, 29 July 1930, p. 3; "Imponente e significativo a sessão civica e hontem do Partido Democratico," *Diario Nacional*, 30 July 1930, p. 1; "Funda-se em S. Paulo a sociedade patriotica 'João Pessoa,'" *Diario Nacional*, 30 July 1930, p. 1; "As demonstrações de pezar em S. Paulo, foram imponentes," *O Combate*, 30 July 1930, p. 1.

104. "Em S. Paulo," *O Estado de S. Paulo*, 2 Aug. 1930, p. 5.

105. "Em S. Paulo," *O Estado de S. Paulo*, 3 Aug. 1930, p. 5; Melo, *Dicionário de autores paulistas*, 211; Assembléia Legislativa, *Legislativo paulista*, 101–4.

106. *O Combate*, 8 Aug. 1930, p. 1; *Diario de S. Paulo*, 8 Aug. 1930 (see esp. photographs on pp. 11, 18); *Diario Nacional*, 8 Aug. 1930, pp. 1, 10; *Diario Nacional*, 10 Aug. 1930, p. 3; *O Estado de S. Paulo*, 8 Aug. 1930, pp. 4–5; *O Estado de S. Paulo*, 12 Aug. 1930, pp. 3, 4; DOPS "Termo de declarações" of Manoel Carlos da Silva, n.d., CEDAE, FPD, pasta DET.61; Laudelino de Abreu to "Ilmo. Sr. Dr. 1° Delegado Auxiliar," São Paulo, 19 Aug. 1930, CEDAE, FPD, pasta DET.61; untitled DOPS document, 8 Aug. 1930, CEDAE, FPD, pasta DET.62; José Augusto Costa, *Criminosos de duas revoluções, 1930–1932* (São Paulo: n.p., 1933), 100–102; A. Leite, *História da civilização paulista*, 186; Aureliano Leite, *Memórias de um revolucionário: A revolução de 1930, pródomos e conseqüências* (n.p., 1931), 10–12; Nogueira Filho, *Ideais e lutas de um burguês progressista*, 2:481–82. The law school maintained an armory for the use of the student militia (*tiro de guerra*).

107. "Partido Democratico," *O Estado de S. Paulo*, 2 Aug. 1930, p. 5; "Em Olympia," *O Estado de S. Paulo*, 3 Aug. 1930, p. 5; "O momento politico," *O Estado de S. Paulo*, 12 Aug. 1930, p. 4.

108. Antonio de Araripe Sucupira to "Chefe de Policia," Araraquara, 29 Aug. 1930 (including attachments), CEDAE, FPD, DET.61; Martins [illegible surname (Lorena?)] to Laudelino de Abreu, Jaboticabal, 13 Sept. 1930, CEDAE, FPD, DET.62; J. Costa, *Criminosos de duas revoluções, 1930–1932*, 104–8; A. Leite, *Memórias de um revolucionário*, chaps. 1–4; A. Leite, *Páginas de uma longa vida*, 52; Nogueira Filho, *Ideais e lutas de um burguês progressista*, 2:482–90; H. Silva, *1930*, 339–41.

109. Vicente Carlos de França Carvalho Filho to "Chefe de Policia," Cafelandia, 4 Sept. 1930, CEDAE, FPD, pasta DET.61; L. B. Mello Monteiro to Laudelino de Abreu, São Paulo, 16 Aug. 1930, CEDAE, FPD, pasta DET.61; Raul Aguiar Leme and Basilio Ribeiro to "Delegado de Policia de Bragança," Bragança, 22 Feb. 1930, CEDAE, FPD, pasta DET.61; Jayme Brasil Simões to "Meu caro Dr. Lorena" [Eduardo Vergueiro de Lorena], no location [likely Pirajuí], n.d., CEDAE, FPD, pasta DET.61; Antonio de Araripe Sucupira to "Chefe de Policia," Araraquara, 29 Aug. 1930 (including attachments), CEDAE, FPD, DET.61; Martins [illegible surname (Lorena?)] to Laudelino de Abreu, Jaboticabal, 13 Sept. 1930, CEDAE, FPD, DET.62; untitled DOPS document, 11 Aug. 1930, CEDAE, FPD, DET.62; A. Leite, *Memórias de um revolucionário*, 16, 23, 32.

110. "Não se cogitou ainda da escolha do futuro inquilino dos Campos Elyseos," *O Combate*, 16 June 1930, p. 1; "Candidaturas e incompatibilidades," *O Combate*, 27 June 1930, p. 1; "Vida alheia . . . ," *O Combate*, 26 July 1930, p. 6.

111. "A renuncia do Cel. Joaquim da Cunha Junqueira provoca uma crise na politica de Ribeirão Preto" (newspaper clipping labeled *Diario da Noite*, 20 March 1930), AESP, AJCDJ, caixa AP174, pasta 2; "Coronel Joaquim da Cunha: O seu afastamento da actividade politica" (newspaper clipping labeled *Correio Paulistano*, 22 March 1930), AESP, AJCDJ, caixa AP174, pasta 2; "Novamente encrencada a politica de Ribeirão Preto," *O Combate*, 17 June 1930, p. 2; "Politica de Ribeirão Preto," *O Combate*, 5 July 1930, p. 3; Altino Arantes Paiva to Joaquim da Cunha Diniz Junqueira, Ribeirão Preto, 25 July 1930, AESP, AJCDJ, caixa AP174, pasta 5; Joaquim da Cunha Diniz Junqueira et al. to "Illmo. Correligionario e Amigo," Ribeirão Preto, 1 Aug. 1930, AESP, AJCDJ, caixa AP174, pasta 1; " 'O Combate' no interior," *O Combate*, 4 Sept. 1930, p. 4; Walker, "Ribeirão Preto, 1910–1960," 63, 74; Cione, *História de Ribeirão Preto*, 245.

112. "Vida alheia . . . ," *O Combate*, 24 Sept. 1930, p. 6; "Vida alheia . . . ," *O Combate*, 30 Sept. 1930, p. 6; "Vida alheia . . . ," *O Combate*, 2 Oct. 1930, p. 6; "Vida alheia . . . ," *O Combate*, 3 Oct. 1930, p. 6; "Vida alheia . . . ," *O Combate*, 7 Oct. 1930, p. 3.

113. "Foi reconhecido o novo directorio politico da Penha" (newspaper clipping labeled *S. Paulo-Jornal*, 23 May 1930), AIHGSP, APD, pacote 61; "Pela politica" (newspaper clipping labeled *Folha da Noite*, 27 May 1930), AIHGSP, APD, pacote 61; "A pacificação politica da Penha" (newspaper clipping labeled *S. Paulo-Jornal*, 28 May 1930), AIHGSP, APD, pacote 61; "Os restos de um partido" (newspaper clipping labeled *Folha da Noite*, 29 May 1930), AIHGSP, APD, pacote 61; "Vida alheia . . . ," *O Combate*, 30 July 1930, p. 6.

114. "Em Campinas," *O Combate*, 29 Aug. 1930, p. 1.

115. "Vida alheia . . . ," *O Combate*, 30 Sept. 1930, p. 6; "Vida alheia . . . ," *O Combate*, 3 Oct. 1930, p. 2; P. Duarte, *Que é que ha?*, 164. Rumors of Krahenbuhl's defection had been circulating since mid-August: "Vida alheia . . . ," *O Combate*, 18 Aug. 1930, p. 2; "Vida alheia . . . ," *O Combate*, 19 Aug. 1930, p. 6.

116. Moreira, *Em face da revolução*, 133.

117. A. Leite, *Memórias de um revolucionário*, chaps. 5–19; A. Leite, *Páginas de uma longa vida*, 52–53; Nogueira Filho, *Ideais e lutas de um burguês progressista*, chap. 9; "Nascimento e seu famoso depoimento," *O Bandeirante*, 28 Oct. 1930, p. 4.

118. DOPS reports in CEDAE, FPD, pasta DET.67; H. Silva, *1930*, 216–21, 342–43; Távora, *Uma vida e muitas lutas*, 2:74.

119. "O sr. Monlevade é democratico, mas é tambem solidario com o governo" (newspaper clipping labeled *A Platea*, 13 Oct. 1930), AIHGSP, APD, pacote 62.

120. C. R. Cameron to Walter S. Washington, "Political Report No. 11," São

Paulo, 21 Oct. 1930, USNARA, RG59, 832.00/688; Paulo de Almeida Nogueira, *Minha vida*, 390; Nogueira Filho, *Ideais e lutas de um burguês progressista*, 2:566.

121. H. Silva, *1930*, 342.

122. "Vida alheia . . . ," *O Combate*, 7 Oct. 1930, p. 3; "Vida alheia . . . ," *O Combate*, 14 Oct. 1930, p. 4; Mauricio de Lacerda, *Segunda republica* (Rio de Janeiro: Freitas Bastos, n.d. [1931]), 195.

123. C. R. Cameron to S. Walter Washington, "São Paulo Political Report No. 6," São Paulo, 9 Oct. 1930, USNARA, RG59, 832.00/679; Arthur G. Parsloe to the Secretary of State, Santos, 11 Nov. 1930, USNARA, RG59, 832.00Revolutions/228; Edwin V. Morgan to the Secretary of State, Rio de Janeiro, 5 Dec. 1930, USNARA, RG59, 832.00/693; Nogueira Filho, *Ideais e lutas de um burguês progressista*, 2:566; Vampré, *São Paulo, terra conquistada*, 60–61.

124. Nogueira Filho, *Ideais e lutas de um burguês progressista*, 2:566; H. Silva, *1930*, 342; "Batalhão academico," *O Combate*, 11 Oct. 1930, p. 1.

125. Vampré, *São Paulo, terra conquistada*, 60–61; Eduardo Etzel, *Um médico do século XX: Vivendo transformações* (São Paulo: Nobel, 1987), 93.

126. Del Picchia, *A longa viagem*, 2: 271, 273; Silva Duarte, *A revolução victoriosa: A marcha heroica dum povo que se liberta* (São Paulo: Livraria Zenith, 1930), 265–68; A. Leite, *Memórias de um revolucionário*, 126–27, 135–37; Paulo de Almeida Nogueira, *Minha vida*, 390–91; Francisco Pati, *A cidade sem portas* (São Paulo: Rêde Latina, 1956), 154; H. Silva, *1930*, 345–46; Vieira, *Na imprensa*, 111–13; Vampré, *São Paulo, terra conquistada*, 53; telegram, C. R. Cameron to the Secretary of State, São Paulo, 24 Oct. 1930, USNARA, RG59, 832.00Revolutions/147; *New York Times*, 25 Oct. 1930, p. 1; *New York Times*, 26 Oct. 1930, p. 2; photograph in Ana Maria Brandão Murakami, *A revolução de 1930 e seus antecedentes* (Rio de Janeiro: Nova Fronteira, 1980), 173.

127. Telegram, C. R. Cameron to the Secretary of State, São Paulo, 24 Oct. 1930, USNARA, RG59, 832.00Revolutions/147; "No 'Correio Paulistano,' " *Diario da Noite*, 24 Oct. 1930, p. 1; C. R. Cameron to the Secretary of State, São Paulo, 25 Oct. 1930, USNARA, RG59, 832.00Revolutions/153; "A heroica jornada de São Paulo," *Diario de S. Paulo*, 25 Oct. 1930, p. 3; *New York Times*, 25 Oct. 1930, p. 1; *New York Times*, 26 Oct. 1930, p. 2; Americano, *São Paulo nesse tempo, 1915–1935*, 391; Brito, *Memórias de um ajudante de ordens*, 41, 183; Del Picchia, *A longa viagem*, 2:271; S. Duarte, *A revolução victoriosa*, 266–68; Jardim, *A aventura e outubro e a invasão de São Paulo*, 143–45; A. Leite, *Memórias de um revolucionário*, 126–27, 142–43, 161; Mello, *Entre índios e revoluções*, 194; Motta Filho, *Contagem regressiva*, 99, 149, 153–54; Paulo de Almeida Nogueira, *Minha vida*, 391; Nogueira Filho, *Ideais e lutas de um burguês progressista*, 2:566; Pati, *A cidade sem portas*, 154–56; Vampré, *São Paulo, terra conquistada*, 55; José Maria Whitaker, *O milagre da minha vida* (São Paulo: Hucitec, 1978), 79; interview with José Gomes Talarico, by Maria Cristina Guido and Reinaldo Roels Júnior, Rio de Janeiro, 27 Sept. 1978, CPDOC, PHO; Trento, *Do outro lado do Atlântico*, 391.

128. Jardim, *A aventura de outubro e a invasão de São Paulo*, 145; A. Leite, *Memórias de um revolucionário*, 142; interview with José Gomes Talarico, by Maria Cristina Guido and Reinaldo Roels Júnior, Rio de Janeiro, 21 Sept. 1978, CPDOC, PHO; interview with José Gomes Talarico, by Maria Cristina Guido and Reinaldo Roels Júnior, Rio de Janeiro, 27 Sept. 1978, CPDOC, PHO; "As roletas do P. R. P. foram destruidas," *A Platea*, 25 Oct. 1930, p. 1; *New York Times*, 26 Oct. 1930, p. 2. A photograph of the crowd gathered around the bonfire in front of the Republican Club is published in Murakami, *A revolução de 1930 e seus antecedentes*, 172.

129. Americano, *São Paulo nesse tempo, 1915–1935*, 392; Jardim, *A aventura de outubro e a invasão de São Paulo*, 145; A. Leite, *Memórias de um revolucionário*, 142; Mello, *Entre índios e revoluções*, 194.

130. C. R. Cameron to the Secretary of State, São Paulo, 25 Oct. 1930, USNARA, RG59, 832.00Revolutions/153; Brito, *Memórias de um ajudante de ordens*, 41; Jardim, *A aventura de outubro e a invasão de São Paulo*, 146; Paulo de Almeida Nogueira, *Minha vida*, 391; Nogueira Filho, *Ideais e lutas de um burguês progressista*, 2:566; Whitaker, *O milagre da minha vida*, 79; Wolfe, *Working Women, Working Men*, 50; interview with Leontina da Silva Raposo, São Paulo, April 1982, in José Aranha de Assis Pacheco, *Perdizes: História de um bairro* (São Paulo: Prefeitura Municipal, 1983), 254.

131. "A heroica jornada de São Paulo," *Diario de S. Paulo*, 25 Oct. 1930, p. 3; "O bom humor do povo," *A Platea*, 25 Oct. 1930, p. 2; "Wild Riots Greeted Brazil Coup d'Etat," *New York Times*, 26 Oct. 1930, p. 2; "Uma tribuna para todos," *O Povo*, 11 Nov. 1930, p. 3; S. Duarte, *A revolução victoriosa*, 268; A. Leite, *Memórias de um revolucionário*, 141.

132. "Vast Damage Done by Sao Paulo Mob," *New York Times*, 27 Oct. 1930, p. 3; Trento, *Do outro lado do Atlântico*, 391. Trento also claims that "Ford and General Motors" were "also devastated," but I have found no evidence that supports this claim.

133. Jardim, *A aventura de outubro e a invasão de São Paulo*, 145; Whitaker, *O milagre da minha vida*, 79; "Effeitos da crise," *O Combate*, 23 Aug. 1930, p. 6.

134. "A heroica jornada de São Paulo," *Diario de S. Paulo*, 25 Oct. 1930, p. 3; "Sao Paulo Mob Destroys Jail, Repeating Taking of Bastile," *New York Times*, 27 Oct. 1930, p. 1; "Nascimento e seu famoso depoimento," *O Bandeirante*, 28 Oct. 1930, p. 4; S. Duarte, *A revolução victoriosa*, 268; A. Leite, *Memórias de um revolucionário*, 142–43; A. Leite, *Páginas de uma longa vida*, 52–53; Mello, *Entre índios e revoluções*, 194; Whitaker, *O milagre da minha vida*, 79; Wolfe, *Working Women, Working Men*, 50; photograph in Murakami, *A revolução de 1930 e seus antecedentes*, 174.

135. C. R. Cameron to the Secretary of State, São Paulo, 25 Oct. 1930, USNARA, RG59, 832.00Revolutions/153; Jardim, *A aventura de outubro e a invasão de São Paulo*, 146; A. Leite, *Memórias de um revolucionário*, 141–42; Nogueira Filho, *Ideais e lutas de um burguês progressista*, 2:566; H. Silva, *1930*, 17,

345; Vampré, *São Paulo, terra conquistada,* 51, 55–56; Whitaker, *O milagre da minha vida,* 79; "Rosna-se mesmo que dos salões do 'Republicano' e do 'Portugal,'" *O Combate,* 21 April 1930, p. 1 (this article dates from the period in which the pro-Prestes, anti-Vargas journalist Jorge Santos was temporarily editor, perhaps while on the payroll of the state machine); untitled article, *O Combate,* 24 July 1930, p. 1; "Vida alheia . . . ," *O Combate,* 28 July 1930, p. 6; "Vida alheia . . . ," *O Combate,* 30 July 1930, p. 6; "Vida alheia . . . ," *O Combate,* 5 Aug. 1930, p. 3; "Vida alheia . . . ," *O Combate,* 13 Sept. 1930, p. 6; "O jogo," *O Combate,* 15 Sept. 1930, p. 1; "Vida alheia . . . ," *O Combate,* 2 Oct. 1930, p. 6; "Vida alheia . . . ," *O Combate,* 7 Oct. 1930, p. 6; "As roletas do P. R. P. foram destruidas," *A Platea,* 25 Oct. 1930, p. 1; *New York Times,* 26 Oct. 1930, p. 2; "É preciso não enfraquecer no combate ao cancro do jogo," *O Povo,* 18 Nov. 1930, p. 4; "Uma tribuna para todos," *O Povo,* 1 Dec. 1930, p. 2.

136. A. Leite, *Memórias de um revolucionário,* 143; "Brazil Is at Peace, Vargas President" and "Vast Damage Done by Sao Paulo Mob," *New York Times,* 27 Oct. 1930, p. 3.

137. Arthur G. Parsloe to the Secretary of State, Santos, 11 Nov. 1930, USNARA, RG59, 832.00Revolutions/228; "A Platéa em Santos," *A Platea,* 20 Nov. 1930, p. 2.

138. Arthur G. Parsloe to the Secretary of State, Santos, 11 Nov. 1930, USNARA, RG59, 832.00Revolutions/228; Leonardo Roitman in Alcindo Gonçalves, *Lutas e sonhos: Cultura política e hegemonia progressista em Santos, 1945–1962* (São Paulo: Ed. da Universidade Estadual Paulista, 1995), 74; F. Santos, *História de Santos, 1532–1936,* 1:328; F. Silva, *Operários sem patrões,* 336–37.

139. Leonardo Roitman in A. Gonçalves, *Lutas e sonhos,* 74; F. Santos, *História de Santos, 1532–1936,* 1:328, 2:96, 2:98; F. Silva, *Operários sem patrões,* 337–38; Arthur G. Parsloe to the Secretary of State, Santos, 11 Nov. 1930, USNARA, RG59, 832.00Revolutions/228.

140. Arthur G. Parsloe to the Secretary of State, Santos, 11 Nov. 1930, USNARA, RG59, 832.00Revolutions/228; Jardim, *A aventura de outubro e a invasão de São Paulo,* 146; Leonardo Roitman in A. Gonçalves, *Lutas e sonhos,* 74; F. Silva, *Operários sem patrões,* 337–38; "A occupação da cidade de Santos pelos revolucionarios," *A Platea,* 30 Oct. 1930, p. 2; "Uma tribuna para todos," *O Povo,* 12 Nov. 1930, p. 2.

141. Arthur G. Parsloe to the Secretary of State, Santos, 11 Nov. 1930, USNARA, RG59, 832.00Revolutions/228; Leonardo Roitman in A. Gonçalves, *Lutas e sonhos,* 74; F. Silva, *Operários sem patrões,* 338.

142. Americano, *São Paulo nesse tempo, 1915–1935,* 390; Love, *São Paulo in the Brazilian Federation,* 297.

143. "São Caetano," *O Povo,* 5 Nov. 1930, p. 1.

144. "Em Rio Claro," *Diario da Noite,* 27 Oct. 1930, p. 4.

145. "A revolução em Ribeirão Preto," *O Povo,* 5 Nov. 1930, p. 4; Walker, "Ribeirão Preto, 1910–1960," 75, 91 (quote on p. 75).

146. "Salve, triumphador!," *O Bandeirante*, 28 Oct. 1930, p. 1; "Miguel Costa reentrou vencedor em S. Paulo," *Diario Nacional*, 29 Oct. 1930, p. 6; *New York Times*, 29 Oct. 1930, p. 10; A. Leite, *Memórias de um revolucionário*, 163–64; Lopes, "Em cima do acontecimento," chap. 2; Nogueira Filho, *Ideais e lutas de um burguês progressista*, 2:560–61; photographs in Murakami, *A revolução de 1930 e seus antecedentes*, 176–77, and in *O Povo*, 29 Oct. 1930, p. 1.

147. C. R. Cameron to the Secretary of State, São Paulo, 30 Oct. 1930, USNARA, RG59, 832.00Revolutions/174; "Vibrante de jubilo e cheio de esperança . . . ," *Diario Nacional*, 30 Oct. 1930, p. 1; "Brazil's New Chief Enters Sao Paulo," *New York Times*, 30 Oct. 1930, p. 3; "Rebel Troops Pour into Rio de Janeiro," *New York Times*, 31 Oct. 1930, p. 9; Americano, *São Paulo nesse tempo, 1915–1935*, 393; P. Duarte, *Que é que ha?*, 73; A. Leite, *História da civilização paulista*, 188; A. Leite, *Memórias de um revolucionário*, 168–69; A. Leite, *Páginas de uma longa vida*, 54–55; Paulo de Almeida Nogueira, *Minha vida*, 391; Nogueira Filho, *Ideais e lutas de um burguês progressista*, 2:580–81; Lopes, "Em cima do acontecimento," chap. 2.

Conclusion and Epilogue

1. Alexandre Marcondes Filho to Sylvio de Campos, São Paulo, July 1926, CPDOC, AMF, doc. 1926.07.00 (emphasis added); "O Partido Nacional" (newspaper clipping labeled *Diario da Noite*, 22 Sept. 1927), AIHGSP, APD, album VIII; Nhôzinho Rato quoted in Motta Filho, *Contagem regressiva*, 203. In the mid-1920s, Monteiro Lobato famously remarked, "No one knows what they want, but no one wants what is," expressing a point of view similar to that of the anonymous *Diário da Noite* writer. See Chaves Neto, *Minha vida e as lutas de meu tempo*, 31.

2. The best of the historians of the period is Boris Fausto, whose works offer a general overview of the historiography as well as an interpretation of the events themselves. See esp. *A revolução de 1930* and his essay "As crises dos anos vinte e a revolução de 1930." in *História geral da civilização brasileira*, part 3, *O Brasil republicano*, vol. 9, *Sociedade e instituições, 1889–1930*, 4th ed., ed. Boris Fausto (Rio de Janeiro: Bertrand Brasil, 1990 [1977]), 401–426. I offer my own analyses of portions of the literature in "History, Sociology, and the Political Conflicts of the 1920s in São Paulo, Brazil," *Journal of Latin American Studies* 37, no. 2 (May 2005): 333–349, and "The Specter of Liberalism: Notes on the Democratic Party of São Paulo and the Historiography of Twentieth-Century Brazil," *Estudios Interdisciplinarios de América Latina y el Caribe* 16, no. 2 (July-Dec. 2005): 153–161, though readers of the two essays will have to suffer through youthful authorial overkill (in the case of the former) and rank editorial incompetence (in the case of the latter [cf. partially corrected version at www.tau.ac.il/eial]). Further examples of the various interpretations of the

political conflicts of the 1920s, in São Paulo and elsewhere in Brazil, include Nícia Vilela Luz, "A década de 1920 e suas crises," *Revista do Instituto de Estudos Brasileiros* 6 (1969): 67–75; Marieta de Moraes Ferreira, "A reação republicana e a crise política dos anos 20," *Estudos Históricos* 11 (Jan.-June 1993): 9–23; Ilan Rachum, "Nationalism and Revolution in Brazil, 1922–1930: A Study of Intellectual, Military and Political Protesters and of the Assault on the Old Republic" (Ph.D. diss., Columbia University, 1970); Vizentini, *Os liberais e a crise da república velha*; Vizentini, *A crise dos anos 20*; Vizentini, *O Rio Grande do Sul e a política nacional*; Antônio Carlos Villaça, "O pensamento brasileiro na década de 20," *Revista do Instituto Histórico e Geográfico Brasileiro* 346 (Jan.-March 1985): 91–105.

3. Villaça, "O pensamento brasileiro na década de 20," 103.

4. Quote from E. V. da Costa, *1932*, 10. See also Love, *São Paulo in the Brazilian Federation*, 164–66; M. Prado, *A democracia ilustrada*, 16–21.

5. On Raphael Sampaio Vidal: Antônio Gontijo de Carvalho, "Rafael Sampaio Vidal," *Digesto Econômico* 211 (Jan.-Feb. 1970): 5–7; Regina Hipólito, "Rafael Sampaio Vidal," in A. Abreu et al., *Dicionário histórico-biográfico brasileiro*, 5:6058–59. On Alcântara Machado: Godinho and Andrade, *Constituintes brasileiros de 1934*, 193–94; Guastini, *Tempos idos e vividos*, 117–42; Hermes Lima, *Travessia: Memórias* (Rio de Janeiro: José Olympio, 1974), 54; Jorge Miguel Mayer, "Alcântara Machado," in A. Abreu et al., *Dicionário histórico-biográfico brasileiro*, 3:3372–74. On Marcondes Filho: Jorge Miguel Mayer, "Marcondes Filho," in Abreu et al., *Dicionário histórico-biográfico brasileiro*, 3:3557–58. On Molinaro: chap. 2; "Pelos bastidores da politica," *O Combate*, 8 Dec. 1927, p. 1; Tan-Tan, "Politicando," *O Pinheirense*, 13 Jan. 1929, p. 1.

6. The comparison with the United States was not lost on contemporaries: "A camara delapida os cofres municipaes e depois augmenta os impostos," *O Combate*, 21 Sept. 1915, p. 1; "Assassinio do Major José Molinaro," *O Estado de S. Paulo*, 28 Dec. 1928, p. 6.

7. At least one PRP ward boss was himself not surprised: "O momento politico," *O Combate*, 24 Oct. 1928, p. 3. See also Love, *São Paulo in the Brazilian Federation*, 165.

8. As has long been clear: Fausto, *A revolução de 1930*, 41, 46–47, 51, 54–55; Edgar de Decca, *1930: O silêncio dos vencidos*, 6th ed. (São Paulo: Brasiliense, 1994 [1981]), part II; Paulo Sérgio Pinheiro, *Política e trabalho no Brasil*, 2nd ed. (Rio de Janeiro: Paz e Terra, 1977 [1975]), 47–48 (see also pp. 71–81); Vera Calicchio, "Centro das Indústrias do Estado de São Paulo," in A. Abreu et al., *Dicionário histórico-biográfico brasileiro*, 2:1309. The CIESP's support for the PRP should not be taken to mean, however, that São Paulo's large industrialists did not form an otherwise conflictive host, that many PD leaders were not invested in industry, or that smaller manufacturers, whose relationships with the grand industrialists of the state capital were not without rancor, did not side with the PD against the PRP.

9. See Carl H. Landé, "The Dyadic Basis of Clientelism," in *Friends, Followers, and Factions: A Reader in Political Clientelism*, ed. Steffen W. Schmidt et al. (Berkeley: University of California Press, 1977), xxx.

10. Corrêa, *A rebelião de 1924 em São Paulo*, 171n.

11. Policia de São Paulo, *Movimento subversivo de julho*, 219–20.

12. Ibid., 194–95.

13. Police delegate of Barretos quoted in Corrêa, *A rebelião de 1924 em São Paulo*, 169n.

14. Policia de São Paulo, *Movimento subversivo de julho*, 150–53; "A nova administração do municipio de Barretos," *O Combate*, 28 Jan. 1926, p. 4.

15. Vavy Pacheco Borges notes the difficulty of studying generational conflict in her *Tenentismo e revolução brasileira* (São Paulo: Brasiliense, 1992), 171 n. 47.

16. "Prestes lembra a longa marcha da coluna," *O Estado de S. Paulo*, 2 July 1978, pp. 7–8 (quotes on p. 8), AIHGSP, AR1924, single box containing contents of caixas 4–6, pasta 7.

17. Figueiredo, *1924*, 221–22.

18. Mesquita Filho, "Os ideais democráticos na revolução brasileira," 95.

19. Jardim, *A aventura de outubro e a invasão de São Paulo*, 16, 128–37 passim; Costa, *Criminosos de duas revoluções, 1930–1932*, 10–11; N. Oliveira, *1924*, 28; Everardo Dias, "Maurício de Lacerda," *Revista Brasiliense*, Jan.-Feb. 1960, p. 152; Augusto Ferreira de Castilho, *Democracia no Brasil: Philosophia, historia e politica da actualidade* (São Paulo: Instituto D. Anna Rosa, 1929), unpag. dedication page; "O pleito do dia 24," *O Combate*, 28 Feb. 1928, p. 6.

20. Melo, *Dicionário de autores paulistas*, 261; Silva Sobrinho, *Santos noutros tempos*, 83–88; Figueiredo, *Memórias de um jornalista*, 201; F. Santos, *História de Santos, 1532–1936*, 2:441–42; Schmidt, "Paulo Gonçalves," 33–42; "Paulo Gonçalves," *O Estado de S. Paulo*, 9 April 1927, p. 2; "Manifesto do Partido da Mocidade à Nação," São Paulo, 19 Nov. 1925, reprinted in Casalecchi, *O Partido Republicano Paulista*, 285–87.

21. Love, *São Paulo in the Brazilian Federation*, 165–66. The PD leaders' median year of birth would be even later if one discounted the party's figurehead, Antônio Prado, whose leadership was described as having been "more honorary than actual." Jardim, *A aventura de outubro e a invasão de São Paulo*, 133.

22. Rubens do Amaral, "Confissões de um jornalista," in *Testamento de uma geração*, ed. Edgard Cavalheiro (Porto Alegre: Livraria do Globo, 1944), 229; Cândido Motta Filho, "Luís de Toledo Piza e Almeida," *Revista do Instituto Histórico e Geográfico de São Paulo* 58 (1960): 1; Plinio Salgado, untitled preface to Motta Filho, *Alberto Torres e o thema da nossa geração*, ii, iv.

23. *O Combate*, 24–29 Sept. 1928; *O Estado de S. Paulo*, 25–29 Sept. 1928; Antonio de Lima to Soares Lara, Santos, 26 Sept. 1928, in AIHGSP, APD, pacote 38; Nogueira Filho, *Ideais e lutas de um burguês progressista*, 1:308; Francisco [Francesco] Frola, *Recuerdos de un antifascista, 1925–1938* (Mexico

City: México Nuevo, 1939), 98–99; C. R. Cameron, Report 167, "Fascism in São Paulo," 29 Oct. 1928, USNARA, RG84, Consular Posts, São Paulo, Brazil, volume 90, 800 series; "Termo de declarações," Gabinete de Investigações, São Paulo, n.d., CEDAE, FPD, DET.61; Laudelino de Abreu to "Ilmo. Sr. Dr. 1º Delegado Auxiliar," São Paulo, 19 Aug. 1930, CEDAE, FPD, DET.61; untitled documents [by Dias Sobrinho], dated 8 Aug. 1930 and 11 Aug. 1930, CEDAE, FPD, DET.62; A. Leite, *Memórias de um revolucionario*, chap. 1, chaps. 18–20; *Diario de S. Paulo*, 8 Aug. 1930 (see esp. photos on pp. 11, 18); "Em São Paulo," *O Estado de S. Paulo*, 25 Oct. 1930, pp. 2–3. In 1930, 170 students matriculated at the São Paulo Law School; up to that point, entering classes had typically consisted of around 70 students. Martins and Barbuy, *Arcadas*, 167.

24. Vieira, *Os grandes ideaes do Partido Democratico*, passim (quotes on p. 5).

25. Ibid.; Vieira, *Na imprensa*, 20–39, wherein the speech's original publication in the *Diario Nacional*, 12 and 13 Sept. 1928, is noted.

26. Vieira, *Os grandes ideaes do Partido Democratico*, passim (quotes on pp. 18, 22, 23).

27. Mario Pinto Serva, "Politica e partidos," in his *O voto secreto, ou a organisação de partidos nacionaes*, 238–39 (emphasis added).

28. Antonio de Sampaio Doria, "Objecções ao voto secreto," in his *O espirito das democracias*, 65–99 (quotes on pp. 76 [emphasis added], 91–92).

29. Antonio de Sampaio Doria, "Democracia," in his *Democracia / A Revolução de 1930* (São Paulo: Nacional, 1930), 4–45. Elsewhere, Sampaio Doria had framed the problem in expressly racial terms (in his *O espirito das democracias*, 13), as had his fellows in Monteiro Lobato's Pro-Secret Ballot League (above, chap. 4).

30. Míriam Lifchitz Moreira Leite, *Outra face do feminismo: Maria Lacerda de Moura* (São Paulo: Ática, 1984); Maria Lacerda de Moura, "O voto e a mulher proletaria," *O Trabalhador Graphico*, 7 Feb. 1923, p. 2; Maria Lacerda de Moura, "O voto feminino," *O Combate*, 8 Dec. 1927, p. 2; "Aspectos e impressões do grande Congresso para a escolha dos candidatos democraticos," *O Combate*, 6 Dec. 1927, p. 1; Waldemar Fleury, "Duas personalidades femininas," *O Combate*, 19 Dec. 1927, p. 3; "O voto feminino em Minas," *O Combate*, 31 Oct. 1928, p. 5; "Como se fundou o Partido Democratico," *A Platea*, 4 Nov. 1930, pp. 1–2. Zoroastro Gouveia, like Condé a leader of the PD's popular wing, remained an opponent of women's suffrage as a delegate to the national constitutional convention of 1933–34, by which time he was an avowed socialist and a vocal opponent of most of the PD's other surviving leaders: Rachel Soihet, "A pedagogia da conquista do espaço público pelas mulheres e a militância feminista de Bertha Lutz," *Revista Brasileira de Educação* 15 (Sept.-Dec. 2000): 104.

31. "Pelo direitos do povo" (newspaper clipping labeled *O Progresso* [Faxina], 10 Aug. 1927), AIHGSP, APD, album VI.

32. "Victoria" (newspaper clipping labeled *O Diario* [Jahu], 7 Dec. 1927), AIHGSP, APD, album IX.

33. Bertho Condé, "Pensamentos," *Folha do Partido Democratico*, published in *O Combate*, 4 Feb. 1927, p. 5, AIHGSP, APD, album V.

34. Propaganda materials, AIHGSP, ALN, pacote 1.

35. Saladino Cardoso Franco to Julio Prestes de Albuquerque, São Bernardo, 27 June 1928, AESP, AJPA, caixa APO7; "O conflicto democratico de S. Bernardo," *O Combate*, 26 June 1928, p. 1.

36. "A reeleição do sr. Marrey Junior" (newspaper clipping labeled *Praça de Santos*, 14 Jan. 1930), emphasis added, AIHGSP, APD, pacote 2 (second series).

37. "A ultima palavra do general Prestes," *O Combate*, 30 Aug. 1929, p. 1; "Voto secreto, voto obrigatorio e justiça unica," *O Combate*, 7 Aug. 1929, p. 1.

38. J. Canuto, "Campanha em pról da unidade nacional," *Diario da Noite* (clipping dated 11 Sept. 1929), AIHGSP, APD, pacote 59.

39. Propaganda poster, "Alistae-vos," AIHGSP, ALN, pacote 1 (this item is reproduced in miniature in Assembléia Legislativa, *Legislativo paulista*, 71); chap. 5, above.

40. Cândido Motta (Pai), quoted in Affonso Henriques, *Vargas, o maquiavélico* (São Paulo: Palácio do Livro, 1961), 172; propaganda poster, "O Candidato Nacional," reprinted in *O Combate*, 1 March 1930, p. 3; Laudemiro Menezes, "A ascendencia de S. Paulo na federação," *O Combate*, 28 April 1930, p. 4.

41. Above, chaps. 2, 3, 4, 5, and 6.

42. The quote is from Mario Pinto Serva, *A reforma eleitoral* (São Paulo: Livraria Zenith, 1931), 225. See also above, chaps. 3, 4, and 5.

43. Lobato et al., *O voto secreto*, 16–17 (quote on p. 17); Mesquita Filho, *A crise nacional*, 57–58, 63–64 (quote on p. 64).

44. Vivaldo Coaracy, *Problemas nacionaes* (São Paulo: Sociedade Impressora Paulista, 1930), 104.

45. *Progress in South America*, 12. See also M. Viotti and Vitaliano Rotellini, *The Press of the State of S. Paulo, Brasil, 1827–1904* (São Paulo: Vanorden & Comp., 1905).

46. Carelli, *Carcamanos e comendadores*, 62; de Luca, *A "Revista do Brasil,"* 38; C. R. Cameron, Report No. 151, "São Paulo Press on the Kellogg Pact," 4 Sept. 1928, USNARA, RG84, Consular Posts, São Paulo, Brazil, 1928, vol. 90, 800 series. The growth of the *Estado*'s readership appears still more spectacular when one considers that in 1888 the most popular newspaper in São Paulo claimed a daily circulation of only 3,300. See Schmidt, *São Paulo de meus amores*, 134–35.

47. Last, *Facts about the State of São Paulo*, 51; "A imprensa no Brasil," *O Combate*, 15 March 1921, p. 1; "Imprensa paulistana," *O Combate*, 24 July 1925, p. 1; M. Albuquerque, *Os jornais de bairro na cidade de São Paulo*, 25–29; Dias, *História das lutas sociais*, 187–89; P. Duarte, *História da imprensa em São Paulo*, 31–32; Rodolfo Mota Lima, "Sintese histórica," in *5 de Julho, 1922–1924* (Rio de Janeiro: Henrique Velho, n.d. [1944]), 143; Mota and Capelato, *História da*

"Folha de S. Paulo," 1921–1981, chap. 1; Nobre, História da imprensa de São Paulo, 229–33; Schmidt, Bom tempo, 318; Sodré, História da imprensa no Brasil, 356, 363, 365–71; Annibal Machado to directorio, São Paulo, 30 Aug. 1926, AIHGSP, APD, pacote 45. On Tacape, A Encrenca, and A Federação, which do not figure in the sources cited (or, as far as I can tell, in the existing historiography of Brazilian print culture), I am drawing on my notes on the issues of 28 April 1928 (Tacape, at the library of the São Paulo Law School); 18 Oct. 1929 and 27 Dec. 1929 (A Encrenca, at the Biblioteca Nacional and the Arquivo Edgard Leuenroth, respectively); and 30 Sept. 1926 (A Federação, at São Paulo's Biblioteca Mário de Andrade).

48. "A imprensa no Brasil," O Combate, 15 March 1921, p. 1.

49. The two quotes are from A. Martins, Revistas em revista, 234 (emphasis suppressed); Afonso Schmidt, "Voltolino," Paulistania, March-April 1949, quoted in Ana Maria de Moraes Belluzzo, Voltolino e as raízes do modernismo (São Paulo: Marco Zero, 1992), 27 (see also p. 48). See also José Aranha de Assis Pacheco, Taquara rachada e outras memórias (São Paulo: by the author, 1989), 136–37, 154.

50. In addition to Marcondes Filho's letter to Sylvio de Campos, cited above, see Jardim's polemic with "The Press and the Demagogues," both of which he charged with responsibility for the events that led to the "invasion" of São Paulo. Jardim, A aventura de outubro e a invasão de São Paulo, 15–21.

51. Americano, São Paulo nesse tempo, 1915–1935, 222; "Manifestação á imprensa," O Combate, 28 Jan. 1916, p. 4; above, chaps. 2, 3, 5, and 6.

52. Motta Filho, Contagem regressiva, 125. Nhôzinho Rato, to say nothing of his friends, was relatively fortunate in that his home county of Una—"no-good land this way, good land this way, a little cattle-raising and a lot of sugar-cane"—was no great prize. In the absence of rival claimants for power, bosses like him were able to maintain power. Ibid., 121, 125.

53. V. Borges, Tenentismo e revolução brasileira, 33–36; M. Prado, A democracia ilustrada, 97–98.

54. V. Borges, Tenentismo e revolução brasileira, chaps. 1–2 (see p. 36 on Costa's nomination as "special inspector"); Vera Calicchio, "Legião Revolucionária de São Paulo," in A. Abreu et al., Dicionário histórico-biográfico brasileiro, 3:3052–53; M. Prado, A democracia ilustrada, 99, 116–17, 120–23; Edwin V. Morgan to State Department, Rio de Janeiro, 10 March 1931, and attachment: "Abstract from Political Report of March 7, 1931," USNARA, RG59, 832.00/717; Cabral, Tempos de Jânio e outros tempos, 13–16; P. Duarte, Que é que ha?, 19, 166; Carlos Castilho Cabral to Paulo Nogueira Filho, [São Paulo?], 17 June 1957, in Paulo Nogueira Filho, A guerra cívica, 1932, 4 vols. in 6 (Rio de Janeiro: José Olympio, 1965–1981), 2:390; Brasil Gerson, "Entre os legionarios e democraticos," O Homem do Povo, 13 April 1931, p. 3; "Sallesopolis na éra revolucionaria," O Povo, 23 July 1931, p. 2.

55. João de Castro Guimarães, Antonio Jacintho Guimarães, and Mario

Moreira, untitled memorandum, São Paulo, 19 Dec. 1930, AIHGSP, APD, pacote 40; "Coisas de S. Caetano," *O Povo*, 1 Dec. 1930, p. 2; M. Prado, *A democracia ilustrada*, 115–16.

56. Vieira, *Na imprensa*, 114 (see also i–v); Charles R. Cameron to Edwin V. Morgan, São Paulo, 13 Feb. 1931, USNARA, RG59, 832.00/771 (mislabeled, filed in 710s).

57. V. Borges, *Tenentismo e revolução brasileira*, 37–49; M. Prado, *A democracia ilustrada*, 99–101, 104–5 (but on pp. 100–101, cf. John D. French's review in the *Hispanic American Historical Review* 69, no. 2 [May 1989]: 360–61); P. Duarte, *Que é que ha?*, 154–55.

58. V. Borges, *Tenentismo e revolução brasileira*, 46–49, 79; De Paula, *1932*, 225–27; H. Lima, *Travessia*, 62–63; M. Prado, *A democracia ilustrada*, 124–27; Harry W. Brown, Current Events Report (Rep. No. 1019), Rio de Janeiro, 31 March 1932, USNARA, RG59, 832.00/787.

59. V. Borges, *Tenentismo e revolução brasileira*, 52, 54; De Paula, *1932*, 88–94; Aureliano Leite, "Causas e objetivos da revolução de 1932," *Revista de História* 25 (1962): 143; H. Lima, *Travessia*, 63, 65–66; M. Prado, *A democracia ilustrada*, 126–27; telegram, Charles R. Cameron to State Department, São Paulo, 23 May 1932 (17h00), USNARA, RG59, 832.00/790; telegram, Charles R. Cameron to State Department, São Paulo, 24 May 1932, USNARA, RG59, 832.00/791; Charles R. Cameron to Edwin V. Morgan, São Paulo, 25 May 1932, USNARA, RG59, 832.00/799.

60. The quotes are from Charles R. Cameron to Walter C. Thurston, São Paulo, 30 July 1932, USNARA, RG59, 832.00/810. Useful introductions to the revolt of 1932 include Maria Helena Capelato, *O movimento de 1932: A causa paulista* (São Paulo: Brasiliense, 1981), and Stanley E. Hilton, *A guerra civil brasileira: A revolução constitucionalista de 1932* (Rio de Janeiro: Nova Fronteira, 1982). Jeziel De Paula's *1932* is an excellent reinterpretation based on surviving photographic evidence. Aureliano Leite, "Bibliografia da revolução constitucionalista," *Revista de História* 25 (1962): 145–66, represents an early attempt at cataloguing the outpouring of published material that the events of 1932 inspired.

61. For "Brazil's Thermidor": John D. Wirth, "Tenentismo in the Brazilian Revolution of 1930," *Hispanic American Historical Review* 44, no. 2 (May 1964): 177.

62. Nogueira Filho, *A guerra cívica, 1932*; M. Prado, *A democracia ilustrada*, chap. 2; F. Santos, *História de Santos, 1532–1936*, chap. 26; Terci, "A cidade na primeira república," 289.

63. Arthur Morgan (pseud., Armando de Arruda Pereira), *Os engenheiros de S. Paulo em 1932: Pela lei e pela ordem* (São Paulo: n.p., 1934), 49–50; Clovis de Oliveira, *A indústria e o movimento constitucionalista de 1932* (São Paulo: Serviço de Publicações do CIESP/FIESP, 1956); Barbara Weinstein, *For Social Peace in Brazil: Industrialists and the Remaking of the Working Class in*

São Paulo, 1920–1964 (Chapel Hill: University of North Carolina Press, 1996), 63–64.

64. Moreira, *Em face da revolução*, 72–73. Any argument for the absolute novelty of the riotous, semi-ritualized sacking of newspaper offices and printing plants runs up against the fact that the practice, and the specific term for it (*empastelamento*), were already in use in the nineteenth century.

65. De Paula, *1932*, 150–60; Barbara Weinstein, "Inventing the *Mulher Paulista*: Politics, Rebellion, and the Gendering of Brazilian Regional Identities," *Journal of Women's History* 18, no. 1 (winter 2006): 22–49; "A installação do Partido Democrático em Itú," *O Combate*, 2 Aug. 1926, p. 4; *O Combate*, 13 Feb. 1930, p. 3; "Casa do soldado," *A Platea*, 10 Nov. 1930, p. 3; P. Duarte, *Que é que ha?*, 161.

66. V. Borges, *Tenentismo e revolução brasileira*, 76.

67. For introductions to these themes in the specific context of 1932, see Katia Maria Abud, "O bandeirante e o movimento de 32: Alguma relação?," in *O imaginário em terra conquistada*, ed. Maria Isaura Pereira de Queiroz (São Paulo: Centro de Estudos Rurais e Urbanos, 1993), 36–44; and esp. Weinstein, "Racializing Regional Difference."

68. Holien Gonçalves Bezerra, *O jogo do poder: Revolução paulista de 32* (São Paulo: Moderna, 1989), 101; V. Borges, *Tenentismo e revolução brasileira*, 70, 91, 129, 187. See also Carlos Castilho Cabral to Paulo Nogueira Filho [São Paulo?], 17 June 1957, in Nogueira Filho, *A guerra cívica, 1932*, 2:390–91.

69. H. Lima, *Travessia*, 72.

70. Luiz Carlos Prestes in *A Manhã* (Rio de Janeiro), 5 July 1935 (second edition), cited in Vitor Manoel Marques da Fonseca, "A ANL na legalidade" (tese de mestrado, Universidade Federal Fluminense, 1986), 236; *Hoje*, 21 Nov. 1945, p. 8; *Hoje*, 26 Nov. 1945, p. 6; Getúlio Vargas, *Ideário político de Getúlio Vargas*, ed. Raul Guastini (São Paulo: n.p., 1943), 99–100, 121–23. See also Guastini's editorial comments in ibid., 100; Cassiano Ricardo, "O Estado Novo e o seu sentido bandeirante," *Cultura Política* 1, no. 1 (Mar. 1941): 110–132.

71. Cabral, *Tempos de Jânio e outros tempos*, 32, makes much of Adhemar's zeal for inaugurating new public works.

72. A. Leite, *Páginas de uma longa vida*, 312, 504; Cunha Motta, *Os rapazes da imprensa: Um pouco da história de São Paulo* (São Paulo: Ateniense, 1990), 161–63 (Roberto de Abreu Sodré is quoted on p. 163). See also Cabral, *Tempos de Jânio e outros tempos*, esp. 52–56. Marrey himself tried starting up his own party, the Popular Sindicalist Party, but it foundered (had it not, perhaps Jânio would not have gone off on his own) and so he allied himself with Adhemar de Barros in preparation for the elections of 1947, in which he received more votes than any other São Paulo city council candidate. In 1950, he allied himself with the PTB for another successful campaign, this one taking him to the federal legislature. Marrey resigned his seat in 1953 to take a cabinet-level position in the city government of São Paulo after Jânio was elected prefeito. Jorge Miguel

Mayer, "José Adriano Marrey Júnior," in A. Abreu et al., *Dicionário histórico-biográfico brasileiro*, 3:3604–5.

73. W. Ferreira, "A Faculdade de Direito na arrancada de 9 de julho de 1932," 416–33 (quotes on pp. 420, 433).

74. Mesquita Filho, "Os ideais democráticos na revolução brasileira," 118–19 (emphases added). This essay, an extended review of João Alberto Lins de Barros's *Memórias de um revolucionário*, was originally published in serial form in *O Estado de S. Paulo* in June and July 1954.

75. Tired of backing losing candidates, the UDN endorsed Jânio Quadros's presidential campaign of 1959–60 and, when he won, the *Estado* waxed enthusiastic, calling his election "the victory of Democracy" and "a defeat of unprecedented proportions for the remains of Getulismo," but the actual relationship between Quadros and the UDN, including the *Estado* group, was far from cordial. *O Estado de S. Paulo*, 6 Oct. 1960, quoted, in translation, in John W. F. Dulles, *The São Paulo Law School and the Anti-Vargas Resistance, 1938–1945* (Austin: University of Texas Press, 1986), 195; Robert J. Alexander, notes on a conversation with Claudio Abramo, São Paulo, 24 April 1956, Robert J. Alexander Papers (microfilmed collection), reel 3, image 425.

76. Clovis Botelho Vieira to Miguel Costa, São Paulo, 6 July 1959, FMC, AEL, pasta 36. See also Vieira's *O general Ataliba Leonel*, most of which was also written in July 1959.

77. Coutinho had also been a subscriber of the PD manifesto of 21 March 1926, and a candidate of the Worker-Peasant Union of Brazil in São Paulo's state elections of 1934. Mário Maia Coutinho, *Quanto custa não ser eleito: Peripécias e decepções de um candidato a deputado* (São Paulo: Edições Patrimônio, 1962), passim (quotes on pp. 49, 75); Nicolau Soares do Couto Esher to Nilo Peçanha, São Paulo, 12 Feb. 1922, MR, ANP, caixa 48; "A sucessão presidencial da republica," *O Combate*, 30 July 1921, p. 1; Serafim Leme da Silva et al., "Ao eleitorado independente de São Paulo," São Paulo, 3 April 1922, in secção livre, *O Combate*, 27 April 1922, p. 2; "Manifesto á nação," *O Estado de S. Paulo*, 22 March 1926, p. 3.

78. Robert J. Alexander, notes on a conversation with Aristides Lobo, São Paulo, 27 Aug. 1959, Robert J. Alexander Papers (microfilmed collection), reel 3, image 862; Del Roio, *A classe operária na revolução burguesa*, 62–67, 141–43, 152–53, 157–58.

79. Abguar Bastos et al., untitled statement, *Revista Brasiliense*, Sept.-Oct. 1955, pp. 1–3. On Afonso Schmidt: above, chap. 4, and his *São Paulo de meus amores*, published in 1954. On Sérgio Milliet: above, chap. 5; Sérgio Milliet to Paulo Duarte, [São Paulo?], 27 June 1933, in P. Duarte, *Memórias*, 2:162–63; L. Gonçalves, *Sérgio Milliet*; and his own works, *Roberto* (see esp. pp. 133–35, 138–39, 151–52 on Roberto/Milliet's disenchantment with Brazil), *Marcha á ré* (São Paulo: n.p., 1936), *Ensaios* (São Paulo: n.p., 1938), "O meu depoimento" (ca. 1942), in Cavalheiro, *Testamento de uma geração*, 239–43, and *De cães,*

gatos, gente (São Paulo: Martins, 1964). On Elias Chaves Neto: above, chap. 2, his *Minha vida e as lutas de meu tempo* (the quotes are on p. 27; the ellipsis is his), and his *A revolta de 1924*.

80. Abguar Bastos et al., untitled statement, *Revista Brasiliense,* Sept.-Oct. 1955, pp. 1–3 (quotes on p. 1); Edgard Cavalheiro, "Monteiro Lobato e a Revista do Brasil," *Revista Brasiliense,* Sept.-Oct. 1955, pp. 5–14.

81. Everardo Dias, "Lutas operárias no estado de São Paulo," *Revista Brasiliense,* Sept.-Oct. 1955, pp. 77, 81; Dias, *História das lutas sociais no Brasil;* "As proximas eleições municipaes e o proletariado," *O Combate,* 29 Oct. 1928, p. 3; "Quem é Everardo Dias," *Folha do Bloco Operario e Camponez,* published as a broadside in *O Combate,* 29 Oct. 1928, p. 5; Nogueira Filho, *Ideais e lutas de um burguês progressista,* 2:486–87; E. Rodrigues, *Os companheiros,* 2:47–48.

82. "Waldemar Belfort de Mattos," *Revista Brasiliense,* Jan.-Feb. 1957, pp. 124–25 (quote on p. 124); Waldemar Belfort de Mattos to Francisco Morato, São Paulo, 20 Feb. 1932, AIHGSP, APD, pacote 46; British Chamber of Commerce of São Paulo and Southern Brazil, *Personalidades no Brasil,* 111–12; Del Roio, *A classe operária na revolução burguesa,* 228; Brazilian Socialist Party electoral slate reprinted in Assembléia Legislativa, *Legislativo paulista,* 114; above, chaps. 3, 4, and 5.

83. "General Miguel Costa," *Revista Brasiliense,* Sept.-Oct. 1959, p. 45.

84. Julio Mesquita (Pai), quoted in Goulart, "Júlio Mesquita," 365 (Goulart takes the quote from *O Estado de S. Paulo,* 16 Dec. 1915); Karl Marx, "The Eighteenth Brumaire of Louis Napoleon," in *The Karl Marx Library,* ed. Saul K. Padover, vol. 1: *On Revolution* (New York: McGraw-Hill, 1971), 246.

Bibliography

Archival Sources

BRAZIL

Campinas
Universidade Estadual de Campinas
    Arquivo Edgard Leuenroth: Coleçaõ Maurício de Lacerda; Fundo
      Miguel Costa
    Centro de Documentação Cultural Alexandre Eulalio: Fundo Paulo
      Duarte

Rio de Janeiro
Casa de Rui Barbosa
    Arquivo de Rui Barbosa
Centro de Pesquisa e Documentação de História Contemporânea do Brasil
    Arquivo Alexandre Marcondes Filho
    Arquivo Getúlio Vargas
    Programa de História Oral: interviews with Paulo Duarte, Jorge Duque
      Estrada, José Gomes Talarico
Museu da República
    Arquivo Nilo Peçanha

São Paulo
Arquivo do Estado de São Paulo
    Arquivo Altino Arantes
    Arquivo Joaquim da Cunha Diniz Junqueira
    Arquivo José Carlos de Macedo Soares
    Arquivo Júlio Prestes de Albuquerque
Arquivo do Instituto Histórico e Geográfico de São Paulo
    Arquivo Aureliano Leite
    Arquivo Liga Nacionalista
    Arquivo Partido Democrático
    Arquivo Revolução de 1924 em São Paulo
Arquivo do Istituto Italiano di Cultura
    Arquivo Antonio Piccarolo

College Park, Maryland
United States National Archives and Records Administration
  Record Group 59, General Records of the Department of State
  Record Group 84, Records of the Foreign Service Posts of the
    Department of State

New Brunswick, New Jersey
Special Collections and University Archives, Rutgers University
  Robert J. Alexander Papers

Washington, D.C.
Oliveira Lima Library, Catholic University of America
  Oliveira Lima Clipping Collection
  Oliveira Lima Correspondence Collection

Periodicals (published in the city of São Paulo
unless otherwise noted)

O Alpha (Rio Claro)
O Bandeirante
Brazil Magazine (Rio de Janeiro)
Braz-Journal
A Capital
O Combate
O Commentario
Commercio da Lapa
Diario da Noite
Diario de S. Paulo
Diario Nacional
A Encrenca
O Estado de S. Paulo
A Federação
Folha da Manhã
Folha da Noite
Hoje
O Homem do Povo
O Libertador
New York Times
O Parafuso
Patria (Ribeirão Preto)
O Pinheirense
A Platea

A Plebe
O Povo
A Provincia de São Paulo
Outlook (New York)
O Regional (Caçapava)
Revista Brasiliense
Revista do Brasil
A Ronda
O Sacy
S. Paulo-Jornal
O Solidario (Santos)
Tacape
O Trabalhador Graphico

Works Cited

Abreu, Alzira Alves de, Israel Beloch, Fernando Lattman-Weltman, and Sérgio
    Tadeu de Niemeyer Lamarão, eds. Dicionário histórico-biográfico brasileiro.
    2nd ed. Rio de Janeiro: Editora da Fundação Getúlio Vargas, 2001 [1984].
Abreu, Diores Santos. Formação histórica de uma cidade pioneira paulista:
    Presidente Prudente. Presidente Prudente: Faculdade de Filosofia, Ciência e
    Letras de Presidente Prudente, 1972.
Abud, Katia Maria. "O bandeirante e o movimento de 32: Alguma relação?"
    In O imaginário em terra conquistada, ed. Maria Isaura Pereira de Queiroz,
    36–44. São Paulo: Centro de Estudos Rurais e Urbanos, 1993.
Adduci, Cássia Chrispiniano. "Nação brasileira e 'mística paulista': Uma
    análise dos memorialistas da rebelião militar de 1924 em São Paulo." Lutas
    Sociais 5 (1998): 7–24.
Aguiar, Marco Alexandre de. Botucatu: Imprensa e ferrovia. São Paulo: Arte e
    Ciência, 2001.
Album de Araras: Documentário histórico, geográfico, ilustrativo do município de
    Araras. Araras: n.p., 1948.
Albuquerque, Júlio Prestes de. 1924: Um depoimento. Edited by Célio Debes.
    São Paulo: Arquivo do Estado, 1981.
Albuquerque, Maria Elisa Vercesi de. Os jornais de bairro na cidade de São
    Paulo. São Paulo: Imprensa Oficial do Estado, 1985.
Alvarenga, José. E o sertão acabou. Osvaldo Cruz, São Paulo: by the author, 1998.
Alvim, Gustavo Jacques Dias. "O Diário": A saga de um jornal de causas.
    Piracicaba: Editora da Universidade Metodista de Piracicaba, 1998.
Amaral, Brenno Ferraz do. Cidades vivas. São Paulo: Monteiro Lobato, 1924.
———. A literatura em São Paulo em 1922. Edited by Pedro Ferraz do Amaral.
    São Paulo: Conselho Estadual de Cultura, 1973.

Amaral, Leopoldo. *Campinas actual*. N.p., n.d.

Amaral, Luis. *A hora da expiação: O momento brasileiro, em synthese*. São Paulo: n.p., 1930.

Amaral, Pedro Ferraz do. *Celso Garcia*. São Paulo: Martins, 1973.

Amaral, Rubens do. "Antônio Prado." In *Homens de São Paulo*, by Aureliano Leite et al., 231–63. São Paulo: Martins, 1954.

Americano, Jorge. *A lição dos factos: Revolta de 5 de julho de 1924*. São Paulo: Saraiva, 1924.

———. *São Paulo naquele tempo, 1895–1915*. São Paulo: Saraiva, 1957.

———. *Stó Paulo nesse tempo, 1915–1935*. São Paulo: Melhoramentos, 1962.

Andrade, Oswald de. *Um homem sem profissão: Memórias e confissões*. Rio de Janeiro: José Olympio, 1954.

Andrews, George Reid. *Blacks and Whites in São Paulo, Brazil, 1888–1988*. Madison: University of Wisconsin Press, 1991.

Aquino, Laura Christina Mello de. *Os "tenentes" estrangeiros: A participação de batalhões estrangeiros na rebelião de 1924 em São Paulo*. João Pessoa: Editora da Universidade Federal de Paraíba, 1998.

Arantes, Altino. *Passos do meu caminho*. Rio de Janeiro: José Olympio, 1958.

Arinos de Melo Franco, Afonso. *Rodrigues Alves: Apogeu e declínio do presidencialismo*. 2 vols. Rio de Janeiro: José Olympio, 1973.

Assembléia Legislativa de São Paulo. *Legislativo paulista: Parlamentares, 1835–1999*. Edited by Auro Augusto Caliman. São Paulo: Imprensa Oficial, 1999.

Azzi, Francisco. *Educação civica*. São Paulo: Weiszflog [&] Irmãos, 1916.

Baptistella, Celma da Silva Lago. "Evolução dos viveiros de citros no Brasil." *Informações Econômicas* 35, no. 4 (April 2005): 75–80.

Barbosa, Alaor. *Um cenáculo na paulicéia: Um estudo sobre Monteiro Lobato, Godofredo Rangel, José Antônio Nogueira, Ricardo Gonçalves, Raul de Freitas e Albino de Camargo*. Brasília: Projecto Editorial, 2002.

Barbosa, Maria Valéria, Nelson Santos Dias, and Rita Márcia Martins Cerqueira. *Santos na formação do Brasil: 500 anos de história*. Santos: Prefeitura Municipal, 2000.

Barbosa, Ruy. *Campanha presidencial, 1919*. Bahia: Livraria Catalina, 1919.

———. *Excursão eleitoral ao estado de S. Paulo*. São Paulo: Casa Garraux, 1909.

———. *A grande guerra*. Edited by Fernando Nery. Rio de Janeiro: Guanabara, 1932.

Barriguelli, José Cláudio, ed. *O pensamento político da classe dominante paulista, 1873–1928*. São Carlos: Arquivo de História Contemporânea, 1986.

Barros, Paulo de Moraes. *Politica do café*. Rio de Janeiro: Imprensa Nacional, 1929.

Barros, Roque Spencer Maciel de. *A evolução do pensamento de Pereira Barreto*. São Paulo: Grijalbo, 1967.

Batista, Eduardo. "Luiz Pereira Barreto." In *Os desbravadores*, ed. Galeno Amorim, 47–58. 2nd ed. Ribeirão Preto: Palavra Mágica 2002 [2001].

Beattie, Peter M. *The Tribute of Blood: Army, Honor, Race, and Nation in Brazil, 1864–1945*. Durham, N.C.: Duke University Press, 2001.

Belluzzo, Ana Maria de Moraes. *Voltolino e as raízes do modernismo*. São Paulo: Marco Zero, 1992.

Berardi, Maria Helena Petrillo. *Santo Amaro*. São Paulo: Prefeitura Municipal, Secretária de Educação e Cultura, 1969.

Bertolli Filho, Claudio. "A gripe espanhola em Sâo Paulo." *Ciência Hoje* 58 (Oct. 1989): 30–41.

Bertonha, João Fábio. *Sob a sombra de Mussolini: Os italianos de São Paulo e a luta contra o fascismo, 1919–1945*. São Paulo: Annablume, 1999.

Bethel, Leslie, ed. *Colonial Brazil*. Cambridge: Cambridge University Press, 1987.

Bezerra, Holien Gonçalves. *O jogo do poder: Revolução paulista de 32*. São Paulo: Moderna, 1989.

Bieber, Judy. *Power, Patronage, and Political Violence: State-Building on a Brazilian Frontier, 1822–1889*. Lincoln: University of Nebraska Press, 1999.

Bilac, Maria Beatriz Bianchini. *As elites políticas de Rio Claro: Recrutamento e trajetória*. Campinas: Editora da Universidade Estadual de Campinas, 2001.

Borges, Dain. "Intellectuals and the Forgetting of Slavery in Brazil." *Annals of Scholarship* 11, nos. 1–2 (1996): 37–60.

Borges, Vavy Pacheco. *Tenentismo e revolução brasileira*. São Paulo: Brasiliense, 1992.

British Chamber of Commerce of São Paulo and Southern Brazil. *Personalidades no Brasil / Men of Affairs in Brazil*. São Paulo: n.p., n.d.

Brito, Luiz Tenorio de. *Memórias de um ajudante de ordens*. São Paulo: Nacional, 1951.

Broca, Brito. *Memórias*. Rio de Janeiro: José Olympio, 1968.

Bueno, Javier. *Mi viaje a América*. Paris: Casa Editorial Garnier Hermanos, 1913.

Cabanas, João. *A columna do morte*. Asunción: Kraus, 1926.

Cabral, C. [Carlos] Castilho. *Batalhões patrioticos na revolução de 1924*. São Paulo: Livraria Liberdade, 1927.

———. *Tempos de Jânio e outros tempos*. Rio de Janeiro: Civilização Brasileira, 1962.

Caldeira, Jorge. "Julio Mesquita, fundador do jornalismo moderno no Brasil." In *A guerra, 1914–1918*, by Julio Mesquita, 1:21–32. São Paulo: Terceiro Nome, 2002.

Camargos, Marcia Mascarenhas, and Vladmir Sacchetta. "Procura-se Peter Pan . . ." In *Minorias silenciadas: História da censura no Brasil*, ed. Maria Luiza Tucci Carneiro, 207–35. São Paulo: Imprensa Oficial, 2002.

Camêu, Francolino. *Politicos e estadistas contemporaneos*. Rio de Janeiro: Officinas Graphicas d' *O Globo*, 1928.

Campos, Zulmiro de. *Vultos de Sorocaba*. São Paulo: Sociedade Editora Olegario Ribeiro, 1921.

Capelato, Maria Helena. *O movimento de 1932: A causa paulista*. São Paulo: Brasiliense, 1981.

Capelato, Maria Helena, and Maria Lígia Prado. *O bravo matutino: Imprensa e ideologia no jornal "O Estado de S. Paulo."* São Paulo: Alfa-Omega, 1980.

Capri, Roberto. *O estado de São Paulo e seus municipios*. 3 vols. in 1. São Paulo: n.p., 1913.

Caputti Sobrinho, Vicente. *Minha terra, minha gente*. Sorocaba: Fundação Ubaldino do Amaral, 1995.

Carelli, Mario. *Carcamanos e comendadores: Os italianos de São Paulo da realidade à ficção, 1919–1930*. Translated by Ligia Maria Pondé Vassallo. São Paulo: Ática, 1985.

Carolo, Alexandre. "Quinzinho da Cunha." In *Os desbravadores*, ed. Galeno Amorim, 59–64. 2nd ed. Ribeirão Preto: Palavra Mágica, 2002 [2001].

Carone, Edgard, and Maria Sílvia Arantes Junqueira. "Atas do Partido Republicano Paulista." *Estudos Históricos* 11 (1972): 135–230.

Carrer, Nelson. "Francisco Schmidt." In *Os desbravadores*, ed. Galeno Amorim, 65–69. 2nd ed. Ribeirão Preto: Palavra Mágica, 2002 [2001].

Carvalho, Afranio. *Raul Soares, um líder da república velha*. Rio de Janeiro: Forense, 1978.

Carvalho, Antônio Gontijo de. "Rafael Sampaio Vidal." *Digesto Econômico* 211 (Jan.-Feb. 1970): 5–7.

Carvalho, Joaquim Nunes de. *A revolução no Brasil, 1924–1925: Apontamentos para a história*. 2nd ed. Rio de Janeiro: Typ. São Benedicto, 1930.

Carvalho, José Murilo de. *A formação das almas: O imaginário da república no Brasil*. São Paulo: Companhia das Letras, 1990.

Casalecchi, José Ênio. *O Partido Republicano Paulista: Política e poder, 1889–1926*. São Paulo: Brasiliense, 1987.

Castilho, Augusto Ferreira de. *Democracia no Brasil: Philosophia, historia e politica da actualidade*. São Paulo: Instituto D. Anna Rosa, 1929.

Cavalheiro, Edgard, ed. *Testamento de uma geração*. Porto Alegre: Livraria do Globo, 1944.

Chasteen, John Charles. *Heroes on Horseback: A Life and Times of the Last Gaucho Caudillos*. Albuquerque: University of New Mexico Press, 1995.

Chaves Neto, Elias. *Minha vida e as lutas de meu tempo*. São Paulo: Alfa-Omega, 1978.

——. *A revolta de 1924*. São Paulo: Officinas Graphicas Olegario de Almeida Filho & Comp., 1924.

Cintra, Assis. *Os escandalos da 1.ª república*. São Paulo: J. Fagundes, 1936.

Cione, Ruben. *História de Ribeirão Preto*. 3rd ed. Ribeirão Preto: IMAG, 1990.

Coaracy, Vivaldo. *Encontros com a vida: Memórias*. Rio de Janeiro: José Olympio, 1962.

——. *Problemas nacionaes*. São Paulo: Sociedade Impressora Paulista, 1930.

Cobb, Richard. "The Revolutionary Mentality in France." In *A Second Identity: Essays on France and French History*, 122–41. London: Oxford University Press, 1969.

Cobra, Amador Nogueira. *Em um recanto do sertão paulista*. São Paulo: Typ. Hennies [&] Irmãos, 1923.

Coelho, Benedito Carlos Marcondes. *O processo político da comunidade guaratinguetaense*. Santos: Secretaria de Estado da Cultura, 1982.

Cohen, Ilka Stern. "Em nome das classes conservadoras: Associação Comercial de São Paulo, 1917–1928." Tese de mestrado, Pontifícia Universidade Católica de São Paulo, 1986.

Condé, Bertho. *Ensaios de politica espirtualista*. São Paulo: Editora O Pensamento, 1927.

Corrêa, Anna Maria Martinez. *A rebelião de 1924 em São Paulo*. São Paulo: Hucitec, 1976.

Costa, Cyro, and Eurico de Goes. *Sob a metralha: Historico da revólta em São Paulo, de 5 de julho de 1924*. São Paulo: Monteiro Lobato, 1924.

Costa, Emilia Viotti da. *The Brazilian Empire: Myths and Histories*. Rev. ed. Chapel Hill: University of North Carolina Press, 2000 [1985].

——. "Liberalismo e democracia." *Anais de História* 7 (1975): 9–30.

——. "New Publics, New Politics, New Histories: From Economic Reductionism to Cultural Reductionism—in Search of Dialectics." In *Reclaiming the Political in Latin American History: Essays from the North*, ed. Gilbert M. Joseph, 17–31. Durham, N.C.: Duke University Press, 2001.

——, ed. *1932: Imagens contraditórias*. São Paulo: Arquivo do Estado, 1982.

Costa, José Augusto. *Criminosos de duas revoluções, 1930–1932*. São Paulo: n.p., 1933.

Costa, Luiz Augusto Maia. "O ideário urbano paulista na virada do século: O engenheiro Theodoro Sampaio e as questões territoriais e urbanas modernas, 1886–1903." Tese de mestrado, Universidade de São Paulo, 2001.

Coutinho, Mário Maia. *Quanto custa não ser eleito: Peripécias e decepções de um candidato a deputado*. São Paulo: Edições Patrimônio, 1962.

Dean, Warren. *The Industrialization of São Paulo, 1880–1945*. Austin: University of Texas Press, 1969.

——. "The Planter as Entrepreneur: The Case of São Paulo." *Hispanic American Historical Review* 46, no. 2 (May 1966): 138–52.

——. *Rio Claro: A Brazilian Plantation System, 1820–1920*. Stanford, Calif.: Stanford University Press, 1976.

Debes, Célio. *Júlio Prestes e a primeira república*. São Paulo: Arquivo do Estado, 1982.

——. *Washington Luís*. Two volumes to date. São Paulo: Imprensa Oficial do Estado, 1994–.

de Decca, Edgar. *1930: O silêncio dos vencidos*. 6th ed. São Paulo: Brasiliense, 1994 [1981].

Del Fiorentino, Teresinha Aparecida. "O operariado campineiro de 1930 a 1945." *Revista da SBPH* 1 (1983): 17–34.

Del Picchia, Menotti. *A longa viagem*. 2 vols. São Paulo: Martins, 1970–72.

———. *Tormenta*. São Paulo: Nacional, 1932.

Del Rios, Jefferson. *Ourinhos: Memórias de uma cidade paulista*. Ourinhos: Prefeitura Municipal, 1992.

Del Roio, Marcos. *A classe operária na revolução burguesa: A política de alianças do PCB, 1928–1935*. Belo Horizonte: Oficina de Livros, 1990.

de Luca, Tania Regina. *A "Revista do Brasil": Um diagnóstico para a (n)ação*. São Paulo: Editora da Universidade Estadual Paulista, 1998.

———. *O sonho do futuro assegurado: O mutualismo em São Paulo*. São Paulo: Contexto, 1990.

Demartini, Zeila de Brito Fabri. "O coronelismo e a educação na 1.ª república." *Educação & Sociedade* 34 (Dec. 1989): 44–74.

De Paula, Jeziel. *1932: Imagens construindo a história*. Campinas: Editora da Universidade Estadual de Campinas, 1998.

Dias, Everardo. *História das lutas sociais no Brasil*. São Paulo: Alfa-Omega, 1977.

Doria, Antonio de Sampaio. *Democracia / A Revoluçaõ de 1930*. São Paulo: Nacional, 1930.

———. *O espirito das democracias*. São Paulo: Monteiro Lobato, 1924.

Downes, Earl Richard. "The Seeds of Influence: Brazil's 'Essentially Agricultural' Old Republic and the United States, 1910–1930." Ph.D. diss., University of Texas, 1986.

Drummond, José Augusto. *A coluna Prestes: Rebeldes errantes*. São Paulo: Brasiliense, 1985.

Duarte, Paulo. *Agora nós*. São Paulo: n.p., 1927.

———. *História da imprensa em São Paulo*. São Paulo: Escola de Comunicações e Artes, Universidade de São Paulo, 1972.

———. *Júlio Mesquita*. São Paulo: Hucitec, 1977.

———. *Memórias*. Vols. 1–9. São Paulo: Hucitec, 1974–79.

———. *Memórias*. Vol. 10. Rio de Janeiro: Paz e Terra, 1980.

———. *Que é que ha? Pequena historia de uma grande pirataria*. São Paulo: n.p., 1931.

Duarte, Silva. *A revolução victoriosa: A marcha heroica dum povo que se liberta*. São Paulo: Livraria Zenith, 1930.

Dulles, John W. F. *Anarchists and Communists in Brazil, 1900–1935*. Austin: University of Texas Press, 1973.

———. *The São Paulo Law School and the Anti-Vargas Resistance, 1938–1945*. Austin: University of Texas Press, 1986.

Egas, Eugenio. *Galeria dos presidentes de São Paulo*. 3 vols. São Paulo: Secção de Obras d' *O Estado de S. Paulo*, 1926–27.

——, ed. *Os municipios paulistas*. 2 vols. São Paulo: Secção de Obras d' *O Estado de S. Paulo*, 1925.

Elias Netto, Cecílio. *Memorial de Piracicaba: Século XX*. Piracicaba: Instituto Histórico e Geográfico de Piracicaba, 2000.

Ellis, Myriam. "As bandeiras na expansão geográfica do Brasil." In *História geral da civilização brasileira*, part 1, *A época colonial*, vol. 1, *Do descobrimento à expansão territorial*, ed. Sérgio Buarque de Holanda, 273–96. São Paulo: Difel, 1960.

Ellis Junior, Alfredo. *Raça de gigantes*. São Paulo: Helios, 1926.

Estado de São Paulo. *Lei e regulamento sobre a qualificação eleitoral do estado de São Paulo*. São Paulo: Typographia do *Diario Official*, 1900.

Etzel, Eduardo. *Um médico do século XX: Vivendo transformações*. São Paulo: Nobel, 1987.

Faria, Teresinha Paiva de, Maria Rosalina Rodarte Carvalho, Célia Maria de Mendonça, and Benedito Carlos Marcondes Coelho. *Decadência do café numa comunidade vale-paraibana*. Guaratinguetá: n.p., 1973.

Farina, Duílio Crispim. *Medicina no planalto de Piratininga*. São Paulo: n.p., 1981.

Fausto, Boris. "Conflito social na república oligárquica: A greve de 1917." *Estudos Cebrap* 10 (1974): 79–109.

——. "As crises dos anos vinte e a revolução de 1930." In *História geral da civilização brasileira*, part 3, *O Brasil republicano*, vol. 9, *Sociedade e instituições, 1889–1930*, ed. Boris Fausto, 401–26. 4th ed. Rio de Janeiro: Bertrand Brasil, 1990 [1977].

——. "Imigração e participação política na primeira república: O caso de São Paulo." In *Imigração e política em São Paulo*, by Boris Fausto, Oswaldo Truzzi, Roberto Grün, and Célia Sakurai, 7–26. São Paulo: Sumaré, 1995.

——. *A revolução de 1930: Historiografia e história*. 16th ed. São Paulo: Companhia das Letras, 1997 [1970].

——. *Trabalho urbano e conflito social, 1890–1920*. 4th ed. São Paulo: Difel, 1986 [1976].

Federici, Hilton. *Símbolos paulistas: Estudo histórico-heráldico*. São Paulo: Secretaria da Cultura, Comissão de Geografia e História, 1981.

Ferrari, Terezinha. "Ensaio de classe: O Centro dos Industriais de Fiação e Tecelagem de São Paulo, 1919–1931; Estudo sobre a organização do empresariado têxtil durante os anos vinte." Tese de mestrado, Pontifícia Universidade Católica de São Paulo, 1988.

Ferreira, Antonio Celso. *A epopéia bandeirante: Letrados, instituições, invenção histórica, 1870–1940*. São Paulo: Editora da Universidade Estadual Paulista, 2002.

Ferreira, Marieta de Moraes. "A reação republicana e a crise política dos anos 20." *Estudos Históricos* 11 (Jan.-June 1993): 9–23.

Ferreira, Waldemar. "A Faculdade de Direito na arrancada de 9 de julho de 1932." *Revista da Faculdade de Direito* 55 (1960): 416–33.

Figueiredo, Antônio dos Santos. *A evolução do estado no Brasil*. Porto: n.p., 1926.

———. *Memórias de um jornalista*. São Paulo: Unitas, 1933.

———. *1924: Episodios da revolução de S. Paulo*. Porto: n.p., 1924.

Fonseca, Vitor Manoel Marques da. "A ANL na legalidade." Tese de mestrado, Universidade Federal Fluminense, 1986.

Forjaz, Maria Cecília Spina. *Tenentismo e Aliança Liberal, 1927–1930*. São Paulo: Polis, 1978.

Freitas, Affonso A. de. *A imprensa periodica de São Paulo desde seus primordios até 1914*. São Paulo: Typographia do *Diario Official*, 1915.

Freitas, Clovis Glycerio Gracie de. *Jornada republicana: Francisco Glycerio*. São Paulo: Plexus, 2000.

French, John D. "Industrial Workers and the Origin of Populist Politics in the ABC Region of Greater São Paulo, 1900–1950." Ph.D. diss., Yale University, 1985.

———. Review of *A democrácia ilustrada*, by Maria Lígia Coelho Prado. *Hispanic American Historical Review* 69, no. 2 (May 1989): 360–61.

Freyre, Gilberto. *New World in the Tropics: The Culture of Modern Brazil*. New York: Alfred A. Knopf, 1959.

———. *Order and Progress: Brazil from Monarchy to Republic*. Translated by Rod W. Horton. New York: Alfred A. Knopf, 1970.

Frola, Francisco [Francesco]. *Recuerdos de un antifascista, 1925–1938*. Mexico City: México Nuevo, 1939.

Gaiarsa, Octaviano A. *Santo André: Ontem, hoje, amanhã*. Santo André: Prefeitura Municipal, 1991.

Gallotta, Brás Ciro. "*O Parafuso*: Humor e crítica na imprensa paulistana, 1915–1921." Tese de mestrado, Pontifícia Universidade Católica de São Paulo, 1997.

Giesbrecht, Ralph Mennucci. *Sud Mennucci: Memórias de Piracicaba, Porto Ferreira, São Paulo. . . .* São Paulo: Imprensa Oficial, 1997.

Gifun, Frederick Vincent. "Ribeirão Prêto, 1880–1914: The Rise of a Coffee County." Ph.D. diss., University of Florida, 1972.

Gitahy, Maria Lucia Caira. "The Port Workers of Santos, 1889–1914: Labor Movement in an Early 20th Century City." Ph.D. diss., University of Colorado, 1991.

———. *Ventos do mar: Trabalhadores do porto, movimento operário e cultura urbana*. São Paulo: Editora da Universidade Estadual Paulista, 1992.

Godinho, Wanor R., and Oswaldo S. Andrade. *Constituintes brasileiros de 1934*. Rio de Janeiro: n.p., 1934.

Gomes, Angela Maria de Castro. *A invenção do trabalhismo*. 3rd ed. Rio de Janeiro: Editora da Fundação Getúlio Vargas, 2005 [1988].

Gonçalves, Alcindo. *Lutas e sonhos: Cultura política e hegemonia progressista em Santos, 1945–1962*. São Paulo: Editora da Universidade Estadual Paulista, 1995.

Gonçalves, João Felipe. " 'As imponentes festas do sol': O jubileu cívico-literário de Rui Barbosa." In *Estudos históricos sobre Rui Barbosa*, by Isabel Lustosa, Eduardo Silva, Antônio Herculano Lopes, Margarida Maria Lacombe Camargo, João Felipe Gonçalves, and Maria Lúcia Horta Ludolf de Melo, 151–204. Rio de Janeiro: Casa de Rui Barbosa, 2000.

———. *Rui Barbosa: Pondo as idéias no lugar*. Rio de Janeiro: Editora da Fundação Getúlio Vargas, 2000.

Gonçalves, Lisbeth Rebollo. *Sérgio Milliet: Crítico de arte*. São Paulo: Editora da Universidade de São Paulo, 1992.

Goulart, Maurício. "Júlio Mesquita." In *Homens de São Paulo*, by Aureliano Leite et al., 305–65. São Paulo: Martins, 1954.

Graham, Richard. *Patronage and Politics in Nineteenth-Century Brazil*. Stanford, Calif.: Stanford University Press, 1990.

Grínberg, Isaac. *História de Mogi das Cruzes: Do começo até 1954*. São Paulo: n.p., 1961.

Guastini, Mário. *Tempos idos e vividos*. São Paulo: Universitária, 1944.

Guimarães, Manoel Luiz Lima Salgado, Paulo Sérgio de Sá, Silvia Ninita de Moura Estevão, and Vera Lúcia Ascenção, eds. *A revolução de 30: textos e documentos*. 2 vols. Brasília: Editora da Universidade de Brasília, 1982.

Hahner, June E. *Poverty and Politics: The Urban Poor in Brazil, 1870–1920*. Albuquerque: University of New Mexico Press, 1987.

Henriques, Affonso. *Vargas, o maquiavélico*. São Paulo: Palácio do Livro, 1961.

Hilton, Stanley E. *A guerra civil brasileira: A revolução constitucionalista de 1932*. Rio de Janeiro: Nova Fronteira, 1982.

Holloway, Thomas H. *Immigrants on the Land: Coffee and Society in São Paulo, 1886–1934*. Chapel Hill: University of North Carolina Press, 1980.

Instituto Astronomico e Geographico de São Paulo. *Carta geral do estado de São Paulo, 1933*. São Paulo: n.p., 1933.

Jardim, Renato. *A aventura de outubro e a invasão de São Paulo*. 2nd ed. Rio de Janeiro: Civilização Brasileira, 1932.

———. *Um libello a sustentar: Additamento ao livro "A aventura de outubro e a invasão de São Paulo"* Rio de Janeiro: Civilização Brasileira, 1933.

———. *Reminiscências: De Resende, estado do Rio, às plagas paulistas, S. Simão, Batatais, Altinópolis e Ribeirão Preto*. Rio de Janeiro: José Olympio, 1946.

Johnson, H. B. "Portuguese Settlement, 1500–1580." In *Colonial Brazil*, ed. Leslie Bethell, 1–38. Cambridge: Cambridge University Press, 1987.

Joseph, Gilbert M. "Reclaiming 'the Political' at the Turn of the Millennium." In *Reclaiming the Political in Latin American History: Essays from the North*, ed. Gilbert M. Joseph, 3–16. Durham, N.C.: Duke University Press, 2001.

Khoury, Iara Aun, ed. *As greves de 1917 em São Paulo e o processo de organização proletária*. São Paulo: Cortez, 1981.

Kipling, Rudyard. *Brazilian Sketches*. New York: Doubleday, Doran and Co., 1940 [1927].

Kirkendall, Andrew J. *Class Mates: Male Student Culture and the Making of a Political Class in Nineteenth-Century Brazil.* Lincoln: University of Nebraska Press, 2002.

Kittleson, Roger. " 'Ideas Triumph Only after Great Contests of Sorrows': Popular Classes and Political Ideas in Porto Alegre, Brazil, 1889–1893." In *Liberals, Politics, and Power: State Formation in Nineteenth-Century Latin America,* ed. Vincent C. Peloso and Barbara A. Tenenbaum, 235–58. Athens: University of Georgia Press, 1996.

———. *The Practice of Politics in Postcolonial Brazil: Porto Alegre, 1845–1895.* Pittsburgh: University of Pittsburgh Press, 2006.

Knight, Alan. "Latin America." In *The Oxford History of the Twentieth Century,* ed. Michael Howard and William Roger Lewis, 277–91. Oxford: Oxford University Press, 1998.

———. *The Mexican Revolution.* 2 vols. Cambridge: Cambridge University Press, 1986.

Lacerda, Mauricio de. *Segunda republica.* Rio de Janeiro: Freitas Bastos, n.d. [1931].

Landé, Carl H. "The Dyadic Basis of Clientelism." In *Friends, Followers, and Factions: A Reader in Political Clientelism,* ed. Steffen W. Schmidt, James C. Scott, Carl H. Landé, and Laura Guasti, xiii–xxvii. Berkeley: University of California Press, 1977.

Last, Gilbert. *Facts about the State of São Paulo.* São Paulo: British Chamber of Commerce of São Paulo and Southern Brazil, 1926.

Leal, Victor Nunes. *Coronelismo: The Municipality and Representative Government in Brazil.* Translated by June Henfrey. Cambridge: Cambridge University Press, 1977 [1949].

Leão, A. [Antonio] Carneiro. *S. Paulo em 1920.* Rio de Janeiro: *Annuario Americano,* 1920.

Leite, Aureliano. "Bibliografia da revolução constitucionalista." *Revista de História* 25 (1962): 145–66.

———. "Causas e objetivos da revolução de 1932." *Revista de História* 25 (1962): 139–44.

———. *Dias de pavor: Figuras e scenas da revolta de S. Paulo.* São Paulo: Monteiro Lobato, 1924.

———. *História da civilização paulista.* São Paulo: Martins, 1946.

———. *Memórias de um revolucionário: A revolução de 1930, pródomos e conseqüências.* N.p., 1931.

———. *Páginas de uma longa vida.* São Paulo: Martins, 1966.

———. *Subsídios para a história da civilização paulista.* São Paulo: Saraiva, 1954.

Leite, Aureliano, Affonso de E. [Escragnolle] Taunay, Fernando Góes, Victor de Azevedo, Rubens do Amaral, Cândido Motta Filho, Maurício Goulart, Flamínio Fávero, Edgard Cavalheiro, and Heitor Ferreira Lima. *Homens de São Paulo.* São Paulo: Martins, 1954.

Leite, Míriam Lifchitz Moreira. *Outra face do feminismo: Maria Lacerda de Moura*. São Paulo: Ática, 1984.

Leme, Ernesto. *A casa de Bragança: Memórias*. São Paulo: Parma, 1981.

———. *Rui e São Paulo*. Rio de Janeiro: Casa de Rui Barbosa, 1949.

Leonel, Jayme, João Gomes Martins Filho, Enéas Cezar Ferreira, Carvalho Sobrinho, Menotti Del Picchia, and Arruda Camargo. *O último dos coronéis: Homenagem dos autores ao grande brasileiro, General Ataliba Leonel, no primeiro centenário do seu nascimento*. São Paulo: n.p., 1975.

Levi, Darrell E. *The Prados of São Paulo, Brazil: An Elite Family and Social Change, 1840–1930*. Athens: University of Georgia Press, 1987.

Levi-Moreira, Silvia. "Ideologia e atuação da Liga Nacionalista de São Paulo, 1917–1924." *Revista de História* 116 (1984): 67–74.

———. "Liberalismo e democracia na dissidência republicana paulista: Estudo sobre o Partido Republicano Dissidente de São Paulo, 1901–1906." Tese de doutorado, Universidade de São Paulo, 1991.

———. "A luta pelo voto secreto no programa da Liga Nacionalista de São Paulo, 1916–1924." *Revista Brasileira de História* 7 (March 1984): 72–80.

Levine, Robert M. *Pernambuco in the Brazilian Federation, 1889–1937*. Stanford, Calif.: Stanford University Press, 1978.

Lewin, Linda. *Politics and Parentela in Paraíba: A Case Study of Family-Based Oligarchy in Brazil*. Princeton, N.J.: Princeton University Press, 1987.

Lima, Hermes. *Travessia: Memórias*. Rio de Janeiro: José Olympio, 1974.

Lima, J. C. [José Custódio] Alves de. *Recordações de homens e cousas do meu tempo*. Rio de Janeiro: Leite Ribeiro, Freitas Bastos, Spicer & Cia., 1926.

Lima, Octaviano Alves de. *Revolução econômico-social*. 2nd ed. São Paulo: Brasiliense, 1947 [1931].

Lima, Rodolfo Mota. "Sintese histórica." In *5 de Julho, 1922–1924*, 139–43. Rio de Janeiro: Henrique Velho, n.d. [1944].

Linhares, Hermínio. *Contribuição à história das lutas operárias no Brasil*. 2nd ed. São Paulo: Alfa-Omega, 1977 [1955].

Lobato, Monteiro. *Cidades mortas*. Various editions. [1919].

Lobato, Monteiro, et al. *O voto secreto: Carta aberta ao exmo. snr. dr. Carlos de Campos*. São Paulo: n.p., 1924.

Lôbo, Pelágio. "O fôro de Campinas do império e na república." In *Monografia histórica do município de Campinas*, 329–44. Rio de Janeiro: Instituto Brasileiro de Geografia e Estatística, 1952.

———. *Recordações das arcadas*. São Paulo: Reitoria da Universidade de São Paulo, 1953.

Lockhart, James, and Stuart B. Schwartz. *Early Latin America*. Cambridge: Cambridge University Press, 1983.

Lopes, Cleide. "Em cima do acontecimento: A revolução de 30 e a imprensa paulista." Tese de mestrado, Pontifícia Universidade Católica de São Paulo, 1988.

Lopreato, Christina Roquette. *O espírito da revolta: A greve geral anarquista de 1917*. São Paulo: Annablume, 2000.

Love, Joseph L. "The Party in Power." Unpublished manuscript chart, n.d.

——. "Political Participation in Brazil, 1881–1969." *Luso-Brazilian Review* 7, no. 2 (Dec. 1970): 3–24.

——. *Rio Grande do Sul and Brazilian Regionalism, 1882–1930*. Stanford, Calif.: Stanford University Press, 1971.

——. *São Paulo in the Brazilian Federation, 1889–1937*. Stanford, Calif.: Stanford University Press, 1980.

Love, Joseph L., and Bert J. Barickman. "Rulers and Owners: A Brazilian Case Study in Comparative Perspective." *Hispanic American Historical Review* 66, no. 4 (Nov. 1986): 743–65.

Love, Joseph L., John Wirth, and Robert Levine. "O poder dos estados: Análise regional." In *História geral da civilização brasileira*, part 3, *O Brasil republicano*, vol. 8, *Estrutura de poder e economia, 1889–1930*, ed. Boris Fausto, 51–151. 6th ed. Rio de Janeiro: Bertrand Brasil, 1997 [1975].

Luebke, Frederick C. *Germans in Brazil: A Comparative Study of Cultural Conflict During World War I*. Baton Rouge: Louisiana State University Press, 1987.

Luz, Nícia Vilela. "A década de 1920 e suas crises." *Revista do Instituto de Estudos Brasileiros* 6 (1969): 67–75.

Machado, Antônio de Alcântara. *Brás, Bexiga e Barra Funda: Notícias de São Paulo*. Repr. ed. Belo Horizonte: Vila Rica, n.d. [1927].

Maffei, Eduardo. *A greve: Romance*. Rio de Janeiro: Paz e Terra, 1978.

——. *Vidas sem norte: Romance do tenentismo*. São Paulo: Brasiliense, 1980.

Mallon, Florencia. *Peasant and Nation: The Making of Postcolonial Mexico and Peru*. Berkeley: University of California Press, 1995.

Manchester, Alan K. "Reminiscences of a Latin American Revolution." *South Atlantic Quarterly* 32, no. 1 (Jan. 1933): 74–84.

Mangabeira, João. *Rui: O estadista da república*. Rio de Janeiro: José Olympio, 1943.

Manor, Paul. "The Liga Nacionalista de São Paulo: A Political Reformist Group in Paulista Academic of Yore, 1917–1924." *Jahrbuch für Geschichte von Staat, Wirtschaft und Gesellschaft Lateinamerikas* 17 (1980): 317–53.

Marcigaglia, Luiz. *Férias de julho: Aspectos da revolução militar de 1924 ao redor do Lyceu Salesiano de S. Paulo*. 2nd ed. São Paulo: Escolas Profissionaes do Lyceu Coração de Jesus, 1927 [1924].

Mariano, Júlio. "História da imprensa em Campinas." In *Monografia histórica do município de Campinas*, 301–13. Rio de Janeiro: Instituto Brasileiro de Geografia e Estatística, 1952.

Marrey Junior, J. A. [José Adriano]. *O Partido Democratico no Congresso Federal*. São Paulo: Secção de Obras d' O Estado de S. Paulo, 1927.

Martins, Ana Luiza. *Revistas em revista: Imprensa e práticas culturais em tempos de república; São Paulo, 1890–1922*. São Paulo: Editora da Universidade de São Paulo, 2001.

Martins, Ana Luiza, and Heloisa Barbuy. *Arcadas: História da Faculdade de Direito do Largo de São Francisco*. São Paulo: Melhoramentos, 1999.

Martins, José de Souza. *São Caetano do Sul em quatro séculos de história*. São Caetano do Sul: Saraiva, 1957.

———. *Subúrbio: Vida cotidiana e história no subúrbio da cidade de São Paulo; São Caetano, do fim do império ao fim da república velha*. São Paulo: Hucitec, 1992.

Marx, Karl. "The Eighteenth Brumaire of Louis Napoleon." In *The Karl Marx Library*, ed. Saul K. Padover, vol. 1: *On Revolution*, 243–328. New York: McGraw-Hill, 1971.

McIntire, Robert Leonard. *Portrait of Half a Century: Fifty Years of Presbyterianism in Brazil, 1859–1910*. Cuernavaca: Centro Intercultural de Documentación, 1969.

Medici, Ademir. *Immigração e urbanização: A presença de São Caetano na região do ABC*. São Paulo: Hucitec, 1993.

Mello, Darcy Siciliano Bandeira de. *Entre índios e revoluções: Pelos sertões de São Paulo, Mato Grosso e Goiás de 1911 a 1941*. São Paulo: Soma, 1982.

Melo, Luís Correia de. *Dicionário de autores paulistas*. São Paulo: n.p., 1954.

Mendes, Cunha. *A psychologia do eleitorado brasileiro*. Rio de Janeiro: Leite Ribeiro, 1926.

Menezes, Raimundo de. *História pitoresca de quarenta cadeiras: Anedotário da Academia Paulista de Letras*. São Paulo: Hucitec, 1976.

Mesquita, Esther. *Um livro de memórias sem importância*. Translated by Lucia de Salles Oliveira. São Paulo: Livraria Duas Cidades, 1982.

Mesquita, Julio. *A guerra, 1914–1918*. 4 vols. São Paulo: Terceiro Nome, 2002.

Mesquita Filho, Julio. *A crise nacional: Reflexões em torno de uma data*. São Paulo: Secção de Obras d' O Estado de S. Paulo, 1925.

———. "Os ideais democráticos na revolução brasileira." In *Política e cultura*, 92–119. São Paulo: Martins, 1969.

Michetti, Heloisa Helena, and M. Antonieta de A. G. Parahyba. "O jôgo das fôrças políticas da vida de Araraquara." *Revista de Ciência Política* 2, no. 3 (July-Sept. 1968): 59–78.

Milliet, Sérgio. *De cães, gatos, gente*. São Paulo: Martins, 1964.

———. *Ensaios*. São Paulo: n.p., 1938.

———. *Marcha á ré*. São Paulo: n.p., 1936.

———. *Roberto*. São Paulo: L. Niccolini & Cia., 1935.

Monbeig, Pierre. *Pioneiros e fazendeiros de São Paulo*. Translated by Ary França and Raul de Andrade e Silva. São Paulo: Hucitec, 1984.

Monsma, Karl, Oswaldo Truzzi, and Silvano da Conceição. "Solidariedade étnica, poder local e banditismo: Uma quadrilha calabresa no oeste paulista, 1895–1898." *Revista Brasileira de Ciências Sociais* 53 (Oct. 2003): 71–96.

Moraes, Aurino. *Minas na Aliança Liberal e na revolução.* Belo Horizonte: Pindorama, 1933.

Moraes, Heitor de. *Patria rediviva: De Pires Ferreira a Martim Francisco.* São Paulo: Secção de Obras d'*O Estado de S. Paulo,* n.d. [1918].

Morato, Francisco. *A desnacionalização do Major Miguel Costa e a irrevogabilidade da naturalização.* São Paulo: n.d., 1928.

Moreira, Rangel. *Em face da revolução.* São Paulo: n.p., 1930.

——. *Fragoa brasileira.* São Paulo: F. Fragale & Cia., 1926.

Morgan, Arthur [Armando de Arruda Pereira]. *Os engenheiros de S. Paulo em 1932: Pela lei e pela ordem.* São Paulo: n.p., 1934.

Mota, Carlos Guilherme, and Maria Helena Capelato. *História da "Folha de S. Paulo," 1921–1981.* São Paulo: Impres, 1980.

Mota, Lourenço Dantas, ed. *A história vivida.* 3 vols. São Paulo: *O Estado de São Paulo,* 1981–82.

Motta, Cunha. *Os rapazes da imprensa: Um pouco da história de São Paulo.* São Paulo: Ateniense, 1990.

Motta, Marly Silva da. *A nação faz cem anos: A questão nacional no centenário da independência.* Rio de Janeiro: Editora da Fundação Getúlio Vargas, 1992.

Motta Filho, Cândido. *Alberto Torres e o thema da nossa geração.* São Paulo: Schmidt, n.d. [between 1931 and 1933].

——. *Contagem regressiva.* Rio de Janeiro: José Olympio, 1972.

——. *Dias lidos e vividos.* Rio de Janeiro: José Olympio, 1977.

——. *Uma grande vida.* São Paulo: Edições de *Politica,* 1931.

——. "Luís de Toledo Piza e Almeida." *Revista do Instituto Histórico e Geográfico de São Paulo* 58 (1960): 1–10.

Motta Sobrinho, Alves. *Gama Rodrigues: Humanista e médico, 1.º deputado municipalista brasileiro.* São Paulo: Sala Euclides da Cunha, 1962.

Moura, Clóvis. *Sacco e Vanzetti: O protesto brasileiro.* São Paulo: Brasil Debates, 1979.

Murakami, Ana Maria Brandão. *A revolução de 1930 e seus antecedentes.* Rio de Janeiro: Nova Fronteira, 1980.

Namier, Lewis. *The Structure of Politics at the Accession of George III.* 2nd ed. London: MacMillan and Co., 1957 [1929].

Neiva, Arthur. *Daqui e de longe . . . Chronicas nacionaes e de viagem.* São Paulo: Comp. Melhoramentos de S. Paulo, 1927.

Nobre, Freitas. *História da imprensa de São Paulo.* São Paulo: Edições Leia, 1950.

Nogueira, Oracy. "Contribuição à história do municipalismo no Brasil." *Revista de Administração* 7, nos. 25–28 (1953): 23–74.

———. *Família e comunidade: Um estudo sociológico de Itapetininga*. Rio de Janeiro: Centro Brasileiro de Pesquisas Educacionais, 1962.

———. "Os movimentos e partidos políticos em Itapetininga." *Revista Brasileira de Estudos Políticos* 11 (June 1961): 222–47.

———. *Negro político, político negro*. São Paulo: Editora da Universidade de São Paulo, 1992.

Nogueira, Paulo de Almeida. *Minha vida: Diário de 1893 a 1951*. São Paulo: Emprêsa Gráfica *Revista dos Tribunais*, 1955.

Nogueira, Paulo de Castro Pupo. "O fôro de Campinas, 1918–1950." In *Monografia histórica do município de Campinas*, 347–58. Rio de Janeiro: Instituto Brasileiro de Geografia e Estatística, 1952.

Nogueira Filho, Paulo. *A guerra cívica, 1932*. 4 vols. in 6. Rio de Janeiro: José Olympio, 1965–81.

———. *Ideais e lutas de um burguês progressista: O Partido Democrático e a revolução de 1930*. 2 vols. São Paulo: Anhambi, 1958.

Noronha, Abilio de. *Narrando a verdade*. São Paulo: Monteiro Lobato, 1924.

Oliveira, Clovis de. *A indústria e o movimento constitucionalista de 1932*. São Paulo: Serviço de Publicações do CIESP/FIESP, 1956.

Oliveira, Ganymédes José Santos de. *Uma vez, Casa Branca. . . .* São Paulo: São Paulo Editora, 1973.

Oliveira, Nelson Tabajara de. *1924: A revolução de Isidoro*. São Paulo: Nacional, 1956.

Oliveira, Percival de. *O ponto de vista do P. R. P.* São Paulo: São Paulo Editora, 1930.

Orsi, Itamir Lello, and Eddy C. Paiva. *Famílias ilustres e tradicionais de Santo André*. N.p., 1991.

Owensby, Brian P. *Intimate Ironies: Modernity and the Making of Middle-Class Lives in Brazil*. Stanford, Calif.: Stanford University Press, 1999.

Pacheco, José Aranha de Assis. *Perdizes: História de um bairro*. São Paulo: Prefeitura Municipal, 1983.

———. *Taquara rachada e outras memórias*. São Paulo: by the author, 1989.

Paes Leme Junior [Júlio da Silveira Sudário]. *Breve notícias históricas sôbre Itápolis*. São Paulo: n.p., 1938.

Pagnocca, Ana Maria Penha Mena. *Crônica dos prefeitos de Rio Claro, 1908–1983*. Rio Claro: Arquivo Público e Histórico, 1983.

Pang, Eul-Soo. *Bahia in the First Brazilian Republic: Coronelismo and Oligarchies, 1889–1934*. Gainesville: University of Florida Press, 1979.

Partido Democratico. *O voto secreto: Collectanea de opiniões, discursos e documentos sobre o assumpto*. Edited by Mario Pinto Serva. São Paulo: Livraria Liberdade, 1927.

Partido Republicano de S. Paulo. *A scisão, 1901*. São Paulo: Typographia da Industrial de S. Paulo, 1901.

Pati, Francisco. *A cidade sem portas*. São Paulo: Rêde Latina, 1956.

———. *O espírito das arcadas*. São Paulo: n.p., 1950.

Paula, Carlos F. de. "Assistência pública." In *Monografia histórica do município de Campinas*, 475–96. Rio de Janeiro: Instituto Brasileiro de Geografia e Estatística, 1952.

Pedroso Júnior, [José Correia], and Nicolau Tuma. *Homenagem postuma* [ao] *constituinte Bertho Condé*. Brasília: Departamento de Imprensa Nacional, 1966.

Penna, Belisario. *Saude e trabalho*. São Paulo: n.p., 1924.

Penteado, Jacob. *Belenzinho, 1910: Retrato de uma época*. São Paulo: Martins, 1962.

———. *Memórias de um postalista*. São Paulo: Martins, 1963.

Perdigão, Reis. "Marco 20." In *5 de Julho, 1922–1924*, 105–7. Rio de Janeiro: Henrique Velho, n.d. [1944].

Pereira, Aloysio, et al. *Rio Claro sesquicentenária*. Rio Claro: Museu Histórico e Pedagógico Amador Bueno da Veiga, 1978.

Pereira, Eduardo Carlos, and Elizabeth Filippini. *Cem anos de imigração italiana em Jundiaí*. São Paulo: Estudio RO, 1988.

Pereira, Maria Apparecida Franco. "O comércio cafeeiro na praça de Santos: O comissário de café, 1870–1920." In *Santos: Café e história*, by Maria Apparecida Franco Pereira et al., 9–34. Santos: Leopoldianum, 1995.

Perissinotto, Renato Monseff. "Estado, capital cafeeiro e crise política na década de 1920 em São Paulo, Brasil." *Hispanic American Historical Review* 80, no. 2 (May 2000): 299–332.

Petrolli, Valdenizo. "História da imprensa no ABC paulista." Tese de mestrado, Instituto Metodista de Ensino Superior (São Bernardo do Campo), 1983.

Pignataro, Lícia Capri. *Imigrantes italianos em Rio Claro e seus descendentes*. 2 vols. Rio Claro: Arquivo Público e Histórico, 1982.

Pinheiro, Paulo Sérgio. *Política e trabalho no Brasil*. 2nd ed. Rio de Janeiro: Paz e Terra, 1977 [1975].

Pires, Mário. *Campinas: Sementeira de ideais*. Limeira: Edição "Letras de Provincia," n.d.

Piza, Moacyr. *Tres campanhas*. São Paulo: Secção de Obras d'*O Estado de S. Paulo*, 1922.

Piza, Wladimir Toledo. *Por quem morreu Getúlio Vargas*. Rio de Janeiro: Ampersand, 1998.

Policia de São Paulo. *Movimento subversivo de julho*. São Paulo: Casa Garraux, 1925.

Prado, Antônio de Almeida. *Crônica de outrora*. São Paulo: Brasiliense, 1963.

Prado, Maria Lígia Coelho. *A democracia ilustrada: O Partido Democrático de São Paulo, 1926–1934*. São Paulo: Ática, 1986.

———. "O Partido Democrático de São Paulo: Adesões e aliciamento de eleitores, 1926–1934." *Revista de História* 117 (1984): 71–85.

——. "O pensamento conservador paulista: O regionalismo de Cincinato Braga." *Anais do Museu Paulista* 31 (1982): 235–45.

Prado, Nazareth, ed. *Antonio Prado no imperio e na republica*. Rio de Janeiro: F. Briguet, 1929.

Prado Junior, Caio. *The Colonial Background of Modern Brazil*. Translated by Suzette Macedo. Berkeley: University of California Press, 1967.

Presidente de São Paulo. *Fala dirigida ao congresso constituinte de S. Paulo pelo governador do estado, Dr. Americo Braziliense de Almeida Mello, no dia 8 de junho de 1891*. São Paulo: n.p., 1891.

——. *Mensagem apresentado ao congresso de S. Paulo, a 7 de abril de 1893, pelo dr. Bernardino de Campos, presidente do estado*. São Paulo: n.p., 1893.

——. *Mensagem apresentada ao congresso legislativo, em 14 de julho de 1927, pelo Dr. Dino da Costa Bueno, presidente do estado de São Paulo*. São Paulo: n.p., 1927.

——. *Mensagem enviada ao congresso legislativo, a 7 de abril de 1897, por Campos Salles, presidente do estado*. São Paulo: n.p., 1897.

Procurador Criminal da Republica. *Successos subversivos de São Paulo: Denuncia apresentada ao exmo. sr. dr. juiz federal da 1ª vara de São Paulo*. Rio de Janeiro: Imprensa Nacional, 1925.

Progress in South America: The Remarkable Growth of the City and State of Sao Paulo. London: Office of *The Sphere*, n.d.

Quaresma, Quélia Holandina. "Electoral Mobilization and the Construction of a Civic Culture in Brazil, 1909–1930." Ph.D. diss., University of Miami, 1998.

Rachum, Ilan. "Nationalism and Revolution in Brazil, 1922–1930: A Study of Intellectual, Military and Political Protesters and of the Assault on the Old Republic." Ph.D. diss., Columbia University, 1970.

Rama, Angel. *The Lettered City*. Translated by John Charles Chasteen. Durham, N.C.: Duke University Press, 1996.

Repartição de Estatistica e Archivo de São Paulo. *Divisão judiciaria e administrativa e districtos eleitoraes do estado de São Paulo em 1926*. São Paulo: Officina do *Diario Official*, 1927.

Ribeiro, Alvaro. *Falsa democracia / A revolta em São Paulo em 1924*. Rio de Janeiro: F. de Piro & Cia., 1927.

Ricardo, Cassiano. "O Estado Novo e seu sentido bandeirante." *Cultura Política* 1, no. 1 (March 1941): 110–32.

Rocha, Osorio. *Barretos de outrora*. São Paulo: n.p., 1954.

Rodrigues, Antonio da Gama. *Gens lorenensis: Do sertão de Guayparé à formosa cidade de Lorena, 1646–1946*. N.p., 1956.

Rodrigues, Edgar. *Os companheiros*. Vols. 1–2. Rio de Janeiro: VJR, 1994–95.

——. *Os companheiros*. Vols. 3–5. Florianópolis: Insular, 1997–98.

——. *Nacionalismo e cultura social, 1913–1922*. Rio de Janeiro: Laemmert, 1972.

——. *Socialismo e sindicalismo no Brasil, 1675–1913*. Rio de Janeiro: Laemmert, 1969.

——, ed. *Alvorada operária: Os congressos operários no Brasil*. Rio de Janeiro: Mundo Livre, 1979.

Sabato, Hilda. "Citizenship, Political Participation and the Formation of the Public Sphere in Buenos Aires, 1850s–1880s." *Past and Present* 136 (Aug. 1992): 139–63.

——. *The Many and the Few: Political Participation in Republican Buenos Aires*. Stanford, Calif.: Stanford University Press, 2001.

——. "On Political Citizenship in Nineteenth-Century Latin America." *American Historical Review* 106, no. 4 (Oct. 2001): 1290–1315.

Salles, Dagoberto. *A vida de um brasileiro, que é uma lição de civismo: Campos Salles*. São Carlos: Typographia Artistica, 1917.

Sampaio, Francisco Ribeiro. *Renembranças*. Campinas: Academia Campinense de Letras, 1975.

Sampaio, João. *O voto secreto*. São Paulo: n.p., 1922.

Sampaio, Teodoro [Theodoro]. *São Paulo no século XIX e outros ciclos históricos*. Edited by Hildon Rocha. Petrópolis: Vozes, 1978.

Santos, Amilcar Salgado dos. *A brigada Potyguara*. N.p., 1925.

Santos, Carlos José Ferreira dos. *Nem tudo era italiano: São Paulo e a pobreza, 1890–1915*. São Paulo: Annablume, 1998.

Santos, Davino Francisco dos. *A coluna Miguel Costa e não coluna Prestes*. São Paulo: Edicon, 1994.

Santos, Francisco Martins dos. *História de Santos, 1532–1936*. 2 vols. São Paulo: Empreza Graphica da *Revista dos Tribunaes*, 1937.

Santos, Wanderley dos. *Antecedentes históricos do ABC paulista, 1550–1892*. São Bernardo: Prefeitura do Município, 1992.

Schmidt, Afonso. *Bom tempo*. São Paulo: Brasiliense, 1958.

——. "Paulo Gonçalves." *Revista da Academia Paulista de Letras* 48 (Dec. 1949): 33–42.

——. *São Paulo de meus amores*. São Paulo: Clube do Livro, 1954.

Schwartz, Stuart B. "Plantations and Peripheries, c. 1580–1750." In *Colonial Brazil*, ed. Leslie Bethell, 67–144. Cambridge: Cambridge University Press, 1987.

Schwartzman, Simon. *São Paulo e o estado nacional*. São Paulo: Difel, 1975.

Seabra, Alberto. *Problemas sul-americanos*. São Paulo: Monteiro Lobato, 1923.

Secretaria da Agricultura, Industria e Commercio de São Paulo. *Os municipios do estado de São Paulo*. São Paulo: n.p., 1933.

Serva, Mario Pinto. *A reforma eleitoral*. São Paulo: Livraria Zenith, 1931.

——. *O voto secreto, ou a organisação de partidos nacionaes*. São Paulo: Imprensa Methodista, n.d.

Shanin, Teodor. *Russia as a "Developing Society."* New Haven, Conn.: Yale University Press, 1985.

Shirley, Robert W. *The End of a Tradition: Culture Change and Development in the Município of Cunha, São Paulo, Brazil.* New York: Columbia University Press, 1971.

Silva, Fernando Teixeira da. *Operários sem patrões: Os trabalhadores da cidade de Santos no entreguerras.* Campinas: Editora da Universidade Estadual de Campinas, 2003.

Silva, Hélio. *1930: A revolução traída.* Rio de Janeiro: Civilização Brasileira, 1966.

Silva, Hélio, and Maria Cecília Ribas Carneiro. *História da república brasileira.* Vol. 7, *Fim da 1ª república.* São Paulo: Três, 1975.

Silva Sobrinho, Costa e. *Santos noutros tempos.* São Paulo: n.p., 1953.

Skidmore, Thomas E. *Black into White: Race and Nationality in Brazilian Thought.* 2nd ed. Durham, N.C.: Duke University Press, 1993 [1974].

———. *Politics in Brazil, 1930–1964: An Experiment in Democracy.* Oxford: Oxford University Press, 1967.

Soares, José Carlos de Macedo. *Justiça: A revolta militar em São Paulo.* Paris: n.p., 1925.

Sodré, Nelson Werneck. *História da imprensa no Brasil.* 4th ed. Rio de Janeiro: Mauad, 1999 [1966].

Soihet, Rachel. "A pedagogia da conquista do espaço público pelas mulheres e a militância feminista de Bertha Lutz." *Revista Brasileira de Educação* 15 (Sept.-Dec. 2000): 97–117.

Souza, Rosa Fátima de. *O direito à educação: Lutas populares pela escola em Campinas.* Campinas: Editora da Universidade Estadual de Campinas, 1998.

Stein, Stanley J. *Vassouras: A Brazilian Coffee County, 1850–1890.* Cambridge, Mass.: Harvard University Press, 1957.

Tavora, Juarez. *Á guisa de um depoimento sobre a revolução brasileira de 1924.* Vol. 1. São Paulo: Editora d' O Combate, 1927.

———. *Uma vida e muitas lutas.* 3 vols. Rio de Janeiro: José Olympio, 1973–76.

Teixeira, Sebastião. *O Jahú em 1900: Repositorio de dados, informações e documentos para a historia do Jahú.* Jahú: Correio do Jahú, 1900.

Telarolli, Rodolpho. *Eleições e fraudes eleitorais na república velha.* São Paulo: Brasiliense, 1982.

———. *Poder local na república velha.* São Paulo: Nacional, 1977.

Terci, Eliana Tadeu. "A cidade na primeira república: Imprensa, política e poder em Piracicaba." Tese de doutorado, Universidade de São Paulo, 1997.

Thiollier, René. *O homem da galeria: Echos de uma epoca.* São Paulo: Depositaria Livraria Teixeira, n.d.

Toledo, Edilene. *Travessias revolucionárias: Idéias e militantes sindicalistas em São Paulo e na Itália, 1890–1945.* Campinas: Editora da Universidade Estadual de Campinas, 2004.

Travassos, Nelson Palma. *Quando eu era menino. . . .* São Paulo: EdArt, 1960.

Trento, Angelo. *Do outro lado do Atlântico: Um século de imigração italiana no*

Brasil. Translated by Mariarosaria Fabris and Luiz Eduardo de Lima Brandão. São Paulo: Nobel, 1988.

Twentieth Century Impressions of Brazil. London: Lloyd's Greater Britain Publishing, 1913.

Vampré, Leven. *São Paulo, terra conquistada*. São Paulo: Sociedade Impressora Paulista, 1932.

Vargas, Getúlio. *Ideário político de Getúlio Vargas*. Edited by Raul Guastini. São Paulo: n.p., 1943.

Vieira, Clovis Botelho. *O general Ataliba Leonel*. São Paulo: n.p., 1959.

———. *A grande guerra e as tradições liberaes do Brasil*. São Paulo: Livraria e Officinas Magalhães, 1918.

———. *Os grandes ideaes do Partido Democratico*. São Paulo: Rossetti, 1928.

———. *Na imprensa*. São Paulo: Irmãos Ferraz, 1931.

Villaça, Antônio Carlos. "O pensamento brasileiro na década de 20." *Revista do Instituto Histórico e Geográfico Brasileiro* 346 (Jan.-March 1985): 91–105.

Viotti, M., and Vitaliano Rotellini. *The Press of the State of S. Paulo, Brasil, 1827–1904*. São Paulo: Vanorden & Comp., 1905.

Vizentini, Paulo Gilberto Fagundes. *A crise dos anos 20: Conflitos e transição*. 2nd ed. Porto Alegre: Editora da Universidade Federal do Rio Grande do Sul, 1998 [1992].

———. *Os liberais e a crise da república velha*. São Paulo: Brasiliense, 1983.

———, ed. *O Rio Grande do Sul e a política nacional: As oposições civis na crise dos anos 20 e na revolução de 30*. 2nd ed. Porto Alegre: Martins, 1985 [1982].

Waddell, Agnes S. "The Revolution in Brazil." *Foreign Policy Association Information Service* 6, no. 26 (4 March 1931): 489–506.

Walker, Thomas W. "Ribeirão Preto, 1910–1960." In *Dos coronéis à metrópole: Fios e tramas da sociedade e da política em Ribeirão Preto no século XX*, by Thomas W. Walker and Agnaldo de Sousa Barbosa, 13–143. Translated by Marina Carla Magri. Ribeirão Preto: Palavra Mágica, 2000.

Weinstein, Barbara. "Brazilian Regionalism." *Latin American Research Review* 17, no. 2 (1982): 262–76.

———. *For Social Peace in Brazil: Industrialists and the Remaking of the Working Class in São Paulo, 1920–1964*. Chapel Hill: University of North Carolina Press, 1996.

———. "Inventing the *Mulher Paulista*: Politics, Rebellion, and the Gendering of Brazilian Regional Identities." *Journal of Women's History* 18, no. 1 (winter 2006): 22–49.

———. "Not the Republic of Their Dreams: Historical Obstacles to Political and Social Democracy in Brazil." *Latin American Research Review* 29, no. 2 (1994): 262–73.

———. "Racializing Regional Difference: São Paulo vs. Brazil, 1932." In *Race and Nation in Modern Latin America*, ed. Nancy P. Applebaum, Anne S. Macpherson, and Karin Alejandra Rosemblatt, 237–62. Chapel Hill: University of North Carolina Press, 2003.

Whitaker, José Maria. *O milagre da minha vida*. São Paulo: Hucitec, 1978.

Wirth, John D. *Minas Gerais in the Brazilian Federation, 1889–1937*. Stanford, Calif.: Stanford University Press, 1977.

———. "Tenentismo in the Brazilian Revolution of 1930." *Hispanic American Historical Review* 44, no. 2 (May 1964): 161–79.

Witter, José Sebastião, and Francisco de Assis Barbosa. "Francisco Glicério, um republicano pragmático." In *Idéias políticas de Francisco Glicério*, ed. José Sebastião Witter, 23–63. Rio de Janeiro: Casa de Rui Barbosa, 1982.

Wolfe, Joel. "Anarchist Ideology, Worker Practice: The 1917 General Strike and the Formation of São Paulo's Working Class." *Hispanic American Historical Review* 71, no. 4 (Nov. 1991): 809–46.

———. *Working Women, Working Men: São Paulo and the Rise of Brazil's Industrial Working Class*. Durham, N.C.: Duke University Press, 1993.

Womack, John, Jr. *Zapata and the Mexican Revolution*. New York: Alfred A. Knopf, 1969.

Woodard, James P. "Coronelismo in Theory and Practice: Evidence, Analysis, and Argument from São Paulo." *Luso-Brazilian Review* 42, no. 1 (2005): 99–117.

———. "History, Sociology, and the Political Conflicts of the 1920s in São Paulo, Brazil." *Journal of Latin American Studies* 37, no. 2 (May 2005): 333–49.

———. "Regionalismo paulista e política partidária nos anos vinte." *Revista de História* 150 (2004): 41–56.

———. "The Specter of Liberalism: Notes on the Democratic Party of São Paulo and the Historiography of Twentieth-Century Brazil." *Estudios Interdisciplinarios de América Latina y el Caribe* 16, no. 2 (July-Dec. 2005): 153–61.

Zweig, Stefan. *Brazil: Land of the Future*. Translated by Andrew St. James. New York: Viking Press, 1941.

Index

Glycerio, Francisco. *See* Leite, Francisco Glycerio de Cerqueira

Gomes, Eduardo, 231

Gonçalves, Paulo (Francisco de Paula Gonçalves), 219, 316 n. 36, 321 n. 70

Goulart, Francisco de Paula, 38

Goulart, Maurício, 205

Gouveia, Zoroastro, 171, 198, 200, 205, 207, 361 n. 30

Gracco, Mário, 105

Guaratinguetá, 22, 36, 47, 94, 103, 197

Guarulhos, 166

Guastini, Mário, 202

Guião, João, 77

Guimarães, Aureliano, 100

Hall, Ricardo, 205

Hummel, Carlos, 211

Ibirá, 52

Iguape, 21, 26, 43, 45

Inácio, "Chico," 51

Indian Protection Service, 20

influenza epidemic of 1918, 71, 88–89, 105

Invisible Society for Political Action, 143, 151, 179

Iporanga, 21, 45, 162, 171, 182, 207

Itapetininga, 19, 22, 51, 67, 87, 190, 272 n. 169, 296 n. 210

Itápolis, 43, 53

Itaquera, 28

Itararé, 21, 92, 169, 208

Itatiba, 48, 52

Itu, 19, 22

Jaboticabal, 68, 121, 161, 306 n. 67

Jacupiranga, 21

Jardim, Renato, 24–25, 123, 127, 219

Jaú, 23, 47, 104–105, 166, 185, 222, 329 n. 133

Joly, Benedito Pires, 212

Jundiaí, 19, 22, 26, 53, 66, 119–122, 165, 209

Junqueira, Francisco da Cunha, 104

Junqueira, Joaquim da Cunha Diniz, 37, 39–40, 43, 45, 48, 67, 69, 91–92, 103, 111, 122, 144, 166, 207, 212, 254 n. 14

"Juo Bananére" (pseud. of Alexandre Ribeiro Marcondes Machado), 156

Krahenbuhl, Pedro, 86, 171, 208, 354 n. 115

Lacerda, Luiz de Queiroz, 158

Lacerda, Maurício de, 184–185, 223

Lafer, Horácio, 157

Lapa, 19, 54, 56, 68, 168, 171, 177

Laranjal, 161

Lascala, Luiz, 105

Leão, Waldemar, 179, 199

Lefevre, Henrique Neves, 316 n. 36

Leite, Aureliano, 117, 207–208, 318 n. 49

Leite, Francisco Glycerio de Cerqueira, 36, 39, 61, 63, 67, 178, 254 n. 15

Leme, 51

Leme, Floriano de, 186

Lemos, Antônio Cajado de, 159, 316 n. 36

Lençóis, 69

Leonel, Ataliba, 37, 172, 207, 267 n. 90

Liberal Alliance, 190, 195–200, 203–204, 345 n. 33

Liberating Party, 154

Lima, Diogenes de, 171

Lima, Octaviano Alves de, 153

Lima, Sylvestre de, 67, 106

Lima, Sylvio Alves de, 153, 316 n. 36

Limeira, 20, 53, 105, 167

Lins, 52, 55

Lins, Manoel Joaquim de Albuquerque, 37, 63, 67–68, 255 n. 20

Lobato, José Bento Monteiro, 18, 94, 124–129, 131, 135, 143–144, 149, 151, 179, 184, 190–191, 197, 214, 236–237, 308 n. 90, 309 n. 57, 358 n. 1

Lobato, Menêmio, 203

Lobo, Aristides, 235

James P. Woodard is an assistant professor of history
at Montclair State University.

LIBRARY OF CONGRESS CATALOGING-IN-PUBLICATION DATA

Woodard, James P.

A place in politics : São Paulo, Brazil, from seigneurial republicanism
to regionalist revolt / James P. Woodard.

p. cm.

Includes bibliographical references and index.

ISBN 978-0-8223-4346-2 (cloth : alk. paper)

ISBN 978-0-8223-4329-5 (pbk. : alk. paper)

1. Political culture—Brazil—São Paulo—History.

2. São Paulo (Brazil)—Politics and government—History.

3. Brazil—Politics and government—1889–

4. Regionalism—Brazil—São Paulo—History.

I. Title.

F2651.S257W66 2009

306.20981'0904—dc22

2008051090